DATA BASE MANAGEMENT

DATA BASE MANAGEMENT

Fred R. McFadden

Department of Business Information Systems
University of Colorado
Colorado Springs, Colorado

Jeffrey A. Hoffer

School of Business
Indiana University
Bloomington, Indiana

The Benjamin/Cummings Publishing Company
Menlo Park, California • Reading, Massachusetts
London • Amsterdam • Don Mills, Ontario • Sydney

To our wives, Evelyn McFadden and Patty Hoffer.

Sponsoring Editor: Susan Nelle
Production Coordinator: Mimi Hills
Copy Editor: Janet Greenblatt
Designer: Gary Head
Illustrations: Art by Ayxa, Ben Turner Graphics

Library of Congress Cataloging in Publication Data

McFadden, Fred R., 1933–
   Data base management.

   Bibliography: p.
   Includes index.
   1. Data base management.   I. Hoffer, Jeffrey A.
II. Title.
QA76.9.D3M395   1985   001.64   84-12388
ISBN 0-8053-6780-2

CDEFGHIJ-HA-898765

The Benjamin/Cummings Publishing Company, Inc.
2727 Sand Hill Road
Menlo Park, California 94025

Preface

This text is designed for an introductory course in data base management. An increasing number of business schools require such a course as part of the information systems curriculum. The text has been used successfully at both undergraduate and graduate levels, as well as for management and professional development programs.

SCOPE OF THE BOOK

Data Base Management was developed to meet an unfilled need. A vast number of data base texts and reference books are available today; however, most of these books are more suitable for computer science courses (or as reference works) than for the business school curriculum. This situation is reflected in industry, where the amount of data base software and techniques far outweighs successful implementation.

This textbook provides a balance between managerial and technical issues. Important topics include:

1. Emphasis on the concept of information as a corporate resource.
2. A separate chapter on strategic data base planning (Chapter 3).

3. Emphasis on data administration, with extensive discussion of its role and organization placement.

4. Emphasis on the role of the data dictionary/directory as a tool in planning and controlling the information resource.

5. Complete discussion of data base design, including normalization and computer-assisted design techniques. Data base design is shown to have a definite link to information systems analysis and design.

6. Discussion of distributed data bases and data base management on minicomputers and microcomputers.

7. Coverage of traditional as well as fourth generation data base management technology.

LEARNING AIDS AND SUPPLEMENTS

To assist the student, *Data Base Management* includes the following learning aids:

- Realistic **Case Examples** illustrate important concepts throughout the text. Two case examples highlight concerns from industry: Pine Valley Furniture Company for the manufacturing sector, and Mountain View Community Hospital for the service sector. Case examples are identified by the symbols shown in the margin.

- A **Summary** at the end of each chapter capsulizes the main concepts of the chapter.

- The **Chapter Review** tests students' knowledge. The **Review Questions** check the students' grasp of new terms and important concepts. **Problems and Exercises** require the students to apply their knowledge to realistic situations, and in some cases to extend this knowledge to new problems and situations.

The text is part of a complete educational package that is designed to provide a high level of support to the instructor:

- The *Instructor's Manual* is a comprehensive, 400-page manual containing numerous instructional resources. First, for each chapter there are 6 to 10 Teaching Suggestions: lecture outlines, teaching hints, and student projects and activities that make use of the chapter content. Second, there are complete solutions to both the Review Questions and the Problems and Exercises in the text. Third, there are 600 multiple-choice and true-false questions (approximately 40 per chapter) with answers. Finally, the Instructor's Manual includes a set of 100 masters for overhead transparencies, with enlarged art from the text as well as supplementary material.

- A separate *Case Book for Data Base Management* contains six realistic cases for course projects. Most of these cases can be solved and the data bases implemented using either mainframe computers, minicomputers, or microcomputers.

ACKNOWLEDGMENTS

We are grateful to the numerous individuals who contributed to the preparation of this textbook. First, we wish to thank our reviewers for their exhaustive reviews and their many excellent suggestions for improving the text. Those who reviewed the text were David Blair, University of Michigan; Marilyn Bohl, IBM, San Jose, CA; David W. Chilson, Bowling Green State University; Jon D. Clark, North Texas State University; Ronald Eaves, California State Polytechnic University, Pomona; Tom Finneran, ITT, Shelton, CT; Bart Simpson, Federal Express, Colorado Springs; Frances L. Grant, California State University, Chico; Richard Heath, St. Cloud, MN; Daniel T. Lee, University of Wisconsin; Charles J. Rogers, California State University, Stanislaus; David Whitney, San Francisco State University, CA; and Margart S. Wu, University of Iowa. Next, we wish to thank our typists, Kathy Abeyta, Kathy Claybaugh, and Patty Hoffer, who were tireless and meticulous in capturing the manuscript on word processing systems so that the inevitable revisions could be accomplished with relative ease. We benefitted from discussions with our colleagues, especially Daniel Couger (University of Colorado) and Ananth Srinivasan (Indiana University).

We are very grateful to the staff of Benjamin/Cummings for their support throughout the project. In particular, we wish to thank Susan Nelle (Editor) and Mimi Hills (Production Coordinator) for their encouragement and support. Our thanks also go to our many students who helped test the manuscript in its various stages. We would like to thank the following students who assisted in preparing the *Instructor's Manual*: Terry Ryan, Kathleen George, Cheryl McKay, Ed Joyner, Laurie Kiracofe, and Li Cheng (Indiana University), and Jackie Gianunzio and Rose Johnston (University of Colorado). To all of these individuals, and to our families, we give our thanks. It hardly needs saying that much of the value of this text is due to their assistance, but we alone bear responsibility for any errors or omissions that remain within these covers.

Fred R. McFadden

Jeffrey A. Hoffer

Contents in Brief

Contents

DATA BASE MANAGEMENT

I

Basic Concepts

The first three chapters of this text present the basic concepts of data base management. In Chapter 1 we introduce the data base environment. Here we contrast the data base approach with conventional file processing, illustrating the potential advantages of the data base approach. We also introduce the major software components of a data base environment, including data base management systems and data dictionary/directory systems.

In Chapter 2 we describe the basic concepts and characteristics of data, introducing the concepts of entities and entity classes. In this chapter we describe the basic associations between data items and other data entities, as well as the three-level ANSI/SPARC data model, which is the underlying model for most data base management systems today.

Chapter 3 is an introduction to data base planning. We explain the importance of planning to successful data base implementation. We describe the steps in data base planning and introduce a simple top-down model that integrates data base planning with overall business system planning. Also, we introduce a case example of a hospital, which is used extensively throughout the remainder of the text.

1

The Data Base Environment

INTRODUCTION

This book is about the data resource of organizations and about the management of that resource. The recognition by management that data (or information) is indeed a resource is a recent development. According to Diebold (1979, 41) "Information, which in essence is the analysis and synthesis of data, will unquestionably be one of the most vital of corporate resources in the 1980s. It will be structured into models for planning and decision making. It will be incorporated into measurements of performance and profitability. It will be integrated into product design and marketing methods. In other words, information will be recognized and treated as an asset."

Two important factors demonstrate management's acceptance of data resource management: firm commitment to the data base approach and successful establishment of the data administration function.

A **data base** is a shared collection of interrelated data designed to meet the varied information needs of an organization. A data base has two important properties: it is integrated and it is shared. By *integrated* we mean that previously distinct data files have been logically organized to eliminate (or reduce) redundancy and to facilitate data access. By *shared* we mean that all qualified users in the organization have access to the same data, for use in a variety of activities.

The data base approach offers a number of important and practical advantages to an organization. Reducing redundancy improves the consistency of data while reducing the waste in storage space. Sharing data often permits new data processing applications to be developed without having to create new data files. In general, less redundancy and greater sharing lead to less confusion between organizational units and less time spent resolving errors and inconsistencies in reports. The data base approach also permits centralized control over data standards, security restrictions, and integrity controls. This facilitates the natural evolution and change of information systems *and* organizations. It permits the use of powerful query languages by users who have no previous programming experience. Finally, the data base approach promotes data independence, which insulates application programs from modifications to the data base itself. All of these advantages are described in the following sections.

DATA AS A RESOURCE

Every organization has a pool of resources that it must manage effectively to achieve its objectives. Although their roles differ, all resources—human, financial, and material—share a common characteristic: they all incur cost and are of value to the organization.

It is now recognized that data are also a resource, since they, too, incur cost and are of value to an organization. In fact, the value of data is unique in that the entire organization depends on its availability for the management of other resources. Any organization that fails to treat data (or information) as a resource and to manage it effectively will be handicapped in how it manages its human, material, and financial resources.

In this text, we will distinguish between data and information. **Data** are facts concerning people, objects, events, or other entities. Data can be financial and quantitative or it can be qualitative and subjective; it can be internal or external; it can be historical or predictive. There are many sources of data in an organization: financial and managerial accounting, production and operations, sales, payroll and personnel, planning, and so on.

Information is data that have been organized or prepared in a form that is suitable for decision making. For example, a list of students and grade point averages in random order is data; but a list of students arranged in order of grade point averages (highest to lowest) represents information to a person responsible for voting an outstanding student award. A pool of carefully organized data can readily be used to produce a variety of information.

To manage their data resources more effectively, many organizations are formally defining their data and placing them into data bases. As we have already said, a data base is an integrated collection of data that is shared by all organizational users. An organization may choose to have a single, large integrated data base; several separate data bases maintained on a central computer; or separate data bases maintained on separate computers within organizational divisions. We will describe the advantages and disadvantages of each of these approaches in later chapters.

Users   Physical data base

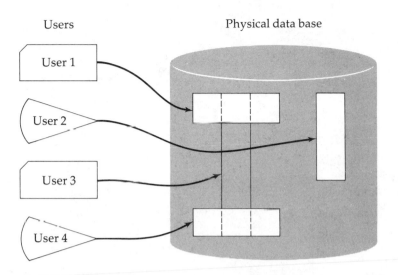

Figure 1-1
A notion of a data base
system.
(Source: Clark 1980, 4.)

The notion of a data base is shown in Figure 1-1. The data base is conceived as a single entity that consists of a collection of interrelated records. Within the data base are stored records of importance to individual users. There can be numerous users sharing the data base. As shown in the figure, some of the users may access the data in batch mode, while other users do so in on-line mode.

We will describe the data base approach and its advantages and disadvantages by means of a realistic case example. In this example, a small company progresses from manual information systems to a small business computer using traditional files and finally to considering the data base approach.

Pine Valley Furniture

CASE EXAMPLE

Pine Valley Furniture Company manufactures high-quality, all-wood furniture and distributes it to stores in a metropolitan area. There are several product lines, including dinette sets, stereo cabinets, wall units, living room furniture, and bedroom furniture. Pine Valley employs about 50 persons at the present time and is experiencing rapid growth.

Pine Valley Furniture was founded about ten years ago by Donald Knotts, its general manager and majority owner. Mr. Knotts had made custom furniture as a hobby and started the business in his own garage. Pine Valley Furniture was operating out of a rented warehouse until five years ago, when it was moved to its present location.

Managing the data resource at Pine Valley Furniture was relatively simple during the first years of its operation. At first, Mr. Knotts kept most of the information needed to run the business in his head, although a few records were kept, mostly for tax purposes. When the business expanded

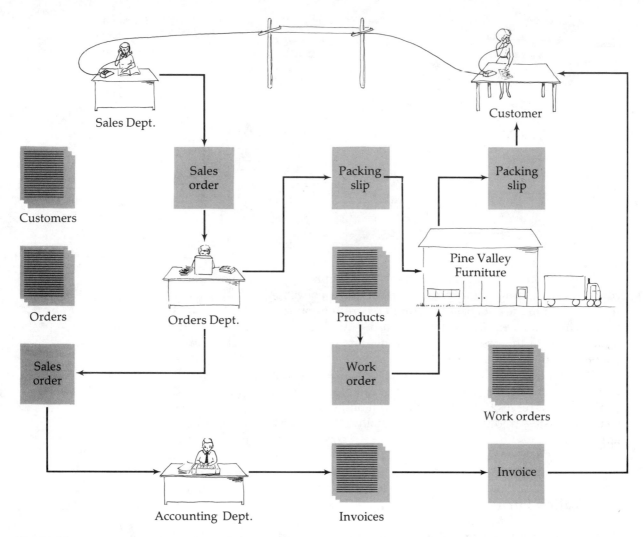

Figure 1-2
Manual information
system (Pine Valley
Furniture).

into the rented warehouse, there were about ten employees. It was then that Mr. Knotts hired a part-time bookkeeper to keep a small set of books. These books included a general ledger and accounts receivable and payable ledgers. The books, in effect, were a small, centralized data base that provided most of the information needed to run the company at that time.

When Pine Valley Furniture moved into its present location, its product line had expanded and its sales volume had doubled in two years. Its work force had grown to over 30 employees. With this organizational growth and complexity, Mr. Knotts found that he could no longer manage the operation by himself. He therefore organized the company into functional areas of responsibility. Manufacturing operations were organized into three main sections: Fabrication, Assembling, and Finishing. Each of these sections had a manager. Also, separate departments were established for several business functions. There was now a Sales Department, an Orders Department, an Accounting Department, and a Purchasing Department. Pine Valley Furniture had emerged from the entrepreneurial mode of operation to a formal organization with functional departments and managers.

When Pine Valley Furniture organized into functional departments, it also changed its approach to managing its data resources. The single set of books that it had used previously were no longer adequate to run the business. Instead, each department now had its own books—files, ledgers, and so on—and formal lines of communication were established to transfer data between departments.

Figure 1-2 shows the manual information system at Pine Valley Furniture. This diagram depicts the flow of data for the mainstream functions—order processing, billing, shipping, and processing work orders. Most customer orders are received in Sales by telephone. The Sales Department refers to a customer file to check the customer's credit and then prepares a sales order. The sales order is then sent to the Orders Department, which checks a products file to determine whether the requested item is in stock. If the item is in stock, the clerk prepares a packing slip. If the item is not in stock (or if the stock level has dropped below a predetermined level), the clerk prepares a work order to manufacture a lot of the item. One copy of the sales order is sent to Accounting, and another copy is filed in the Orders Department. The Accounting Department prices the sales order and prepares an invoice for items shipped to the customer. A packing slip is also included with each customer shipment.

Notice in Figure 1-2 that each department has a separate file (or files) to support its operations and answer its questions. The files shown in Figure 1-2 and typical user questions that might be answered by referring to these files are shown in the following table:

Department	File	Typical Questions
Sales	Customer	What is customer ABC's address and credit limit?
Orders	Products	How many tables (product #123) do we have in stock?
Accounting	Invoices	How much does customer ABC owe us on invoice #567?
Manufacturing	Work Orders	How many units of product #123 are we scheduled to build today?

In addition, other departments also have files to support their operations. For example, Purchasing has a file of purchase orders to indicate what materials are currently on order from vendors.

The information system portrayed in Figure 1-2 is a manual system. In this system, the data files are decentralized, and each department works with a portion of the organization's data. Although the system works, it has a number of deficiencies or disadvantages:

1. A constant stream of paperwork (in the form of memos, reports, transactions, and so on) and telephone calls is required to communicate changes and keep the files synchronized.

2. The system cannot easily provide answers to more complex operational questions. For example, to answer the question "What invoices are outstanding for order #123 from customer ABC?" will probably require some research on the part of the Orders Department.

3. Managers cannot easily obtain summary information required for decision making.

4. Duplicate data exist throughout the organization, resulting in lack of consistency. For example, information concerning customer orders is maintained in the Sales, Orders, Accounting and Shipping departments at Pine Valley Furniture.

It is tempting to assume that a computer would help eliminate many of these typical shortcomings of a manual information system. True, a computer will often permit data to be processed faster and more accurately. However, in the traditional file processing environment that has prevailed for decades, many of the preceding problems remain or may even be amplified. The reason for this is that in file processing systems, the designer essentially seeks to automate existing manual systems, as we will explain in the following section.

TRADITIONAL FILE PROCESSING SYSTEMS

The traditional approach to information systems design focuses on the data processing needs of individual departments in the organization. The information systems (or IS) group responds to user requests by developing (or acquiring) new computer programs, often one at a time, for individual applications such as accounts receivable, payroll, and inventory control. Each application program or system that is developed is procedure-oriented and is designed to meet the needs of a particular department or user group. That is, there is no overall map, plan, or model to guide the growth of applications.

Each new computer application is typically designed with its own set of data files. Much of the data in these new files may already be present in existing files for other applications. However, to meet the needs of a new application, the existing files would have to be restructured. This, in turn, would require that existing programs that use these same files would have to be revised or completely rewritten. It is often far simpler (and also less risky) to design new files for each application.

In these traditional systems, file and record descriptions are placed within each individual program. For example, if you have ever written a COBOL program, you know that you were required to code a Data Division that described each file, record, and data item (or field) used by that program. As a result, each application program "owns" its data files, and the program logic is dependent on (or closely interwoven with) the data formats and descriptions.

File Processing Systems at Pine Valley Furniture

Three years ago, Pine Valley Furniture Company acquired a small business computer. The company had been experiencing numerous operating problems, including declining customer service and increasing inventory levels. Although the company had grown rapidly, profits had failed to keep pace. Mr. Knotts decided that the manual information system that existed at that time (illustrated in Figure 1-2) was no longer sufficient to manage a fast-growing business. After some evaluation, a small business computer was selected and installed at Pine Valley Furniture.

Most of the applications that have subsequently been installed on the computer are in the accounting and financial areas. At the present time, these applications include order filling, invoicing, accounts receivable, inventory control, accounts payable, payroll, and general ledger. Most of these application programs were purchased from a software vendor who modified the programs to meet the requirements of Pine Valley Furniture Company.

Three of the computer applications at Pine Valley Furniture are depicted in Figure 1-3. The systems being illustrated are order filling, invoicing, and payroll. The figure shows the major data files associated with each application system. We will now define each of the terms illustrated in Figure 1-3.

An **application system** is an integrated set of application programs, data files, and procedures that performs a business process or function. For example, the Invoicing System prepares an invoice for each shipment of furniture to a customer of Pine Valley Furniture.

An **application program** (or simply **program**) performs one task (or a related set of tasks) associated with an application. For example, program B in the invoicing application is a Pricing Program that records a unit price for each item, extends the price for the number of items ordered, and computes a total price for the invoice.

A **data file** (or simply **file**) is a collection of records. These records are often (but not always) of the same type. For example, the Customer Master File contains one record for each of Pine Valley Furniture's customers.

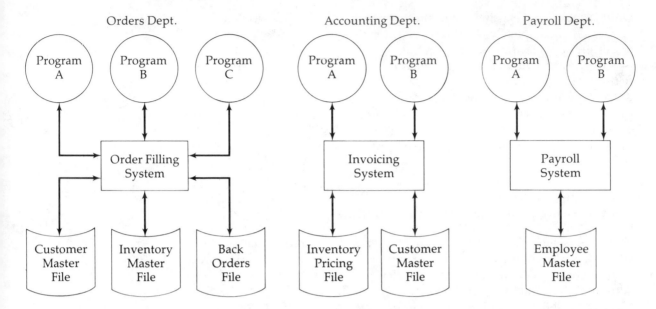

Figure 1-3
Three application systems
at Pine Valley Furniture.

A **logical record** (or simply **record**) is a collection of data items that describes a particular object or entity. For example, each Customer Master Record contains the following data items: CUSTOMER#, NAME, BILLING ADDRESS, SHIP-TO ADDRESS, CREDIT RATING, and DISCOUNT RATE.

A **data item** is a unit fact concerning some object. It is the smallest named unit of data in an information system.

Notice that each application system in Figure 1-3 has its own data files. This is typical of traditional applications. Some of the files contain duplicate (or redundant) data. For example, the Inventory Master File used by the Order Filling System and the Inventory Pricing File used in the Invoicing System both contain data describing products sold by Pine Valley Furniture. Also, these two application systems both use a Customer Master File. Is this, in fact, one file or two distinct files with duplicate information? In this case the software vendor designed the two applications to share a single Customer Master File. However, there remains a considerable amount of duplicated data in the files used in the various applications at Pine Valley Furniture.

You may notice the similarity in design between the computer systems at Pine Valley Furniture and the earlier manual systems they replaced (compare Figures 1-2 and 1-3). In each case, the approach was to develop procedures and associated data files to solve data processing problems for individual functional departments. With the computer systems, the data files are no longer physically located within the individual departments, as in the manual system. However, they are tailored to the needs of each application or department and are generally regarded as "belonging" to that department or application, rather than as a resource to be shared by all departments or users.

The computer applications at Pine Valley Furniture have generally been successful. They have allowed the company to reduce its paperwork burden and to improve its response to customer orders. They have also provided management with better information concerning costs, sales, and profits. Nevertheless, managers at Pine Valley are dissatisfied with several aspects of the new computer system. While the applications have helped improve the operations management function they have had little impact on middle management and still less on top management. Mr. Knotts and the other managers at Pine Valley Furniture have come to realize that there are basic limitations to traditional file processing systems.

Disadvantages of File Processing Systems

The basic disadvantages of file processing systems are uncontrolled redundancy, inconsistent data, inflexibility, limited data sharing, poor enforcement of standards, low programmer productivity, and excessive program maintenance.

Uncontrolled Redundancy. In file processing systems, each application has its own files. This approach inevitably leads to a high level of data redundancy. There are several disadvantages to recording the same data item in multiple files. First, valuable storage space is wasted. Second, the same data may have to be input several times to update all occurrences of a data item. Third, inconsistencies (or various versions) often result, which require time to resolve and correct.

Inconsistent Data. When the same data are stored in multiple locations, inconsistencies in the data are inevitable. For example, several of the files at Pine Valley Furniture contain customer data. Suppose that there is an address change for one of the customers. If the files are to be consistent, this change must be made simultaneously (and correctly) to each of the files containing the customer address data item. Since the files are controlled by different users, there is a strong likelihood that some files will reflect the old address, while others reflect the new address.

Inconsistencies in stored data are one of the most common sources of errors in computer applications. They lead to inconsistent documents and reports and undermine the confidence of users in the integrity of the information system. For example, the outdated customer address just described may lead to a customer invoice being mailed to the wrong location. As a result, the invoice may be returned and the customer payment delayed or lost.

Inflexibility.   A file processing system resembles a mass production facility. It produces numerous documents and reports routinely and efficiently, provided that these outputs were anticipated in the original design of the system. However, such systems are often quite inflexible and cannot easily respond to requests for a new or redesigned "product." In other words, an application system cannot readily satisfy demands for information in a new format that wasn't anticipated in the original design. This often leads to considerable frustration on the part of the users, who cannot understand why the computer system cannot give them information in a new format when they know it exists in the application files.

For example, the Order Filling System at Pine Valley Furniture contains three files: Customer Master, Inventory Master, and Back Orders (see Figure 1-3). Suppose that the Orders Department manager wants to obtain a list of back-ordered items for a given customer. Unless this request had been anticipated when the system was designed, it will be difficult to satisfy the request. If the request represents a new requirement, a new application program may be required to extract the required records from each file and produce the desired report.

Limited Data Sharing.   With the traditional applications approach each application has its own private files and there is little opportunity for users to share data outside of their own applications. Referring to Figure 1-3, you will notice that users in the Accounting Department have access to the Invoicing System and its files. However, they may not have access to the Order Filling System files, which are used primarily by the Orders Department.

One consequence of limited data sharing is that the same data may have to be entered several times to update files with duplicate data. For example, at Pine Valley Furniture, a change in the description for an inventory item would have to be entered separately into the Order filling and Invoicing systems, since each contains its own version of an inventory file.

Another consequence of limited data sharing is that in developing new applications, the designer often cannot (or does not) exploit data contained in existing files. Instead, new files are designed that duplicate much of the existing data. Suppose that the manufacturing manager at Pine Valley Furniture requests a new system for scheduling production orders. Such a system would undoubtedly require an inventory file to provide economical order quantities, status of existing orders, and related inventory information. Of course, an Inventory Master File already is being used in the Order Filling System. However, a redesign of this file would be required to meet the requirements of the scheduling application. This, in turn, would probably require a complete rewrite of Programs A, B, and C in the Order Filling System (see Figure 1-3). Instead, the designer would specify a new Inventory File for the Production Scheduling System. In file processing systems, the cycle of limited data sharing and redundancy are perpetuated in this manner.

Poor Enforcement of Standards.   Every organization requires standard procedures and methods so that it may operate effectively. Within information systems, standards are required for data names, formats, and access restrictions. Unfortunately, data standards are difficult to make known and enforce in a traditional file processing environment, mainly because of the decentralized responsibility for system design and operation. Two types of inconsistencies may result from poor enforcement of standards: synonyms and homonyms. A **synonym** results when two different names are used for the same data item, for example, student number and matriculation number. A **homonym** is a single name that is used for two different data items. For example, in a bank the term *balance* might be used to designate a checking account balance in one department and a savings account balance in a different department.

Enforcement of standards is particularly difficult in larger organizations with decentralized responsibility and decision making. Without centralized control or coordination, users in various departments may purchase their own computers and develop their own private applications without regard for compatibility or sharing of data. However, even in a small company, the achievement of standards is often difficult in an applications environment. At Pine Valley Furniture, the individual applications that were purchased from the software vendor were of a stand-alone variety and were not really compatible with one another (although all the applications were integrated with the Accounting General Ledger System). The various application programs often used different names and formats for the same data items, which made modifications more difficult and precluded the sharing of data.

Low Programmer Productivity.   In traditional file processing systems, the programmer must design each record and file used by a new application program and then code the data definitions in the program. The programmer must also select the file access method to be used and write procedural input/output statements in the program. This burden of designing files and records, describing data, and writing procedural input/output statements is repeated for each application program and constitutes a major portion of the system development effort. As a result, it is a major factor contributing to low programmer productivity, which continues to plague the data processing industry. Low programmer productivity, in turn, increases software costs, such as for the packaged software products purchased by Pine Valley Furniture.

Excessive Program Maintenance.   In file processing systems, descriptions of files, records, and data items are embedded within individual application programs. Therefore, any modification to a data file (such as a change of data name, format, or method of access) requires that the program (or programs) be modified. To illustrate, suppose that the data item CUSTOMER NAME had to be expanded from a 20-character field to a 25-character field in the

Customer Master File at Pine Valley Furniture. As a result of this simple change, several programs in the Order Filling System and Invoicing System would have to be modified.

The process of modifying existing programs is referred to as **program maintenance**. In many organizations today, 80% or more of the programming effort is devoted to this activity. Much of the shortage of computer programmers and the large backlog of new applications can be attributed to the burden of maintaining programs in file processing systems.

The disadvantages discussed here were especially pronounced in first- and second-generation application systems. In third-generation systems, a number of powerful support packages and tools have been introduced to help overcome (or at least minimize) some of the disadvantages. These software support packages include access methods for secondary keys, generalized file management and report writers, on-line query processing, transaction processing systems, data dictionaries, and high-level programming languages. However, even with these facilities, there remain the fundamental deficiencies of file processing systems: redundant data, low sharing of data, lack of standards and control, and low productivity.

DATA BASE APPROACH

The data base approach represents a different concept in information resource management. Data are viewed as an important, shared resource that must be managed like any other asset, such as people, materials, equipment, and money. According to Everest (1976), the data base concept is rooted in an attitude of *sharing* common data resources, *releasing control* of those data resources to a common responsible authority, and *cooperating in the maintenance* of those shared data resources.

The data base itself is the subject of this approach. According to Martin (1981, v), "A data base is a shared collection of interrelated data, designed to meet the needs of multiple types of end users. The data are stored so that they are independent of the programs that use them. A common and controlled approach is used in adding new data and modifying and retrieving existing data. A data base is not only shared by multiple users, but it is perceived differently by different users."

Data Base Approach for Pine Valley Furniture

Pine Valley Furniture Company has not yet attempted to implement any data bases. However, Mr. Knotts is aware of the data base approach and some of its potential advantages. Let's look at how the furniture company's applications system would be designed from a data base approach.

A model of the important data relationships at Pine Valley Furniture is illustrated in Figure 1-4. The model shown in this figure is called a **concep-**

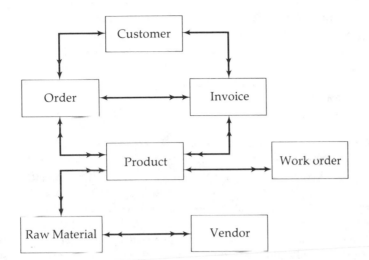

Figure 1-4
Conceptual data model
(Pine Valley Furniture).

tual model. Each rectangle in the model represents an entity. An **entity** is a person, place, object, event, or concept about which the organization wishes to record data. Arrows between entities represent relationships between those entities. A **relationship** is a logical association between two entities. For example, the arrow from "Customer" to "Order" in Figure 1-4 indicates that a given customer may have several outstanding orders with Pine Valley Furniture at any given time. Also, the arrow from "Order" to "Invoice" indicates that each customer order may have one or more invoices, each representing a partial shipment (an arrow with two heads means a "many" relationship—we will explain such relationships in Chapter 2).

At this point, we will merely illustrate a conceptual model. In later chapters, we will explain detailed procedures for deriving such models.

Benefits of the Data Base Approach

The data base approach offers a number of important advantages, compared to traditional approaches. These benefits include minimal data redundancy; consistency of data; integration of data; sharing of data; enforcement of standards; ease of application development; uniform security, privacy, and integrity controls; data accessibility and responsiveness; data independence; and reduced program maintenance.

Minimal Data Redundancy.   With the data base approach, previously separate (and redundant) data files are integrated into a single, logical structure. In addition, each data item occurrence is ideally recorded in only one place in the data base. For example, the fact that the SHIP-TO ADDRESS for a specific customer of Pine Valley Furniture is 328 Acacia Street might be recorded in four separate files in a file processing system (see Figure 1-3). But in a data base system, this fact will normally be recorded once.

We are not suggesting that *all* redundancy can or should be eliminated. Sometimes there are valid reasons for storing multiple copies of the same data (e.g., data access efficiency, data validation checks). However, in a data base system, redundancy is *controlled*. It is designed into the system to improve performance (or provide some other benefit), and the system is (or should be) aware of the redundancy.

Consistency of Data. By eliminating (or controlling) data redundancy, we greatly reduce the opportunities for inconsistency. For example, if each SHIP-TO ADDRESS is stored only once, we cannot have disagreement on the stored values. When controlled redundancy is permitted in the data base, the data base system itself should enforce consistency by updating each occurrence of a data item when a change occurs. If the data item SHIP-TO ADDRESS is stored in two separate records in the data base, then the data base system should update this data value in both records whenever a change occurs. Unfortunately, many systems today do not enforce data consistency in this manner.

Integration of Data. In a data base, data are organized into a single, logical structure, with logical relationships defined between associated data entities. In this way, the user can easily relate one item of data to another related item. For example, take another look at Figure 1-4. Suppose the user identifies a particular Product. Since this entity is logically related to the Raw Material entity, the user can easily determine what raw materials are required to build the product. Also, the user can check to see what raw materials are on order from a vendor, since the Raw Material entity is logically related to the Vendor entity. Data management software (described later) performs the function of associating logically related data items, regardless of the physical organization or location of the items in the data base.

 Sharing of Data. A data base is intended to be shared by all authorized users in the organization. For example, if Pine Valley Furniture implemented a data base, it would be designed to satisfy the information needs of Accounting, Sales, Manufacturing, Purchasing, and other departments. The company could essentially return to the "single set of books" that it had when it was first founded. Most data base systems today permit multiple users to share a data base concurrently, although certain restrictions are necessary, as described in later chapters.

In a data base system, each functional department is provided with its own view (or views) of the data base. Each such departmental view (or **user view**) is a subset of the conceptual data base model. For example, Figure 1-5 shows three possible user views for Pine Valley Furniture. The first user view is for the Sales Department and shows the relationship between the Customer and Order entities. The second user view is for the Accounting Department and shows the relationships among the Customer, Order, and

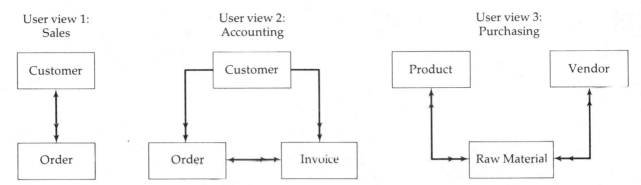

Figure 1-5
Three possible user views (Pine Valley Furniture).

Invoice entities. The third user view is for the Purchasing Department and shows the relationships among the Product, Vendor, and Raw Material entities. These user views simplify the sharing of data, since they provide each user with the precise view of data required to make a decision or perform some function without making the user aware of the overall complexity of the data base.

Enforcement of Standards. Establishing the data administration function is an important part of the data base approach. This organizational function has authority for defining and enforcing data standards. If a data administration function existed at Pine Valley Furniture, this office would approve all data names, formats, and data usage throughout the company. Moreover, all changes to data standards would have to be approved by data base administration. Data base administration is discussed in Chapter 10.

Ease of Application Development. A major advantage of the data base approach is that the cost and time for developing new business applications are greatly reduced. Studies show that once the data base has been designed and implemented, a programmer can code and debug a new application at least two to four times faster than with conventional data files (even greater improvements are possible with high-level languages). The reason for this improvement is that the programmer is no longer saddled with the burden of designing, building, and maintaining master files. Thus, the cost of software development is reduced, and new applications are available to the user in a much shorter time span.

Uniform Security, Privacy, and Integrity Controls. The data administration function has complete jurisdiction over the data base and is responsible for establishing controls for accessing, updating, and protecting data. Centralized control and standard procedures can offer improved levels of data base protection, compared to a dispersed data file system. However, if proper controls are not applied, a data base probably will be *more* vulnerable than conventional files, since a larger user community is sharing a common resource. We describe measures for data base security, privacy, and integrity in Chapter 11.

Data Accessibility and Responsiveness. A data base system provides multiple retrieval paths to each item of data, giving a user much greater flexibility in locating and retrieving data than with inflexible data files. Retrieval of data can cross traditional departmental boundaries. To illustrate, refer to the conceptual model for Pine Valley Furniture (Figure 1-4). Suppose that a customer calls requesting information about several items that have been back-ordered. While on the phone, the salesperson can look up the Customer record, then display the particular Order in question. The salesperson can then display the Product record for each item on that order. Finally, the salesperson can display the Work Order status for each back-ordered item to determine its completion date.

This example represents a routine (planned) sequence of retrievals. But a data base system can also satisfy certain ad hoc (one-time) requests for data without the need for an application program. For example, a manager might request a special summary of sales by size of store or by geographical location. Such requests can often be satisfied through the use of a user-oriented query language or report writer that is compatible with a data base system. Although some of these features may be provided in application systems, data base systems are generally much more responsive to changing information requirements.

Data Independence. The separation of data descriptions from the application programs that use the data is called **data independence**. As a result, an organization's data can change and evolve (within limits) without necessitating a change in the application programs that process the data. Data independence is one of the major objectives of the data base approach.

In traditional systems, application programs are *dependent* on their data files. That is, the descriptions of the data and the logic for accessing those data are built into each individual application program. Any change to the data file therefore requires modifying or rewriting the application program.

With the following example King (1981, 128–129) vividly illustrates the problems of data dependence:

> In a particular organization, data integration is proposed between payroll and personnel departments. Reading the latest literature on data base, the DP manager convinces user management to share their data requirements and the benefits are outlined. Program development progresses for the two application areas, and the development effort results in the successful implementation of both applications with all the expected benefits. Personnel is then asked by management to encourage the employees to carpool. This new function requires that new data elements (map coordinates, carpool request, carpool driver) be added to the data base. After careful consideration of the requirement, it is discovered that 15 bytes of new information will have to be added to the personnel record. Since this increase in record length will be added to the physical record, in conventional systems it must be added to the record length description in each program that accesses the record. The

DP manager is now faced with asking the payroll department to fund changes in all the payroll programs, when the payroll department is uninterested in the new data. The personnel department would like to accommodate the new requirement with a minimum of impact as well. In conventional systems, both application areas would have to change all programs that reference that record type. It is standard to encounter resistance on the part of user management when they are asked to accommodate data requirements for departments other than their own.

As this example illustrates, data dependence in a traditional data file environment discourages users from sharing data. Instead, independent data files are established for each new application program. The greater the number of programs and files that exist, the more reluctant is the DP department to respond to the latest needs of end users because of the costs of modifying programs and data.

Reduced Program Maintenance.   Stored data must be changed frequently for a variety of reasons. New data item types are added, data formats change, new storage devices or access methods are introduced, and so on. In a data file environment, these changes require modifying the application programs that access the data. The term *maintenance* refers to modifying or rewriting old programs to make them conform to new data formats, access methods, and so forth.

In a data base system, data are independent of the application programs that use them. Within limits, either the data or the application programs that use the data can be changed without necessitating a change in the other factor. As a result, program maintenance can be significantly reduced in a data base environment.

In this section, we have identified ten major benefits of the data base approach, explaining how they improve the information systems function in the organization. However, many of the stated benefits can also be translated into business terms, since they result in reduced costs of programming new applications, reduced costs of program maintenance, improved quality of managerial decisions, and reduced costs of waiting for information and/or postponing decisions.

When Can an Organization Justify Data Base?

Implementing the data base approach requires a large investment of organizational resources. An investment in new software products, additional hardware, and new personnel skills are normally required. Management commitment and time are also needed. Other costs include education and training, conversion, and documentation. To justify the conversion to data base, an organization should perform an extended analysis of benefits and costs. McFadden and Suver (1979) describe techniques for performing an analysis of data base costs and benefits.

A quick indication of whether data base is justified can often be obtained by considering the information systems context in a firm. The following factors favor the data base approach in an organization (U.S. Department of Commerce 1980):

1. Application needs are constantly changing, with considerable uncertainty as to the important data elements, expected update or processing functions, and expected volumes to be handled.

2. Rapid access is frequently required to answer ad hoc questions.

3. There is a need to reduce long lead times and high development costs in developing new application systems.

4. Many data elements must be shared by users throughout the organization.

5. There is a need to communicate and relate data across functional and departmental boundaries.

6. There is a need to improve the quality and consistency of the data resource and to control access to that resource.

7. Substantial dedicated programming assistance is not normally available.

COMPONENTS OF THE DATA BASE ENVIRONMENT

The major components of a typical data base environment have been identified by Clark (1980). By studying these components and their relationships, you will gain a better understanding of the data base approach and its advantages. The six components shown in Figure 1-6 are described briefly in the following list. Each component is described in greater detail in subsequent chapters.

1. *User group.* The user group consists of all requesters of data. There are three basic categories of user requests: read only, add/delete, and modify. All user requests for data are made through the data base management system.

2. *Data base management system, or DBMS.* The DBMS is a software system that receives and satisfies all requests for data. Normally, the DBMS provides concurrent access to multiple data base users. Also, the DBMS must be able to recover or restore a damaged data base from backup copies and logs or audit trails of data base activity.

3. *Data base.* The data base is the physical repository of all user data. For example, student information is contained within a university data base.

4. *Data dictionary/directory, or DD/D.* The DD/D is a repository of all *definitions* of data used by the organization. For example, all data item names,

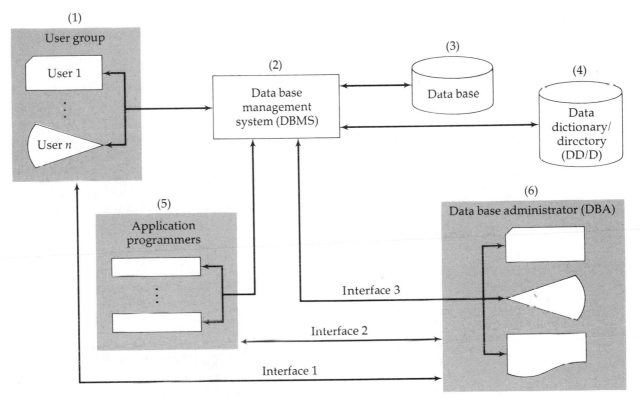

Figure 1-6
DBMS operational environment.
(Source: Clark 1980, 6.)

lengths, and representations are stored in the DD/D. As we will see in later chapters, the DD/D is a key tool in managing the data resource.

5. *Application programmers.* Application programmers write code to process user requests for data. For example, an accounts receivable program written in COBOL by an application programmer may be used to update customer accounts in a data base. With the increasing use of high-level fourth-generation languages, end users are often able to request data without using application programs.

6. *Data base administrator, or DBA.* The data base administrator is a manager who is responsible for the cost-effective definition of an organization's data. Responsibilities of the DBA include working with users to define the data they use, modeling the data, designing data bases, developing adequate controls, and evaluating new data base technologies. We define these responsibilities in detail in Chapter 10.

In addition to the operational entities, several critical interfaces between entities are defined in Figure 1-6. Following is a brief description of the three interfaces emphasized in the figure.

1. *User-DBA interface.* The DBA defines user rights and responsibilites in retrieving data and mediates any conflicts that might arise. Also, the DBA trains users in data base technology so they can exploit its advantages.
2. *Programmer-DBA interface.* The DBA controls all data definitions and establishes standards for all application programs that access the data base. The DBA also trains programmers in using the DBMS.
3. *DBA-DBMS interface.* The DBA monitors operational performance of the DBMS and initiates changes that may be necessary to improve response time or other operational characteristics.

In summary, the DBMS operational environment shown in Figure 1-6 is an integrated system of hardware, software, and people that is designed to facilitate the storage, retrieval, and control of the information resource (Clark 1980).

RELATIONSHIP OF DATA BASE TO MIS AND DSS

Information systems (and data bases) must satisfy the information needs of all levels of management in an organization—operational, middle, and top management. However, the information needs at the various levels are quite different. In fact, it is often said that an organization requires two types of information systems—operational and management.

Operational information systems support everyday operations of the organization. They provide detailed information such as status reports, action documents, and displays. The primary objectives in operational information systems are accuracy and rapid response.

Management information systems (MIS) provide information required by managers for planning and decision making. They provide summary information to managers (especially at higher levels). The emphasis in management information systems is on flexibility and ease of use.

Traditional information systems have essentially been operational in their orientation, and attempts to structure these systems to provide management information have met only limited success. However, the emergence of data bases, high-level languages, personal computers, and other technology has finally made it possible to provide systems that truly support management planning and decision making. In fact, these systems are often called decision support systems.

A **decision support system** (DSS) is a collection of resources designed to support managerial decision making. A DSS will normally include the following components:

1. A terminal (often a personal computer) located in a manager's office or other convenient location.

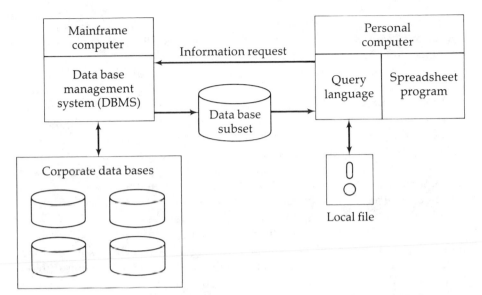

Figure 1-7
Example of a simple
decision support system
(DSS).

2. A DBMS for building, accessing, and manipulating local files or data bases.
3. A powerful, user-friendly language for retrieving and manipulating data.
4. Modeling tools (such as forecasting and simulation) for evaluating various alternative decisions.

A simple (but very common) example of a DSS is shown in Figure 1-7. In this example, a personal computer (used by a manager) is linked to the organization's mainframe computer. The mainframe computer uses a DBMS to maintain the organization's data bases, which contain operational-level data.

The manager using the personal computer uses a high-level query language to formulate English-language requests for data relevant to a particular decision-making situation. These requests are passed to the mainframe computer, which uses the DBMS to extract the requested data from the data base. These data are passed to the personal computer, where they may then be displayed or summarized and stored as a local file or data base. Also, the manager may use the data in a model (in this case, a financial spreadsheet program) to evaluate various alternatives. Thus, we see that the organizational data bases can be used as a source of data for a DSS.

SUMMARY

In this chapter, we have presented data as an important organizational resource, deserving of top management planning and control. The traditional approach to managing this resource—through dispersed data files—

often results in redundant and inconsistent data, inflexible systems, and exorbitant maintenance costs. The net result is systems that exceed cost estimates yet are not responsive to management needs.

The data base approach represents a completely different approach to managing data resources. With this approach, the overall information needs of the organization are defined before individual application programs are designed and implemented. Advantages of the data base approach include minimum data redundancy, maximum data sharing, and reduced maintenance costs. Many of these advantages are the result of data independence, which insulates end user views (and application programs) from changes to the data base itself. To achieve these benefits, a number of additional costs must be incurred. These include the costs of new software and hardware, skilled personnel, training, and conversion to data base.

Major components of a data base system include the data base management system (DBMS), which is used to manage the user data base, and the data dictionary facility, which is used to manage the data dictionary/directory. Data administration is the organizational function primarily responsible for managing the data resource.

CHAPTER REVIEW

Review Questions

1. Define each of the following terms:
   a. data
   b. information
   c. data base
   d. application system
   e. application program
   f. data file
   g. record
   h. data item
   i. data independence
   j. data base management system (DBMS)

2. Contrast the following terms:
   a. data dependence; data independence
   b. data base management system; decision support system
   c. user data base; data dictionary/directory
   d. operational information system; management information system
   e. user group; application programmers
   f. data; information

3. List and briefly describe seven disadvantages of many traditional application systems.

4. Explain why data redundancy is so common in traditional application systems.

5. List and briefly describe ten benefits that can often be achieved with the data base approach, compared to traditional application systems.

6. Briefly describe six major components in a data base environment.

7. List seven factors that, if present, would favor the data base approach in an organization.

Problems and Exercises

1. Draw a conceptual model (similar to Figure 1-4) for each of the following:
   a. Football team: entities are Team, Coaches, Agents, Players, Games.
   b. Family: entities are Mother, Father, Children, Cars.
   c. Bank: entities are Branches, Customers, Tellers, Accounts, Transactions.

2. Add the entity Employee to the conceptual model in Figure 1-4. Assume that a given work order may require one or more employees.

3. Pine Valley Furniture wants to create a production scheduling application. Draw a diagram of an application system (see Figure 1-3). Assume that this system requires information about products, work orders, and raw materials. Also assume that three application programs will be required.

4. Show a user view (similar to those in Figure 1-5) for a production scheduling system at Pine Valley Furniture. Assume that the company has implemented a data base using the conceptual model shown in Figure 1-4. This application requires information about products, work orders, and raw materials.

5. Visit an organization that has installed the data base approach. Talk to the person in data administration and determine each of the following:
   a. Which of the benefits of the data base approach have been realized by the organization?
   b. What major components of a data base system (Figure 1-6) are present in this organization?
   c. Does the organization have a conceptual model? In what form is it represented?

References

Auerbach Publishers, eds. 1981. *Practical Data Base Management*. Princeton, N.J.: Auerbach Publishers.

Clark, Jon D. 1980. *Data Base Selection, Design, and Administration.* New York: Praeger Publishers.

Diebold, John. 1979. "IRM: New Directions in Management." *Infosystems* (October).

Everest, Gordon C. 1976. "Database Management Systems Tutorial." In *Readings in Management Information Systems,* ed. Gordon B. Davis and Gordon C. Everest. New York: McGraw-Hill.

King, Judy M. 1981. *Evaluating Data Base Management Systems.* New York: Van Nostrand Reinhold.

McFadden, Fred R., and James D. Suver. 1979. "Costs and Benefits of a Data Base System." *Harvard Business Review* (January-February): 131–139.

Martin, James. 1981. *An End-User's Guide to Data Base.* Englewood Cliffs, N.J.: Prentice-Hall.

Synott, William R., and William H. Gruber. 1981. *Information Resource Management.* New York: Wiley-Interscience.

U.S. Department of Commerce. National Bureau of Standards. 1980. *Guideline for Planning and Management of Database Applications.* FIPS Publication 77. Washington, D.C.

## 2

Data Concepts and Characteristics

INTRODUCTION

In his book *The Third Wave*, Alvin Toffler (1980) describes the emergence of a new era, which he terms the age of the information society. According to Toffler, the information society represents a "third wave" in societal evolution, displacing the earlier agricultural and industrial societies. The information society is bringing about fundamental changes in work patterns, organizational arrangements, and individual life styles.

To most persons in a modern, computerized society, this "third wave" is already becoming a fact of life. We are practically submerged in information at work, at home, and at most places in between. Personal computers are invading our homes as well as our offices and factories. Managers and other professionals are often bombarded by more information than they can assimilate or use effectively.

Despite our first-hand familiarity with data and information, most of us have a rather simplistic and one-dimensional view of these commodities. To understand data as an organizational resource, we must have accurate definitions and understand the concepts and characteristics of data. In this chapter, we describe the nature of data and develop many of the basic definitions. We also describe the views of data required by its various users and the concept of data independence.

DATA VERSUS INFORMATION

The terms *data* and *information* are often used interchangeably. In this section, we will distinguish between these two terms.

Data are facts concerning people, places, events, or other objects or concepts. We will assume that data are recorded on some computer-processable medium such as magnetic ink or optical characters, magnetic disk surface, or computer semiconductor memory. Data are often relatively useless to human decision makers until they have been processed or refined in some manner.

Information is data that have been processed and refined and then displayed in a format that is convenient for decision making or other organizational activities. For example, a report listing customers whose credit accounts are past due by 60 days or more contains information that is useful to a credit manager.

In practice, the distinction between data and information is often difficult to maintain. Data become information when used in the context of making a specific decision or when applied to the solution of a particular problem. Thus, the definition depends on how the data (or information) are used, rather than on inherent properties of the data. As a result, in the context of information systems, it is common to use the terms interchangeably.

In this text, we will use the term *data* when referring to the facts recorded in a data base. However, we will often use the term *information* to refer to the overall "information resource" of an organization. Today, organizations frequently extract selected portions of one data base, summarize, and then store in a separate data base (often on a personal computer). We will not distinguish this second, derived data base by a separate term.

NATURE OF DATA

In this section, we will provide the basic definitions of data. As shown in Figure 2-1, there are three realms, or levels of abstraction, that must be considered in describing data. These realms are reality (the real world), metadata ("information about data"), and the actual data.

Reality

Reality consists of the organization itself, the various components of the organization, and the environment in which the organization operates. Any organization is a collection of people, facilities, and artifacts (or objects) that are organized to satisfy certain goals. Each organization interacts with its environment and both influences and is influenced by that environment.

An **entity** is any object or event about which the organization chooses to collect and store data. An entity may be a tangible object, such as an employee, a product, a computer, or a customer, or it may be an intangible item, such as a bank account, a cost center, a part failure, or an airline flight. Examples of entities at Pine Valley Furniture Company include customers, products, sales orders, work centers, and employees.

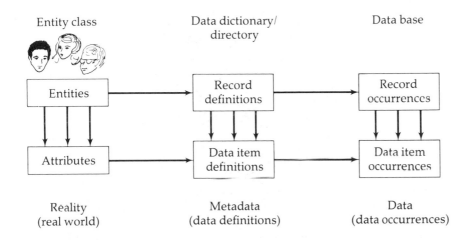

Figure 2-1
Three realms used to
describe data.

An **entity class** is a collection of entities that possess similar charac-teristics. Examples of entity classes are Customers, Students, and Patients. Entity classes are sometimes referred to as entity sets or entity types.

Entities are grouped into entity classes for convenience. In general, each entity is assigned to one, and only one, entity class. However, the definition of entity classes, as well as the assignment of an entity to an entity class, can be somewhat arbitrary. For example, consider the Employee entity class. Does this consist of persons who are full-time employees only, or does it also include part-time employees? And, what entities constitute the entity class Work Center? Individual machines, machine groups, or entire departments? Questions such as these must be resolved before appro-priate models of organizational data can be developed.

The number of entity classes for an organization depends on the size and complexity of that organization. For example, a medium-sized corpora-tion typically defines several hundred entity classes, whereas a small com-pany such as Pine Valley Furniture would probably have less than 100 entity classes.

Pine Valley Furniture

CASE EXAMPLE

For each entity class, there are a number of attributes of interest to an organization. An **attribute** is a property of an entity that we choose to record. For example, two entity classes at Pine Valley Furniture Company are Customers and Products. Here are some of the attributes for these entities:

Customers	Products
Customer number	Product number
Name	Description
Address	Finish
Telephone number	Price
Credit limit	Weight
Balance	

For each entity class, ten or more attributes are typically defined. Therefore, an organization with several hundred entity classes may expect to define several thousand attributes.

Each entity in an entity class must possess at least one attribute (or several in combination) that distinguishes it from other entities in that class. This unique property of an entity is called an **identifier.** For example, a Social Security number is an identifier for an employee, and a product number is an identifier for a product. The quantity of a particular product may be identified on a customer invoice by a combination of invoice number and product number. The entity identifier must be unique; no two entities in an entity class may have the same value for this attribute.

Attributes are properties of individual entities. Another type of property that we are interested in is the **association,** which is some form of relationship between two (or more) entities. Associations may exist between entities of the same entity class or between entities from two (or more) entity classes. Here is an example of each type of association at Pine Valley Furniture:

1. In the Employee entity class, some employees are managers while the remainder are workers. An association called Manages allows us to determine the workers reporting to a given manager (or the manager of a given worker).

2. There is an entity class called Customers and another called Orders. By defining an association called Open Orders between entities from these two entity classes, we can determine all outstanding orders for a given customer.

Entities are components of the real world of the organization and its environment. However, it is usually impractical for a manager (or other employee) to make decisions or take actions based on direct observation of these entities. Imagine a manager having to walk to a warehouse and count the items in a bin whenever an inventory action is required, or having to call a customer to obtain the shipping address prior to dispatching each shipment. Instead of direct observation, the organization relies on a model of the entities in the form of data that describe their properties. This brings us to the second realm of data: metadata.

Metadata

Metadata is information about the data in an organization. It is used by data administrators and others to develop logical models of an organization's entities and the associations between those entities. Metadata is stored and maintained in the organization's data dictionary/directory.

Corresponding to each entity class in the real world, there is normally one record type defined in the metadata realm. Also, corresponding to each attribute, there is a data item type defined in the metadata realm (see Figure 2-1).

A **data item** is a unit fact. It is the smallest named unit of data in a data base and therefore the smallest unit of data that has meaning to a user. Examples of data items are EMPLOYEE-NAME, STUDENT#, and ORDER-DATE (we often use # as an abbreviation for NUMBER, as in STUDENT#). Information that is normally catalogued in the data dictionary/directory for each data item type includes the data item name, length, type (or representation), and a brief narrative description.

A **data aggregate** is a collection of data items that is named and referenced as a whole. For example, a data aggregate called NAME might be composed of the data items LAST-NAME, FIRST-NAME, and MIDDLE-INITIAL. Also, a data aggregate called SALES might consist of four data items: SALES-FIRST-QUARTER, SALES-SECOND-QUARTER, SALES-THIRD-QUARTER, and SALES-FOURTH-QUARTER. When data aggregates are used, they must be defined in the data dictionary/directory. Metadata that are recorded for each data aggregate type include the data aggregate name, description, and names of the included data items. In COBOL, data aggregates are referred to as group items.

Data items are sometimes called data elements, fields, or attributes. However, we prefer to use the term *data item* when referring to a unit of data. *Field* is a physical, rather than logical, term that refers to the column positions within a record where a data item is located. We have already defined *attribute* as a property of a real-world entity rather than as a data-oriented term. However, since there is a data item for each attribute, the two terms are often used interchangeably. In fact, in the relational model (presented in Chapter 6), the term *attribute* is used instead of *data item*. The term *data element* is simply a synonym for *data item*, but is used less frequently.

A **record** is a named collection of data items and/or data aggregates. Most organizations define one record *type* for each entity class. Thus, if there is an entity class called Sales Orders, we might choose to define a record type called SALES-ORDER-RECORD. Metadata defining each record type are catalogued in the data dictionary/directory. These metadata include the record name, description, size (or length), component data items and aggregates, and identification of primary and secondary keys (described shortly).

In addition to records describing entities, some records describe associations (relationships) between entities. Often this type of record (called an **intersection** record) arises when some event has occurred involving the associated entities.

A **key** is a data item used to identify a record. There are two basic types of keys: primary keys and secondary keys.

A **primary key** is a data item that uniquely identifies a record. The primary key of a record corresponds to the identifier of a real-world entity. For example, STUDENT# would normally be the primary key for STUDENT records. As with identifiers, there may be several possible (or candidate) primary keys for the same record. Also, two or more data items may be required to identify a record.

A **secondary key** is a data item that normally does not uniquely identify a record but identifies a number of records in a set that share the same property. For example, the data item MAJOR might be used as a secondary key for STUDENT records. Of course, this data item does not identify a unique record; for example, many students will have business as a major. However, the secondary key does identify a subset of students who are business majors. Secondary keys arise when data are referenced by categories (this will be explained in Chapter 5).

Data

The third (and last) realm in Figure 2-1 consists of data **occurrences**. For each entity in the real world, there is normally a record occurrence that contains data item values describing that entity. For example, at Pine Valley Furniture, there are 50 employees in the Employee entity class. Thus, there are 50 Employee record occurrences in the data base. However, there is only one definition of this record type in the metadata.

A **file** is a named collection of all occurrences of a given record type. For example, the Employee file at Pine Valley Furniture Company consists of 50 Employee records at the present time.

Notice the important distinction between metadata (data definitions) and data (data occurrences). Metadata (such as data item definitions) are not stored in the data base. Conversely, occurrences of user data are not stored in the data dictionary/directory.

A file may be visualized as a two-dimensional array, called a **flat file**. An example of a flat file arrangement of data is shown in Figure 2-2. The table, or two-dimensional array, shown in this figure contains sample product data for Pine Valley Furniture Company. Thus, the data correspond to the Product entity class. Each column of the table contains values for a particular data item. The data item names at the top of the table correspond to product attributes. Each row of the table represents a record occurrence and corre-

Data items

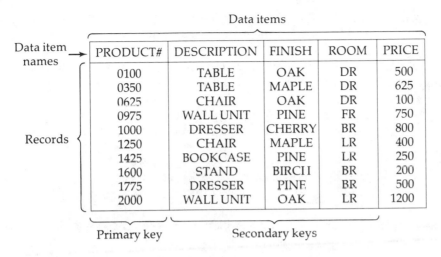

PRODUCT#	DESCRIPTION	FINISH	ROOM	PRICE
0100	TABLE	OAK	DR	500
0350	TABLE	MAPLE	DR	625
0625	CHAIR	OAK	DR	100
0975	WALL UNIT	PINE	FR	750
1000	DRESSER	CHERRY	BR	800
1250	CHAIR	MAPLE	LR	400
1425	BOOKCASE	PINE	LR	250
1600	STAND	BIRCH	BR	200
1775	DRESSER	PINE	BR	500
2000	WALL UNIT	OAK	LR	1200

Data item names

Records

Primary key   Secondary keys

Figure 2-2
Flat file representation of data.

sponds to one product entity. Notice that there is only one value at the intersection of each row and column. This is an important property of flat files.

The primary key for the PRODUCT records is PRODUCT#. A particular value of PRODUCT# (such as 1250) uniquely identifies a record occurrence. The data items DESCRIPTION, FINISH, and ROOM have been designated as secondary keys. A particular value for one of these keys designates a subset of records (rather than a particular record). For example, the description "wall unit" identifies two records (product numbers 0975 and 2000).

To complete the description of the three realms in Figure 2-1, we may define a **data base** as a named collection of interrelated files. Thus, a data base contains data occurrences that describe one or more entity classes and the associations between those entity classes.

ASSOCIATIONS BETWEEN DATA ITEMS

In this section, we describe simple graphical techniques for representing data items and the associations between data items. Later we will show how associations arise between records. Each type of data item is represented by an ellipse (or "bubble") with the data item name enclosed, as follows:

An **association** is a logical, meaningful connection between data items. An association implies that values for the associated data items are in some way dependent on each other.

A data base contains hundreds (or even thousands) of data items. If there are N data items, then there are $N(N-1)$ possible associations between the data items. Fortunately, many of these possible associations are meaningless and of no interest to the organization. For example, there is no meaningful association between the following two data items:

However, there is an important association between these two data items:

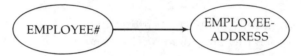

The association results from the observation that each employee has an address. We will represent associations by arrows connecting the data items, as in the previous illustration.

Types of Associations

Suppose that we have two data items, A and B. From data item A to data item B there are two possible associations, or mappings: one-to-one and one-to-many. We will represent these associations with the following notation:

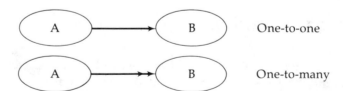

A **one-to-one association** from data item A to data item B means that for a specified period of time, a given value of A has one and only one value of B associated with it. That is, if we know the value of A, then the value of B is implicitly known. We represent a one-to-one association with a single-headed arrow. Assuming that at a given period of time each employee has exactly one address, the following mapping is one-to-one:

A **one-to-many association** from data item A to data item B means that at each period in time, a given value of A has zero, one, or an arbitrary number of values of B associated with it. We represent a one-to-many mapping with a double-headed arrow. Assuming that for a specified period of time each employee may have taken zero, one, or more than one training course, the following mapping is one-to-many:

There is another type of association between data items, called a conditional association, which is a variation of those already described. With a **conditional association,** for a given value of data item A there are two possibilities: either there is exactly one value of data item B, or there is no value of data item B. We diagram a conditional association as a one-to-one association with a zero recorded on the arrow:

Here is an example of a conditional association in a hospital environment:

That is, each hospital bed will be assigned to one patient or, at some instant in time, will be unassigned.

Reverse Associations

If there is an association from data item A to data item B, there is also a reverse association from B to A. This leads to three possible associations between data items: one-to-one, one-to-many, and many-to-many. These associations are diagrammed as follows:

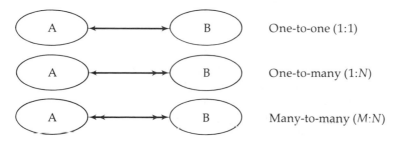

Figure 2-3
Examples of associations
between data items.

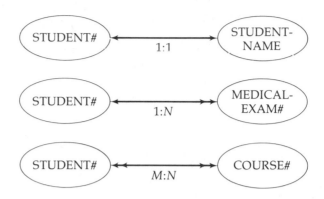

A **one-to-one association** means that at a given instant in time, each value of data item A is associated with exactly one value of data item B. Conversely, each value of B is associated with one value of A.

A **one-to-many association** means that at a given instant in time, each value of data item A is associated with zero, one, or more than one value of data item B. However, each value of B is associated with exactly one value of A. The mapping from B to A is said to be many-to-one, since there may be many values of B associated with one value of A.

A **many-to-many association** means that at a given instant in time, each value of data item A is associated with zero, one, or many values of data item B. Also, each value of B is associated with zero, one, or many values of A.

Examples of these three associations are shown in Figure 2-3. If we assume that no two students have the same name, then the association between STUDENT# and STUDENT-NAME is 1:1 (in reality, duplicate student names must be expected). The association between STUDENT# and MEDICAL-EXAM# is 1:N (each student may take several medical exams, but each exam pertains to a particular student). Finally, the association between STUDENT# and COURSE# is M:N (each student registers in many courses, and each course has many students registered).

In modeling an organization's data, we are not always interested in a given reverse association. If a particular reverse association is not of interest, the arrowheads are simply omitted in the link from data item B to data item A.

Bubble Charts

The notation we have introduced for representing data items and associations can be used to develop complex data models. We will use the term *bubble charts* to refer to data models that are expressed using this notation. Bubble charts are useful for grouping data items into records and for deriving more complex data models.

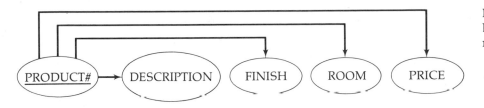

Figure 2-4
Bubble chart of Product
record.

PRODUCT#	DESCRIPTION	FINISH	ROOM	PRICE

(a)

0975	WALL UNIT	PINE	FR	750

(b)

Figure 2-5
Representing record types
and occurrences.
(a) Product record type.
(b) Product record
occurrence.

Grouping Data Items. A record is a collection of data items that represents a particular entity. Each record has a primary key that uniquely identifies the record. Therefore, there is a one-to-one association from the primary key of a record to the remaining data items in the record. For example, consider the Product records for Pine Valley Furniture Company (see Figure 2-2). A bubble chart showing the structure of these records appears in Figure 2-4. The data item PRODUCT# is underlined to indicate that it is the primary key for this record type.

Data items are grouped into records (such as in Figure 2-4) using a technique called **normalization.** This is a step-by-step procedure for analyzing the associations between data items. We describe normalization in Chapters 6 and 7.

We will represent record types by rectangles containing the names of the data items included in the record. Again, the primary key is underlined. A representation of the Product record type is shown in Figure 2-5a, while Figure 2-5b shows one occurrence of this record type.

Bubble charts also provide insight into the nature of secondary keys. Assume that a secondary key does not uniquely identify a record (the usual case). Therefore, there is a one-to-many association from that secondary key to the primary key of the record, since there may be many primary key values associated with a given value of the secondary key. For example, FINISH is a secondary key for the Product record type. Therefore, there is a one-to-many association from FINISH to PRODUCT# (see Figure 2-6a). Figure 2-6b shows one occurrence, where the secondary key value is OAK. There are three associated product numbers: 0100, 0625, and 2000.

Secondary keys provide a powerful technique for retrieving selected data records without searching an entire file. In the Product file, we can list

Figure 2-6
Representing secondary keys.
(a) Bubble chart with secondary key (finish).
(b) Occurrences for a particular value (oak).

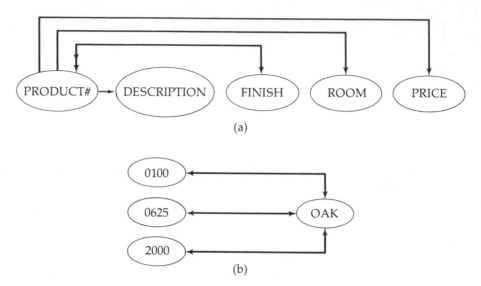

(a)

(b)

all products whose DESCRIPTION is WALL UNIT or whose FINISH is OAK (or a combination of these two factors). In Chapter 5 we describe how secondary keys are represented and used.

Sometimes, secondary keys are unique. In this case, the secondary key could be used as a primary key; however, the user has chosen some other data item as the primary key. We refer to a unique secondary key as an **alternate key.** For example, an automobile may be uniquely identified by either its license plate number or its engine number. If the license plate number is chosen as the primary key, then the engine number is an alternate key.

Modeling Data Structures.   In addition to grouping data items into records, we can use bubble charts to develop more complex data structures. We begin with simple user views of data and progressively combine these into more complex data models. For example, Figure 2-7 shows two user views for Pine Valley Furniture. User view 1 contains data for the Customer entity class and is required by the Sales Department to obtain information about individual customers (the data item called CUSTOMER DETAILS actually represents several data items such as SHIP-TO-ADDRESS, PHONE#, and so on). User view 2 is required by the Orders Department to look up details of customer orders (ORDER# is the primary key).

Figure 2-7c shows how these two views are combined into a single view. Since CUSTOMER# in user view 2 is already contained in user view 1, it is not repeated in the combined view.

The process of combining user views to obtain an overall data model is described in Chapter 8. Since an organization often must structure a data model with several hundred (or even several thousand) data items, data base design software packages are frequently used to assist this process.

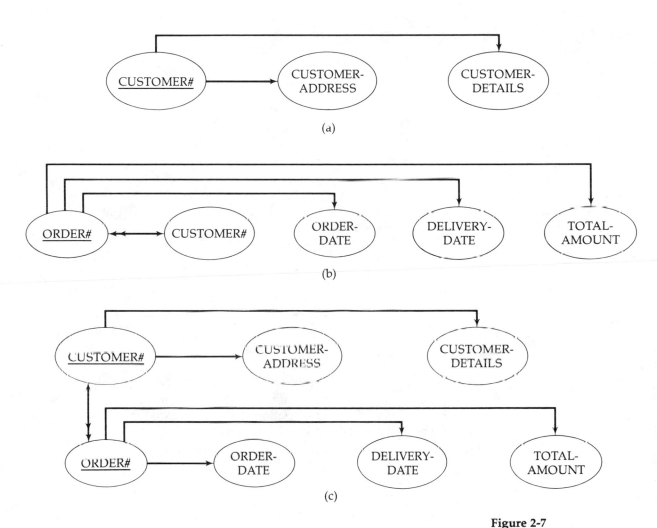

(a)

(b)

(c)

Figure 2-7
Data modeling:
combining user views.
(a) User view 1: Sales.
(b) User view 2: Orders.
(c) Combined views.

ASSOCIATIONS BETWEEN RECORDS

When the data model has been expressed in the form of a bubble chart (as in Figure 2-7), the next step is to group the data items into records. When this is done, the result is a set of record types with associations between them. For example, Figure 2-8 shows the result of grouping the data items in Figure 2-7c into records. There are two resulting record types: Customer and Order. Since the association between the primary keys (CUSTOMER# and ORDER#) is 1:N, the association between the record types is also 1:N. This reflects the fact that in the real world, at a given instant in time, a customer may have zero, one, or more than one outstanding order.

Figure 2-8
Association between two
record types.

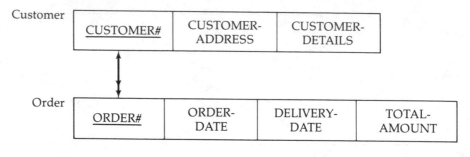

Figure 2-9
Types of associations.

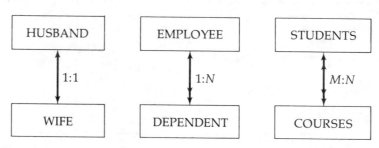

Types of Associations

Between any two record types there are three possible associations: one-to-one, one-to-many, and many-to-many. Examples of these associations are shown in Figure 2-9. The associations between record types have the same meanings as the associations between data items.

Data Structure Diagrams

When a data model has been completed, the resulting chart may contain dozens (or hundreds) of record types. The associations between the record types are also shown. We refer to a chart representing a data model as a **data structure diagram** (the term *Bachman diagram* is also used, named after the person who first proposed this technique).

A data structure diagram for a portion of the data base at Pine Valley Furniture Company is shown in Figure 2-10. This diagram contains four record types: CUSTOMER, ORDER, PRODUCT, and ORDER LINE. Three of these record types (PRODUCT, ORDER, and CUSTOMER) represent real-world entities. The ORDER LINE record type represents the association between Orders and Products, as we will see shortly. All the associations shown in the data structure diagram are one-to-many. In large, complex data structure diagrams, it is often useful to label each association arrow with a meaningful name, as illustrated in the figure.

One occurrence of this data structure is shown in Figure 2-11. Customer #B324 has two outstanding orders: #221 and #316. Order #221 is for two dressers (product #1000) and one bookcase (product #1425). The total

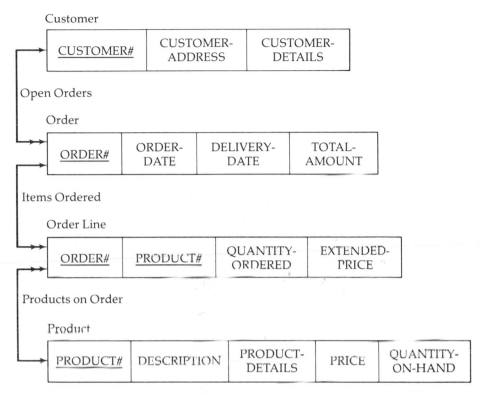

Figure 2-10
Data structure diagram
(Pine Valley Furniture).

amount of this order is $1850. Order #316 is for one dresser (product #1000) and three chairs (product #0625). The total amount of this order is $1100. Notice that product #1000 appears on two separate orders for the same customer.

The data structure diagram in Figure 2-10 provides a logical model of the data required for the "demand side" of business operations at Pine Valley Furniture Company. By providing a primary key value, a user can obtain data about a particular customer, order, or product. Also, by providing a secondary key value, a user can display a group of records that share a certain property (for example, all customers whose credit limit is $5000). Finally, by using the associations between records, a user can obtain much additional information, such as all outstanding orders for a given customer, all products (or line items) on a given order, and all outstanding orders for a given product. Of course, a full data structure diagram for this company would include many more data items, record types, and associations.

The links between records in Figure 2-10 represent logical associations between records (and their associated entities). They do not represent "pointers" or other physical means of implementing associations or relationships. We describe techniques for implementing such associations in Chapter 5.

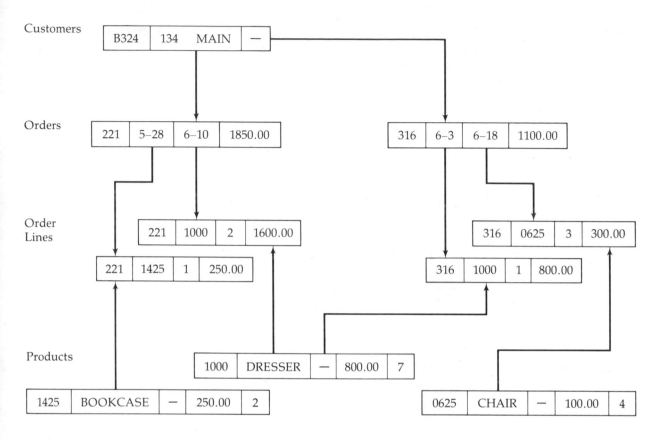

Figure 2-11
An occurrence of a data structure.

Concatenated Keys

Some data items cannot be uniquely identified by a simple primary key that consists of one data item. A primary key that consists of two or more data items is required to identify these data items. Such a key is called a **concatenated key** (the term *concatenated* means "joined together"). The term *composite key* is also sometimes used.

In Figure 2-10, the ORDER LINE record type has a concatenated key consisting of ORDER# joined with PRODUCT#. Each occurrence of this record type represents one line on a particular customer order. Both ORDER# and PRODUCT# are required to identify the QUANTITY-ORDERED and therefore the EXTENDED-PRICE. Neither ORDER# nor PRODUCT# by itself is sufficient to identify these items. For example, Figure 2-11 shows that for product #1000, the order quantity on order #221 is 2, while on order #316 it is 1.

On a bubble chart we will show a concatenated key as a single bubble with the data items that compose the key joined by a plus sign, +. Here is an example:

Many-to-Many Associations. Actually, the concatenated key in ORDER LINE (ORDER#+PRODUCT#) has a deeper meaning. There are no many-to-many associations expressly shown in Figure 2-10; only one-to-many associations are shown. Yet it seems that there should be a many-to-many association between Orders and Products: each customer order may request several products, while at a given instant each product may have zero, one, or many outstanding orders.

The association between the Order entity class and the Product entity class is indeed many-to-many, as shown in Figure 2-12. However, this association has been resolved into two one-to-many associations by the creation of a third record type called ORDER LINE (Figure 2-12b). The

Figure 2-12
Resolving many-to-many associations.
(a) A many-to-many association.
(b) Two one-to-many associations.

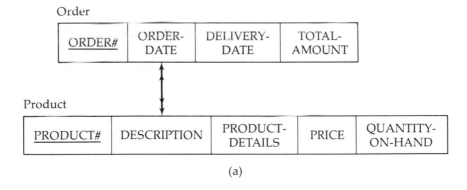

(a)

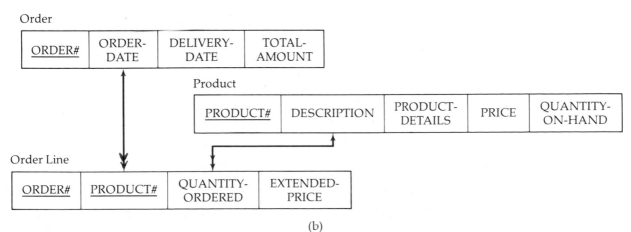

(b)

ORDER LINE record type contains data about the association between the ORDER record type and the PRODUCT record type (namely, QUANTITY-ORDERED and EXTENDED-PRICE). A record that contains such data is called an **intersection record**. The primary key of such a record is the concatenation of the associated primary keys (in this case, ORDER# + PRODUCT#).

If a data base has been properly designed, the data structure diagram will rarely contain many-to-many associations. During the process of normalization (described in Chapters 6 and 7), these associations will be resolved into appropriate 1:N associations, as in the preceding example. Notice that the design shown in Figure 2-12b is superior to that shown in Figure 2-12a. The intersection data in ORDER LINE is a more natural way for the user to view the data.

It might seem that resolving a many-to-many association is accomplished at the cost of additional redundancy. After all, the data items ORDER# and PRODUCT# are repeated in ORDER LINE. However, we must remember that a data structure diagram is a *logical* (not physical) representation of the data. Separate occurrences of the data items ORDER# and PRODUCT# may or may not be physically stored in the ORDER LINE record occurrences. We describe physical data representations in Chapters 4 and 5.

Deeply Concatenated Keys.   In the preceding example, the intersection record allowed us to form an association between two entity classes—Orders and Products. Sometimes we wish to form an association between three or more entity classes. Again, we can use an intersection record for this purpose.

Suppose that a company orders parts from several different suppliers. These parts are stocked at several different warehouses. Thus, we have a many-to-many association between three entity classes: Suppliers, Parts, and Warehouses. At a given instant in time, the quantity of parts on order (QTY-ON-ORDER) depends on three data items: PART#, SUPPLIER#, and WHSE#. We express the relationship between these data items as follows:

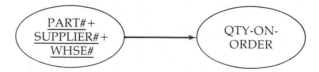

The associations between entity classes are shown in Figure 2-13. There are two intersection records: INVENTORY and ORDER. The INVENTORY record type contains the data item QUANTITY-ON-HAND, which represents the quantity of parts on hand at a particular warehouse (once a part is in inventory, the identity of the supplier is no longer of interest). The ORDER record type contains the QUANTITY-ON-ORDER, which depends on three data items as described earlier. This record type allows us to convert an *M:N* association between three entity classes into three 1:N associations.

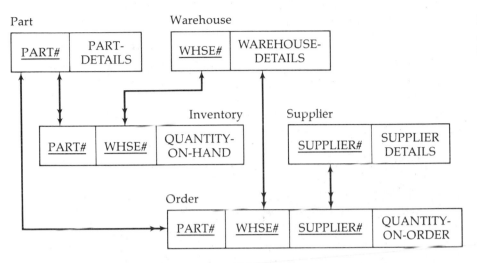

Figure 2-13
Associations between
multiple record types.

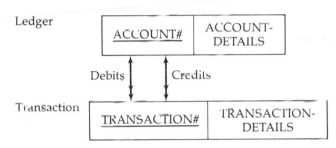

Figure 2-14
Multiple associations
between two record types.

Multiple Associations Between Two Record Types

In data modeling, it is sometimes appropriate to define two or more associations between the same two record types. For example, Figure 2-14 shows the data structure diagram for a simple accounting application. There are two record types: LEDGER and TRANSACTION. In the Ledger file, there is one record occurrence for each numbered account in the general ledger. The Transaction file contains recent transactions that are posted to the general ledger accounts. There are two one-to-many associations between Ledger and Transaction, called DEBIT and CREDIT. At a given instant in time, DEBIT associates all transactions, if any, that cause a debit entry to a particular ledger account. CREDIT provides a similar association between a given ledger account and transactions that result in credit entries.

When there are two or more associations between two record types, as in this example, each association must be named or labeled so that the nature of each association is clear to the users. It is often desirable to name single associations between record types in a data structure diagram, since this tends to improve user understanding of the data model.

Recursive Associations (Loops)

So far, we have described associations between two different entity classes (and therefore record types). In data modeling, we frequently need to describe associations between entities in the same entity class (for example, Students or Employees). An association between entities in the same entity class is called a **recursive association** (or **loop**). There are two types of recursive associations: one-to-many and many-to-many.

One-to-Many.   In a one-to-many recursive association, in a specified time period each entity is formally associated with zero, one, or many entities in the same entity class. However, in the reverse association there is a 1:1 relationship. For example, Figure 2-15 shows the usual MANAGES association among employees in the Employee entity class. If we assume that each employee has only one manager, then MANAGES is a 1:N association. Since there is only one record type, the link appears in the form of a loop (Figure 2-15a).

Two occurrences of this data structure are shown in Figure 2-15b. In a loop, or recursive association, a given entity can be both a "parent" and a "child." For example, the employee MIKE manages two employees (PAUL

Figure 2-15
Recursive association (1:*M*).
(a) Data structure.
(b) Two occurrences.

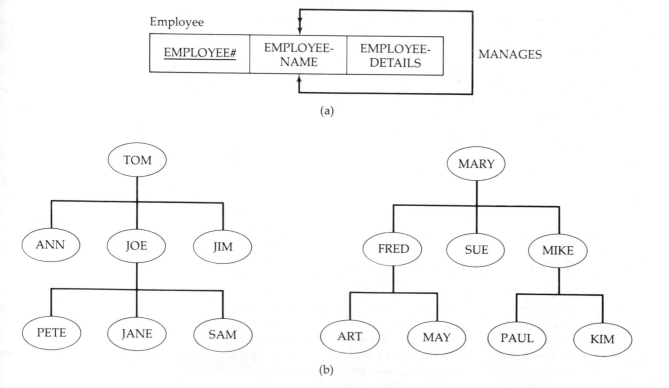

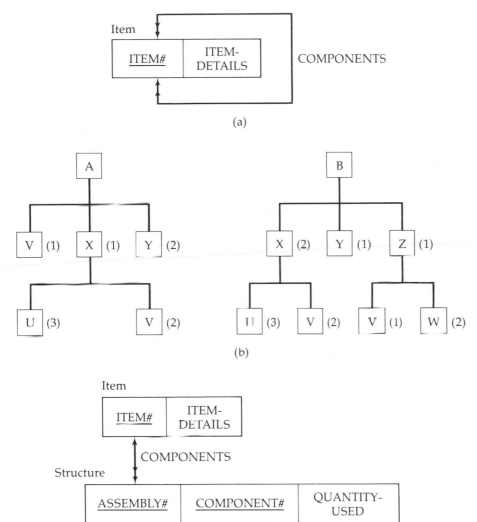

Figure 2-16
Bill of materials recursive
association.
(a) Data structure (*M:N*).
(b) Two occurrences.
(c) Data structure (1:*N*).

and KIM) and is managed by another employee (MARY). A recursive relation can encompass an arbitrary depth (number of levels).

Many-to-Many. In some organizations, each employee may have more than one manager (this is often referred to as a "matrix" form of organization). In this case, the MANAGES association among employees is *M:N*, since each employee both manages and is managed by several employees. This is an example of a many-to-many recursive association.

The most frequently used many-to-many recursive association in data bases is the bill of materials structure (see Figure 2-16). Many products are made of subassemblies, which in turn are composed of other subassemblies, parts, and so on. As shown in Figure 2-16a, the bill of materials data structure is an *M:N* recursive association between entities we call Items. Two occurrences of such a structure are shown in Figure 2-16b. Each of these diagrams shows the immediate components of each item as well as the quantities of each component. For example, item X consists of item U (quantity 3) and item V (quantity 2).

Notice that the associations in Figure 2-16 are in fact *M:N*. Several of the items have more than one component type (for example, item A has three immediate component types: V, X, and Y). Also, several of the items are used in different higher-level assemblies. For example, item X is used in both item A and item B.

A many-to-many recursive association is usually reduced to one (or more) one-to-many associations by using an intersection record type. In Figure 2-16c, an intersection record type called STRUCTURE is shown. There is one such intersection record for each *immediate* component of an item. The primary key of the STRUCTURE record is the concatenation of ASSEMBLY# (the parent item number) and COMPONENT# (the component item number). The intersection data contained in the record is QUANTITY-USED, the quantity of each component. For example, referring to Figure 2-16b, item X uses item V (quantity 2). The intersection record for this combination appears as follows:

LEVELS (OR VIEWS) OF DATA

A data base is a resource that is shared by all qualified users in an organization. Yet each of these users typically requires a different view of the data. In a hospital, for example, the medical staff requires a view of patient medical data, while the administrative staff requires a view of financial and administrative data. Only data base administration typically requires a view of the entire data base.

To satisfy these needs, most data base management systems today permit the organization's data base to be viewed at three levels of abstraction. These three levels, shown in Figure 2-17, are the conceptual model, the internal model, and multiple external models (called views). We have added a fourth level (the physical data organization) in Figure 2-17 to represent the way the data are actually organized on physical storage devices.

The model in Figure 2-17 was developed in 1972 by the Standards Planning and Requirements Committee (SPARC) of the American National Standards Institute (ANSI). Thus, it is referred to as the ANSI/SPARC model. The objective of this study group was to make recommendations

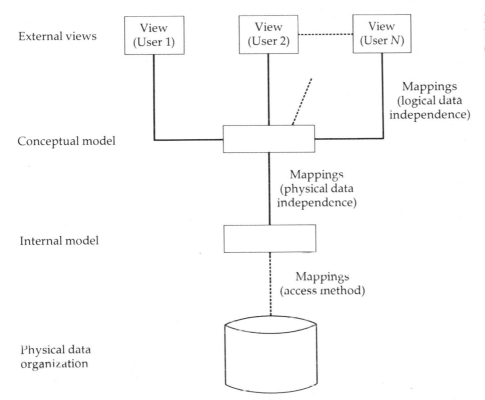

Figure 2-17
Levels, or views, of data
(ANSI/SPARC model).

concerning standards for data base technology (Tsichritzis and Klug 1978). The ANSI/SPARC model has had a strong influence on the development of contemporary data base management systems.

In studying the ANSI/SPARC model in Figure 2-17, we must realize that only the physical data base (the lowest level) actually exists. The three models—internal, conceptual, and external—are simply abstractions that allow various users to view the physical data base in different ways.

Conceptual Model

The **conceptual model (conceptual view)** defines the entire information resource at an abstract level. This view includes all the entities represented in the data base, the relationships between these entities, and other features such as security restrictions, audit controls, and validation procedures. The conceptual model does *not* contain any implementation details, such as file organizations, access methods, or hardware device descriptions.

A conceptual model for Pine Valley Furniture Company is shown in Figure 2-10. This conceptual model is not yet complete—additional record types and associations will be added later. Nevertheless, Figure 2-10 shows how a conceptual model can be represented in the form of a data structure diagram.

External Models (Views)

Each user view is a subset of the conceptual model, defined and formatted according to that user's needs. One user view for Pine Valley Furniture Company is shown in Figure 2-8. This view is derived from the conceptual model shown in Figure 2-10.

Internal Model

The **internal model** is a definition of the physical implementation of the data base by the DBMS. It defines the data base as a collection of logical records, called "internal" or "stored" records. It describes the methods by which these records are interrelated—for example, by pointers or indexes. We describe alternative data structures in Chapter 5.

Physical Data Organization

The lowest level of data representation in Figure 2-17 is the physical data organization. This level includes a description of the physical devices that are used, the grouping of records into blocks, addressing techniques, and similar details. We describe techniques for physical data organization in Chapter 4.

DATA INDEPENDENCE

What is the purpose of the three-level architecture shown in Figure 2-17? As we have already said, this architecture provides views of the organization's data that are tailor-made for each data base user. Another important advantage is that the three-level architecture provides data independence, which we described as a major advantage of the data base approach in Chapter 1. Data independence allows various changes to be made to a data base with minimum impact to its users.

As shown in Figure 2-17, there are mappings (translations) between each of the various levels of the data base model. The DBMS provides the mappings between the external user view and the conceptual model. It also provides the mappings between the conceptual model and the internal model. Finally, the computer system access method provides the mappings between the internal model and the physical data base. In effect, these mappings translate a user request for logical data into requests for the physical data to answer that request. (We describe the details of how a DBMS operates in Chapter 10.)

There are two levels of data independence: physical data independence and logical data independence. These two levels are provided by the mappings in the ANSI/SPARC model (Figure 2-17).

Physical Data Independence

Physical data independence allows the internal model to be modified without affecting either the conceptual model or the external views. For example, a file organization could be changed from indexed sequential to direct to speed up access to individual records. Or a list organization could be replaced by an inverted file organization. Physical data independence permits the data base administrator to "tune" the physical data base, while permitting application programs to run as if no changes had occurred.

Logical Data Independence

Logical data independence means that the conceptual model can be modified or extended without changing the external views. For example, different types of entities can be added to the data base, or new attributes can be added to existing entities. Logical data independence permits the data base to change and evolve without affecting existing user views or programs.

The important types of logical and physical data independence are presented in Table 2-1. The left-hand column in this table shows the type of data independence provided. The right-hand column provides examples of the types of changes that can be made without affecting user views or application programs. Although data base management systems differ in the level and amount of data independence provided, some contemporary systems provide most of the levels shown in Table 2-1.

Table 2-1
Important Types of Data Independence

Level of data independence	Examples of changes
Logical	
Data item format	Data item type, length, representation, or unit of measure
Data item usage	How a data item is derived, used, edited, or protected
Logical record structure	How data items are grouped into logical records
Logical data structure	Overall logical structure or conceptual model
Physical	
Physical data organization	How the data are organized into stored records
Access method	What search techniques and access strategies are used
Physical data location	Where data are located on storage devices
Storage device	Characteristics of the physical storage devices used

SUMMARY

In this chapter, we have described the nature of data (or information, which is data that have been processed and displayed for a decision maker). Data exist in three realms: reality (representing entities and their properties), metadata (representing record types and data item types), and data (representing actual stored data values).

We described techniques for representing data in this chapter. These techniques include bubble charts (for representing associations between data items) and data structure diagrams (for representing associations between record types).

To provide data independence, most data base management systems provide a three-level architecture for visualizing an organization's data base. The three levels in this model (called the ANSI/SPARC model) are the conceptual model, the external models (or views), and the internal model. This model provides two levels of data independence: physical, which insulates a user from changes to the internal model, and logical, which insulates a user from changes to the conceptual model.

CHAPTER REVIEW

Review Questions

1. Define each of the following terms:

   a. entity
   b. entity class
   c. association
   d. metadata
   e. attribute
   f. data item
   g. data aggregate
   h. record
   i. file
   j. primary key
   k. secondary key

2. Contrast the following terms:

   a. physical data independence; logical data independence
   b. primary key; secondary key
   c. conceptual model; external model
   d. attribute; data item
   e. entity; entity class

3. Give at least one synonym for each of the following terms:

   a. data item
   b. association
   c. entity class
   d. data aggregate
   e. data structure diagram

4. What is a recursive association? What are the two types of recursive associations?

5. Briefly describe each of the following:
   a. conceptual model
   b. external model
   c. internal model

6. Briefly describe the three realms used in describing data.

Problems and Exercises

1. Consider each of the following changes to a data base. Assuming that an application program is unaffected by the change, indicate whether it is an example of logical or physical data independence.
   a. Move the data to newer, faster storage devices.
   b. Change a data item called ZIP-CODE from a five-digit field to a nine-digit field.
   c. Change from indexed sequential access method (ISAM) to virtual sequential access method (VSAM).
   d. Add a new data item called CARPOOL to an existing Employee record type.
   e. Add a new record type called TEXTBOOK to an instructional data base.

2. Give two examples (other than those in the text) of each of the following associations between two entities:
   a. one-to one
   b. one-to-many
   c. many-to-many
   d. recursive one-to-many
   e. recursive many-to-many
   f. multiple associations

3. Examine the PRODUCT data in Figure 2-2 and answer the following questions.
   a. What items are designated bedroom (BR) furniture? (Give the item numbers.)
   b. What items have PINE finish?
   c. What items have a PRICE that is $500 or less?
   d. What items of pine bedroom furniture sell for $500 or less?

4. An EMPLOYEE record type has the following attributes: EMPLOYEE#, NAME, JOB-TITLE, DATE-OF-BIRTH. Show typical data for six employees using a flat file representation (similar to Figure 2-2).

5. List five attributes for each of the following entity classes:
   a. Patient
   b. Student
   c. Car
   d. Video Game
   e. Textbook

6. List five entity classes for each of the following attributes:
   a. Name
   b. Color
   c. Weight
   d. Price

7. Draw a bubble chart (similar to Figure 2-6b) for the secondary key value ROOM='LR' in Figure 2-2.

8. Draw a bubble chart showing the associations between the following data items (make any assumptions that are necessary): STUDENT#, STUDENT-NAME, TELEPHONE#, COURSE#, COURSE-NAME, UNITS, INSTRUCTOR-NAME, INSTRUCTOR-OFFICE#.

9. Combine the following user views into a single view:

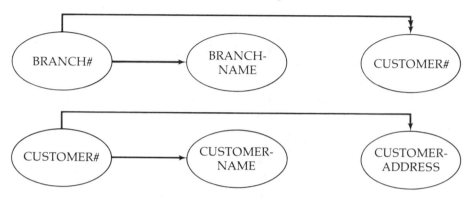

10. Draw an occurrence of each of the following:
    a. data structure diagram in Figure 2-13
    b. data structure diagram in Figure 2-14
    c. data structure diagram in Figure 2-16c

11. Draw a data structure diagram for each of the following associations.
    a. A given course can have several prerequisite courses, and a given course can be a prerequisite for several other courses.
    b. A student can register in several courses, and a course can have many students registered.
    c. A computer can run a number of software packages, and each software package can run on zero, one, or many computers.
    d. A student can have zero, one, or many roommates (who are also students).

References

Date, C. J. 1981. *An Introduction to Database Systems*. 3d ed. Reading, Mass.: Addison-Wesley.

Katzan, Harry. 1975. *Computer Data Management and Data Base Technology*. New York: Van Nostrand Reinhold.

Martin, James. 1983. *Managing the Data-Base Environment*. Englewood Cliffs, N.J.: Prentice-Hall.

Toffler, Alvin. 1980. *The Third Wave*. New York: William Morrow.

Tsichritzis, D. C., and A. Klug, eds. "The ANSI/X3/SPARC DBMS Framework: Report of the Study Group on Data Base Management Systems." *Information Systems*, 3.

Data Base Planning

INTRODUCTION

Data base systems were first installed in business enterprises during the late 1960s. Since that time, thousands of organizations have converted to this approach. Yet today, the promise of data base is largely unrealized. According to Voell (1980):

> Data base and data administration have, by and large, not lived up to the expectations and promises made in most writings. The corporate data base integrated to reduce redundancy, accessible to multiple applications, protected from the unauthorized, and controlled so that it contains only valid information is a myth. Today, data base is largely just an access method. Similarly, the data administration function is not controlling a global view of information. The real promise and benefits of a corporate data base are valid, but are yet to be realized.

Why have so many enterprises failed to realize the potential of the data base approach? No doubt there are many reasons. However, comparison of successful and unsuccessful organizations reveals that lack of adequate planning for data base is the most common and pervasive shortcoming.

IMPORTANCE OF DATA BASE PLANNING

Traditionally, information systems have not really been planned or designed at all, but have evolved in a "bottom-up" fashion as stand-alone systems to solve isolated organizational problems. In effect, traditional information systems ask the question "What procedure (application program) is required to solve this particular problem as it exists today?" The problem with this approach is that the required organizational procedures are likely to change over time as the environment changes. For example , a company may decide to change its method of billing customers, or a university may change its procedures for registering students. When such changes occur, it is usually necessary to modify existing application programs.

In contrast, data resource management essentially asks the question "What are the data base requirements to satisfy the information needs of the enterprise today and well into the future?" A major advantage of this approach is that an organization's data are less likely to change (or will change more slowly) than its procedures. For example, unless an organization changes its business fundamentally, its underlying data structure will remain reasonably stable over a ten-year period. However, the procedures used to access and process the data will change many times during that period. Thus, the challenge of data resource management is to design stable data bases that are relatively independent of the languages and programs that are used to update the data base.

To benefit from this approach, the organization *must* analyze its information needs and plan its data base carefully. If a data base approach is attempted without such planning, the results may well be disastrous. The resulting data base may support individual applications, but will not provide a resource that can be shared by users throughout the enterprise. The DBMS becomes just a costly access method that provides the same structured reports and displays as the previous systems. Program maintenance problems continue to plague the data processing organization.

With the acceptance of data as a valuable organizational resource, an entirely different planning approach is required. The organization must develop strategic plans for its data resources, just as it develops strategic plans for its human, financial, and material resources. The planning process must be "top-down," so that information systems and data base planning are integrated with basic enterprise objectives. The result is a comprehensive data base plan that will provide a road map for data base design and implementation.

This chapter presents a framework for data base planning. Although there is no single methodology or standard approach that is used for this purpose, the techniques presented are representative of those being used by successful organizations. According to Holland (1980): "A very few organizations are superimposing a data model over their business systems plan. These are the electronic organizations of the future that will significantly reduce their maintenance costs, provide program and data independence, add new applications with ease and enjoy an effective user environment."

ORGANIZATIONAL ENVIRONMENT

A major objective of data base planning is to develop a **strategic data model.** This data model should be a model of the information needs of the entire organization, both today and well into the future—say ten years or more.

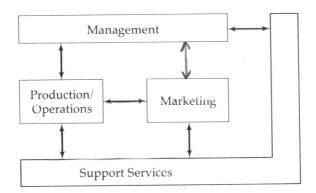

Figure 3-1
Functional overview of a
business enterprise.
(Source: Robert H.
Holland, "Data Base
Stability," *ICP Interface
Data Processing
Management*, Spring
1981, p. 32.)

The data model should be understood and supported by the various functional areas of the organization. A high-level overview of the functions common to most organizations is shown in Figure 3-1. The four functional areas shown in this figure are Marketing, Production/Operations, Management, and Support Services. As the diagram shows, each of the functions has an interface with the others.

Marketing (sometimes referred to as the "demand side" of the organization) is responsible for creating and/or identifying the demand for products and services. Marketing may be further broken down into Sales, Advertising, Market Research, Distribution, and related activities. Production/Operations (the "supply side") is responsible for providing the products and services. This function may consist of materials management, production scheduling and control, production operations, and so on. Support Services consists of functions such as engineering, accounting, personnel, and main tenance. Management is responsible for the overall planning and direction of the organization.

It is usually not practical for an organization to implement its data base all at once or over a short time span. Instead, the data base is implemented in stages over a period of time—perhaps several years. The end result might be a single large data base or, more likely, several smaller data bases. For this reason, it is important that the organization have a strategic data base plan and data model to guide the implementation. Without such a plan, the data base will evolve in a haphazard fashion and will fail to yield its intended benefits.

Anthony (1965) has identified three levels of management planning and control in an organization: strategic, tactical, and operational (see Figure 3-2). **Strategic planning** is the process of deciding on organizational goals and objectives, determining the resources that will be required, and deciding on the policies that are to govern the acquisition, use, and disposition of these resources. Strategic managers are responsible for overall performance of the enterprise.

As suggested in Figure 3-2, strategic management relies on data in a highly summarized form. For example, the chief executive officer of a company would most likely be concerned with return on investment or

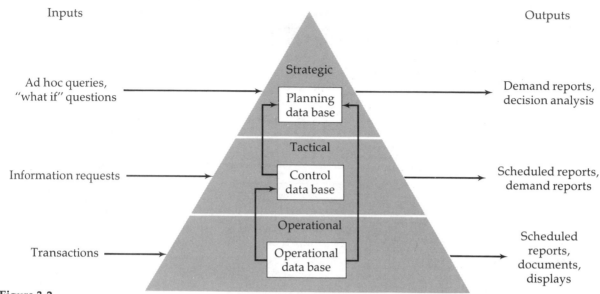

Inputs   Outputs

Ad hoc queries,   Demand reports,
"what if" questions   decision analysis

Information requests   Scheduled reports,
                                                                          demand reports

Transactions   Scheduled
                                                                          reports,
                                                                          documents,
                                                                          displays

Strategic — Planning data base

Tactical — Control data base

Operational — Operational data base

Figure 3-2
Typical information needs
by management level.

market share growth rather than the performance of a particular department or product line. A manager at this level often requires a decision support system (described in Chapter 1) that can respond to ad hoc queries for information and simulate various planning alternatives. Also, top managers require considerable external data such as business forecasts, economic data, and competitive information.

Tactical management is concerned largely with management control. This is the process by which managers ensure that resources are obtained and used effectively and efficiently in the accomplishment of enterprise objectives. Management control is concerned with balancing the use of resources, measuring progress against plans, and taking corrective action when necessary.

As shown in Figure 3-2, tactical managers require information in the form of summaries of operational data and management control reports such as budget summaries. This information must be made available in response to ad hoc requests as well as in the form of periodic reports.

Operational control focuses on the execution of specific tasks and activities. It is concerned with scheduling and controlling individual jobs, procuring materials, and taking specific personnel actions.

Data required for operational control is detailed and frequently non-monetary. It is based on transactions such as patient registrations, material receipts, and personnel assignments. The operational control system must produce operating documents and displays that are immediately useful for operational decision making.

DATA BASE PLANNING PROCESS

The purpose of data base planning is to develop a strategic, or long-range, plan for a data base environment that will support the organization's information needs, both today and in a planned future. The data base plan is a subset of the organization's information systems (IS) plan, which, in turn, is a subset of the overall corporate plan. Thus, we visualize the planning process as hierarchical, or top-down, in nature. An alternative approach is bottom-up, in which the planner extrapolates from existing systems and information needs. However, with this approach, there is no assurance that the data base plan will be in agreement with higher-level plans.

Data base planning should be established as a formal project within the organization. A project team consisting of somewhere between four and eight members (depending on the size and complexity of the organization) seems to work well in practice. Team members should represent a cross section of end users (managers) as well as data processing personnel. The team leader should be chosen carefully and should be a strong candidate for the data administrator position. The project team should report in a staff relationship to the IS director or to a higher-level manager.

Tasks in Data Base Planning

The major tasks in planning for a data base environment are shown in Figure 3-3. The feedback arrows on the left of Figure 3-3 indicate that data base planning is not strictly a sequential process. Refinements within certain tasks are often necessary as an organization learns more about its data requirements.

Initiate Study (Task 1).   The first task of the project team is to define the goals and objectives of the data base approach in the organization. First, the project team should identify the problems and limitations of the present environment. Next, the team should identify the benefits to be achieved with the data base environment (we identified the major benefits in Chapter 1). The anticipated benefits are then stated in the form of goals and objectives that mesh with the organization's long-range plans.

Establish the Data Administration Function (Task 2).   The functions and responsibilities of data administration (or data base administration) should be defined early in the planning process. The person who is data administrator (or a leading candidate for this position) should assume a leadership role in the subsequent planning steps. Tools, such as a data dictionary/directory system, should be acquired to support the remaining tasks.

Perform Business Systems Analysis (Tasks 3–6).   The study team identifies and documents the business functions, processes, activities, and entities.

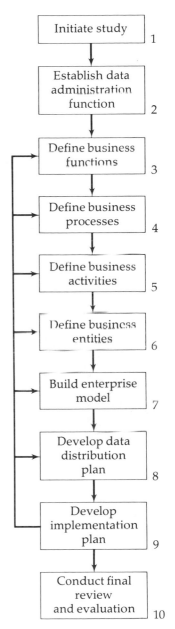

Figure 3-3
Tasks in strategic data base planning.

Figure 3-4
Top-down planning
versus bottom-up design.

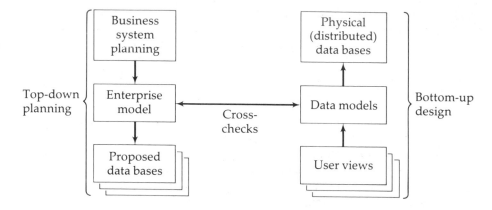

Build Enterprise Model (Task 7). Building an enterprise model is the central step in the entire strategic planning process. The enterprise model portrays the major entity classes for the organization and the associations between those entities.

Develop Data Distribution Plan (Task 8). If data will be distributed in several physical data bases, the study team develops a plan for data distribution. (Distributed data bases are described in Chapter 15.)

Develop Implementation Plan (Task 9). The team establishes a timetable and responsibilities for data base implementation. Priorities are established so that the strategic data base plan ties in with overall IS plans.

Conduct Final Review and Evaluation (Task 10). The project team prepares a final report and reviews all components to ensure that they are consistent. The report is presented to top management, and responsibility for updating the plan is assigned.

Top-Down Planning Versus Bottom-Up Design

As shown in Figure 3-4, developing corporate data bases requires both top-down planning and bottom-up design. Top-down planning, which is the topic of this chapter, starts with basic organizational goals and objectives. Using business system planning, we analyze organizational functions, processes, activities, and entities. We then develop an **enterprise model,** which is a diagram showing the major entities of the organization and the associations between those entities. The enterprise model, which is also called an entity chart, is *not* a detailed data model, but a planning document. By analyzing the enterprise model, we can divide the overall effort into several proposed data bases.

Detailed data base design is a bottom-up process (see Figure 3-4). Analysts begin with user views of data and apply normalization techniques to develop detailed data models (data base design is described in Part 3). In data base design, the data models are cross-checked against the enterprise model to ensure that they are complete and accurate. Thus, the top-down enterprise model plays three important roles:

1. It provides an overall, integrative view of corporate entities and data.

2. It provides a basis for segmenting the overall corporate data model into a number of manageable data base projects.

3. During detailed data base design, it provides a cross-check and means of integrating individual data bases into the overall corporate framework.

DATA BASE PLANNING METHODOLOGY

In this section, we describe a methodology for top-down data base planning. This methodology is based on the Business System Planning (BSP) approach developed by IBM to assist organizations in establishing a system architecture plan. Business System Planning is a top-down approach that has as its basic assumption that "an information system plan for a business must be integrated with the business plan and should be developed from the point of view of top management and with their active participation" (*Business System Planning* 1975, 1). The methodology presented here combines some of the features of BSP with other related data base planning approaches. Data base planning is part of overall system planning.

There are four main phases in the BSP process. They are identifying the business environment, business planning, business systems analysis, and data base analysis (see Figure 3-5).

Identifying the Business Environment

Indentifying the business environment means identifying the internal and external environments in which the firm now exists and will exist over the strategic planning horizon. The external environment includes customers, competitors, suppliers, government, technology, and economic conditions. The internal environment includes policies, practices, and constraints.

Business Planning

Business planning considers the forecasted business environment and develops organizational goals and objectives, strategies (competitive approaches), resource requirements, policies, and constraints. The business

Figure 3-5
Business System Planning
process.

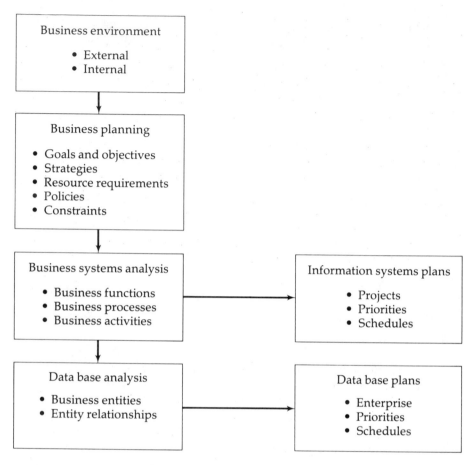

plan (sometimes called the master plan) is the fundamental planning document for the organization. It must be carefully documented and communicated to key managers throughout the organization. Also, the business plan must be revised and updated as conditions change.

Business Systems Analysis

The foundation of a comprehensive data base plan is business systems analysis. The goal of this process is to analyze the basic functions and subfunctions of the organization, identifying present and future information needs to support these functions. This analysis of business functions is independent of existing organizational lines. A top-down graphical approach is used to identify organizational functions. First, the major functions of the organization are identified. Each of these functions is then divided into a group of subfunctions, called processes. Each process, in turn, is divided (where appropriate) into a set of elementary subfunctions called activities. Also, the business entities required by each of the processes are identified during the analysis. An example of such an analysis in a manufacturing firm is shown in Figure 3-6 in the form of a simple chart, called a **business chart.**

Business functions are broad groups of closely related activities and decisions that contribute to a product or service life cycle. In Figure 3-6, the functions are identified as follows: planning, materials, production planning, production operations, and quality assurance. Several additional functions would normally be identified in a manufacturing firm (see chapter exercises). A small company such as Pine Valley Furniture Company may have from five to ten functions, while a large corporation such as IBM might have 20 or more functions.

A business function may correspond to an existing organizational unit, or it may cut across several existing units. For example, the quality assurance business function in Figure 3-6 may actually be spread across several organizational units, such as engineering, purchasing, and quality control. It is far better to relate data base design to basic organizational functions and processes than to organizational units, since the latter are subject to frequent change.

Business processes are decision-related activities that occur within a function and often serve to manage people, money, material, or information. In Figure 3-6, the materials function has been subdivided into the following processes: requirements planning, purchasing, receiving, inventory accounting, and warehousing. Business processes should again reflect related activity groupings rather than existing departmental functions. Each business function within an organization can often be modeled with some three to ten processes.

Business activities are specific actions required to carry out a process. In Figure 3-6, the purchasing process was subdivided into the following activities: evaluate vendors, select vendor, generate purchase orders, and process invoices.

Business actions are procedure-oriented activities. For example, the action of generating purchase orders is a transaction that is initiated by a buyer, perhaps using an on-line terminal. These actions result in data being updated or added to or deleted from the data base.

Business entities are persons, objects, or events about which information is recorded in the data base. We can determine the entities required by each of the processes by examining the activities for that process and asking what entities are required for input, processing, and output for each activity. For example, consider the purchasing process in the business chart (Figure 3-6). By reviewing the activities and discussing the purchasing process with users, we discover that the following entities are required: Vendor, Purchase Order, Invoice, Buyer, and Inventory Item.

Figure 3-6
Business chart for a
manufacturing company.

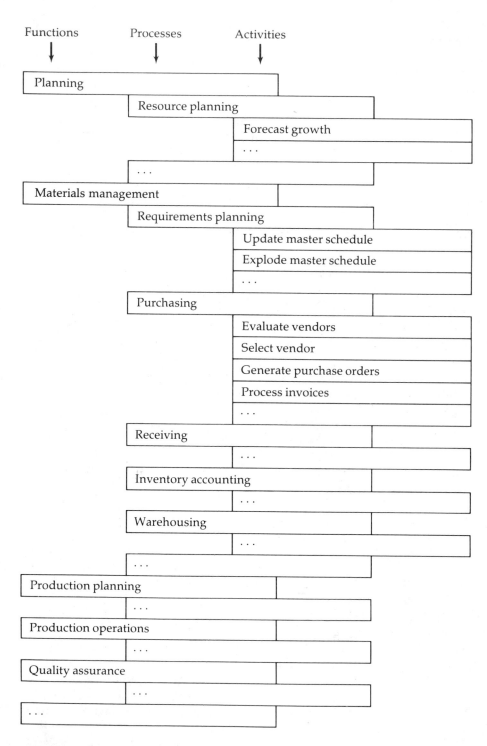

Data Base Analysis

Data base analysis is the last phase of the BSP process (see Figure 3-5). Business entities were identified in the previous phase. The purpose of data base analysis is to identify the relationships between these entities and to develop a conceptual model for the organization. We refer to the conceptual model developed during this stage as the enterprise model. As shown in Figure 3-5, data base priorities and schedules are also developed during this phase. This is important because the data base plans must support overall IS priorities and schedules.

A portion of an enterprise model for a purchasing data base is shown in Figure 3-7. This model contains the following entities: VENDOR, BUYER, PURCHASE ORDER, INVENTORY ITEM, and INVOICE. These entities were identified for the purchasing process, and while other entities may be required for this process, we will not consider them here. Here are the relationships between the various entities:

- VENDOR to PURCHASE ORDER is a one-to-many relationship: for each vendor, there may be many outstanding purchase orders at a given time; however, for a given purchase order there is only one vendor.

- BUYER to PURCHASE ORDER is one-to-many: each buyer may be responsible for several outstanding purchase orders, however, a given purchase order is the responsibility of only one buyer.

- PURCHASE ORDER to INVOICE is one-to-many: for each purchase order, there may be several invoices submitted by the vendor; however, a given invoice is applied to only one purchase order.

- PURCHASE ORDER to INVENTORY ITEM is many-to-many: each purchase order may order several items; also, each inventory item may have several purchase orders outstanding at any given time.

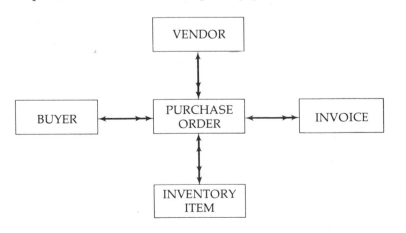

Figure 3-7
Data model for a purchasing data base.

Other Components of BSP

A full Business Systems Planning study would include additional techniques that are beyond the scope of this chapter. For example, BSP recommends the use of matrices, where the organizational processes are mapped against data files and data bases. Through detailed analysis of these matrices, the data analyst can group entities into proposed data bases. This refines the process of segmenting the enterprise model into a set of proposed data bases. For more information on these techniques, see *Business System Planning* (1975) and Martin (1980).

CASE EXAMPLE   Mountain View Community Hospital

The principles of data base planning can be illustrated with the case example of a hospital, an organization familiar to most people. Although the example is hypothetical, it does contain many of the elements of a real hospital environment. The same case is used in later chapters to illustrate detailed data base design and implementation.

Mountain View Community Hospital is a not-for-profit, short-term, acute general hospital. It is a small to medium-sized hospital, with 100 beds at the present time. Mountain View Community is the only hospital in the city of Mountain View, a rapidly growing city with a population of about 25,000 people in the heart of the Rocky Mountains.

An organizational chart for Mountain View Community Hospital is shown in Figure 3-8. As with most hospitals, Mountain View Community is divided into two organizational groups. The physicians, headed by Dr. Browne (chief of staff) are responsible for the quality of medical care provided their patients. The group headed by Ms. Baker (administrator) provides the nursing, clinical, and administrative support required by the physicians to serve their patients.

Business Planning

Mountain View Community has a long-range plan that was prepared with the assistance of a management consulting firm two years ago. The plan, which covers a ten-year horizon, defines the hospital's service area and its forecasted growth, identifies basic goals and objectives for the hospital, and identifies the capacity and resources that will be required to meet future needs.

Although most admissions to Mountain View Community Hospital are from the city of Mountain View, some patients are also admitted from the

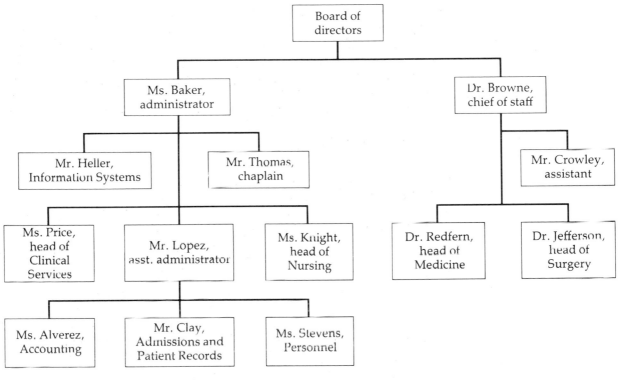

Figure 3-8
Organization chart for
Mountain View
Community Hospital.

surrounding rural areas. As a result, the entire county in which Mountain View is located (Mesa County) was defined as the hospital's service area. The population of Mesa County is about 40,000 at present and has been growing at an annual rate of 8%, a trend that is expected to continue for several years.

The basic goal of Mountain View Community Hospital is to continue to meet the needs of Mountain View and Mesa County for high-quality health care, while containing costs that have been rising in accordance with national trends in recent years.

To support the expected demand for services, the long-range plan calls for expansion and modernization of facilities. These plans include the addition of a new wing in five years, with expansion from the present 100 to 150 beds. Adequate land already exists for this expansion, as well as for additional parking facilities. Also, several existing facilities are to be renovated, including the Admitting and Outpatient registration areas. Two new service facilities are planned over a five-year period: Ultra Sound and Occupational Therapy.

Existing Information Systems

Mountain View Community has a minicomputer that was leased two years ago. The system has 256 KB central memory and 64 MB on-line disk storage capacity. Plans call for adding a faster processor and additional memory and disk storage capacity during the coming year. However, the extent of these additions has yet to be determined.

Present information systems are batch-oriented and include application programs for patient accounting, billing and accounts receivable, and financial accounting. These application packages were obtained from a software vendor specializing in hospital applications.

Mr. Heller, who was recently appointed manager of Information Systems, identified the following deficiencies with the present systems:

1. The systems do not support the medical staff by recording or reporting the results of laboratory tests and procedures.

2. Since the systems are batch-oriented, they do not support on-line procedures such as patient registration or inquiries regarding billing.

3. The system does not accumulate costs by department or cost center.

4. The system is inflexible and does not respond well to changing management needs or to the frequent changes in reporting requirements of external health agencies.

Management at Mountain View Community had for some time recognized that the present information systems were not responsive to their needs. Mr. Lopez (assistant administrator), who had previous experience with data base systems in a large city hospital, had advocated that Mountain View Community investigate this approach. Mr. Heller was hired as manager of Information Systems partly because of his experience with data base systems. A new systems analyst (Mr. Helms) also was recently hired. Mr. Helms had experience in data base design, and it was expected that he would be a candidate for the data base administrator position if and when it was approved by the board of directors.

At a meeting of the board of directors, Mr. Heller explained the concept of data resource management. Ms. Baker (hospital administrator) proposed that Mountain View Community adopt this approach and that Mr. Helms be appointed data base administrator. The board of directors agreed with the concept, but insisted that a study be conducted to estimate costs and benefits as well as develop an overall data base plan. Ms. Baker formed a study team with the following members: Mr. Lopez, assistant administrator (leader); Ms. Knight, head of nursing; Mr. Crowley, assistant chief of staff; Mr. Heller, manager of Information Systems; and Mr. Helms, systems analyst. An outside consultant was hired to assist them. The consultant spent two days helping the team outline the study approach and establish schedules.

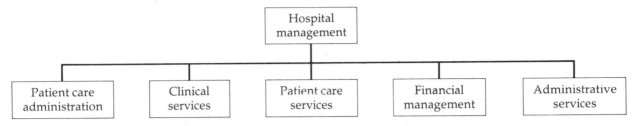

Figure 3-9
Hospital business
functions.

Business Systems Analysis

The study team reviewed Mountain View Community Hospital's long-range plan and proceeded with a business systems analysis. First, the team identified the basic functions of a small general hospital. The functions, which are illustrated in Figure 3-9, consist of the following:

- *Patient care administration*, to manage the logistical and record-keeping aspects of patient care.
- *Clinical services*, to provide laboratory testing and procedures and patient monitoring and screening.
- *Patient care services*, to provide patients with medical care and support services.
- *Financial management*, to manage the financial resources and operations of the hospital.
- *Administrative services*, to provide general management and support services.

Having identified the basic functions, the next step was to define the processes for each function. The project team spent considerable time interviewing other managers to clarify the process definitions. A business chart showing the functions, processes, and some of the activities is shown in Figure 3-10. In total, 22 processes were identified for Mountain View Community Hospital.

As the processes and activities were defined, the study team also identified ten basic business entities required by the processes (see Figure 3-11). The study team recognized that additional entities would be identified during detailed data base design. However, the team felt that these ten entities define the basic data resources of the hospital.

The study team completed their business systems analysis in about one month, at which time they made a brief presentation of their results to the board of directors. The hospital directors were impressed with the integrated approach to information systems planning. Ms. Baker recommended that the study team proceed to develop a data base plan, a recommendation that was endorsed by the board of directors.

Figure 3-10
Business chart (Mountain View Community Hospital).

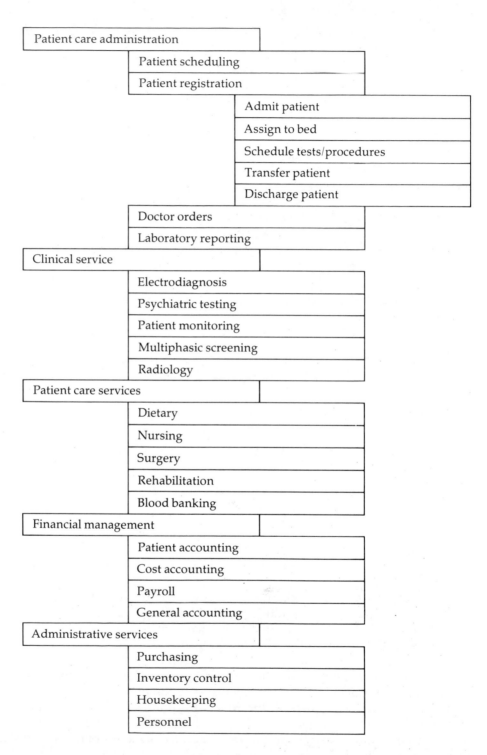

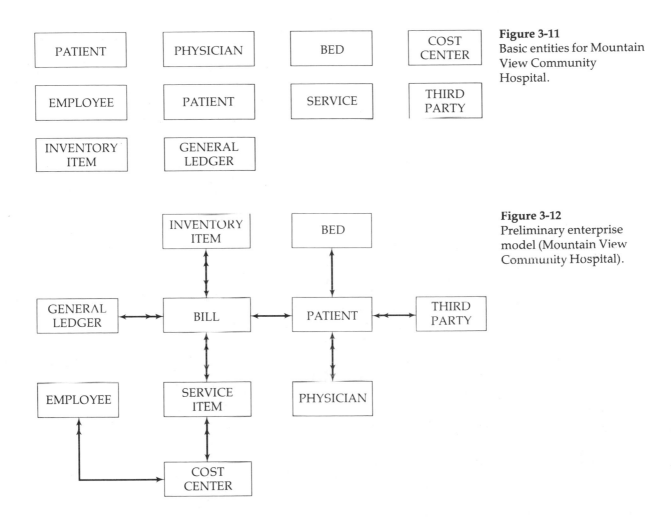

Figure 3-11
Basic entities for Mountain View Community Hospital.

Figure 3-12
Preliminary enterprise model (Mountain View Community Hospital).

Data Base Planning

The study team reviewed the business entities for Mountain View Community Hospital. With some assistance from the outside consultant, the team identified the associations between the entities. The team then constructed a preliminary enterprise model for the hospital, shown in Figure 3-12. Following are the associations contained in the enterprise model:

- PATIENT to BED is a one-to-one relationship: at a given time, each patient is assigned to one BED and vice versa.
- PATIENT to BILL is one-to-one: each PATIENT has one BILL, and each BILL is associated with one Patient.

- COST CENTER to SERVICE ITEM is one-to-many: each COST CENTER (such as Radiology) provides several SERVICE ITEMS, but a given SERVICE ITEM is associated with only one COST CENTER.

- THIRD PARTY to PATIENT is one-to-many: each THIRD PARTY insurer has many registered PATIENTS, but each PATIENT is assumed to have only one THIRD PARTY insurer (this assumption may need to be reexamined later).

- GENERAL LEDGER to PATIENT BILL is one-to-many: the GENERAL LEDGER Accounts Receivable account has many outstanding PATIENT BILLS, but each PATIENT BILL is associated with only one account (Accounts Receivable).

- PHYSICIAN to PATIENT is many-to-many: each PHYSICIAN has many PATIENTS, while a given PATIENT may be assigned more than one PHYSICIAN (for example, if a specialist is involved).

- PATIENT BILL to SERVICE ITEM is many-to-many: each PATIENT BILL consists of several SERVICE ITEMS, while a given SERVICE ITEM will be reflected in several PATIENT BILLS at a given time.

Constructing an enterprise model such as the one shown in Figure 3-12 requires an in-depth analysis of the organization, the "business rules" or procedures that govern its operations, and the resulting associations between entities. It requires the involvement of both experienced data base analysts and users who understand their business and the data required to operate it effectively.

Final Report

The study team then prepared a final report summarizing the data base plan for Mountain View Community Hospital. The report included a business chart; a description of hospital functions, processes, activities, and entity classes; an enterprise model; a list of benefits and costs of the data base

Figure 3-13
Data base implementation schedule for Mountain View Community Hospital.

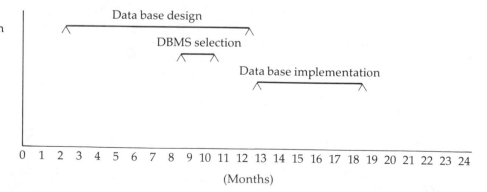

approach; and a two-year plan for data base design and implementation at Mountain View Community Hospital (see Figure 3-13).

The study team presented the data base plan to the board of directors at their regular meeting the following month. The board endorsed the plan and shortly thereafter approved the creation of the data base administrator position. Ms. Baker appointed Mr. Helms to this position, to report initially to Mr. Heller.

SUMMARY

Data base planning is essential if the benefits of data resource management are to be realized. The data base plan must support the overall information systems plan as well as basic organizational goals and objectives.

A methodology for data base planning was presented in this chapter. The methodology uses a top-down approach and is performed by a study team sponsored by top management. The basis for the planning effort is the business plan, which is an overall statement of enterprise goals, objectives, policies, and constraints. The methodology presented is patterned after IBM's Business System Planning, which uses a top-down approach to define enterprise functions, processes, activities, and events.

A major objective of data base planning is to develop a preliminary conceptual data model. This model, called the enterprise model, shows the relationships between the important business entities. The data base plan also includes an overall schedule for data base design and implementation. This chapter illustrates the data base planning process with a realistic case example of a hospital.

CHAPTER REVIEW

Review Questions

1. Concisely define each of the following terms:
   a. business function
   b. business process
   c. business activity
   d. business entity
   e. enterprise model
   f. strategic planning
   g. operational control

2. Contrast the following terms:
   a. top-down planning; bottom-up design
   b. business plan; business system plan
   c. strategic planning; tactical management
   d. business processes; business activities

3. Briefly describe the ten tasks in data base planning.

4. Define four basic functions common to most enterprises.

5. Describe three levels of management planning and control and the typical inputs and outputs for each level.

6. Why is a data dictionary system valuable during the data base planning process?

7. Describe three uses for the enterprise model.

8. When should the data base administration function be established? Why?

9. Explain how the results of both top-down planning and bottom-up design can be used to develop an enterprise data model.

10. Many organizations attempt to implement data bases without performing the planning described in this chapter. What results would you expect from this approach? Why?

Problems and Exercises

1. A family can be regarded as a small business organization.
   a. Define the major functions, processes, and activities for a family and draw a business chart.
   b. Define the entities and draw an enterprise model.

2. Examine the business chart for a manufacturing firm (Figure 3-6).
   a. List three additional functions that would be included in the business chart for a typical manufacturing firm.
   b. List three processes that would be included in the quality assurance function. (*Hint:* Consider various points in a manufacturing firm where quality must be planned or measured.)
   c. List three activities that would be included in the receiving process.

3. Examine the business chart for Mountain View Community Hospital (Figure 3-10). List three activities for each of the following processes:
   a. nursing
   b. payroll
   c. housekeeping

4. List three additional entities that might appear in the enterprise model for Mountain View Community Hospital (Figure 3-12).

5. Draw a preliminary business chart for Pine Valley Furniture Company. In doing this, perform the following steps:

   a. Review the Pine Valley Furniture case (see Chapter 1).

   b. Review the business chart for a typical manufacturing firm (Figure 3-6).

   c. Make (and state) any assumptions you believe necessary.

6. A professional football team is a business organization.

   a. Define several functions, processes, and activities and draw a preliminary business chart.

   b. Define several entity classes and draw a tentative enterprise model.

7. Expand the enterprise model for Pine Valley Furniture Company (Figure 1-4) by adding the following entity classes: EMPLOYEE, WORK CENTER, and PURCHASE ORDER. (Make any assumptions that are necessary.)

8. Consider a high school as a business enterprise.

   a. Define several functions, processes, and activities and draw a business chart.

   b. Define several entity classes and draw an enterprise model.

9. Examine the business chart for Mountain View Community Hospital (Figure 3-10). List three activities for each of the following processes:

   a. patient accounting

   b. blood banking

   c. rehabilitation

10. Visit an organization that is using the data base approach. Evaluate the state of data base planning in that organization—organizational commitment to planning, the methods used, and their effectiveness.

References

Anthony, Robert N. 1965. *Planning and Control Systems: A Framework for Analysis.* Cambridge, Mass.: Harvard University Press.

Business System Planning: Information System Planning Guide. 1975. Pub. no. GE20-0527-1. White Plains, N.Y.: IBM Corporation.

Holland, Robert H. 1980. "Data Base Planning Entails Return to Basics." *Computerworld* (October 27).

————. 1981. "Data Base Stability." *ICP Interface Data Processing Management* (Spring).

Martin, James. 1982. *Strategic Data Planning Methodologies.* Englewood Cliffs, N.J.: Prentice-Hall, Inc.

Meurer, Thomas F. 1980. "Solving the Mystery of Data Base Design." *Computerworld* (September 17).

Voell, Ronald F. 1980. "Data Base Planning." In *Advances in Data Base Management,* Vol. 1, ed. Thomas A. Rullo. Philadelphia: Heyden.

II

Data Base Architecture

The three chapters in Part II provide a detailed description of the physical and logical data organizations most often used in data base systems.

Chapter 4 is an introduction to physical data organization. We review the characteristics of secondary storage devices, principally magnetic disks. We describe the file organizations used in data base applications, with emphasis on the indexed and hashed organizations. Advantages and disadvantages of each type of physical organization are described.

Chapter 5 describes the data structures used to build and manage data bases. Data structures are used to represent associations between data entities. Some of the important data structures described in this chapter are queues, stacks, sorted lists, rings, multilists, inverted lists, and B-trees. It is essential that you understand the various data structures, since they are building blocks of data management systems.

Chapter 6 introduces data models. Data models are concerned with the way data look to the user, rather than with their physical representations. Three basic data models are described: hierarchical, network, and relational. Also, data manipulation commands are described and illustrated for each of the three models.

4

Physical Data Organization

INTRODUCTION

In this chapter, we will examine the basic techniques used for storing and accessing data on secondary storage devices. Physical data organization represents the lowest level in the ANSI/SPARC model introduced in Chapter 2 (see Figure 4-1). It is important to realize that this is the only level at which an organization's data base exists in physical form (if we can regard a series of magnetized spots as a physical form!). All the remaining levels in the ANSI/SPARC model are abstract views of the physical data base.

At the physical level, a data base may be viewed as a collection of stored records and files. Here are typical operations we may want to perform on a file:

1. Fetch an arbitrary record from the file.

2. Insert a record into the file.

3. Modify a record in the file.

4. Read the entire file.

5. Read the next record in the file.

6. Delete a record from the file.

7. Reorganize the file.

In selecting a physical data organization (or file organization), the system designer must consider a number of important factors, including the physical characteristics of the secondary storage devices to be used, the

Figure 4-1
ANSI/SPARC
architecture.

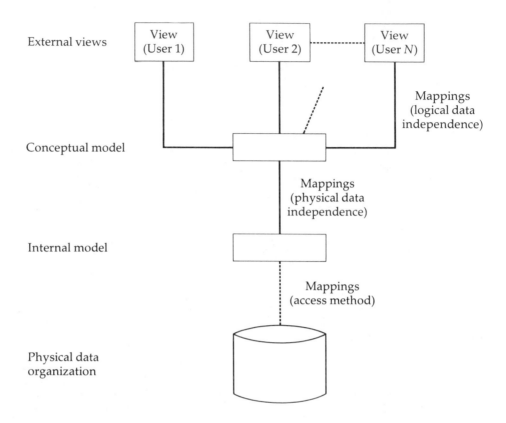

operating system and file management software (or access methods) available, and the set of criteria that reflect user needs for storing and accessing data.

The criteria that are normally important in selecting a file organization include fast access for retrieval, high throughput for processing transactions, efficient use of storage space, protection from failures or data loss, and security from unauthorized use. Often these objectives are conflicting, and the designer must select a physical data organization that provides a reasonable balance among the criteria within the resources that are available.

In this chapter, we will describe only basic file organizations, where storage and retrieval of records are based on a single key (the primary key). In the next chapter, we will describe multiple-key file organizations.

DIRECT ACCESS STORAGE DEVICES

Physical organization of data is strongly influenced by the characteristics of the devices on which the data are stored. In this section, we will review the important characteristics of direct access storage devices. We will concentrate on magnetic disk storage, since this is by far the most important type of secondary storage used today. However, most of the concepts described here will apply to newer storage devices that may emerge in the future.

There are two broad classes of secondary storage devices, or media: sequential devices and direct access devices.

Sequential devices require that records be stored and processed in linear sequence. Individual records are not addressable on these devices. Magnetic tape is the principal type of sequential medium used in computer systems. Tape media range from high-density, reel-mounted tapes used on large computer systems to the small cassettes and cartridges used on micros and personal computers. Magnetic tapes are used primarily to hold backup copies of a data base and logs and audit trails of data base updates, as a protection against system failure, and as a basis for data base recovery.

In a **direct access storage device** (DASD), the entire storage space is divided into a number of discrete locations, much like bins in a warehouse. Each location is individually addressable. As a result, a record can be stored or retrieved directly from a storage location without extensive scanning of other records.

Figure 4-2
Removable-media disk.
(Courtesy DEC.)

Types of Magnetic Disks

Two types of disk media are frequently used for data base applications: removable media (or disk packs) and fixed media (or Winchester disks).

Removable media refer to disk packs that are designed to be inserted into or removed from a disk drive. A **disk pack** is a set of disks that are mounted together in a stack. The disk pack is placed on a spindle in a disk drive, which rotates the disks at high speed. The major advantage of removable media is that the disk packs can be removed from the disk drive and used to store backup copies of the data or interchanged among disk drives for maximum flexibility.

An example of a disk drive that uses removable media (Digital RA60) is shown in Figure 4-2. The disk pack shown in this figure has a capacity of 205 million bytes (MB) of user data. There are three drives mounted in a cabinet, with a total capacity of 615 MB.

Fixed-media devices are those in which the disks are permanently mounted in the disk drive and cannot normally be removed. These devices are often referred to as **Winchester disks**, after the technology that was initially developed by IBM. With Winchester disks, the magnetic disks and access mechanism are sealed into a single unit called the **head-disk assembly**, or HDA. This unit is sealed in a clean-room environment, and it protects the recording media from external contaminants. Although Winchester disks are usually fixed-media devices, there are also removable Winchester disks.

Winchester disks range in size from the standard 14-inch-diameter units used in large computers to the 5¼-inch-diameter units frequently used in personal computers. Even smaller, more compact units (approximately 3 inches in diameter) are being introduced.

Winchester disks offer two important advantages over removable disks: improved data reliability, a result of eliminating contaminants that cause head-disk interference; and higher recording density, which results in higher data transfer rates and lower cost per megabyte of storage. In 1972, a megabyte of disk storage cost about $1000; ten years later it cost less than $40.

The only disadvantage of fixed-media disks is that since the disks cannot be removed, special provisions must be made to provide backup copies of data. Magnetic tape is often used to copy data files from Winchester disks for this purpose.

A fixed-media disk unit (IBM 3380) is shown in Figure 4-3. Each such disk drive has a total storage capacity of about 1260 MB. We will use this disk unit to illustrate many of the examples in the following sections.

Basic Magnetic Disk Concepts

Whether fixed or removable media are used, certain terms are used to describe disk units and their subdivisions. The major terms of interest are illustrated in Figure 4-4.

A **volume** is a physical storage unit such as a removable disk pack, fixed head-disk assembly, or reel of magnetic tape. Each disk surface in a volume is served by one (or more) read/write heads that are attached to access arms (see Figure 4-4). The access mechanism moves the heads in or out (relative to the center of the disks) and positions the heads at a specific track on the recording surface. All the recording heads move in unison, but only one read/write head may actually read or write data at any one time. The disk drive shown in Figure 4-3 uses two independent read/write actuators per disk drive, so that one actuator can be reading data while the other is "seeking" an address.

A **track** is a circular recording position on a disk surface that rotates under a read/write head. All the data recorded on a track may be read by a single read/write head without changing the position of the head.

A **cylinder** consists of the set of tracks that can be read without moving the read/write mechanism. In most disk units, a cylinder consists of the set of tracks from the various surfaces that are in the same radius (thus, the tracks are vertically aligned, as shown in Figure 4-4). In some current disk drives, a cylinder consists of several adjacent tracks on the same surface; however, we will assume a vertical arrangement in the following discussion.

Here are the physical characteristics for the disk drive shown in Figure 4-3:

Tracks per cylinder: 15

Cylinders per drive: 1770

Track capacity (bytes): 47,476

Thus, the total capacity of each cylinder is 15 tracks × 47,476 bytes per track, or 712,140 bytes. The total capacity of the disk drive is 1770 cylinders × 712,140 bytes per cylinder, or 1,260,487,800 bytes (1.26 gigabytes).

Figure 4-3
Fixed-media disk.
(Courtesy IBM.)

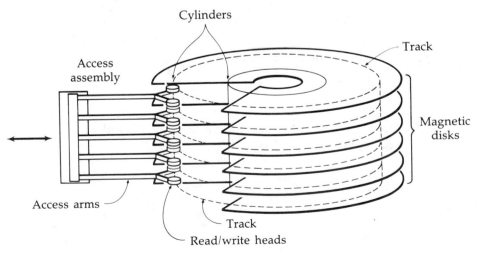

Figure 4-4
Components of a disk module.

This capacity is sufficient to store the text for nearly 1000 textbooks such as this one.

Disk Performance Factors

The time required to locate and transfer a block of data between disk and main memory depends on three factors: seek time, rotational delay, and transfer time. We will illustrate these factors using the IBM 3380 disk (shown in Figure 4-3) as an example.

Seek time (S) is the time required to move the access arm to a desired cylinder. The seek time may vary from zero (when the arm is already positioned at the correct cylinder) to some maximum value (when the arm must be moved between the first and last cylinders). For timing purposes, the *average* seek time (which is characteristic of the disk model) is usually used. The average seek time for the IBM 3380 disk unit is 16 milliseconds (msecs).

Rotational delay is the time required following a seek for the required data block to rotate to a position under a read/write head. The minimum time is zero, while the maximum time is that required for one complete revolution of the disk (R). The *average* rotational delay is $R/2$.

The IBM 3380 disk unit rotates at 3600 revolutions per minute (rpm). Thus, the time required for one complete revolution (R) is $60 \times 1000/3600$, or 16.7 msecs. The average rotational delay for this unit is $16.7/2$, or about 8.3 msecs.

Transfer time is the time required to transmit a block of data between disk and main memory. This factor depends on the data transmission rate (s) and the size of the data block in bytes (B) to be transmitted. The nominal data transmission rate for the IBM 3380 disk is 3 MB per second, or 3000 bytes per millisecond.

Random Access Times.   The average time (T) required to locate and transmit a random block of data is given by the formula

$$T = \text{seek time} + \text{rotational delay} + \text{transfer time}$$

$$= S + \frac{R}{2} + \frac{B}{s}$$

For example, for the IBM 3380, the average time to randomly locate and transmit a 3000-byte data block is

$$T = 16 + \frac{16.7}{2} + \frac{3000}{3000}$$

$$= 16 + 8.3 + 1$$

$$= 25.3 \text{ msec}$$

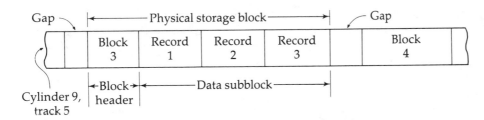

Figure 4-5
Physical storage block on
magnetic disk.

Sequential Access Times. When data blocks are accessed sequentially (rather than randomly), the access arm is positioned at a given cylinder and all data records on that cylinder are read (or written) without further access arm movement. Thus, for sequential access, the seek time is negligible and may be ignored. The average time to locate and transmit a record in this mode is approximately equal to the average rotational delay. For the IBM 3380, the average sequential access time is 8.3 msec.

DATA STORAGE ON DISKS

A disk volume is essentially a very large electronic filing cabinet. Instead of drawers with dividers, it is subdivided into cylinders, tracks, and blocks. In this section, we will examine the techniques for storing data records on disks.

Physical Storage Blocks

A physical storage block is the smallest addressable unit of data on a disk. We will refer to this unit simply as a **block** (the term *physical record* is also sometimes used). Normally, each track contains (or is subdivided into) a number of blocks. In some disk units, the size of a block is fixed by hardware considerations, while in other units, blocks are formatted by software so that the user can choose the block size. In the latter case, the same block size is normally used for an entire file.

A generalized diagram of a physical storage block is shown in Figure 4-5. Notice that the block is divided into two sections—a block header and a data subblock.

The **block header** contains data that allow the system to locate and identify the block. These data usually include a unique block number and the length of the data subblock that follows. (In Figure 4-5 we simply show the block number.) The contents of the block header differ from one disk model to another and also depend on the particular data format chosen by the user. We will illustrate some of the more common formats shortly.

The **data subblock** consists of the stored records that are contained in the block. Each stored record contains user data and may also contain overhead data (such as pointers) that are used to logically relate that particular record to other stored records. The data subblock is the unit of data that is transmitted between computer main memory and the disk volume in response to an input or output command. This means that the block header is *not* transmitted—it is maintained and used by the system to locate and identify data subblocks.

Addressing Storage Blocks

The address of a physical storage block is specified by three factors: cylinder number, track number (which specifies the surface), and block number. Thus, the address of the block shown in Figure 4-5 is given as follows:

Cylinder number: 9

Track number: 5

Block Number: 3

Given this block address, the computer can access the block directly. For example, it can execute a command such as the following: "Fetch the data subblock in block 3, track 5, cylinder 9." This command will cause the disk unit to locate that block and read the data subblock into an area of main memory.

The combination of cylinder, track, and block number is referred to as a **physical disk address**. To locate a specific record on magnetic disk, the disk control unit must pass a physical address to the disk unit. However, physical addresses are awkward for purposes of data management. For example, if the data file is reorganized or moved to another area on the disk volume, then the physical addresses of the data blocks must be changed. For this reason, relative (rather than physical) disk addresses are normally used for data management. With **relative disk addresses**, each address specifies a storage block's position relative to the start of the file. Thus, the first block in the file is viewed to have address 0, the second block address 1, and so on (see Figure 4-6).

For the remainder of this text, we will assume that relative disk addresses are used to locate physical storage blocks. That is, we will imagine that for each file stored on disk, the disk volume is organized into a series of physical blocks with relative addresses as shown in Figure 4-6. We will assume that the computer file management system being used converts the relative disk addresses to the necessary physical addresses.

Record Blocking

The number of data records contained in a data subblock is called the **blocking factor**. As shown in Figure 4-7, there are three options: unblocked records, blocked records, and spanned records.

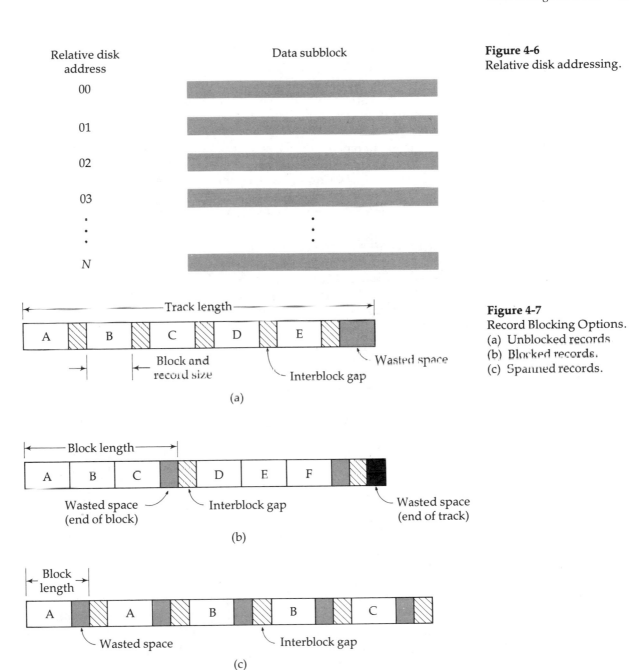

Figure 4-6
Relative disk addressing.

Figure 4-7
Record Blocking Options.
(a) Unblocked records
(b) Blocked records.
(c) Spanned records.

Unblocked Records. With unblocked records, each data subblock corresponds to one data record. If the length of the data subblock is the same as the length of a data record (as shown in Figure 4-7a), there is no wasted space within each subblock. However, depending on the length of a data subblock compared to the track length, there may be wasted space at the end of each track, as shown in the figure.

Blocked Records.   With blocked records, several data records are grouped into each data subblock (see Figure 4-7b). Depending on the block length relative to record length, there may or may not be wasted space within each data subblock. Also, there may be wasted space at the end of each track. The designer must choose the block size and blocking factor so as to avoid excess wasted space.

The main advantage of blocked records (compared to unblocked records) is that they speed up input/output operations. This is because a group of records is read or written with each input or output operation. Blocked records also conserve storage space, since there is one block header and interrecord gap for each block of records rather than for each record.

Spanned Records.   With spanned records, each data record is split into two or more segments. Each segment is stored in a separate data subblock (see Figure 4-7c). Spanned records are used only when the length of a record exceeds that of a fixed-length data subblock. Since spanned records complicate input/output operations, they are not widely used in data base applications.

Typical Data Formats

In this section, we will briefly describe three data formats frequently used in contemporary disk systems. The first two (count-data and count-key-data formats) are used in IBM (and IBM-compatible) disk drives, including the one shown in Figure 4-3. The third (sector addressing) is used in many other disk systems, including the one shown in Figure 4-2.

IBM Data Formats.   The two IBM data formats are shown in Figure 4-8. The designer may decide to use either approach, depending on the nature of the application.

The **count-data format** (Figure 4.8a) resembles the format shown in Figure 4-5. The count subblock (which corresponds to the block header) contains the relative address of the physical storage block on the track. The first block on each track has address 0, the second address 1, and so on. This relative address (or block number) is used to locate a specific block. The count-data format is used for sequential files and relative-addressed files.

The **count-key-data format** is shown in Figure 4-8b. With this format, the block header contains two subblocks: a count subblock and a key subblock. The count subblock contains the relative block address on the track (as in the count-data format). The key subblock contains the primary key of the *last* record in the block (that is, the record in that block with the largest primary key value). The count-key-data format allows the system to search a track until a block containing a record with a desired key is located. For example, in Figure 4-8b, the system could determine that block 3 con-

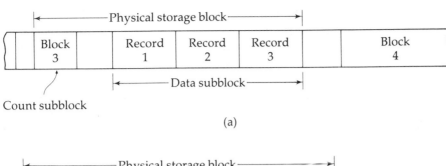

(a)

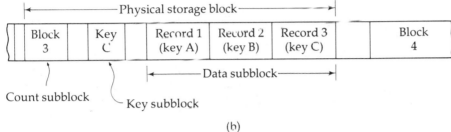

(b)

Figure 4-8
Common data formats
(IBM).
(a) Count-data format.
(b) Count-key-data
format.

tains the record with key equal to C (or less) before reading that block. The count-key-data format is used with indexed file organizations.

Sector Addressing.   With the **sector-addressing format**, each track is subdivided into a number of fixed length sections called **sectors**. A common sector size is 512 bytes (this is the sector length used in the disk unit shown in Figure 4-2). Each sector is addressable. With sector addressing, a physical storage block may consist of one sector or (in some units) two or more sectors linked together.

Throughout this text, we will assume that the IBM data formats are being used, although the principles are much the same when sector addressing is used.

Disk Storage Capacity

A typical problem in file design is to estimate the amount of disk capacity required for each file. This calculation depends on a number of factors: the characteristics of the disk volume, the number of records in the file, the record size, the blocking factor, and the data format to be used. We will illustrate the approach using the IBM 3380 disk unit as an example.

Suppose that an organization wants to create a file of customer records on magnetic disk. This file contains fixed-length records and has the following characteristics:

Number of records: 10,000   Blocking factor: 10 records per block

Record length: 200 bytes   Data format: count-key-data

The number of records that will fit on a track can be calculated using formulas or tables provided by the manufacturer. A track capacity table for the IBM 3380 disk is shown in Table 4-1. If we know the size of each data subblock and the data format to be used, we can look up the number of blocks per track.

The size of a data subblock is equal to the record size times the blocking factor. In our example this is 2000 bytes (200 bytes per record times 10 records per block). Referring to the columns for count-key-data format in Table 4-1, this number falls in the range from 1909 to 2068 bytes. According to the table, the number of blocks per track is 17 (the numbers 1909 and 2068 represent the minimum and maximum data subblock sizes with 17 blocks per track).

The number of records per track in this example will be 170 (since the blocking factor is 10). Thus, the file will require 10,000/170, or 59 tracks (rounded to the nearest integer). Earlier we stated that for the IBM 3380 disk there are 15 tracks per cylinder. Thus, the customer file will require 59/15, or 4 cylinders.

The total capacity of an IBM 3380 disk volume is 1770 cylinders. Thus, the customer file will require 4/1770, or less than one-fourth of 1%, of the capacity of the disk. Clearly, other files will be stored on the disk in addition to the customer file. This leads us to define two additional terms: extent and directory.

An **extent** is a collection of physical storage blocks that are contiguous on a magnetic disk. Normally, a file is allocated to a single extent; however, if enough contiguous blocks are not available, multiple extents may be used. A single extent for the customer file would consist of 1000 blocks and, as we have seen, will require four cylinders.

A disk **directory** is an index to the contents of a disk volume. Since each volume typically contains a number of files, a directory is necessary to identify and locate each file. The directory, which is located at the beginning of a volume, usually consists of two components: a home block and file headers. (Various terms are used in different systems.)

The **home block** contains information concerning the entire volume, including the volume name, a code indicating the owner of the volume, volume protection information, and a master index to the file headers.

Each **file header** identifies one file on the volume. It contains information such as a file name or identifier, file ownership, creation date, and protection factors. Most importantly, the file header contains a list of the extents that make up the file, the number of blocks in each extent, and the physical location of each extent. Thus, the directory provides the file management system the information required to locate the beginning of each file that is stored on the volume. When a file is created, extended, relocated, or otherwise changed, the system updates the disk directory to reflect these changes.

Table 4-1
IBM 3380 Track Capacity Table

Count-Data Format		Count-key Data Format		Blocks per Track
Data Subblock (bytes)		Data Subblock (bytes)		
Min.	Max.	Min.	Max.	
23,477	47,476	23,221	47,220	1
15,477	23,476	15,221	23,220	2
11,477	15,476	11,221	15,220	3
9,077	11,476	8,821	11,220	4
7,477	9,076	7,221	8,820	5
6,357	7,476	6,101	7,220	6
5,493	6,356	5,237	6,100	7
4,821	5,492	4,565	5,236	8
4,277	4,820	4,021	4,564	9
3,861	4,276	3,605	4,020	10
3,477	3,860	3,221	3,604	11
3,189	3,476	2,933	3,220	12
2,933	3,188	2,677	2,932	13
2,677	2,932	2,421	2,676	14
2,485	2,676	2,229	2,420	15
2,325	2,484	2,069	2,228	16
2,165	2,324	1,909	2,068	17
2,005	2,164	1,749	1,908	18
1,877	2,004	1,621	1,748	19
1,781	1,876	1,525	1,620	20
1,685	1,780	1,429	1,524	21
1,589	1,684	1,333	1,428	22
1,493	1,588	1,237	1,332	23
1,397	1,492	1,141	1,236	24
1,333	1,396	1,077	1,140	25
1,269	1,332	1,013	1,076	26
1,205	1,268	949	1,012	27
1,141	1,204	885	948	28
1,077	1,140	820	884	29
1,045	1,076	789	820	30

MANAGEMENT OF INPUT AND OUTPUT

We will now describe the hardware and software components used to manage input/output operations. Our purpose is to describe each component in just enough detail to explain its contribution to input/output (I/O) processing.

Figure 4-9
Major hardware
components.

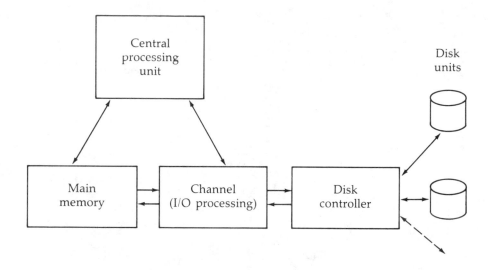

Figure 4-10
Major software
components.

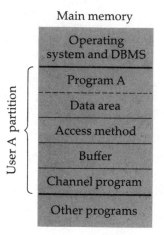

Hardware Components

The major hardware components of a computer with magnetic disk storage devices are shown in Figure 4-9. The arrows in this diagram represent the flow of both data and control information between the various devices.

The **central processing unit** (CPU) performs all calculations and logical operations and supervises all operations of the remaining computer components.

Main memory consists of a large number of addressable storage locations that are used to store both program instructions and data items. Data that are stored on magnetic disk must be transferred to main memory before they can be processed by a user program.

An **input/output processor** (or **channel**) is a device that executes input and output instructions under control of the CPU. An I/O processor is essentially a mini- or microcomputer that frees the CPU for other tasks by executing I/O instructions.

A **disk controller** controls the actual operation of one or more disk units. The disk controller handles all the specific characteristics of each disk unit, such as instructions to read tracks and cylinders. Most disk controllers today are programmable devices that help optimize disk performance and perform error recovery functions.

A microcomputer or personal computer would not contain all the components shown in Figure 4-9. The disk controller is often a chip or card and is normally packaged with the disk drive rather than as a separate unit. Also, most micros do not have channels; instead, the disk and controller are connected to the CPU through a simple port or interface.

Software Components

The major software components in a disk file management system are shown in Figure 4-10.

An **operating system** is the overall supervisory and control program of a computer. The operating system allocates memory, controls the execution of tasks, and provides a variety of utility and support functions.

Most computers today (except some small micros and minis) use a multiprogramming operating system. **Multiprogramming** is a technique whereby several programs are placed in main memory at the same time, *giving the illusion* that they are being executed simultaneously (they are, in fact, being executed consecutively). When a program requests an input or output operation (such as to read or write a record), the CPU interrupts execution of that program and hands the I/O task to an I/O processor. The CPU then executes another program until it, too, requires an input or output operation. Multiprogramming greatly improves the productivity of a computer, since the slower I/O operations are overlapped with other processing tasks.

A multiprogramming operating system allocates a **partition**, or area of main memory, to each user. The contents of a typical partition (shown in Figure 4-9) are a user application program (with its data area), an access method, a buffer, and a channel program.

An **application program** is a program that performs processing tasks for user functions such as accounts receivable, inventory, and student registration. An application program may insert new records in a data base or may modify or delete existing records. Most application programs are allocated a **data area** for the temporary storage of input and output records and program data.

A **buffer** is an area of memory used to receive a block of stored records from a storage device or used to transmit a block of records to that device. A

Figure 4-11
Input/Output processing.

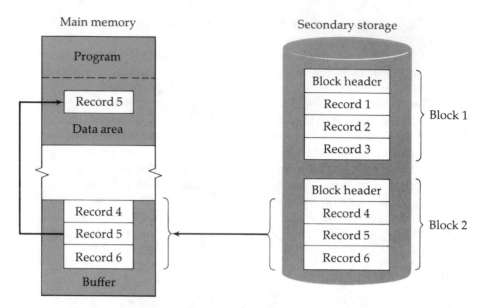

buffer must be large enough to contain an entire data subblock that is stored on a secondary storage device. In the example using customer records in the previous section, the size of a data subblock (and the corresponding buffer size) is 2000 bytes.

An **access method** is a file management subprogram provided by the operating system. When the CPU is executing an application program and a READ or WRITE instruction is reached, the CPU switches execution to the access method. A copy of the access method being used by a program may be maintained in the user partition or maintained in the system library and linked to user programs.

A **channel program** is a special program provided by the operating system and executed by an I/O processor. Executing a channel program causes a data subblock to be transmitted between secondary storage and a buffer.

Input/Output Processing

Now let us see how these hardware and software components are coordinated to transmit data records between secondary storage and a user program (see Figure 4-11). Suppose that a user program is being executed in a partition, as shown in the figure. This program accesses data records that are stored on a magnetic disk file (the blocking factor is 3 in this example). When an instruction to READ a record from this file is encountered, the CPU transfers control to the access method. The access method checks to see if the required record is located in the buffer in the program's partition. If the record is located in the buffer, then the access method transfers it from the buffer to the program data area and execution continues. (In Figure 4-11, record 5 has just been transmitted to the program data area.)

If the required record is not in the buffer, the access method passes a request for this record to the operating system. The operating system then builds a channel program to access the required data subblock on magnetic disk. The I/O processor executes this channel program and sends instructions to the disk controller, which activates the disk read/write mechanism as necessary. The required data subblock is read and transmitted to the buffer in main memory. While these input (or output) tasks are being performed, the operating system has transferred control to another user program. The sequence of events for a WRITE instruction is essentially the reverse of those for a READ instruction.

The type of I/O processing just described—where records are moved from a buffer to a program data area before they are processed—is called **move mode** processing. Some systems (and languages) also permit **locate mode** processing, in which records are processed in the buffer without moving them to a program data area. Although locate mode processing is more efficient, it is not available with all systems and is not used as frequently as move mode processing.

From our discussion, we see that the access method (a subprogram of the operating system) is responsible for delivering a single stored record to or from an application program. A program may request a record with a READ command or store a record with a WRITE command. The access method normally provides the following services, which are transparent to the application programmer: blocking and deblocking of records, locating and accessing required data subblocks and transmitting them between main memory and disk storage, and handling exceptions and error conditions. When a data base management system (DBMS) is used, the standard access methods are still normally used to provide these record-handling functions. However, it is the DBMS, acting on behalf of a user program, that initiates the READ or WRITE.

Virtual Storage

Early multiprogramming operating systems assigned a fixed-size memory partition to each user (this is the approach we have assumed in the previous discussion). This approach presented problems of space management and program design. A large program either had to be assigned to a large memory partition or had to be segmented to operate in a smaller partition. To overcome these problems, most multiprogramming operating systems today use an approach called virtual storage (see Figure 4-12).

The term **virtual storage** refers to the fact that an application program can be much larger than main memory. As shown in Figure 4-12, with virtual storage, a user program (and its associated access routines and data

Figure 4-12
Virtual storage.

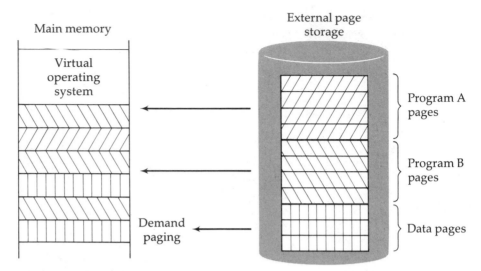

areas) resides in a partition of external storage (rather than a main memory partition). This storage is called **external page storage** and may be a high-performance disk unit or a mass-storage semiconductor device.

As shown in Figure 4-12, application programs and data files are divided into segments called **pages** (a typical page size is about 4000 bytes). At a given instant, only those pages required for program execution reside in main memory. When the CPU requires a page not in main memory, the virtual operating system causes this page to be read into main memory. This process of transmitting required pages is called **demand paging** and is managed by the virtual operating system. While a new program page is being read from external page storage, the operating system will have the CPU execute a page of another user program.

FILE ORGANIZATION

A **file organization** is a technique for physically arranging the records of a file on a secondary storage device (we will continue to assume the use of magnetic disks). An overview of the basic file organizations is shown in Figure 4-13. Three file organizations are shown: sequential, indexed, and direct. In an indexed organization, the records may be sequential (in which case a block index is used), or nonsequential (in which case a full index is required). We will consider only the indexed sequential case in this chapter (indexed nonsequential is described in Chapter 5).

In a direct file organization, two addressing schemes are frequently used: relative addressing, and hash addressing. When hash addressing is used, the addressing algorithm usually generates a relative address (this is indicated by an arrow from "hash-addressed" to "relative-addressed" in Figure 4-13).

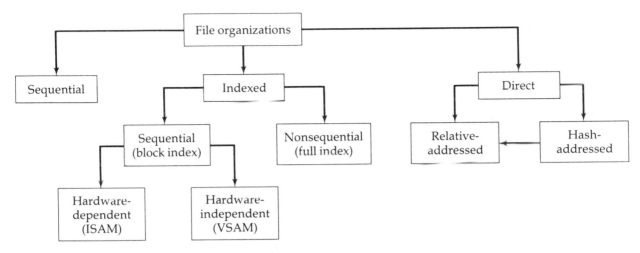

Figure 4-13
Overview of basic file organizations.

Comparison of Basic File Organizations

All the file organizations shown in Figure 4-13 (except indexed-nonsequential) consist of records whose only key is the primary key. A brief comparison of these organizations is presented in Figure 4-14.

In a **sequential** file organization (Figure 4-14a), the physical order of records in the file is the same as that in which the records were written to the file. Normally, this is in ascending sequence of the primary key (as shown in the example, which consists of the names of popular video games). A given record can be accessed only by first accessing all records that physically precede it.

In an **indexed sequential** organization (Figure 4-14b), the records are also stored in physical sequence according to the primary key. The file management system, or access method, builds an index, separate from the data records, that contains key values together with pointers to the data records themselves. This index permits individual records to be accessed at random without accessing other records. The entire file can also be accessed sequentially in an indexed sequential organization.

We will use the term *relative organization* to refer to a direct file organization in which relative addressing is used. In a *relative* organization (Figure 4-14c), each record can be retrieved by specifying its relative record number. The **relative record number** is a number from 0 to n that gives the position of the record relative to the beginning of the file. For example, a program can issue a command such as "read the fourth record in the file." It is the responsibility of the user (or application program) to specify the relative location of a desired record. Records in a relative file are often loaded in primary key sequence (as shown in Figure 4-14c) so that the file may be processed sequentially. However, the records may also be in random sequence, which occurs when the relative file organization is used in conjunction with hash addressing.

Figure 4-13
Overview of basic file organizations.

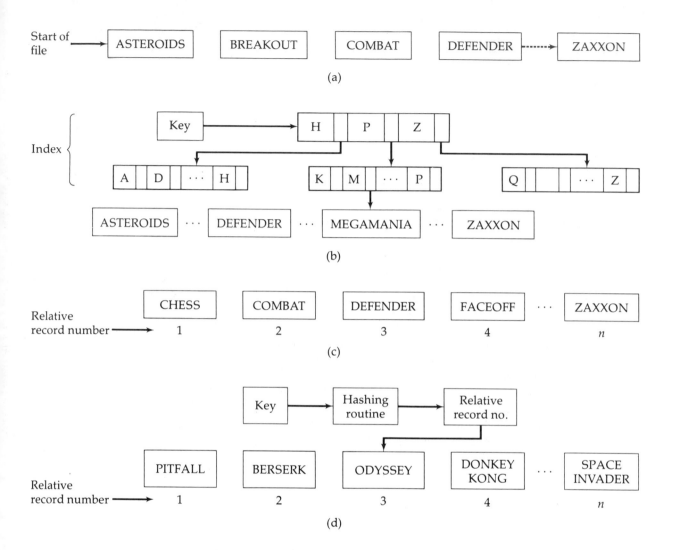

Figure 4-14
Comparison of file organizations.
(a) Sequential organization.
(b) Indexed sequential organization.
(c) Relative organization.
(d) Hashed organization.

The term *hashed organization* is used to refer to a direct file organization in which hash addressing is used. In a **hashed** organization (Figure 4-14d), the primary key value for a record is converted by an algorithm (called a **hashing routine**) into a relative record number. The record is then located by its relative record number, as for a relative organization. The hashing algorithm scatters the records throughout the file, and they are normally not in primary key sequence.

Record Access Modes

You may ask why there is a need for the various file organizations shown in Figure 4-13 (as well as the more complex organizations described in Chapter

Table 4-2
File Organizations and Record Access Modes

File organization	Record access mode	
	Sequential	Random
Sequential	Yes	No (impractical)
Indexed sequential	Yes	Yes
Direct-relative	Yes	Yes
Direct-hashed	No (impractical)	Yes

5). To answer this, we must review how the records in a file may need to be accessed in different applications. There are two basic modes for accessing records: sequential access and random access.

In **sequential access**, record storage or retrieval starts at a designated point in the file (usually the beginning) and proceeds in linear sequence through the file. Each record can be retrieved only by retrieving all the records that physically precede it. Sequential access is generally used for copying files and for sequential batch processing of records.

In **random access**, a given record is accessed "out of the blue" without referencing other records in the file. Unlike sequential access, random access follows no predefined pattern. Random access is typically used for on-line updating and/or retrieval of records.

A file organization is established when the file is created, and it is rarely changed. However, a record access mode can change each time the file is used. Thus, a file may be processed using the sequential-access mode one time and the random-access mode the next time. (In fact, the access mode may change from one record access to another.) It is therefore important to choose a file organization that permits efficient access according to the record access modes that will be required. Table 4-2 shows the combinations of file organizations and record access modes that are permitted in most systems.

As shown in the table, all the file organizations except sequential permit random access. Also, all the organizations except hashed permit sequential access. (Although physical sequential access to a hashed file is technically possible, it is not practical, since the records are not in logical sequential order.) Thus, two of the file organizations—indexed sequential and relative—permit access in both the sequential and random modes.

CASE EXAMPLE   Pine Valley Furniture

In the following sections, we will describe the indexed sequential and hashed organizations in greater detail. To illustrate each organization, we will use a portion of the Product file for Pine Valley Furniture Company (see Table 4-3). To simplify the presentation, only four data items are shown— PRODUCT# (the primary key), DESCRIPTION, FINISH, and ROOM.

Notice that there are gaps in the product number values in Table 4-3. As a result, it would not be practical to use a relative organization for this file, with product number as the relative record number, since there would be massive gaps in the storage file. (For example, the record for product# 100 would be followed by 24 empty record slots, then the record for product# 125.) This is a typical problem with primary key values, and it indicates why "primary key equals relative address" is not often an acceptable addressing technique for direct files.

INDEXED SEQUENTIAL ORGANIZATION

For several years, the indexed sequential file organization has been the "workhorse" organization for files that are stored on direct access storage devices. The reason is that this organization allows access to records in both the sequential and random modes. Most vendors supply access methods that support indexed sequential organizations and automatically maintain the indexes used to randomly access individual records.

The type of index used in an indexed sequential organization is referred to as a block index. In a **block index**, each index entry refers to a block of records (rather than a single record). This simplified index structure is made possible by the fact that the records within each block are in primary key sequence. To locate a specific record, we search the index to locate a block of records, then scan the block until the desired record is found.

If we are willing to maintain a file of records sorted by key values, we can always take advantage of this known order and use a block index to locate a given record quickly. For example, the white pages of an ordinary telephone directory represent an indexed sequential organization. In the upper left-hand corner of each page is the name of the first person listed on that page. By using this block index, we can quickly locate the page that contains a particular name. We then scan the names on that page until the desired name is located.

There are two basic implementations of the indexed sequential organization: hardware-dependent and hardware-independent. In IBM systems, the access methods that support these organizations are called, respectively, indexed sequential access method (ISAM) and virtual sequential access

Table 4-3
Product File (Pine Valley Furniture Company)

Product#	Description	Finish	Room	(Other data)
100	Stereo Cabinet	Maple	LR	
125	Coffee Table	Walnut	LR	
153	Hutch	Maple	DR	
207	Wall Unit	Oak	LR	
221	Stereo Cabinet	Pine	FR	
252	Dining Table	Maple	DR	
286	Desk	Birch	O	
314	Chair	Pine	FR	
363	Room Divider	Walnut	LR	
394	Dining Table	Oak	K	
418	Hutch	Birch	DR	
434	Bookcase	Pine	FR	
488	Lamp Table	Cherry	LR	
500	Computer Desk	Pine	O	
515	Bookcase	Maple	LR	

method (VSAM). Most other vendors provide similar access methods or file management systems. The hardware-independent version, or VSAM, is newer and more powerful and has replaced ISAM in many applications.

Hardware-Oriented Implementation (ISAM)

A diagram of an indexed sequential file that uses a single index is shown in Figure 4-15. The product records are stored in ascending product number sequence, three records per track. For simplicity, we assume that the records are unblocked, so that there is one product record per data subblock. The count-key-data format is used for indexed sequential (in Figure 4-15, only the key and data subblocks are shown). An overflow area is shown that will be used to hold new product records that may be added to the file.

A simple track index is shown with the product file in Figure 4-15. For each track, this index contains one entry, the highest key for a product record contained on that track. To locate a specific product record, we search the track index (using "highest key" as the argument) until we find a value that equals or exceeds the target product number. For example, suppose we wish to locate the record for product #418. Searching the track index, we find that this record must be located on track 4. Track 4 may then be scanned to locate record 418 (the count-key-data format allows the computer to search for a record with a specific key).

Figure 4-15
Simple indexed sequential
organization.

Track index

Track no.	Highest key
1	153
2	252
3	363
4	434
5	515

Track	Key	Record	Key	Record	Key	Record
1	100	Rec 100	125	Rec 125	153	Rec 153
2	207	Rec 207	221	Rec 221	252	Rec 252
3	286	Rec 286	314	Rec 314	363	Rec 363
4	394	Rec 394	418	Rec 418	434	Rec 434
5	488	Rec 488	500	Rec 500	515	Rec 515
6	Overflow area					

ISAM Architecture.   Most files require the use of more than one cylinder of a disk volume. When this occurs, the access method (ISAM) maintains a cylinder index that directs the search for a record to the cylinder on which it is located (see Figure 4-16). For large files, the cylinder index itself is split into several segments and a master index (or index to the index) is maintained. The master index may require one or more levels, depending on the size of the file.

The architecture of an indexed sequential file organization is shown in Figure 4-16. Indexed sequential files are normally composed of three areas:

1. The **prime area**, which contains the data records and the track index. (An index to the tracks of each cylinder is stored at the beginning of each cylinder.)

2. An **overflow area**, used for records that are added to the file but will not fit in the prime area.

3. An **index**, which contains the master index and cylinder indexes.

The use of the multilevel index is illustrated in Figure 4-16. Each arrow in this diagram represents a pointer from one index to a lower-level index. Suppose we wish to locate the record for product #500. Referring first to the master index, we are directed to the first cylinder index. Searching that index, we see that record #500 will be contained on cylinder 1 (if it is in the file). At this point, the disk access mechanism is moved to cylinder 1 (if

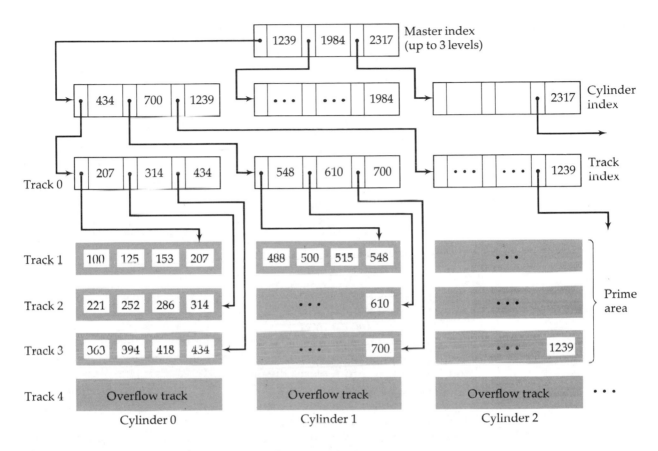

necessary) and the track index for that cylinder is read into main memory (we assume that the track index is contained on track 0). Searching the track index, we find that the desired record is on track 1 of that cylinder. The target record can then be read by scanning track 1.

In Figure 4-16, the records are unblocked. In most applications, however, it is much more likely that the records would be blocked (several records per data subblock). However, this would not change the index structure or search procedure shown in the figure. Once the track containing a particular record is identified, the track is searched for a physical block that contains that record. The search is straightforward, since in the count-key-data format, each subblock of records is preceded by a key subblock that contains the highest record key in the data subblock (see Figure 4-8).

Processing ISAM Files. When records are first loaded onto an ISAM file, the access method creates the indexes such as those shown in Figure 4-16. During subsequent processing of the file, searching and maintenance of this index are also carried out by the access method and are completely transparent to the program that accesses the file. For example, a program can request a particular record by specifying its primary key value. The access

Figure 4-16
Indexed sequential architecture.

Figure 4-17
Managing overflows in
ISAM.

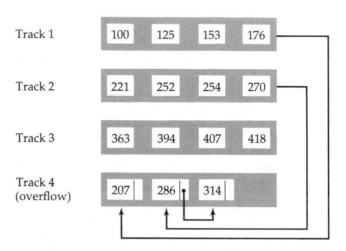

method (not the program) searches the indexes and delivers the requested record to the program data area.

To update a record in an ISAM file, the data subblock containing the record is read into main memory using either the sequential- or random-access mode. The record is modified, then written on top of the old record (thus, the new record replaces the old record).

Records to be deleted from an ISAM file are normally not physically removed (or erased) from the file immediately. Instead, a special delete character is placed in the first character position of each deleted record. This character is then used in subsequent accesses to inform a program that the record has been logically deleted from the file.

Inserting new records into an ISAM file (or any sequential file) presents special problems. To maintain the records in key sequence, it might seem necessary to push all the records down beyond the point of insertion. However, this is not a practical solution. Instead, two techniques are used to handle insertions.

With the first technique, some free space is left on each track (not shown in Figure 4-16). This free space will allow occasional insertions but cannot accommodate insertions of clusters of records (e.g., many new product records).

With the second method, overflow areas are reserved for records that overflow tracks in the prime area. Several tracks are usually reserved at the end of each cylinder for this purpose. Also, an independent overflow area may be reserved to receive records that overflow the cylinder overflow areas.

The method of handling overflows in ISAM is illustrated in Figure 4-17. First, record #176 was inserted into the file shown in Figure 4-16. To maintain key sequence, this record was inserted on track 1, replacing record 207, which was moved to the overflow track. A pointer was created from track 1, giving the address of the first overflow record for that track. (In reality, the pointer is placed in the track index, but we will not consider this technical detail.) Next, records numbered 254 and 270 were inserted into the file on track 2. The records they replaced (286 and 314) were moved to the overflow track. These records are chained together, as shown by the arrow from record 286 to record 314. Thus, the records in the prime area are maintained in logical sequence by physical position, while the records in the overflow area are maintained in logical sequence by means of pointers.

Over a period of time, the number of records in the overflow areas of an ISAM file will increase. As this occurs, the performance will decline, since more accesses are required on the average to retrieve each record. Thus, an ISAM file needs to be reorganized periodically. In reorganization, the entire file is reloaded and records in the overflow areas are moved to their proper location in the prime area. Also, the indexes are updated as necessary at this time.

Performance Factors.   A major advantage of indexed sequential files is that they permit rapid sequential access, which is the mode used for batch retrieval or updating. Since the records are in primary key sequence (or chained in an overflow area), an entire cylinder may be read without moving the access arm. The average access time for sequential processing is therefore equal to the average rotational delay. For the IBM 3380 (or any other disk drive that rotates at 3600 rpm), the average access time for this mode is about 8.3 msec.

In comparison, the average time for random access to an ISAM file is relatively slow. Although the master index to a file is often moved to main memory when the file is opened, the lower levels of a large index normally reside on disk. Thus, two or three disk accesses are required to search the index for random retrieval of a record. Also, when the target track is searched, it may turn out that the search must continue to an overflow area.

As a general rule of thumb, random access to a particular record in ISAM for a large file may be expected to require an average of about three disk accesses. In an earlier section we computed the average access time (seek time plus rotational delay) for the IBM 3380 disk drive as 25.3 msec. Therefore, the average random access time for a given record is about 3×25.3, or 75.9 msec. Thus, the maximum rate for random accesses to a large file is about 790 accesses per minute, computed as follows:

$$\frac{60 \times 1000}{75.9} = 790$$

In practice, the performance (measured in response time) of a system will decline rapidly well before the access rate reaches this theoretical maximum. We may therefore conclude that indexed sequential files can support a moderate volume of transactions that require random access. However, for high-volume applications (such as airline and other reservation systems), other file organizations (such as direct with hash addressing) are required to provide acceptable performance.

The access times for indexed sequential files (both ISAM and VSAM) can be improved by carefully locating the indexes. As we have already said, the track indexes in ISAM are located in the prime area (usually on the first track of each cylinder). This allows the system to avoid a seek (access arm movement) in going from a track index to the associated data records.

For optimum performance, the cylinder indexes in ISAM should not be interspersed with the data. Ideally, they should be located on a separate disk volume (preferably on a high-performance disk drive). This location permits index searching to proceed on one disk volume in parallel with data searching in the prime areas. However, if the higher-level indexes are located on the same volume as the data, they should *not* be stored on the first cylinder of the file. If the frequency of accesses to the data is fairly evenly distributed across the file, the optimum placement of the cylinder indexes is near the center of the prime data area.

Advantages and Disadvantages of ISAM.   The major advantages of an ISAM organization are that the file can be processed in both sequential and random modes, new records can be inserted in the middle of the file and processed either randomly or sequentially, and most vendors provide an access method that supports an indexed sequential organization.

The disadvantages of this file organization are that the file must be reorganized periodically to "clean up" overflow records and deleted records, random access to individual records is relatively slow, and the indexes are organized by hardware boundaries (tracks and cylinders). Because of this last item, when a file is transferred to a new disk volume (say with greater track capacity), the indexes must be completely reorganized.

Hardware-Independent Implementation (VSAM)

Virtual sequential access method (VSAM) is a more powerful and flexible access method than ISAM. It supports an indexed sequential organization with multilevel indexes that is similar in concept to ISAM. However, where ISAM organizes records (and therefore indexes) around tracks and cylinders, VSAM is free of these hardware boundaries.

VSAM Architecture.   The basic architecture of VSAM is shown in Figure 4-18. In an ISAM file, the basic indexed group of records is the collection of records on a track (the records may be blocked or unblocked). In a VSAM file, the basic indexed group is called a **control interval** (which may be considered a virtual track). The size of a control interval is chosen by the file designer and may be less than, equal to, or greater than the length of a track. Just as tracks on a disk are grouped into cylinders, control intervals in VSAM are grouped into **control areas** (or virtual cylinders).

Figure 4-18 shows some of the product records loaded on a VSAM file. As with an ISAM file, the records are loaded in primary key sequence in the

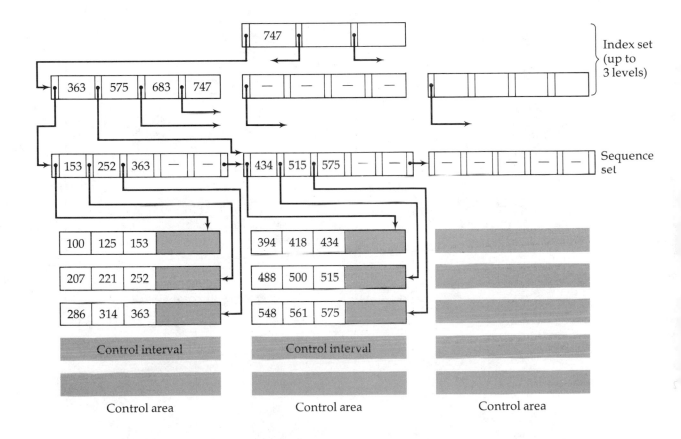

Figure 4-18
Architecture of VSAM.

control intervals. Notice that space for insertion of new records is reserved automatically at the end of each control interval. This is called **distributed free space**. Also, some control intervals in each control area are left empty. The amount of empty space in each control interval and the number of empty control intervals in a control area are specified by the file designer.

The index structure in VSAM is similar to that in ISAM. As shown in Figure 4-18, the index is divided into two components: the index set (up to three levels) and the sequence set. As with ISAM, locating a random record proceeds by starting with the highest level in the index set and progressively searching the index until the target control interval is identified. The control interval is then scanned to locate the desired record.

Record Insertions.   The method of handling record insertions in VSAM is more refined (and efficient) than in ISAM. When a new record is inserted, if the appropriate control interval is not full, the existing records are moved to the right by the access method and the new record is inserted in key sequence. This is illustrated in Figure 4-19, where record 350 has been inserted into control inverval 02. To make room for this new record, record 363 is moved back in the control interval.

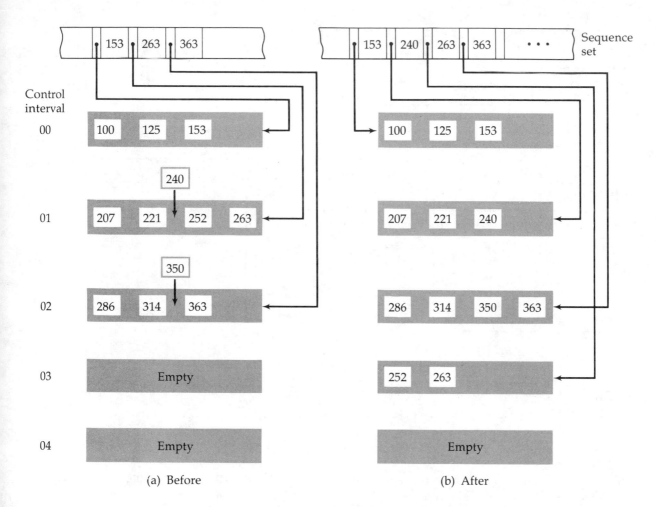

Figure 4-19
Managing record
insertions in VSAM.

Figure 4-19 also illustrates how insertions are managed when a control interval is full. Suppose we wish to insert record #240 into the file. This record should be placed in control interval 01, between records 221 and 252. However, control interval 01 is already full. Therefore, the access method (VSAM) performs a **control interval split**. About half the records in control interval 01 are placed into an empty control interval. In Figure 4-19, records 252 and 263 are placed in control interval 03, while records 207, 221, and 240 remain in control interval 01. A new entry is also placed in the sequence set so that this new control interval can be accessed.

Records are always maintained in sequence within each control interval. However, after a control interval split, the records are no longer in sequence within the control area as a whole. In our example, to access the records sequentially after the split, we would have to access the control intervals in the following order: 00, 01, 03, 02. However, notice that the entries in the associated sequence set *are* in sequence. Thus, the sequence set is used to maintain the logical order of records in a control area.

Following a large number of record insertions, a control area may become full. When this happens, it is no longer possible to perform another control interval split for further insertions, since all the control intervals are now full. In this case, VSAM performs a **control area split**, allocating a new control area to the file. Approximately half the records in the control area that has become full are moved to the new control area. The indexes are adjusted to reflect the new file structure.

The splitting of control intervals and control areas in an expanding VSAM file resembles the division of cells in a biological organism. No periodic reorganization of the file is required (unlike ISAM), since in essence the file is reorganized incrementally as splits occur.

Processing VSAM Files.　The sequence set is used for sequential processing of VSAM files. As a result of interval and area splits, the records are not in primary key sequence on the file (except immediately after the file is first loaded). However, the entries in the sequence set are in primary key sequence. Also, the components of the sequence set are chained together horizontally (see Figure 4-18). Therefore, by processing the sequence set from left to right, VSAM can access the records in logical order.

Random access to records in VSAM is similar to that for ISAM. The search begins at the highest level of the index set and proceeds to lower levels until the control interval containing the target record has been located. As with ISAM, the random-access time may be relatively slow owing to the levels of index that must be traversed.

Advantages of VSAM.　VSAM offers three major advantages over ISAM. First, periodic file reorganization is not required, since the file can grow indefinitely by means of the splitting process. Second, the file organization is independent of hardware characteristics. (Thus, a file can be moved to a different volume without restructuring the indexes.) And finally, some versions of VSAM support secondary keys (which are described in Chapter 5).

HASHED FILES

In most on-line systems, the dominant (or exclusive) mode of file access is random. Typical of these are reservation systems (e.g., airline, hotel, and car rental) and information retrieval systems (e.g., library and stock market quotation). In these systems, both updating and retrieval are accomplished in the random mode, and there is rarely a need for sequential access to the data records.

In such applications, a hashed file organization is often preferred. A hashed file organization provides rapid access to individual records, since it is not necessary to search indexes. The major disadvantage of this organization is that sequential processing is not convenient because the records are

Figure 4-20
Major components of
hashed files.
(Source: Severance and
Duhne 1976.)

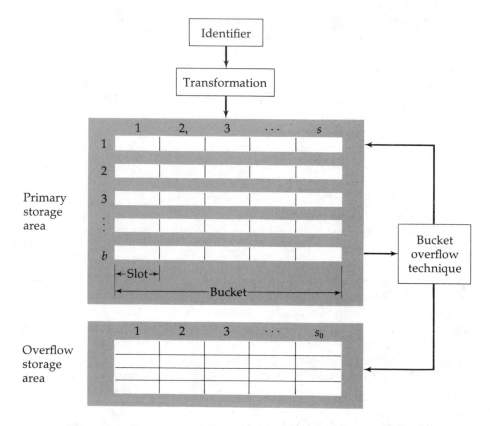

not stored in primary key sequence. However, this is not an important
consideration for many on-line applications.

Hashed File Principles

The major components and terms associated with hashed files are shown in
Figure 4-20. The primary storage area is divided into a number of addressable locations, called **buckets**. Each bucket consists of one or more **slots**
where records may be stored. An addressing algorithm transforms each
record identifier into a relative address (or bucket number), and the record is
stored in that bucket if there is an empty slot. If all slots in the bucket are full,
then the record is stored in a bucket in an overflow area.

In terms of the IBM architecture that we have been assuming throughout this chapter, a bucket is simply a physical storage block. The count-data
format (shown in Figure 4-8a) is used for hashed files. With this format, the
file management system can search for a particular physical storage block (or
bucket).

Hashing Routines. Records are assigned to buckets by means of a **hashing
routine**, or transformation, which is an algorithm that converts each primary

key value into a relative disk address. Ideally, the hashing routine that is chosen should distribute the records as uniformly as possible over the address space to be used. This provides two important benefits. First, collisions are minimized. (A **collision** is the assignment of two or more records to the same bucket.) And second, file space is utilized as efficiently as possible.

Of the numerous hashing algorithms that have been proposed (see Martin 1977 for a summary), the one that consistently performs best under most conditions is the **division/remainder method**. The steps used in this procedure are as follows:

1. Determine the number of buckets to be allocated to the file.

2. Select a prime number that is approximately equal to this number.

3. Divide each primary key value by the prime number. (Note that if the primary key value is alphanumeric, it must first be converted to numeric form.)

4. Use the remainder as the relative bucket address.

Figure 4-21 shows the results of applying this hashing routine to the product file. In part (a) of this figure, a bucket size of 1 is used, while in part (b), the bucket size (or record blocking factor) is 2. To simplify the illustration, only the primary key values (rather than the complete records) are shown in each bucket.

Since there are 15 product records (that is, no more than 15 exist at any one time), with a bucket size of 1 at least 15 buckets will be required. In designing a hashed file, it is best to allow some free space (we will discuss this later). In this example, 19 buckets (numbered 00 to 18) are allocated. This results in a file load factor of 15/19, or about 80%. The hashing routine consists of dividing each product number by 19 (a prime number) and saving the remainders.

The first product number (100) is divided by 19, with the following result:

$$19{\overline{\smash{\big)}\,100}} \begin{array}{r} 5 \\ \underline{95} \\ 5 \end{array}$$

Since the remainder is 5, this record is stored in bucket 05. Next, this procedure places record 125 in bucket 11 and record 153 in bucket 01. This procedure continues until we reach record 252. When 252 is divided by 19, the remainder is 5. Since bucket 05 is already full, we have our first collision. A common procedure is to place a record that will not fit in its "home" address into the next available empty bucket (this is called **open overflow**). In this case, record 252 could be placed in bucket 06. However, this might

Figure 4-21
Hashed files for product
records.
(a) Bucket size=1.
(b) Bucket size=2.

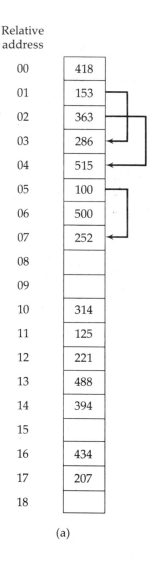

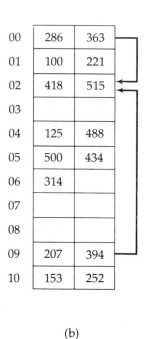

(a)   (b)

displace another record (yet to be loaded) whose hashed address is 06. To
avoid this, record 252 is set aside until all other records have been loaded in
their home addresses.

    The result of loading this file is shown in Figure 4-21a. The records were
loaded in two passes. In the first pass, all records that fit in their home
addresses were stored. In the second pass, the records that created collisions
in the first pass were stored in the first available address following their
home address. Although the hashing routine distributed the records fairly
uniformly throughout the file, there were three collisions: records 252, 286,
and 515. For each of these displaced records, a pointer is placed in the home
bucket to indicate its overflow location. This technique is called **chained
overflow**.

In Figure 4-21b, a hashed file with a bucket capacity of 2 is shown for the same product records. In this case, 11 buckets (numbered 00 to 10) were used. Each product number was hashed by dividing by the prime number 11 and saving the remainder. As in the previous example, the records were loaded in two passes. Two collisions resulted, for records 418 and 515. Since the home address for record 515 is bucket 09, the search for an available space for this record resulted in the record being placed in bucket 02 (in this case, the search "spilled over" to the beginning of the file).

To retrieve a record in a hashed file, the hashing algorithm is applied to the primary key value to calculate the relative bucket address. If the record is located at its home address, then only one disk access is required. If it is in an overflow area, then two (or more) accesses are required. Referring to Figure 4-21a, 12 of the records will require one disk access, while the other 3 records will require two accesses. Assuming that the frequency of accesses to these records is equal, the **average search length** (or number of accesses per record) is 1.2, computed as follows:

$$\text{Average search length} = \frac{(12 \times 1) + (3 \times 2)}{15} = 1.2$$

For an IBM 3380 disk unit, the average access time for this file is 1.2 accesses per record $\times$ 25.3 msec (average access time), or 30.36 msec. The theoretical maximum access rate is slightly less than 2000 accesses per minute.

Managing Overflows

As illustrated in the preceding examples, collisions and overflows are inevitable with hashed files. It is therefore necessary to devise methods for storing and retrieving records that exceed a bucket's capacity. Normally, there is a choice of the chaining technique as well as the type of overflow area to be used.

Chaining Technique. Overflow records may simply be placed in the next available empty slot (open overflow). However, some form of chaining (or use of pointers) is normally used to reduce the number of accesses required to locate an overflow record. As shown in Figure 4-22, there are two types of overflow chaining: coalesced and separate.

With **coalesced chaining**, a record that overflows its home bucket is placed in a free slot in any unfilled bucket. A pointer chain is established for the synonym records. For example, in Figure 4-22a, assume that the home bucket for record D is bucket 1. Since bucket 1 is full, record D is placed in an empty slot in bucket 2. Now an attempt is made to place record Z in bucket 2 (its home address). Since bucket 2 is now full, this record overflows to bucket 3. Notice that with coalesced chaining, overflow from one primary bucket may cause premature overflow in another primary bucket. With

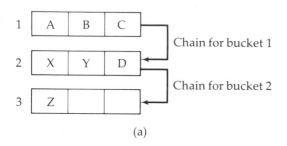

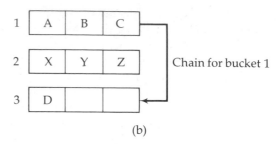

(a)   (b)

Figure 4-22
Types of overflow chaining.
(a) Coalesced chaining.
(b) Separate chaining.

coalesced chains, record retrieval times increase as a file load factor grows.

With **separate chaining**, overflow records are relocated to avoid the merging of synonym chains. For example, in Figure 4-22b, record D is initially placed in bucket 2. However, when an attempt is made to place record Z in bucket 2, record D is relocated to bucket 3. Notice that only one pointer chain is now required, instead of two chains in the coalesced case. Thus, separate chains have faster retrieval than coalesced chains; however, overhead is required to relocate records.

Separate Overflow Area.   Overflow records may be placed in empty slots in the primary storage area or in an independent overflow storage area (shown in Figure 4-20). An independent overflow storage area provides three important advantages: it avoids coalesced chains, thereby avoiding an increase in average retrieval times; it avoids the overhead required to relocate overflow records from primary buckets when those buckets are required as home addresses; and it permits orderly and inexpensive file expansion.

In summary, with hashed files, it is usually preferable to place overflow records in buckets in an independent overflow area, with pointers in the home buckets to the overflow buckets.

Hashed File Design

In designing hashed files, the primary objective is to provide fast random access to records. Thus, the average search length must be kept as close to 1 as possible. Other considerations such as efficient use of storage space are of secondary importance.

There are three factors that will reduce collisions and minimize the average search length in hashed files:

1. Use a hashing routine that distributes the records as evenly as possible over the available address space (the division/remainder method should normally be used).

2. Select a low load factor (assign more disk capacity than is required for the file).

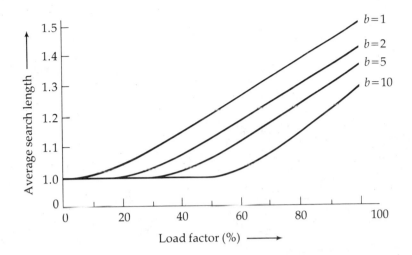

Figure 4-23
Average search length
versus load factor.
(Source: James Bradley,
*File and Data Base
Techniques*, New York,
Holt, Rinehart & Winston,
1982.)

3. Use a larger bucket capacity (blocking factor).

Load Factor. The **load factor** is the percentage of the space allocated to the file that is taken up by records in the file. For example, the load factor in the file shown in Figure 4-21b is 15/22, or about 68%.

A low load factor reduces the number of records that overflow their home addresses. This, in turn, reduces the average search length. In practice, load factors between 50% and 80% should normally be used. If the file is expected to grow, then a lower load factor should be used initially, since it will increase as insertions occur.

Bucket Capacity. Increasing the bucket capacity will also reduce the number of overflows and hence the average search length. This is true because with a bucket capacity greater than 1, some collisions can occur before overflow becomes necessary. Unfortunately, using a bucket capacity greater than 1 can complicate the programming task, as we will soon see.

Given the load factor and bucket capacity, we can use formulas or curves to estimate the average search length. The curves shown in Figure 4-23 show the average search length versus load factor for bucket sizes of 1, 2, 5, and 10 (chained overflow is assumed). For a load factor of 100% and a bucket capacity of 1, the average search length is about 1.5. Notice that for a given load factor (say 80%), we can reduce the average search length by increasing the bucket capacity.

Managing Hashed Files

A comparison of hashed files in a traditional file environment and in a data base environment is shown in Figure 4-24. This figure helps explain why hashed files are more widely used in a data base environment.

Figure 4-24
Managing hashed files
in a traditional file
environment versus a
data base environment.
(a) Traditional file
    environment.
(b) Data base
    environment.

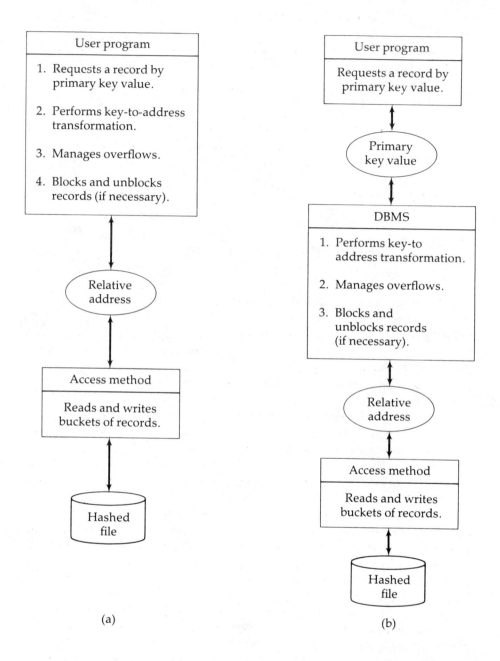

(a)

(b)

File Environment.   Most access methods (or file management systems) do
not directly support hashed files. Instead, the access method supports a
relative file organization. Therefore, as shown in Figure 4-24a the programmer writing a program that will manipulate hashed files must code many of
the file management functions. For example, in writing a COBOL program,
the programmer must code the hashing routine (or else cause a routine to be

copied from a common library). Also, the programmer is responsible for coding the overflow management routines (such as progressive chained overflow). Finally, if records are blocked (bucket capacity is greater than 1), the programmer must write instructions to block and unblock records. The coding task becomes quite complex, and as a result, hashed files are used only when absolutely necessary.

Data Base Environment. Most data base management systems today directly support hashed files. As shown in Figure 4-24b, the file management functions—hashing routines, overflow management, and record management—are built into the DBMS. As a result, the application programmer is relieved of coding these routines and can write instructions that request a record by its primary key value. The DBMS transforms this value to a relative address, which is then passed on to the access method. In fact, the ease of using direct hash-addressed file organizations is one of the major advantages of a data base management system.

Advantages and Disadvantages

Hashed files offer two major advantages over indexed sequential organizations: random access is faster (nearly three times as fast as ISAM), and insertions and deletions are more easily handled.

On the other hand, hashed files have three disadvantages: sequential access is impractical; disk space is not as efficiently utilized (because of lower load factors); and the programming task may be more complex (not true when a DBMS is used).

SUMMARY

This chapter presented a review of the basic principles and methods of file organization. A file organization is a technique for organizing and accessing records on secondary storage devices.

Throughout the chapter, we have assumed the use of magnetic disk storage devices. We reviewed the basic hardware terms and performance factors associated with magnetic disks—tracks, cylinders, sectors, access times, and so on. Also, basic data formats, such as count-key-data and count-data, were described.

Vendor-supplied access methods insulate the user from many of these hardware details. They allow us to visualize a file extent as a series of storage locations. Each storage location can hold one or more records and can be addressed by specifying its location relative to the beginning of the file. The access method translates this relative address to the necessary hardware address and manages other hardware-dependent details.

Three basic file organizations are frequently used: sequential, indexed, and direct. Indexed sequential organizations (the most common of all) are used when both sequential and random access to a file are required. Direct files with hashed addressing are frequently employed in on-line data base applications when fast random access to records is required for updating and retrieval. Sequential file organizations are used primarily in making backup copies of data bases.

CHAPTER REVIEW

Review Questions

1. Give concise definitions for each of the following terms:
   a. volume
   b. extent
   c. buffer
   d. multiprogramming
   e. virtual storage
   f. hashing routine
   g. block index
   h. control interval
   i. bucket
   j. collision
   k. load factor

2. Contrast the following terms:
   a. removable media; fixed media
   b. physical address; relative address
   c. count-data format; count-key-data format
   d. access method; channel program
   e. ISAM; VSAM
   f. separate chaining; coalesced chaining

3. Prepare a table showing the major advantages of each of the following:
   a. sequential file organization
   b. indexed sequential file organization
   c. hashed file organization

4. Briefly describe three typical magnetic disk data formats.

5. What information is typically contained in each of the following?
   a. Home block
   b. File header

6. What hardware device normally performs the following function?
   a. Stores instructions and data at execution time.
   b. Executes I/O instructions under CPU control.
   c. Performs calculations and logical operations.
   d. Optimizes disk performance and performs error recovery.

7. Describe three techniques for reducing collisions in hashed files.

8. Give two examples (other than those presented in the text) of everyday occurrences of indexed sequential files.

9. Describe two techniques for managing overflows from a home address in hashed files.

10. With respect to the physical areas of a disk, list in decreasing order of desirability the areas you would use to store overflow from a home address.

Problems and Exercises

1. The inventory file for Apex Manufacturing Company contains 40,000 records. Each record contains 500 bytes (fixed length). The records are to be stored on an IBM 3380 disk volume using the count-key data format.
   a. How many cylinders will be required if the blocking factor is 2?
   b. How many cylinders will be required if the blocking factor is 10?
   c. If the records are stored as a VSAM file, what will be the average time to access a record at random (assume that three disk accesses are required)?

2. Redraw the VSAM file in Figure 4-19b to show the effect of inserting the following records:
   a. primary key value 248   b. primary key value 337

3. Redraw the ISAM file in Figure 4-17 to show the effect of inserting the following records (create an additional overflow track if necessary):
   a. primary key value 215   b. primary key value 328

4. A hashed file is to have a capacity of approximately 1000 buckets. The prime number 997 will be used as a divisor in the hashing routine. What addresses will be generated for records with the following key values: 762, 20439, 618472?

5. Redraw the hashed file in Figure 4-21a to show the effect of inserting the following records:
   a. primary key value 170   c. primary key value 40
   b. primary key value 695

6. What is the average search length for the file shown in Figure 4-21b?

7. The disk unit shown in Figure 4-2 has the following characteristics:

Sector size: 512 bytes	Cylinders per disk pack: 1600
Sectors per track: 43	Average seek time: 41.7 msec
Tracks per cylinder: 4	Rotational speed: 3600 rpm

   a. What is the total capacity (in bytes) for each disk pack?
   b. What is the average access time?

8. Refer to the disk unit described in Problem 7.

   a. What is the average sequential access time to records in an ISAM file?

   b. What is the average random access time to records in an ISAM file?

   c. What is the average random access time to records in a hashed file? Assume that each sector (or bucket) contains one record and that a load factor of 75% is used.

9. Refer to the file described in Problem 1. Suppose that this file is to be loaded on the disk unit described in Problem 7. Assume that records do not span sectors (therefore, there will be only one record per sector).

   a. How many cylinders will be required for the data records of this file?

   b. What percent of the total capacity of a disk pack will be required for the data records of this file?

10. The disk unit described in Problem 7 is to be used to store a file containing 10,000 records. A hashed file organization is to be used. The size of each record is 100 bytes. Since the sector size is 512 bytes, five records will be stored per sector (thus, the bucket size is 5).

    a. If an average search length of 1.3 is acceptable, what load factor should be used?

    b. Given your answer to part (a), how many buckets (or sectors) should be allocated to this file?

    c. Given your answer to part (b), how many tracks should be allocated to this file? How many cylinders?

11. Refer to the ISAM file shown in Figure 4-16. On what cylinder and track are each of the following records located?

    a. product #573

    b. product #685

12. A disk drive for a personal computer has the following characteristics:

    Bytes per track: 5000
    Tracks per cylinder: 8
    Cylinders per disk pack: 100
    Average rotational delay: 10 msec
    Average seek time: 30 msec

    a. What is the total capacity of the disk drive?

    b. A sequential file with 5000 records is placed on this unit. Each track can contain 20 records. How many cylinders are required for this file?

13. Visit a computing center that processes commercial applications.

    a. What access methods are available with this computer and its operating system?

    b. Identify examples of each of the file organizations described in this chapter.

    c. Discuss the factors that are considered in designing files.

References

Bradley, James. 1982. *File and Data Base Techniques*. New York: Holt, Rinehart & Winston.

Katzan, Harry, Jr. 1975. *Computer Data Management and Data Base Technology*. New York: Van Nostrand Reinhold.

Martin, James. 1977. *Computer Data Base Organization*. 2d ed. Englewood Cliffs, N.J.: Prentice-Hall.

Severance, Dennis, and Ricardo Duhne. 1976. "A Practioner's Guide to Addressing Algorithms." *Communications of the ACM* 19 (June): 314-326.

Ullman, Jeffrey D. 1982. *Principles of Database Systems*. 2d ed. Rockville, Md.: Computer Science Press.

5

Data Structures

INTRODUCTION

Data structures are the combination of brick, mortar, and glue that hold data bases together. In Figure 5-1 (reproduced from Figure 4-1), data structures apply to the internal model level in the ANSI/SPARC model introduced earlier. This means that data structures are primarily used by data management technologies (like data base management systems, operating system access methods, and application development packages) and are often transparent to application or end user programming.

The efficiency of an application program, such as an Inventory Master File update program for Pine Valley Furniture, depends on the use of a well-chosen data management technology. Occasionally, application designers and programmers need to design a new data structure for some specialized requirement; usually, however, the responsibility of the information systems designer is to understand the data processing required and to choose appropriate technologies, including data structures. To make this choice, we need to know how data structures work, which is the purpose of this chapter.

Data structures are used to represent associations between elements of data. These elements could be data items, records, or "data about data," such as the ISAM track index entries in Figure 4-15. For example, data structures can be used to link a Product# to its Description and to also connect a Customer record to its associated Open Order records.

In general, data structures connect one element of data to another. This can be viewed in a graphical form, as depicted in Figure 5-2. Here each element of data (data item, record, or overhead data) is a node. Links

122

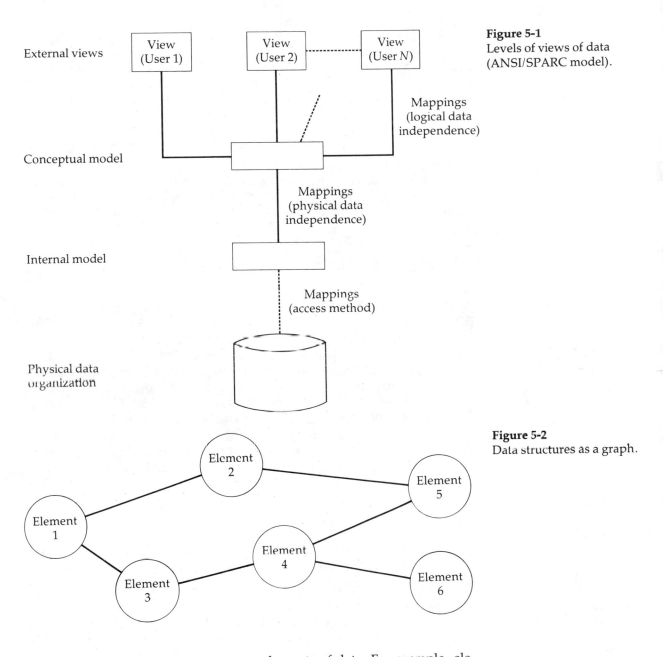

Figure 5-1
Levels of views of data
(ANSI/SPARC model).

External views

View (User 1) View (User 2) View (User N)

Mappings
(logical data
independence)

Conceptual model

Mappings
(physical data
independence)

Internal model

Mappings
(access method)

Physical data
organization

Figure 5-2
Data structures as a graph.

Element 2

Element 5

Element 1

Element 4

Element 3

Element 6

represent an association between two elements of data. For example, element 1 might stand for a Customer record and element 2 might represent an Order record; then the link between them means that the relationship between a Customer and his or her Orders is represented explicitly in the data structure. The links on the graph give the graph its structure, or architecture. It is the particular structure of graph and the way these links are implemented that distinguish one data structure from another.

A data structure is static and "comes to life" only through use. It is as important to discuss how to process (sometimes called "traverse") data structures as it is to discuss their form. Some data structures process updates efficiently with modest data retrieval speed; other structures provide very rapid retrieval, but maintenance is very costly. Both form and process will be covered in this chapter.

Data structures can basically be described by two characteristics: the method used to connect one data element to an associated data element and the architecture of the data structure graph that can be constructed. The first characteristic, called the location method, seems to be more fundamental, and this is where we will begin. We will discuss the second characteristic, architecture, later in the chapter.

BASIC LOCATION METHODS

All data structures assume that data is to be organized so that one element of data precedes another, and so on. Thus, terms like PRIOR/NEXT or PREDE-CESSOR/SUCCESSOR are frequently used when talking about locating data. That is, finding data is relative to having already found some other piece of data. Data are also assumed to have a natural, logical sequence or sorting rule (like ascending on part number). Basic location methods are used to connect given data to their predecessors and successors in this sequence. Location methods involve both connection mechanisms and methods for relative placement of actual data. Together, the alternatives for both connection and placement can be used to describe the traditional sequential, linked list, and inverted data structures, as well as various other basic structures and hybrids.

There are only two basic methods for *connecting* elements of data, as outlined by Severance (1974):

Figure 5-3 (opposite)
Basic location methods.
(a) Address sequential connection (sequential).
(b) Pointer sequential connection (simple chain or list).
(c) Address sequential, data indirect connection ("inverted").
(d) Pointer sequential, data indirect connection ("list inverted").

1. An **address sequential** (AS) connection, in which a successor element is placed and located in the physical memory space immediately following the current element (see Figures 5-3a and c).

2. A **pointer sequential** (PS) connection, in which some additional data (called a pointer) are explicitly stored in the current element to identify the location of the successor element (see Figures 5-3b and d).

Also, there are only two basic methods for *placement* of data relative to the connection mechanism:

1. **Data direct** (DD) placement, in which the connection mechanism links an item of data directly with its successor (and/or predecessor) item (see Figures 5-3a and b).

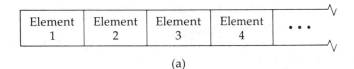

(a)

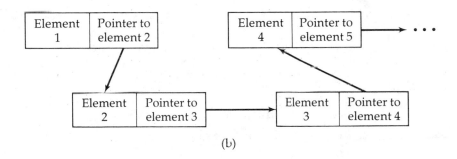

(b)

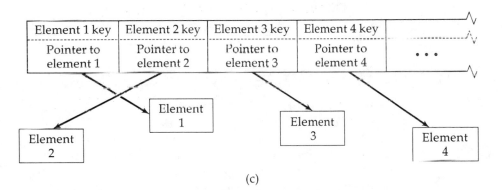

(c)

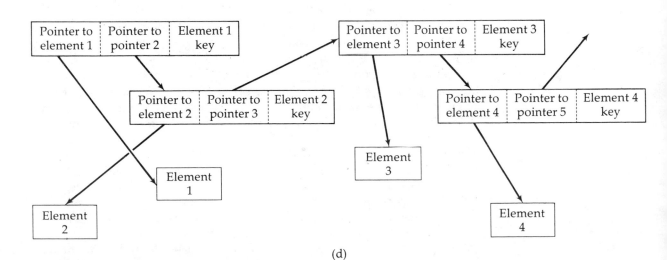

(d)

2. **Data indirect** (DI) placement, in which the connection mechanism links pointers to the data, not the data themselves (see Figures 5-3c and d).

Address Sequential Connection

Address sequential data direct (ASDD, or simply sequential) was described in Figure 4-15a when we were discussing file organizations. It is simple, easy to understand and process, uses no extra storage space above that required for data, and it supports efficient sequential access. Now let's take another look at the list of typical data base operations for record processing introduced at the beginning of Chapter 4 and reproduced below:

1. Fetch an arbitrary record from the file.
2. Insert a record into the file.
3. Modify a record in the file.
4. Read the entire file.
5. Read the next record in the file.
6. Delete a record from the file.
7. Reorganize the file.

Sequential performs rather well for operations 3, 4, and 5, but is cumbersome, if not impractical, for the others.

   With ASDD, arbitrary (randomly selected) records cannot be found without possibly extensive scanning of the data structure. For example, consider a typical business file of 100,000 records and sequential access time (conservatively, we will use only average rotational delay) of 8.3 msec (as calculated in Chapter 4 for an IBM 3380 disk drive). We will assume for simplicity here that each record access requires a physical file access (i.e., no record blocking) and that there is a random application program record processing time between record reads. Access to an arbitrary record (by physical sequential scanning) would be from 8.3 msec (to access the first record) to 830 seconds ($13^5/_6$ minutes to access the last physical record), with an average of 6 minutes and 55 seconds (access to middle record of file). These calculations also assume that each access will require a rotational delay and that seeks occur infrequently so that seek time can be ignored.

   Insertion of a new element in an ASDD data structure requires that all subsequent elements be moved, which can be time-consuming. Modification is easy if we can simply write the new element values over the old, but sequential data storage media like magnetic tape require the whole set of data to be rewritten. Element deletion itself is simple if we only mark the deleted element as purged and do not immediately recover this now unused space. Depending on the amount of deletion activity, this practice of only marking deletions can lead to excessive wasted space and frequent data

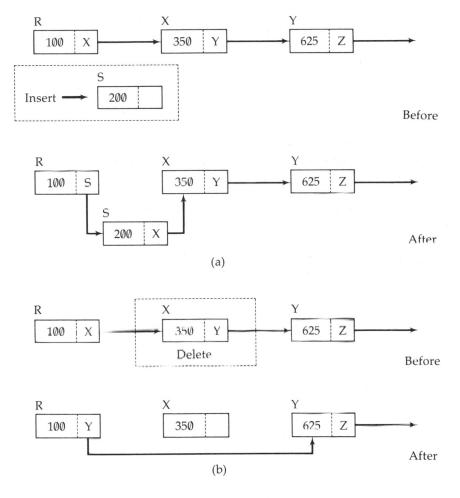

Figure 5-4
Maintenance of pointer
sequential data structure.
(a) Insertion into a
    pointer sequential
    data structure.
(b) Deletion from a
    pointer sequential
    data structure.

reorganizations. Reorganization requires the costly act of rewriting the whole set of elements.

Pointer Sequential Connection

Pointer sequential data direct (PSDD, or list) data structures greatly decrease the cost of performing insertion and deletion of new elements; but fetching random elements is not less costly than with ASDD. Figures 5-4a and b, respectively, illustrate how new product numbers can be added to and deleted from a PSDD data structure for the Pine Valley Furniture Product Master File. For insertion of product# 200, once space for the new product record is located (which can be *anywhere* in the file where there is an available record slot), then insertion only requires changing two pointers, the pointer in the predecessor record of product# 200 (i.e., 100 at location R) and the pointer in the product# 200 record itself (set to the location of the successor of

100 prior to the insertion). The remainder of the data structure is independent of this change. This can be viewed as adding a new link to a chain. In a later section ("Linear Interrecord Data Structures"), we will present pseudocode for insertion (and deletion) procedures of several pointer sequential data structures. At this point, concentrate on understanding what has to be done to maintain pointer sequential connections, not *how* (in computer programming terms) to perform such maintenance.

Deletion of an element from a PSDD data structure is even simpler and can be viewed as welding two links of a chain together. In Figure 5-4b, the successor of the element being deleted (product# 625 at location Y) is to become the new direct successor of the predecessor element to the one being deleted (100 at location R). Only the one pointer value has to be changed. The pointer associated with product# 350 does not have to be changed. Special provisions are often necessary when deleting from (or inserting into) an empty pointer sequential data structure. In a later section we will address this issue.

It should be explicitly noted that pointer sequential connection requires "overhead" space beyond meaningful data. This overhead space may seem small, but practice has shown that in total, for all uses of pointers in a data base (in key indexes, record chains, synonym chains, and so on), 100% overhead is not uncommon!

Retrieval of a random record in a pure PSDD data structure is even more time-consuming than in an ASDD structure. The same arbitrary record will be in the same relative sequential position in each set. The greater time for PSDD is due to the fact that each movement from node to node (e.g., record to next record in sequence) will be at least as far physically as the equivalent step for ASDD. With ASDD, this move is to an adjacent physical location; with PSDD, the move could require disk head movement.

Indirect Data Placement

Besides connection methods (AS and PS), data structures are also characterized by the relative placement of data and the connection mechanism. Either indirect or direct placement and access to the actual data can be employed.

Indirect placement (see Figures 5-3c and d) usually makes scanning a data structure more efficient (than with data direct), since the connection nodes are often smaller than the actual data being managed and hence can be scanned more quickly and possibly kept in main computer memory for long periods of time.

Consider again the Pine Valley Furniture Product Master File. Each product record may be as much as 300 characters long, which means that only one record will fit in one 300-character data block. If a pointer and a product number are each only 4 characters long, then 37 pointer and key nodes will fit per block in the case of address sequential data indirect (ASDI, or inverted file) implementation. If, as before, we assume 100,000 records in this file, then the average time to scan the pointers will be $1/37$ of what it was when we calculated this earlier, or 11.2 seconds. One more access would be required to retrieve the data (at a cost of an additional random record access time of roughly 25 msec). Because the pointer nodes are so compact compared to the actual data records, many of these pointers can be kept in computer main memory while the file is being used. This means that frequently a physical read of secondary memory to retrieve pointers will not have to be made. Finally, because all the connections are stored in these compact blocks, insertions and deletions are more efficient than with the data direct (DD) counterparts in Figure 5-3.

Summary of Basic Location Methods

The four alternatives of ASDD (sequential), PSDD (chain), ASDI (inverted), and PSDI (list inverted) are all extreme points and "pure" situations. Hybrids, or combinations, frequently occur in one structure. A reexamination of Figure 4-15 on the ISAM structure will demonstrate how ISAM uses address sequential connection within primary data tracks, pointer sequential connection to handle overflows, and data indirect connections via use of multiple indexes.

TYPES OF POINTERS

The previous discussion indicated that pointers are often used to connect two elements of data. A **pointer** is a field associated with one piece of data used to identify the location of another piece of data. That is, a pointer contains some type of address that can be used to locate associated data. In this section, we will introduce the three types of pointers and discuss their relative capabilities.

There are physical, relative, and logical pointers. Figure 5-5 illustrates the basic differences between them. *Physical* and *relative* refer to the types of disk addressing outlined in Chapter 4. A **physical (address) pointer** resolves absolutely where the associated data reside, since it includes the disk cylinder, track, and block numbers of the data to which we are pointing.

A physical pointer is the fastest type of pointer, since it does not need to be further manipulated to specify data location. It is, however, the most restrictive. If the associated data change location in any way (e.g., because of reorganization of a file), then the pointer must be changed. The pointer value has no alphanumeric relationship to meaningful data base contents, so once a pointer is destroyed, it can be difficult to reconstruct. Physical pointers are of fixed size (the length of disk addresses) and usually rather short (e.g., 4 to 8 bytes).

Figure 5-5
Types of pointers.
(a) Physical address
    pointer.
(b) Relative address
    pointer for *R*th record
    in file.
(c) Logical key pointer for
    record with key.

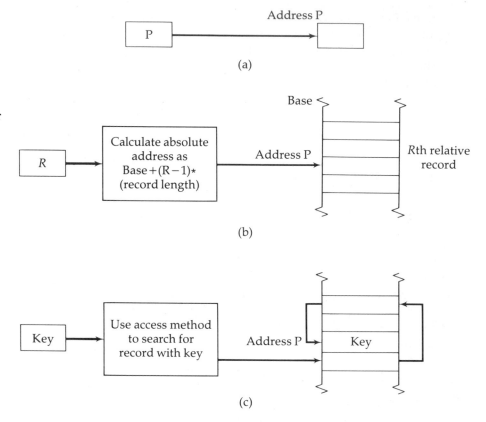

A **relative (address) pointer** contains the relative position (or "offset") of the associated data with respect to the beginning of the data structure in which the associated data are located. This could indicate a certain byte position within a record, a certain relative record number within a file, or a certain relative block within a file. The reference can be from one file to another. For example, a pointer in a Customer record could connect that record to an associated Order record in the Orders file.

Relative pointers require marginally more computer time (several microseconds) to access the associated data, since the relative address must be translated into a physical address either by data management software or by the operating system access method (disk controllers understand only absolute, physical addresses). This translation process has to "look up" such values as record length and blocking factor to perform this calculation.

The primary advantage of relative pointers is that when the *whole* data structure changes location and all relative data placement within the structure is preserved, relative pointer values into that structure need not change. For the preceding example, the Orders file can be moved from one disk device to another to better distribute disk activity, and the relative pointers in the Customer file need not be modified. Relative pointers are difficult to reconstruct, since they have no alphanumeric relationship to meaningful data. The length of a relative pointer varies between applications but is less than the length of a physical pointer, since a relative address must be no larger than the largest physical address. The length depends on the range of possible relative positions in the data structure. For instance, given a 10,000-record Order file, a relative pointer in the Customer file to link a customer to an associated order would have to be at least 14 bits long (or, more likely, a whole 2 bytes).

A **logical (key) pointer** contains meaningful data (i.e., content of the data base) about the associated element of data. Logical pointers are useful only if the associated data have some additional structure (like an ISAM index) that supports key access on pointer values. Logical pointers are used when very rapid, direct access is not required and meaningful data exist anyhow. For example, an Order file record is likely to contain the Customer# found on the order sales form. This field is included directly in Order file records so that it is readily available to print on shop orders, invoices, status reports, and the like. Occasionally, other customer data (name, address, and so on) are also required. To access these additional data, the Customer# is used to locate the Customer file record via its primary key ISAM index or hashing function on Customer#.

Logical pointers require the most computer time to actually retrieve the associated record because a purely hardware-independent value is used. This value must be transformed into a relative or physical pointer via table lookup, index searching, or a mathematical calculation. In any case, this translation time may include several physical file accesses to retrieve key synonyms or several index blocks. But use of this hardware-independent value means that data can be moved; even relative placement within a structure can be changed, and logical pointers need not change. The cost to accomplish this location independence includes both time and space to maintain the key access method.

Logical pointers tend to be the longest type of pointer. Most data keys are relatively long compared to the length of a relative pointer (which must hold the value of the number of records in a file) or compared to the length of a disk address (for physical pointers). For example, the Pine Valley Furniture Product Master File in Figure 2-2 has only ten active records with logical pointers (keys) that are, say, 4 bytes long. In this case, a physical pointer might be 4 bytes (depends on computer addressing scheme), but only a single-byte relative pointer is required. A distinct advantage of logical pointers is that they do have real-world meaning. If destroyed on computer media, they can be readily reconstructed from business documents and other computerized data. Finally, logical pointers can be said to be data that are in common between two nodes (e.g., records). This common data view is inherent (even required) in the relational data model developed in Chapter 6.

Table 5-1
Comparison of Types of Pointers

Characteristic	Type of pointer		
	Physical	Relative	Logical
Speed of access	Fastest	Medium	Slowest
Sensitivity to data movement	Most	Only sensitive to relative position changes	Least
Sensitivity to destruction	Very	Very	Often can be easily reconstructed
Space requirement	Fixed, usually short	Varies, usually longer	Varies, usually longest

Table 5-1 summarizes our comparison of types of pointers. The remainder of this chapter and subsequent chapters will rely on the basic data structures and pointer types discussed here.

INTRARECORD DATA STRUCTURES

At the conceptual and enterprise levels of the ANSI/SPARC model (see Figure 5-1), each (logical) record is viewed as one address sequential data direct (ASDD) structure. This is quite adequate, since functional content is what is being designed or understood at these levels. At the internal level, however, efficiency issues of access speed, update time, and storage space become important. This is why many data management technologies choose to compress or split records into forms that are not simple ASDD. The common phenomena of insignificant leading decimal digits, trailing blanks in alphanumeric strings, and missing data can be handled in special ways to make data processing more efficient. Often, one logical record can be broken into several physical records to improve processing that only requires segments of the logical record.

The data structures used to connect fields within a single record are called **intrarecord (data) structures**. Five frequently used intrarecord structures are discussed in the next section, followed by a section on how and

(a)

PRODUCT#	DESCRIPTION	FINISH	ROOM	PRICE
0 1 0 0	T A B L E	O A K	D R	5 0 0
0 9 7 5	W A L L U N I T	P I N E	F R	7 5 0
1 7 9 5	C H A I R		L R	

(b)

```
100$TABLE$OAK$DR$500$
975$WALL UNIT$PINE$FR$750$
1795$CHAIR$$LR$$
```

(c)

3	8	11	13	16	100TABLEOAKDR500
3	12	16	18	21	975WALL UNITPINEFR750
4	9	9	11	11	1795CHAIRLR

(d)

```
(P)100(D)TABLE(F)OAK(R)DR($)500(X)
(P)975(D)WALL UNIT(F)OAK(R)DR($)750(X)
(P)1795(R)LR(D)CHAIR(X)
```

(e)

```
0 1 0 0 0 0 T A B L E 0 0 O A K       0 0 D R 0 0 5 0 0 0 0
0 9 7 5 0 0 W A L L   X X P I N E     0 0 F R 0 0 7 5 0 0 0
1 7 9 5 0 0 C H A I R 0 0              0 0 L R 0 0         0 0
```

```
XX
UNIT $
```

Figure 5-6
Intrarecord structures.
(a) Positional intrarecord structure.
(b) Relational intrarecord structure.
(c) Indexed intrarecord structure.
(d) Labeled intrarecord structure.
(e) Fixed-with-overflow intrarecord structure.

why a record may be broken into several parts, even with purposeful duplication of data, to achieve improved data base performance. Later, in Chapter 9, we will illustrate how judicious choice of an intrarecord structure relates to physical data base record design.

Managing Record Space

The five frequently used intrarecord structures are illustrated for the Pine Valley Furniture Product Master File in Figure 5-6. These structures are called positional, relational, indexed, labeled, and fixed-with-overflow (Maxwell 1973).

Positional Storage.   The **positional** structure (see Figure 5-6a) has every field in a fixed, relative location within a record. Each field has a fixed length, since a fixed amount of space is preestablished for each field. Each field is easily accessed, since it is in a predetermined position. And each field is allocated space for its longest possible value. This means that wasted space can occur, and will occur frequently for fields with highly variable length (such as narrative descriptions). To counter this, data base designers will often force narrative fields to be abbreviated or coded to fit into a reasonably small maximum length.

Space for a new positional record is easily allocated, since each is of fixed length. A contiguous pool of record slots will allow deleted record space to be easily recovered because all new records will fit *exactly* into unused space. This process of allocating and deallocating space to records as they are inserted and deleted is called **space management**. The positional structure is by far the most frequently found, owing to its simplicity of field access and ease of space management.

Relational Storage.   The **relational** structure (see Figure 5-6b) uses a special symbol, called a **delimiter**, to indicate the end of each field. Each field is of variable length, depending on the number of significant alphanumeric characters that exist. Even the maximum allowable length can be changed without requiring reloading of data. Missing fields, such as Finish and Price for Product# 1795, are indicated by adjacent delimiters. The relative sequence of fields is, however, fixed. The total record length is usually variable, as shown in Figure 5-6b; however, this need not be the case (here or in the case shown in Figure 5-6c or d as well). If a fixed length for a record can be determined such that it is not possible (or even that it is highly unlikely) that the actual total variable record length (sum of all variable- and fixed-length fields) would exceed this value, then fixed-length records are possible. This greatly facilitates space management, since space is easily reused.

A problem with variable-length structures is that space for a small record that is deleted can go unused for a long period until another small record is created (unless the file is reorganized). This effect of blocks of used and unused memory cells is called the **checkerboard effect**. Further, records that shorten in length can create small, wasted spaces that can remain wasted for long periods owing to the small probability of extremely short records; and records must be moved to a larger space and a "hole" created if the record length expands.

Accessing fields within a relational record requires scanning the record and counting delimiters. For example, to retrieve the Finish of Product# 0975 would actually require scanning 14 characters until encountering the second delimiter to find the beginning of PINE. Further scanning is necessary to discover the complete Finish value (scan until next delimiter). This process can be expedited by using a combination of fixed- and variable-length fields and by coding fields into fixed lengths whenever possible. For example, the delimiter after each Room value could be deleted, since the coded Room field is of fixed length.

An additional (potential) penalty with the relational intrarecord structure is the extra space required for delimiters. This space must be traded-off with the possible savings in space from useless characters that are eliminated. If the values of all fields are permitted to have only a typical alphanumeric range, then the delimiter can be eliminated. In this case, one can simply add (or subtract) a constant from the value of the last digit/character of each field, thus making the character out of the acceptable range (e.g., 128 would work for the ASCII character set). The relational structure is normally used in situations with highly variable field lengths but relatively fixed length once a value is entered and in cases of significant missing data.

Indexed Storage.   The **indexed** structure (see Figure 5-6c) records the end of each field (relative character pointer) in an index or field directory that is usually stored at the beginning of each record. The advantage here over the relational structure is that this index can be used as a lookup table, and a desired field can be directly retrieved without scanning the record. For example, the index for product# 0975 implies that the Finish (field 3) of this product is in positions 13–16 (i.e., starts one position after the end of field 2 and continues until the end of field 3). Missing fields are indicated by adjacent index pointers having the same value (see the index for product# 1795 in Figure 5-6c). Field values can be missing for numerous reasons, but missing values occur frequently in recently entered records.

An indexed intrarecord structure exhibits the same record space management issues of the relational structure when records are of variable length. The space required for each record, in comparison to relational, depends on the evaluation of delimiter and pointer space. The space required for a delimiter, usually 1 byte, is also sufficient to store any of 256 relative character pointer values. If the record length exceeds 256 bytes, the space for a record index entry will be greater than the overhead space for a delimiter in the relational structure. This evaluation not withstanding, the indexed structure is used most frequently for long, variable-length records to save scanning costs.

Labeled Storage.   The **labeled** structure (see Figure 5-6d) uses unique, short identification codes preceding each field value. These codes, or labels, like delimiters, must not be a legitimate character value in any field. Unlike delimiters, a *different* code is used to label the start of each field.

Labels provide two distinct advantages. First, field values can be written in any order (e.g., values for previously missing values are simply added to the end of the record). And second, no space (even for delimiters) is required when a field is missing. Disadvantages are that records must be scanned (as with relational) to find individual fields, and label length may be greater than delimiter length if there are many fields in a record. The labeled structure is most frequently considered in those situations where many missing values occur.

Fixed-with-Overflow Storage.   Finally, the **fixed-with-overflow** structure (see Figure 5-6e) combines the concept of fixed-length record with variable-length fields. Each field is allocated a fixed length that is chosen to balance wasted space with frequency of overflow. If the actual field length is no greater than the space allocated, a zero pointer value (called **null**) signifies no overflow on that field. If the actual field is longer than reserved field space (as in the case of WALL UNIT in Figure 5-6e), then the pointer indicates the position of the overflow characters and a delimiter shows the end of the overflow.

With the fixed-with-overflow structure, the start of each field is known exactly, so fields are as easily accessed as in positional and indexed structures. Space requirements are reduced compared to positional structure *if* pointer space is less than the space eliminated (which is *not* the case in Figures 5-6a and 5-6e). Primary data space is easy to manage and reuse, since these records are of fixed length. This structure is slightly more complex because of the need to access the separate overflow area, but it combines several advantages of the other structures.

Data Item Partitioning and Clustering

What does the phrase "Don't put all your eggs in one basket" mean? It may have been motivated by several factors. First, if all the eggs are in one basket and the basket is lost, stolen, or damaged, then all the eggs can become unusable. That is, we want to protect and secure the investment in eggs. If we divide the eggs into several baskets and one basket is damaged, we still have many useful eggs. Second, since sometimes we want to use large eggs, other times small eggs, sometimes brown eggs, and other times white eggs, all the eggs in one basket would force us to sort through all our eggs each time we wanted to use only a subset. That is, our usage of eggs is selective and we can more quickly find the eggs we want if we divide our supply into separate, categorized baskets.

This egg analogy has direct relevance to intrarecord data structures. By putting data into more usage-oriented physical files, we can improve the performance of a data base and better safeguard the valuable data resource.

The process of dividing a logical record into distinct physical parts is called **data item clustering** (we are actually clustering together into one physical record data that have some common data processing usage). If these different physical parts are not allowed to have common data items (data redundancy), then this special case is called **data item partitioning**. (See Hoffer and Severance [1975] and Schkolnick [1977] for more detail.)

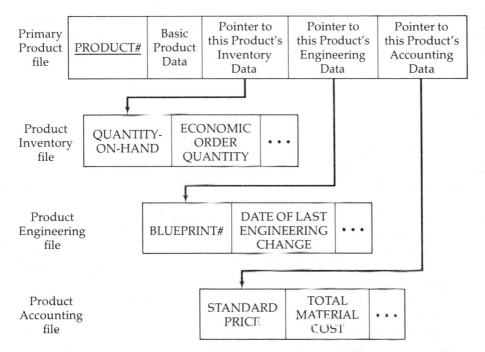

Figure 5-7
Example of data item partitioning.

Pine Valley Furniture

Figure 5-7 shows one way the total logical PRODUCT record for Pine Valley Furniture could be partitioned into application-oriented segments and separate files. The conceptual PRODUCT record would still be viewed as one comprehensive record. Many external views would conceive of the PRODUCT record as all or even only a subset of the data elements in just one of the partitions. Other external views would see one logical record that was composed of data elements from multiple partitions. The point is that it is only at the internal level that the distinction between partitions needs to be managed. In Chapter 6, we will discuss other human factor reasons why it may be best to break one logical record into clusters. The choice to partition or cluster is made by the data base designer during development of the internal data model from the conceptual data model and information on data usage by application programs.

In Figure 5-7, pointers are used to connect the primary record segment to the others. The primary segment contains basic data about a product that are used in many applications. When additional data are required (e.g., on-hand inventory balance or order quantity for inventory control applications), then the appropriate secondary segments are accessed via the pointers from the primary segment or physical record. Alternatives to the structure shown in Figure 5-7 allow direct access into each physical partition via hashing, an ISAM index, or some other file organization on *each* physical file.

LINEAR INTERRECORD DATA STRUCTURES

Interrecord data structures are used to connect different, related records in the same or separate files. Such structures can be used to represent logical orderings of records within the same file (e.g., Product Master Records in Product# numerical order or in Finish alphabetic sequence). These structures can also be used to group together records that have a common characteristic (e.g., all the Product Master Records with a missing price). In addition, these structures can be used to link related records of different types (e.g., a Product Master Record with all the Order records that indicate a customer order for the same product).

A **linear interrecord structure** is one for which there is only one NEXT data element emanating from each element in a given data structure. In some cases, however, there may be *several* linear data structures for the same set of data elements. One example of this, called multilist, will be covered later in this section.

We will also present in this section a detailed account of procedures for processing data structures. An understanding of how to process a data structure is important because some data base management systems require procedural language programs written in COBOL, for example, to initiate some of the detailed movement from one data element to another. Further, the more a programmer or data base designer knows about how a DBMS works (e.g., how it inserts new records into a data base), the better prepared these application people are for selecting data management technologies appropriate for the application at hand.

Basic Linear Data Structures

Three basic linear data structures are presented here: stacks, queues, and sorted lists/files. Each can be implemented using address sequential or pointer sequential connections. When pointer sequential connections are used, these structures are collectively called linked lists, or more descriptively, chains.

Stacks. One basic structure is a stack. A **stack** has the property that all insertions (addition of new records) and deletions (removal of no longer needed records) are made at the same end of the data structure. Stacks exhibit a last-in-first-out (LIFO) property. A common example of a stack is a vertical column of plates in a cafeteria line that are in a push-down, pop-up rack. In business data processing, stacklike structures are useful in maintaining a set of unprioritized or unsorted records. For example, Figure 5-8 illustrates a pointer sequential or chained stack structure for ORDER-LINE records, all of which are related to a common ORDER record (this example is based on Figure 2-10).

In this example, the ORDER record acts as the head-of-chain or start node of the data structure. The value of the FIRST-ORDER-LINE field is a pointer to the first ORDER-LINE record. The sequence of ORDER-LINE records is immaterial; consequently, new ORDER-LINE records can simply be inserted at the "top" of the stack. ORDER-LINE records are deleted in LIFO fashion as they are filled for shipment.

The value 0 in the ORDER-LINE record for PRODUCT# 1425 in Figure 5-8a is called a **null pointer** and signifies the end of the data structure (i.e., no more ORDER-LINE records for ORDER# 1234). To insert the new ORDER-LINE record for PRODUCT# 0625, one would simply put the value X (relative record number pointer) into NEXT-ORDER-LINE for this new record and change FIRST-ORDER-LINE to R. This is shown in Figure 5-8b.

This insertion of a new record can be written in the form of a general insertion procedure or algorithm. If we let NEW be the relative record number of the ORDER-LINE record to be inserted and let START be the relative record number of the ORDER record for this new ORDER-LINE, then the following pseudocode procedure accomplishes the insertion:

(1) NEXT-ORDER-LINE(NEW) ←FIRST-ORDER-LINE(START)
(2) FIRST-ORDER-LINE(START) ←NEW

In this procedure (and others to follow), the symbol ← means that the value of the field to the left of the symbol is replaced by the value of the field to the right of the symbol. Field names followed by a variable in parentheses should be read much like an array subscript in many programming languages. For example, NEXT-ORDER-LINE(NEW) should be read as "the value of field NEXT-ORDER-LINE stored in the NEW-th relative record in the ORDER-LINE file," and FIRST-ORDER-LINE(START) should be read as "the value of field FIRST-ORDER-LINE stored in the START-th relative record in the ORDER file."

The reader should note that this procedure will work correctly when we insert the first ORDER-LINE instance for a given ORDER. In this special case, FIRST-ORDER-LINE(START) will be 0 before the insertion and step 1 will properly result in a null pointer for NEXT-ORDER-LINE of the new record. In developing such procedures, the designer should take care to account for all special conditions (such as empty chains).

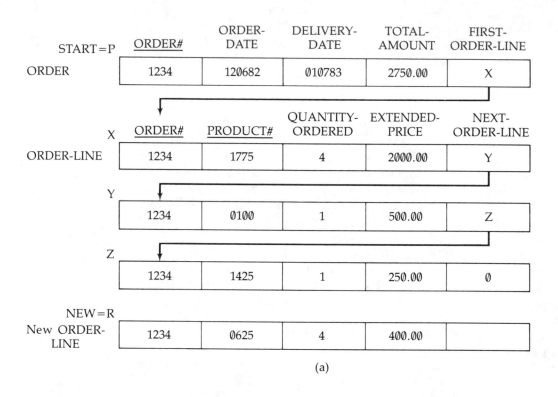

	ORDER#	ORDER-DATE	DELIVERY-DATE	TOTAL-AMOUNT	FIRST-ORDER-LINE
START=P ORDER	1234	120682	010783	2750.00	X

	ORDER#	PRODUCT#	QUANTITY-ORDERED	EXTENDED-PRICE	NEXT-ORDER-LINE
X ORDER-LINE	1234	1775	4	2000.00	Y
Y	1234	0100	1	500.00	Z
Z	1234	1425	1	250.00	0
NEW=R New ORDER-LINE	1234	0625	4	400.00	

(a)

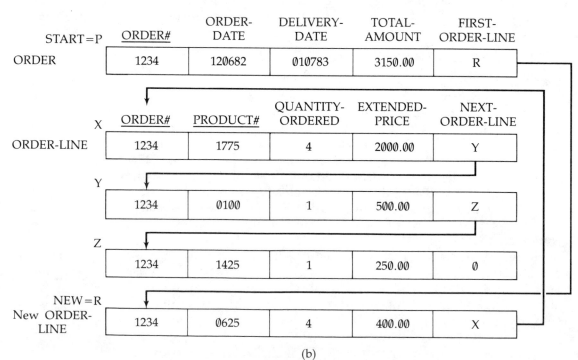

	ORDER#	ORDER-DATE	DELIVERY-DATE	TOTAL-AMOUNT	FIRST-ORDER-LINE
START=P ORDER	1234	120682	010783	3150.00	R

	ORDER#	PRODUCT#	QUANTITY-ORDERED	EXTENDED-PRICE	NEXT-ORDER-LINE
X ORDER-LINE	1234	1775	4	2000.00	Y
Y	1234	0100	1	500.00	Z
Z	1234	1425	1	250.00	0
NEW=R New ORDER-LINE	1234	0625	4	400.00	X

(b)

Queues. The second basic linear data structure presented here is the queue. A **queue** has the property that all insertions occur at one end and all deletions occur at the other end. A queue exhibits a first-in-first-out (FIFO) property. A common example of a queue is a check-out line at a grocery store. In business data processing, queuelike structures are often used to maintain lists of records in chronological order of insertion. For example, Figure 5-9 illustrates a pointer sequential, or chained, queue of ORDER-LINE records kept in order of arrival (and, hence, filling sequence) for a common PRODUCT record (this example is based on Figure 2-10).

This example also introduces the concept of a bidirectional chain or list structure (to make queue maintenance easier). A **bidirectional chain** has both "forward" and "backward" pointers emanating from each element of data (record in this case). The benefit of having both forward and backward (NEXT/PRIOR) pointers is that when processing a chain in one direction (forward), you do not have to remember or find the immediate predecessor (which often must be updated during insertions and deletions), since it is known directly from the pointer (backward).

In this example, the OLDEST-ORDER-LINE field in the PRODUCT record serves as the head-of-chain pointer for filling orders (deletions), since orders will be filled in first-come-first-served order. The NEWEST-ORDER-LINE field serves as the head-of-chain pointer for entering new orders (insertions), since new orders have the lowest priority to be filled. It is assumed that records are inserted as orders are received so that order receipt sequence is the same as the insertion sequence.

To insert the new ORDER-LINE for ORDER# 3168 (similarly to the method used with a stack), we put Z into PRIOR-ORDER-LINE for this new record, put 0 into the NEXT-ORDER-LINE field of the new ORDER, put R into the NEXT-ORDER-LINE field of the previously newest relative record (Z), and change NEWEST-ORDER-LINE to R. This result is shown in Figure 5-9b. This process can be written into a general insertion procedure as follows:

(1) PRIOR-ORDER-LINE(NEW) ←NEWEST-ORDER-LINE(START)
(2) NEXT-ORDER-LINE(NEW) ←0
(3) NEXT-ORDER-LINE(NEWEST-ORDER-LINE(START)) ←NEW
(4) NEWEST-ORDER-LINE(START) ←NEW

This procedure works fine when there is at least one ORDER-LINE record for PRODUCT# 0100. The case of an "empty queue" can be handled by changing only step 3 to be conditionally applied when the queue is non-empty, replacing step 3 with

(3′) If NEWEST-ORDER-LINE(START) ≠ 0 then
    NEXT-ORDER-LINE(NEWEST-ORDER-LINE(START)) ←NEW

You can verify that the other steps work properly with an empty queue.

Figure 5-8 (opposite) Example of a stack.
(a) Before New ORDER-LINE inserted.
(b) After New ORDER-LINE inserted.

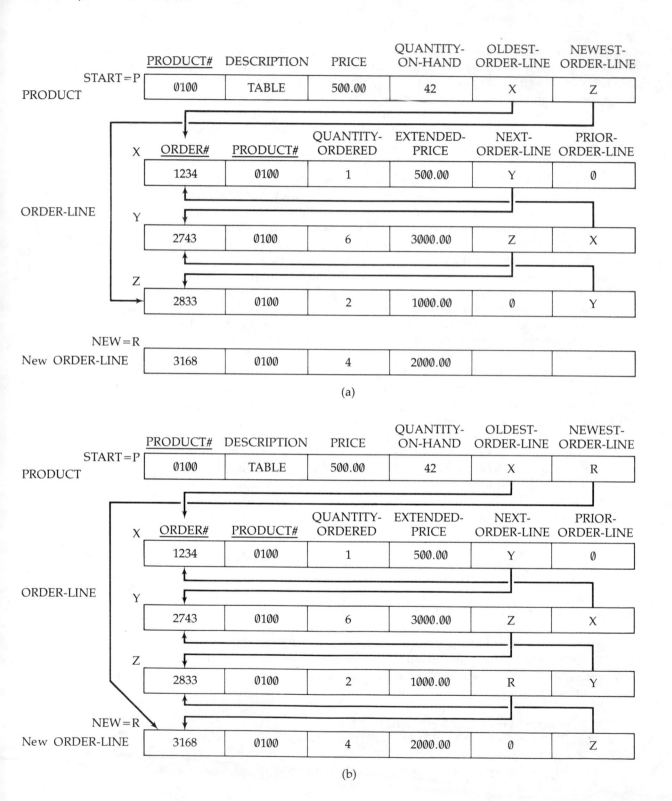

(a)

(b)

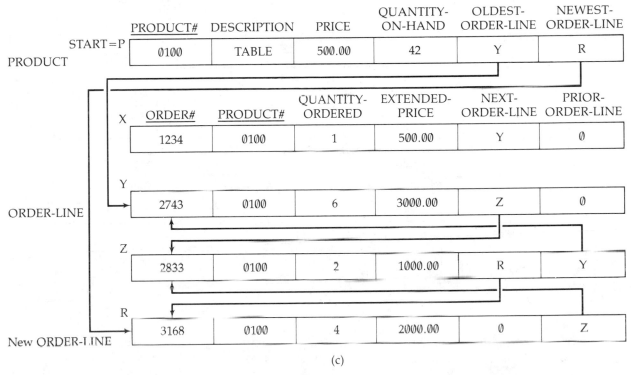

(c)

Figure 5-9
Example of a queue with bidirectional pointers.
(a) Before New ORDER-LINE insertion or deletion of OLDEST-ORDER-LINE.
(b) After New ORDER-LINE insertion.
(c) After both New ORDER-LINE insertion and OLDEST-ORDER-LINE deletion.

Deletion follows a simpler process in which two links are "welded" together. In the example of Figure 5-9, deletion would occur when the oldest order on file for PRODUCT# 0100 can be filled. This would be accomplished by changing OLDEST-ORDER-LINE to Y and indicating that the ORDER-LINE for ORDER# 2743 is now the oldest ORDER-LINE by changing its PRIOR-ORDER-LINE value to 0. The result of these changes is shown in Figure 5-9c. This process can be written into a general deletion procedure:

(1) OLDEST-ORDER-LINE(START) ←
        NEXT-ORDER-LINE(OLDEST-ORDER-LINE(START))
(2) PRIOR-ORDER-LINE(OLDEST-ORDER-LINE(START)) ←0

This deletion procedure works fine when deleting the last ORDER-LINE record of an order, so special logic is not required to handle this situation. In general, insertion and deletion (and retrieval) procedures have to be carefully written to consider extreme situations (especially "empty" chains). Finally, it should be noted that both stacks and queues perform quite efficiently regardless of data structure length (e.g., number of records on a chain). This is because all activity occurs at the ends, which can be directly

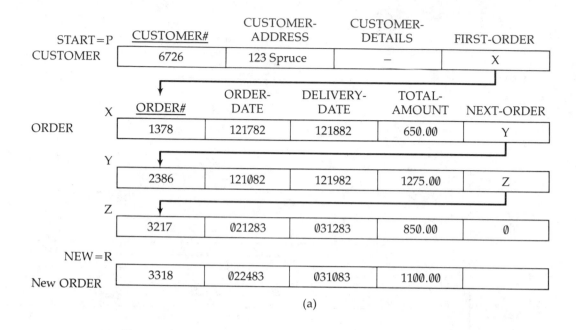

START=P CUSTOMER	CUSTOMER#	CUSTOMER-ADDRESS	CUSTOMER-DETAILS	FIRST-ORDER
	6726	123 Spruce	–	X

X ORDER	ORDER#	ORDER-DATE	DELIVERY-DATE	TOTAL-AMOUNT	NEXT-ORDER
	1378	121782	121882	650.00	Y
Y	2386	121082	121982	1275.00	Z
Z	3217	021283	031283	850.00	0

NEW=R New ORDER					
	3318	022483	031083	1100.00	

(a)

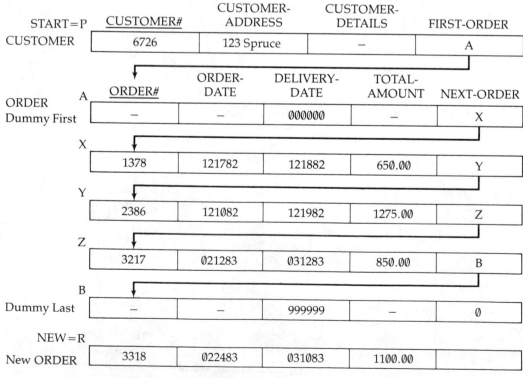

START=P CUSTOMER	CUSTOMER#	CUSTOMER-ADDRESS	CUSTOMER-DETAILS	FIRST-ORDER
	6726	123 Spruce	–	A

A ORDER Dummy First	ORDER#	ORDER-DATE	DELIVERY-DATE	TOTAL-AMOUNT	NEXT-ORDER
	–	–	000000	–	X
X	1378	121782	121882	650.00	Y
Y	2386	121082	121982	1275.00	Z
Z	3217	021283	031283	850.00	B
B Dummy Last	–	–	999999	–	0

NEW=R New ORDER					
	3318	022483	031083	1100.00	

Figure 5-9
(continued).

(b)

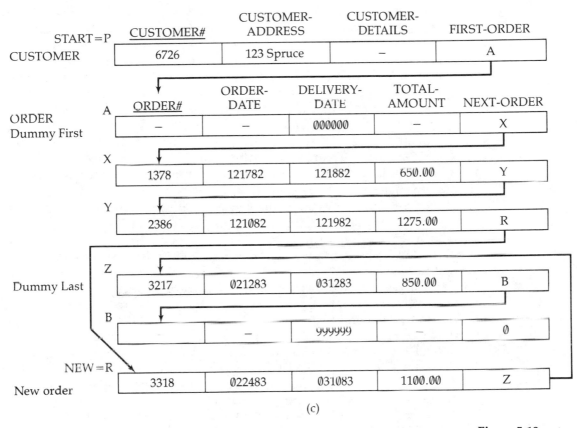

	CUSTOMER#	CUSTOMER-ADDRESS	CUSTOMER-DETAILS	FIRST-ORDER
START=P CUSTOMER	6726	123 Spruce	–	A

	ORDER#	ORDER-DATE	DELIVERY-DATE	TOTAL-AMOUNT	NEXT-ORDER
ORDER Dummy First A	–	–	000000	–	X
X	1378	121782	121882	650.00	Y
Y	2386	121082	121982	1275.00	R
Dummy Last Z	3217	021283	031283	850.00	B
B		–	999999	–	0
NEW=R New order	3318	022483	031083	1100.00	Z

(c)

Figure 5-10
Example of a sorted list.
(a) Before New ORDER insertion and without Dummy First and Dummy Last ORDERS.

(b) Before New ORDER insertion and with Dummy First and Dummy Last ORDERS.

(c) After New ORDER insertion.

accessed from head-of-chain pointers. This efficiency independence from data structure length is not true for the next data structure.

Sorted Lists. The last basic linear data structure to be introduced is the sorted list. A **sorted list** has the property that insertions and deletions may occur anywhere within the list; elements of data are maintained in logical order based on a key field value, and elements are inserted or deleted by specifying the key value involved. A common example of a sorted list is a telephone directory. In business data processing, sorted lists occur frequently. For example, Figure 5-10 illustrates a pointer sequential, or chained, sorted list (often referred to as "the" list data structure) of ORDER records related to a typical CUSTOMER record. The ORDER records are maintained in a single, unidirectional sorted order by DELIVERY-DATE, with the oldest ORDER on the "top" of the list (this example is based on Figure 2-10). Sorted lists are maintained to avoid resorting a set of data (records) each time the oldest, newest, or all in sequence are desired.

In this example, the FIRST-ORDER field serves as the head-of-chain pointer, and it points to the ORDER record for the given CUSTOMER that has the earliest DELIVERY-DATE. The process of inserting the new record for ORDER# 3318 is much more complex than in prior linear data structures. The greater complexity is due to having to scan the chain to find the proper position in which to place the new record. Special logic is required if this place happens to be on either end of the chain or is into an empty chain. To guarantee that insertion (and later deletion) will always be in the interior of the chain, "dummy" first and last records are often included in the chain. This is shown in Figure 5-10b. Although these dummy records require additional space and must be skipped in scanning, the savings in insertion and deletion speed and ease are usually considered more advantageous.

Figure 5-10c shows the result of inserting the record with ORDER# 3318 into the sorted list of Figure 5-10b. The list is scanned starting from the relative record number in FIRST-ORDER. If duplicate key values are not permitted, then the process must check at each "visit" of an ORDER record that the key there does not match the key for the new ORDER. This type of check is not required in the situation in Figure 5-10, since duplicate key values are allowed (the key is a secondary key). The correct position of the record with ORDER# 3318 is found when the first DELIVERY-DATE greater than 031083 is encountered; this is when the scan reaches the record with ORDER# 3217. This ORDER now becomes the successor of the record with ORDER# 3318, so the NEXT-ORDER pointer of the record with ORDER# 3318 is set to value Z. The tricky part is to remember the predecessor (without the aid of backward pointers).

In the following chained sorted list insertion procedure, position variables PRE and AFT are used to hold the values of the predecessor and successor, respectively, of the new ORDER record. Step 4 is included in brackets to indicate where a check for duplicate keys would appear if required. The insertion procedure is:

(1) PRE ←FIRST-ORDER(START)
(2) AFT ←NEXT-ORDER(FIRST-ORDER)
(3) DO WHILE DELIVERY-DATE(AFT) < =DELIVERY-DATE(NEW)
    (4) [If DELIVERY-DATE(AFT)=DELIVERY-DATE(NEW) then indicate a Duplicate Error]
    (5) PRE ←AFT
    (6) AFT ←NEXT-ORDER(AFT)
(7) ENDDO
(8) NEXT-ORDER(PRE) ←NEW
(9) NEXT-ORDER(NEW) ←AFT

Step 3 says that if we have not yet found a DELIVERY-DATE in the chain that is greater than the DELIVERY-DATE of the new ORDER, then skip ahead one link in the chain and continue to test for the desired position to insert.

Deletion from a chained sorted list is left as an exercise at the end of the chapter.

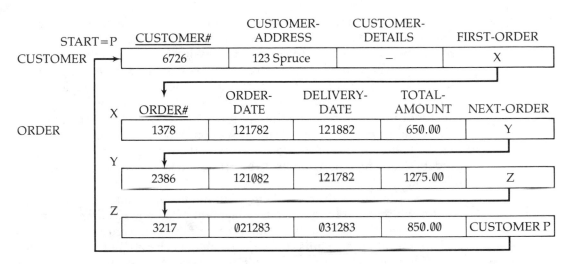

Figure 5-11
Ring data structure.

Other Linear Structures.   A variation on basic linear data structures is called a ring. A **ring** is a closed loop data structure in which the end of the chain (and the front, too, in the case of bidirectional chains) points to the head-of-chain element. A ring variation on Figure 5-10a is shown in Figure 5-11. Rings are useful in that they permit us to move to any other chain member from any given chain element. For example, if we had accessed the ORDER record with ORDER# 2386 via, say, hashing on its primary key of ORDER#, then we could still find all the ORDERs for the customer of the order record with ORDER# 2386. Note that with this ring, the NEXT-ORDER pointer in the last record of the chain must clearly indicate that it points to the CUSTOMER file, not the ORDER file.

As you might expect, many other variations on these basic linear data structures have been invented, and many of these are used in modern data management technologies (see Knuth 1973 for an excellent survey). Some of these variations will be presented in Chapters 12 and 13. This section should provide the fundamentals necessary to cope with these other structures later in the book.

Multilist Data Structure

An annoying characteristic of address sequential data structures is their inflexibility. Not only must related data follow one another in physical sequence (which causes a lot of work to maintain), but also only *one* sequence (sorted order or association) can be supported with these structures. A chained linear data structure, like those presented in the prior section, avoids the problem of maintaining physical sequential placement. But these basic structures are still limited to representing a *single* logical ordering.

Often in business data processing, and certainly in a data base environment, the same data will be associated in several groups, or several sorted sequences will be desired to support processing of shared data. Consider, for example, the same set of Customer Orders that need to be connected to their associated Customer record, maintained in order date sequence for auditing purposes, and that also need to be grouped together by delivery date for producing reports for the shipping dock. It would be desirable to be able to maintain all these associations without having to duplicate or triplicate the voluminous Order records (a goal of data management). The multilist data structure, among others to be presented later, is a means to achieve this goal.

A **multilist data structure** (better, but not usually, called multichain) is one for which more than one NEXT element of data may emanate from a given element. Thus, multiple pointers (multiple chains) are employed, one each for the different "paths" through the data. Each path links records with a common characteristic or in a different sequence. With multilist, it is possible to be "walking" through one association and in the middle decide to follow another. For example, while accessing the Order records for a given Customer (one chain), we could find all the Orders to be delivered on the same day of one of those Orders (another chain) so as to anticipate possible shipping delays due to a bottleneck (excess work load) on the shipping dock. A multilist data structure for this situation is depicted in Figure 5-12a.

Multilist is a basic building block for implementation of the CODASYL network data model presented in Chapter 13. As a preview of what we will see in that chapter, consider the data structure depicted in Figure 5-12b. In this example, ORDER-LINE records for the same ORDER are linked via one list, and ORDER-LINE records for the same PRODUCT are linked via another list. Thus, the same ORDER-LINE data can be shared by both product management and order processing applications. Note that ORDER-LINE records are sorted by PRODUCT# within an ORDER list and ORDER-LINE records are sorted by DUE-DATE within a PRODUCT list.

Hazards of List Structures

The disadvantage of any list (chain) structure arises with long chains. Scanning a long chain can take an enormous amount of time, since each movement from, say, record to record, may require a disk cylinder change. With single lists, it is often possible to cluster the associated data together into the same cylinder, but with multiple lists, it is very difficult to place each element of data in relatively close proximity to each of its associated data. Long chains also cause a problem when we try to find one or a few records that fall into some category or range of key values. For example, we may want to know what Orders to be shipped today were entered one week ago (because data entry errors have been discovered in other Orders entered that same day and we wish to take precautions so as to correctly ship today).

Figure 5-12 (opposite) Examples of multilist structures.
(a) General multilist structure.
(b) ORDER-LINE with two lists.

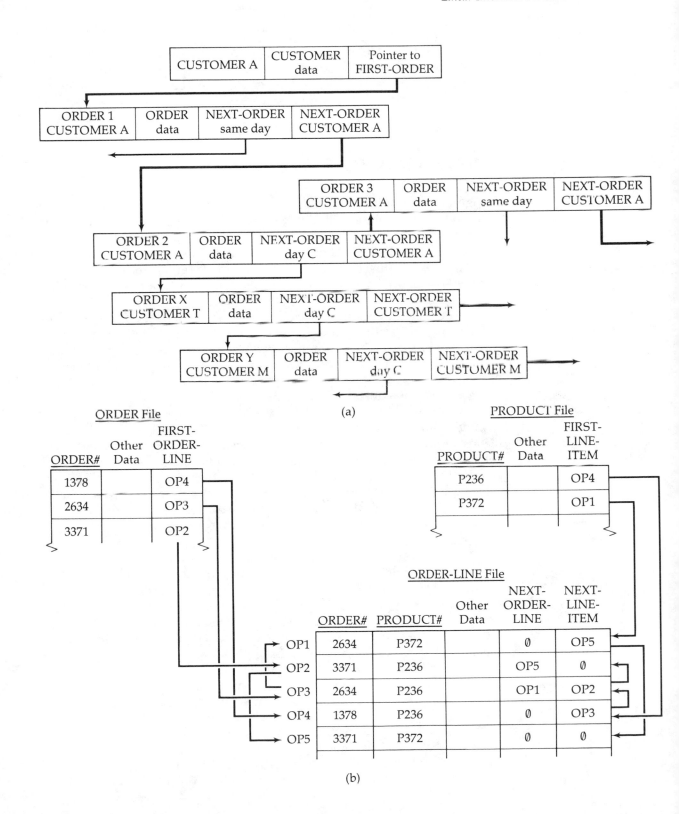

(a)

(b)

To answer this question could require scanning two long lists of Orders (for order date and delivery date sequences). The next data structure we are going to discuss is designed to handle this so-called multiple-key kind of query more efficiently than multilist.

INVERTED LISTS

A student preparing a term paper for an economics course needs some additional information. She knows that economist Milton Friedman has written on the topic for which she needs information and that she has already found all relevant Friedman publications, except for those printed in the last six months. She also knows that only certain terms adequately describe (identify, categorize, or are associated with) the kind of information now needed.

The student goes to the university library, where she finds three indexes of periodical literature. One index identifies publications by author name, another identifies economics publications by date of publication, and the third identifies key word topical groupings. Each index identifies (or addresses) a publication by common pieces of data—the periodical name, the publication date, and the page numbers (if you are finding this analogy helpful, you will see the similarity of these data to a disk address!). The student quickly scans each index and writes down three lists of "addresses": those from the first index for Milton Friedman, those from the second index for economics publications in the last six months, and those from the third index for the relevant topical key words. She then compares the three lists and finds that only four papers meet all the search criteria. Finally, she walks (physically) through the library to retrieve the few relevant publications, having avoided very time-consuming browsing of many publications through the library stacks.

The student in this example has used inverted lists to significantly speed up a multiple-key search of the library. An **inverted list** is a table, list, index, or directory of data addresses that indicates all the data (records) that have a common property. The address sequential data indirect data structure covered earlier in this chapter is a convenient way to view this table. In the next section, we will see that data structures other than ASDI are usually used to manage an index in business applications.

Figure 5-13 views a possible inverted list structure for the PRODUCT file of Pine Valley Furniture (this figure is based on Figure 2-2). Indexes are created to speed processing, usually for qualified access questions that use secondary keys. Secondary keys were defined in Chapter 2 to be data items that normally do not uniquely identify a record, but identify a number of records that share the same property.

Although in Figure 2-2 DESCRIPTION, FINISH, and ROOM were all identified as secondary keys, indexes on only DESCRIPTION and ROOM

DESCRIPTION	Addresses
BOOKCASE	7
CHAIR	3, 6
DRESSER	5, 9
STAND	8
TABLE	1, 2
WALL UNIT	4, 10

DESCRIPTION
Index
(secondary key)

ROOM	Addresses
BR	5, 8, 9
DR	1, 2, 3
FR	4
LR	6, 7, 10

Room index
(secondary key)

PRODUCT#	Address
0100	1
0350	2
0625	3
0975	4
1000	5
1250	6
1425	7
1600	8
1775	9
2000	10

PRODUCT# index
(primary key)

Address	PRODUCT#	DESCRIPTION	FINISH	ROOM	PRICE
1	0100	TABLE	OAK	DR	500
2	0350	TABLE	MAPLE	DR	625
3	0625	CHAIR	OAK	DR	100
4	0975	WALL UNIT	PINE	FR	750
5	1000	DRESSER	CHERRY	BR	800
6	1250	CHAIR	MAPLE	LR	400
7	1425	BOOKCASE	PINE	LR	250
8	1600	STAND	BIRCH	BR	200
9	1775	DRESSER	PINE	BR	500
10	2000	WALL UNIT	OAK	LR	1200

PRODUCT
data file

Figure 5-13
Inverted list structure.

were created in Figure 5-13. This is because the cost to maintain a FINISH index (which is incurred as new records are added, as old records are deleted, or as FINISH values are modified) was more than the retrieval savings from use of a FINISH index compared to the alternative of physically *scanning all* PRODUCT records to find those with the specified FINISH. Also, it was observed that questions involving FINISH were not very discriminating; that is, *many* records satisfied queries on FINISH. A general rule of thumb is that if more than 10% of the records in a file satisfy a key qualification, an index on that key is not very helpful — a complete file scan is equally or more efficient.

Indexes are more compact than the data records they reference. Often, indexes can be kept in computer main memory for extended periods so that secondary memory access costs to retrieve indexes can be reduced. However, indexes for files with a large number of records can also be very large. An index, then, can be viewed as a file itself on which an index can be created, and so on. This is what we saw earlier with ISAM and VSAM.

Not all secondary keys need to be indexed, as noted earlier. But before a data base designer can decide which indexes to create, all secondary keys must be identified. When all data processing is known in advance, then computer program specifications provide an excellent source to identify secondary keys. Before these program specifications are developed or when significant ad hoc data base queries are anticipated, some general guidelines are required to assist in identifying secondary (and even alternative primary) keys. Guidelines for identifying secondary (and primary) keys can be found in Table 5-2. This table summarizes this taxonomy and indicates examples from the Pine Valley Furniture data base for each key type.

TREES

It was observed in the prior section that an index with a large number of entries can itself present an interesting index data structuring problem. If an index is helpful in storing and searching through data records, then could an index help to organize another index? ISAM, VSAM, and other file organizations, as well as a host of other data structures, all are based on this approach of recursively indexing indexes. This type of hierarchy of data and pointers to data is generalized by the tree data structure. Trees can be used to organize data directly or organize indexes into data.

A **tree data structure** has the property that each element of the structure (except the root) has only one path coming in (i.e., there is only one pointer that points to any given element), but there may be zero or many paths coming out of an element (i.e., there can be several pointers in any given element pointing to other elements). This set of pointers may be address sequential or pointer sequential connected. A **binary tree** permits at most two paths coming out of an element.

Table 5-2
Primary and Secondary Key Taxonomy

Key type	Description and motivation	Example from Pine Valley Furniture
Simple primary key	This is one data item whose values are unique to each record in a file; frequently required in on-line applications	PRODUCT# for Product records
Partial value key	A data item with long values may be cumbersome to index. The first n characters may be very discriminating, but not unique	PRODUCT-DESCRIPTION for Product records
Concatenated primary key	Records that contain data about (the relationship between) two entities are identified by a combination of the related entity primary keys	ORDER# and PRODUCT# for Order-Line records
Concatenated retrieval key	Although lists of addresses from two separate indexes can be intersected to answer queries with AND conditions, a combined key index can avoid this cost	FINISH and ROOM for Product records
Simple category key	Frequently, records are sought that have a common characteristic (single, nonunique value or range of values)	FINISH for Product records
Complex category key	Often, queries arise that simply ask which records exist with specified interdata item characteristics	QUANTITY-ON-HAND less than REORDER-POINT for Product records
Existence/ count key	Some queries only ask if any record exists or how many exist with specified properties; these can be answered from just an index	DELIVERY-DATE of today for Order records
Intrafile concatenated key	Complex relationships can exist between records within the same file, such as Bill-of-Materials; a key that is a concatenation of these related record keys can speed access	Parent PRODUCT# and component PRODUCT# for Bill-of-Materials in Product file

continued

Table 5-2
Primary and Secondary Key Taxonomy (continued)

Key type	Description and motivation	Example from Pine Valley Furniture
Missing value key	This is a special case of the simple category key in which the characteristic sought is the null value	PRICE for Product records
Interfile key	This is an inverted list equivalent to a chain structure. Here records are identified by a common characteristic that is also the primary key of another file	PRODUCT# for Order-Line records
Audit/change key	Frequently, data processing audit and control procedures need to know which records have been modified, added, or deleted during the most recent period	PRODUCT# for Product records (e.g., to tag records with price changes)
Sort key	An index can be used to maintain a sorted order to avoid sorting records before every batch reporting	CUSTOMER-ZIPCODE for Customer records

There is a great deal of specialized terminology associated with trees, some of which has already been introduced. Figure 5-14 graphically depicts many of the terms. We may view trees genealogically. The **root** is the element (node) with no parents. All the direct offspring of a common parent are collectively called a **filial set**; each member (node) of a filial set is a **sibling**. All the offspring (both direct descendents and all future generations) form a **subtree**. All terminal elements that have no offspring are called **leaves**. **Level** refers to the distance from the root in terms of number of branches to backtrack to return to the root. In addition, the term **degree** signifies the maximum number of offspring from an element; a binary tree is a tree of degree (or order) 2.

Binary Sequence Trees

Figure 5-15 illustrates one type of binary tree, called a sequence tree, for the PRODUCT file of Pine Valley Furniture. In a **sequence tree**, all the data elements (subtree) accessible starting from the left pointer (branch) of an

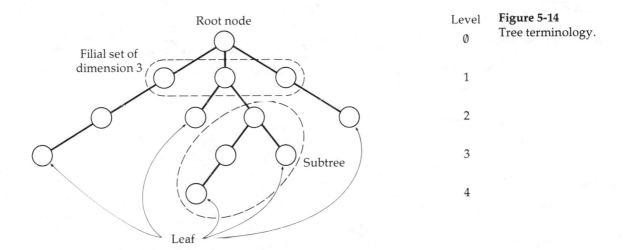

Figure 5-14
Tree terminology.

element have key values less than the key for the given element of data, and similarly, the right pointer leads to elements with key values greater than the given element. In box 11 of Figure 5-15, the record for PRODUCT# 1000 is at the root, the element that has no pointers pointing to it. Records for PRODUCT# 0100, 0625, 1425, and 1775 are leaves, those elements that do not point to any other elements. The boxes within Figure 5-15 show the evolution of the sequence tree as each key is inserted in the file. Exercise 9 at the end of the chapter defines a situation for retrieval of records from a tree.

Properties of Trees

Sequence trees, like most trees, often appear in business data processing as a method of providing fast primary key access to records in a file. Sequence trees introduce several important properties that should be considered with *all* trees:

In a sequence tree, some records are closer to the root than others. This means that a different number of comparisons and branches will be required to access different records. If frequently accessed records could be placed close to the root, then overall data base performance could be improved. Some types of trees do build **uniform accessibility** by placing *all* records in leaves and requiring that all leaves be an equal distance from the root (VSAM has this property). This factor of distance from root will be extremely important later when we consider the hierarchical data model in Chapter 6.

The evolution of the tree in Figure 5-15 was dependent on the order in which records were inserted. If, for example, PRODUCT# 1600 had been inserted first, it would have become the root, and the whole structure of the tree would have changed. The worst case here is when the records are loaded in ascending or descending primary key order! Many trees that store

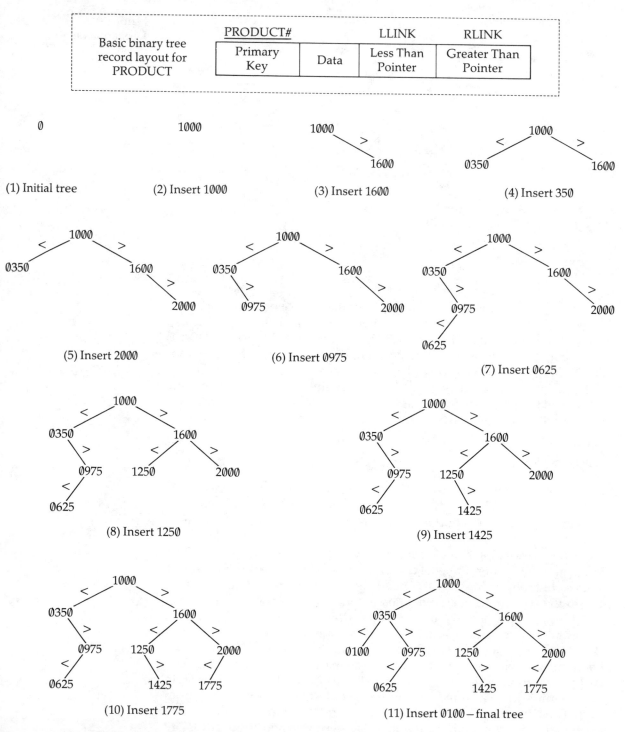

Figure 5-15 Example of a sequence tree.

data records only in leaves do not exhibit this insertion dependence property. But if the type of tree being used can become pathological in shape with certain insertion sequences, care should be taken in loading records. In general, bushy trees provide the best performance.

Many "varieties" of trees have been developed. Three characteristics are especially useful in distinguishing between trees:

1. **Branching factor** or **degree**—the maximum number of children allowed per parent.

2. **Sibling connection**—the type of connection between siblings (choices are parent index, address sequential, and pointer sequential).

3. **Depth**—the maximum number of levels in the tree.

Large branching factors, in general, create broader, more shallow trees. Since access time in a tree is often more dependent on depth than on breadth, and since movement between levels means a disk access, it is usually advantageous to have bushy, shallow trees.

The preceding remarks are qualified because tree search time also depends on the type of sibling connection. A **parent index** is a set of pointers in an element, one pointer for each of the offspring. This method provides rapid access to each offspring at the expense of storage space for the pointers. Further, since a pointer to each offspring could lead to various parts of a disk, access to *all* offspring could be time-consuming. A parent index allows easy answering of questions like "Does a given record have any children records?" or "How many offspring does a given record have?"

One way to speed up access to the whole filial set is to store the whole set as a block and connect siblings via address sequential. In this case, the parent only needs one pointer to the beginning of the block for the filial set. Space is conserved (few pointers) and all siblings are rapidly accessed as a group. The problem is to manage updates (insertions and deletions) to filial sets. When pointer sequential connection between siblings is used, space management is easier but access time is slower. The general rule is to use pointer sequential when there is a small filial set, address sequential when the size of the filial set is stable, and parent index otherwise.

B-Trees

The ISAM and VSAM file organizations presented in the preceding chapter are both based on tree data structures. Both use trees to structure an index into records that are stored only at the leaves. Device independence and dynamic index reorganization were the primary distinguishing characteristics of VSAM. VSAM is based on a tree data structure called a B-tree (B for balanced, meaning all leaves are the same distance from the root). B-trees guarantee a predictable efficiency that many other types of trees do not. For

Figure 5-16
B-tree nonleaf node
structure.

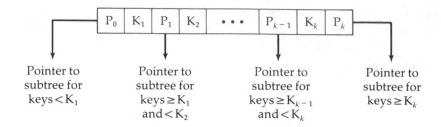

Pointer to
subtree for
keys $< K_1$

Pointer to
subtree for
keys $\geq K_1$
and $< K_2$

Pointer to
subtree for
keys $\geq K_{k-1}$
and $< K_k$

Pointer to
subtree for
keys $\geq K_k$

example, with a B-tree of degree 199, any record in a file as large as 1,999,998 records can be retrieved in three accesses! Although hashing may yield fewer accesses for random record retrieval, hashing does not support sequential retrieval and B-trees do. Not only VSAM, but also many data base management systems, now use B-trees as the principal method for primary and secondary key access.

A **B-tree of degree** *m* has the following properties:

1. Every node has less than or equal to *m* children (*m* greater than or equal to 3 and usually odd).

2. Every node, except the root and leaves, has at least *m*/2 children.

3. All leaves are at the same level and only contain pointers to the actual data records.

4. A nonleaf node that has *k* children will contain *k* − 1 keys.

Figure 5-16 illustrates the general structure of nonleaf nodes in a B-tree, and Figure 5-17a shows an example B-tree of degree 3 (very small for illustrative purposes only) for the Product Master File of Pine Valley Furniture (developed from Figure 2-2). The leaves only contain pointers to the actual records identified by their PRODUCT#.

Maintaining B-Trees. Insertions and deletions of records from the Product file must preserve the B-tree properties. Consider the insertion of PRODUCT# 0800. Figure 5-17b shows the resultant tree. Since the node labeled A still has no more than three children, no restructuring is required. Now consider insertion of PRODUCT# 1500. Node B in Figure 5-17b is "full" with three (*m*) children. The B-tree answer to this is to split node B into two nodes. To split will require choice of a key (PRODUCT#) to be moved to the parent of B (i.e., C) to indicate the boundaries for the split of node B. This new key in C will also make node C overflow, so C will also be split and a new key moved into D. Figure 5-17c shows one possible result of these splits. (Different trees can result from different choices on which key to move up a level; we usually choose a key to divide nodes as evenly as possible and to permit an equal expansion capacity in all nodes.) Note that no other nodes, besides those on a path from the leaf that needs to be split to the root, can be

Figure 5-17 (opposite)
Example of B-tree
maintenance.
(a) Initial B-tree.
(b) B-tree after insertion
   of PRODUCT# 0800.
(c) B-tree after insertion
   of PRODUCT# 1500.
(d) B-tree after deletion of
   PRODUCT# 0975.
(continued on p. 160)

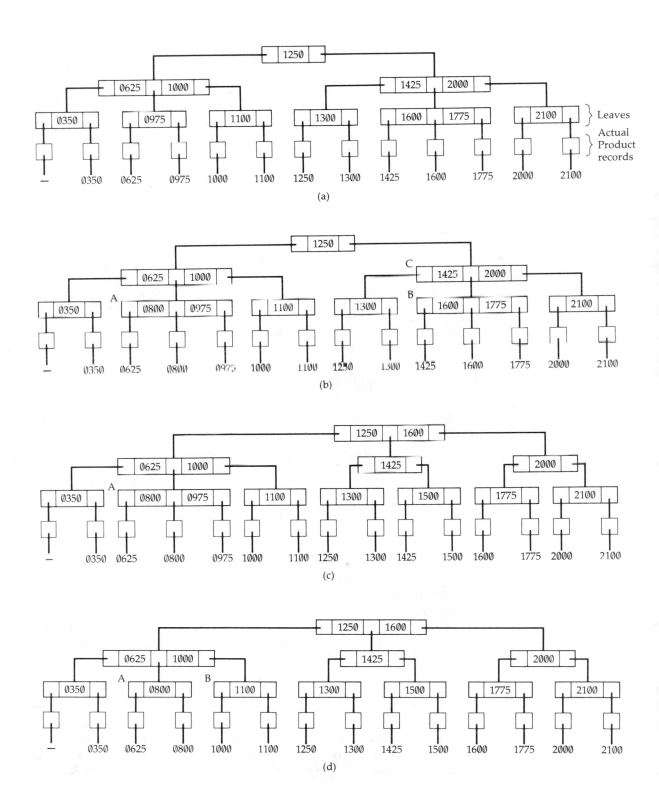

(a)

(b)

(c)

(d)

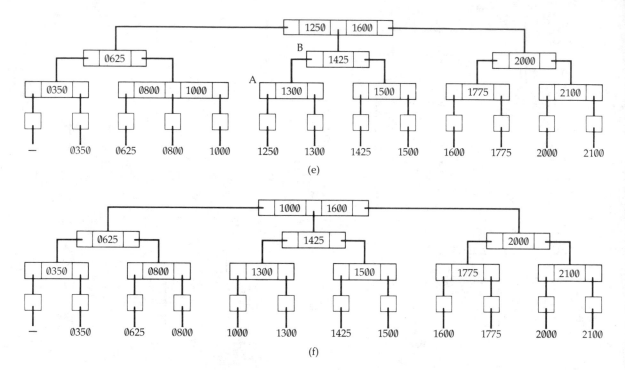

(e)

(f)

Figure 5-17 (continued)
(e) B-tree after deletion of PRODUCT# 1425.
(f) B-tree after deletion of PRODUCT# 1250.

changed. If the root overflows, it is split and a new level is formed with a new root above the split.

As can be seen from Figure 5-17, not only are all records equally accessible in B-trees, but also the shape of a B-tree is dependent on loading sequence.

Deletion from B-trees can be as simple as insertion; sometimes it can be more complex (when deletion causes B-tree properties to be violated). Consider the deletion of PRODUCT# 0975 from Figure 5-17c. Since this would leave two pointers in node A (still above the minimum of $^3/_2$, or 1.5, children), and key 0975 does not appear in any parent node to A, deletion is simple; the result appears in Figure 5-17d. Now consider deleting PRODUCT# 1100 from node B in Figure 5-17d. Deleting the key will violate properties of B-trees, and the parent of node B will have to be changed, since it refers to PRODUCT# 1100. Figure 5-17e shows the result of this deletion.

The most extensive type of deletion from a B-tree is illustrated by the deletion of PRODUCT# 1250 from Figure 5-17e. In this case, deletion will affect both node B (since it will no longer have at least $m/2$ children) and the root (because key 1250 exists there and because node B will change). Since all leaves are at the same level of the tree, we cannot simply get rid of node B and have the root point directly to a leaf. Extensive tree rearrangement is required. Various reorganizations are possible; the reorganization goals are to retain B-tree properties, to keep subtrees as uniform in shape as possible, and to keep reorganization work to a minimum. One solution, "rotating"

PRODUCT# 1000, seems to satisfy all these criteria. This solution is illustrated in Figure 5-17f.

Review of Trees

The preceding discussion of trees has illustrated that they can permit rapid retrieval of data for both random and sequential processing. The examples shown here all have dealt with access to records within one file based on primary keys. These examples can easily be changed to work with secondary keys. When tree structures are used to connect records in different files, another name is used—the hierarchical data model, which is covered in the next chapter. Trees are special cases of a more general data structure called networks. Since networks are used in data base management primarily to connect records in different files, we will delay consideration of the network data model until the next chapter.

SUMMARY

In this chapter, we presented various data structures as groundwork for understanding data base structures. We have tried to show the most fundamental components and their impact on data base processing and performance. Address sequential and pointer sequential connection have been shown to be basic building blocks of all data structures. File organizations like ISAM and VSAM have been explained in terms of their underlying data structure.

We have demonstrated that each data structure exhibits its own performance. Some structures manage small sets of data better than large, other structures provide very rapid data retrieval but are costly to maintain. A data base designer must carefully match the characteristics of the data processing to be performed (sequential processing, random record retrieval, quantity of record insertions and deletions, and so on) with an appropriate, efficient data structure. Most of the time this matching is done by selecting operating system access methods and data base management systems that best satisfy the data processing requirements.

We have also identified three types of pointers—physical, relative, and logical—and their comparative characteristics. We have shown how these pointers and also address sequential connection can be used to build physical records in intrarecord data structures and to represent associations between records in interrecord data structures.

Interrecord data structures were described as basic linear (such as stacks, queues, and sorted lists), multilist (a technique to permit multiple associations to be maintained concurrently among the same data), inverted lists (an indexing technique that supports rapid multiple-key qualification retrieval), and trees (a hierarchical set of indexes and record connections).

The next chapter utilizes these data structures to describe different architectural forms, called data models, for data bases.

CHAPTER REVIEW

Review Questions

1. Define each of the following terms:

   a. data structure
   b. successor element of data
   c. address sequential connection
   d. pointer sequential connection
   e. data direct access
   f. data indirect access
   g. pointer
   h. physical pointer
   i. relative pointer
   j. logical pointer
   k. intrarecord data structure
   l. space management
   m. data item partition
   n. linear interrecord structure
   o. stack
   p. queue
   q. sorted list
   r. bidirectional chain
   s. multilist data structure
   t. inverted list data structure
   u. tree data structure
   v. binary tree
   w. root
   x. leaf
   y. B-tree

2. List and explain at least three criteria that could be used to measure the efficiency of data structures.

3. Summarize the relative advantages and disadvantages of the three types of pointers.

4. Explain the data structure(s) used in the ISAM file organization.

5. Define and critically compare the different types of intrarecord data structures.

6. Discuss the relative advantages and disadvantages of multilist and inverted list structures for managing multiple associations and answering multiple-qualification questions.

7. Give at least one example of each type of secondary key from a situation of your choice (but different from Pine Valley Furniture).

8. Explain why it may be beneficial to divide one logical record into several physical records.

9. Explain why a B-tree is such an appealing data structure.

10. Discuss how bidirectional pointers can make chain maintenance simpler.

11. What is the purpose of "dummy" nodes at the front and end of a list data structure?

Problems and Exercises

1. Redraw Figure 2-10 to show the use of single directional pointers (chains) to manage the associations in this figure. Show the additional "data about data" (pointers) required in each record type.

2. Consider the following questions processed using the Pine Valley Furniture data base depicted in Figure 2-10.

   a. List all customers with an order due for delivery today.

   b. Count the number of times PRODUCT# 1425 has been ordered in the past year.

   c. List the price of each of the products with a DESCRIPTION of TABLE (Pine Valley makes more varieties of tables than all other types of products combined!).

   Identify the secondary keys used in these queries and for each, explain whether an inverted index would be advantageous.

3. Consider the following data item specifications for a Customer record at Pine Valley Furniture:

   CUSTOMER: fixed length, always present/known

   CUSTOMER-ADDRESS: highly variable length, always present/known

   DOLLAR-SALES-YTD: fixed length, not present for prospective customers

   CREDIT-LIMIT: fixed length, not present for prospective customers

   SALES-COMMENTS: highly variable length, not present for prospective customers

   Design an intrarecord structure for this Customer record and justify your design.

4. For the Customer record defined in Problem 3, discuss a situation that would suggest the need to partition or cluster data items from this record into several physical records.

5. Consider the stack in Figure 5-8. Write a pseudocode record deletion procedure for this stack structure.

6. The queue record insertion procedure of this chapter was facilitated by the use of bidirectional pointers. In Figure 5-9a, delete the head-of-chain pointer NEWEST-ORDER-LINE and the PRIOR-ORDER-LINE pointer and then rewrite the queue insertion procedure. (*Hint:* The null pointer, 0, indicates the end of a chain.)

7. Write a sorted list deletion procedure to delete an ORDER record with key value DELKEY using the sorted list depicted in Figure 5-10b. (*Hint:* First list any possible error conditions, similar to duplicate key, that can occur during deletion, and build checks for these errors into your procedure.)

8. Consider the B-tree in Figure 5-17c. Modify this B-tree to handle the following record updates. Show the resultant B-tree after each modification and process the changes in exactly the order given. The updates are:

   (1) Insert 1100
   (2) Insert 1150
   (3) Delete 0625
   (4) Insert 0750
   (5) Delete 2000
   (6) Delete 1600

9. Consider the sequence tree in Figure 5-15. Let LLINK(X) be a pointer to the left subtree of the Product record at relative address X. Let RLINK(X) be similarly defined for the right subtree. Assume that the address of the root of the tree is stored in variable ROOT. Let PRODUCT#(X) be the product number in the Product record at relative address X, and let KEY contain the product number to be retrieved. Write a tree search procedure to locate a record with the product number stored in KEY. Your procedure should place the address of the record sought into variable ADDR. Your procedure should be designed to start searching at the root and proceed in the most efficient path. Place a value of 0 in ADDR if no record with product number KEY exists.

References

Hoffer, Jeffrey A., and Dennis G. Severance. 1975. "The Use of Cluster Analysis in Physical Data Base Design." *Proceedings of First Very Large Data Base Conference*, Framingham, Mass., September (available from Association for Computing Machinery), 69–86.

Knuth, Donald. 1973. *The Art of Computer Programming.* Vol. 3, *Sorting and Searching.* Reading, Mass.: Addison-Wesley.

Maxwell, William L., and Dennis G. Severance. 1973. "Comparison of Alternatives for the Representation of Data Item Values in an Information System." Technical report no. 199, September, Dept. of Operations Research, Cornell University.

Schkolnick, Mario. 1977. "A Clustering Algorithm for Hierarchical Structures." *ACM-TODS* 2 (March): 27–44.

Severance, Dennis G. 1974. "Identifier Search Mechanisms: A Survey and Generalized Model." *ACM-Computing Surveys* 6 (September): 175–194.

6

Data Models

INTRODUCTION

A **model** is a representation of real-world objects, events, and their associations. It is an abstraction from reality (i.e., in a different form) and often is simplified for ease of understanding and manipulation. Model airplanes that allow aeronautical engineers to design better airplanes, mathematical models that allow business analysts to improve the operation of an enterprise, and model people (dolls) that allow children to practice the responsibilities of parenthood all suitably represent some real-world situation.

A **data model** is an abstract representation (a description) of the data about entities, events, activities, and their associations within an organization. More liberally, a data model represents (describes) an organization itself, since, for example, it is the association between customers and the orders they submit that leads to associations between Customer records and Order records.

The purpose of a data model is twofold: first, to represent data and second, to be understandable. If a data model accurately and completely represents required data and is understandable (and easy to use), then it can be used in some application, just as a model airplane can be used in a wind tunnel for testing design features.

Careful thought on the model airplane analogy will suggest that there are three types of airplane models for different applications:

1. There are those models (or submodels) that each "user" of an airplane conceives. For example, the pilot sees the airplane as a set of instruments and equipment for maneuvering the plane; and the aeronautical engineer sees the plane in terms of shapes, lines, and aerodynamics. These are called **external models**.

2. There is the model that consolidates the aerodynamics, the internal cockpit physical layout, and other views to check for inconsistencies (e.g., there may be fine aerodynamic features but not enough passenger capacity to be economical). This model is used by a general design engineer responsible for the overall architecture and objectives of the project (this design engineer in the data base realm is called a data administrator). This model is called a **conceptual model**.

3. There is a fabrication model that puts every part in its place in some abstract form (often a blueprint) so that the airplane can actually be constructed and used. This model is useful to an assembly foreman, construction project manager, and workers responsible for production and daily operations (the blueprint in the data base realm is developed by a data base designer or administrator and is used by programmers and others who build application programs). This model is called an **internal model**.

CASE EXAMPLE   **Pine Valley Furniture**

Figure 6-1 is a version of Figure 2-17 that shows the correspondence between levels of data models in Pine Valley Furniture and the levels of airplane models just presented. At the external level, models or user views are used by systems analysts and users to elicit data requirements. They are used in training to explain to new employees how to use an information system. Here, user understanding is very important, so the model clearly conveys only what a given user wants from a data base. One form of a data model in this level may be flowcharts or data flow diagrams (see DeMarco 1978). Bubble charts, introduced in Chapter 2, can also be helpful here. Data models to be presented in this chapter can also be used to depict user views. End users may also interact with a data base by using a query language or problem-oriented language. Thus, there are also external data models used to depict the data being used by a user via a specific data processing technology. This latter type of external model is often called a **subschema**.

   With a conceptual data model, we need to be able to consolidate user views, check for consistency (e.g., do all users refer to the same data item by the same name?), and validate that all data and relationships have been identified. It is important at this level to capture the semantics about data. For example, one user may mean *all* customer orders when she says "orders," and to another user this term may only refer to those orders that still have products to be delivered. Further, information about who can do what with data must be captured and represented for subsequent use in develop-

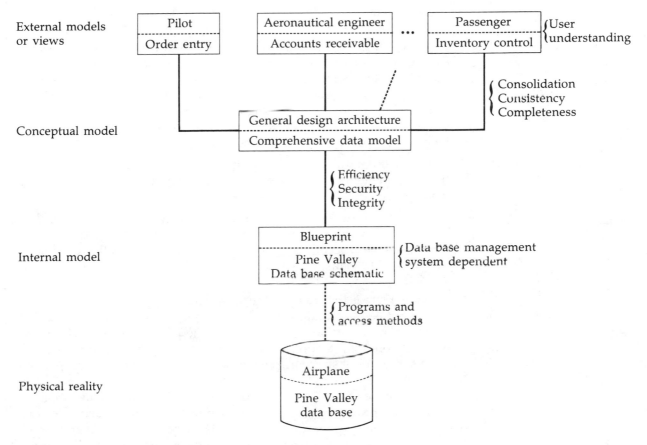

External models or views

| Pilot | Aeronautical engineer | ... | Passenger | {User understanding |
| Order entry | Accounts receivable | | Inventory control | |

{Consolidation
Consistency
Completeness

Conceptual model

General design architecture
Comprehensive data model

{Efficiency
Security
Integrity

Internal model

Blueprint
Pine Valley
Data base schematic

{Data base management system dependent

{Programs and access methods

Physical reality

Airplane
Pine Valley
data base

Figure 6-1
Levels of data models compared to airplane models.

ing the data base. Finally, the conceptual model, since it is the basis for design of the internal data base, should be supplemented with information about usage and maintenance of the data base so that an efficient internal structure can be devised.

The final model of data, the internal model (often called a **schema**), provides the interface with computer technologies: data base management systems, operating system access methods, and other programs. This model type uses data structures to build complex architectures for organizing data. Whereas the data structures covered in Chapter 5 primarily dealt with organization of and access to single files of data, the internal data model (as the other levels) relates data from different files (e.g., Customer to Order). Because this data model type deals with specific technologies, we will see that each DBMS can have its own unique internal data model or schema architecture.

Thus, we have outlined three categories of data models:

1. External data models, of which there *may* be two subcategories: (a) logical external data models or views used to elicit and describe data requirements in a technology-independent manner; and (b) subschema data models, which describe only the data required for a given data processing task but which are defined using a technology-dependent style (like a COBOL Data Division, FORTRAN dimension statements, data definition language [DDL] of a DBMS, and so on).

2. Conceptual data models, used to comprehensively define all the data base requirements of all users into a consistent and singular data base description.

3. Internal data models, used to comprehensively define the whole data base using a technology-dependent style (i.e., models limited by the capabilities of the technology and that explicitly state how the technology will be used to manage data).

In addition, there is the reality of the objects and events of an organization. We mask out certain characteristics from reality, since we determine that these are not necessary in the abstraction. Good data base design depends significantly on a good application area systems analysis to establish the suitable subset for abstraction. This process will be addressed, in part, in Chapters 7 and 8.

The purpose of this chapter is to review various data model architectures that have proved to be appropriate at different levels of abstraction of a data base. We will see that some data models can be applied at several levels, whereas others have been especially designed for specific levels. Chapters 7 and 8 will demonstrate the process of using external and conceptual data models for data base design. As already noted, because the internal data model used to specify the detailed structure of a data base depends on the DBMS being used, this chapter will only present some families of internal data models. Specific implementations of these families are covered in Chapters 12 to 14. This separation of generic data model from implementation emphasizes that any given data model is not the exclusive property of any one DBMS and that a data model can be used to represent data before the appropriate data base technology is selected.

THE HIERARCHICAL DATA MODEL

A hierarchy is a familiar structure. Organizations have always been viewed as a hierarchy of positions and authority; computer programs have relatively recently been viewed as a hierarchy of control and operating modules;

and various taxonomies of animal and plant life view elements in a hierarchical set of relationships.

Definitions

The **hierarchical data model** represents data as a set of nested one-to-many (1:M) and one-to-one (1:1) relationships (see "Types of Associations" in Chapter 2 for a review of these terms), as depicted in Figure 6-2 for the Pine Valley Furniture data base from Figure 2-10. There is a single record type, in this case CUSTOMER, that "owns" ORDER, which in turn "owns" ORDER-LINE, which in turn "owns" PRODUCT. No single occurrence of a record type may have more than one "parent" (record type or occurrence) in the hierarchy. Because of the similarity of hierarchies and tree data structures, terminology like root, level, and leaf are also used when discussing hierarchies.

Relationships in a Hierarchy

The hierarchical rule of only one parent does not cause a problem as long as relationships are truly 1:M from parent to child throughout the hierarchy. A review of Figure 2-10 will indicate that the 1:1 Products-in-Order relationship in Figure 6-2 is the reverse of the 1:M Products-on-Order relationship in Figure 2-10. That is, a given PRODUCT record is associated with many ORDER-LINE records, not just one. But the hierarchical data model rule will not support an M:1 relationship.

Figure 6-3 shows via a record instance diagram what must occur to implement the hierarchy rule. The result is *redundancy*. Data concerning PRODUCT# X is associated with three ORDER-LINE records. Since an occurrence of PRODUCT# X can only have one ORDER-LINE parent instance, this PRODUCT# X data must be repeated under each associated ORDER-LINE instance. Each time PRODUCT# X's DESCRIPTION, PRICE, or other data change, application program logic has to guarantee that all copies of these data will be updated (and at approximately the same time to avoid potential data base inconsistencies).

Is there any way to avoid this redundancy? Since PRODUCT can also be viewed to "own" all these data, then why not invert the hierarchy? (In fact, Figure 6-2 is the view of the data from the perspective of the customer order processing function; PRODUCT would not be their focus or root; the CUSTOMER would be.)

In Figure 6-4, we show the result of placing PRODUCT as the root of the hierarchy, which might be the perspective of a product sales management function. Now the problem is that the hierarchy rule will force redundancy of *both* ORDER (since different ORDER-LINEs apply to the same ORDER) and CUSTOMER (since different ORDERs are placed by the same CUSTOMER). Without actually comparing the amount of physical data that

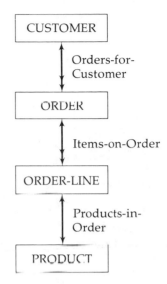

Figure 6-2
Example of hierarchical data model for Pine Valley Furniture.

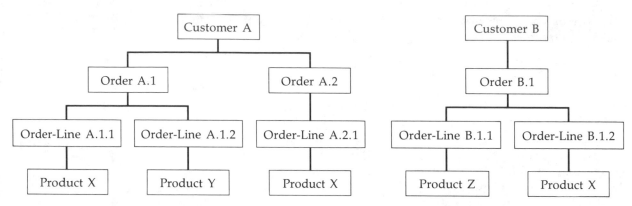

Figure 6-3
Instance diagram for data base in Figure 6-2.

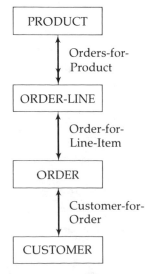

Figure 6-4
Example of product-oriented hierarchy for Pine Valley Furniture.

would be repeated, this hierarchy in Figure 6-4 seems to be less desirable than the one in Figure 6-2.

We can improve the hierarchy of Figure 6-3 slightly if we recognize that 1:1 relationships serve no useful purpose and that no information is lost or further repeated (*or* repeated less) if we combine into *one* record two records that have a 1:1 relationship. Figure 6-5 shows what would happen to Figure 6-3 if we combined ORDER-LINE and PRODUCT record data into one consolidated record type. The result is to save one level in the hierarchy, which will likely mean one fewer disk access to collect together all the data along one path from a root to a leaf.

Hierarchies are very explicit structures. If one record type is not directly below another in the hierarchy, then no direct relationship (nor any direct accessing) between those record types is possible. For example, there clearly is an association between all the ORDER-LINE and PRODUCT records for the same PRODUCT#. But this type of lateral relationship is not possible in a hierarchy.

Multiple subtree hierarchies are also permitted. Figure 6-6 shows what might result from expanding the role of the data base depicted in Figure 6-2 to also support shipping. In this situation, the SHIPMENT-LINE record may contain some data items duplicated from associated ORDER-LINE and PRODUCT records.

Figure 6-6 also suggests another limitation, besides redundancy, of the hierarchical data model. This limitation concerns integrity control and semantics. A SHIPMENT-LINE record should exist *only* when there is an associated ORDER-LINE (we should not ship what has not been ordered). Also, an order cannot be deemed closed until all ORDER-LINEs have been shipped. Because there is no direct relationship between ORDER-LINE and SHIPMENT-LINE in this hierarchy, these integrity constraints cannot be enforced by the data model or a DBMS built on the hierarchical data model.

Sometimes in hierarchies, empty relationship record types exist for the sole purpose of relating other record types. Consider Figure 6-6 again and assume that for this data base there is no use for ORDER-DATE, DELIVERY-

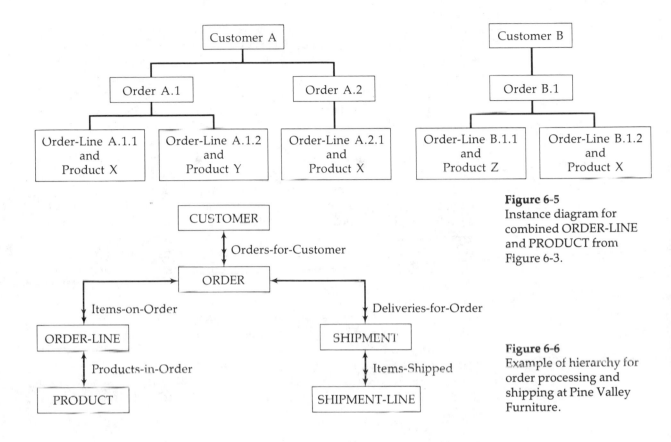

Figure 6-5
Instance diagram for
combined ORDER-LINE
and PRODUCT from
Figure 6-3.

Figure 6-6
Example of hierarchy for
order processing and
shipping at Pine Valley
Furniture.

DATE, and so on, which might be found in the ORDER record. But assume that we do wish to know what was ordered and what has been shipped. In this case, we could still create a relationship ORDER record (sometimes called a dummy record), void of meaningful content, just to link ORDER-LINE records with associated SHIPMENT records.

Data Processing with the Hierarchical Data Model

Hierarchies have the advantage that they are familiar structures for which there are many examples of data and relationships that follow such an architecture. Any record occurrence within a hierarchy implicitly contains all the data in record occurrences above it. Hierarchies show "each" relationship explicitly (i.e., each relationship implemented) and require some of the least sophisticated data management technology to manipulate. Any nested relationship present in the hierarchy implies that data can be efficiently retrieved via that relationship.

Hierarchies are, in general, entered at the root, and scanning records to answer questions must begin there. For the query presented earlier, every CUSTOMER record would have to be retrieved and then, in recursive fashion, each associated ORDER and ORDER-LINE would have to be re-trieved (scanning could stop on CUSTOMER-related records as soon as a PRODUCT# X record is found for that customer). The hierarchy of Figure 6-4 would support more efficient retrieval of records for this query, since there, all desired customer data are under one PRODUCT parent; other PROD-UCT records and associated ORDERS do not have to be accessed for any purpose to answer this question. This type of sensitivity of hierarchical record placement to data processing requirements will be addressed in more detail in Chapters 8 and 9 on data base design and in Chapter 12 on data base management systems that use the hierarchical data model.

The style of processing a hierarchical data base is distinct. First, with some data base management technologies, a data base is limited to only one hierarchy, so programs cannot be written to report on data directly from two hierarchies. Second, some query programming languages may require spe-cial statements or clauses to virtually rearrange the data base hierarchy in order to write a query for certain questions. This virtual rearrangement may be to invert a hierarchy in order to place qualified data items (PRODUCT#) above other data to be retrieved (CUSTOMER-NAME); this rearrangement could also be to move all the data used in the query into a common path from lowest level to highest level referenced. An example of this last requirement can be found in Figure 6-6. Some query languages would require a special phrase to virtually move SHIPMENT data into its associated ORDER record so as to write a program to answer a question such as "What orders for PRODUCT# Y have been shipped in the past week?" (e.g., to trace defective goods).

Implementation of the Hierarchical Data Model

Hierarchical data base management systems frequently use inverted index-ing as a way to avoid extensive data base scanning (see "Inverted Lists" in Chapter 5). If, in the data base of Figure 6-6, we could index PRODUCT records (a leaf of the hierarchy) on PRODUCT# and then could efficiently find the parent of any record, then the hierarchy of Figure 6-2 could be made to act like the hierarchy of Figure 6-4 to answer the query on the customers of PRODUCT# X. That is, we would enter the hierarchy directly on PROD-UCT# X records without having to search for them starting at the root and visiting many immaterial intermediate record instances.

The hierarchy rule of only one parent implicitly means that a record can only participate explicitly in *one* relationship as the target of that rela-tionship. Consider the Orders-for-Customer relationship in Figure 6-2. A Customer could "own" proposed/tentative orders, open orders, and closed orders, to name a few. The hierarchical data model does not permit three relationships in this case. The hierarchical model forces one of two imple-mentations. One approach is to put an additional data item, STATUS, in the ORDER record to distinguish the different types of records. Queries would have to scan all ORDERS to find selected types or a secondary index would have to be created. The second approach is to create three separate record types and have each type below CUSTOMER in the hierarchy. This causes unnecessary and redundant data definitions and may cause significant maintenance work: when an order changes status, we have to move a whole subtree from, say, a proposed subtree to an active subtree, which requires work for subtree removal and reinsertion (possibly reentry of data) with some data base management systems.

Hierarchies are usually implemented using tree type data structures and extensive use of pointers. Each record type in a hierarchy can have any or all of the following pointers:

1. Pointer to the *first* dependent child record for each record type directly below the record (head-of-chain pointer). For example, in Figure 6-2, an ORDER record instance might contain a pointer to the first ORDER-LINE instance for that ORDER.

2. Pointer to the next record of the same type under a common parent (sibling or twin pointer). For example, an ORDER-LINE record instance might have a pointer to the next ORDER-LINE on the same ORDER; a null pointer would be used to signify the end of the list.

3. Pointer to parent record (parent pointer). For example, an ORDER-LINE record instance might have a pointer to the ORDER instance on which it is a line item.

4. Pointer to *each* dependent child record for each record type directly below the record (children pointer array); either this or (1) and (2) above, but usually not both, are implemented. For example, an ORDER record instance might contain *n* pointers, each pointing to each of the ORDER-LINE instances for line items on that ORDER.

5. Pointer to next record of the same type in order by primary key or as part of a primary key access method like a sequence tree (primary key pointer). For example, an ORDER record instance might contain a pointer to the ORDER instance with the next ascending or descending ORDER# key value.

Figure 6-7 illustrates the possible contents of the ORDER record from Figure 6-6 for the examples just given.

A second form of hierarchy implementation uses address sequential connection to cluster together related hierarchical records into one file. This clustering can be viewed logically in Figure 6-8 for the hierarchy of Figure 6-5. This is a logical view, since each record would typically be broken into several fixed-length data blocks owing to the highly variable and long length of this record structure.

In Figure 6-8, components of the hierarchy are arranged in what is called a preorder, depth-first sequence. That is, we store the data in the record as soon as it is encountered in the hierarchy of Figure 6-5. We proceed

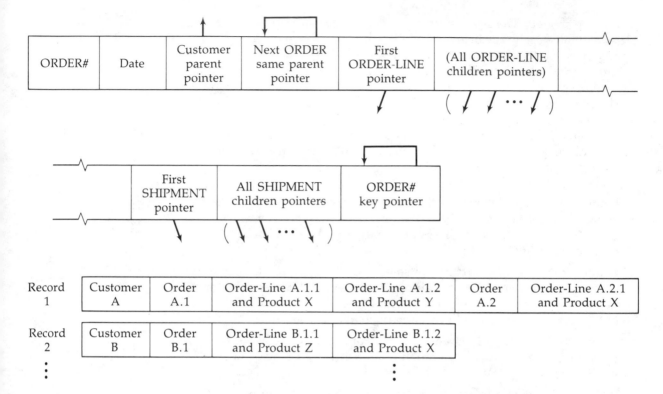

Figure 6-7 (top)
Example of possible order
record contents in a
hierarchy with pointer
sequential connection.

Figure 6-8 (bottom)
Preorder, depth-first
hierarchical record layout.

to build the record by starting at a root instance (e.g., segment for Customer A) and continue by first taking the leftmost branch from a segment. When we reach a leaf, we pop back up to the prior level (e.g., from Order-Line A.1.1 and Product X we return to Order A.1) and attempt to take the next branch out of the prior level. When we exhaust branches, as with a leaf that has no branches, we return to the prior level. Each time we visit a segment for the *first* time, we append these new data to the record being built. Each root instance defines another record instance.

Summary of the Hierarchical Data Model

The hierarchical data model has had a major influence on data management. Its similarity to data structures in programming languages like COBOL and PL/I has made it easy for many programmers to understand. It can be a very efficient structural form when data relationships follow a purely nested 1:*M* pattern. Data base management systems like System 2000 and IMS, based on the hierarchical data model, continue to be popular products (see MRI System Corp. 1981 and IBM 1982). Even considering its limitations that cause undesirable redundancy, the hierarchical model is well established in practice.

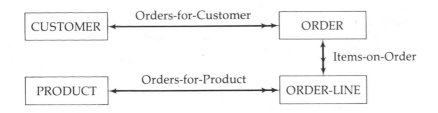

Figure 6-9
Example of a simple
network data model for
Pine Valley Furniture.

THE NETWORK DATA MODEL

It was stated in the previous section that the single-parent rule of the hierarchical data model forces redundant and excessive data and structure. When this rule may be violated, we can create a network data model and further eliminate redundancy.

The network model permits as much or as little structure as is desired. We can even create a hierarchy (a special case of a network) if that is what is needed. As with the hierarchical data model, if a certain relationship is not *explicitly* included in the data base definition, then it cannot be used in data base processing.

Definitions

The **network data model** represents data as a set of record types and pairwise relationships between record types. Relationships that involve more than two record types (e.g., a relationship between PRODUCT, VENDOR, and WAREHOUSE) are not *directly* permitted (we will return to this point in the next section). Figure 6-9 is a diagram of a network data model for the Pine Valley Furniture data base from Figure 2-10 (you may want to compare Figure 6-9 with Figure 6-2).

There are three types of network data models. The **simple network data model** (the most common because of the efforts of the CODASYL Data Base Task Group [DBTG] in defining a proposed standard for this type of network [CODASYL 1975; CODASYL Data Description Language Committee 1978]) does not permit $M:N$ relationships directly in a data base. For example, the simple network model does not permit a direct linkage of ORDER with PRODUCT in Figure 6-9, which would be an $M:N$ relationship. The CODASYL network model will be discussed in Chapter 13. In this chapter, we address the general characteristics of network data models without restriction to any particular implementation or standard (like CODASYL).

The **complex network data model** permits $M:N$ relationships to be represented. For example, we could enhance Figure 6-9 to include vendor information on those products that Pine Valley Furniture simply buys and resells under their label. This expanded complex network data base is

Figure 6-10
Example of complex and simple network data models.
(a) Example of a complex network data model.
(b) Example of a simple network equivalent to the complex network using a link record.
(c) Example of a simple network equivalent to the complex network using a cycle.

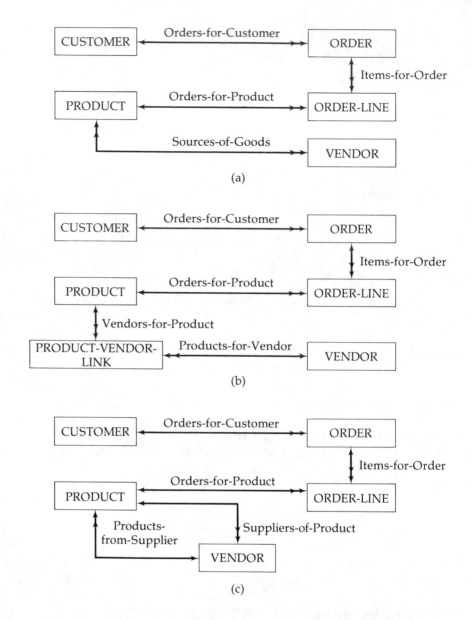

(a)

(b)

(c)

shown in Figure 6-10a; Figures 6-10b and 6-10c illustrate two alternative equivalent simple network data models.

The PRODUCT-VENDOR-LINK record in Figure 6-10b is called a **link record** and serves only to relate PRODUCTs to VENDORs; it has no meaningful contents. ORDER-LINE, on the other hand, is called an **intersection record** and its meaningful contents are called **intersection data**. In practice, pure link records are rare, since there is usually some data about the relationship to be retained. For example, we probably want to know not only the PRODUCT-VENDOR association, but also the PRODUCT-PRICE from

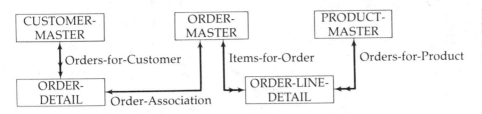

Figure 6-11
Example of a limited
network data model for
Pine Valley Furniture.

each VENDOR; PRODUCT-PRICE would be stored in the intersection record.

Figure 6-10c shows an approach that will work (if cycles are permitted by the DBMS) when intersection data will never be needed. This cycle approach can present an integrity problem in some data base management systems that control insertion of new records based on existence of current records (see Chapter 13). The link record approach provides greater record independence, since each record type exists on its own.

Very few data base management systems have implemented the complex network data model; one DBMS that has is MDBS III (Micro Data Base Systems, Inc. 1981), which is available on a variety of mini- and microcomputers.

The **limited network data model** divides all record types into two sets: primary or master record type and secondary, detail, or transaction record type. All relationships are from a master to a detail. The data base management systems TOTAL (CINCOM Systems, Inc. 1982) and IMAGE (Hewlett-Packard 1979) are the primary commercial products to adopt this network model. Figure 6-11 illustrates a limited network model for the simple network data base of Figure 6-9. An additional detail record type (called ORDER-DETAIL) is necessary since ORDER cannot be both a child of CUSTOMER and a parent of ORDER-LINE.

A limited network permits the same detail record type to be a detail in two or more relationships (e.g., ORDER-LINE-DETAIL) and the same master record type to be a master for two or more relationships (e.g., ORDER-MASTER). All master record types are accessed via a primary key. To be able to retrieve the ORDER-MASTER in Figure 6-11 once an ORDER-DETAIL is retrieved, we may have to redundantly store the ORDER# in both order record types. The remainder of the ORDER data can be stored in either record. Access from master to detail is assumed to be via a chain.

Relationships in a Network

All network models support the use of multiple 1:*M* relationships between the same pair of record types (with the limited model, all relationships must be in the same direction). Consider, as in the last section, three relationships from CUSTOMER to ORDER for proposed/tentative, open and closed orders. With a network model, we would simply define three relationships between CUSTOMER and ORDER.

Figure 6-12
Example of a disconnected
network data base.

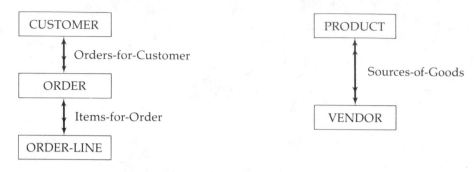

The primary feature of the complex network is its ability to support one record instance (e.g., VENDOR instance) being "owned" by more than one record instance of some other type (e.g., PRODUCT instances). Other network data models do not support multiple parent records of the same type (i.e., *M:N* relationships). In a simple network, we would have to create two 1:*M* relationships, one from PRODUCT to VENDOR (or to a link record) and the other from VENDOR to PRODUCT (or to a link record) to represent such an *M:N* relationship. The problem with this solution is that two relationships have had to be defined, and update of both is the responsibility of the application program, rather than being synchronized by the DBMS. The complex network data model is quite suitable for describing a conceptual data base and for depicting external data bases used for requirements analysis. For the internal data base or for an external subschema data base definition, the relationship capabilities of the DBMS (complex versus simple) must be considered.

It is even possible with networks to create disconnected segments of a data base, as shown in Figure 6-12. In this figure, we have not chosen to implement the relationship from PRODUCT to ORDER-LINE. That is, we will not be able to use a programming language or query language to *simply* retrieve, for example, all the orders for products that are priced greater than $2000 (assuming that PRICE is in the PRODUCT record only). There are, however, ways around this that are not "simple" or not as efficient to program. We could write one program or one program module to find and save the PRODUCT#'s of all PRODUCT records with PRICE greater than $2000. If ORDER-LINE records had a secondary index on PRODUCT#, then another program or module could take the list of PRODUCT#'s, access the ORDER-LINE records for these PRODUCT#'s via the secondary index, and then find the parents of the accessed ORDER-LINE records.

The preceding example emphasizes the true meaning, at the internal data model level, of a relationship. A relationship here really is a direct-access path that does not use key access to the target record. In a conceptual or external network data base model, *how* an association is implemented is of no concern. This explicitness is, however, helpful. It clearly informs us what can be economically answered. We will see in a following section that in the case of the relational data model, all relationships are implicit, and which

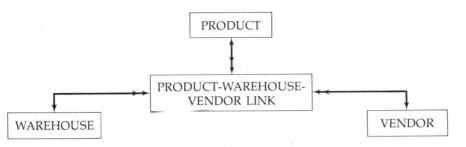

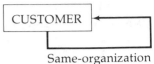

Same-organization

Figure 6-14
Example of a loop relationship in a conceptual or external network data model.

Figure 6-13 Example of a network model structure for a three-way relationship.

questions can be answered efficiently and which are very costly to answer cannot be predicted from only the data model.

As was mentioned earlier, the network data model cannot be used to represent *directly* three-way or higher order relationships. An example of a three-way relationship is what PRODUCTs are supplied to what WAREHOUSEs by what VENDORs. Figure 6-13 illustrates a network structure for *indirectly* representing this three-way relationship, which again uses a link or an intersection record type. A link or intersection record must be created for *each* three way relationship instance. That is, if there were three VENDORs, two PRODUCTs and four WAREHOUSEs and each PRODUCT could be shipped to each WAREHOUSE by each VENDOR, there would have to be $3 \times 2 \times 4$ or 24 link or intersection record instances.

Intrafile relationships, sometimes called **loops**, can also arise in data modeling. At the logical external and conceptual data model levels, loops can be shown by a relationship line that exits and enters the same record type, as depicted in Figure 6-14. This example is for a relationship that groups customers together when several customers are subunits of the same organization (e.g., different divisions of General Motors). For the internal network data model, loops can be handled in one of two ways. First, if possible, a secondary index can be created on a data item within the CUSTOMER record on PARENT-ORG. A second approach is to create a separate record type on ORGANIZATION and a 1:*M* relationship from ORGANIZATION to CUSTOMER.

Another example of an intrafile loop is a **logical sequence** of records within a file. We could illustrate this by substituting CUSTOMER-ZIPCODE sequence for the Same-Organization relationship in Figure 6-14. Such record sorts are only useful in preparing output from data base processing (avoids postretrieval sorting of records or report lines) and hence need to be included only in an internal data model. The typical construct to represent record sequences is called a **singular** or **system relationship**. In this case, the loop relationship is a path that links all the records together in sequence. A pointer chain is usually used to implement this.

Figure 6-15
Examples of cycles in a network.
(a) Example of an efficiency-oriented cycle.
(b) Example of a nonimplied cycle.

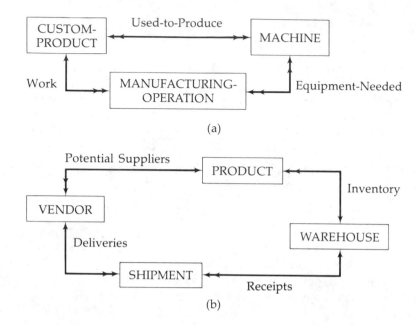

(a)

(b)

Still another type of relationship that can be represented in all but the limited network data model is a **cycle**, or series of relationships that begin and end with the same record type. Cycles can be created to avoid long access paths through a network and hence are redundant.

Consider the custom furniture business at Pine Valley Furniture. Figure 6-15a illustrates data relevant for managing the custom furniture projects. In this diagram, a cycle has been used to shorten the path from a MACHINE to the CUSTOM-PRODUCTs it is used to produce. The Used-to-Produce relationship could be used to reduce the cost to find associated CUSTOM-PRODUCT records for a given MACHINE (since intermediate MANUFAC-TURING-OPERATION records do not have to be accessed). But data base maintenance activities are now redundant (and can be inconsistent); it is possible that a maintenance program would associate a MACHINE with the proper MANUFACTURING-OPERATION, which in turn is associated with the correct CUSTOM-PRODUCT, but the maintenance program could fail to make the proper association from MACHINE to CUSTOM-PRODUCT.

Cycles that are not redundant and not implicit can also occur. In Figure 6-15b the Potential Suppliers relationship is not implied from other data and relationships, since other VENDORs, besides those that *have* shipped products to the firm, could also be possible suppliers.

One additional type of relationship that can occur and can be represented in network data models is called a **class relationship**. Consider the example shown in Figure 6-16, in which ORDERs, INVOICEs, and PAY-

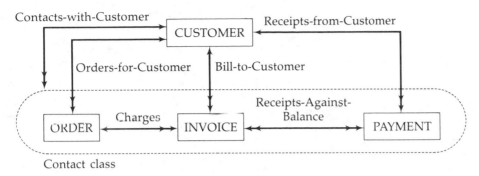

Figure 6-16
Example of a class
relationship in a network
data model.

MENTs for a CUSTOMER are all shown, as well as individual relationships between the record types. The set of all ORDER, INVOICE, and PAYMENT records form a class of records for CONTACT that Pine Valley Furniture has had with a CUSTOMER. It is possible with some network data base management systems to also define the Contacts-with-Customer relationship, which could be used to produce a chronological history of all customer activities with Pine Valley Furniture. Frequently, class relationships arise when one user does not conceive of different record types (a contact is a contact) and other users conceive of different entities.

Data Processing with the Network Data Model

Network model data bases are often associated with record-level programming languages like COBOL and PL/I, so-called **host languages**. As we will see in Chapter 13, retrieval with most network systems begins by accessing an "owner" record via some entry point (primary key) into the data base. Then the program "walks" through relevant data base records by getting the "first" or "next" record in relationships. Keeping track of where we are in the data base is a chore of diligence. This type of data base processing has been termed **navigation**, since we must maneuver carefully to avoid becoming lost.

The data required for reporting is collected in stages as each related record is retrieved. Records that do not contain required data may have to be accessed in the process. Maintenance of the data base often requires updating of numerous chains; establishing the proper parent record in each chain for insertion (and deletion) is tedious and prone to subtle mistakes.

Recently, vendors of network-type data base management systems have developed high-level query and maintenance languages that relieve a programmer, especially a nonprofessional, from this kind of detail. Examples of such languages will be presented in Chapter 13 for CODASYL network data base management systems.

Figure 6-17
Example of a bit map
implementation for a
Sources-of-Goods
relationship in a network.

Sources-of-Goods

		VENDOR				
		1	2	...	Y	...
PRODUCT	1	1	0	...	0	...
	2	0	0	...	1	...
	:	:	:	:	:	:
	X	1	0	...	1	...
	:	:	:	:	:	:

Implementation of the Network Data Model

Networks are usually implemented using pointer sequential connections and a multilist-type structure (see Chapter 5). Each record type in a network can have a combination of the following pointers defined (similar to those for a hierarchy in Figure 6-7):

1. Pointer to the first record of each target record type (arrowhead) for which the given record is at the source (arrow tail) of a relationship (head-of-chain pointer).

2. Pointer to the next (prior) record of the set of records that are all the target of a common source record of a relationship (sibling or twin pointer).

3. Pointer to the source record for each relationship in which the given record is a target record (parent pointer).

4. Pointer to each target record for which the given record is the source (children pointer array); pointer types (1) and (2) or this, but usually not both, is used.

A second form of network implementation, especially useful for *M:N* relationships, is called a bit map, which is depicted in Figure 6-17 for the Sources-of-Goods relationship from Figure 6-10a. A **bit map** is a matrix created for each relationship. Each row corresponds to the relative record number of a source record, and each column corresponds to the relative record number of a target record of a relationship. A 1 bit in a cell for row X and column Y means that the records corresponding to row X and column Y are associated in this relationship; a zero means no association. For example, Figure 6-17 indicates that PRODUCT with relative record number X is related to VENDORs with relative record numbers 1 and Y (and possibly others not shown). Bit maps are powerful data structures for the following reasons:

1. Any record type(s) can be included in rows or columns.

2. 1:1, 1:*M*, *M:N*, and *M*:1 relationships can all be represented.

3. Rows and columns can be logically manipulated by Boolean operators ("and," "or," "not") to determine records that satisfy complex associations (e.g., any record that has both parent S and parent T).

4. A bit map is compact and can be manipulated equally as well in either a row or column access (all the row records for a common column *or* all the column records for a common row).

Summary of the Network Data Model

We have seen that the network data model, in its three forms, can represent a wide variety of data bases. The complex network data model is quite useful for describing an external or conceptual data base because many relationship types can be easily depicted and each relationship and record type is explicitly stated. The simple and limited network models are primarily useful at the internal data base level or with an external data model used for programming (subschema). In both cases, the purpose of the data model is to convey what is *implemented* in the data base.

On the other hand, some have argued that the network model is complex and difficult to use. Network diagrams, unless thoughtfully arranged, frequently look like an explosion at a spaghetti factory. Networks are also criticized because they have typically been implemented in ways to be consistent with record-at-a-time processing languages, like COBOL; some believe that such data base processing is unnecessarily difficult.

Later in this chapter, we will briefly review how easy or difficult it is to use different data models based on reported experience and research. But the general claim by some is that the network model is just "not natural."

THE RELATIONAL DATA MODEL

The choice of many data base designers and users is the relational data model. As we will see, the relational model is different from network and hierarchical models not only in architecture but also in the following ways:

1. Implementation independence: the relational model logically represents all relationships implicitly, and hence, one does not know what associations are or are not *physically* represented by an efficient access path (without looking at the internal data model).

2. Terminology: the relational model has been developed with its own set of terminology, most of which has equivalent terms in other data models.

3. Logical key pointers: the relational data model uses primary (and secondary) keys in records to represent the association between two records;

because of this model's implementation independence, however, it is conceivable that the physical data base (totally masked from the user of a relational data base) could use address pointers or one of many other methods.

4. Normalization theory: properties of a data base that make it free of certain maintenance problems have been developed within the context of the relational model (although these properties can also be designed into a network data model data base).

5. High-level programming languages: programming languages have been developed specifically to access data bases defined via the relational data model; these languages permit data to be manipulated as groups or files and not procedurally one record at a time.

Definitions

The relational data model uses the concept of a relation to represent what we have previously called a file. A **relation** is viewed as a two-dimensional table. Three examples of relations for Pine Valley Furniture are shown in Figure 6-18. A relation has the following properties:

1. Each column contains values about the same attribute, and each table cell value must be simple (i.e., a single value).

2. Each column has a distinct name (attribute name), and the order of columns is immaterial.

3. Each row is distinct; that is, one row cannot duplicate another row for selected key attribute columns.

4. The sequence of the rows is immaterial.

A **tuple** is the collection of values that compose one row of a relation. A tuple is equivalent to a record instance. An *n-tuple* is a tuple composed of *n* attribute values. PRODUCT is an example of a 4-tuple.

A **domain** is the set of possible values for an attribute. For example, the domain for QUANTITY-ON-HAND in the PRODUCT relation is all integers greater than or equal to zero. The domain for CITY in the VENDOR relation is a set of alphabetic character strings restricted to the names of U.S. cities.

We can use a short-hand notation to abstractly represent relations (or tables). The three relations in Figure 6-18 can be written in this notation as

PRODUCT (PRODUCT#,DESCRIPTION,PRICE,
             QUANTITY-ON-HAND)

VENDOR(VENDOR#,VENDOR-NAME,VENDOR-CITY)

SUPPLIES(VENDOR#,PRODUCT#,VENDOR-PRICE)

Figure 6-18
Example of a relational
data model.

PRODUCT relation   Attributes

	PRODUCT#	DESCRIPTION	PRICE	QUANTITY-ON-HAND	Relative record#
	0100	TABLE	500.00	42	1
Tuples	0975	WALL UNIT	750.00	0	2
	1250	CHAIR	400.00	13	3
	1775	DRESSER	500.00	8	4

Primary key

VENDOR relation

VENDOR#	VENDOR-NAME	VENDOR-CITY
26	MAPLE HILL	DENVER
13	CEDAR CREST	BOULDER
16	OAK PEAK	FRANKLIN
12	CHERRY MTN	LONDON

SUPPLIES relation

VENDOR#	PRODUCT#	VENDOR-PRICE
13	1775	250.00
16	0100	150.00
16	1250	200.00
26	1250	200.00
26	1775	275.00

In this form, that attribute (or attributes in combination) for which no more than one tuple may have the same (combined) value is called the **primary key**; the primary key attribute(s) is (are) underlined for clarity. Although several different attributes (called **candidate keys**) might serve as the primary key, only one (or one combination) is chosen. These other keys are then called **alternate keys**.

The SUPPLIES relation in Figure 6-18 has two attributes required in combination to identify uniquely each tuple. A composite or *concatenated* key is a key that consists of two or more attributes appended together. Concatenated keys appear frequently in a relational data base, since intersection data, like VENDOR-PRICE, must be uniquely identified by a combination of the primary keys of the related entities. Each component of a concatenated key can be used to identify tuples in another relation. In fact, values for all component keys of a concatenated key must be present, although nonkey attribute values may be missing. Further, the relational model has been enhanced by some (e.g., Hammer and McLeod [1978]) to indicate that a tuple (e.g., for PRODUCT) logically should exist with its key value (e.g., PRODUCT#) if that value appears in a SUPPLIES tuple.

We can relate tuples in the relational model only when there are common attributes in the relations involved. We will expand on this idea in the next section. The SUPPLIES relation also suggests that an *M:N* relationship requires the definition of a third relation, much like a link or intersection record in the simple network model.

E. F. Codd (1970) popularized the use of relations and tables as a way to model data. At first glance, this view of data may seem only to be a different perspective on the network data model (all we have done is replace address pointers with logical pointers and eliminate lines from the data base diagram). Several debates have essentially argued this point (see "The Data Base Debate" 1982 and Olle 1975). Codd and many others have shown that relations are actually formal operations on mathematical sets. Further, most data processing operations (e.g., printing of selected records and finding related records) can also be represented by mathematical operators on relations. The result of mathematical operations can be proved to have certain properties. A collection of operations, called normalization, has been shown to result in data bases with desirable maintenance and logical properties. This mathematical elegance and visual simplicity has made the relational data model one of the driving forces in the information systems field.

Relationships in the Relational Data Model

The relational data model is as rich as the complex network model in its ability to represent directly, without much redundancy, a wide variety of relationship types. However, unlike the network model, relationships are implicit; that is, there is no diagrammatic convention (arcs, or links) used to explicitly show a relationship between two relations (i.e., relationship between entities).

The basic construct for representing a relationship in the relational data model is to place a common attribute in each related relation. To see how this works, consider the following set of relations that define a relational data base for the complex network of Figure 6-10a:

CUSTOMER(<u>CUSTOMER#</u>,CUSTOMER-ADDRESS,
        CUSTOMER-DETAILS)

ORDER(<u>ORDER#</u>,CUSTOMER#,ORDER-DATE,
        DELIVERY-DATE,TOTAL-AMOUNT)

PRODUCT(<u>PRODUCT#</u>,DESCRIPTION,PRICE,
        QUANTITY-ON-HAND)

ORDER-LINE(<u>ORDER#</u>,<u>PRODUCT#</u>,
        QUANTITY-ORDERED,EXTENDED-PRICE)

VENDOR(<u>VENDOR#</u>,VENDOR-NAME,VENDOR-CITY)

SUPPLIES(<u>VENDOR#</u>,<u>PRODUCT#</u>)

In this example, CUSTOMER, PRODUCT, and VENDOR are basic relations that exist independently from all other data. The ORDER relation, too, can exist independently, but one of its attributes, CUSTOMER#, called a **cross-reference** (or **foreign**) **key**, implements the Orders-for-Customer relationship from Figure 6-10a. The attribute CUSTOMER# in the ORDER relation could have any name (say, ACCOUNT#). As long as the domain of values and the meaning of CUSTOMER# and ACCOUNT# are the same, then proper linking of related tuples can occur. The problem with using different names in different relations for the same attribute is that a "reader" of a relational data base definition may not readily understand that these two attributes can be used to link related data. In most cases, use of a cross-reference key in the relational data model means that, for example, any value of CUSTOMER# found in an ORDER tuple logically should exist as a CUSTOMER# in some unique existing CUSTOMER tuple.

The ORDER relation has its own unique key, ORDER#. An alternate key might be the combination of CUSTOMER# and ORDER-DATE (if customers do not submit two or more orders in a day). If ORDER# was not an essential piece of data for applications of this data base, then the following SALE relation would be sufficient:

SALE(<u>CUSTOMER#</u>,<u>ORDER-DATE</u>,DELIVERY-DATE,
        TOTAL-AMOUNT)

Here the cross-reference key appears as (part of) the primary key in each related record (tuple). This is a common phenomenon in relational data bases.

The ORDER-LINE and SUPPLIES relations exist because of *M:N* relationships. ORDER-LINE is like the intersection record of a network data base where QUANTITY-ORDERED and EXTENDED-PRICE are the intersection data. The concatenated key is composed of the keys of the related relations. The SUPPLIES relation is like the link record of a simple network data base. In this data base, we do not care to know anything about this *M:N* relationship other than the PRODUCT and VENDOR associations themselves.

Three-way and higher order relationships are represented in a way similar to Figure 6-13 for the network model. The relational version of Figure 6-13 is

PRODUCT(<u>PRODUCT#</u>,DESCRIPTION,PRICE,
  QUANTITY-ON-HAND)
VENDOR(<u>VENDOR#</u>,VENDOR-NAME,VENDOR-CITY)
WAREHOUSE(<u>WAREHOUSE#</u>,W-CITY,W-CAPACITY)
P-W-V(<u>PRODUCT#</u>,<u>WAREHOUSE#</u>,<u>VENDOR#</u>,LEAD-TIME)

LEAD-TIME is included to show how intersection data would appear in this case. It is important to note that the relational data model here includes only four relations, whereas the equivalent network model included four record types and three relationships in the representation/definition. The difference, as always, is that relationships are implicit from common attributes in the relational data model.

An intrafile loop (intrarelation) relationship is represented in the relational model by including as an additional attribute the relation's primary key. For example, a relationship that groups customers from a common parent organization would be shown with the following modification of the CUSTOMER relation previously given:

CLIENT(<u>CUSTOMER#</u>,CUSTOMER-ADDRESS,
  PARENT-CUSTOMER#)

Here both CUSTOMER# and PARENT-CUSTOMER# have the same domain of values.

The properties of a table/relation in the relational data model do prohibit a logical sequence relationship. The relational model assumes that sequence is not a natural characteristic of data but only has relevance when data are manipulated. This emphasizes again the application independence of the relational model. Sequencing will be produced by a data manipulation language during reporting.

Cycles can also be represented in the relational model. In a cycle, relations A and B have a common attribute, relations B and C a common attribute, and so on, until the cycle is completed with relations X and A with a common attribute. Because logical pointers (common attributes) are used to link related tuples, maintenance is not a problem as it was for cycles in the network model. As long as proper logical key values are entered, the correct physical linkages will be made by the DBMS.

A class relationship can also be depicted in a relational data base. Consider the following relational data model for the class relationship example of Figure 6-16:

CUSTOMER(<u>CUSTOMER#</u>,CUSTOMER-DETAILS)
ORDER(<u>ORDER#</u>,CUSTOMER#,ORDER-DETAILS)
INVOICE(<u>INVOICE#</u>,CUSTOMER#,ORDER#,INVOICE-DETAILS)
PAYMENT(<u>JOURNAL#</u>,CUSTOMER#,PAYMENT-DETAILS)
I-P(<u>INVOICE#</u>,<u>JOURNAL#</u>,AMT-APPLIED,I-P DETAILS)

The common attribute CUSTOMER# allows a user to deal with all contact entities for the same customer, although a single CONTACT entity (relation) has not been created. Some relational data base management systems support definition of a "view" that could be used to define such a class relation as a merger of attribute values from each of the component CONTACT relations. The JOIN relational operator, to be introduced in the next section, can also be used to create such a merged table.

Any table that satisfies the four properties presented in the previous section can be a relation. In fact, a table with these properties is said to be in **first normal form**. Experience has shown that although sufficient for data processing, first normal form (1NF) relations can still have some undesirable data maintenance properties. In general, these problems are inconsistencies that can occur in a data base after records are inserted, deleted, or modified. The process of ridding a data base definition of these problems or anomalies is called **normalization**. Because it is a process of data base design, normalization will be covered in Chapters 7 and 8. What we will present here are the desirable relationships between *attributes* that are the basis for normalization.

A relationship between attributes is called a **functional dependency**. Attribute B is functionally dependent (or simply dependent) on attribute A if at each point in time, each value of A has only one value of B associated with it. For example,

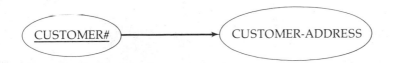

illustrates that CUSTOMER-ADDRESS is dependent on CUSTOMER#.

The primary key (single or concatenated) in a relation uniquely identifies the tuple and hence each of the remaining attributes in the relation. The ORDER and ORDER-LINE relations from the beginning of this section can be illustrated using such a dependency diagram (called a bubble diagram) as follows:

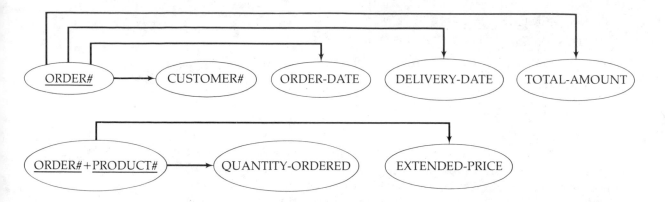

These bubble diagrams indicate that each of the ORDER relation nonkey attributes depends on ORDER# and *only* ORDER#. Further, it is shown that all nonkey attributes of the ORDER-LINE relation depend only on the *whole* concatenated key of ORDER# and PRODUCT#. This example suggests two other relation properties (in addition to the four already given):

5. *All* nonkey attributes should be *fully dependent* on the *whole* key.
6. Each nonkey attribute should be dependent only on the relation's key, not on any other nonkey.

Property (5) is associated with second normal form (2NF) and property (6) with third normal form (3NF). Chapters 7 and 8 demonstrate how to produce relations with these and other properties as part of a data base design process. The purpose here is to introduce the concept of interattribute functional dependencies as an important, practical component of the relational data model. Second, third, and so forth, normal forms are not essential parts of the relational model, but the relational model has been the context for the discovery of these desirable data base design properties. These same properties can be included in a network data base.

Data Processing with the Relational Data Model

The basic component of the relational data model is a relation. Not surprisingly, it is relations, *not* tuples, that are referenced when accessing a data base via a relational DBMS. For this reason, data processing with a relational data base is called file-at-a-time, not record-at-a-time. Whereas processing with the network model involves *repetitively* accessing a record and all its related records, data processing with the relational model involves manipulating a series of *groups* (relations) of qualified records, each group as a whole.

Two classes of special-purpose relational data manipulation languages (DMLs) characterize most available methods for processing relational data bases: relational algebra and relational calculus. Chapter 14 will present detailed examples in each of these classes and examples of a few other unique relational languages. Although some relational data base management systems permit programs written in procedural languages to access a relational data base, the standard practice is to use one of the high-level special-purpose DMLs.

Relational algebra manipulates one or two relations as operands and produces a new relation as the result. Relational algebra was the first DML proposed for the relational data model. The basic operators were presented in one of E. F. Codd's (1970) first publications on the relational model. We will introduce three of these relational algebra operators here (SELECT, PROJECT, and JOIN) to suggest the style of data processing; other operators will be reviewed in Chapter 14.

Following are examples of the three basic relational algebra operators for the data base of Figure 6-18:

(a) SELECT PRODUCT WHERE PRODUCT#='0975' GIVING RESULT

(b) SELECT PRODUCT WHERE PRICE < 550.00 GIVING RESULT

(c) SELECT PRODUCT WHERE DESCRIPTION = 'TABLE' AND
QUANTITY-ON-HAND > 12 GIVING RESULT

(d) PROJECT SUPPLIES OVER (PRODUCT#, VENDOR-PRICE) GIVING
RESULT

(e) PROJECT PRODUCT OVER (DESCRIPTION) WHERE PRICE > 600.00
GIVING RESULT

(f) JOIN VENDOR AND SUPPLIES OVER VENDOR# GIVING RESULT

(g) JOIN VENDOR OVER VENDOR# AND SUPPLIES OVER SUPPLIER#
GIVING RESULT

The first operator, SELECT, retrieves all tuples of a specified relation that satisfy a certain condition and constructs a new table that contains the selected tuples. The qualification in example (a) is on a primary key, so the RESULT relation will contain only one tuple. In example (b), it is possible that many tuples have a value of PRICE less than 550, so RESULT here could contain many tuples. PRICE is a secondary key. It is assumed that a primary key access method has been implemented to make query (a) efficient to process. In the next section, we will see why query (b) may or may not be costly to answer. Example (c) demonstrates that tuple selection conditions may be made complex by connecting basic conditions by Boolean operators ("and," "or," "not").

The SELECT operator constructs a new table by taking a *horizontal* subset of an existing table. That is, it selects those whole rows that satisfy a stated condition. In contrast, the PROJECT operator forms a *vertical* subset of an existing table by extracting specified columns (attributes) from all tuples to form a new table. If only some of the key attributes are extracted,

Figure 6-19
RESULT table for
example (d).

RESULT relation

PRODUCT#	VENDOR-PRICE
1775	250.00
0100	150.00
1250	200.00
1775	275.00

the resultant table could contain duplicate rows. Different relational algebra DMLs handle this violation differently. Some automatically eliminate redundancy; some leave elimination of redundant rows as an option for the programmer/user.

Example (d) illustrates the typical form of a command with the PROJECT operator. Figure 6-19 shows the RESULT table of this command for the SUPPLIES relation of Figure 6-18. Note that the RESULT table has one fewer tuples than the SUPPLIES relation, since PROJECTion resulted in duplicate rows. Example (e) demonstrates that PROJECT can include an implicit SELECT by use of a WHERE clause.

The third basic operator, and the one most unique and fundamental to relational algebra, is JOIN. The JOIN operator combines the data from two relations based on values for a common attribute. As with SELECT and PROJECT, the result of JOIN is also a relation.

Example (f) illustrates the JOIN operator. In this JOIN, the rows of the VENDOR and SUPPLIES relations are scanned. Whenever a tuple from each has the same value for VENDOR#, the two tuples are concatenated to form a new relation tuple. Figure 6-20 is the RESULT relation for this JOIN. Note that there is no RESULT tuple for VENDOR# 12, since this value is *not* in common between the VENDOR and SUPPLIES relations. Tables produced from a JOIN may not have one or more of the six properties discussed previously; the RESULT table for this example violates property (5), which states that all nonkey attributes must be fully dependent on the key. Example (g) shows how each relation in the JOIN can use different names for the same attribute on which the tables are being JOINed. The only requirement is that the two names have the same meaning (domain). In this case, VENDOR# and SUPPLIER# are called **role names**.

The type of JOIN just illustrated is called the **equi-join**. The equi-join makes all matches for tuples with common values. Chapter 14 will discuss other types of JOINs.

The second major category of relational DMSs is relational calculus. **Relational calculus** manipulates relations implicitly by specifying condi-

RESULT relation				
VENDOR#	PRODUCT#	VENDOR-NAME	VENDOR-CITY	VENDOR-PRICE
13	1775	CEDAR CREST	BOULDER	250.00
16	0100	OAK PEAK	FRANKLIN	150.00
16	1250	OAK PEAK	FRANKLIN	200.00
26	1250	MAPLE HILL	DENVER	200.00
26	1775	MAPLE HILL	DENVER	275.00

Figure 6-20
RESULT table for example (f).

tions that can involve attributes from several relations. Relational calculus combines the three algebra operators into one operator, called RETRIEVE, and a WHERE clause for SELECT and JOIN. For example, a relational calculus type of command for example (f) would be

RETRIEVE(VENDOR.VENDOR-NAME,VENDOR.VENDOR-PRICE)
INTO RESULT WHERE VENDOR.VENDOR#=SUPPLIES.VENDOR#

Since several relations can be referenced in one query and the same attribute name can be used in each of these, it is necessary to prefix each attribute name with the relation name that applies to the question and that attribute. This example shows how a WHERE clause is used to imply a JOIN. A JOIN literally means where the common attribute values are equal, create a new tuple. Also, this example shows that PROJECT is replaced in the syntax by listing the attributes that are to be included in the table being created (the INTO table).

Very comprehensive existence statements can be made in relational calculus that essentially combine several JOINs into one statement. Suppose that a snowstorm has made transportation from Denver to Pine Valley Furniture impossible. Pine Valley management realizes that some of its primary suppliers ship from Denver. The Pine Valley purchasing manager poses the following question: "What products supplied by any vendor in Denver have a quantity on hand less than ten units (considered a critically low value)?" Relational calculus would structure the question in the following way:

RETRIEVE (PRODUCT.PRODUCT#) INTO RESULT
    WHERE PRODUCT.QUANTITY-ON-HAND < 10 AND
        PRODUCT.PRODUCT#=SUPPLIES.PRODUCT# AND
        SUPPLIES.VENDOR#=VENDOR.VENDOR# AND
        VENDOR.VENDOR-CITY='DENVER'

The WHERE clause provides the equivalent of two JOINs, two attribute value SELECT clauses, and a PROJECT. The equivalent relational algebra would be

JOIN PRODUCT AND SUPPLIES OVER PRODUCT# GIVING X

JOIN X AND VENDOR OVER VENDOR# GIVING Y

SELECT Y WHERE QUANTITY-ON-HAND < 10 AND
             VENDOR-CITY = 'DENVER' GIVING Z

PROJECT Z OVER(PRODUCT#) GIVING RESULT

A relational calculus statement can become very complicated, but it can state in one language command the equivalent of many relational algebra commands.

Other relation-processing languages have been developed. Examples of other unique DMLs will be presented in Chapter 14.

Implementation of the Relational Data Model

As stated earlier, the relational data model is a purely logical view of data. Unlike the hierarchical and network models, whose structure and diagrammatic conventions imply specific physical linkages, in the relational model, we do not know *what* relationships have been implemented with an efficient access path and we do not know *how* a relationship has been implemented. We might conclude that in practice, a wide variety of data structures would be used. Surprisingly, this is not the case.

By far, the most common data structure for implementing a relational data base is the use of tree-structured indexes (often B-trees) on primary and selected secondary keys. Any attribute that is used to select tuples in a PROJECT or WHERE clause is a possible candidate for indexing. Attributes used to JOIN relations can be indexed; frequently, this greatly reduces the cost to perform a JOIN. To JOIN relations VENDOR and SUPPLIES from Figure 6-18 without an index (or without sorting both relations into order by values for the common attribute), we would have to follow the following procedure:

1. Do Until end of VENDOR table.
    2. Read next VENDOR tuple.
    3. Scan the *whole* SUPPLIES relation, and if a tuple has the same VENDOR# as the current VENDOR tuple, then create a new RESULT tuple.
4. End Do.
5. Eliminate redundant tuples from relation RESULT.

With an index, step (3) is made much more efficient, since only the SUP-PLIES tuples with the same VENDOR#, if any exist, need to be retrieved (which is probably a very small percentage for each value of VENDOR#).

Some relational data base management systems use clever schemes to reduce the cost of using key indexes. Each query to be processed is para-phrased into a special form. This form, **disjunctive normal form** (DNF) (see Wong and Chiang [1971]), structures the WHERE clauses of a query into a set of conjunctions with only OR operators between conjunctions and only AND and NOT operators within a conjunction. Any query can be rewritten into DNF.

Consider the following WHERE clause:

WHERE (PRICE > 700 OR PRICE < 520) AND DESCRIPTION = 'TABLE'

This can be rewritten into DNF as

WHERE (PRICE > 700 AND DESCRIPTION = 'TABLE') OR
      (PRICE < 520 AND DESCRIPTION = 'TABLE')

In DNF, each phrase in parentheses is a conjunction. Recall from Chapter 5 that AND operators cause items from two inverted lists to be intersected and OR operators cause items from two inverted lists to be merged. Given the data base of Figure 6-18, the following three lists would be constructed from indexes on PRICE and DESCRIPTION:

LIST 1	LIST 2	LIST 3
PRICE > 700	PRICE < 520	DESCRIPTION = 'TABLE'
2	1	1
	3	
	4	

This WHERE clause means

(LIST 1 AND LIST 3) OR (LIST 2 AND LIST 3)
({2} AND {1})   OR ({1,3,4} AND {1})
   (null)   OR   (1)
                      1

The only record (tuple) that satisfies the query is the one in relative record 1, or PRODUCT# 0100.

Some relational data base management systems do not process the AND operators; thus, not all attributes used in WHERE clauses need to be indexed. For example, a DBMS can be designed to recognize that within a conjunction, the result of the ANDing will be a subset of the smallest list.

The DBMS will then take the shortest list from each conjunction (*each conjunction must be processed, since the result will include any record that satisfies any of the conjunctions*) and merge the shortest lists together. This avoids the cost of intersecting sets while incurring the cost of accessing additional tuples that fail some qualifications within a conjunction. These extra tuples will have to be eliminated through the evaluation of values within the tuples retrieved. Hopefully, these "false drops" will be few and the extra cost to access these will be less than the cost to access additional indexes and intersect lists.

Indexes appear to be the data structure chosen for relational data bases because of the similarity of Boolean SELECT/WHERE clauses to inverted list intersection and merger. Manipulating index entries is like manipulating the tuples to which the entries point. Trying to determine an efficient pointer sequential network path for a query would cause a lot of overhead. Relational data base management systems are often used for highly interactive on-line information systems, which may have many ad hoc queries. Fast response, at the expense of extra index space, seems to be the popular choice.

Summary of the Relational Data Model

We have described the fundamentals of the relational data model. Because of its independence from the physical data base, the relational model has become an effective tool not only for managing data via a DBMS but also for conceptual and external data modeling. Normal forms, easily checked within the relational model, are often used as rules of data base design. Data manipulation languages based on relational algebra and calculus are often called "user-friendly" and are the model for fourth-generation programming languages (to be discussed in later chapters).

The relational data model does have some caveats. First, the relational model redundantly shows keys as logical pointers for implementing relationships. If these key attribute values are actually represented in all tuples in which they appear, this can lead to considerable redundancy. Further, if key values change, then the data base requires extensive maintenance. For example, if PRODUCT# appears in both the PRODUCT and SUPPLIES relations, then PRODUCT#'s must be carefully changed in two relations when products are recoded. If, on the other hand, a SUPPLIES tuple has an address pointer (physical or relative record number) to its associated PRODUCT tuple, then the SUPPLIES tuples are independent of changes in PRODUCT#'s. Since values of primary relation keys are usually tightly controlled (e.g., cannot change PRODUCT# without deleting tuples and inserting new ones) and infrequently change value, most practitioners are not concerned with this caveat. Further, because of the implementation independence of the relational model, logical keys may not be used in the physical data base.

The second caveat is associated with the efficiency of relational data base management systems. The data processing community has found the relational DBMS most attractive for information retrieval applications, characterized by multiple-key qualification queries. High-volume transaction processing and data maintenance applications are still frequently performed with hierarchical and network systems. For those situations that exhibit information processing against a "production" data base, two alternative data base environments have been created. In the first, portions of the transaction/production data base are periodically extracted and loaded into a separate data base managed by a relational DBMS. This solution provides specialized service to two diverse applications and keeps the unstructured information processing from interfering with the main data base. In this way, the main data base performance can be tuned to high-volume applications, where efficiency is crucial. The information processing data base can be used without retarding production performance. More and more, this information processing data base is being placed on a microcomputer to provide even computer independence. Chapter 15 will discuss this development in the data base field.

In the second data base environment for information processing against a production data base, the DBMS used for transaction processing is enhanced to support a relational like query language. In this way, users can view the data base as a set of flat files and process it at the file level. Many commercial nonrelational data base management systems provide such facilities.

The final caveat, which in some measure has been dealt with by the relational data base management systems, is a lack of semantic quality control in the relational data model. For example, since each table exists on its own, there is no guarantee that a cross-reference key will reference an existing tuple, since the relational model has no construct or property to force this matching. Consider VENDOR# in the SUPPLIES relation of Figure 6-18. The basic relational model does not state that a value here must correspond to a value of VENDOR# that exists in the VENDOR relation. Many relational data base management systems have included an INTEGRITY clause on relations to specify validation rules on attribute values; for some systems, these rules can include checks on cross-reference keys.

As has been stated, the relational data model, because of its implementation independence and normalization theory, is used during the process of data base design, even for internal network or hierarchical data bases. To separate conceptual and external data base design totally from the DBMS technology (not bias the choice of technology to relational), other data models have been developed. The Entity-Relationship Model (see Chen 1976, 1977) and the Semantic Data Model (see Hammer and McLeod 1978) are two such conceptual data models. These models are presented in the next section. This chapter will then conclude with a review of data models, including consideration of human factors of various models (error proneness, understandability, user satisfaction).

TECHNOLOGY-INDEPENDENT DATA MODELS

The hierarchical, network, and relational data models have proved to be effective notations for representing organizational data. With a few limitations (especially for hierarchical), data and a wide variety of relationships can be easily modeled using these architectures. This means that at the internal data model level, we can build data bases to support data processing efficiently for a wide range of data, as well as support query and maintenance processing.

Some people in the data base field, however, have argued that for external and conceptual data modeling, it is better to use data base description conventions that are independent of the particular internal implementation that will be or could be used. In this way, a data base designer can specify data base requirements without indicating a bias (albeit subtle) toward use of a particular DBMS.

Unique data model forms have been developed for external and conceptual levels. Their purpose has been to enhance other data models with additional information particularly relevant at these logical data levels and to provide tools that are independent of technologies used for implementing the conceptual design. Two such data models will be introduced here. They are the Entity-Relationship and Semantic data models.

The Entity-Relationship Data Model

Basically, the Entity-Relationship (E-R) data model (originated by Chen 1976, 1977) augments the network model by introducing a special symbol, the diamond, to explicitly indicate each relationship. Figure 6-21 illustrates this by depicting in E-R notation the complex network data model of Figure 6-10a. Each diamond represents a relationship type; this diamond exists for both 1:*M* and *M:N* relationships between entities (rectangles). Letters on lines between an entity rectangle and a relationship diamond specify the number of entities (e.g., 1 CUSTOMER) associated with each instance of the relationship (e.g., Orders-for-Customer).

Further, a diamond (e.g., Sources-of-Goods) exists whether or not intersection data are present. This means that an E-R diagram does not have to be redrawn, as would a complex network diagram, if such intersection data (e.g., the vendor's price for a product) were recognized. In this way, an E-R diagram acts like a simple network data model (see Figure 6-10b). Thus, it is easy to translate from an E-R data model into a simple network data model for implementation.

An E-R data model can also be supplemented to indicate data elements, as shown in Figure 6-22. Note in this case that both entities and relationships may have data element bubbles associated with them. Data element bubbles for a relationship are intersection data. When an E-R data model is being

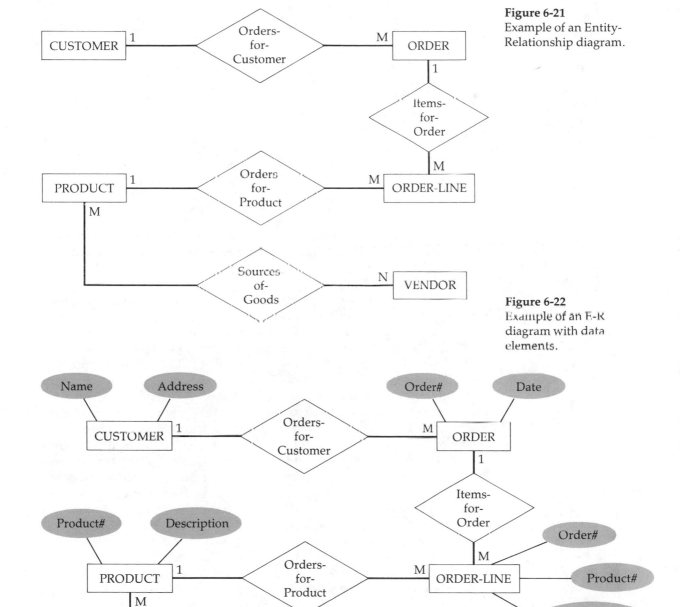

Figure 6-21
Example of an Entity-
Relationship diagram.

Figure 6-22
Example of an E-R
diagram with data
elements.

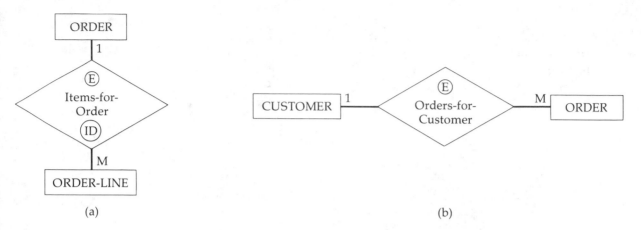

Figure 6-23
Semantic controls in E-R diagrams.
(a) Example of existence and ID dependencies.
(b) Example of an existence dependency only.

implemented, diamonds (relationships) with no associated data bubbles (e.g., Orders-for-Customers) do not have to appear as separate "record" types; a diamond with bubbles requires implementation as a distinct record (relation) type.

Another feature of the E-R data model is the ability to signify special semantic controls on entities and relationships. One such situation is called an **existence dependency**, which is illustrated in Figure 6-23a. Here an ORDER-LINE cannot exist without an associated ORDER. Further, if an ORDER is canceled, then all associated ORDER-LINEs must also be purged. The "E" inside a relationship diamond explicitly indicates an existence dependency. This figure also illustrates a second semantic property, an identifier **(ID) dependency**. Here the ORDER-LINE entity uses the Order# as part of its identifier. If, for some reason, an Order# changes, then the ID dependency explicitly indicates that ORDER-LINE entities associated with such an ORDER also have to be updated. An "ID" in a relationship diamond is used to indicate an ID dependency. Although in this case an existence dependency implies an ID dependency, this is not always true. Figure 6-23b illustrates that an ORDER cannot exist without a CUSTOMER, but each ORDER is identified by an independent primary key (Order#).

Because relationships can have associated data, the E-R data model poses an interesting dilemma: Is a relationship (diamond) really an entity "in sheep's clothing"? Consider Figure 6-24, which also depicts the complex network data base of Figure 6-10a. Compare Figures 6-22 and 6-24. Note that in Figure 6-22, ORDER-LINE is depicted as an entity, but in Figure 6-24, it is a relationship. Because there is associated data with ORDER-LINE, a relation or record type would appear in an internal implementation, so in this case the distinction between entity and relationship is simply a matter of how one views the data.

Whether or not an entity or relationship results in a record type or relation in an internal implementation basically depends on two factors: whether there are any data associated with the entity or relationship and the capabilities of the internal data model to be used. For example, in Figure

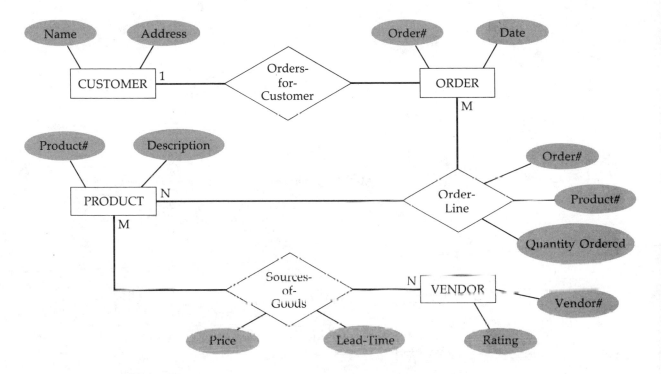

Figure 6-24
E-R diagram with an ORDER-LINE relationship.

6-24, since the ORDER-LINE relationship has associated data, it will result in a record or relation. On the other hand, Sources-of-Goods would not require a record type in a complex network internal data model, but would for simple network or relational.

Another interesting situation of implementation of an E-R data model is shown in Figure 6-25. Here, since all we know about DEPENDENTs of an EMPLOYEE are their names, network and relational data model implementations are different. A network would simply have two record types associated by a relationship (called a set in Chapter 13), in which the DEPENDENT record would contain Dependent-Name. A relational implementation would not represent dependents as a relation, but would only represent essentially the Relatives relationship. If DEPENDENT were also ID-dependent on EMPLOYEE, then Employee# would also be part of the RELATIVES relation key in the relational implementation.

The Semantic Data Model

As was stated earlier, the purpose of data modeling at the external and conceptual levels is to capture an understanding of data in an organization. Emphasis should be on meaning, not structure, so that the data base requirements can be identified. Thus, a data model that concentrates on documenting the meaning of data would incorporate much of the information needed for subsequent structuring of data.

Figure 6-25
Example of implementation of an E-R diagram.

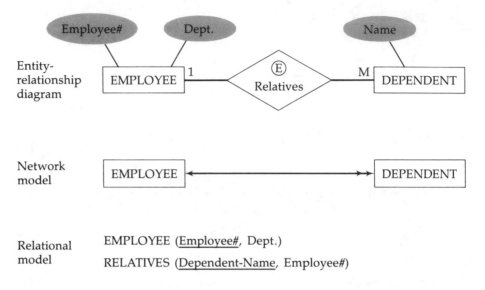

Several sources (Hammer and McLeod 1978; Teorey and Fry 1982) suggest information necessary to give meaning to entities and relationships. Some of these items are as follows:

1. Relationship membership rules: each entity may exist independently of the other; the existence of one is dependent on the existence of the other (these two rules were incorporated in the E-R model); the association is conditional on some criteria (only Customer Orders, not Shop or Build-to-Stock Orders, are linked to Customers); an entity is permanently associated with another entity, and association cannot be switched (an Order is always for a given Customer until the Order is deleted); entity association is temporal (employee assignment to a department); and entities are selectively associated (a warehouse contains products or raw materials, but not both).

2. Entity abstractions: entities, instances of which are generalizations or types of other entities (e.g., a WORK-ORDER entity, instances of which are different types of ORDERs such as Customer and Build-to-Stock; each WORK-ORDER entity instance could have attributes such as Total-$-Value and Number-of-Orders-Active).

3. Entity aggregations: entities, instances of which are a collection of other entities (e.g., PRODUCT-LINE entity, an instance of which is a set of PRODUCT entity instances, such as an instance of a set of Early American PRODUCTs).

4. Entity subsets: a group of entity instances that are a subset of instances of another entity type (e.g., CLOSED-ORDERS, which are a subset of

ORDERS and which have their own additional data elements of Date-Closed and Date-Billed).

With this perspective in mind, Hammer and McLeod (1978) developed the Semantic Data Model to specify this and other descriptive information about entities. The Semantic Data Model (SDM), like the relational model, is not actually a diagrammatic model, but a definitional model. An example of an SDM for part of the data base of Figure 6-10a, with some enhancements to illustrate the extensive descriptive clauses of the SDM, is shown in Figure 6-26. The SDM is extensive, and not all definitional clauses are shown here; only some are included to indicate the richness of this data model.

This figure shows that each entity (class) can be defined by a name (e.g., CUSTOMER), a description, an interclass connection (in the case of entity class, CUST-ORDER), and a set of member attributes. The interclass connection for CUST-ORDER specifies that instances of this entity are a subset of ORDER entities, specifically those that are Build-to-Stock Orders. The member attributes of an entity (class) are described by a name and a set of clauses that indicate the range of permissible values (e.g., Name of CUSTOMER must come from a set of values called NAMES, defined elsewhere). In addition, attributes can be given a more precise meaning by indicating if values may change, if they may be missing/null, whether they are related to values in other entities (the inverse clause), and if they are nonsimple fields of multiple values (e.g., Contact attribute of CUSTOMER, which is a list of CUST-ORDER references). An entity class itself, as well as instances of the entity class, may have attributes. For example, the CUST-ORDER class as a whole is characterized by Total-$-Value, which is a sum of the Value attributes across all instances of this subclass, and Number-of-Orders-Active, which is a count of the number of active CUST-ORDERs.

As can be seen from this example, the SDM is capable of representing almost any characteristic of data and relationships a data base designer could imagine. In fact, the SDM can be customized to include any descriptive clause desired. An SDM data base description can become quite long because of this richness of information. It is therefore the most complete data model available for defining a data base at external and conceptual levels. When a data base designer requires a method to consolidate various levels of data abstraction, the SDM seems appropriate because of its ability to interconnect the meanings of different entity classes. The SDM is certainly one data-modeling tool that should be in the toolbox of any data base designer.

FACTORS IN SELECTING A DATA MODEL

The diversity of data models presented in this chapter would indicate that the developer of a data base has a difficult choice in selecting an appropriate

Figure 6-26
Example of the semantic
data model.

CUSTOMER
> Description: all people and organizations that have purchased
>> products from Pine Valley Furniture
> Member attributes:
>> Name
>>> Value class: NAMES
>>> Not changeable
>>> May not be null
>> Address
>>> Value class: ADDRESSES
>> Contact
>>> Value class: CUST-ORDER
>>> Inverse: Client
>>> Multivalued

ORDER
> Description: all orders for products by customers and orders
>> written to build inventory
> Member attributes:
>> Order#
>>> Value class: ORDER-NUMBERS
>>> Not changeable
>>> May not be null
>> Date
>>> Value class: DATES
>> Type
>>> Value class: ORDER-TYPES
>> Value
>>> Value class: MONEY
>> Status
>>> Value class: STATUS-VALUES

CUST-ORDER
> Description: all orders for products by customers
> Interclass connection: subclass of ORDER where Type=CUST
> Member attributes:
>> Client
>>> Value class: NAMES
>>> Inverse: Contact
>>> Not changeable
> Class attributes:
>> Total-$-Value
>>> Value class: MONEY
>>> Derivation: Sum of all Values across all members
>> Number-of-Orders-Active
>>> Value class: INTEGERS
>>> Derivation: number-of-members of this entity class
>>>> where Status=Active

data model. No single choice is best in all situations; in fact, the evidence suggests that the best choice is to use several data models, each for different purposes.

The choice of an appropriate internal data model should not be made until the conceptual data base is described, since the nature of the data base (types of relationships present, data processing requirements, and so on) will dictate the best internal data model. Basically, this choice is coupled with the selection of a DBMS and will be made primarily on adequacy of implementing the conceptual data base, efficiency of DBMS product, vendor support, price, and various other technical and managerial factors. Chapter 11 will review this choice in more detail. For our purposes here, however, it will be useful to concentrate on one multifaceted factor that could be called ease of use as a perspective on evaluating any data model.

For an internal data model, ease of use primarily relates to the programming interface with a data base. Reisner (1981) has reviewed a broad set of research on data base query languages. These studies have defined ease of use via such precise, quantitative variables as number and severity of errors made during programming, correctness of interpreting the true meaning of a query statement, correctness of specifying the result of a query against a sample data base, training time to reach a specific level of expertise, time to write queries, and confidence that queries written were correct. Most of these studies have been conducted over short time periods, so long-term retention and the effects of prolonged use of query languages or the data models they use are still unknown.

Although these studies reported by Reisner have done much to structure an approach to evaluating query languages and data models, the results have been inconclusive. Some studies have recognized that inexperienced computer users are able to perform better with relational query languages both before and after minimal exposure to such languages than with query languages associated with hierarchical or network data base management systems. More seasoned computer users, those with training in procedural languages, were able to deal with all languages equally well after minimal exposure. Studies have concluded that it is difficult to separate the effects of the query language from the underlying data model; thus, we are not certain whether problems are in the syntax and grammar of query languages or in the internal data models themselves.

One specific study by Brosey and Shneiderman (1978) tried to isolate the effects of the data model by measuring the results of manually using a sample data base. Their results indicated that a hierarchical model was easier for beginners to use, with no difference for more experienced subjects. However, these researchers readily admitted that the data base used in the study had a "natural tree structure." Related, fundamental research in psychology on human information organization has shown similar results. People are able to use a variety of data organizations effectively, as long as they are not forced to use a structure incapable of capturing the true meaning of data. Thus, it would appear that the "natural" structure of data, more than individual, personal preferences, is what matters.

Another study (Hoffer 1982) basically confirms this observation in an environment more akin to conceptual data modeling than programming. In an experiment in which subjects were asked to represent a data base for a situation described in narrative form, a wide variety of data models were used, and often hybrids were developed. Although relational-like architectures were used more frequently than network or hierarchical, the most popular was flow diagrams! Again, more questions were raised than were answered, but several conclusions from this and other work are apparent. First, no one data model dominates others in understandability or any sense of ease of use. Second, since different people with different skills and experience are able to use different data models with various abilities, a data base practitioner must be able to use a variety of data models appropriate for the data base and the user. Finally, data modeling is closely tied to information systems modeling (flowcharts), and the true meaning of data comes from understanding the whole data processing environment. That is, data modeling is part of information systems modeling and data base design is part of information systems design.

SUMMARY

This chapter has reviewed the major data models that influence the data management field. These models have been reviewed separate from their technological implementations. It is important to recognize that data models are distinct from data base management systems.

Hierarchical, network, and relational data models have been defined and discussed as architectures for external, conceptual, and internal data modeling. The Entity-Relationship and Semantic data models were reviewed as tools for external and conceptual data modeling.

These data models have been defined with no bias toward any best alternative. In fact, experience and research suggests that each of these models can be effective as long as their use is not forced into an "unnatural" situation. That is, it is safe to predict that all of these, and probably future models as well, will be used to model data and provide DBMS structure for years to come.

The challenge to data base and data processing professionals is to learn each of these data models in order to be able to use each as the situation dictates. This chapter has addressed the ability of these data models to represent data and relationships. Further, this chapter has addressed these data models independent of particular data base management systems (to be covered in Chapters 11 to 14) so that these principles can be applied in the use of any DBMS.

CHAPTER REVIEW

Review Questions

1. Define each of the following terms:

a.	data model	n.	relational data model
b.	relationship	o.	relation
c.	external data model	p.	*n*-tuple
d.	conceptual data model	q.	normalization
e.	internal data model	r.	functional dependency
f.	subschema data model	s.	join
g.	hierarchical data model	t.	disjunctive normal form
h.	network data model	u.	Entity-Relationship data model
i.	intersection record	v.	existence dependency
j.	loop or intrafile relationship	w.	ID dependency
k.	system relationship	x.	Semantic data model
l.	cycle	y.	relationship membership rule
m.	class relationship	z.	entity subset

2. Match the terms in each column that are the most similar from the network and relational data models:

relation	value set
tuple	field
attribute	file
value	data item
role	record
domain	record data name

3. Briefly explain the differences between the simple, complex, and limited network data models.

4. Define a bit map and explain how it can be used to implement relationships.

5. Define first, second, and third normal forms in terms of data base properties associated with each.

6. Think of a question (query) involving several relations in a university data base. Formulate this question in both relational algebra and relational calculus.

7. Explain why some relational data base management systems do not make use of all indexes that could be used to find the tuples that satisfy a query.

8. Explain why relationships are called explicit in the hierarchical and network data models and implicit in the relational data model.

9. Many people have trouble distinguishing an entity from a relationship. For example, do you regard marriage as a relationship or an entity? Why?

10. Explain why it is desirable to use a technology-independent data model for external or conceptual data modeling.

11. Provide an example of an existence dependency and an example of an ID dependency in a university data base.

12. Explain the purpose of the inverse clause in the semantic data model.

Problems and Exercises

1. Consider the entities of Vehicle, Buyer, Owner, Sales Invoice, and Service Visit for an automobile dealership. Design a hierarchical, a network (both simple and complex), a relational, and an Entity-Relationship data base model for this situation. Assume any data items you need to give this situation meaning to you.

2. For each of the following relations, determine if there is a violation of a relation property. If not, explain why not. If so, identify which rules are violated and state exactly what part of the relation causes the violation.
   a. MENU(FOOD-ID,FOOD-NAME,PRICE,RECIPE#, NUMBER-OF-PORTIONS)
   b. EMPLOYEE(EMPLOYEE#,SOC-SEC-#,NUMBER-OF-DEPENDENTS)
   c. DAILY-TIPS(DATE,EMPLOYEE#,AMOUNT,EMPLOYEE-NAME)
   d. WORK-SCHEDULE(DATE,SHIFT,EMPLOYEE#)

3. Consider the entities of Agent, Policy, Client, Beneficiary, and Insurance Company in an independent insurance agency. Define two alternative hierarchical data base designs for this situation and compare their relative efficiencies.

4. This chapter described two ways to implement a hierarchy. One of these methods used address sequential connection between records in a common hierarchy instance. Take one of your hierarchies from Problem 3 and show the physical data arrangement for it using this physical hierarchy implementation method.

5. Consider the entities of Project, General Task, and Employee in a project management or job shop organization. Specify relations with typical attributes to represent these entities and the relationships between them.

6. The Bureau of Motor Vehicles can issue an individual several types of driver's licenses: passenger car, chauffeur, farm vehicle, motor bicycle, and so on. If the bureau ever wanted to consider the LICENSE entity class, what should be done in a relational model for its data base?

7. Consider the relation
   STOCK-TRACE(STOCK-CODE,DATE,HIGH,LOW,CHANGE)
   and the relational calculus statement
   RETRIEVE (STOCK-CODE,CHANGE) INTO RESULT
     WHERE STOCK-TRACE.DATE>831012

Besides creating a new table RESULT with tuples from STOCK-TRACE and with only STOCK-CODE and CHANGE attributes for recent daily stock activity, will the relational DBMS have to perform any other function to make RESULT a relation with all of its properties?

8. Consider the following two tables:

Airport

LOC CODE	NUMBER-OF-RUNWAYS	CONTROLLER	RADIO-FREQUENCY
LAX	6	YES	122.65
ORD	8	YES	111.78
ITH	2	NO	130.50
SPR	2	YES	117.55

Schedule

AIRLINE	FLT#	LOC-CODE	ARRIVAL
EA	123	ORD	0923
TW	1173	LAX	1106
BT	6	ORD	1000
CT	12	SPR	1400
EA	123	SPR	1145

Write a set of relational algebra statements to place FLT# and RADIO-FREQUENCY into a relation called CONTACT, to contact a controller for all scheduled flights. Complete a table with values for the resultant CONTACT relation.

9. Many commercial data processing products claim to use the relational data model. What criteria would you apply to evaluate such a claim? That is, what characteristics must the product have to warrant the relational title?

10. Figure 6-26 shows part of an SDM for the Pine Valley Furniture network data base of Figure 6-10a. Fill in the missing elements of this SDM description.

References

Brosey, M., and B. Shneiderman, 1978. "Two Experimental Comparisons of Relational and Hierarchical Database Models." *International Journal of Man-Machine Studies* 10 625–637.

Chen, Peter P-S. 1976. "The Entity-Relationship Model—Toward a Unified View of Data." *ACM-TODS* 1 (March): 9–36.

———. 1977. *The Entity-Relationship Approach to Logical Data Base Design.* Wellesley, Mass.: Q.E.D. Information Sciences, Inc., Data Base Monograph Series No. 6.

CINCOM Systems, Inc. 1982. *TOTAL Reference Manual.* Cincinnati: CINCOM Systems, Inc.

CODASYL. 1975. *Data Base Task Group Report, 1971*. Available from the Association for Computing Machinery, New York.

CODASYL Data Description Language Committee. 1978. *DDL Journal of Development*. Hull, Canada: CODASYL.

Codd, E.F. 1970. "A Relational Model of Data for Large Shared Data Bases." *Communications of the ACM*. 13 (June): 77–387.

"The Data Base Debate." 1982. In *Computerworld*, a transcript of part of Data Base '82, a portion of the Wang Institute of Graduate Studies' short summer course.

DeMarco, Thomas. 1978. *Structured Analysis and System Specification*. New York: Yourdon Press.

Hammer, Michael, and Dennis McLeod. 1978. "The Semantic Data Model: A Modelling Mechanism for Data Base Applications." *Proceedings of ACM-SIGMOD Conference 1978*, Austin, Tex.

Hewlett-Packard. 1979. *IMAGE Data Base Management System Reference Manual: HP3000*. Part no. 32215-90003. Cupertino, Calif.: Hewlett-Packard, September.

Hoffer, Jeffrey A. 1982. "An Empirical Investigation into Individual Differences in Database Models." *Proceedings of Third International Information Systems Conference*. Ann Arbor, Mich., December 1982.

IBM. 1982. *IMS/VS General Information Manual*. Form no. GH20-1260. White Plains, N.Y.: IBM.

Micro Data Base Systems, Inc. 1981. *Application Program Reference Manual: MDBS-DMS*. Lafayette, Ind.: Micro Data Base Systems.

MRI System Corp. 1981. *System 2000 Reference Manual*. Austin, Tex.: MRI System Corp.

Olle, T. William. 1975. "A Practitioner's View of Relational Data Base Theory." *ACM-SIGMOD FDT-Bulletin* 7 (3–4): 29–43.

Reisner, Phyllis. 1981. "Human Factor Studies of Database Query Languages: A Survey and Assessment." *Computing Surveys* 13 (March): 13–31.

Teorey, Toby J., and James P. Fry. 1982. *Design of Database Structures*. Englewood Cliffs, N.J.: Prentice-Hall.

Wong, Eugene, and T. C. Chiang. 1971. "Canonical Structure in Attribute Based File Organization." *Communications of the ACM* 14 (September): 593–597.

III

Data Base Design and Administration

Data base design is the process of analyzing the information needs of an organization and developing a conceptual data model that reflects those needs. We describe the process of data base design in Chapters 7 through 9. Chapter 10 then describes the ongoing process of data base administration.

Chapter 7 identifies the four major steps in data base design: requirements analysis, conceptual design, implementation design, and physical design. Requirements analysis is covered in this chapter. Also, the techniques of normalization are introduced in Chapter 7. Normalization is used to construct a conceptual data model from user views of data.

Conceptual design is described in Chapter 8. Conceptual design starts with user requirements for data and produces a data model independent of data base management systems or other physical considerations. We illustrate this process in Chapter 8 by using the hospital case introduced in Chapter 3.

Chapter 9 describes implementation and physical design. Implementation design is concerned with mapping the conceptual data model to a particular DBMS. Physical design deals with selecting record formats, access methods, security design, and related considerations. We describe a number of the trade-offs that must be considered during this process.

Chapter 10 introduces data base administration. We describe functions of data base administration and its importance to success with data base in the organization. Alternatives for organizational placement of data base administration are described.

7

Introduction to Data Base Design

INTRODUCTION

This is the first of three chapters devoted to the important topic of data base design. In this chapter, we introduce the basic steps in data base design and describe normalization, which is fundamental to the design process. In Chapter 8, we will describe logical data base design, while physical data base design is described in Chapter 9.

Data base design is the process of developing data base structures from user requirements for data. It starts with requirements analysis, which identifies user needs (present and future) for data. It then proceeds by translating these user requirements into first a conceptual, then a physical, data base design. The resulting design must satisfy user needs in terms of completeness, integrity, performance constraints, and other factors.

Data base design is a complex and difficult process. It requires the commitment and participation of the entire organization. Also, it requires the use of an organized approach or methodology. Until recently, such methodology did not exist, and data base design was often a haphazard process. However, a number of tools and techniques (including computer-assisted design) are now available to facilitate data base design. We describe a number of such techniques in these chapters.

STEPS IN DATA BASE DESIGN

Teorey and Fry (1982) have developed a general model for data base design, defining four major steps in the design process. These steps, shown in Figure 7-1, are requirements formulation and analysis, conceptual design,

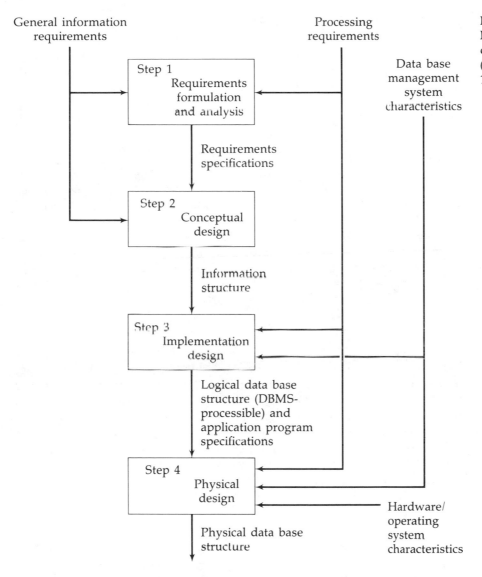

Figure 7-1
Major steps in data base design.
(Source: Teorey and Fry 1982.)

implementation design, and physical design. The interconnections (or inputs and outputs) for each of the design phases are also shown in the figure.

Requirements Formulation and Analysis

The purpose of requirements formulation and analysis is to identify and describe the data that are required by the organization. As shown in Figure 7-1, the major inputs to this process are user information requirements (especially the data items that are used and the associations between those data items) and processing requirements (report frequencies, response-time requirements, and so on). These requirements are identified through interviews with users. As data are defined, the metadata are stored and catalogued in a data dictionary/directory. The output from requirements formulation and analysis (hereafter called requirements analysis) is a set of requirements specifications for conceptual design. We will describe requirements analysis shortly.

Conceptual Design

The purpose of conceptual design is to synthesize the various user views and information requirements into a global data base design. This design is called the conceptual data model (also called the conceptual schema) and may be expressed in one of several forms: entity-relationship diagram, semantic data model, normalized relations, and so on. The conceptual data model describes entities, attributes, and relationships and is independent of specific data models and data base management systems. We will describe conceptual design in Chapter 8.

Implementation Design

The purpose of implementation design is to map the conceptual data model into an internal model (or schema) that can be processed by a particular DBMS. First, the conceptual data model is mapped into a hierarchical, network, or relational data model. Then DBMS-processible schema and subschemas are developed using the data description language for the DBMS to be used. Implementation design is considered an intermediate step between logical and physical data base design. We will describe this activity in Chapter 9.

Physical Design

Physical design is the last stage of data base design. It is concerned with designing stored record formats, selecting access methods, and deciding on physical factors such as record blocking. Physical design is also concerned with data base security, integrity, and backup and recovery. We will describe the steps in physical design in Chapter 9.

Stepwise Refinement

The steps in data base design are pictured in Figure 7-1 as proceeding in sequential fashion. In reality, however, there is much repetition between the steps. For example, during conceptual design, it may be discovered that there are gaps in the data definitions, pointing out the need for additional requirements formulation and analysis. The entire design process is best viewed as one of stepwise refinement, where the design at each stage is progressively refined through this type of iteration. Design reviews should be performed at the end of each stage before proceeding to the next stage.

REQUIREMENTS ANALYSIS

Requirements analysis is the process of identifying and documenting what data the users require in the data base to meet present and future information needs. During this phase, the data base analyst studies data flows and decision-making processes in the organization and works with users to answer the following questions:

1. What user views of data are required (present and future)?
2. What data elements (or attributes) are required in these user views?
3. What are the primary keys that uniquely identify entities in the organization?
4. What are the relationships between data elements?
5. What are the operational requirements such as security, integrity, and response time?

During requirements analysis, the analyst identifies not only what data are used, but how they are used. For example, in a bank, does the data element CUSTOMER# uniquely identify a customer, even if that customer has accounts at more than one branch of that bank? Is CUSTOMER-NAME an alternate key, or is CUSTOMER# the only candidate key? Who has the authority to update a customer BALANCE? Rules concerning the meaning and usage of data are referred to as **semantic rules**, and they must be identified during requirements analysis.

Steps in Requirements Analysis

In traditional systems, a process-oriented approach is used for requirements analysis, focusing on data flows and processes or transformations. The principal tool of requirements analysis for traditional systems is the data flow diagram.

A quite different approach to requirements analysis is necessary for data base design. This approach, which might be called a data-oriented approach, focuses on the data that must be included in the data base to satisfy user requirements. The principal tools are user view analysis, data definition and description, and normalization.

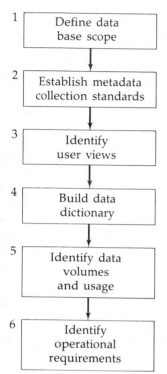

Figure 7-2
Steps in requirements analysis.

Actually, both the process-oriented and data-oriented approaches can be used for requirements analysis. The analysts may develop data flow diagrams to help them understand user procedures and data flows and at the same time analyze user views and requirements for information. Together, these two approaches can be used to check for completeness. However, the analysts should be aware that the data flow diagrams reflect existing procedures that are likely to change drastically in a data base environment. We describe structured techniques for developing procedures to access and update data bases in Chapter 9.

Compared to the other steps in data base design, requirements analysis is a relatively unstructured process. The major steps that are normally required are shown in Figure 7-2. They are as follows:

1. Identify the scope of the data base design effort.

2. Develop metadata collection standards and procedures.

3. Identify user views and data requirements.

4. Build a dictionary of data definitions and relationships.

5. Identify data volumes and usage patterns.

6. Establish operational requirements (steps 5 and 6 may be performed after conceptual design is completed).

Define Scope of the Data Base

Ideally, an organization would design and implement a single global data base that would support all of its functions. However, in most organizations, such a data base would be prohibitively large, complex, and costly to develop. As a result, a better strategy is to design and implement several smaller data bases, all within the context of an overall plan as described in Chapter 3.

A strategy for partitioning the data base design effort should be part of the overall strategic data base plan. The study team should review the organization's information systems plan before proceeding with the requirements analysis. This plan should include business charts, an enterprise model, and data base priorities and implementation plans (see Figures 3-10 through 3-13). These plans should be used as an overall framework for data base design.

Establish Data Collection Standards

The major tasks of requirements analysis involve identifying user needs for data and collecting and recording metadata. The requirements analysis team must interview all managers and key operating personnel in the areas within the scope of the data base design effort. The persons to be interviewed can be determined through discussions with key managers and supervisors. In a larger organization, a questionnaire requesting job titles and descriptions may be sent to each supervisor.

Structured interview techniques should be used during this process, including standardized data collection forms and follow-up procedures. In most cases, at least one follow-up interview with each user is required.

Identify User Views

Data collection initially focuses on user views of data. A **user view** is a subset of data required by a particular user to make a decision or carry out some action. A user view corresponds to an external schema in the ANSI/SPARC model. We identify user views by reviewing tasks that are performed or decisions that are made by users and by reviewing the data required for these tasks and decisions. Existing reports, files, documents, and displays are important sources of information about user views, and the analysts should collect sample copies of all such documents and formal information sources. Also, the analysts must probe to determine the semantic rules that govern the use of data. And in addition to formal information sources, informal sources should be identified, such as telephone calls and personal contacts. Also, it is important that future requirements for data be anticipated where possible.

An example of a user view is shown in Figure 7-3. This is a simple grade report that is mailed to the students of Mountain View College at the end of each semester. Semantic rules are summarized by the data associations shown in the figure. We use this view later in the chapter to illustrate the principles of normalization, since it is a view that is familiar to all students.

Data analysts should use a standard form for recording information about user views. A sample form for this purpose is shown in Figure 7-4. Metadata from the student grade report are recorded on the form to illustrate its usage. Each organization will design its own forms for recording information about user views.

In attempting to evaluate future information needs, the analysts must allow for proposed business or organizational changes. When they can be anticipated, it is generally simpler to incorporate future data needs into the data base design. However, not all needs can be anticipated, and so the data base system must be sufficiently flexible to handle growth and change without undermining existing applications.

Build a Data Dictionary

Each data item type that appears in a user view must be defined and described in detail. A standard form should be used for this purpose to ensure uniformity in data collection. A typical form for describing data items

Figure 7-3
Example of a user view.

MOUNTAIN VIEW COLLEGE
GRADE REPORT
FALL SEMESTER 198X

STUDENT#: 38214   MAJOR: INFO. SYSTEMS
STUDENT-NAME: JANE BRIGHT

COURSE#	COURSE-TITLE	INSTRUCTOR-NAME	INSTRUCTOR-LOCATION	GRADE
IS 350	DATA BASE	CODD	B104	A
IS 465	SYSTEMS ANALYSIS	KEMP	B213	B

Data Associations:
STUDENT# ←——→ STUDENT-NAME, MAJOR
STUDENT# ←——→→ COURSE-NUMBER
COURSE# ←——→ COURSE-TITLE, INSTRUCTOR-NAME,
            INSTRUCTOR-LOCATION
INSTRUCTOR-NAME ←——→ INSTRUCTOR-LOCATION
(STUDENT#, COURSE#) ←——→ GRADE

Figure 7-4
Typical form for
describing user views.

User View

USERVIEW# __4__   NAME __Grade Report__
DESCRIPTION __Mailed to each student at the end of__
__a semester__
PRIMARY USER:
   NAME __MVC students__   LOCATION __n/a__
   ORGANIZATION __n/a__   PHONE __n/a__
DATA ELEMENTS:

NUMBER	NAME	NUMBER	NAME
1	STUDENT#	4	COURSE#
2	STUDENT-NAME	5	COURSE-TITLE
3	MAJOR	(etc.)	

(or elements) is shown in Figure 7-5. Some of the attributes (or metadata) that are recorded on this form are data element number (or identification), name, description, type, length, and allowable range. If the data item is an identifier, the name of the entity type that it identifies is also recorded. The form in Figure 7-5 contains entries for the data item STUDENT#, which

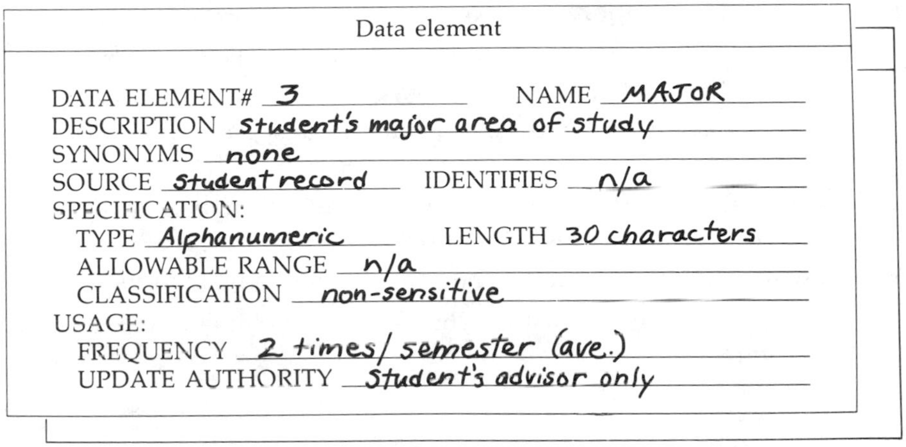

```
                          Data element

   DATA ELEMENT# _3_____          NAME _MAJOR_____
   DESCRIPTION _Student's major area of study_____
   SYNONYMS _none_____
   SOURCE _student record_  IDENTIFIES _n/a_____
   SPECIFICATION:
      TYPE _Alphanumeric___  LENGTH _30 characters_
      ALLOWABLE RANGE _n/a_____
      CLASSIFICATION _non-sensitive_____
   USAGE:
      FREQUENCY _2 times/semester (ave.)_____
      UPDATE AUTHORITY _Student's advisor only____
```

Figure 7-5
Typical form for describing data elements.

appears on the Grade Report. Notice that this item is defined as an identifier for the Student entity type.

If an automated data dictionary system is used (which is recommended), forms such as the one shown in Figure 7-5 are furnished by the system vendor. These preprinted forms are used by the analysts to record metadata for entry into the data dictionary. If an automated system is not available during requirements analysis, the organization should design forms such as the one in Figure 7-5 for data collection.

As each data item is defined, it is recorded in the data dictionary. Any inconsistencies that arise are resolved by the analysts. For example, two (or more) names are often found to be used for the same data item (synonyms). In other cases, a single name may be in use for two data items (homonyms). The end result of this effort is a dictionary of standard data definitions and descriptions.

Identify Data Volume and Usage

Information concerning data volumes and usage patterns is required for physical data base design. Collecting these data is another step in requirements analysis. However, it is best performed after a preliminary version of the conceptual data model has been completed, since the analysts and users can then refer to the entities in the data model. We illustrate this step with an example later in the chapter.

Identify Operational Requirements

The analysts must also collect information concerning user operational requirements for data. This includes requirements for each of the following areas:

1. Security: Who is authorized to access and modify the data?

2. Integrity: What are the editing rules and rules for keeping data items mutually consistent?

3. Response times: What are reasonable limits for response times in accessing data?

4. Backup and recovery: What are the parameters for backing up and recovering the data base in the event of loss?

5. Archiving: How long must data be retained, and in what form?

6. Growth projections: How will data bases grow in volume and complexity in the future?

Data Flow Diagrams

Data flow diagrams are widely used in process-oriented systems analysis. They are also useful in supplementing the data-oriented analysis that we describe in this chapter. Data flow diagrams help analysts understand an existing system and provide an excellent tool for communicating with users.

 A simple data flow diagram is shown in Figure 7-6. This diagram portrays the data flows for the patient accounting process at Mountain View Community Hospital. Data flows are shown by arrows, while processes (or transformations) are shown by circles. Files (or "data stores") are portrayed by open rectangles (symbols used in data flow diagrams are not yet standardized). For extended discussions of data flow diagrams and their use, see Weinberg (1979).

NORMALIZATION

In the process of requirements analysis, we identify and describe a number of user views (present and planned) like the one in Figure 7-3. Depending on the scope of the data base, there may be several dozen, or even several hundred, user views such as this one. Each user view, in turn, is typically composed of a number of data items or types. For example, the Grade-Report view contains eight data item types: STUDENT#, STUDENT-NAME, MAJOR, COURSE#, COURSE-TITLE, INSTRUCTOR-NAME, IN-STRUCTOR-LOCATION, and GRADE. These data items pertain to several entity classes such as Students, Courses, and Instructors.

The basic problem of logical data base design can be stated as follows. Given the mass of metadata that has been collected and organized by requirements analysis, how do we design a conceptual data model that represents these metadata naturally and completely? In other words, how

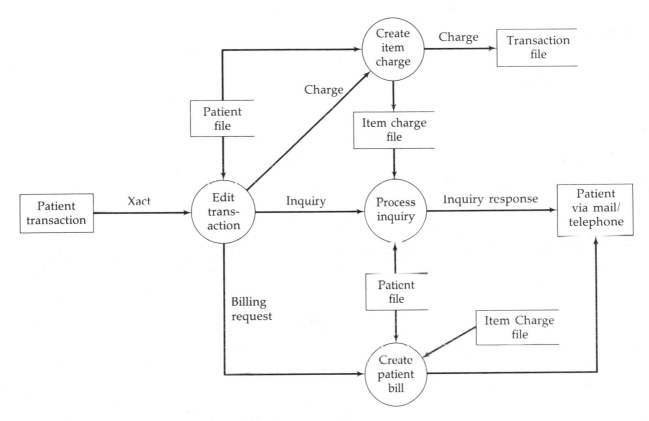

Figure 7-6
Data flow diagram for
patient accounting
(Mountain View
Community Hospital).

should the data item types be combined to form relations (or record types) that describe entities and the relationships between entities?

Until recently, data base specialists have lacked a comprehensive technique for logical data base design. As a result, data base design has historically been an intuitive and often haphazard process. However, the techniques of normalization now provide a foundation for logical data base design. **Normalization** is the analysis of functional dependencies between attributes (or data items). The purpose of normalization is to reduce complex user views to a set of small, stable data structures. Experience clearly shows that normalized data structures are more flexible, stable, and easier to maintain than unnormalized structures.

Steps in Normalization

The basic steps in the normalization process are shown in Figure 7-7. First, user views are identified. Next, each user view is converted to the form of an unnormalized relation. Any repeating groups are then removed from the unnormalized relation; the result is a set of relations in first normal form (1NF). Next, any partial dependencies are removed from these relations; the

Figure 7-7
Steps in normalization.

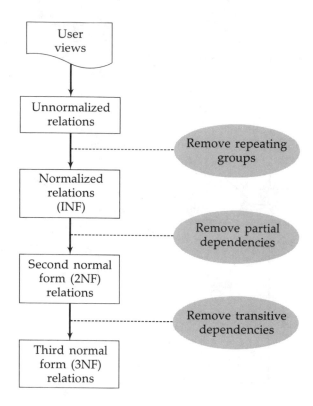

result is a set of relations in second normal form (2NF). Finally, any transitive dependencies are removed, creating a set of relations in third normal form (3NF).

Intuitively, normalization "untangles" the complex relationships between data items that exist in a typical user view (such as the one in Figure 7-3). Each user view is reduced to a set of simple relations (described in Chapter 6), each of which either describes an entity class (such as Student or Instructor) or describes an association between two or more entity classes.

Unnormalized Relations

The analyst visualizes the data in each user view as if they were laid out in tabular form. Figure 7-8 shows a relational view of Grade-Report. We will refer to this view as the GRADE-REPORT relation. Notice that sufficient data have been recorded in GRADE-REPORT to clarify its structure.

GRADE-REPORT is an example of an unnormalized relation. An **unnormalized relation** is a relation that contains one or more repeating groups. As a result, there are multiple values at the intersection of certain rows and columns. Since each student takes more than one course, the course data in GRADE-REPORT constitutes a repeating group within student data. For

GRADE-REPORT

STUDENT#	STUDENT NAME	MAJOR	COURSE#	COURSE-TITLE	INSTRUCTOR NAME	INSTRUCTOR LOCATION	GRADE
38214	BRIGHT	IS	IS 350	DATA BASE	CODD	B104	A
			IS 465	SYS ANAL	KEMP	B213	C
69173	SMITH	PM	IS 465	SYS ANAL	KEMP	B213	A
			PM 300	PROD MGT	LEWIS	D317	B
			QM 440	OP RES	KEMP	B213	C
...							

Figure 7-8
Example of an unnormalized relation.

example, there are two entries in each column for STUDENT# 38214 starting with the attribute COURSE#.

In an unnormalized relation, a single attribute cannot serve as a candidate key. For example, in GRADE-REPORT suppose we examine STUDENT# as a candidate key. The relationships between STUDENT# and the remaining attributes are as follows:

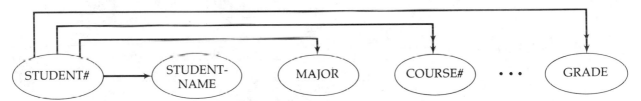

There is a one-to-one relationship from STUDENT# to STUDENT-NAME and MAJOR. However, the relationship is one-to-many from STUDENT# to COURSE# and the remaining attributes. Therefore, STUDENT# is not a candidate key, since it does not uniquely identify all the attributes in this relation.

The main disadvantage of unnormalized relations is that they contain redundant data. In GRADE-REPORT, for example, information containing the course IS465 is contained in multiple locations (two tuples in the sample data shown in Figure 7-8). Suppose that we want to change the COURSE-TITLE for this course from SYS ANAL to SYS ANAL & DES. To make this change, we would have to search the entire GRADE-REPORT relation to locate all occurrences of COURSE# IS465. If we failed to update all occurrences, the data would be inconsistent.

A shorthand notation for the unnormalized relation GRADE-REPORT is as follows:

GRADE-REPORT (STUDENT#, STUDENT-NAME, MAJOR,
(COURSE#, COURSE-TITLE, INSTRUCTOR-NAME,
INSTRUCTOR-LOCATION, GRADE))

In this notation, the inner set of parentheses designates the repeating group.

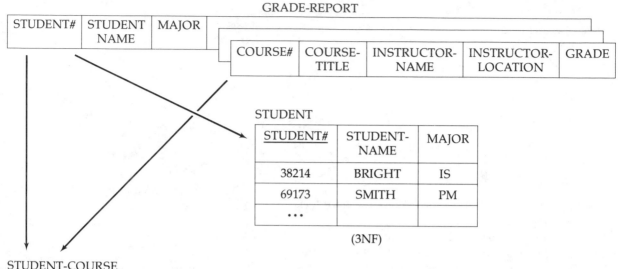

GRADE-REPORT

STUDENT#	STUDENT NAME	MAJOR					

	COURSE#	COURSE-TITLE	INSTRUCTOR-NAME	INSTRUCTOR-LOCATION	GRADE

STUDENT

STUDENT#	STUDENT-NAME	MAJOR
38214	BRIGHT	IS
69173	SMITH	PM
...		

(3NF)

STUDENT-COURSE

STUDENT#	COURSE#	COURSE-TITLE	INSTRUCTOR-NAME	INSTRUCTOR-LOCATION	GRADE
38214	IS 350	DATA BASE	CODD	B104	A
38214	IS 465	SYS ANAL	KEMP	B213	C
69173	IS 465	SYS ANAL	KEMP	B213	A
69173	PM 300	PROD MGT	LEWIS	D317	B
69173	QM 440	OP RES	KEMP	B213	C
...					

(1NF)

Figure 7-9
Normalizing a relation by removing the repeating group.

Normalized Relations: First Normal Form

A **normalized relation** is a relation that contains only elementary (or single) values at the intersection of each row and column. Thus, a normalized relation contains no repeating groups.

To normalize a relation that contains a single repeating group, we remove the repeating group and form two new relations. This process is illustrated for GRADE-REPORT in Figure 7-9. The two new relations formed from GRADE-REPORT are the following:

1. The relation STUDENT, which contains those attributes that are not part of the repeating group: STUDENT#, STUDENT-NAME, and MAJOR. The primary key of this relation is STUDENT#. This relation is in third normal form, as we will see.

2. The relation STUDENT-COURSE, which contains those attributes from the repeating group. The primary key of this relation is a composite key: STUDENT# plus COURSE#. STUDENT# is the primary key in the first relation, while COURSE# is an attribute that identifies each course repeating group for a given student. Notice that it is necessary to use this composite key, since both STUDENT# and COURSE# are needed to uniquely identify a student's GRADE.

The STUDENT-COURSE relation in Figure 7-9 is in first normal form (1NF). A relation is in **first normal form** if it contains no repeating groups. Such a relation does not have to meet any other constraints, as we will soon see.

Although the STUDENT-COURSE relation is in first normal form, it is still not an ideal representation of these data. A glance at the sample data in this relation (Figure 7-9) reveals that there is considerable data redundancy. If we leave the data in this form, we will encounter anomalies (problems or inconsistencies) in inserting, deleting, and updating data.

Insertion Anomaly. Suppose we want to insert data in this relation for a new COURSE# and COURSE TITLE. For example, we may want to insert BA 200, INTRO DP. We cannot insert these data until at least one student has registered for this course, since STUDENT# is part of the composite key. Similar anomalies occur in attempting to insert new instructor data.

Update Anomaly. Suppose we want to change the course title for IS465 from SYS ANAL to SYS ANAL & DES. Since the title of this course appears in STUDENT-COURSE a number of times, the user will have to search through all tuples in this relation and update the course title each time it occurs. This procedure will be inefficient and can result in inconsistencies if all occurrences are not correctly updated.

Deletion Anomaly. Suppose that only one student is enrolled in a course (perhaps an independent study). If the student drops that course (or leaves school), we want to delete that tuple from the data base. Unfortunately, this will result in our losing information about the title and instructor of that course.

The reason for these anomalies in STUDENT-COURSE is that several of the nonkey attributes in this relation are dependent only on COURSE# and not on the full primary key (STUDENT# plus COURSE#). This is shown in Figure 7-10. Figure 7-10a shows the dependencies of the nonkey attributes in tabular form, while Figure 7-10b shows a dependency diagram depicting the same information.

Figure 7-10
Dependencies of nonkey
attributes on the
composite primary key.
(a) Student-Course
    relation.
(b) Dependency diagram.

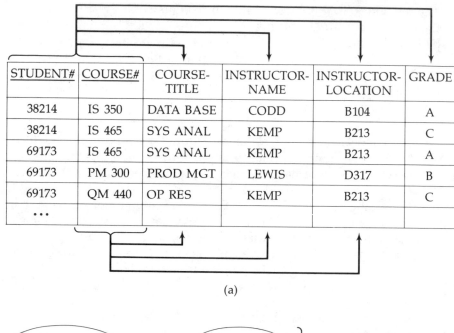

STUDENT#	COURSE#	COURSE-TITLE	INSTRUCTOR-NAME	INSTRUCTOR-LOCATION	GRADE
38214	IS 350	DATA BASE	CODD	B104	A
38214	IS 465	SYS ANAL	KEMP	B213	C
69173	IS 465	SYS ANAL	KEMP	B213	A
69173	PM 300	PROD MGT	LEWIS	D317	B
69173	QM 440	OP RES	KEMP	B213	C
...					

(a)

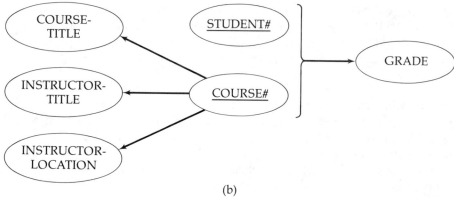

(b)

Notice that GRADE is the only attribute that is dependent on both STUDENT# and COURSE#. This is because we must know both the student and the course taken to determine a grade. An attribute that depends on the full composite key (rather than part of that key) is said to be **fully dependent** on that key.

The remaining nonkey attributes (COURSE-TITLE, INSTRUCTOR-NAME, and INSTRUCTOR-LOCATION) are dependent only on COURSE#, and not on the combination STUDENT# plus COURSE#. These attributes are said to be **partially dependent** on the primary key.

STUDENT-COURSE

STUDENT#	COURSE#	COURSE-TITLE	INSTRUCTOR-NAME	INSTRUCTOR-LOCATION	GRADE

REGISTRATION

STUDENT#	COURSE#	GRADE
38214	IS 350	A
38214	IS 465	C
69173	IS 465	A
69173	PM 300	B
69173	QM 440	C
...		

(3NF)

COURSE-INSTRUCTOR

COURSE#	COURSE-TITLE	INSTRUCTOR-NAME	INSTRUCTOR-LOCATION
IS 350	DATA BASE	CODD	B104
IS 465	SYS ANAL	KEMP	B213
PM 300	PROD MGT	LEWIS	D317
QM 440	OP RES	KEMP	B213
...			

(2NF)

Figure 7-11
Conversion of a relation to second normal form by removing partial functional dependency.

Second Normal Form

To eliminate the anomalies of the first normal form, we must remove partial functional dependencies. A relation is in **second normal form** if it is already in first normal form and any partial functional dependencies have been removed.

To convert a relation with partial dependencies to second normal form, we create two new relations, one with attributes that are fully dependent on the primary key and the other with attributes that are dependent on only part of that key. This process is illustrated in Figure 7-11 for the STUDENT-COURSE relation, where the following new relations are created:

1. A REGISTRATION relation, with composite key STUDENT# plus COURSE#. The nonkey attribute GRADE is fully dependent on the primary key. This relation is in third normal form.

2. A COURSE-INSTRUCTOR relation, with the primary key COURSE#. The nonkey attributes (COURSE-TITLE, INSTRUCTOR-NAME, and INSTRUCTOR-LOCATION) are those that are dependent only on COURSE# (as shown in Figure 7-11).

The anomalies described earlier for first normal form have been eliminated in these new relations. Notice that each course is described only once in the COURSE-INSTRUCTOR relation. As a result, any update to course data (such as a change in title) is confined to a single tuple. Also, since course data are separated from student data, new course data can be inserted or old course data deleted without reference to student data.

Although second normal form represents an improvement, additional refinement is required, since data concerning the entity INSTRUCTOR are "hidden" within the COURSE-INSTRUCTOR relation. A diagram of the dependencies within this relation appears as follows:

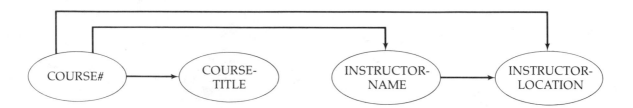

Notice that each of the nonkey attributes is dependent on COURSE#. However, INSTRUCTOR-LOCATION is also dependent on INSTRUC-TOR-NAME. That is, there is a unique location (or office number) for each instructor. This is an example of a transitive dependency. A **transitive dependency** occurs when one nonkey attribute (such as INSTRUCTOR-LOCATION) is dependent on one or more nonkey attributes (such as INSTRUCTOR-NAME). A simple transitive dependency appears as follows:

In this case, there is a transitive dependency between the primary key and attributes A and B. Transitive dependencies result in insertion, deletion, and update anomalies, similar to those for partial dependencies.

Insertion Anomaly.   Suppose we want to insert data for a new instructor in the COURSE-INSTRUCTOR relation (Figure 7-11). Since instructor data are dependent on COURSE#, we cannot insert instructor data until an instructor has been assigned to teach at least one course. For example, in Figure 7-11, we cannot insert data for the instructor Smith until one or more courses have been assigned to Smith.

Update Anomaly.   Instructor data occur multiple times in the COURSE-INSTRUCTOR relation (for example, instructor KEMP has two occurrences). As a result, any change to instructor data (such as a new instructor location) requires searching the entire relation to locate the desired occurrences and then updating each occurrence. The number of such occurrences in a relation will vary over time.

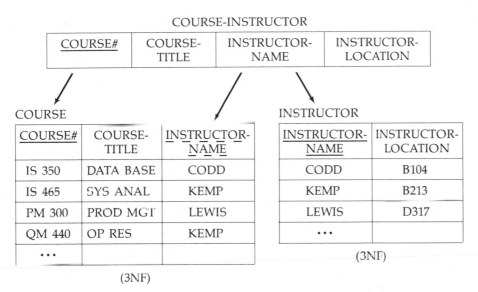

Figure 7-12
Conversion of a relation to third normal form by removing transitive dependency.

Deletion Anomaly. Deleting the data for a particular course may result in the loss of instructor data. For example, deleting the data for the course IS350 will cause the loss of data concerning the instructor CODD.

To eliminate these anomalies, a further normalization step is necessary. This step converts a relation to third normal form by removing transitive dependencies.

Third Normal Form

A relation is in **third normal form** (3NF) if it is in second normal form and contains no transitive dependencies. A relation in third normal form has the following simple dependency relationships:

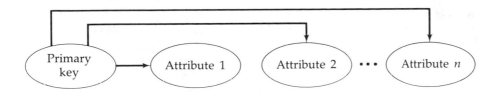

That is, each nonkey attribute is fully dependent on the primary key, and there are no transitive ("hidden") dependencies.

The process of removing a transitive dependency is illustrated for the COURSE-INSTRUCTOR relation in Figure 7-12. The nonkey attributes that

Figure 7-13
Summary of 3NF relations
for GRADE-REPORT.

STUDENT#	STUDENT NAME	MAJOR
38214	BRIGHT	IS
69173	SMITH	PM
...		

STUDENT (STUDENT#, STUDENT-NAME, MAJOR)

INSTRUCTOR-NAME	INSTRUCTION-LOCATION
CODD	B104
KEMP	B213
LEWIS	D317
...	

INSTRUCTOR (INSTRUCTOR-NAME, INSTRUCTOR-LOCATION)

COURSE#	COURSE-TITLE	INSTRUCTOR-NAME
IS 350	DATA BASE	CODD
IS 465	SYS ANAL	KEMP
PM 300	PROD MGT	LEWIS
QM 440	OP RES	KEMP
...		

COURSE (COURSE#, COURSE-TITLE, INSTRUCTOR-NAME)

STUDENT#	COURSE#	GRADE
38214	IS 350	A
38214	IS 465	C
69173	IS 465	A
69173	PM 300	B
69173	QM 440	C
...		

REGISTRATION (STUDENT#, COURSE#, GRADE)

participate in the transitive dependency (INSTRUCTOR-NAME and IN-STRUCTOR-LOCATION) are removed to form a new INSTRUCTOR relation. The primary key of this relation is INSTRUCTOR-NAME, since we assume that this attribute uniquely identifies INSTRUCTOR-LOCATION. The data base analyst would have to investigate this assumption to ensure its validity, since names are often not unique.

Although the attribute INSTRUCTOR-NAME becomes the primary key in the new INSTRUCTOR relation, it is also a nonkey attribute in the new COURSE relation (see Figure 7-12). INSTRUCTOR-NAME is said to be a foreign key in the COURSE relation. A **foreign key** is a nonkey attribute in one relation (such as COURSE) that also appears as a primary key in another relation (such as INSTRUCTOR). In this example, the foreign key allows us to associate a particular course with the instructor who teaches that course. We indicate a foreign key by underlining it with a dashed line, as in Figure 7-12.

The normalization process is now completed. The Grade-Report user view (Figure 7-3) has been transformed through a series of simple steps to a set of four relations in third normal form. The 3NF relations are summarized in Figure 7-13, both in tabular form and in shorthand notation.

These 3NF relations are free of the anomalies described earlier. Since each entity is described in a separate relation, data concerning that entity can

ST-MAJ-ADV

STUDENT#	MAJOR	ADVISOR
123	PHYSICS	EINSTEIN
123	MUSIC	MOZART
456	BIOL	DARWIN
789	PHYSICS	BOHR
999	PHYSICS	EINSTEIN

(a)

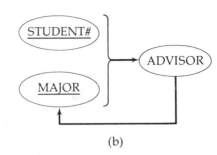

(b)

Figure 7-14
Boyce–Codd normal form.
(a) Relation in 3NF with anomalies.
(b) Dependency diagram.
(c) Relations in BCNF.

ST-ADV

STUDENT#	ADVISOR
123	EINSTEIN
123	MOZART
456	DARWIN
789	BOHR
999	EINSTEIN

ADV-MAJ

ADVISOR	MAJOR
EINSTEIN	PHYSICS
MOZART	MUSIC
DARWIN	BIOL
BOHR	PHYSICS

(c)

easily be inserted or deleted without reference to other entities. Also, updates to the data for a particular entity are easily accomplished, since they are confined to a single tuple (row) within a relation.

In the process of normalizing Grade-Report, no information is lost from the original user view. In fact, the Grade-Report in Figure 7-3 can be recreated by combining the data from the 3NF relations in Figure 7-13 using relational algebra (described in Chapter 6).

BEYOND THIRD NORMAL FORM

Relations in third normal form are sufficient for most practical data base design problems. However, 3NF does not guarantee that all anomalies have been removed. Recent research has identified additional normalization steps that can be performed to remove any remaining anomalies. Although these refinements are not often required, you should be aware of them and the conditions under which they may be required.

Boyce–Codd Normal Form

When a relation has more than one candidate key, anomalies may result even though the relation is in 3NF. For example, consider the ST-MAJ-ADV relation shown in Figure 7-14a. The primary key of this relation is the composite key (STUDENT#, MAJOR). The semantic rules for the relation are as follows:

1. Each student may major in several subjects.
2. For each major, a given student has only one advisor (this condition must be true if STUDENT#+MAJOR is the primary key).
3. Each major has several advisors.
4. Each advisor advises only one major.

A dependency diagram summarizing these rules is shown in Figure 7-14b. The relation is clearly in 3NF, since there are no partial functional dependencies and no transitive dependencies. Nevertheless, there are still anomalies in the relation. For example, suppose that student #456 changes her major from BIOL to MATH. When the tuple for this student is updated, we lose the fact that DARWIN advises in BIOL (update anomaly). Also, suppose we want to insert a tuple with the information that WATSON advises in COMPSCI. This, of course, cannot be done until at least one student majoring in COMPSCI is assigned WATSON as an advisor (insertion anomaly).

In the ST-MAJ-ADV relation, there are two candidate keys: (STUDENT#, MAJOR) and (STUDENT#, ADVISOR). Although the first of these candidate keys was chosen as the primary key, the second could equally well have been chosen. Notice that the two candidate keys overlap, since they have STUDENT# in common. The type of anomalies that exist in this relation can only occur when there are two or more overlapping candidate keys. Thus, the situation is relatively rare, but nevertheless can occur.

R. F. Boyce and E. F. Codd identified this deficiency and proposed a stronger definition of 3NF that remedies the problem. Their definition relies on the concept of a determinant. A **determinant** is any attribute (simple or composite) on which some other attribute is fully functionally dependent. For example, in the ST-MAJ-ADV relation, the attribute ADVISOR is a determinant, since the attribute MAJOR is fully functionally dependent on ADVISOR (see Figure 7-14b). We say that a relation is in Boyce-Codd normal form (BCNF) if and only if it is in 3NF and every determinant is a candidate key.

Applying the Boyce–Codd rule, we see that ST-ADV-MAJ is not in BCNF (even though it is in 3NF) because even though ADVISOR is a determinant, it is not a candidate key (one ADVISOR may advise many students). To overcome this problem, we project the original 3NF relation into two relations that are in BCNF. The result of this operation for ST-MAJ-ADV is shown in Figure 7-14c. The first of these two relations (called ST-ADV) contains the attributes STUDENT# and ADVISOR, which form the primary key. The second relation (called ADV-MAJ) contains ADVISOR (the primary key) and MAJOR (a nonkey attribute). You should check that these relations are in BCNF by applying the basic definition.

COM-PAC-OUT

COMPUTER	PACKAGE	OUTLET
APPLE	VISICALC	COMPUTERLAND
APPLE	APPLESTAR	COMPUTERLAND
APPLE	VISICALC	BYTE SHOP
ZENITH	WORDSTAR	COMPUTERSHOP
ZENITH	SUPERCALC	COMPUTERSHOP
ZENITH	WORDSTAR	BYTE SHOP

(a)

Figure 7-15
Fourth normal form.
(a) Example of
   multivalued
   dependencies.
(b) Relations in fourth
   normal form.

COM-PAC

COMPUTER	PACKAGE
APPLE	VISICALC
APPLE	APPLESTAR
ZENITH	WORDSTAR
ZENITH	SUPERCALC

COM-OUT

COMPUTER	OUTLET
APPLE	COMPUTERLAND
APPLE	BYTE SHOP
ZENITH	COMPUTERSHOP
ZENITH	BYTE SHOP

(b)

Fourth Normal Form

Consider the relation COM-PAC-OUT illustrated in Figure 7-15. This relation contains information about computers, software packages, and outlets. We assume the following:

1. For each COMPUTER, there may be several PACKAGES and several OUTLETS.
2. PACKAGES and OUTLETS depend only on COMPUTER and are independent of each other.

There are no determinants in the relation COM-PAC-OUT. Therefore, the three attributes (COMPUTER, PACKAGE, OUTLET) form a composite key, and the relation is in BCNF. However, this is a form of dependence between the attributes. For each COMPUTER, there is a well-defined set of PACKAGES and a well-defined set of OUTLETS. We can diagram these relationships as follows:

The type of dependence shown in this example is called a multivalued dependence. A **multivalued dependency** exists when there are three attributes (e.g., A, B, and C) in a relation, and for each value of A there is a well-defined set of values of B and a well-defined set of values of C. However, the set of values of B is independent of set C, and vice versa.

Referring to Figure 7-15a, we can see that there are a good deal of redundant data in a relation when there are multivalued dependencies, despite the fact that the relation is in BCNF. As usual, this results in update anomalies. For example, suppose that ZENITH decides to drop the COM-PUTERSHOP outlet. In this case, two tuples must be deleted, one for the WORDSTAR package and one for the SUPERCALC package (deletion anomaly). Also, suppose that APPLE decides to add a package called SU-PERFILE. We must search the relation and insert a new tuple for each APPLE outlet (in the example, two tuples would be added).

To remove these anomalies, we split the relation COM-PAC-OUT into two relations, as shown in Figure 7-15b. The resulting relations contain the associations between COMPUTERS and PACKAGES and between COM-PUTERS and OUTLETS. These relations have no multivalued dependencies and are said to be in fourth normal form. A relation is in **fourth normal form** (4NF) if it is in BCNF and contains no multivalued dependencies.

Additional Normal Forms

Other normal forms (beyond 4NF) have been defined. We describe them only briefly here, since they appear to be mostly of research interest. For an extended discussion of these normal forms, see Date (1981).

Fifth Normal Form. This normal form is designed to cope with a type of dependency called join dependency. A relation that has a join dependency cannot be decomposed by projection into other relations without spurious results. Fifth normal form (5NF) provides a definition for removing join dependencies if they exist and can be discovered. However, according to Date (p. 263), "it is tempting to think that such relations are pathological cases and likely to be rare in practice."

Domain-Key Normal Form. Fagin (1981) has proposed a conceptually simple normal form called the domain-key normal form (DK/NF). According to this definition, a relation is in DK/NF if and only if every constraint on the relation is a logical consequence of key constraints and domain constraints. Fagin shows that if a relation is in DK/NF, it cannot have insertion or deletion anomalies.

Fagin's definition is an important contribution, since it provides a completely general definition of normal forms. Unfortunately, it does not provide a methodology for converting a given relation to DK/NF.

Interrelation Constraints. All the normal forms that we have described have been concerned with individual relations. The object has been to refine relations into higher normal forms so that they would not contain redundant data and therefore be subject to modification anomalies. But we have not yet mentioned interrelation constraints—constraints imposed on attributes that exist in two or more relations.

For an example of an interrelation constraint, examine the 3NF relations for GRADE-REPORT (Figure 7-13). The attribute INSTRUCTOR-NAME appears in two relations: COURSE and INSTRUCTOR. A reasonable inter-relation constraint for this situation is the following: Do not insert an instructor name in the COURSE relation unless it already appears in the INSTRUCTOR relation. With an **interrelation constraint**, the value (or existence) of an attribute in one relation depends on some condition in another relation.

Interrelation constraints are very important, since they allow us to control the integrity of data bases. Unfortunately, at the present time, many DBMS products do not allow interrelation constraints to be defined or automatically enforced. Therefore, enforcing interrelation (or interrecord) constraints is the responsibility of the application programmer (usually, they are simply not enforced). Interrelation constraints are now being introduced in some new products. Chapters 13 and 14 will discuss some of these products and how they handle interrelation constraints.

Limits of Normalization. The objective of normalization is to reduce redundancy and produce a set of stable data structures. In most applications, the use of third normal form is adequate to achieve these objectives, but sometimes, further refinement to BCNF or 4NF is warranted.

It should be remembered that the normalization steps described in this chapter are only guidelines to be used by the data base designer. The designer's skill and experience also play a role, and sometimes the designer may choose not to normalize "all the way" to third normal form (or higher). For example, consider the following CUSTOMER relation:

CUSTOMER (<u>NAME</u>, STREET, CITY, STATE, ZIP)

The primary key of this relation is NAME. However, the relation is in 2NF because there is a "hidden," or transitive, dependence. A ZIP code uniquely identifies the CITY and STATE, so that within the CUSTOMER relation, we have the following functional dependence:

Normalization theory would suggest that we convert CUSTOMER to two relations in 3NF. These two relations are:

CUSTOMERDATA (<u>NAME</u>, STREET, <u>ZIP</u>)
LOCATION (<u>ZIP</u>, CITY, STATE)

However, in practice the designer would most likely choose *not* to decompose CUSTOMER into the two relations because the attributes STREET, CITY, STATE, and ZIP are almost always used together as a unit. Although conceptually correct, decomposing CUSTOMER into two relations would require the user to logically associate the CUSTOMERDATA and LOCATION data each time they are referenced. Thus, the designer should use judgment and common sense in applying normalization theory. However, any departures from 3NF should be justified and carefully documented. The use of normalization should be enforced for both network and relational implementations.

DATA VOLUME AND USAGE

The last step in requirements analysis is to collect information concerning data volume and usage patterns. This step is most easily accomplished after the conceptual schema is completed, as we will see. When the conceptual schema is completed, the data base designers should conduct a design review with users. At this same time, information can be gathered concerning data volume and usage.

We will illustrate the techniques of data volume and usage analysis with the conceptual schema for GRADE-REPORT. However, you should keep in mind that this schema was derived from a single user view. We illustrate the techniques for an extended example in the next chapter.

Conceptual Data Model

The four normalized relations for GRADE-REPORT shown in Figure 7-13 are a perfectly valid representation of a conceptual schema, and no additional transformation is necessary. However, it is often useful to map the relations into a data structure diagram so that users can easily see the associations between entities. Also, the resulting data structure diagram (sometimes called a relational map) is useful to data base designers if the conceptual schema is to be implemented as a network or hierarchical model.

The conceptual data model for GRADE-REPORT, expressed as a data structure diagram, is shown in Figure 7-16. Each relation is represented by a rectangle containing the names of its attributes (primary keys are underlined). The one-to-many association from STUDENT to REGISTRATION is the consequence of the composite key (<u>STUDENT#</u>, <u>COURSE#</u>) in REGISTRATION. This composite key implies that a given student registers in several courses. For the same reason, there is a one-to-many association from COURSE to REGISTRATION. Finally, the foreign key <u>INSTRUCTOR-</u>

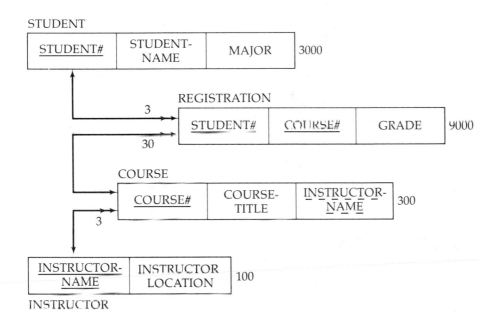

Figure 7-16
Conceptual data model
(GRADE-REPORT).

NAME in COURSE implies the association between INSTRUCTOR and COURSE. (This association is one-to-many, since each instructor teaches several courses.)

Data Volumes

Data volume figures are superimposed on the conceptual schema shown in Figure 7-16. These data volumes are necessary for physical data base design (described in Chapter 9). The figures shown in Figure 7-16 are based on the following assumptions:

1. There are 3000 students.
2. Each student registers for an average of 3 courses (thus, there are 9000 registration entries).
3. There are 100 instructors.
4. Each instructor teaches an average of 3 courses (thus, there are 300 courses).
5. Each course has an average of 30 registrants ($9000 \div 300 = 30$).

In collecting such data volume figures, the analysts must allow for future growth. Often, two sets of figures are collected—one set representing current volumes, the other representing forecasted volumes for a future time frame (say, five years later).

Figure 7-17
Another user view
(CLASS-LIST).

MOUNTAIN VIEW COLLEGE CLASS LIST FALL SEMESTER 198X			
COURSE#: IS 350 COURSE-TITLE: DATA BASE INSTRUCTOR-NAME: CODD INSTRUCTOR-LOCATION: B104			
STUDENT#	STUDENT-NAME	MAJOR	GRADE
38214	BRIGHT	IS	A
40875	CORTEZ	CS	B
51893	EDWARDS	IS	A
...			

Data Usage Analysis

The last step in requirements analysis is to define how the data are to be used. This step requires that the following two tasks be performed:

1. Define data base transactions. A **transaction** is a record of an event, or a request for information, that causes certain actions be taken against a data base.

2. Define the logical data base accesses required to process each transaction (expressed as a logical access map).

We will illustrate this process with another user view based on the GRADE-REPORT data base. Figure 7-17 shows a view called Class-List, which provides a list of students registered in each class at Mountain View College. The list is produced three times each semester: after registration, at midsemester, and when the semester is ended (GRADES are recorded in the final version only).

Now let us define the transaction CREATE-CLASS-LIST. This transaction is a request for information, namely, to produce one version of the CLASS-LIST view. This transaction will require the following logical steps:

1. Read the next COURSE record (or tuple).

2. Read the INSTRUCTOR record for that COURSE.

3. Print (or display) the report header.

Figure 7-18
Logical access map
(CREATE-CLASS-LIST).
(a) Preliminary map.
(b) Final map.

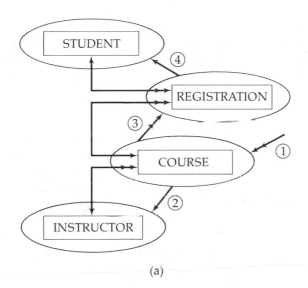

(a)

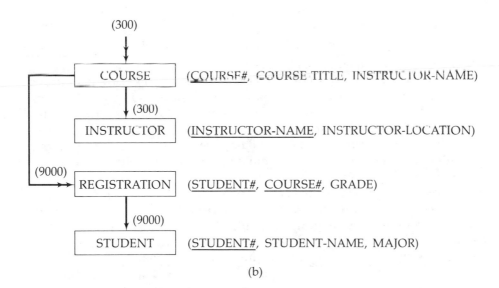

(b)

4. Read the next REGISTRATION record for that COURSE.

5. Read the STUDENT record corresponding to that REGISTRATION.

6. Print a detail line for the report.

7. Repeat steps 4 through 7 for each REGISTRATION for the COURSE.

A **logical access map** (LAM) is a diagram showing the sequence of logical accesses to conceptual data base records (or relations). An LAM for the transaction CREATE-CLASS-LIST is shown in Figure 7-18. Figure 7-18a shows a preliminary LAM superimposed on the conceptual schema. Figure 7-18b shows the same map arranged in the logical sequence in which the records are accessed. This LAM also shows the total number of accesses that will be required for each conceptual record type to produce the entire set of 300 class lists. This information is also necessary for physical data base design, for example, in selecting file organizations and access methods.

The LAM in Figure 7-18b can be used directly to specify a procedure to create the class lists. We describe procedure design in Chapter 9.

Figures 7-3 and 7-17 illustrate how two different user views (or external schemas) may be derived from the same conceptual schema. Figure 7-16 is simply a different view of the same data. In fact, we could have created the conceptual schema by normalizing the data in Class-List (we ask you to do this in the chapter exercises).

SUMMARY

In this chapter, we have presented an introduction to data base design. First, we described the major steps, which are requirements formulation and analysis, conceptual design, implementation design, and physical design. Next, we described requirements formulation and analysis, which is the process of determining user requirements for data. Requirements analysis consists of defining the scope of the data base, establishing data collection standards, identifying user views, building the data dictionary, and identifying data volumes and usage patterns.

We also described normalization, which is the cornerstone of modern data base design. Normalization is the step-by-step process of removing unwanted dependencies from relations, thereby eliminating data redundancy and the resultant anomalies in modifying data. Normalization should result in simple data structures that are easy to maintain.

We described a number of normal forms in this chapter. Third normal form is adequate for most practical data base design problems. However, 3NF relations should be checked to determine if there are any remaining unwanted dependencies. When such dependencies exist, there will be redundancy in the relations. These dependencies can be removed by applying the definitions of BCNF or 4NF.

When the conceptual schema is completed, it should be reviewed with users to ensure that all semantic rules have been followed and that no important data have been omitted from the model. At this time, additional information concerning data volumes and usage patterns should be collected and superimposed on the conceptual schema.

CHAPTER REVIEW

Review Questions

1. Define each of the following terms concisely:

   a. data base design
   b. user view
   c. semantic rules
   d. normalization
   e. determinant

   f. multivalued dependence
   g. interrelation constraint
   h. logical access map
   i. unnormalized relation

2. Contrast the following terms:

   a. unnormalized relation; normalized relation
   b. full dependence; partial dependence
   c. process-oriented approach; data-oriented approach
   d. transitive dependence; multivalued dependence
   e. insertion anomaly; deletion anomaly
   f. primary key; foreign key

3. Briefly define each of the following:

   a. first normal form
   b. second normal form
   c. third normal form
   d. Boyce–Codd normal form
   e. fourth normal form
   f. domain-key normal form

4. Describe the procedure required for each of the following:

   a. To convert an unnormalized relation to 1NF.
   b. To convert a 1NF relation to 2NF.
   c. To convert a 2NF relation to 3NF.
   d. To convert a 3NF relation to BCNF.
   e. To convert a BCNF relation to 4NF.

5. Why are interrelation constraints significant?

6. Briefly describe the four major steps in data base design.

7. Briefly describe five steps of requirements analysis.

8. What is the significance of domain-key normal form (DK/NF)?

9. What are semantic rules? Why are they important?

10. Explain how procedure formation for data bases differs from that for conventional application programs.

Problems and Exercises

1. Draw a data flow diagram representing the registration procedure at your school.

2. Derive a set of 3NF relations for the Class-List user view (Figure 7-17). Use the assumptions stated in Figure 7-3. Compare your results with Figure 7-13.

3. The transaction CREATE-GRADE-REPORT is a request to produce the Grade Report shown in Figure 7-3.
   a. List the logical steps required to process this transaction.
   b. Draw a logical access map representing the logical data base accesses.

4. Write a sequence of relational algebra commands to create Grade-Report (Figure 7-3) from the 3NF relations in Figure 7-13. Refer to Chapter 6 for a discussion of relational algebra.

5. Classify each of the following relations as unnormalized, 1NF, 2NF, or 3NF (state any assumptions you make).
   a. EMPLOYEE (<u>EMPLOYEE#</u>,EMPNAME,JOBCODE)
   b. EMPLOYEE (<u>EMPLOYEE#</u>,EMPNAME,(JOBCODE, #YEARS))
   c. EMPLOYEE (<u>EMPLOYEE#</u>,EMPNAME,JOBCODE,JOBDESCRIPTION)
   d. EMPLOYEE (<u>EMPLOYEE#</u>,EMPNAME,<u>PROJECT#</u>,HRS-WORKED)

6. For each of the following relations, do the following:
   a. State the normal form in its present state.
   b. Identify any unwanted dependencies.
   c. Give an example of an insertion and deletion anomaly.
   d. Further normalize the relation, stating what definition you are using.

EMPLOYEE

EMP#	COURSES	INTERESTS
123	COMM. I	BOWLING
123	COMM. II	BOWLING
456	Q.C.	SKIING
456	Q.C.	BOWLING

EMP# ←→ COURSES
EMP# ←→ INTERESTS

FOOTBALL

PLAYER	POSITION	COACH
EARL	FB	JOE
JOHN	G	ED
TONY	FB	PETE
CARL	T	JIM
MACK	FB	JOE

COACH ←→ POSITION

CUSTOMER ORDER			
ORDER#: 61384			DATE: 11/4/8X
CUSTOMER#: 1273			
CUSTOMER NAME: CONTEMPORARY DESIGNS			
CUSTOMER ADDRESS: 123 OAK ST.			
CITY-STATE-ZIP: AUSTIN, TX. 28384			
PRODUCT#	DESCRIPTION	QUANTITY ORDERED	UNIT PRICE
M-128	BOOKCASE	2	150
B-381	CABINET	1	725

ORDER# ←——→ CUSTOMER#
PRODUCT# ←——→ DESCRIPTION

Figure 7-19
CUSTOMER ORDER
(Pine Valley Furniture).

7. A customer order form for Pine Valley Furniture Company is shown in Figure 7-19.

   a. Derive a set of 3NF relations.

   b. Create a data structure diagram.

8. Do the following for the conceptual data model derived for the user view in Figure 7-19:

   a. Add data volumes to the conceptual data model, using the following assumptions:

      (i)   200 customers
      (ii) 2 orders per customer (average)
      (iii) 3 products per order (average)
      (iv) 300 products

   b. Create a logical access map for the transaction CREATE-CUSTOMER-ORDER.

9. Refer to the conceptual data model for Grade-Report (Figure 7-16). Draw a logical access map for the transaction CREATE-GRADE-REPORT (Figure 7-3).

10. Obtain a user view such as a credit card statement of account, a phone bill, or some other common document. Perform the following:

    a. Fill out a user view form (Figure 7-4).

    b. Fill out a data element form (Figure 7-5) for a data item that identifies some entity.

    c. Derive a set of 3NF relations.

    d. Draw a data structure diagram.

References

Date, C.J. 1981. *Introduction to Database Systems*. 3d ed. Reading, Mass.: Addison-Wesley.

Fagin, Ronald. 1981. "A Normal Form for Databases that is Based on Domains and Keys." ACM *Transactions on Database Systems* 6 (September): 387–415.

Martin, James. 1983. *Managing the Data-Base Environment*. Englewood Cliffs, N.J.: Prentice-Hall.

Teorey, T.J., and J.P. Fry. 1982. *Design of Database Structures*. Englewood Cliffs, N.J.: Prentice-Hall.

Weinberg, Victor. 1979. *Structured Analysis*. New York: Yourdon Press.

## 8

Conceptual Design

INTRODUCTION

Before starting construction on a new house, a builder must consult a set of architectural plans. The architect who designs these plans determines the present and future needs of the prospective homeowner. In addition, any constraints of the owner as well as the natural environment are taken into account. Similarly, before creating a data base, an organization must develop an "architectural plan" to ensure that the data base will meet its present and future information needs.

Conceptual data base design is the process of developing a detailed "architectural plan" for the data base. We will refer to this plan as the conceptual data model (it is also called a conceptual schema). The conceptual data model represents the entities of the organization, the attributes of those entities, and the relationships between entities. It is defined by the data themselves and is entirely independent of application programs, computer hardware, the data base management system, or any other physical considerations.

Conceptual design is the second step in data base design, following requirements analysis. As shown in Figure 8-1, the major inputs to this activity are the requirements specifications representing user needs for data. Much of the metadata required for conceptual design should be organized in the data dictionary. The output of conceptual design is a conceptual data model that represents the information structure of the organization.

Figure 8-1
Position of conceptual design in the data base design process. (Source: Teorey and Fry 1982.)

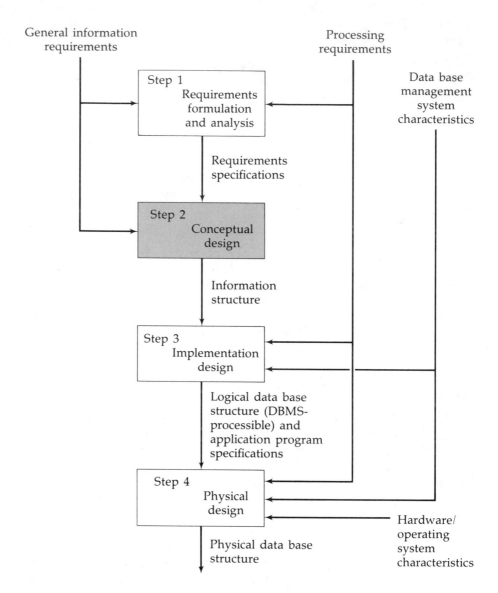

General information requirements

Processing requirements

Data base management system characteristics

Step 1
Requirements formulation and analysis

Requirements specifications

Step 2
Conceptual design

Information structure

Step 3
Implementation design

Logical data base structure (DBMS-processible) and application program specifications

Step 4
Physical design

Physical data base structure

Hardware/ operating system characteristics

TRADE-OFFS IN CONCEPTUAL DESIGN

The data base designer must perform a series of trade-offs during conceptual data base design. How these trade-offs are resolved will have an important bearing on the overall success of the data base project. Following is a brief description of several such trade-offs (Auerbach Publishers 1980).

Scope of the Design

Should an organization attempt to design a single large global data base to meet its information needs? Or should the organization design a separate data base for each of its applications? Perhaps there is an intermediate approach that is superior to either of these two extremes.

With the **global approach**, the designer attempts to design a single integrated data base to meet the organization's present and future information needs. This approach is basically the "total systems" approach that was widely advocated during the 1960s. However, the global approach has seldom proved successful. The design task is so complex and the time and resources required are normally so large that the global approach becomes quite risky. Any benefits from data base implementation are delayed for months or years, so that the project is in danger of losing organizational commitment and momentum.

With the **application approach**, the designer performs a requirements analysis and designs a separate data base for each new application. This reduces the design task to a manageable size. However, there are two major disadvantages. First, there is no assurance that the various data bases will ever be integrated or shared. Second, the application data bases will probably be designed to resemble conventional application files with extensive data redundancy and lack of data independence. Thus, the application approach is just as risky (perhaps riskier) than the global approach.

An intermediate design approach seems preferable to either the global or individual application approach. With this approach, the designers sketch a high-level enterprise model (see Chapter 3) based on an analysis of business processes and functions. This model shows the major entities that must be described in the data base and the relationships between those entities. The enterprise model is then used to partition the overall data base design into several smaller, more manageable data bases (or segments of a global data base). Each smaller data base should represent a natural grouping of data entities rather than a specific application or functional unit of the organization. The data base designers then develop a detailed logical design for each of these smaller data bases, using the strategic data model as an integrating framework. Davis (1974) refers to this approach as a federation of systems.

We do not rule out the global data base approach. That approach has been used successfully by a number of smaller organizations where the information structures are not unduly complex and where there was unquestioned organizational commitment. However, when these conditions are not present, we recommend the "partitioned" or "federated" approach.

Design Approach

The designer must choose between two possible design approaches: top-down and bottom-up. This choice is closely related to the design scope we have just described.

Figure 8-2
Bottom-up conceptual
design process.

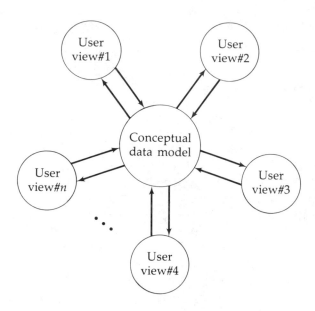

With the top-down approach (also called *entity analysis*), the designer starts with the enterprise model and adds detail to that model until a satisfactory conceptual design has been achieved. For example, the designer decides what attributes to associate with each entity, chooses primary keys, and so on. The main disadvantage of this approach is that there is no assurance that all user requirements will be represented in the model.

The other major approach to data base design employs a bottom-up analysis (also called *attribute synthesis*). With this approach, the analyst performs a detailed requirements analysis and models each user view separately. The relations for each user view are then merged to form a conceptual schema, as shown in Figure 8-2. Each user view in turn can be derived from this conceptual data model.

Actually, both the top-down and bottom-up approaches can be used, with each approach providing a check on the other. However, we stress the bottom-up approach in this chapter.

DBMS Dependency

Should the data base management system be selected and its features and constructs introduced early during the conceptual data base design process? Or should conceptual design proceed without reference to features of the DBMS to be used?

We strongly recommend the latter approach. Although introducing the DBMS early may spread the overall implementation effort, it will greatly reduce flexibility. A data model expressed in the constructs of one DBMS cannot be mapped easily into the constructs of another DBMS. Therefore, we recommend that the conceptual design be completed before DBMS features are considered. In fact, the completed conceptual design is most useful in evaluating what DBMS features are required by the organization.

One major difficulty may arise in postponing the DBMS software decision until conceptual design is completed. In discussing requirements analysis (Chapter 7), we recommended that the organization use an automated data dictionary facility to record metadata. Yet a mainstream trend in data management systems is to integrate the data dictionary with the DBMS and other data management software (we describe these software products in Chapter 11). Therefore, as a practical matter, an organization may be forced to choose its data management software before conceptual design begins if it is going to use the data dictionary to support requirements analysis. This compromise is acceptable (indeed, necessary), provided that conceptual design is performed without reference to the DBMS that is going to be used. The conceptual schema is mapped to a DBMS-dependent schema during implementation design.

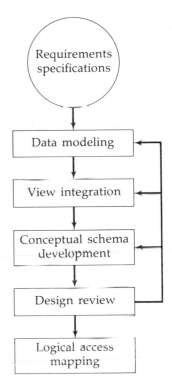

Figure 8-3
Steps in conceptual design.

STEPS IN CONCEPTUAL DESIGN

A number of different approaches and methodologies are used for conceptual data base design. The detailed steps, or tasks, are naturally dependent on the approach or methodology that is used. However, the steps shown in Figure 8-3 represent the major tasks that must be performed.

Data Modeling

Data modeling is the process of identifying and structuring the relationships between data elements. The analyst starts with the user views that are identified during requirements analysis and normalizes these data using the steps described in the previous chapter. The result of data modeling is a set of relations in third normal form for each user view.

View Integration

View integration is the process of merging the relations for each user view into a single set of relations in third normal form. The result of view integration is a conceptual data model for the organization's data base expressed in the form of normalized relations.

To illustrate how relations are merged, suppose that modeling a user view results in the following 3NF relation:

EMPLOYEE1 (<u>EMPLOYEE#</u>, NAME, ADDRESS, PHONE)

Modeling a second user view might result in the following relation:

EMPLOYEE2 (<u>EMPLOYEE#</u>, NAME, ADDRESS, PHONE, JOBCODE, #YEARS)

Since these two relations have the same primary key (EMPLOYEE#), they describe the same entity and may be merged into one relation. The result of merging the relations is the following relation:

EMPLOYEE (<u>EMPLOYEE#</u>, NAME, ADDRESS, PHONE, JOBCODE, #YEARS)

Notice that an attribute that appears in both relations (such as NAME in the preceding example) appears only once in the merged relation.

When merging two relations, the data base analyst should be aware that a transitive dependency may be introduced into the merged relation. For example, suppose that we have two relations with the following dependency diagrams:

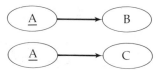

Since these two relations have the same primary key, they can be merged into a single relation. However, attribute C may be functionally dependent on attribute B. If so, we have introduced a transitive dependency into the merged relation, as shown in the following diagram:

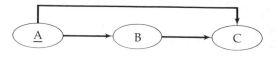

To resolve this dependency, the analyst can create the following two relations:

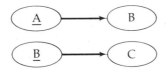

Conceptual Data Model Development

As we have indicated, when view integration is completed, the conceptual data model is expressed in the form of normalized relations. For better user understanding (and also for subsequent design steps), we may wish to transform these 3NF relations into a graphical model. We illustrated this process in Chapter 7, where the 3NF relations for Grade-Report (Figure 7-13) were transformed into a data structure diagram (Figure 7-16). The conceptual data model may be expressed in several different forms: a data structure diagram, an entity-relationship model, or a semantic data model. It may be drawn manually or by computer graphics.

A conceptual data model for a small to medium-sized company may comprise some 50 to 100 entities. For example, Figure 8-4 shows a conceptual data model for a medium-sized distributor. There are some 50 entities in the diagram (a manufacturing company would typically define more entities). Notice that the entities fall into natural clusters or groups. Thus, there is a Product cluster, a Parts cluster, a Dealer cluster, and a Financial cluster. Each of these clusters might be physically implemented as a separate data base (Martin 1983 refers to these clusters as "subject" data bases).

Design Review

When the initial version of the conceptual data model is developed, it should be subjected to a formal design review. All managers and key users should evaluate the conceptual data model and suggest changes or improvements before the next step (implementation design) is attempted. The conceptual data model should be evaluated from two points of view: accuracy and completeness. Does the conceptual data model accurately reflect the organization's data and their relationships? For example, is the association between Suppliers and Materials one-to-many, or should it really be many-to-many? And is the data model complete, or are there important entities, attributes, or relationships that should be added?

A report or questionnaire posing specific questions about the conceptual data model should be prepared by the design team before the review is held. An example of such a questionnaire for a Customer Information data base is presented in Figure 8-5 (see Teorey and Fry 1982 for a discussion of alternative conceptual design techniques).

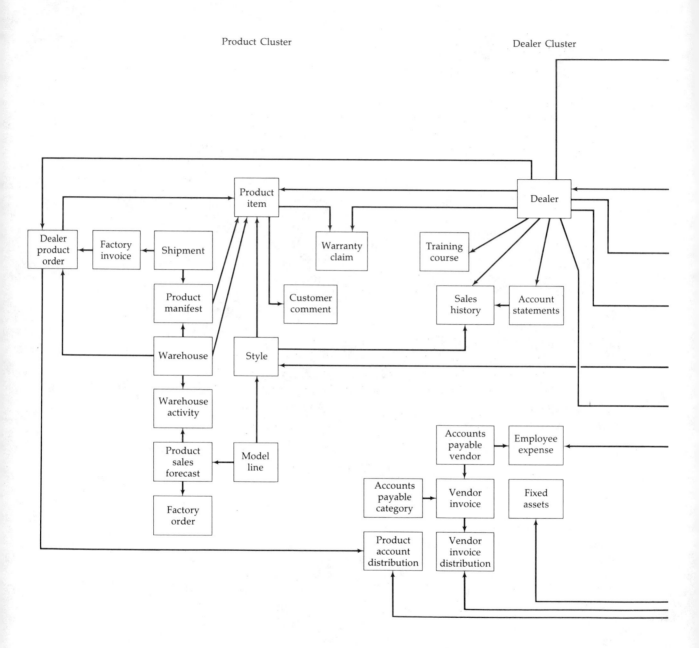

Figure 8-4
Sample conceptual data model.
(Courtesy Peat, Marwick, Mitchell & Co.)

Logical Access Mapping

Logical access maps (introduced in Chapter 7) are diagrams showing the logical sequence of accessing the conceptual records that are required to process transactions. LAMs provide a basis for developing data base pro-

Parts Cluster

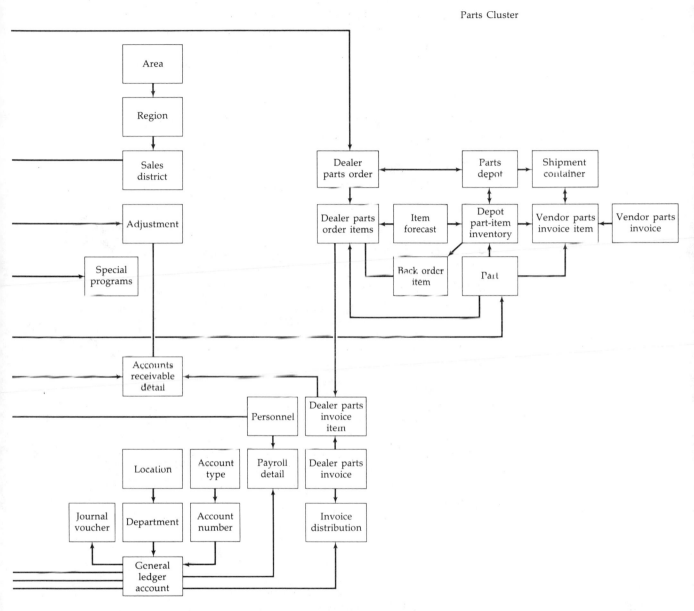

Financial Cluster

cedures and are also used to estimate the frequency of logical accesses to records.

Logical access mapping may be considered part of conceptual design or a step in implementation design. We will regard logical access mapping as the last step in conceptual design, as shown in Figure 8-3.

Figure 8-5
Sample design review
questionnaire.
(Source: Donna L.S.
Rund in Teorey and Fry
1982.)

CUSTOMER INFORMATION

Statements About How Customer Information Is and Is Not Used in the Current Operating Environment

1. Each customer must be assigned to a salesperson before an account may be established.
COMMENTS: _____
_____

2. All orders must be from customers with established accounts.
COMMENTS: _____

3. Each customer can be served by only one salesperson.
COMMENTS: _____

4. Each customer may have an unlimited number of orders.
COMMENTS: _____

5. If a salesperson is replaced, all customers must be immediately reassigned to a new salesperson and all sales agreements renegotiated.
COMMENTS: _____

6. If a customer is deleted or inactivated, all of the customer's current orders will be removed and sales agreements nullified.
COMMENTS: _____

7. Customers have no direct relationship to invoices, vendors, item numbers, or warehouses.
COMMENTS: _____

8. More than one customer may be on a given order.
AGREE _____
DISAGREE _____

9. A customer buys from a warehouse and not a salesperson. Consequently, each customer may have a sales agreement with each warehouse.
AGREE _____
DISAGREE _____

CASE EXAMPLE   Mountain View Community Hospital

We can illustrate the various steps of conceptual design by continuing the case of Mountain View Community Hospital, which was introduced in Chapter 3. We include requirements analysis in the following discussion.

Conceptual data base design at Mountain View Community Hospital was performed under the direction of Mr. Helms, the data base administrator. Mr. Helms was assisted in this effort by Mrs. Green, whose title was

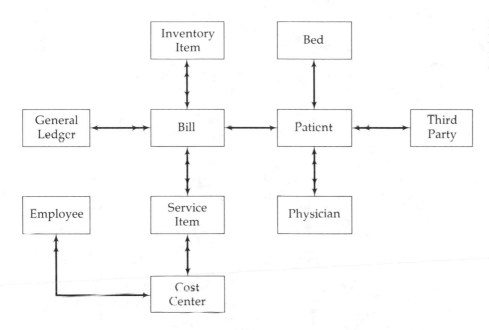

Figure 8-6
Preliminary enterprise model (Mountain View Community Hospital).

data analyst. Mrs. Green was previously a systems analyst with Mountain View Community Hospital and had attended a seminar on data base analysis and design. A data base consultant assisted in organizing the design effort and answered some technical questions. However, the analysis was performed almost entirely by the design team of Mr. Helms and Mrs. Green.

Conceptual data base design (together with requirements analysis) at Mountain View Community Hospital required approximately five months. This period was broken down as follows:

Requirements analysis: 2 months
Data modeling: 1 month
View integration: 1 month
Conceptual data model development: 2 weeks
Final review with users: 2 weeks

Enterprise Model

An enterprise model was developed for Mountain View Community Hospital in Chapter 3. This strategic model is shown again in Figure 8-6 for ease of reference.

Remember that the enterprise model was developed using a top-down process, proceeding from business functions and processes. It identifies the major business entities and their relationships. The design team at Mountain View Community Hospital used the strategic data model as a guide in

Figure 8-7
Sample metadata
(Mountain View
Community Hospital).

```
┌─────────────────────────────────────────────────────────────┐
│                         User View                            │
│  ┌─────────────────────────────────────────────────────────┐│
│  │ User view ____/____        Name _Patient Bill_          ││
│  │ Description _Itemized statement mailed to patient at_   ││
│  │   _end_ _of month following discharge_                   ││
│  │ Primary User:                                            ││
│  │   Name _Mary Ann Stevens_    Location _A 128_           ││
│  │   Organization _Accounts Receivable_  Phone _Ext. 2300_ ││
│  │ Data Elements:                                           ││
│  │   Number      Name          Number       Name           ││
│  │   _100_   _Patient Number_   _200_   _Item Code_        ││
│  │   _101_   _Patient Address_  _201_   _Description_      ││
│  │   _102_   _City-State-Zip_   _250_   _Charge_           ││
│  └─────────────────────────────────────────────────────────┘│
└─────────────────────────────────────────────────────────────┘
```

```
┌─────────────────────────────────────────────────────────────┐
│                       Data Element                           │
│  Data Element# _100_          Name _Patient Number_         │
│  Description _Identifying number assigned to a patient on admission_ │
│  Synonyms _Patient ID_                                       │
│  Source _Admissions_          Identifies _Patient entity_    │
│  Specification:                                              │
│    Type _Integer_             Length _5 digits_             │
│    Allowable range _00000 - 99999_                          │
│  Programming language name _PATIENT-NBR_                     │
│  Usage:                                                      │
│    Frequency _daily_                                         │
│    Update authority _Admissions_                            │
└─────────────────────────────────────────────────────────────┘
```

developing a conceptual data model. However, they expected the conceptual data model to be more detailed and to contain more relationships than the enterprise model.

Requirements Analysis

The design team interviewed users throughout Mountain View Community Hospital, including nurses, doctors, administrators, and clerks. Samples of existing reports and other operating documents were obtained.

As the design team accumulated these user views, they documented the data elements that were used throughout the organization. The meaning and usage of each data element were recorded, and any inconsistencies were resolved with the users. Information concerning each data element (metadata) was then recorded in the hospital's data dictionary system. Sample metadata collected during requirements analysis are shown in Figure 8-7.

Figure 8-8
User views for Mountain
View Community
Hospital.

When requirements analysis was nearly completed, the design team drew an overview diagram identifying the various user views to be used in designing a conceptual data model. Part of this overview diagram is shown in Figure 8-8. It identifies four significant user views of data for Mountain View Community Hospital: Patient Bill, Room Utilization Report, Patient Display, and Physician Report.

When the overview diagram was completed, the design team reviewed it with users to ensure that all relevant user views had been considered. There were other user views in addition to the four we named. However, we will use these four views in the following discussion to illustrate the design of a conceptual data model for Mountain View Community Hospital.

User View 1: Patient Bill

The first user view is that of the Patient Bill (see Figure 8-9). Charges incurred by each patient are accumulated during that patient's stay at the hospital. After the patient is discharged, a statement is sent to the patient in the format shown in Figure 8-9.

The Patient Bill consists of header information for the patient, followed by an itemized list of patient charges. If we view the Patient Bill as a relation, this itemized list constitutes a repeating group. To express the Patient Bill in shorthand notation, we list the attributes as follows:

Figure 8-9
User view 1: Patient Bill.

Mountain View Community Hospital 200 Forest Dr. Mountain View, Co.

Statement of account for:

Patient name: Baker, Mary
Patient address: 300 Oak St.
City-State-Zip:
  Mountain View, Co. 80638

Patient#: 3249
Date admitted: 09-10-8X
Date discharged: 09-14-8X

Item Code	Description	Charge
200	Room semi-pr	150.00
205	Television	10.00
307	X-ray	25.00
413	Lab tests	35.00
	Balance Due	220.00

BILL (PATIENT#, PATIENT-NAME, PATIENT-ADDRESS,
    CITY-STATE-ZIP, DATE-ADMITTED, DATE-DISCHARGED
    (ITEM-CODE, DESCRIPTION, CHARGE))

This is an unnormalized relation, since it contains a repeating group (designated by the inner parentheses). To normalize this relation, we remove the repeating group, thus creating the following two new relations:

3NF: PATIENT (<u>PATIENT#</u>, PATIENT-NAME, PATIENT-ADDRESS,
    CITY-STATE-ZIP, DATE-ADMITTED, DATE-DISCHARGED)

1NF: DETAIL(<u>PATIENT#</u>, <u>ITEM-CODE</u>, ITEM-DESCRIPTION,
    CHARGE)

In the PATIENT relation, PATIENT# is the primary key, since it uniquely identifies a patient (PATIENT-NAME is assumed not to be a candidate key, since it may not be unique). In the DETAIL relation, the primary key is the composite of PATIENT# and ITEM#.

PATIENT is in third normal form. However, DETAIL is in first normal form, since it contains a partial dependency, as shown in the following diagram:

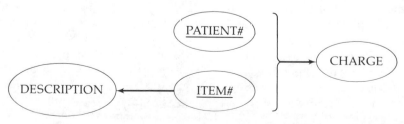

Room Utilization Report Date: 10-15-8X				
Location	Accom	Patient#	Patient Name	Exp Discharge Date
100-1	PR	6213	Rose, David	10-17-8X
101-1	PR	1379	Cribbs, John	10-15-8X
102-1	SP			
102-2	SP	1239	Miller, Ruth	10-16-8X
103-1	PR	7040	Ortega, Juan	10-19-8X

Figure 8-10
User view 2: Room Utilization Report.

We assume that a particular CHARGE depends on both PATIENT# and ITEM#. However, the ITEM-DESCRIPTION depends only on ITEM#.

To convert DETAIL to 2NF, we remove the partial dependency, creating two new relations:

3NF: LIST (PATIENT#, ITEM CODE, CHARGE)

3NF: ITEM (ITEM-CODE, DESCRIPTION)

Each of these relations is in 3NF, so the normalization steps are completed. The set of 3NF relations for the Patient Bill are shown below.

1. (PATIENT#, PATIENT-NAME, PATIENT-ADDRESS, CITY-STATE-ZIP, DATE-ADMITTED, DATE-DISCHARGED)

2. (ITEM-CODE, DESCRIPTION)

3. (PATIENT#, ITEM-CODE, CHARGE)

User View 2: Room Utilization Report

The Room Utilization Report (Figure 8-10) is a daily report that provides information about the current patient in each location. LOCATION specifies the room and bed numbers (e.g., 102-2 is room 102, bed 2). If a LOCATION is not assigned to a patient when the report is printed, then PATIENT#, PATIENT-NAME, and EXP-DISCHARGE-DATE are left blank (see the entry for 102-1 in Figure 8-10). This report is used by the hospital staff for room scheduling and utilization studies.

This user view is expressed as the following relation:

2NF: ROOM (LOCATION, ACCOM, PATIENT#, PATIENT-NAME, EXP-DISCH-DATE)

Notice that the attribute DATE (top of the Room Utilization Report) is omitted in the preceding relation. This is because DATE is assumed to be

Figure 8-11
User view 3: Patient
Display.

> Patient#: 3249
> Patient Name: Baker, Mary
> Patient Address: 300 Oak St.
> City-State-Zip: Mountain View, Co. 80638
> Date Admitted: 09-12-8X
> Date Discharged: XX-XX-XX
> Location: 437-2
> Extension: 529
> Third Party: Blue Cross

supplied by the system and need not be included in the conceptual view of the data base.

The ROOM relation does not contain any repeating groups and therefore is in 1NF. Also, since the primary key is a single attribute (LOCATION), there cannot be a partial dependency. Therefore, ROOM is already in 2NF.

Inspection of the ROOM relation reveals transitive ("hidden") dependencies involving patient information. Both PATIENT-NAME and EXP-DISCH-DATE depend on PATIENT# as well as on LOCATION. A diagram of this dependency follows:

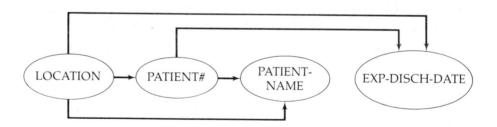

To convert this relation to 3NF, we create two new relations, with PATIENT# the primary key of the relation containing patient data and a foreign key in the other relation.

4. (<u>LOCATION</u>, ACCOM, <u>PATIENT</u>#)
5. (<u>PATIENT#</u>, PATIENT-NAME, EXP-DISCH-DATE)

User View 3: Patient Display

The Patient Display (Figure 8-11) is presented on demand to any nurse or other qualified staff member who uses a visual display. We will assume that the user must enter the PATIENT# to display data for a particular patient.

Figure 8-12
User view 4: Physician
Report.

```
            Mountain View Community Hospital
                    Physician Report

 Date:  10-17-8X                  Physician ID:  Wilcox
                                  Physician Phone:  329-1848

   Patient#      Patient Name      Location      Procedure

    6083        Brown, May          184-2        Tonsillectomy
    1239        Miller, Ruth        102-2        Observation
    4139        Majors, Carl        107-3        Chemotherapy
```

The Patient Display appears in relational form as follows:

2NF: PATIENT (<u>PATIENT#</u>, PATIENT-NAME, PATIENT-ADDRESS, CITY-STATE-ZIP, DATE-ADMITTED, DATE-DISCHARGED, LOCATION, EXTENSION, THIRD-PARTY)

This relation is in second normal form (you should verify this statement). There is a "hidden" dependency in this relation, since LOCATION determines EXTENSION (a particular bed location has a unique telephone extension). Removing this transitive dependency results in the following two 3NF relations:

6. (<u>PATIENT#</u>, PATIENT-NAME, PATIENT-ADDRESS, CITY-STATE-ZIP, DATE-ADMITTED, DATE-DISCHARGED, <u>LOCATION</u>, THIRD-PARTY)

7. (<u>LOCATION</u>, EXTENSION)

User View 4: Physician Report

The Physician Report is prepared daily for each physician treating patients at Mountain View Community Hospital (see Figure 8-12). It lists all patients currently in the hospital and the procedures that have been performed or prescribed by the physician. To simplify the presentation, we assume that a given patient's name does not appear more than once on the report for each physician.

The relational view of this report in shorthand notation is as follows:

DOCTOR (PHYSICIAN-ID, PHYSICIAN-PHONE, (PATIENT#, PATIENT-NAME, LOCATION, PROCEDURE))

This is an unnormalized relation, since there is a repeating group for patient information. Removing the repeating group results in the following relations:

> 3NF: DOCTOR (<u>PHYSICIAN-ID</u>, PHYSICIAN-PHONE)

> 1NF: PATIENT (<u>PHYSICIAN-ID</u>, <u>PATIENT#</u>, PATIENT-NAME, LOCATION, PROCEDURE)

The PATIENT relation is in 1NF, since the patient data in this relation depend only on PATIENT# and not on PHYSICIAN-ID. Removing this partial dependency results in these two relations:

> 3NF: PATIENT (<u>PATIENT#</u>, PATIENT-NAME, LOCATION)

> 3NF: TREATMENT (<u>PHYSICIAN-ID</u>, <u>PATIENT#</u>, PROCEDURE)

These relations are now in 3NF. The set of relations for the Physician Report is therefore as follows:

8. (<u>PHYSICIAN-ID</u>, PHYSICIAN-PHONE)
9. (<u>PATIENT#</u>, PATIENT-NAME, LOCATION)
10. (<u>PHYSICIAN-ID</u>, <u>PATIENT#</u>, PROCEDURE)

View Integration

At this point we have developed a set of ten 3NF functions from the four user views used to illustrate logical data base design at Mountain View Community Hospital. However, several of these relations have duplicate primary keys and therefore may be merged. Relations 1, 5, 6, and 9 all have PATIENT# as a primary key. All these relations are merged to form a single PATIENT relation with PATIENT# as the primary key. Similarly, relations 4 and 7 are merged, since they both have LOCATION as the primary key.

The final set of 3NF relations for Mountain View Community Hospital is shown in Figure 8-13. There is now a total of six relations representing the four user views. An analysis of each of these six relations indicates that no unwanted dependencies exist and they are actually in 4NF.

Conceptual Data Model

After carefully checking the normalized relations, the design team developed a graphical version of the conceptual data model. A preliminary version of the conceptual data model for the four user views considered in this analysis is shown in Figure 8-14.

PATIENT (<u>PATIENT#</u>, PATIENT-NAME, PATIENT-ADDRESS, CITY-STATE-ZIP, DATE-ADMITTED, DATE-DISCHARGED, EXP-DISCH-DATE, <u>LOCATION</u>, THIRD-PARTY)

ROOM (<u>LOCATION</u>, ACCOM, EXTENSION, <u>PATIENT#</u>)

PHYSICIAN (<u>PHYSICIAN-ID</u>, PHYSICIAN-PHONE)

ITEM (<u>ITEM-CODE</u>, DESCRIPTION)

TREATMENT (<u>PHYSICIAN-ID</u>, <u>PATIENT#</u>, PROCEDURE)

CHARGES (<u>PATIENT#</u>, <u>ITEM-CODE</u>, CHARGE)

Figure 8-13
3NF relations for Mountain View Community Hospital.

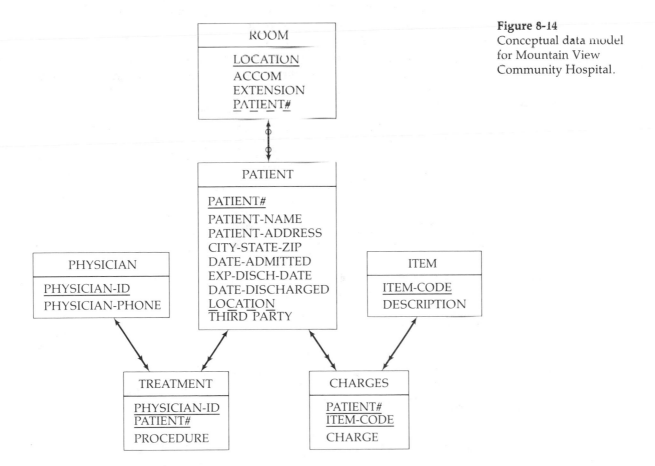

Figure 8-14
Conceptual data model for Mountain View Community Hospital.

Here are the rules for forming a graphical model from 3NF relations:

1. A relation that has a composite key represents an association between two or more entities. The graphical model shows the association between such a relation and the relations that contain the composite key.

2. A relation that has a foreign key has an association with another relation that uses this foreign key as its primary key.

The relation CHARGES has a composite key: (<u>PATIENT#</u>, <u>ITEM-CODE</u>). Therefore, there is an association between the PATIENT and CHARGES relations and between the PATIENT and ITEM relations. The association is one-to-many from PATIENT to CHARGES, since each patient will be charged for several items. Similarly, there is a one-to-many association from ITEM to CHARGES.

The relation TREATMENT represents the association between physicians and patients. There is a 1:M association between PHYSICIAN and TREATMENT and a 1:M association between PATIENT and TREATMENT.

The association between ROOM and PATIENT is a conditional association in both directions (the conditional association was introduced in Chapter 2). The association from ROOM to PATIENT is conditional because at a given time, a hospital bed may be assigned to a patient or it may be unassigned. Also, the association from PATIENT to ROOM is conditional since at a given time a patient may or may not be assigned to a hospital bed (for example, the person may be an outpatient or may have already been discharged from the hospital). These conditional associations are designated by an arrow with circles in Figure 8-14.

COMPUTER-ASSISTED DB DESIGN

Developing a conceptual data model by synthesizing individual user views is clearly a time-consuming process. A conceptual data model for a medium-sized corporation may contain hundreds (or even thousands) of attributes or data items. Fortunately, computer-based design tools are available to assist the design process. These software tools accept descriptions of individual normalized relations and synthesize them into corporatewide data models.

In this section, we briefly describe one such design tool, DATA DESIGNER (see Database Design Inc.), illustrating its use by applying it to the design of the conceptual data model for Mountain View Community Hospital.

Using DATA DESIGNER

Input to DATA DESIGNER consists of relations in 3NF. Each 3NF relation is encoded using a standard input language, with each entry representing an attribute or data item. The following symbols are used:

K designates a primary key attribute.
1 designates a one-to-one relationship.
M designates a one-to-many relationship.
C designates a concatenated key.

To illustrate, let us suppose that we want to encode the following relationship:

The input in DATA DESIGNER is coded as follows:

    K, STUDENT#
    1, STUDENT-NAME

Now let us expand the diagram as follows:

This is coded as follows:

    K, STUDENT#
    1, STUDENT-NAME
    M, COURSE#

A concatenated key is encoded using the symbols K and C. For example, consider the following:

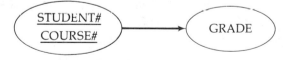

    K, STUDENT#
    C, COURSE#
    1, GRADE

Coding the Hospital Data

With this brief description of DATA DESIGNER, we can now describe coding the input data for Mountain View Community Hospital. These input data are shown in Figure 8-15. The data were input in batch mode; however, DATA DESIGNER will also support on-line mode.

The input data were coded directly from the four views (Figures 8-9 through 8-12). First, data from the Patient Bill (Figure 8-9) were encoded. The symbol V in line 100 of Figure 8-15 stands for "view" and introduces a new data group. The symbols F (line 200) and T (line 300) are used for recording physical characteristics of the data. They are not used in this example and so are encoded with zeros.

Line 400 states that the key of this relation is PATIENT#. Lines 500 through 900 describe the remaining items in the header of the Patient Bill that are dependent on PATIENT# (remember that the symbol 1 designates a 1:1 relationship).

Line 1000 introduces a new group of data items, representing the line items that appear in the body of the Patient Bill. Line 1300 designates ITEM-CODE as a key attribute, and line 1400 indicates that ITEM-DESCRIPTION is dependent on this key. Lines 1800 and 1900 define the concatenated key PATIENT# plus ITEM-CODE, and line 2000 indicates that ITEM-CHARGE was dependent on this concatenated key (as assumed in the text description of the Patient Bill). This completes the encoding of the data items for Patient Bill.

Notice that in encoding the data from the user view, the analyst is continuously normalizing the data. The data from the user views are presented to DATA DESIGNER in third normal form (or higher normal forms, if appropriate).

The data items for the Room Utilization Report (Figure 8-10) are encoded in lines 2100 through 2900. First, LOCATION is designated a key (line 2400). ACCOM is dependent on LOCATION (line 2500). In line 2600, it was assumed that there may be only one patient associated with a given LOCATION. In line 2700, PATIENT# is designated as a key, followed by the attributes PATIENT-NAME, and EXP-DISCH-DATE that are dependent on it. In specifying PATIENT# as a key, the analyst is removing a transitive, or "hidden," dependency.

The data items for the remaining two views are also encoded in Figure 8-15. You should study each of these views (Figures 8-11 and 8-12) and note how the data are encoded in Figure 8-15.

DATA DESIGNER Output

DATA DESIGNER synthesizes the user views into an integrated data model. It produces a variety of reports and graphical outputs that describe the resulting data model.

DATA DESIGNER grouped the input data items for the hospital into six groups. These data groups correspond to the six 3NF relations shown in

```
DDDG0008I THIS IS BATCH MODE.
   >FILE
FILE NAME                                              TYPE
―――――――――――――――――――――――――――――――――――――――――――――――――――――――――
MNTVIEW                                                $DIC
MTNVIEW                                                $SUB
      >LIST MTNVIEW
         0: $VAL
       100: V    STMT-OF-ACCT-PATIENT
       200: F    0000
       300: T    0000
       400: K    PATIENT#
       500: 1    PATIENT-NAME
       600: 1    PATIENT-ADDRESS
       700: 1    CITY-STATE-ZIP
       800: 1    DATE-ADMITTED           4400: F    0000
       900: 1    DATE-DISCHARGED         4500: T    0000
      1000: V    STMT-OF-ACCT-ITEMS      4600: K    PHYSICIAN ID
      1100: F    0000                    4700: 1    PHYSICIAN-PHONE
      1200: T    0000                    4800: M    PHYSICIAN-ID
      1300: K    ITEM-CODE               4900: C    PATIENT#
      1400: 1    ITEM-DESCRIPTION        5000: K    PHYSICIAN-ID
      1500: V    STMT-OF-ACCT-CHARGES    5100: C    PATIENT#
      1600: F    0000                    5200: 1    PROCEDURE
      1700: T    0000                    5300: V    PHYSICIAN-REPORT-PATIENT-INFO
      1800: K    PATIENT#                5400: F    0000
      1900: C    ITEM-CODE               5500: T    0000
      2000: 1    ITEM-CHARGE             5600: K    PATIENT#
      2100: V    ROOM                    5700: 1    PATIENT-NAME
      2200: F    0000                    5800: 1    LOCATION
      2300: T    0000                DDLS0114I THE FILE WAS LISTED.
      2400: K    LOCATION                >LIST MNTVIEW
      2500: 1    ACCOM                    100: ACCOM
      2600: 1    PATIENT#                 200: CITY-STATE-ZIP
      2700: K    PATIENT#                 300: DATE-ADMITTED
      2800: 1    PATIENT-NAME             400: DATE-DISCHARGED
      2900: 1    EXP-DISCH-DATE           500: EXP-DISCHARGE
      3000: V    PATIENT-DISPLAY          600: EXTENSION
      3100: F    0000                     700: ITEM-CHARGE
      3200: T    0000                     800: ITEM-CODE
      3300: K    LOCATION                 900: ITEM-DESCRIPTION
      3400: 1    EXTENSION               1000: LOCATION
      3500: 1    PATIENT#                1100: PATIENT-ADDRESS
      3600: K    PATIENT#                1200: PATIENT-NAME
      3700: 1    PATIENT-NAME            1300: PATIENT#
      3800: 1    PATIENT-ADDRESS         1400: PHYSICIAN-ID
      3900: 1    CITY-STATE-ZIP          1450: PHYSICIAN-PHONE
      4000: 1    DATE-ADMITTED           1500: PROCEDURE
      4100: 1    DATE-DISCHARGED         1600: THIRD-PARTY
      4200: 1    THIRD-PARTY         DDLS0114I THE FILE WAS LISTED.
      4300: V    PHYSICIAN-REPORT        >VALIDATE MTNVIEW MNTVIEW
```

Figure 8-16
Data groups produced by
DATA DESIGNER.

REPORT 001: DATA GROUP LINKS

FROM DATA GROUP	TO DATA GROUP	LINK TYPE
1 (PATIENT)	3	MANY
	4	ONE
	6	MANY
2 (ITEM)	3	MANY
3 (CHARGES)	1	ONE
	2	ONE
4 (ROOM)	1	MANY
5 (PHYSICIAN)	6	MANY
6 (TREATMENT)	5	ONE
	1	ONE

Figures 8-13 and 8-14. A DATA DESIGNER report showing the six data groups and the links between the data groups is shown in Figure 8-16. We have added the name of each relation (from Figure 8-14) to each data group so that you may readily identify it. You should compare the DATA DE-SIGNER output (Figure 8-16) with Figure 8-14 to verify that they are in agreement.

DATA DESIGNER also produces a detailed report showing the composition of each group. Typical output showing the first two groups is given in Figure 8-17. The output shows the primary key for each group, followed by the "owned" data items. The links between groups are also indicated.

Although not shown here, DATA DESIGNER can also produce graphical output portraying the conceptual data model.

DATA VOLUME AND USAGE ANALYSIS

The conceptual data model completes the "architectural plan" (logical design) of the data base. However, once the design has been completed, the designer should return to the user and collect additional data concerning the prospective use of the model. In effect, data volume and usage analysis is an additional step in requirements analysis that is best postponed until after the conceptual model has been completed. In addition to providing useful data, this analysis may reveal inconsistencies in the conceptual model that need to be corrected.

Figure 8-17
Two hospital data groups
(DATA DESIGNER).

REPORT 002: GENERATED CANONICAL SCHEMA

DATA GROUP 1

KEY OR CONCATENATED KEY
PATIENT-NUMBER

OWNED DATA ITEMS	ACCESS TRAFFIC	RESPONSE TIME WT.	MIN	MAX
PATIENT-NO.	0	0.0	0	0
PATIENT-NAME	0	0.0	0	0
PATIENT-ADDRESS	0	0.0	0	0
CITY-STATE-ZIP	0	0.0	0	0
DATE-ADMITTED	0	0.0	0	0
DATE-DISCHARGED	0	0.0	0	0
THIRD-PARTY	0	0.0	0	0
EXP-DISCHARGE	0	0.0	0	0

LINKS TO OTHER DATA GROUPS

LINK TO DATA GROUP	3 (MANY)
LINK TO DATA GORUP	4 (ONE)
LINK TO DATA GROUP	6 (MANY)

REPORT 002: GENERATED CANONICAL SCHEMA

DATA GROUP 2

KEY OR CONCATENATED KEY.

ITEM CODE

OWNED DATA ITEMS	ACCESS TRAFFIC	RESPONSE TIME WT.	MIN	MAX
ITEM-CODE	0	0.0	0	0
ITEM-DESCRIPTION	0	0.0	0	0

LINKS TO OTHER DATA GROUPS

LINK TO DATA GROUP	3 (MANY)

Figure 8-18
Conceptual data model
with volumes and ratios.

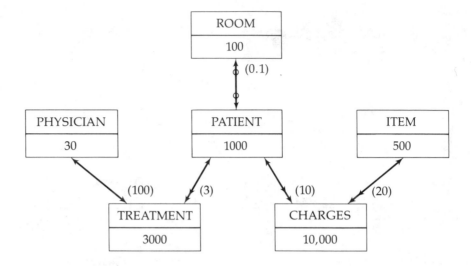

Data volume analysis is concerned with estimating the number of each type of logical entity that must be represented in the data base, both now and in the future. For example, how many PATIENT data entities or records must be stored? **Data usage analysis** is concerned with estimating the frequencies with which each data entity will be accessed, given the various transactions that will be required to access and update the data base. The statistics collected during data volume and usage analysis are vital inputs to the physical data base design process.

Data Volume Analysis for Mountain View Community Hospital

A simplified picture of the conceptual data model for Mountain View Community Hospital is shown in Figure 8-18. Each entity is represented by a rectangle, but the attributes have been omitted. Inside each rectangle is a number representing the estimated average volume for that entity. For example, it is estimated that an average of 1000 PATIENT entities must be accommodated in the data base at any one time. The numbers adjacent to the arrowheads are estimates of the average number of a given entity type associated with a related entity type. For example, Figure 8-18 indicates that there is an average of ten CHARGES associated with each PATIENT at any given time.

The data base design team at Mountain View Community Hospital made the estimates in consultation with users. Since there are 100 beds at the hospital, the maximum number of admitted patients at any one time is limited to 100. However, the accounting staff indicated that the records for an average patient would probably be kept active for about 30 days. Since the average length of stay for a patient is 3 days, the total number of active patient records is expected to be 100×30/3, or 1000. After an average period of 30 days, a Patient record would be archived.

Further discussions with the hospital accounting staff revealed that each patient incurs an average of 10 CHARGES during a hospitalization. Thus, the number of CHARGE entities is expected to be 10×1000, or 10,000. Also, there are 500 separate ITEMS (treatments, pharmacy items, and so forth) that may appear on a patient's bill. Thus, the average number of CHARGES outstanding for a given ITEM is 10,000/500, or 20, as shown in Figure 8-18.

The design team also conferred with the medical staff and discovered that each patient receives an average of 3 treatments. Thus, the average number of TREATMENT entities in the data base is 3×1000, or 3000. Since Mountain View Community Hospital has a staff of 30 physicians who treat patients, the average number of TREATMENT entities for each PHYSICIAN is 3000/30, or 100.

Data Usage Analysis for Mountain View Community Hospital

In data usage analysis, the analyst identifies the major transactions required against the data base. Each transaction is then analyzed to determine the access paths used and the estimated frequency of use. When all transactions have been analyzed, the composite load map is then prepared, showing the total usage of access paths on the conceptual model.

At Mountain View Community Hospital, a systems analyst (Mr. Thomas) was assigned to work with the design team in analyzing user transactions. The data administrator felt that there were three advantages in having an applications specialist assist the design team during this phase of the study. First, the systems analyst could assist the team in identifying access paths for each transaction. Second, the information developed during this phase would be a starting point for designing transaction-processing programs. And finally, having a systems analyst work with the design team would foster cooperation between the data base group and the rest of the information systems organization.

The data base design team used a form for analyzing each transaction at the hospital. Figure 8-19 shows the use of this form for the analysis of the transaction Create Patient Bill. This transaction causes a Patient record to be read along with the detail of patient charges and also causes a bill to be produced in the format of Figure 8-9. After talking with persons in accounting, the analysts estimated an average transaction volume of 2 per hour and a peak volume of 10 per hour.

The number of logical references per transaction and per period are recorded on the form. Create Patient Bill requires only one PATIENT reference per transaction. At peak volume, this translates to 10 references per hour. Each PATIENT has an average of 10 CHARGES. Therefore, the average number of times the PATIENT-CHARGES path is used per transaction is

Figure 8-19
Analysis of the
transaction Create Patient
Bill.

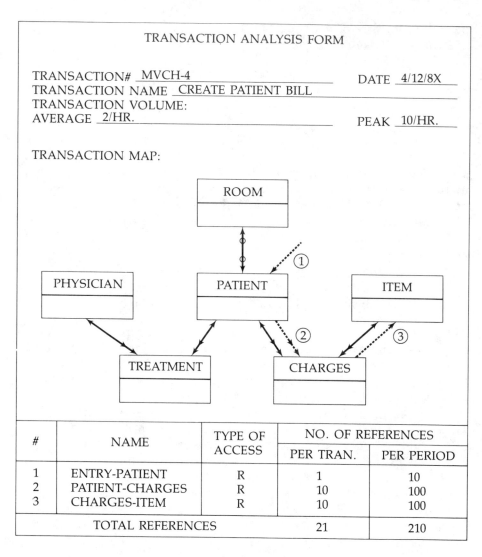

TRANSACTION ANALYSIS FORM

TRANSACTION# _MVCH-4_   DATE _4/12/8X_
TRANSACTION NAME _CREATE PATIENT BILL_
TRANSACTION VOLUME:
AVERAGE _2/HR._   PEAK _10/HR._

TRANSACTION MAP:

#	NAME	TYPE OF ACCESS	NO. OF REFERENCES	
			PER TRAN.	PER PERIOD
1	ENTRY-PATIENT	R	1	10
2	PATIENT-CHARGES	R	10	100
3	CHARGES-ITEM	R	10	100
TOTAL REFERENCES			21	210

10; this translates to a peak volume of 10×10, or 100, per hour. Since the CHARGES-ITEM path is traversed once for each CHARGE, this also results in a peak usage of 100 per hour. The analysts chose to use peak volumes to estimate references per period, since this would measure the maximum load on the data base.

Logical Access Map.   A map for the transaction Create Patient Bill is shown in the middle of Figure 8-19. The dashed line that is superimposed on the conceptual model shows the access path for this transaction. The entry point is at the PATIENT entity, then to the entity CHARGES, then from each CHARGE to ITEM to pick up the description for that CHARGE.

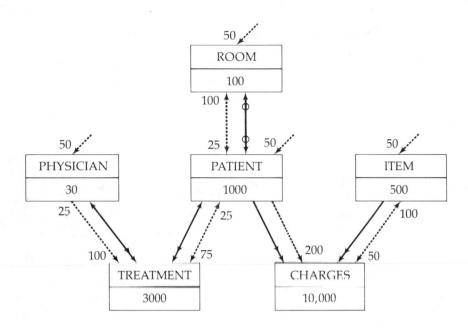

Figure 8-20
Composite usage map
(Mountain View
Community Hospital).

A detailed analysis of each step in the access path is entered at the bottom of the form. The "type of access" to each entity is recorded using the following codes:

R designates to read an entity.
I designates to insert a new entity.
U designates to update an entity.
D designates to delete an entity.

For the Create Patient Bill transaction, each access is coded with an R, since this transaction requires "read" only.

Composite Usage Map. There are many other transactions for the data base in addition to Create Patient Bill, such as Record New Treatment, Record New Patient Charge, and Display Patient Data. When all these transactions have been analyzed, the analysts can combine the data and display them in the form of a composite usage map. A sample composite usage map for Mountain View Community Hospital is shown in Figure 8-20. The number in each rectangle shows the estimated number of entities of that type (e.g., 1000 patients). The number at the head of each dashed arrow is an estimate of the total number of references on a given access path at a peak volume. For example, the number of references to the entity TREATMENT from the entity PATIENT is estimated at 75 per hour. Also, the number of references to PATIENT from outside the model is estimated at 50 per hour.

The composite usage map is a concise reference to the estimated volume and usage of data in the data base. It provides a basis for physical data base design, during which the analysts must design storage structures and access strategies to optimize performance.

SUMMARY

In this chapter, we have introduced conceptual data base design, the second task in the overall data base design process. The steps in conceptual design include data modeling, view integration, conceptual schema development, design review, and logical access mapping. The major products (or deliverables) from this process are the conceptual data model, logical access maps for each transaction, and a composite usage map.

The information systems plan (described in Chapter 3) provides an overall framework for conceptual design. The enterprise model shows the major entities of the organization and their relationships. Also, the business charts delineate the functions, processes, and activities of the organization (see Figure 3-6), thereby helping to identify the transactions required to process the data base.

CHAPTER REVIEW

Review Questions

1. Give concise definitions for each of the following terms:
   a. conceptual data model
   b. entity analysis
   c. attribute synthesis
   d. data modeling
   e. view integration

2. Briefly describe five steps in conceptual design.

3. Describe four different forms in which the conceptual data model can be represented.

4. In the design review, the conceptual data model should be evaluated from two points of view. What are they?

5. Briefly summarize the rules for forming a graphical data model from a set of 3NF relations.

6. What conflict arises when an organization attempts to defer selecting a data base management system until after conceptual design is completed?

7. What is a composite usage map? What is its purpose?

8. What is the disadvantage of expressing the conceptual data model in the format of a particular DBMS?

9. Why is data volume and usage analysis performed after the conceptual data model is completed?

10. Why is a bottom-up approach favored over a top-down approach in conceptual design?

11. Contrast the following terms:
    a. global approach; application approach
    b. entity analysis; attribute synthesis
    c. data volume analysis; data usage analysis
    d. logical access map; composite usage map

Problems and Exercises

1. Examine the sample conceptual data model for a distributing company (Figure 8-4).
   a. Draw a simplified version of this model by selecting between 10 and 15 of the most important entities. Use the convention for drawing arrows that we have used throughout the text. This simplified model might correspond to a planning-level data model (or enterprise model).
   b. Suppose that the company represented in the model shown in Figure 8-4 decides to implement each cluster as a separate data base. Draw lines (or boxes) indicating the boundary of each data base.
   c. Discuss how an association between entities in different data bases might be implemented. For example, in Figure 8-4, there is an association between Style (Product cluster) and Part (Parts cluster).

2. Draw a logical access map for the Create Patient Bill transaction using the format shown in Figure 7-18.

3. Record sample metadata (such as those shown in Figure 8-7) for the Physician Report (Figure 8-12).

4. Expand the conceptual data model for Mountain View Community Hospital by including Third Party information. We want to include the following attributes: THIRD-PARTY-ID, ADDRESS, PHONE#. Assume that a given Patient may subscribe to zero, one, or many third parties.

5. Examine the TREATMENT entity for Mountain View Community Hospital (Figure 8-14). Suppose that the composite key (PHYSICIAN-ID, PATIENT#)

does not uniquely identify a PROCEDURE (i.e., a given physician may perform more than one procedure on a given patient on a given day). Suggest how the TREATMENT entity could be modified to accommodate this situation. How would the Physician Report (Figure 8-12) have to be modified to reflect this change?

6. Devise a design review questionnaire (such as the one in Figure 8-5) for the Mountain View Community Hospital conceptual data model (Figure 8-14).

7. Draw logical access maps for each of the following transactions:
   a. Admit Patient.
   b. Transfer Patient (to a different room).
   c. Create Room Utilization Report (Figure 8-10).
   d. Create Physician Report (Figure 8-12).

8. The relations shown in Figure 8-13 are in 3NF. Examine each relation and state whether it is (or is not) also in:
   a. BCNF
   b. 4NF

9. Examine the transaction Create Patient Bill (Figure 8-19). Suppose that during the design review, the transaction volume figures are revised as follows:
   Average: 5 per hour
   Peak: 15 per hour
   Revise the number of references in the diagram to reflect this change.

10. Following are several 3NF relations. Merge these relations to produce a new set of relations, also in 3NF. Then draw a graphical model of the merged relations.
   a. STUDENT (ST#, STNAME, PHONE#)
   b. COURSE (CRS#, NAME)
   c. MAJOR (ST#, MAJOR)
   d. ENROLL (ST#, CRS#, SECTION#)
   e. UNITS (CRS#, NAME, UNITS)
   f. TEXT (CRS#, SECTION#, TEXTNAME)
   g. LOCATION (CRS#, SECTION#, ROOM#)

11. An invoice form used by Pine Valley Furniture Company is shown in Figure 8-21. One such invoice is submitted to a customer for each shipment. There may be one or more shipments for each customer order (multiple shipments result when items must be back-ordered).
   a. Derive a set of 3NF relations for this document (user view).
   b. Merge the 3NF relations for the invoice with the 3NF relations for the customer order (Figure 7-19).
   c. Develop a conceptual data model (graphical form) for the merged relations.
   d. Encode the two views in DATA DESIGNER input language.

Figure 8-21
Customer invoice (Pine
Valley Furniture).

CUSTOMER NO: 1273   INVOICE NO: 06389

NAME CONTEMPORARY DESIGNS   DATE: 11/5/8X

ADDRESS: 123 OAK ST.   ORDER NO: 61384

CITY-STATE-ZIP: AUSTIN, TX. 28384

PRODUCT NO.	DESCRIPTION	QTY ORD.	QTY SHIP.	QTY BACK.	UNIT PRICE	TOTAL PRICE
B381	CABINET	2	2		150.00	300.00
M128	BOOKCASE	4	2	2	200.00	400.00
R210	TABLE	1	1		500.00	500.00
				TOTAL AMOUNT		1200.00
				5.0% DISCOUNT		60.00
				AMOUNT DUE		1140.00

12. For the conceptual data model developed in Problem 11, develop logical access maps for the following transactions:

   a. Enter New Customer Order.

   b. Create Customer Invoice.

13. Express the conceptual data model for Mountain View Community Hospital as an Entity-Relationship diagram (similar to the one in Figure 6-22).

References

Auerbach Publishers. 1980. *Practical Database Management*. Princeton, N.J.: Auerbach Publishers.

Couger, J. Daniel, Mel A. Colter, and R.W. Knapp. 1982. *Advanced System Development/Feasibility Techniques*. New York: Wiley.

Database Design Inc. Information on DATA DESIGNER© is available from Database Design Inc., 2020 Hogback Rd., Ann Arbor, Mich. 48104.

Davis, Gordon B. 1974. *Management Information Systems: Conceptual Foundations, Structure, and Development*. New York: McGraw-Hill.

Hubbard, George V. 1981. *Computer-Assisted Data Base Design*. New York: Van Nostrand Reinhold.

Martin, James. 1983. *Managing the Data-Base Environment*. Englewood Cliffs, N.J.: Prentice-Hall.

Teorey, T.J., and J.P. Fry. 1982. *Design of Database Structures*. Englewood Cliffs, N.J.: Prentice-Hall.

9

Implementation and Physical Design

INTRODUCTION

The conceptual data model described in Chapter 8 is a model of the organization and its data, completely independent of any data base management system or any other software or hardware considerations. That model must then be refined so that it can be implemented on the DBMS used by the organization.

As shown in Figure 9-1, the refinement of the conceptual data model occurs in two stages: implementation design and physical design. **Implementation design** is concerned with mapping the conceptual data model into a DBMS-processible logical model or schema. The logical model is usually in the form of a network, relational, or hierarchical data model (or some combination of these models). **Physical design** is concerned with selecting file organizations, access methods, and related factors.

Implementation design and physical design are the last steps in the data base design process and must be performed carefully, since they affect performance, integrity, security, and a number of other factors that have a direct impact on users.

IMPLEMENTATION DESIGN

Implementation design starts with the conceptual data model and maps (or transforms) that model into a logical model that conforms to a particular DBMS. Also, specifications for programs to access the data base can be formulated during implementation design.

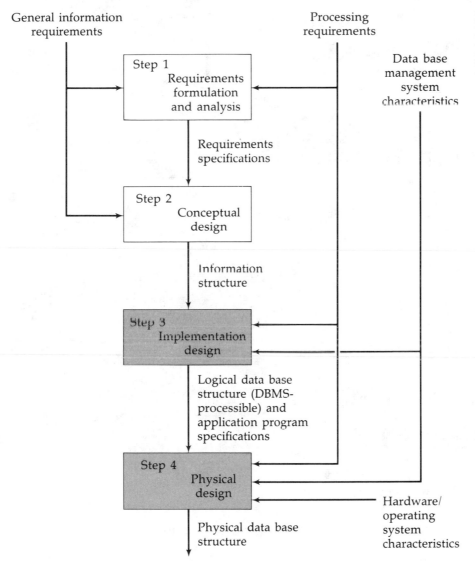

Figure 9-1
Implementation and physical design.
(Source: Teorey and Fry 1982.)

Components of Implementation Design

The major components (inputs and outputs) of implementation design are shown in Figure 9-2.

Inputs. Here are the major inputs to implementation design (Teorey and Fry 1982):

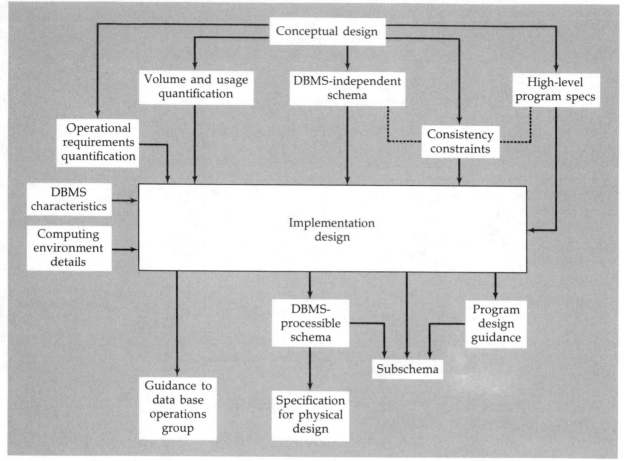

Figure 9-2
Implementation design
process.
(Source: Teorey and Fry
1982.)

1. DBMS-independent schema: the conceptual data model, described in Chapter 8.

2. Operational requirements quantification: specifications for response times, security, integrity, recovery, and archiving of data. These specifications are developed during requirements analysis (Chapter 7).

3. Volume and usage quantification: data volumes and usage figures, which are superimposed on the conceptual data model (described in Chapters 7 and 8).

4. Consistency constraints: rules for keeping data items mutually consistent, both within and between records.

5. High-level program specifications: definitions of access patterns for data base transactions. These definitions may be expressed in the form of logical access maps (described in Chapters 7 and 8).

6. DBMS characteristics: the logical constructs and data definition language of the DBMS to be used.

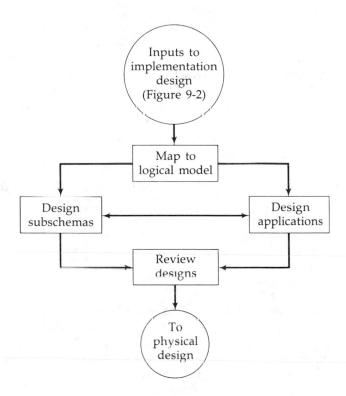

Figure 9-3
Major steps in
implementation design.

Outputs. Here are the major outputs of implementation design (Teorey and Fry 1982):

1. DBMS-processible schema: a schema (or data model) that can be implemented directly on the chosen DBMS.

2. Subschemas: DBMS-processible external views and security constraints on these views.

3. Specifications for physical design: fully documented schemas, subschemas, and volume and usage information.

4. Program design guidance: skeleton program designs, which may be expressed in the form of data base action diagrams (described later).

5. Guidance to data base operations: summary of requirements and constraints for data administration and operations.

Steps in Implementation Design

The major steps in implementation design are shown in Figure 9-3. Although the steps are shown in the general sequence in which they are performed, the process is actually one of progressive refinement with feedback among the various steps.

Mapping to a Logical Model.   The most important step in implementation design is to map the conceptual data model into a DBMS-processible data model, which we will call a **logical model** (also referred to as a **schema**). The magnitude of this effort will depend on the form of expression of the conceptual data model and the logical model to which it is mapped.

The conceptual data model may be expressed in any one of several forms, the most typical being the entity-relationship model, the semantic data model, the data structure diagram (or relational map), and a set of relations in third normal form. On the other hand, most contemporary data base management systems support one or more of the following logical models: hierarchical, network, relational, and inverted file (a relational-like model). Thus, the mapping task may range from complex (such as mapping from an entity-relationship model to a hierarchical model) to trivial (such as when the conceptual and logical models are both relational).

We will illustrate mapping a conceptual data model to the hierarchical, network, and relational data models in the next section.

Designing Subschemas.   A **subschema** is a working subset of the schema (logical model). A large number of subschemas are normally defined on a given schema. Each subschema represents a user view and provides an interface that allows a user application program to access the data base. To design subschemas, we start with the individual user views and map them into logical data submodels.

Designing Programs.   As each subschema is defined, the designers can develop outlines of program logic to process data represented in that subschema. The program designs can be most effectively expressed in structured forms referred to as data base action diagrams. We describe and illustrate data base action diagrams later in the chapter.

Conducting a Design Review.   When the preceding steps have been completed, a thorough review of the implementation design should be conducted. Any omissions or inconsistencies should be corrected before proceeding with the physical design.

MAPPING TO A LOGICAL DATA MODEL

The process of mapping to a logical data model depends on the form of the conceptual data model and the form of the target logical model. It may be performed manually, or it may employ computer-assisted design techniques.

Mountain View Community Hospital

We will use the case of Mountain View Community Hospital to illustrate mapping to a logical data model. A conceptual data model based on four user views was developed for this organization in Chapter 8. This model (expressed as a data structure diagram) is repeated in Figure 9-4.

One of the user views used to develop this conceptual data model was the Patient Bill (see Figure 8-9). Consider the set of 3NF relations that was derived from this user view in Chapter 8:

> PATIENT-BILL (<u>PATIENT#</u>, PATIENT-NAME, PATIENT-ADDRESS,
> CITY-STATE-ZIP, DATE-ADMITTED, DATE-DISCHARGED)
> ITEM (<u>ITEM-CODE</u>, DESCRIPTION)
> CHARGES (<u>PATIENT#</u>, <u>ITEM-CODE</u>, CHARGE)

The conceptual model for these relations is shown in Figure 9-5. We refer to this model as the conceptual user view. It is a subset of the conceptual data model that provides the user all the information required to create a patient bill. Like the conceptual model, each conceptual user view must be mapped to a logical model (or subschema) for the DBMS to be used.

Mapping to a Relational Model

The conceptual data models shown in Figures 9-4 and 9-5 are expressed in the form of relations connected by arrows. Therefore, mapping the conceptual models onto a relational model is a straightforward process. Each box in the conceptual model becomes a relation, and attributes in the boxes are attributes of the relations. Arrows in the conceptual data model are simply ignored, since they convey associations that are usually recorded as data within the relations. Thus, when the conceptual data model shown in Figure 9-4 is mapped to a relational model, there are six relations: ROOM, PATIENT, PHYSICIAN, ITEM, TREATMENT, and CHARGES. Also, when the external view in Figure 9-5 is mapped to a relational model, there are three relations: PATIENT-BILL, ITEM, and CHARGES. These two sets of relations are described to the relational DBMS using the schema and external view data definition languages, respectively. We give examples of these languages in Chapter 14.

For the relational model, external views (or user views) are usually expressed in the form of tables. External views for the Patient Bill are shown in Figure 9-6. Each table contains sample data to assist the user in understanding and using that view.

Figure 9-4
3NF relations and
conceptual data model
(Mountain View
Community Hospital).

PATIENT (<u>PATIENT#</u>, PATIENT-NAME, PATIENT-ADDRESS, CITY-STATE-ZIP, DATE-ADMITTED, DATE-DISCHARGED, EXP-DISCH-DATE, <u>LOCATION</u>, THIRD-PARTY)

ROOM (<u>LOCATION</u>, ACCOM, EXTENSION, <u>PATIENT#</u>)

PHYSICIAN (<u>PHYSICIAN-ID</u>, PHYSICIAN-PHONE)

ITEM (<u>ITEM-CODE</u>, DESCRIPTION)

TREATMENT (<u>PHYSICIAN-ID</u>, <u>PATIENT#</u>, PROCEDURE)

CHARGES (<u>PATIENT#</u>, <u>ITEM-CODE</u>, CHARGE)

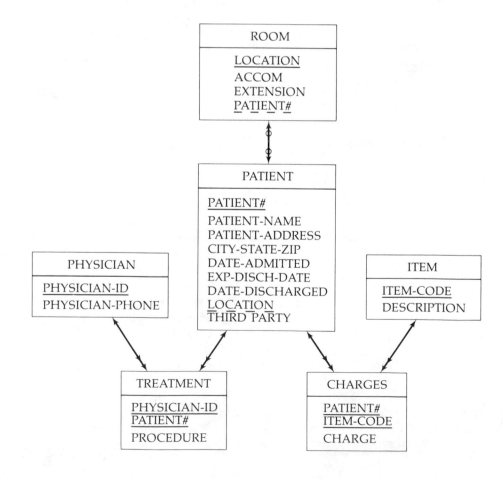

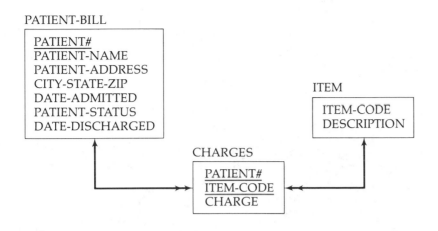

Figure 9-5
Conceptual user view
(Patient Bill).

PATIENT#	PATIENT-NAME	PATIENT-ADDRESS	CITY-STATE-ZIP	DATE ADMITTED	DATE DISCHARGED
3249	BAKER, MARY	300 OAK ST.	MT. VIEW, CO. 80638	09-10-8X	09-14-8X
1837	THOMAS, WM.	137 PINECREST	DENVER, CO. 80180	09-13-8X	09-21-8X
6251	MOORE, ANN	650 VADLE LN	ASPEN, CO. 83149	10-01-8X	10-06-8X
...					

(a)

ITEM-CODE	DESCRIPTION
200	ROOM SEMI-PR
307	X-RAY
413	LAB TESTS
...	

(b)

PATIENT#	ITEM-CODE	CHARGE
3249	200	150.00
3249	307	25.00
1837	307	35.00
...		

(c)

Figure 9-6
External views (Patient
Bill).
(a) Patient Bill view.
(b) Item view.
(c) Charges view.

Mapping to a Network Model

Since the conceptual data model in Figure 9-4 is expressed in the form of a network data structure diagram, mapping to a network data model is also relatively straightforward. However, some additional steps are required. Assuming that the popular CODASYL data model (described in Chapter 13) is to be used, the following steps are usually required:

1. Define record types and associations.

2. Define sets (owner-member relationships).

3. Eliminate redundant keys (if unneeded).

4. Define record access strategies.

Figure 9-7
Network data model.

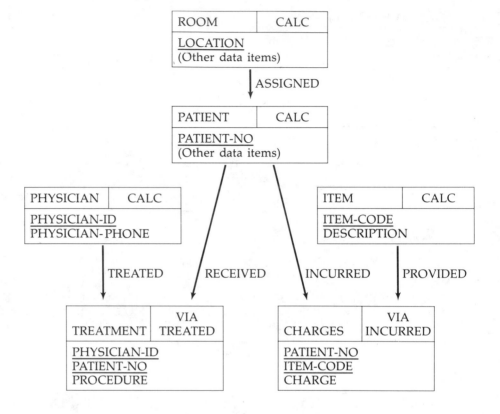

Figure 9-7 shows the result of transforming the conceptual data model (Figure 9-4) to a network data model. Notice that only relatively minor changes have been made in this mapping.

Defining Record Types.   Each box in the conceptual data model becomes a CODASYL record type. For example, there is a PATIENT record type in Figure 9-7. The primary keys are underlined, just as in the conceptual data model. Notice that the data item name PATIENT# in Figure 9-4 has been changed to PATIENT-NO in Figure 9-7 to conform to CODASYL specifications (we explain such details of the CODASYL model in Chapter 13).

In the CODASYL model, a one-to-many association between record types is usually represented by an arrow with a single head. We use this convention in Figure 9-7. For example, there is a 1:*M* association from PHYSICIAN to TREATMENT.

The conditional associations between ROOM and PATIENT in the conceptual model (Figure 9-4) present a problem in mapping to a network model. The CODASYL data model does not explicitly provide for conditional associations. However, a 1:*M* association from entity A to entity B does permit zero, one, or more occurrences of entity B to be associated with each occurrence of entity A. Therefore in Figure 9-7 we show the association from ROOM to PATIENT as a 1:*M* association.

Defining Sets. The set is the basic building block in the CODASYL model. A **set** is a one-to-many association between two record types, where the first record type is called the **owner** and the second record type is called the **member**. Each set type is given a unique name.

In mapping to a network data model, we define a set for each 1:*M* association in the conceptual data model. For example, in Figure 9-7, the 1:*M* association between PHYSICIAN and TREATMENT is defined as a CODASYL set with the name TREATED. PHYSICIAN is the owner record type for this association, while TREATMENT is the member record type. For each occurrence of a PHYSICIAN record type, there may be zero, one, or many associated occurrences of the TREATMENT record type.

In the conceptual data model (Figure 9-4), the association between ROOM and PATIENT is conditional. This means that each patient is either assigned to a room location or else is not assigned (the converse is also true). In the CODASYL model, there is no provision for directly representing conditional associations. However, the CODASYL set does permit each owner record occurrence to have zero or one or more member record occurrences. Therefore, by defining a set (called ASSIGNED) between ROOM and PATIENT, we allow the patient/room association to be represented (however, CODASYL will not enforce only one assignment per location).

Additional properties and constraints of CODASYL sets are defined in Chapter 13.

Eliminating Redundant Keys. In the conceptual data model, composite keys and foreign keys are normally redundant. For example, in Figure 9-4, the composite key for CHARGES is (PATIENT#, ITEM-CODE). Each of these data items is contained in the "parent" record type (in this case, PATIENT and ITEM). Also, the PATIENT relation (or record type) contains the foreign key LOCATION, which is the primary key of the ROOM relation.

When mapping to a CODASYL data model, these duplicate keys are candidates for elimination. For example, the composite key (PATIENT#, ITEM-CODE) can be eliminated from the CHARGES record type, and the LOCATION data item can be eliminated from the PATIENT record type. These duplicated keys can be eliminated because the associations they represent are implied by the CODASYL sets.

Whether keys should in fact be eliminated (to avoid redundancy) is a design decision. In general, keys should *not* be eliminated if either of the following two conditions holds:

1. The key in question is required for direct access to a record (e.g., the composite key (PATIENT#, ITEM-CODE) could be used for direct access to CHARGES records if this is a requirement).

2. The key in question is normally required for reference purposes and if removed will often necessitate referencing the owner record occurrence.

To illustrate the second situation, suppose that in examining an occurrence of a PATIENT record, we normally need to identify the patient's location. If LOCATION were removed from the PATIENT record type, we would have to reference a ROOM record occurrence (owner record) to determine this information. Or suppose that we eliminated (PATIENT#, ITEM-CODE) from the CHARGES record type. In examining a CHARGES record for a particular patient, the user could not determine the item code without referencing an ITEM record occurrence.

In summary, deciding whether or not to eliminate keys requires a trade-off between redundancy and performance. The designers must consider the anticipated usage patterns (identified during requirements analysis) to evaluate each individual case. In Figure 9-7, we have retained the redundant data items so that they can be used for reference purposes.

Defining Record Access Strategies.   The last major step in mapping to a network model is to define the basic techniques to be used to access occurrences of each record type in the model. Although there are many variations, there are two basic record access strategies in the CODASYL model:

1. CALC: we access records directly by supplying a primary key value.

2. VIA: we access records through a set relationship; that is, we first access an owner record occurrence (often using CALC), and then we access each set member occurrence for that owner.

The access strategies to be used depend on the way data will be accessed by various users and their applications. These usage patterns are expressed in the form of a composite usage map (described in Chapter 8). A composite usage map for Mountain View Community Hospital was shown in Figure 8-20. Referring to this map, we see that four record types are normally accessed directly (i.e., from outside the model). These record types are PATIENT, ROOM, PHYSICIAN, and ITEM. The remaining two record types (TREATMENT and CHARGES) are normally accessed by following set relationships. As shown in Figure 8-20, TREATMENT record occurrences are accessed from their owner PHYSICIAN records (100 references per period) and from their owner PATIENT records (75 references per period). Similarly, CHARGES records are accessed from PATIENT records (200 references per period) and from ITEM records (50 references per period).

Based on this information, the access strategies for the record types in the network data model are shown in Figure 9-7. The CALC (or random access) technique is used for PATIENT, PHYSICIAN, ITEM, and ROOM records. TREATMENT records are accessed VIA the TREATED set type, since the frequency of access is greater than for the RECEIVED set type (100 references per period versus 75 references per period). For the same reason, CHARGES records are accessed VIA the INCURRED set.

The VIA clause defines the primary access path to records. Records can also be accessed through secondary access paths. For example, TREAT-MENT records can be accessed using the RECEIVED set relationship, as well as using the TREATED set relationship. However, secondary access paths are nearly always slower and less efficient. We describe the details of various CODASYL access strategies in much more detail in Chapter 13.

Ideally, record access strategies would not be defined during implementation design but during physical design. By defining these strategies during implementation design (and therefore in the schema), we lose some data independence. Thus, if we later decide to change the access strategy for a particular record type (say, from VIA to CALC), this will require that we alter the schema. What is worse, changing the schema often requires that application programs be modified, since application logic often varies with the access strategies that are used.

In essence, the CODASYL approach to data base implementation provides efficient, rapid access, provided that predefined access paths are used. However, the CODASYL approach is somewhat less flexible and therefore more resistant to change than some other models (especially the relational model).

CODASYL Subschemas. We obtain each CODASYL subschema by mapping the conceptual user view to a network model. Figure 9-8 shows the network user view that is obtained by mapping the conceptual user view for Patient Bill. Notice that the only difference in these two models is that the set names INCURRED and PROVIDED have been added in Figure 9-8. Record access strategies (CALC and VIA) are not specified in the subschema, since they are the same as in the logical model (Figure 9-7).

Mapping to a Hierarchical Model

Since the hierarchical data model has several restrictions, mapping a conceptual model to a hierarchical model often presents some problems. Several arbitrary choices must be made, and there is no "correct" result. The mapping is usually performed in two stages: mapping the conceptual model to a DBMS-independent hierarchical model and then mapping the hierarchical model to conform to a particular hierarchical DBMS.

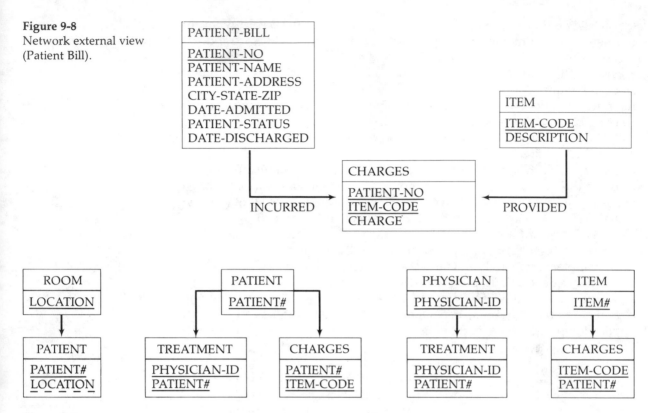

Figure 9-8
Network external view
(Patient Bill).

Figure 9-9
Hierarchical structures.

Hierarchical Data Model. In mapping to a hierarchical model, each box in the conceptual model (Figure 9-4) becomes a "node type" in a hierarchy (or tree structure). Recall from Chapter 5 that each node type in a hierarchy can have only one parent node type. Therefore, it is necessary to refine the conceptual data model by identifying root node types and resolving multiple parentage.

Four hierarchical structures derived from the conceptual data model (Figure 9-4) are shown in Figure 9-9. In this diagram, only the keys are shown; other data items are omitted to simplify the diagram.

Identifying Root Node Types. Each root node type in a hierarchical model defines a data base and provides an entry point to that data base. In Figure 9-9, we have selected four root node types—ROOM, PATIENT, PHYSICIAN, and ITEM—that define four distinct data bases. Thus, a user may access data by starting at any one of these four entry points.

Resolving Multiple Parentage. Since each node type can have only one parent node type, it is necessary to resolve instances of multiple parentage. In Figure 9-4, TREATMENT and CHARGES each have two parents.

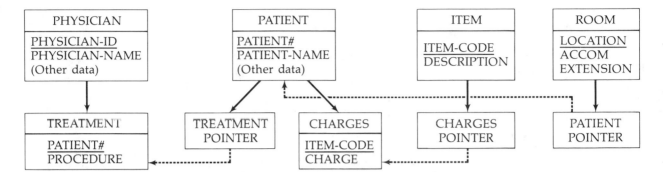

Figure 9-10
Structuring an IMS data base (incorrect version).

To resolve multiple parentage, we must introduce redundancy. One approach is to combine a child node with its parent node. For example, in Figure 9-4, we could combine the TREATMENT node with the PHYSICIAN node. An alternative approach is to repeat node types under two or more parents.

In Figure 9-9, we have resolved multiple parentage by repeating child node types under their parent node types. Thus, TREATMENT appears under both PATIENT and PHYSICIAN, and CHARGES appears under both PATIENT and ITEM. This solution is undesirable, since a great deal of redundancy has been introduced. However, we must remember that Figure 9-9 portrays a logical (not physical) model. Depending on the DBMS used, it may be possible to implement these data bases without excessive redundancy.

DBMS Implementation. The hierarchical structures in Figure 9-9 must be mapped onto a data model for a particular DBMS. A number of hierarchical DBMS products are available. Of these, the most frequently used is IBM's Information Management System (IMS). We illustrate the mapping to an IMS data base in this section, and a detailed description of IMS is provided in Chapter 12.

In IMS, each node is called a **segment**. Although IMS supports a hierarchical data model, it does permit a limited networking capability. Each segment type in IMS can have two parents: a physical parent and a logical parent. The **physical parent** is the parent segment type in the hierarchy. The **logical parent** is a segment type in another hierarchy (or IMS data base) that has a parent/child relationship with the given segment. The logical parent relationship is implemented by means of a **logical pointer**, which is a segment that contains the addresses of logical child segments (but no actual data).

A first attempt at structuring IMS data bases from the hierarchical models is shown in Figure 9-10. Four IMS data bases are shown in the figure, with root segments PHYSICIAN, PATIENT, ITEM, and ROOM. Rather than duplicating the TREATMENT, PATIENT, and CHARGES data (as in Figure 9-9), the logical parent feature of IMS is used in Figure 9-10. For example, the

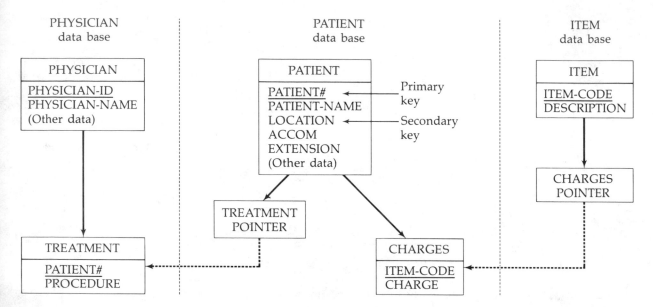

Figure 9-11
Structuring an IMS data base (revised version).

TREATMENT segment type (which appears only once) has PHYSICIAN as its physical parent. PATIENT is the logical parent of TREATMENT, and this relationship is implemented by the logical pointer called TREATMENT POINTER. By using these relationships, a user can access TREATMENT segments using either PHYSICIAN or PATIENT segments as entry points.

Similarly, logical parent relationships are used to avoid duplicating PATIENT and CHARGES data in Figure 9-10. Unfortunately, the structure shown in Figure 9-10 is not feasible, since it violates an important rule of IMS: a logical child cannot itself have a logical child. In Figure 9-10, PATIENT is a logical child of ROOM. But PATIENT, in turn, has a logical child of TREATMENT. Therefore, the structure must be modified. But how? We cannot eliminate the problem by rearranging the logical child relationships.

One solution to the problem is to combine the ROOM and PATIENT segment types into a single segment type. In Figure 9-11, data from the ROOM segment (LOCATION, ACCOM, EXTENSION) have been combined with PATIENT data. This introduces very little redundancy, since the association between PATIENT and LOCATION is 1:1. However, it apparently introduces a new problem: to access room information, it is now necessary to provide a patient number (LOCATION is no longer an entry point).

Fortunately, IMS does provide a facility for secondary keys. As shown in Figure 9-11, PATIENT# is the primary key for the PATIENT segment type, while LOCATION is a secondary key. This allows the user to access a PATIENT segment by providing either a patient number or a location.

The IMS data base shown in Figure 9-11 is now feasible. It contains three data bases, called PHYSICIAN, PATIENT, and ITEM. There are two logical parent relationships: PATIENT is the logical parent of TREATMENT, and ITEM is the logical parent of CHARGES. For each data base, the root node type and its offspring are referred to as a **physical data base record**. For example, in Figure 9-11 the PATIENT, CHARGES, and TREATMENT POINTER segments constitute a physical data base record type.

In structuring an IMS data base, keys that appear in a parent segment (or any segment higher in the hierarchy) are not repeated in a child segment. For example, in Figure 9-11, the item PATIENT# does not appear in the CHARGES segment, since PATIENT# is the primary key of PATIENT, which is the physical parent of CHARGES. However, a key that appears in a logical parent (such as ITEM-CODE) *is* repeated in the logical child segment (in this case, CHARGES).

Alternative Designs.   The data bases shown in Figure 9-11 could have been structured differently. For example, CHARGES could have been made a physical child of ITEM and a logical child of PATIENT. How do designers make these choices? The answer is that in structuring an IMS data base, they make some assumptions about how the data will be used. Access to a physical child segment is usually faster than access to a logical child segment (because of less overhead). Therefore, physical parent/child relationships are used for frequently used access paths, while logical parent/child relationships are used for secondary access paths. In Figure 9-11, the assumption is that CHARGES segments are most often accessed via PATIENT segments (as in preparing a patient bill). However, they may also be accessed from ITEM segments if necessary.

As we have seen, in designing an IMS (or other hierarchical) data base, the designer is forced into making some decisions about how the data will be used. This results in some loss in data independence; if the assumptions are wrong (or the usage patterns change), then the data base structure itself may have to be modified to improve performance. In Figure 9-11, for example, we may have to move the TREATMENT segment type so that it is a physical child of PATIENT and a logical child of PHYSICIAN. Such changes inevitably require changes to application programs.

IMS External Views.   An IMS external view is called a **logical data base record**. A logical data base record has the following properties:

1. It may represent a subset of a physical data base record.
2. It may span two or more physical data base records.

An external view (or logical data base record) for Patient Bill is shown in Figure 9-12. This view contains segments from two physical data base records: PATIENT and ITEM. It uses the logical parent relationship between ITEM and CHARGES shown in Figure 9-11. However, notice that the

Figure 9-12
IMS external view (Patient Bill).

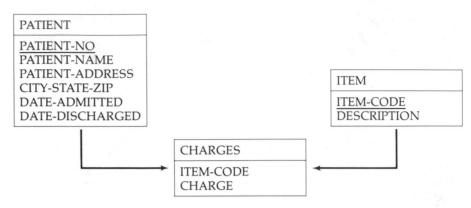

CHARGES POINTER segment is not shown in the external view. The user is unaware of the pointer segments used to implement logical parent relationships in IMS. The Patient Bill (Figure 8-9) can be created by manipulating the segments in the logical data base record in Figure 9-12, as we will show in Chapter 12.

DESIGNING APPLICATIONS

In this section, we describe a structured technique for designing data base applications. This technique, called data base action diagrams, is an extension of the logical access maps (LAMs) introduced in Chapters 7 and 8. Data base action diagrams are much easier to use than conventional structured program design techniques and in fact may be applied by end users with minimal training or experience.

Data Base Applications

The types of applications (or processes) required in a data base environment are shown in Figure 9-13. The data base is stored and maintained with data management software (described in Chapter 11). The processes on the left in Figure 9-13 are used to create and update the data base. These processes must include adequate controls to ensure the accuracy of input data. The applications on the right of Figure 9-13 generate routine documents (such as purchase orders and invoices), produce summary reports, and respond to management requests for information. The data base shown in the figure may be distributed, and users may interact with the data via remote terminals.

One of the most significant developments in software today is the emergence of high-level languages for data base users. Many of these languages can be used by end users with little or no data processing experience to create, access, and update their own data bases. With such lan-

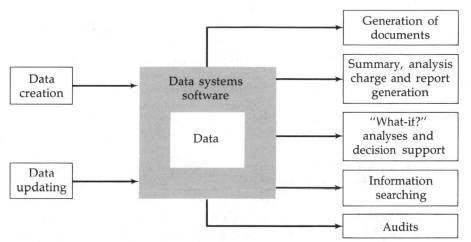

Figure 9-13
Types of data base
applications.
(Source: James Martin
1983.)

guages, users can perform many of the functions shown in Figure 9-13 without having to write conventional application programs. For example, report generators (such as Mark IV and RPG) can be used to generate routine reports; query languages (such as Query-by-Example and Easytrieve) can be used for information searching and retrieval; spreadsheet programs (such as VisiCalc and Multiplan) can be used for analysis and decision support; and application generators (such as Mapper and Ramis II) can be used to develop complete application programs to perform specified functions. We describe several of these languages in later chapters.

With many of these high-level languages, data base action diagrams are not required. Instead, the user simply describes what information is required by "filling in the blanks" or writing simple English-language commands. However, some data base applications do require more complex procedures for processing data, and data base action diagrams are an effective tool for designing such applications.

Data Base Action Diagrams

A **data base action diagram** (DAD) is a map that shows a sequence of actions to be performed on a data base. The data base action diagram is normally drawn alongside a logical access map, extending the logical access map by defining the actions (including control structures) that are to be taken.

Actions.   An **action** is a step that is applied to one instance of one normalized record (Martin 1983). There are four basic types of action: Create, Read, Update, and Delete. In a DAD, an action is drawn with an oblong symbol, as follows:

A3

Actions may be numbered (as in the preceding example) for human reference purposes. However, action numbers are not necessary, since one action never references another.

Each action symbol contains a simple English-language declaration of the action to be taken. For a simple action, this declaration starts with one of the verbs Create, Read, Update, or Delete. The name of the record to which the action applies is written *above* the symbol. Here are two examples:

CUSTOMER

CREATE CUSTOMER RECORD

STUDENT

UPDATE STUDENT GPA

Compound Actions. Sometimes we wish to perform the same action against multiple instances of a given record type. For example, we may want to sort a file of records or select all records that satisfy a certain condition. Such actions are referred to as **compound actions**. A compound action is indicated by a double bar, as follows:

A4

Here are two examples of compound actions:

PRODUCT

SORT RECORDS
BY PRODUCT NAME

STUDENT

SELECT RECORDS
WHERE GPA > 3

Compound action symbols are used mostly with relational data bases, since each compound action can be implemented by a single relational command such as SELECT or JOIN.

Control Structures. Three basic control structures are used in structured programming: sequence, selection, and iteration. These three structures are represented in data base action diagrams by a few additional symbols, as shown in Figure 9-14. This figure also shows notation for representing set relationships.

We indicate a **sequence** of actions by drawing the action symbols in top-to-bottom sequence in the order in which they are to be executed. **Selection** (or IF/THEN condition) is indicated by a partitioned bracket, as shown in Figure 9-14. The condition is shown at the top of the bracket. **Iteration** (or DO WHILE) is indicated by a bracket with a double line. The actions contained within the bracket are executed repeatedly as long as the condition at the top of the bracket is true.

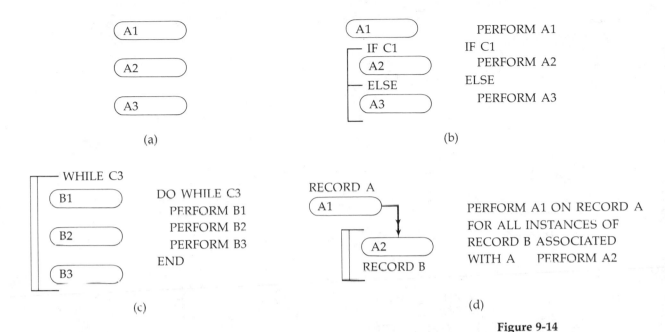

Figure 9-14
Basic control structures.
(a) Sequence.
(b) Selection.
(c) Iteration.
(d) Set relationships.

A **set relationship** is a one-to-many association between two record types. In a data base action diagram, we may wish to indicate that a particular action (or set of actions) is to be performed against all occurrences of records in this association. This is indicated by a double-headed arrow, as shown in Figure 9-14d.

The symbols in Figure 9-14 are nested, or combined, as necessary to express the actions in a data base action diagram. For a more complete discussion of data base action diagrams, see Martin (1983).

Correspondence of LAMs and DADs

Data base action diagrams are usually drawn alongside logical access maps. The LAM shows the sequence of accesses to data base records to process a transaction or produce a desired result. The corresponding DAD simply elaborates the LAM and shows the specific actions that are required.

An example showing this correspondence between the LAM and DAD can be seen in Figure 9-15. The logical access map shows the sequence of accesses required to produce a class list. This logical access map was developed in Chapter 7 (see Figure 7-18). The corresponding DAD shows the actions and control structures needed to perform this task. Notice that each access in the LAM has a corresponding action (in this case READ) in the

Figure 9-15
Correspondence between
logical access map and
data base action diagram.

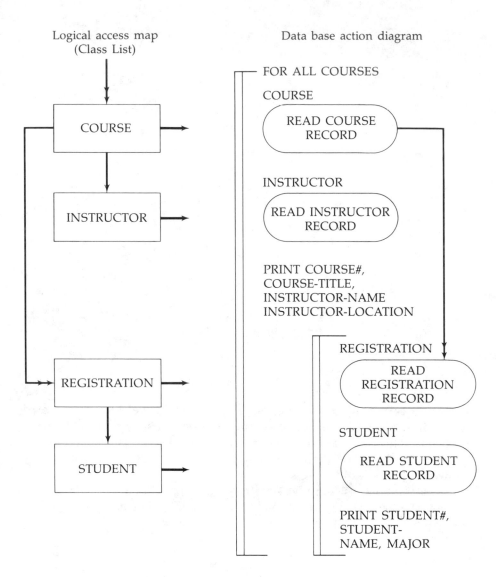

DAD. There is one set relationship in the diagram, representing the one-to-many association between COURSE and REGISTRATION.

There are nested brackets in Figure 9-15. The outer bracket causes repetition of the entire sequence of actions for each course. The inner (or nested) bracket causes a repetition of the actions to read and print student data. Print statements are embedded in the DAD at appropriate locations to produce the class list.

Data base action diagrams are normally related to external views. A logical map is drawn from the external view, and then a DAD is prepared. That is why in Figure 9-3 we show the "design application" step interfaced with the "design subschema" (or external view) step.

We will now illustrate this procedure for Mountain View Community Hospital. A network data model for this organization (mapped from the conceptual data model) is shown in Figure 9-7 and one external view (representing the Patient Bill) is shown in Figure 9-8.

Suppose that we wish to develop an application called "Create Patient Bill." First, we draw a logical access map based on the external view (see Figure 9-16). The LAM is simply a rearrangement of the external view, showing in vertical arrangement the necessary sequence of accesses to the logical records.

The data base action diagram for this process is also shown in Figure 9-16. The outer bracket causes a record to be retrieved for each patient. If the patient has been discharged, the remaining steps are performed. If the patient is not discharged, a bill is not prepared (we assume that patients are not billed until after they are discharged). The inner bracket causes individual charges to be retrieved, printed, and accumulated for each patient. At the end, the total amount owed by the patient is printed.

Converting DADs to Program Code

A data base action diagram is an outline for an application program. It resembles structured English but is generally easier to understand because it is in graphical form. The DAD is language-independent and may be converted to any third- or fourth-generation language.

An example showing the conversion of the DAD in Figure 9-16 to a fourth-generation language (MANTIS) is given in Figure 9-17. Notice that with such a powerful fourth-generation language, there is approximately a one-for-one correspondence between actions and program language statements.

PHYSICAL DESIGN

Physical design is the process of developing an efficient, implementable physical data base structure. It is concerned with how the data are stored on physical devices rather than how they appear to the user. The major inputs to physical design are the logical structures (schemas and subschemas) from implementation design, characteristics of the DBMS and operating system to be used, and user operational requirements. Outputs of physical design

Figure 9-16
Data base action diagram
for CREATE PATIENT
BILL.

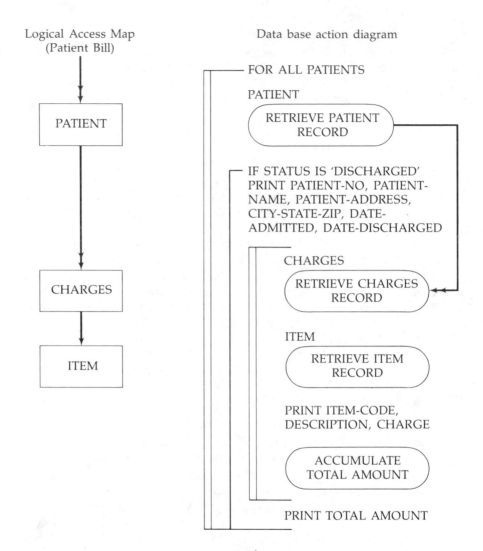

Logical Access Map
(Patient Bill)

Data base action diagram

FOR ALL PATIENTS

PATIENT

RETRIEVE PATIENT
RECORD

IF STATUS IS 'DISCHARGED'
PRINT PATIENT-NO, PATIENT-
NAME, PATIENT-ADDRESS,
CITY-STATE-ZIP, DATE-
ADMITTED, DATE-DISCHARGED

CHARGES

RETRIEVE CHARGES
RECORD

ITEM

RETRIEVE ITEM
RECORD

PRINT ITEM-CODE,
DESCRIPTION, CHARGE

ACCUMULATE
TOTAL AMOUNT

PRINT TOTAL AMOUNT

PATIENT

CHARGES

ITEM

Figure 9-17
Application code
(MANTIS) for CREATE
PATIENT BILL.

```
WHILE PATIENTS > 0
• DO PATIENT-INQUIRY
• IF PATIENT-STATUS = 'DISCHARGED'
•• PRINT PATIENT-NO, PATIENT-NAME, . . .
•• WHILE CHARGES > 0
••• DO CHARGES-INQUIRY
••• DO ITEM-INQUIRY
••• PRINT ITEM-CODE, DESCRIPTION, CHARGE
••• TOTAL-AMOUNT = TOTAL-AMOUNT + CHARGE
•• END
•• PRINT TOTAL-AMOUNT
• END
END
```

are specifications for stored record formats, record placement, and access methods to be used.

As shown in Figure 9-1, physical design is the last stage in the data base design process. In terms of the three-level ANSI-SPARC model, physical design is concerned with the internal model (see Figure 2-17). The major objective of physical design is to provide an optimum balance between performance and operational costs.

There are three major steps in physical design: stored record design, record clustering, and access method selection. As with previous design stages, the steps are performed interactively rather than in linear sequence as shown in Figure 9-18.

Stored Record Design

In the internal model, a data base is viewed as a collection of stored records. A **stored record** is a collection of related data items that corresponds to one or more logical records. In addition to data items, a stored record includes any necessary pointers and other overhead data, such as record length indicators. Thus, a stored record format represents data as they are actually stored on physical devices.

It is important to understand the difference between logical records and stored records. This difference is illustrated in Figure 9-19. As shown in Figure 9-19a, there are three levels, or views, of records: conceptual, external, and stored (or internal). A **conceptual record** is a collection of related data items (the conceptual record in Figure 9-19a has four data items: A, B, C, and D). An **external record** is a subset of the conceptual record and represents a local user view. Several external records may be derived from the same conceptual record. (Although not shown in the figure, an external record may also be derived from two or more conceptual records.) In addition to data items, a **stored record** contains pointers and other overhead data, as shown in Figure 9-19a.

Figure 9-19b shows an example of this three-level architecture. The PATIENT record is a conceptual record that appears in the conceptual data model (see Figure 8-14). PATIENT-BILL is an external record that is derived from PATIENT and appears in a user view (see Figure 9-5). And PATIENT-STORED is a stored record version of the PATIENT record type. It contains two pointer fields: CHARGES-POINTER and TREATMENT-POINTER. These fields contain addresses of occurrences of related records (CHARGES and TREATMENT, respectively). The pointer fields are unknown to users, since they do not appear in the logical record descriptions (conceptual or external).

A **physical data base** is a collection of one or more types of stored records. For example, the collection of all stored records for Mountain View Community Hospital constitutes a physical data base.

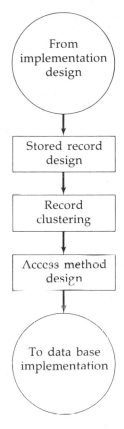

Figure 9-18
Steps in physical design.

Figure 9-19
Contrast between logical and stored records.
(a) Three levels (ANSI/ SPARC model).
(b) Examples of logical and stored records.

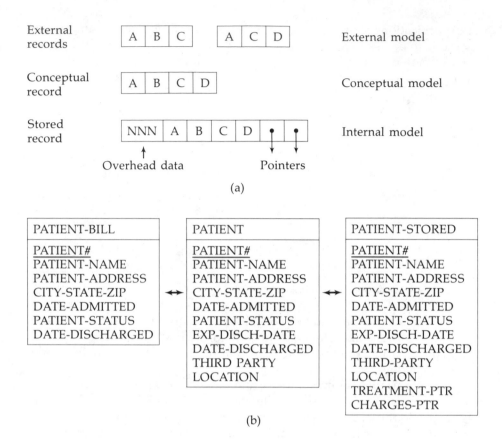

(a)

(b)

Designing stored record formats essentially consists of deciding how to map the logical records to stored records. The stored records may closely resemble the corresponding conceptual records. For example, in Figure 9-19b, the PATIENT-STORED record format is the same as PATIENT, with the addition of two pointer fields. On the other hand, several options exist for modifying stored records to improve performance, including data item storage techniques, data compression, and record partitioning. The specific options available in a given application will depend on the DBMS being used.

Data Item Storage Techniques.   Four basic techniques are available for representing data in stored records: positional, relational, indexed, and labeled (see Figure 9-20). The positional technique is a fixed-length record representation, while the remaining three techniques support variable-length records.

With the **positional technique**, fixed-length fields are used for each data item. Thus, each field must be sufficiently large to accommodate the longest

ELWAYbbbbbbbJbRbbQBbbb83

(a)

ELWAY#JbR#QB#83

(b)

ELWAYJRQB83

(c)

LNELWAYINJRPOQBYR83

LN=last name
IN=initials
PO=position
YR=year started

(d)

Figure 9-20
Data item representation techniques.
(a) Positional technique.
(b) Relational technique.
(c) Indexed technique.
(d) Labeled technique.

anticipated data item value. When data item values are stored, they are right- or left-justified, and blanks are used to pad unused space. (In Figure 9-20, the values are left-justified and the symbol b is used to represent blank space.) The positional technique is the most widely used technique for storing data items, since it simplifies programming and data management tasks. However, it tends to waste storage space, which can be costly, especially for very large data bases.

With the **relational technique**, a special character (not valid in the stored data) is used to delimit data item values. In Figure 9-20, the symbol # is used for this purpose. The special symbol eliminates strings of blanks and therefore conserves space.

The **indexed approach** uses pointers to specify the beginning of each data item value in the record. The pointers normally specify the relative displacement of each value within the record. As with the relational technique, the use of pointers supports variable-length records and eliminates wasted space.

With the **labeled technique**, each data item value is preceded by a label indicating the data item type. This approach allows only certain data items to be included within each record; unwanted data items are simply omitted. The labeled approach is efficient for unstructured data or when a record has many defaulted data item values.

The physical designer may or may not be able to choose the data item storage technique, depending on the DBMS being used. When a choice exists, one of the variable-length record techniques (relational, indexed, or labeled) can be used to conserve storage space if this is an important consideration. However, variable-length records usually complicate the programming task and slow down input/output operations.

Data Compression. Data compression is the process of reducing the length of data item values in stored records. Several techniques are used, the three

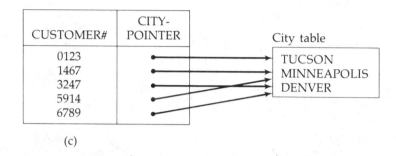

Original data: ATARIbbbbbbb120000
Compressed data: ATARI#712@4

(a)

Original data	Compressed data
TRS8093000X	@93#X
TRS8091000Y	@91#Y
TRS8094000Z	@94#Z

Pattern Table

TRS80	@
000	#

(b)

Original data

CUSTOMER#	CITY
0123	TUCSON
1467	MINNEAPOLIS
3247	DENVER
5914	MINNEAPOLIS
6789	DENVER

CUSTOMER#	CITY-POINTER
0123	
1467	
3247	
5914	
6789	

City table

TUCSON
MINNEAPOLIS
DENVER

(c)

Figure 9-21
Data compression techniques.
(a) Null suppression.
(b) Pattern substitution.
(c) Indexing.

most popular being null suppression, pattern substitution, and indexing (see Figure 9-21).

Null suppression techniques suppress blanks and zeros. One common technique that is used for zero suppression is a simple extension of the relational technique already described. A special character is used to indicate the beginning of a sequence of blanks or zeros (in Figure 9-21a, the symbol # represents the beginning of a sequence of blanks, the symbol @ the beginning of a sequence of zeros). The special character is followed by a digit that represents the length of the sequence. Thus, in Figure 9-21a, the symbol @4 is the compressed version for a sequence of four zeros. Null suppression is an effective technique for compressing "sparse" data that are dominated by zeros or blanks.

Pattern substitution is a technique in which sequences of characters that occur repeatedly in the data are recognized and then represented by shorter codes. An example of this technique is shown in Figure 9-21b.

In this example, two character strings (TRS80 and 000) were identified as patterns in the sample data. These values were stored in a pattern table and coded with the characters @ and #, respectively. The compressed data then appear with these codes replacing the character strings. Notice that this type of data compression requires additional accesses to the pattern table to store and retrieve data. However, pattern substitution is an effective means of data compression when frequent patterns exist in the data.

Indexing is a variation of pattern substitution. Instead of using a code to replace patterns, a pointer is used for each data item value. For example, in Figure 9-21c there is considerable redundancy in the CITY data item values, since each city name is repeated (if there were 10,000 records, each city name would appear many times). To compress the data, a separate CITY table is

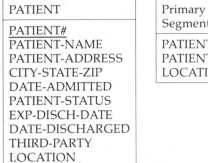
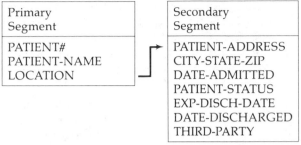

Figure 9-22
Example of record
partitioning.

created. City names are then replaced by pointers that point to the appropriate names in the table (the pointer values must be shorter than the city names for compression to occur).

Some data base management sytems automatically compress stored data. For example, ADABAS (DBMS from Software AG) has a compression algorithm that automatically suppresses trailing spaces on alphanumeric fields and leading zeros on numeric fields, packs numeric data, and compresses null-value fields to a single character. The net result is that an ADABAS file typically requires only about 50% to 65% of the space required for the raw data (Software AG 1982).

Record Partitioning.   The last aspect of stored record design that we will consider is record partitioning. **Record partitioning** (or segmentation) is the process of splitting stored records into separate segments and then allocating those segments to separate physical devices or separate extents on the same device. The reason for partitioning records is that some data items are accessed far more frequently than others. In fact, the so-called 80-20 rule often applies: approximately 20% of the data items often account for about 80% of the input/output activity. We can improve performance by locating the active data items on fast devices (such as fixed-head disks) or in readily accessible locations (such as the middle cylinders on a disk pack).

The simplest form of record partitioning divides a stored record into two segments: the **primary segment** (with the most active data items) and the **secondary segment** (with the less active data items). An example of this segmentation for the PATIENT record at Mountain View Community Hospital is shown in Figure 9-22. The three most active data items (which account for about 80% of all requests) are located in the primary segment: PATIENT#, PATIENT-NAME, and LOCATION. The remaining PATIENT data items are located in the secondary segment. The primary segment might be stored for fast access, with the secondary segment stored on a slower device. In reality, the PATIENT records would probably not be segmented at all, since the data base for this hospital is relatively small. However, record partitioning may be an effective means of improving performance for large data bases.

Notice that the primary and secondary segments are connected by a pointer so that they can be retrieved together when necessary. All user requests for data first generate an access to the primary segment. If the data are not found, then another access to the secondary segment is made. Record partitioning occurs at the physical level and is not visible to data base users.

Record partitioning is part of the more general process of clustering data items into stored records. A cluster analysis technique called the **bond energy algorithm** has been developed to identify natural groupings that occur in large data arrays. Hoffer and Severance (1975) have applied the bond energy algorithm to the process of record partitioning. Their algorithm measures the "bond," or cohesiveness, between data items and groups data items that are used together into physical subfiles. As with all clustering techniques, the bond energy algorithm requires detailed analysis concerning the way that data are used.

Record Clustering

A physical data base consists of a collection of stored records of different types. **Record clustering** is the process of physically grouping these records according to the dominant access paths, thereby minimizing access times. For example, all stored records of a given type may be grouped together in a physical extent. However, it is often more efficient to group occurrences of different record types together when they are frequently accessed together. Optimum record clustering is a complex problem for large, integrated data bases.

Clustering in Hierarchical Data Bases.   In a hierarchical data base, record clustering is the process of grouping segment occurrences into physical blocks or extents. See Figure 9-23, for example. Figure 9-23a shows a physical data base record that consists of the four segment types A, B, C, and D (A is the root segment). Figure 9-23b shows one clustering option, where occurrences of each segment type are grouped together. This grouping is not likely to be efficient, since segments in a hierarchy are often retrieved in top-down, left-to-right sequence.

Another approach to grouping the segments is shown in Figure 9-23c. In this case, occurrences of segments A and B are grouped together (occurrences of segment B are grouped immediately following their parent segment occurrences). This grouping will probably be efficient if root segment (type A) occurrences are normally accessed sequentially with their child (type B) occurrences and if segments C and D are normally accessed sequentially. Certainly, many other groupings are possible even in this simple example.

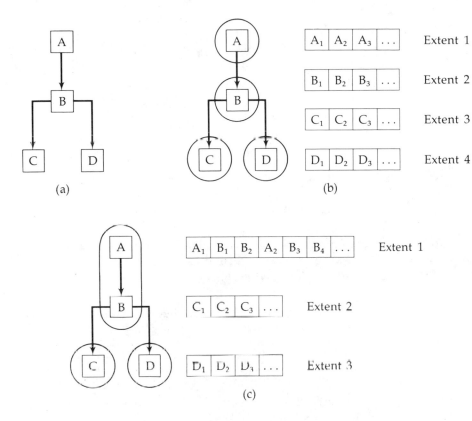

Figure 9-23
Record clustering in a
hierarchical data base.
(a) Sample physical data
base record.
(b) Grouping individual
segments.
(c) Alternative grouping.

Schkolnick (1977) has developed an algorithm for optimum clustering of segments in a hierarchical data base. This algorithm minimizes the expected number of I/O accesses for a given set of user applications by computing a distance function for each clustering option (nonoptimal clusterings are eliminated from further consideration). For details of this algorithm, see Teorey and Fry (1982) and Schkolnick (1977).

The IMS hierarchical data base for Mountain View Community Hospital is shown in Figure 9-10. The primary access path for TREATMENT segments is by means of PHYSICIAN segments, since PHYSICIAN is the root segment. Therefore, TREATMENT segment occurrences will be clustered with their PHYSICIAN parent segment occurrences in an IMS implementation of this data base. For the same reason, CHARGES segment occurrences will be clustered with their PATIENT parent segment occurrences. If the usage patterns for this data base change over time, it may become necessary to revise this clustering scheme.

Clustering in Network Data Bases. In a CODASYL (network) data base, the physical data base structure (or internal model) is specified in the Data Storage Description Language (DSDL). The DSDL is used to define the

Figure 9-24
Example of record
clustering.

PHYSICIAN RECORD# 1	TREATMENT RECORD A	TREATMENT RECORD B
TREATMENT RECORD C		
PHYSICIAN RECORD# 2	TREATMENT RECORD D	TREATMENT RECORD E
PHYSICIAN RECORD# 3	TREATMENT RECORD F	

format of each stored record, the number and size of areas, and the placement of records in areas.

Record placement (or clustering) in a CODASYL data base is controlled by a PLACEMENT clause in the DSDL. For each CODASYL record type, one of three placement modes may be chosen:

1. CALC: A data item value (record key) is hashed to produce a storage address. This results in record occurrences being dispersed randomly throughout a storage area (or extent).

2. CLUSTERED VIA SET: Member record occurrences in a set are clustered together, usually with their owner record occurrence.

3. SEQUENTIAL: Occurrences of a given record type are stored in sequential order according to their primary key.

Referring to the network data model for Mountain View Community Hospital (Figure 9-7), there are two instances where the CLUSTERED VIA SET option will be used in the DSDL. CLUSTERED VIA SET TREATED will be specified for the TREATMENT record type. This clause will cause occurrences of TREATMENT records to be clustered with their PHYSICIAN owner record occurrences (see Figure 9-24). Also, a CLUSTERED VIA SET INCURRED will cause CHARGES record occurrences to be clustered with their PATIENT owner record occurrences.

Design Access Methods

We have described the first two steps in physical design: record design and record clustering. The last step is to select the access methods to be used for the stored records. An **access method** is a technique for storing and retrieving records. Access methods have two major components: a data structure and a search strategy. A **data structure** is a technique for physical data organization. Some important data structures (which are described in Chapter 5) are linear lists, multilists, inverted lists, and trees. A **search strategy** is a technique used to define an access path and locate a specific stored record.

Examples include sequential search, binary search, and hashing (or random access).

The choice of access methods for stored records is a relatively complex process, requiring considerable knowledge of how the data will be used by various applications, as well as technical knowledge of the DBMS being used and the access methods that it supports. Some DBMS products support a wide variety of access methods, while other products constrain the user to a limited set of options. There are numerous formulas for predicting performance (such as average access times) for various access methods. For a detailed discussion of access methods and related performance measures, see Teorey and Fry (1982), Martin (1977), and Wiederhold (1977).

A detailed discussion comparing the performance of various access methods is beyond the scope of this text. However, a classification scheme proposed by Severance and Carlis (1977) can be used to simplify this process. They describe three classes of user applications and the type of access methods best suited to each class. The three classes are as follows:

1. GET ALL or MANY: This class of applications requires access to a significant proportion of the data base, usually between 10% and 100%. Examples of such applications are batch updating and report preparation. Sequential organizations are most efficient for this class of applications.

2. GET UNIQUE: Access is normally to a single target record. Organizations based on primary keys (such as hashing and B-trees) are most efficient for this class of applications.

3. GET SOME: This class of applications requires access to several records (but less than 10% of the data base) on each occasion. The most common example is ad hoc queries that traverse several records. Organizations based on secondary keys (such as inverted files and multilists) are most efficient.

A summary of the three application classes and the most efficient access methods for each class are shown in Table 9-1. The table also groups records from the network data model for Mountain View Community Hospital (Figure 9-7) into the classes, based on the anticipated dominant mode of usage for those records. Four of the record types in Figure 9-7 (ROOM, PATIENT, PHYSICIAN, and ITEM) have a CALC record placement mode. This indicates that the dominant access mode for these records is GET UNIQUE, as shown in Table 9-1. These records can be organized as a hashed file or, if sequential access is also required, as an indexed sequential file. The remaining two record types (TREATMENT and CHARGES) normally require a GET SOME discipline and may therefore be organized using inverted file or multilist techniques.

Table 9-1
Classification of Access Methods

Application class	Typical access methods	Hospital record type
GET ALL or MANY (10%–100%)	Sequential (physical or linked)	None
GET UNIQUE (one)	Random (hashed); Indexed sequential; B-tree	PATIENT; ROOM; PHYSICIAN; ITEM
GET SOME (0%–10%)	Inverted file; multilist	TREATMENT; CHARGES

SUMMARY

In this chapter, we described the final two stages of data base design—implementation design and physical design. Implementation design is concerned with mapping the conceptual model (described in Chapter 8) to a logical data base structure. This logical structure is usually expressed in the form of a hierarchical, network, or relational data model, or some combination of these models. The logical structure is expressed in the form of a DBMS-processable schema. Implementation design is also concerned with mapping conceptual user views into logical views. These logical views are then expressed in the form of DBMS-processable subschemas. Data base action diagrams that express program logic can also be developed during implementation design.

Physical design, which occurs at the level of the internal model, is concerned with developing an efficient, implementable physical data base structure. Several decisions that must be made during physical design concern stored record formats, record clustering, and selection of efficient access methods. Several trade-offs among access times, storage requirements, and data redundancy must typically be made during physical design.

When physical design is completed, the data base is ready to be implemented. In the following chapters, we describe and illustrate this implementation using several types of data base management systems.

CHAPTER REVIEW

Review Questions

1. Concisely define each of the following terms:

   a. logical model
   b. schema
   c. subschema
   d. set
   e. segment

   f. action
   g. stored record
   h. data compression
   i. physical data base

2. Contrast the following terms:

   a. physical design; implementation design
   b. conceptual model; logical model
   c. owner; member
   d. CALC; VIA
   e. physical parent; logical parent
   f. positional technique; relational technique
   g. null suppression; pattern substitution
   h. record clustering; record partitioning
   i. GET ALL; GET SOME

3. List the major steps for each of the following:

   a. implementation design
   b. physical design

4. List four steps in mapping a conceptual model to a CODASYL model.

5. Briefly describe four techniques for representing data in stored records.

6. Describe three techniques for data compression.

7. Describe three general classes of user applications in terms of their access patterns.

8. What is the difference in IMS between a physical data base record and a logical data base record?

9. Why should data access strategies be defined during physical design rather than during implementation design?

10. What is the relationship between LAMs and DADs?

Problems and Exercises

Problems 1 to 5 are based on a conceptual data model (abbreviated version) for Pine Valley Furniture Company. This data model, shown in Figure 2-10, is repeated below.

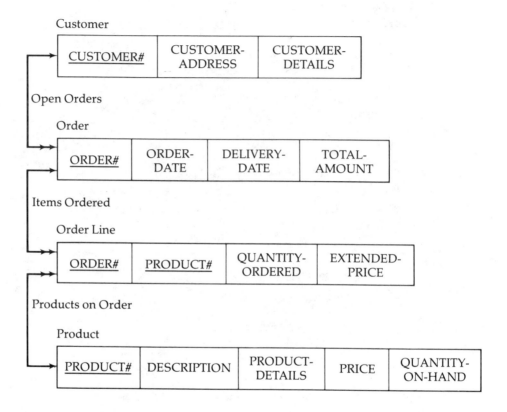

Customer

CUSTOMER#	CUSTOMER-ADDRESS	CUSTOMER-DETAILS

Open Orders

Order

ORDER#	ORDER-DATE	DELIVERY-DATE	TOTAL-AMOUNT

Items Ordered

Order Line

ORDER#	PRODUCT#	QUANTITY-ORDERED	EXTENDED-PRICE

Products on Order

Product

PRODUCT#	DESCRIPTION	PRODUCT-DETAILS	PRICE	QUANTITY-ON-HAND

In answering the following questions, assume that the dominant access patterns for the record types are as follows:

    (i)   CUSTOMER: GET UNIQUE

    (ii) ORDER: GET UNIQUE

    (iii) ORDER-LINE: GET SOME (retrieve all ORDER-LINE occurrences for a given Order occurrence)

    (iv) PRODUCT: GET UNIQUE (GET ALL sometimes required)

1. Map the model to a relational data model. Show sample data.

2. Map the model to a network (CODASYL) data model (similar to the one in Figure 9-7).

3. Map the model to a hierarchical (IMS) data model (similar to the one in Figure 9-11).

4. Suggest an efficient access method for each of the four record types in the data models.

5. Create a logical access map and data base action diagram for a procedure that will create a new customer order. The following steps are performed:
    (i) Create ORDER record occurrence.
    (ii) Retrieve CUSTOMER record.
    (iii) Check customer credit (contained in CUSTOMER record). If credit OK, proceed; otherwise, print message and stop.
    (iv) Create ORDER-LINE record occurrence for each product on the order.
    (v) Retrieve PRODUCT record occurrence for each ORDER-LINE occurrence.
    (vi) Multiply PRICE (PRODUCT record) by QUANTITY (ORDER-LINE), giving EXTENDED-PRICE (ORDER-Line).

6. One of the user views for Mountain View Community Hospital is the Physician Report (see Figure 8-12).
    a. Referring to the hospital data model (Figure 8-14), draw a logical access map for the procedure CREATE-PHYSICIAN-REPORT.
    b. Draw a data base action diagram for the preceding LAM.

7. Consider the following data:
    APPLEbbbbbVISICALC60000
    APPLEbbbbbVISICLONE70000
    a. Show these data with null suppression (use the same symbols as in Figure 9-21).
    b. Show these data with pattern substitution.

8. Refer to the conceptual data model (Figure 8-14) and Room Utilization Report (Figure 8-10) for Mountain View Community Hospital.
    a. Derive a conceptual user view (such as the one in Figure 9-5) by normalizing the relation in Figure 8-10.
    b. Draw a logical access map for the procedure CREATE-ROOM-UTILIZATION-REPORT using the views developed in part (a).
    c. Draw a data base action diagram for the LAM in part (b).

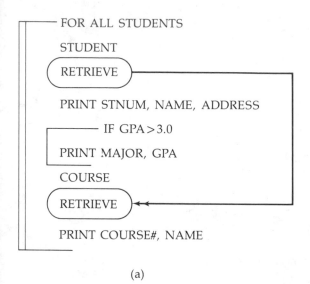

(a)

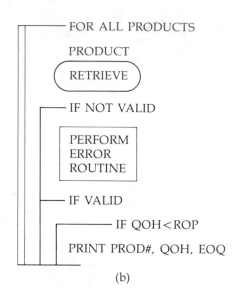

(b)

9. Express each of the following data base action diagrams in structured English (or pseudocode).

10. A simplified conceptual data model for a purchasing data base is shown in Figure 9-25. Map this conceptual model to a CODASYL logical model. Assume the following access patterns:

   (i)   SUPPLIER, BUYER, and PURCHORDER are normally GET UNIQUE.

   (ii) INVOICE is normally GET SOME. There are two cases:

   • Retrieve a PURCHORDER occurrence, then retrieve all associated IN-VOICE occurrences.

   • Retrieve all INVOICE occurrences that have a particular DUE-DATE value.

11. Map the conceptual data model shown in Figure 9-25 to a hierarchical model (see assumptions in Problem 10).

12. Based on the assumptions stated in Problem 10, how are the records shown in Figure 9-25 likely to be clustered in a CODASYL data base?

References

Hoffer, J.A., and D.G. Severance. 1975. "The Use of Cluster Analysis in Physical Data Base Design." *Proceedings of First Very Large Data Base Conference*. September.

Martin, James. 1977. *Computer Data Base Organization*. 2d ed. Englewood Cliffs, N.J.: Prentice-Hall.

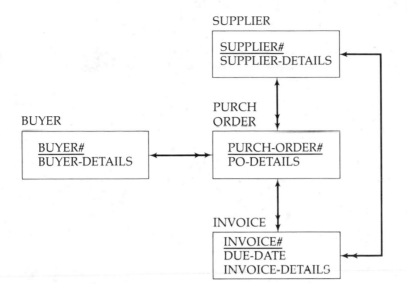

Figure 9-25
Purchasing data base.

————. 1983. *Managing the Data-Base Environment*. Englewood Cliffs, N.J.: Prentice-Hall.

Maxwell, W.L., and D.G. Severance. 1973. "Comparison of Alternatives for the Representation of Data Item Values in an Information System." *Proceedings Wharton Conference Res. Computer Organ. Oper. Res.* 20(5).

Schkolnick, M. 1977. "A Clustering Algorithm for Hierarchical Structures." *ACM Transactions on Database Systems* (March): 27–44.

Severance, D.G., and J.V. Carlis. 1977. "A Practical Approach to Selecting Records Access Paths." *ACM Computing Surveys* 9(4): 259–272.

Software AG. 1982. *ADABAS, Effective Data Base Management for the Growing Corporate Environment*.

Teorey, Toby J., and James P. Fry. 1982. *Design of Database Structures*. Englewood Cliffs, N.J.: Prentice-Hall.

Wiederhold, G. 1977. *Database Design*. New York: McGraw-Hill.

10

Data Base Administration

INTRODUCTION

The need to manage an organization's data resource has resulted in the creation of a new function called data base administration (DBA). The person who heads this function is called the manager, data base administration or, more popularly, the data base administrator (also abbreviated DBA). The term *DBA* is used in this chapter to mean both the person and the function.

Actual experience with computer data bases has established a fundamental principle: the data base administration function is *essential* to the success of managing the data resource. Establishing this function is an indication of top management's commitment to data resource management. When the DBA function is not established, or when it is weakly established, the chances of success of the data base approach are significantly diminished.

The data base is a shared resource, belonging to the entire enterprise. It is not the property of a single function or individual within the organization. The data base administrator is "custodian" of the organization's data, in much the same sense that the controller is custodian of the financial resources. Like the controller, the DBA must develop procedures to protect and control the resource. Also, the DBA must resolve disputes that may arise when data are centralized and shared among users.

Data base administration is responsible for a wide range of functions, including data base planning, design, implementation, maintenance, and protection. Also, the DBA is responsible for improving data base performance and for providing education, training, and consulting support to users. The data base administrator must interact with top management, users, and computer applications specialists.

Selecting the data base administrator and organizing the DBA function are extremely important considerations. The data base administrator must possess a high level of managerial skills and must be capable of resolving differences that normally arise when significant change is introduced into an organization. The DBA should be a respected, senior-level middle manager selected from within the organization, rather than a technical computer expert or a new individual hired for the DBA position.

DATA BASE ADMINISTRATION VERSUS DATA ADMINISTRATION

The manager of the DBA function requires both managerial and technical skills. On the one hand, this person must be capable of enlisting cooperation from users, who may at first be hostile to the idea of "giving up" their "private" data to a shared data base. Also, these users must be convinced of adhering to a set of standard procedures for accessing and protecting the data base. On the other hand, the DBA must be capable of managing a technical staff and dealing with technical issues in designing and managing the data base.

To resolve the managerial versus technical complexity of the DBA function, some organizations are distinguishing between data administration and data base administration. When this distinction is made, **data administration** is regarded as a high level management function (perhaps a corporate vice-president) with responsibility for determining overall information needs from a management perspective. The data administration is "responsible for developing and administering the policies, procedures, practices, and plans for the definition, organization, protection, and efficient utilization of data within a corporate enterprise" (Guide International 1977). This function encompasses all corporate data, whether or not they are part of a stored data base. **Data base administration** is considered a "work group within an organization charged with managing the firm's data resource" (Canning 1972). Data base administration is normally responsible only for computer data bases. It usually reports within the data processing organization.

The process of describing and separating these two functions continues, and in all likelihood, standard definitions (and standard industry practice) will not be adopted for some time to come. In the meantime, the term *data base administration* is most widely used today (and is used in this text) to refer to both the managerial and technical functions of data resource management. The question of organizational placement of the DBA function is addressed later in this chapter.

Figure 10-1
Stages in the data base
system life cycle.

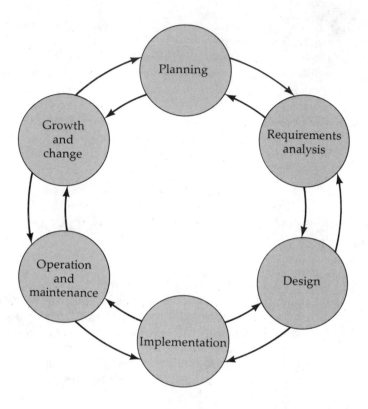

DATA BASE SYSTEM LIFE CYCLE

Data base administration is responsible for managing the data base system life cycle. Therefore, to understand the DBA functions, it is necessary to gain an understanding of that life cycle. As shown in Figure 10-1, there are six stages in the life cycle of a typical data base system:

1. planning
2. requirements formulation and analysis
3. design
4. implementation
5. operation and maintenance
6. growth and change

Normally, these stages are performed in the order given here. However, iteration is often required between the various stages. For example, the design stage may reveal that some data have been inadequately defined, which would lead to further requirements analysis.

Data Base Planning.　The purpose of data base planning is to develop a strategic plan for data base development that supports the overall organizational business plan. Although the responsibility for developing this plan rests with top management, data base administration provides major inputs to the planning process. Data base planning is described in detail in Chapter 3.

Requirements Formulation and Analysis.　The process of requirements formulation and analysis is concerned with identifying data elements currently used by the organization, precisely defining these elements and their relationships, and documenting the results in a form that is convenient to the design effort that is to follow. In addition to identifying current data, requirements formulation and analysis attempts to identify new data elements (or changes to existing data elements) that will be required in the future. We described requirements formulation and analysis in Chapter 7.

Design.　The purpose of data base design is to develop a data base architecture that will meet the information needs of the organizaton, now and in the future. As we described in Chapter 7, there are three stages in data base design: conceptual design, implementation design, and physical design. Although data base administration is responsible for data base design, the DBA group must work closely with users and systems specialists in performing these design activities.

Implementation.　Once the data base design is completed, the implementation process begins. The first step in implementation is the creation (or initial load) of the data base. The data base is simply an empty superstructure until it has been "populated" with actual data values. Data base administration manages the loading process and resolves any inconsistencies that arise during this process.

Operation and Maintenance.　Data base operation and maintenance is the ongoing process of updating the data base to keep it current. Examples of updating include adding a new employee record, changing a student address, and deleting an invoice.

　　Updating the data base is not the responsibility of data base administration. Rather, users are responsible for data base maintenance. However, DBA is responsible for developing procedures that ensure that the data base is kept current and that it is protected during update operations. Specifically, the DBA must perform the following functions:

1. Assign responsibility for data collection, editing, and verification.
2. Establish appropriate update schedules.
3. Establish an active and aggressive quality assurance program, including procedures for protecting, restoring, and auditing the data base.

Growth and Change

The data base is a model of the organization itself. As a result, it is not static, but instead reflects the dynamic changes in the organization and its environment. The DBA function must plan for change and take whatever corrective actions are required to maintain a high level of performance.

FUNCTIONS OF DATA BASE ADMINISTRATION

The major functions of data base administration are summarized in Figure 10-2 according to the data base system life cycle. Some of these functions have been described in previous chapters and are therefore discussed only briefly in this chapter. Functions that have not been covered in previous chapters are described in greater detail.

Planning Functions

Data base administration is responsible for developing a set of plans for data base implementation. Here are some of the major functions that are performed during this stage of the life cycle:

1. Define data base goals.
2. Analyze costs and benefits.
3. Develop implementation plan.
4. Evaluate and select software and hardware.
5. Assess impact of changes in technology.

All of these activities were described in Chapter 3, except for the analysis of costs and benefits. The DBA should assist users in analyzing the prospective costs and benefits of a data base system. Although many of the benefits may seem intangible, they should be quantified as much as possible. These estimates provide a baseline for evaluating performance as data base implementation proceeds.

A list of some of the important costs and benefits of data bases is presented in Table 10-1. The costs are divided into nonrecurring (one-time) and recurring costs and include hardware, software, and personnel additions. The benefits are divided into cost reduction (or avoidance) and value enhancement. The latter category is more difficult to quantify, since it includes improved resource utilization, more timely reports, and improved decision making.

Life cycle phase

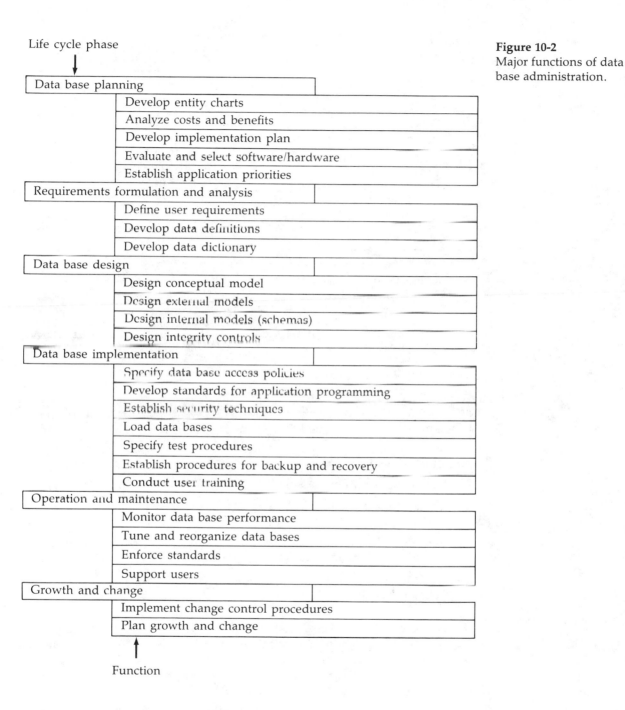

Figure 10-2
Major functions of data
base administration.

Function

Requirements Formulation and Analysis

We described the process of requirements formulation and analysis in
Chapter 7. This is the period of greatest interaction between data base

Table 10-1
Major Costs and Benefits of Data Bases

Data base costs	
Nonrecurring:	Recurring:
Data base software	Personnel costs (DBA)
Hardware	Software lease, maintenance
Data communications equipment	Hardware lease, maintenance
Site and facility	Travel and training
Travel and training	Supplies and utilities
Data conversion	Support services
Studies (analysis, design)	Overhead

Data base benefits	
Cost reduction/avoidance:	Value enhancement:
Reduced program maintenance	Improved resource utilization
Reduced error rates	More timely reports
Reduced loss/fraud	Improved data accessibility
	Improved decision making

administration and user groups. As shown in Figure 10-2, here are the major functions performed by the DBA group during this stage:

1. Define user requirements.
2. Develop data definitions.
3. Develop data dictionary.

The result of requirements formulation and analysis is a complete set of data definitions that are recorded in the data dictionary.

Data Base Design

As already noted, data base design consists of three major phases: conceptual design, implementation design, and physical design. Data base administration is responsible for managing these three phases of the design cycle. Conceptual design is concerned with modeling the organization's data; therefore, during this phase, there is heavy interaction between the DBA group and users throughout the organization. Implementation and physical design is DBMS-dependent, so that there is less interaction with users. However, during this phase, DBA personnel may interact with other system specialists in the data processing organization.

Data Base Implementation

As shown in Figure 10-2, data base administration is responsible for implementing data bases and must perform a number of significant functions in supporting this phase of the life cycle.

Specifying Data Base Access Policies.   In implementing a data base, previously independent application files are consolidated into a corporate data base. Data base administration does not own these data, but instead acts as a custodian. The DBA must determine the rights and duties of the user community concerning use of the data base. For example, some users are responsible for updating certain data, while other users may only be allowed to access (but not update) the data. Still other users may not be permitted to access the same data. In general, the DBA should allocate to users only those rights that are necessary to satisfy their responsibilities.

Developing Standards for Application Programming.   A data base management system provides a number of new facilities, such as high-level languages, application development systems, and security mechanisms. If properly used, these facilities can greatly improve the productivity of application programmers. Data base administration must develop and enforce programming standards to ensure that these facilities are used consistently and correctly.

Establishing Security Techniques.   Since data are shared by many users, a data base tends to increase the vulnerability of data to improper use. Data base administration is responsible for developing adequate security measures, such as passwords, access tables, and encryption facilities. We describe such security techniques in Chapter 11.

Loading Data Bases.   Initial loading of a data base requires significant computer resources, including processor time, input/output channels, and disk storage units. Also, people are required to supervise, reconcile, and verify the process. Careful planning of these resources is required to minimize disruptions to normal operations. A schedule for data base loading must be worked out between DBA and computer operations. The data base load program must provide for checkpoints from which restarts can occur. Elapsed time is minimized by eliminating all unnecessary operator intervention such as disk mounts and dismounts. Finally, audits (random samples) of the newly created data base should be made to verify the loading process.

In most cases, creating a data base involves combining data from a number of existing master files. Frequently, special application programs must be written to extract data from relevant files and load the data into data base records. Since the same data often exist in multiple files maintained by different users, inconsistencies in the data element values are bound to exist.

For example, an employee may be listed as having two different addresses in two separate files. Data base administration must anticipate and reconcile such inconsistencies.

Specifying Test Procedures.   New application programs must be carefully tested before they are allowed to go on-line with a data base. The DBA group is responsible for establishing policies concerning test procedures, coordinating with application programmers, end users, and operations personnel in carrying out these tests.

Establishing Procedures for Backup and Recovery.   As custodian of corporate data, data base administration is responsible for establishing procedures for data base backup and recovery. These procedures include transaction logs, backup copies of the data base, and recovery mechanisms. We describe backup and recovery in detail in Chapter 11.

Conducting User Training.   An important function of data base administration is to provide training in using the data base system to various user groups such as managers, other end users, and systems personnel. The DBA group should evaluate the training needs of these various user groups and should then schedule vendor-conducted training courses or conduct on-site training, as appropriate.

Operation and Maintenance

During the operation and maintenance phase, DBA functions center on monitoring, control, and user support. As shown in Figure 10-2, the DBA group monitors data base performance and responds to user complaints or suggestions. If necessary, the DBA "tunes" or reorganizes the data base for improved performance. Also, the DBA group performs a quality assurance function in checking that standards and procedures are being enforced. Finally, the DBA group actively seeks out ways to support users, for example, by suggesting new data base applications.

Growth and Change

Three major types of change may occur with data bases:

1. Change in size: addition of more data of the kind already contained in the data base (e.g., adding student records as the number of students increases).
2. Change in content or structure: adding new data types or data relationships through the implementation of new applications (e.g., imple-

Table 10-2
Responses to Data Base Change and Growth

Type of change	Method of detection	Possible response(s)
Size	Analysis of space utilization	Additional space allocation; space reallocation
Content/structure	New application requests	Altering logical and physical structure
Usage pattern	Performance monitoring	Reorganization; altering access methods; new hardware

menting a new purchasing application might require adding a new Vendor record type or association).

3. Change in usage pattern: changes in the relative frequency of accessing a particular record type or combinations of record types (e.g., a sudden increase in the frequency of access to Arrest records in a criminal justice data base).

These three major types of growth and change in a data base are summarized in Table 10-2, along with the methods of detecting change and the responses to change available to data base administration (see Lyon 1976 for an extended discussion).

Changes in Size.   Changes in size are detected by analyses of storage space utilization. Most data base management systems include a facility for measuring space utilization. Also, as space utilization increases, performance often tends to decrease. Two measures are available to the DBA to accommodate growth: allocation of additional space (e.g., more cylinders on a disk volume) and reallocation of existing space (requires an unload and reload of the data base).

Changes in Structure.   Changes in content and/or structure result from requests for new applications that cannot be met by the existing data base. The DBA must consult the data dictionary to verify that the required data are not available. Assuming that the request is to be satisfied, the response is to alter both the logical and physical data base structures. Hopefully, this type of change will be minimized by careful data base planning. However, the DBA must be open to change, since change reflects the normal dynamic growth of the organization. In any event, the impact of such changes will be minimized if the DBMS provides a strong measure of data independence.

Changes in Usage Patterns.   Changes in usage patterns are detected by a performance-monitoring system or (in its absence) by degraded performance. For example, average terminal response times may increase from 2 seconds to 2 minutes (or more!). Several responses are available.

Reorganization is one possible response, that is, altering the physical characteristics of the data base. Examples include reassigning frequently accessed records to faster devices, changing the relative placement (or clustering) of records, and altering the content of records. Reorganization normally requires that the data base (or a portion of it) be unloaded and then reloaded.

Altering the access methods is another possible response, for example, changing from a sequential organization to a random organization. This process usually requires unloading and reloading the data base.

If the first two techniques do not improve performance, it may be necessary to resort to a third response, that of providing additional, higher-performance hardware devices (disk drives, controllers, and so on).

Performance in a data base environment is a joint responsibility. Data base administration must work with computer operations, systems programmers, and users to seek ways to improve performance.

INTERFACES OF DATA BASE ADMINISTRATION

Additional insight into the functions of data base administration can be gained by studying the interfaces between DBA and other major groups in the enterprise. As shown in Figure 10-3, data base administration interfaces with four major groups: management, users, application systems, and operations.

Communications with Management

Data base administration has a number of important communications with top management. If the data resource management concept is in practice, the data base administrator may well be a top manager, or at least will report to a top manager.

Management communicates to the DBA function a continuing commitment to the data resource management concept. Hopefully, this includes the necessary budgetary support. Also, management communicates its business plans, goals, priorities, and constraints, which are the basis for data base planning. If there are any major contingencies, such as a reorganization or acquisition, these must also be communicated to the DBA.

The DBA, in turn, communicates to management its budget requirements and data base plans and schedules. The DBA should provide frequent status reports concerning data base projects. Often, the DBA is responsible for performing cost/benefit analyses of specific proposals.

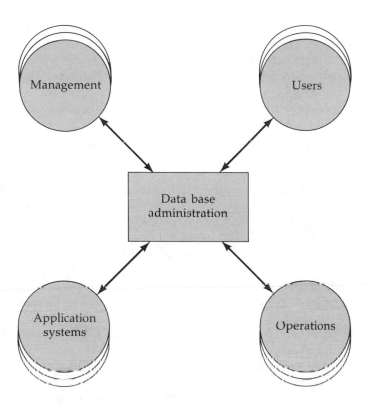

Figure 10-3
Major interfaces of data
base administration.

One way for data base administration to sustain top management support is to show these managers how they can use the data base system to improve their own decision making. The DBA should make recommendations to management concerning the use of high-level query languages, graphic displays, simulation modeling, and other areas of decision support.

Communications with Users

The term *users* is a generic term, referring to any person in the organization who uses the data base. Thus, users may be managers (at any level), clerical personnel, shop workers, or computer personnel. The DBA provides users with the information they require to maintain and protect the data base and to develop new applications. This information includes data definitions, data relationships, and other information stored in the data dictionary. However, the DBA does not provide users with a "hard-copy" listing of the complete data dictionary—but only that portion for which there is a "need to know."

One of the many advantages of the data dictionary is the ability to perform impact studies. This is the ability to show the impact that a data base change will have on programs and data processing (e.g., the change by the Postal Service from a five-digit to a nine-digit zip code). The DBA also consults with users regarding education and training needs, new applications, and methods for improving performance.

During the requirements analysis stage, users provide the DBA with their data requirements—data element descriptions, user views, priorities, access limitations, frequency of updating, and so on. Also, users must keep data base administration informed of possible future data base applications.

Communications with Application Systems

The application systems group includes the analysts and programmers who are responsible for developing user application programs. Data base administration must develop and enforce standards for programs that interface with the data base. These standards include programming techniques, program documentation, and quality assurance. For example, a portion of the standards should address what data manipulation language commands must be used (or are recommended) to access and manipulate the data base. These standards are necessary both to protect the data base and for performance reasons.

For each new application program, the DBA provides the application designer with the controls required by the user. At the same time, the DBA keeps users informed about the data base itself, as well as providing documentation concerning the DBMS as needed.

Application systems provides the DBA with the required application view of data for each new program. Application systems also keeps the DBA informed of priorities and schedules, as well as the status of projects.

It is important that each new application program be carefully tested with test data before attempting to interface it with the "live" data base. The application specialist must communicate the test plan to the DBA, and the two groups must work together to ensure that an adequate plan is developed.

Communications with Operations

Computer operations is concerned with the physical aspects of data processing—hardware operations, shift scheduling, security, tape and disk library, and so on. Operations is also concerned with the operating system and is often assigned technical support (systems programmers) to maintain this software.

Data base administration must provide operations with schedules and standard operating procedures for routine operations, such as updating, backup, and archiving. The DBA also provides operations with standard procedures for protecting the data base and for recovering from errors or abnormal conditions. It should be noted that these are not one-way communications between the DBA and operations; many of the issues must be worked on and resolved jointly. However, the DBA is responsible for the final results.

Operations provides the DBA with standard reports concerning data base usage, system performance, and any errors or problems encountered. Also, operations should provide periodic verification that the standard procedures are being implemented.

USING THE DATA DICTIONARY/DIRECTORY SYSTEM

The data dictionary/directory system (DD/DS) is an essential tool for data base administration and it is used by the data base administrator throughout the entire data base system life cycle. In this section, we describe how the DD/DS is used to support the various activities during this life cycle. Additional details of the DD/DS are provided in Chapter 11.

The uses of the DD/DS during each stage of the life cycle are shown in Figure 10-4. There are four major types of usage:

1. Documentation support: recording, classifying, and reporting metadata.
2. Design aid: documenting the relationships between data entities and performing impact analyses.
3. Metadata generation: generating metadata in formats required by other software components of the data management system (such as DBMS and application programs).
4. Change control: enforcing standards, evaluating the impact of proposed changes, and implementing changes (such as adding new attributes or record types).

Use During System Planning

The DD/DS should be used to document the various "products" of data base planning described in Chapter 3. These products include the business functions, processes, activities, entities, and transactions of the organization. As each of these objects is defined and described, it should be recorded in the DD/DS.

The DD/DS should also be used as a high-level design aid during data base planning. As we describe in Chapter 3, one of the major objectives of this phase is to develop a strategic data model or entity chart, such as the one for Mountain View Hospital shown in Figure 3-12. The DD/DS is used to document the associations among the entities and also may be used to map other associations, such as the relationships between transactions and business activities.

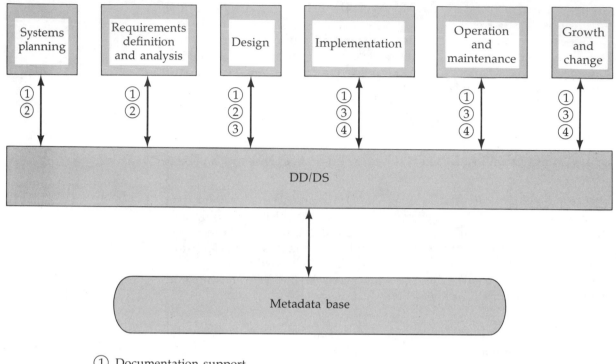

① Documentation support
② Design aid
③ Metadata generation
④ Change control

Figure 10-4
Using the DD/DS during
the data base system life
cycle.
(Source: Leong-Hong and
Plagman 1982. Adapted
with permission.)

Use During Requirements Formulation and Analysis

During requirements formulation and analysis, analysts collect detailed information from users concerning existing and future uses of data. Data items are defined and described. Also described are existing documents, reports, displays, and other user views of data. All the data are associated with the business functions and activities that require their use. Thus, a vast amount of detailed metadata is collected and analyzed during requirements formulation and analysis. As shown in Figure 10-4, the DD/DS is used as a documentation tool and design aid during this phase.

Use During Design

Data base design consists of three phases: conceptual design, implementation design, and physical design. For each data base, the design effort results in a logical and physical design that can be implemented on a target data base management system. The DD/DS is used as a design aid and as a tool to document the logical and physical designs. The DD/DS is also used to generate metadata such as DBMS control blocks or COBOL file descriptions. Finally, the DD/DS can be used to generate user manuals and other forms of documentation.

Use During Implementation

During implementation, the data base is initially loaded and tested. New application programs for loading and updating the data base are also developed and tested. The DD/DS is used during this phase for documentation support, metadata generation, and change control.

The DD/DS is used to produce documentation for all users during implementation. For example, programmers require descriptions of data elements, record types, and other metadata in developing application programs. The DBA uses the DD/DS to resolve inconsistencies (such as synonyms and homonyms or conflicting data types) when loading the data base. Also, the DD/DS is used to enforce standards during implementation. For example, editing criteria and security locks or other mechanisms should be incorporated in the DD/DS. In addition, the DD/DS can be used to generate test data that are used to test various system components during implementation.

Use During Operation and Maintenance

The operation and maintenance phase represents the ongoing updating, operation, and maintenance of the data base. The DD/DS is the basic tool used by the DBA for documentation and control during this phase. For example, the DD/DS is used to enforce standards for security, data integrity, and backup and recovery. Also, the DD/DS is used to collect usage statistics and may be used as the basis for data base auditing and control.

Use During Growth and Change

During the last phase of the life cycle, the DBA monitors the usage and performance of the data base and plans for growth and change. Again, the DD/DS is the primary tool that supports these activities. For example, it can be used for **impact analysis**, determining the impact of a proposed change such as adding a new data item type, record type, or association. In addition, the DD/DS is used to analyze and record changes in business functions, processes, activities, and entities—thus completing the system life cycle.

ORGANIZING THE DBA FUNCTION

This section addresses three key management issues that arise in organizing the DBA functions. The means by which top management resolves these issues is a good indication of their acceptance of data resource management. The three issues are selection of the data base administrator, placement of the DBA function in the organization, and staffing of the DBA functions.

Selecting the DBA

This chapter is essentially an extended job description for the position of data base administrator. A review of the functions of the DBA (see Figure 10-2) indicates that the DBA must possess an unusual collection of managerial, analytical, and technical skills. However, in reviewing the full range of responsibilities, it is apparent that the job is more managerial than technical. The DBA must perform the following typical managerial functions:

1. Planning: developing a comprehensive plan for the organization's data resource.
2. Organizing: organizing and staffing the DBA function.
3. Supervising: supervising the DBA staff.
4. Communicating: communicating with managers, users, and computer specialists.
5. Controlling: developing procedural controls for maintaining and protecting the data resource.

Thus, the organization should define the data base administrator position as a management position. The ideal candidate is a person with at least middle management experience (line or staff), a broad knowledge and a "sense" of the enterprise (including its politics), and stature as a manager. Such a person requires some familiarity with computer-based information systems, but does not have to be a computer or data base expert.

Other candidates for the DBA position might include business analysts, user-oriented systems analysts, or a DBA with relevant experience in another, similar organization. However, a manager with experience in the enterprise is usually preferred.

Highly technical computer specialists such as system programmers are not usually good candidates for data base administrator. Selecting such persons normally results from an overly narrow, technical definition of the DBA position. Most of these individuals do not have the managerial experience, aptitude, or desire to be a data base administrator. However, computer specialists might be assigned to the DBA staff.

Placement of the DBA Function

In most organizations today, the DBA function is placed within the information systems (or data processing) organization. Where the DBA function is placed within the EDP organization varies from one firm to another, depending on the role and tasks assigned to data base administration. Weldon (1981) has identified five common locations within EDP for the DBA function. These locations (shown in Figure 10-5) are described by their orientation (project or functional) and by the nature of the DBA role (advisory, support, consultant, or management).

Advisory DBA.   The advisory DBA is a small staff group (one or more persons) that reports directly to the EDP manager (Figure 10-5a). The functions of the advisory DBA are generally limited to planning, research, and policy formulation. This approach may be used during the early planning stages for a data base approach. Once a DBMS has been introduced, this organization is usually replaced by one of the other forms described here.

Project/Support DBA.   The project/support DBA organization reports to an applications project manager (see Figure 10-5b). The DBA supports the project team by performing data base design tasks and by supporting data base operation and control. In large organizations that follow this approach, it is not unusual to find more than one DBA group, each reporting to a different project team. This organizational approach is generally not effective, since the DBA group should be concerned with an organization-wide view of data, rather than a single application area.

Functional/Support DBA.   The functional/support DBA reports to the manager of support services (Figure 10-5c). The DBA's services are available in a supporting role to all project groups, as needed. This organizational approach is generally not effective, since the DBA has no real input on application priorities or control over the data base.

Consultant DBA.   The consultant DBA reports in a line responsibility to the EDP manager along with the project managers (see Figure 10-5d). At this level, the DBA participates in decision making across all applications and makes recommendations to data processing management. The consultant DBA is the most common organizational position for the DBA today, according to Weldon (1981).

Management DBA.   The management DBA reports directly to the EDP manager and is located higher in the organization than project managers (see Figure 10-5e). In this position, the DBA is able to promulgate and

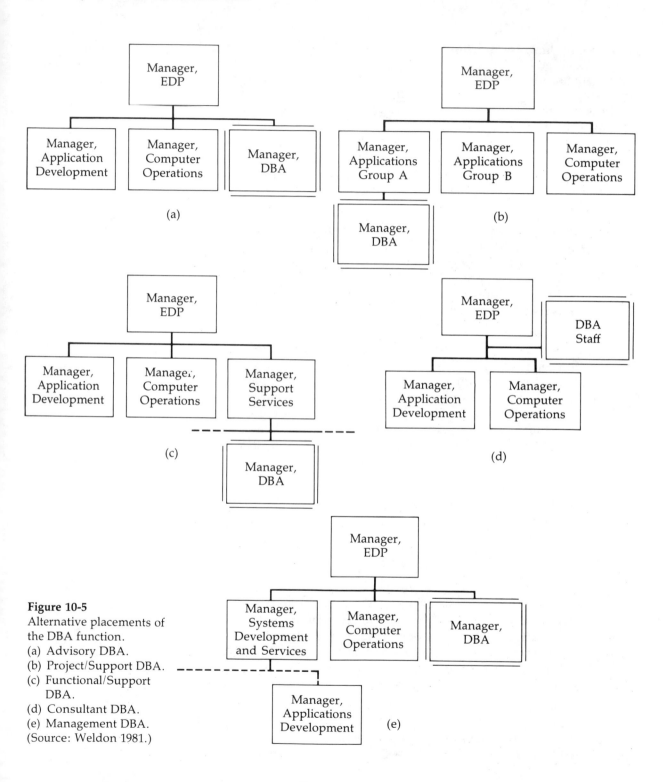

Figure 10-5
Alternative placements of
the DBA function.
(a) Advisory DBA.
(b) Project/Support DBA.
(c) Functional/Support
DBA.
(d) Consultant DBA.
(e) Management DBA.
(Source: Weldon 1981.)

enforce standards for system development and data control. The management DBA is the preferred approach among those described here, since it represents a strong commitment by the company to a data base approach.

The DBA Function in a Decentralized Organization

An advantage of establishing the DBA function is the centralization of numerous data management functions. Tasks such as data base planning, design, operation, and control (which were previously fragmented) are centralized under the DBA. However, this may also lead to conflict in organizations where data processing is decentralized. Fortunately, several organizational arrangements can be used to resolve (or at least minimize) this conflict. Three typical methods of organizing the DBA function in a decentralized environment are shown in Figure 10-6 (for an extended discussion see Weldon 1981).

Decentralized DBA. In organizations where all hardware and system development activities are decentralized, decentralized DBA groups may be formed as needed within each organization (see Figure 10-6a). If there is a corporate system group, a DBA liaison may be established to coordinate among the several DBA groups. This approach will promote the move toward organization-wide standards and knowledge sharing. Lack of such coordination will likely result in incompatible systems and much "reinventing the wheel."

One technique for improving compatibility and avoiding excessive duplication of effort is to designate one of the sites as a "pilot project." As the data base development projects at the pilot site are completed, relevant portions may be transferred to the remaining sites. Also, DBA personnel at the pilot site may act as consultants to the other decentralized DBA groups. However, overall progress is likely to be slow, and there is no assurance that the resulting systems will be compatible.

Centralized DBA. With this approach, the DBA function is centralized within corporate systems (Figure 10-6b). The centralized DBA acts in a support, consultant, or management role to decentralized system development groups.

Partially Decentralized DBA. With this approach, the central DBA staff is partitioned and assigned, as needed, to local organizations. Typically, technical DBA staff (such as DBMS support) remain at the central location. Data base designers are separated and report to local operations managers, with a dotted-line responsibility to the DBA manager (see Figure 10-6c). This alternative is a compromise between the preceding approaches and provides a good balance between flexibility and control.

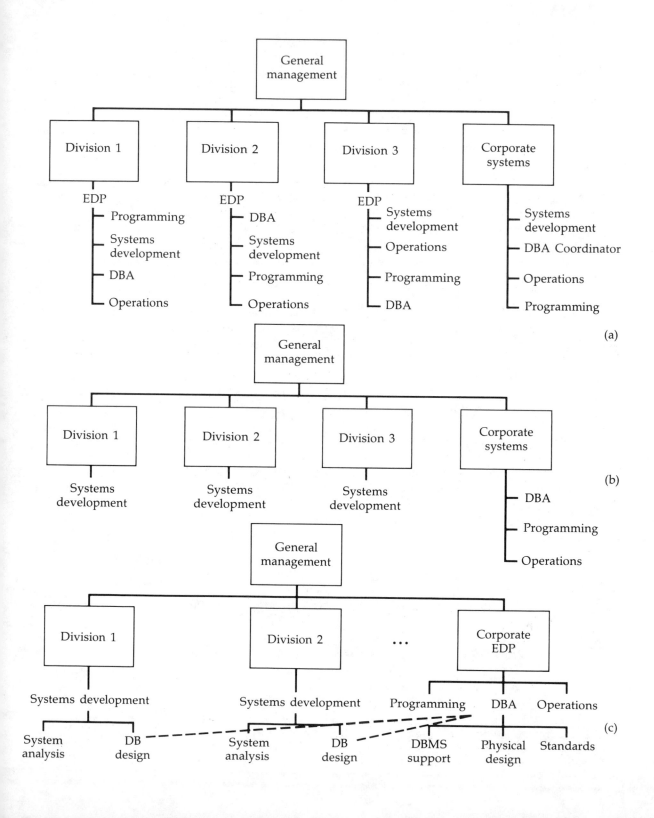

(a)

(b)

(c)

Types of DBA Organizations

The DBA group can be organized along functional or project lines. Weldon (1981) has described a number of alternative organizations for the DBA function. Four typical organizations are shown in Figure 10-7.

Flat DBA Organization.   The flat DBA organization (shown in Figure 10-7a) is typically used in the early stages of DBA development. The organization consists of a few individuals who report directly to the DBA manager. These individuals share the specialized tasks required, such as logical design, physical design, and data dictionary maintenance.

Functional DBA Organization.   As the DBA group becomes larger, it is necessary to organize along functional lines. A typical organization is shown in Figure 10-7b, where there are three functional groups: DB design, data dictionary, and DB operation and control. Each of these groups is headed by a manager who reports to the DBA manager. Data base planning tasks are either assumed by the DBA manager, or (as shown) a separate planning function may be established, as needed.

Project-Oriented DBA.   With a project-oriented DBA, the DB designers are assigned to individual applications or project areas (Figure 10-7c). Other support groups (such as DBMS and data dictionary) continue to report directly to the DBA manager. This approach allows data base designers to become thoroughly familiar with the requirements of a given area. However, it tends to discourage integration among the various areas and, as a result, is generally dysfunctional.

Matrix Organization.   In a matrix DBA organization, certain DBA tasks (such as design and support) are assigned to groups outside the DBA organization. These groups could be system development project groups, end user organizations, or even computer operations (see Figure 10-7d). The assigned groups maintain a dotted-line (indirect) reporting relationship to the DBA manager.

   A matrix organization for the DBA function provides the advantage of flexibility: data base administration can easily adapt to immediate organizational needs. However, there are also two important disadvantages. First, the dual reporting relationship becomes a source of confusion and conflict. Second, the power of the DBA manager is eroded, since a portion of the DBA staff reports directly to other managers. Unless the company routinely (and effectively) uses a matrix form of organization, a matrix organization for the DBA function should be avoided.

Figure 10-6 (opposite) DBA organizations in a decentralized environment.
(a) Decentralized DBA.
(b) Centralized DBA.
(c) Partially decentralized DBA.
(Source: Weldon 1981.)

Figure 10-7
Typical internal DBA
organizations.
(a) Flat DBA
    organization.
(b) Functional DBA
    organization.
(c) Project-oriented DBA.
(d) DBA with matrix
    organization.
(Source: Weldon 1981.)

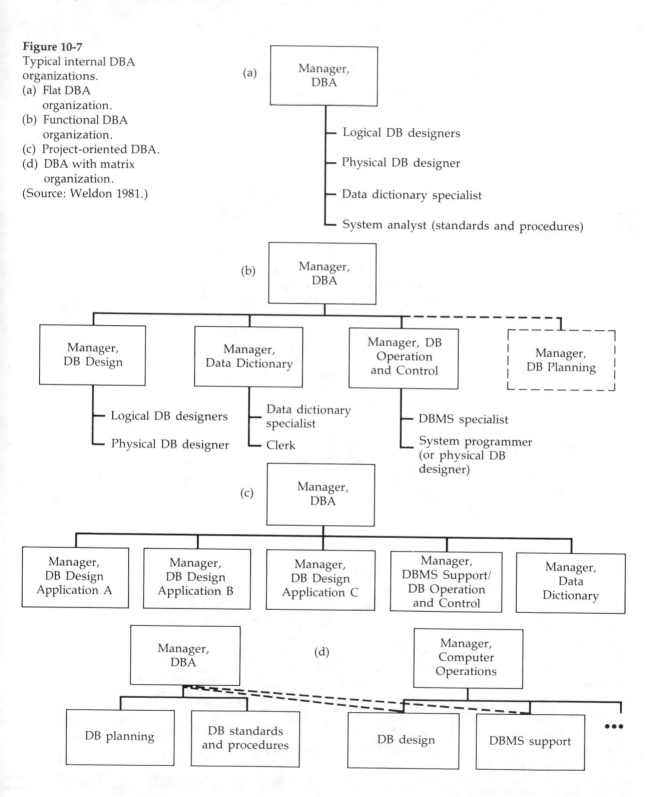

Mountain View Community Hospital

At Mountain View Community Hospital, Mr. Helms was appointed Data Base Administrator following the initial planning study (described in Chapter 3). Mr. Helms was a systems analyst who was a new employee at Mountain View Community, but had previous experience in data base design.

Mr. Helms reports to Mr. Heller, who is Manager of Information Systems (an organization chart for Mountain View Community is shown in Figure 3-8). In turn, a Data Analyst (Mrs. Green) reports to Mr. Helms. The placement of the DBA function at Mountain View Community is an example of the Consultant DBA approach, since the DBA reports directly to the MIS manager, along with two other project managers. As the data base becomes operational, another employee will probably be added to data base administration. However, a flat organization is likely to be used for the foreseeable future.

SUMMARY

Data base administration is essential to managing the organization's data resource. The DBA function is responsible for managing the data base system life cycle. This life cycle consists of data base planning, requirements analysis, data base design, implementation, maintenance, and growth and change. The actual operations of maintaining and updating the data base are the responsibility of the users. However, the DBA function is responsible for developing procedures and controls that ensure that these operations are performed so as to protect the integrity and security of the data base.

Data base administration is a resource management function. It should be assigned at a sufficiently high level within the organization to resolve any potential disputes among users of the data base. Ideally, data base administration should be assigned at a general management level, to an administrative or executive vice-president or to the chief executive officer's staff. However, many organizations assign the DBA initially to report to the manager of information systems.

The manager, data base administration (or data base administrator) should be defined as a management (rather than technical) position. The person selected for this position should have significant management experience within the enterprise. The DBA staff can then be filled out with the necessary technical skills appropriate to the maturity of the DBA function.

CHAPTER REVIEW

Review Questions

1. Contrast data administration and data base administration.

2. List and briefly describe six stages in the data base system life cycle.

3. What are the four major interfaces of data base administration? Summarize the major types of communications with each of these groups.

4. Describe four types of usage of the data dictionary/directory system by DBA.

5. Describe five typical placements (or locations) of the DBA function in actual organizations. Which placement is preferred?

6. Describe three basic types of changes that occur with data bases, and describe the responses available to DBA.

7. a. Where should data base administration be assigned when the function is first created?
   b. Where should it be assigned as the DBA function evolves?

8. Describe four alternative organizations for the DBA function.

Problems and Exercises

1. Customcraft, Inc., is a mail-order firm specializing in the manufacture of stationery and other paper products. Annual sales of Customcraft are $25 million and are growing at a rate of 15% per year. After several years' experience with conventional data processing systems, Customcraft has decided to organize a data base administration function. At present, they have four major candidates for the data base administrator position:

   • John Bach, a senior systems analyst with three years' experience at Customcraft who has attended recent seminars in structured systems design and data base.

   • Margaret Smith, who has been production control manager for the past two years after a year's experience as programmer/analyst at Customcraft.

   • William Rogers, a systems programmer with extensive experience with TOTAL and ADABAS, the two data base management systems under consideration at Customcraft.

   • Ellen Reddy, who is currently data base administrator with a medium-sized electronics firm in the same city as Customcraft.

   Based on this limited information, rank the four candidates for the DBA position, and state your reasons.

2. Evaluate the selection and organizational assignment of the data base administrator for Mountain View Community Hospital. Can you suggest a better candidate for the DBA position than the one selected?

3. Visit an organization that has implemented the data base approach. Evaluate each of the following:

   a. The functions performed by data base administration in the organization.

   b. The organizational placement of the DBA function.

   c. The background of the person chosen for data base administrator.

   d. The DBA staff and its functions.

4. List the major costs and benefits of a data base system at Mountain View Community Hospital.

5. List the major costs and benefits of a data base system at Pine Valley Furniture Company.

6. A major electronics firm has its corporate headquarters on the East coast. There are manufacturing plants located throughout the country. Each plant has its own computer and data processing organization. Describe three alternative ways for organizing the DBA function in this company.

References

Canning, R.G. 1972. "The 'Data Administrator' Function." *EDP Analyzer* 10 (November): 1–14.

Guide International. 1977. "Establishing the Data Administration Function." Chicago: Guide International.

Leong-Hong, B.W., and Bernard K. Plagman. 1982. *Data Dictionary/Directory Systems: Administration, Implementation, and Usage.* New York: Wiley-Interscience.

Lyon, John K. 1976. *The Database Administrator.* New York: Wiley-Interscience.

McFadden, Fred R., and James D. Suver. 1978. "Costs and Benefits of a Data Base System." *Harvard Business Review* 56 (January–February): 131–139.

Perry, William E. 1982. *Evaluating the Cost/Benefits of Data Bases.* Wellesley, Mass.: Q.E.D. Information Sciences, Inc.

Weldon, J.L. 1979a. "The Changing Role of Data Base Administration." Center for Research on Information Systems, New York University.

———. 1979b. "Organizing for Data Base Administration." Center for Research on Information Systems, New York University.

———. 1981. *Data Base Administration.* New York: Plenum Press.

IV

Data Base Implementation

Part IV consists of four chapters in which we describe a number of implementations of data base management systems. These systems are illustrated and compared using common examples.

Chapter 11 presents an introduction to data management software. We describe the various components of a modern data management system, including data base management systems, data dictionary/directory systems, teleprocessing monitors, and query languages. Important functions of a data management system are described, including metadata management, security, backup and recovery, and concurrency control.

Chapter 12 describes implementations of the hierarchical data model. Much of the emphasis is placed on IBM's Information Management System, or IMS. A brief description is also presented of System 2000, another hierarchical DBMS.

Chapter 13 presents a description of the network (or CODASYL) implementation. The various components of CODASYL are described in detail, including the data description language (DDL) and data manipulation language (DML).

Chapter 14 describes several implementations of the relational data model. Some of the languages described in this chapter are SQL/DS, NOMAD, and QUERY-BY-EXAMPLE.

11

Data Management Systems

INTRODUCTION

Choosing the right software for data management is a key ingredient in managing the data resource successfully. In making this choice, the organization should place the highest priority on the productivity of its human resources. These resources take precedence over hardware, whose price and performance are expected to continue to improve dramatically over at least the next decade. Many progressive organizations today are selecting software products that allow end users to take greater responsibility in creating and managing their own data. The "information center" concept, whereby users do their own computing, portends the future.

We describe the major components of data management software in this chapter. Desirable features of these components are noted, and the interrelationships among the components are described. More detailed descriptions of individual products are presented in the following chapters.

DATA MANAGEMENT SOFTWARE COMPONENTS

An overview of the software components in a modern data management system is shown in Figure 11-1. This diagram shows the product line for Cullinet's IDMS data base management system (other vendors use a similar approach). Notice that the various software products and languages are organized around a common data dictionary/directory (called the Integrated Data Dictionary).

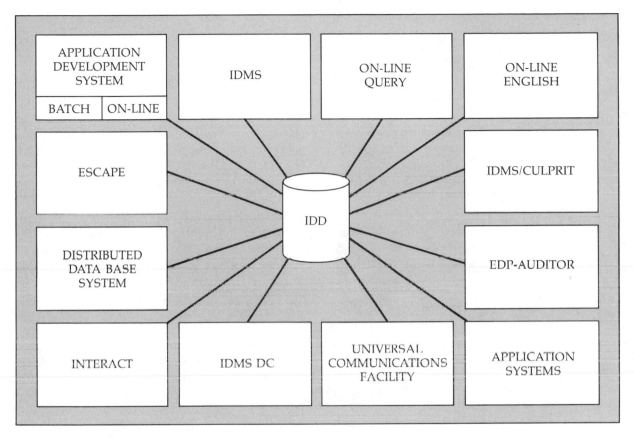

Figure 11-1
Integrated data
management products.
(Courtesy Cullinet.)

Following are the major components of Cullinet's data base management software that are found in most integrated software systems today.

Data Base Management System (DBMS). A DBMS is a generalized software system that is used to manage data bases. The Cullinet DBMS (Integrated Database Management System, or IDMS) supports both centralized and distributed data bases.

Data Dictionary/Directory System. A data dictionary/directory system is a software facility that manages the organization's metadata. The Cullinet Integrated Data Dictionary (IDD) is used to manage all the data management products, as shown in Figure 11-1.

Teleprocessing Monitor. A TP monitor manages all communications with remote terminals. IDMS provides two facilities: IDMS-DC, which is a fully integrated TP monitor, and Universal Communications Facility, which is an interface that allows IDMS applications to communicate with TP monitors developed by other vendors.

Query Language Processor (QLP).   A query language processor provides an interactive retrieval system based on high-level English-language commands. With this facility, users who have no training in procedural languages (such as BASIC and COBOL) can easily retrieve information that is stored in the data base. IDMS provides two query languages: ONLINE QUERY and ONLINE ENGLISH.

Report Generator.   With a report generator facility, a user can design a new report without writing application code. The report generator facility provided by Cullinet (CULPRIT) includes EDP-AUDITOR, a library of routines for auditing the data base.

Application Development Facility (ADF).   An application development facility is a set of program modules and commands for on-line program development. The CULLINET facility (called INTERACT) also includes facilities for text editing and word processing.

Although not shown in Figure 11-1, the data management system will normally include a number of tools to support data base administration. Some of these tools include restart/recovery utilities, data base design aids, and data base performance monitors.

The trend in data management software today is toward an integrated set of software products (such as those shown in Figure 11-1) organized around a common data dictionary/directory. The data dictionary/directory provides all the metadata (or data definitions) that are used by the various software components. We describe many of these software products and their interaction with the data dictionary/directory in subsequent sections.

DBMS FUNCTIONS AND ARCHITECTURE

A **data base management system** (DBMS) is a generalized software system which manages the data base, providing facilities for organization, access, and control (Auerbach Publishers 1981). The term *generalized* means that the DBMS is independent of individual applications and therefore can be employed by any user requiring access to the data base.

DBMS Functions

According to Codd (1982), a comprehensive DBMS provides eight major functions.

Data Storage, Retrieval, and Update.   A data base may be shared by many users. Thus, the DBMS must provide multiple user views and allow users to store, retrieve, and update their data easily and efficiently.

Data Dictionary/Directory. In Chapter 1, we defined the data dictionary/directory as the repository of all information about an organization's data. The DBMS must maintain a user-accessible data dictionary/directory. (This service may be provided by a module of the DBMS itself or by an independent software package, as we will see shortly.)

Transaction Integrity. A **transaction** is a sequence of steps that constitute some well-defined business activity. Examples of transactions are "Admit Patient" (in a hospital) and "Enter Customer Order" (in a manufacturing company).

Normally, a transaction requires several actions against the data base. For example, consider the transaction "Enter Customer Order." When a new customer order is entered, the following steps may be performed by an application program:

1. Input order data (keyed by user).
2. Read Customer record (or insert record if a new customer).
3. Accept or reject the order (if BALANCE-DUE plus ORDER-AMOUNT does not exceed CREDIT-LIMIT, accept the order; otherwise, reject it).
4. If the order is accepted:
   a. Increase BALANCE-DUE by ORDER-AMOUNT.
   b. Store the updated Customer record.
   c. Insert the accepted Order record in the data base.

In processing a transaction, we want the changes to the data base to be made only if the transaction is processed successfully, in its entirety. In this case, we say that the changes are **committed**. If the transaction fails at any point, we say that it has **aborted** and we do not want any of the changes to be made. For example, suppose that the program accepts a new customer order, increases BALANCE-DUE, and stores the updated Customer record. However, suppose that the new Order record is not inserted successfully (perhaps there is a duplicate ORDER# key, or perhaps there is insufficient file space). In this case, we want the transaction to abort and the changes not committed.

To maintain transaction integrity, the DBMS must provide facilities for the user or application programmer to define **transaction boundaries** — that is, the logical beginning and end of transactions. The DBMS should then commit changes for successful transactions and reject changes for aborted transactions.

Recovery Services. The DBMS must be able to restore the data base (or return it to a known condition) in the event of some system failure. Sources of system failure include operator error, disk head crashes, and program errors. Measures for data base recovery are described later.

Concurrency Control.   Since a data base is shared by multiple users, two or more users may attempt to access the same data simultaneously. If two users attempt to update the same data record concurrently, erroneous results may occur, since the transactions may interfere with each other. Safeguards must be built into the DBMS to prevent or overcome the effects of such interference. We will discuss this issue later.

Security Mechanisms.   Data must be protected against accidental or intentional misuse or destruction. The DBMS provides mechanisms for controlling access to data and for defining what actions (such as read-only or update) may be taken by each user.

Data Communications Interface.   Users often access a data base by means of remote terminals in a telecommunications network. A telecommunications monitor is used to process the flow of transactions to and from the remote terminals. The DBMS must provide an interface with one or more telecommunications monitors so that all the necessary functions are performed and the system will assist, rather than place a burden on, the end user.

Integrity Services.   The DBMS must provide facilities that assist users in maintaining the integrity of their data. A variety of edit checks and integrity constraints can be designed into the DBMS and its software interfaces. These checks are normally administered through the data dictionary/directory.

Most contemporary data base management systems provide all the functions named here, at least to some degree (although most do not yet provide a comprehensive set of integrity services). However, DBMS products differ in the manner in which the functions are performed. With some user-friendly products, the functions are performed more or less automatically by the DBMS, with little or no user involvement. With other products, the DBMS provides some facilities or interfaces, but the user must take major responsibility for defining the functions (either directly or through application programs). Thus, an organization must evaluate its needs and select its data management software carefully.

Data Base Definition

A DBMS must provide users with language facilities for describing their data bases. A **data definition language** (DDL) is a vocabulary, or set of commands, that is used to describe a data base to the DBMS. The data base specialist uses the DDL to describe data items, records, primary and secondary keys, and record relationships. In some systems, the DDL is also used to define integrity constraints and access controls.

Schemas.   A **schema** is a specification (or definition) of a data base using the DDL. In Chapter 2, we introduced the ANSI/SPARC three-level data base model (see Figure 2-17). This model allows us to view any data base at three levels of abstraction: the conceptual model, the internal (storage) model, and the external views. Thus, we see that a DBMS that supports the ANSI/SPARC model must allow the user to express three types of schemas: a conceptual schema, an internal schema, and one or more external schemas. Separate data definition languages are often used to express each of these types of schemas.

DBMS Families.   The data definition languages that are used vary from one DBMS product to another. However, there are similarities among **families** of DBMS products. Following are the major DBMS families and the entities that are described in the DDL for each family:

1. Hierarchical family: schemas are used to describe fields, segments, data base records, and data bases; examples are provided in Chapter 12.

2. Network family: schemas are used to describe data items, records, sets, and user views (called subschemas); examples are provided in Chapter 13.

3. Relational family: schemas are used to describe attributes, domains, relations, and views; examples are provided in Chapter 14.

Conceptual Schema.   The conceptual schema defines a global model of the data base. The underlying data model may be hierarchical, network, or relational. Ideally, the data model should make no reference to how the data model is implemented (inverted list, multiple linked lists, and so on) or how the data are physically stored or accessed.

Pine Valley Furniture   CASE EXAMPLE

A simple model for a data base is shown in Figure 11-2 (this model was extracted from a more comprehensive model for Pine Valley Furniture Company). The conceptual model shown in Figure 11-2a (called ORDER-ACCOUNTING) has two record types, Customer and Order. There is a one-to-many association between these record types. Figure 11-2b shows sample data for this model, expressed in the form of the relations CUSTOMER and ORDER.

Figure 11-2c shows a sample relational schema for this data base. The relations are defined by means of CREATE TABLE commands. The attributes in each table are named in the command, and their types and lengths are specified. The schema is user-oriented and contains no information about physical implementation.

Figure 11-2
Conceptual model and
schema.
(a) Conceptual model
    (ORDER-
    ACCOUNTING).
(b) Sample data.
(c) Sample schema
    (relational).

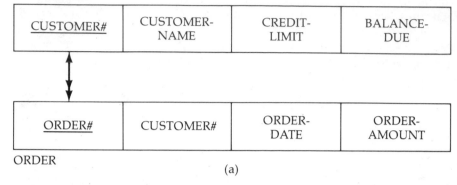

CUSTOMER

CUSTOMER#	CUSTOMER-NAME	CREDIT-LIMIT	BALANCE-DUE

ORDER#	CUSTOMER#	ORDER-DATE	ORDER-AMOUNT

ORDER

(a)

CUSTOMER#	CUSTOMER-NAME	CREDIT-LIMIT	BALANCE-DUE
S298	SUSAN'S PLACE	10,000	6,000
C039	CONTEMP DES	15,000	10,000
A123	CASUAL FURN	5,000	4,000

CUSTOMER

ORDER#	CUSTOMER#	ORDER-DATE	ORDER-AMOUNT
816	A123	12/20/8X	4,000
713	C039	12/8/8X	7,000
942	S298	1/12/8X	5,000
629	C039	12/2/8X	3,000
867	S298	12/28/8X	1,000

ORDER

(b)

```
CREATE TABLE CUSTOMER    (CUSTOMER#          (CHAR(4), NONULL),
                          CUSTOMER-NAME      (CHAR(20)),
                          CREDIT-LIMIT       (INTEGER),
                          BALANCE-DUE        (FLOAT))

     CREATE TABLE ORDER   (ORDER#             (INTEGER, NONULL),
                          CUSTOMER#          (CHAR(4)),
                          ORDER-DATE         (CHAR(8)),
                          ORDER-AMOUNT       (FLOAT))
```

(c)

External Schemas.   External schemas are derived from the conceptual
schema. They define subsets, or views, of the real data. Many external
schemas are defined for a single conceptual schema.

  The DDL used to define external views depends on the data model
being used. Normally, the data model used to define external schemas is the
same as the one used in the conceptual schema (e.g., both are network).

CUSTOMER#	CREDIT-LIMIT
S298	10,000
C039	15,000
A123	5,000

Figure 11-3
External schemas.
(a) User view 1.
(b) User view 2.

DEFINE VIEW USERVIEW1 (CUSTOMER#, CREDIT-LIMIT)
AS SELECT CUSTOMER#, CREDIT-LIMIT FROM CUSTOMER

(a)

CUSTOMER-NAME	ORDER#	ORDER-AMOUNT
CASUAL FURN	816	4,000
CONTEMP DES	713	7,000
SUSAN'S PLACE	942	5,000
CONTEMP FURN	629	3,000
SUSAN'S PLACE	867	1,000

DEFINE VIEW USERVIEW2 (CUSTOMER-NAME, ORDER#, ORDER-AMOUNT)
AS SELECT CUSTOMER-NAME, ORDER#, ORDER AMOUNT FROM CUSTOMER, ORDER
WHERE CUSTOMER. CUSTOMER#=ORDER. CUSTOMER#

(b)

However, some DBMS products allow the conceptual schema to be defined with one data model and the external schemas defined with a different data model. In fact, IDMS (pictured in Figure 11-1) allows users to define their external views using either the CODASYL (network) model or the relational model.

Two external views for ORDER-ACCOUNTING and the associated external schemas are shown in Figure 11-3. These views are derived from the conceptual model by specifying relational algebra commands that are applied to the relations CUSTOMER and ORDER. Each view (or external schema) is defined by a DEFINE VIEW clause followed by a list of attributes that appear in that view. We define the first user view by selecting two attributes (CUSTOMER# and CREDIT-LIMIT) from the CUSTOMER relation. The second user view requires a join of the CUSTOMER and ORDER relations over the CUSTOMER# attribute. Three attributes (CUSTOMER-NAME, ORDER#, and ORDER-AMOUNT) are then selected to form the user view. The language used to form these user views simply names the necessary attributes and relations, but does not express their physical characteristics.

Internal Schema.   The internal schema (or storage schema) for a data base defines the storage files that contain the actual data records for the data base.

Figure 11-4
Index entries for internal
schema.

CREATE UNIQUE INDEX CUSTNO-INDEX ON CUSTOMER (CUSTOMER#)
CREATE INDEX CUSTNAME-INDEX ON CUSTOMER (CUSTOMER-NAME)
CREATE UNIQUE INDEX ORDERNO-INDEX ON ORDER (ORDER#)
CREATE INDEX CNBR-INDEX ON ORDER (CUSTOMER#)

Normally, there is one storage file for each conceptual file or relation described in the conceptual schema. Also, the internal schema defines the
details of the data structures that are used by the DBMS to locate records and
to establish associations between records. For example, inverted lists that
are used to implement secondary keys are defined in the internal schema, as
are pointer fields used to link records.

For the ORDER-ACCOUNTING data base we have been describing,
there are two stored files: a Customer file and an Order file. The characteristics of these files (including the names, types, and lengths of the data
items or attributes) are specified in the conceptual schema (see Figure 11-2)
and do not need to be repeated in the internal schema. However, the
internal schema must specify the indexes used to locate records.

For each of the stored files, we have created two indexes: a primary key
index (specified by CREATE UNIQUE INDEX) and a secondary key index
(specified by CREATE INDEX). The index entries are shown in Figure 11-4.
The first entry in this index is the following:

CREATE UNIQUE INDEX CUSTNO-INDEX ON CUSTOMER
(CUSTOMER#)

This statement instructs the DBMS to create an index (called CUSTNO-
INDEX) for the primary key CUSTOMER# in the CUSTOMER file. This
index will allow users direct access to customer records, given a value for
CUSTOMER#.

The last entry in Figure 11-4 is the following:

CREATE INDEX CNBR-INDEX ON ORDER (CUSTOMER#)

This entry causes the DBMS to create a secondary key index (called CNBR-
INDEX) for the Order records. With this index, a user can provide a customer number (such as C039) and obtain a list of all outstanding orders for
that customer (for customer C039 there are two orders: 629 and 713).

Notice that the internal model does *not* specify any details of physical
data organization. For example, the Customer file may be organized as a
hash file, while the Order file may be organized as an indexed sequential file.
These details (as well as the record blocking factors) are specified to the
access method and are often unknown to the DBMS. On the other hand, the
indexes and list organizations specified in the internal schema are created
and maintained by the DBMS and are unknown to the access methods.

Data Independence

The main reason for using the three-level DBMS architecture that we have just described is that it provides a high level of data independence. In Chapter 2, we defined data independence as being able to change the structure of data without having to modify application programs. There are two types of data independence—logical and physical—and we will now illustrate each type for the ORDER-ACCOUNTING data base.

Logical Data Independence.   Logical data independence is the property that allows us to change the conceptual schema (or overall logical structure of the data base) without changing external schemas or application programs. This property is vital because it allows the data base to grow and change without inflicting excessive maintenance costs.

Consider the following two changes to the conceptual schema for ORDER-ACCOUNTING (Figure 11-2):

1. Data item change: Suppose that it is necessary to change the length of the data item CUSTOMER-NAME from 20 to 30 characters. This is accomplished by changing the specification from CHAR(20) to CHAR(30) in the conceptual schema. Since data item characteristics are not specified in the external schemas (see Figure 11-3), no changes to these views or the programs that use them are required.

2. New data item: Suppose that we wish to add a data item called YTD-SALES to the Customer relation. Again, this change is introduced in the conceptual schema. Any existing views that are derived from the conceptual schema are unaffected by the change.

Physical Data Independence.   Physical data independence is the property that allows us to change physical data organization or access without changing the logical structure. This property is vital, since it permits us to improve performance without having to modify existing programs or user views.

Let us consider two examples of physical data independence for ORDER-ACCOUNTING:

1. Change in implementation procedure: Suppose we want to implement the secondary key CUSTOMER# in the Order records by linked list rather than by an index. This requires a simple change to the internal schema (Figure 11-4), in which the CREATE INDEX clause is replaced by a CREATE LINKED LIST clause. The conceptual schema (and therefore the external schemas) are unaffected by this change.

2. Change in access method: Suppose (for performance reasons) that we want to change the organization of the Customer file from hashed to

indexed sequential. This change is specified in the access method specification (or job control language). No changes to the schemas are required and the DBMS is unaware of the change.

Schema Generation and Translation

In a system that does not use a data dictionary, the three schemas (Figures 11-2 through 11-4) are coded by a data base programmer. However, when a data dictionary/directory system is used, these schemas are generated by the DD/DS using data definitions stored in the data dictionary/directory (DD/D). We describe the data dictionary/directory in the next section.

The source versions of the three schemas (whether coded by hand or generated from the DD/D) are translated by a software module of the DBMS called the DDL translator. The translated versions of the schemas are stored in a library for use by run-time modules of the DBMS (see Figure 11-10).

DATA DICTIONARY/DIRECTORY SYSTEM

The data dictionary/directory system (DD/DS) is the cornerstone of a modern data management system. This system stores and manages all metadata (or "data about data") used by the organization. (We described metadata in Chapter 2; see Figure 2-1.) As we mentioned in Chapter 10, the data dictionary/directory is the principal tool used by data base administration in managing the information resource. Also, as shown in Figure 11-1, an integrated data dictionary/directory interfaces with all other software components of the data management environment.

Components of a DD/DS

A DD/DS has two major components: the data dictionary/directory and the data dictionary/directory manager.

The **data dictionary/directory** (DD/D) is the repository for all organizational metadata, such as data definitions, relationships, and authorities. In other words, the DD/D is a data base of metadata (in fact, it is sometimes referred to as a "metadata base").

The **data dictionary/directory manager** is a software module (or set of modules) used to manage the DD/D. Just as the data base management system is used to manage the user data base, the DD/D manager is used to manage the metadata base.

We can think of the DD/D as being divided into two sections: the data dictionary and the data directory. The **data dictionary** contains definitions of records, data items, relations, and other data objects that are of interest to users or required by data management software. These definitions are employed by users to answer the question, "What data are contained in the organization's data bases, and what are their characteristics?" The same definitions are used by the DD/D manager to generate conceptual and external schemas (such as those shown in Figures 11-2 and 11-3) that are required by the DBMS to access user data bases.

On the other hand, the **data directory** contains information about where data are stored. For example, the internal schemas (such as the one shown in Figure 11-4) are contained in the data directory. Also, the indexes maintained by the DBMS (such as CUSTNO-INDEX and CNAME-INDEX) are stored in the data directory. If the data base is distributed over several geographical locations, the data directory contains information about what data are stored at each node (or location). Thus, the data directory contains information that is used exclusively by data management software rather than by users.

In the discussion that follows, we will emphasize the data dictionary section of the DD/D. However, both types of metadata are always included in the DD/DS.

Structure and Content of the DD/D

The data dictionary contains information about data entities and the relationships between those entities. Thus, the data dictionary is itself a complex data base. A diagram of the structure and contents of a typical data dictionary is shown in Figure 11-5. In this data structure diagram, the data dictionary is organized using a network data model (this is the most common approach). However, data dictionaries are sometimes organized using either the hierarchical or relational data models.

Some 14 types of entities are shown in the diagram in Figure 11-5 (additional entity types can often be created as needed). These entity types can be classified as data entities, system entities, and physical entities.

Data entities describe data objects in the user environment. The data entities included in Figure 11-5 are Element (or Data Item), Group, Record, File, Relationship, Subschema, and Data Base. In a relational data base environment, the data objects would be relations, domains, attributes, and views.

System entities describe objects that process or are otherwise related to data entities. System entities included in Figure 11-5 are Transaction, Report, and Process (a process is a program or program module).

Physical entities are real-world objects that use or are otherwise associated with the data and system objects. The physical entities included in Figure 11-5 are User, Processor, Line, and Terminal.

The associations shown between entities in Figure 11-5 are all one-to-many (however, many-to-many associations can also be represented). The Process entity has a recursive association, since one process (or program) may "call" other processes. The Group (or data aggregate) entity also has a

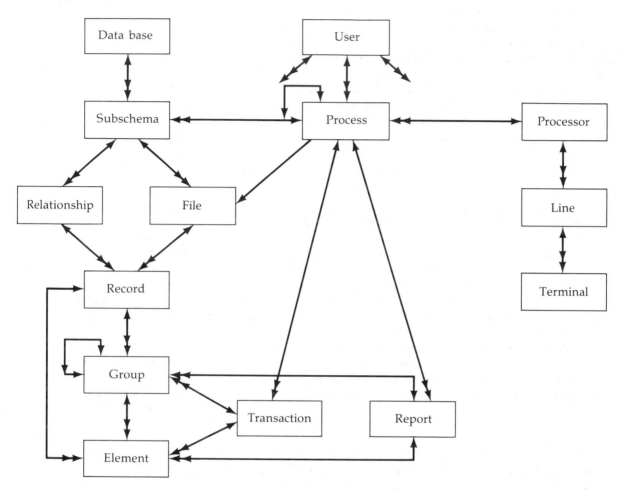

Figure 11-5
Logical structure of a data
dictionary.
(Source: Allen, Loomis,
and Mannino 1982.)

recursive association, since one group may contain other groups. The User
entity may have an association with nearly any other entity type in the
diagram.

A sample occurrence of the logical structure of this data dictionary is
shown in Figure 11-6. This occurrence is for the ORDER-ACCOUNTING
data base. Notice that there is one record occurrence in the data dictionary
for each subschema, one record for each data element type, and so on. The
associations between entities allow us to easily determine what data objects
(such as elements) are used by other objects (such as records or
transactions).

A typical DD/DS allows the user to define numerous attributes for each
entity included in the DD/D. For example, typical attributes for an Element
entity are shown in Table 11-1. The attributes are illustrated for the data item
CREDIT-LIMIT. Notice that in addition to describing the data item, the
attributes contain important editing criteria. Using these metadata, the

Data Base

Subschema
(external views)

Relationship

Record

Element

File

Transaction

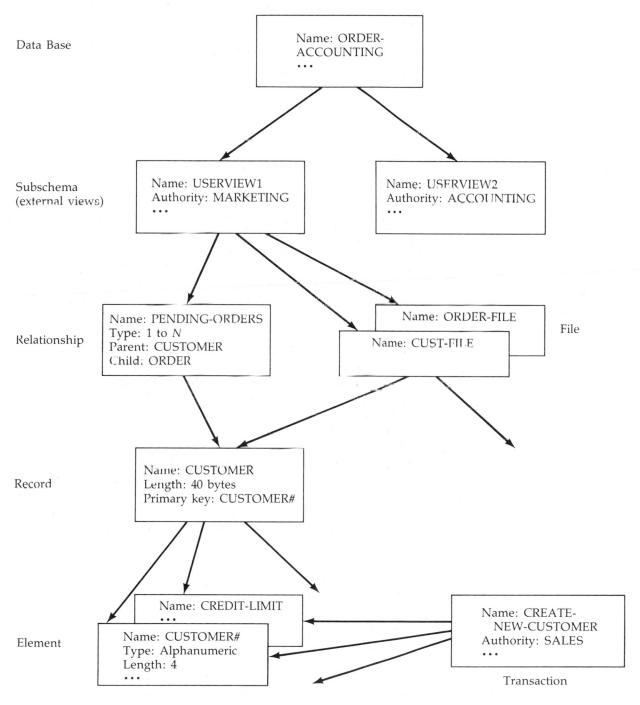

Figure 11-6
An occurrence of DD/D
logical structure.

Table 11-1
Typical Attributes for an Element Entity

Attribute	Example
User name	CREDIT-LIMIT
Type	Numeric
Length	8 bytes
Representation	Packed decimal
Lower limit	0
Upper limit	100,000
Default value	1000
Internal name	CRED-LIM
Display format	ZZZ,ZZ9.99
Description	Maximum unpaid balance for an approved credit customer

DBMS can enforce the editing criteria when users input data. For example, the DBMS should reject any attempt to input a credit limit value that is not numeric, that exceeds 8 bytes, that is negative, or that exceeds the value 100,000.

A typical medium-sized company may have several thousand data items to describe. There will be one record in the data dictionary for each data item that is defined. Each record will contain the attributes shown in Table 11-1 (in reality, additional attributes may be used).

The entities shown in Figure 11-5 and the attributes given in Table 11-1 are typical of those provided in commercial data dictionary/directory systems. However, most vendors provide an **extensibility** feature that allows users to define additional entities, relationships, and attributes as needed. For example, with this feature, a user could define a new entity type called DEPARTMENT to be included in Figure 11-5. The user would define the attributes used to describe DEPARTMENT and the associations between this new entity and other entities in the figure.

Functions of the DD/D Manager

As we have seen, the data dictionary/directory is a complex data base that resembles any other data base in the organization in structure, but not in content (the DD/D contains metadata values rather than data values). Therefore, to manage the data dictionary/directory, the DD/D manager must provide many of the functions of a data base management system (these functions were given earlier in the chapter).

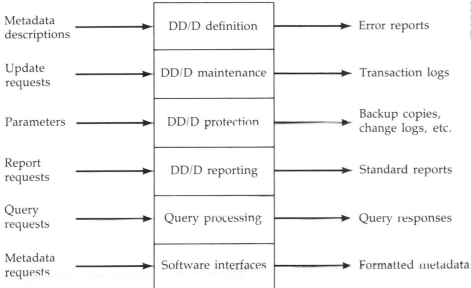

Figure 11-7
Major functions provided
by DD/D manager.

Six major functions normally provided by the DD/D manager are shown in Figure 11-7. Following are brief descriptions of these functions.

DD/D Definition.   The DD/D manager must provide a data definition language for describing entities, relationships, and attributes. We illustrated data definition languages in the previous section (see Figures 11-2 through 11-4).

DD/D Maintenance.   The DD/D manager must also provide language facilities for creating the DD/D and for adding, changing, and deleting its contents. This is normally an interactive language that allows the user to easily access the DD/D from a terminal.

DD/D Protection.   The DD/D manager must provide facilities for protecting the DD/D. Features that are required include security, concurrency control, and backup and recovery (all of these features are described later).

DD/D Reporting.   The DD/D manager must provide a facility for extracting metadata and producing reports describing the organization's data. The DD/D manager may include a report processor module or it may provide an interface to a standard report writer included in the data management system. For example, with Cullinet's data management system (Figure 11-1), the CULPRIT Report Generator is used to produce reports from the Integrated Data Dictionary.

DATA

  DATA BASE   HUMAN RESOURCE

THE HUMAN RESOURCE DATA BASE CONTAINS THE INFORMATION RELATED
TO PERSONNEL, PAYROLL, SKILLS, AND BENEFITS. IT IS MAINTAINED
BY THE VARIOUS SUBSYSTEMS THAT MAKE UP THE HUMAN RESOURCES
APPLICATION SYSTEM. IT IS USED FOR REPORTING BY THESE SAME
SUBSYSTEMS AS WELL AS THE MANAGEMENT REPORTING SYSTEM AND
ACCOUNTING REPORTING SYSTEM.

    AREA   PAYROLL

THE PAYROLL AREA CONSISTS OF THE PAYROLL MASTER FILE AND
CONTAINS INFORMATION REGARDING ALL PAY UNITS. IT IS MANAGED
BY THE PAYROLL DEPARTMENT.

      FILE   PAYROLL–MASTER

THE PAYROLL MASTER FILE CONTAINS A RECORD FOR EACH EMPLOYEE
INCLUDING ACTIVE EMPLOYEES, TERMINATED EMPLOYEES, AND
SUSPENSIONS.

        RECORD   PAYROLL

THE PAYROLL RECORD CONTAINS EMPLOYEE NUMBER,
HIS/HER PAY CODE, AND RATE OF PAY, WHICH ALSO INCLUDES
TAX INFORMATION

          KEY   PAYROLL NUMBER

THE EMPLOYEE NUMBER KEY IS USED TO RANDOMLY ACCESS
PAYROLL RECORDS FOR IDENTIFICATION AND TAX REPORTING
PURPOSES. ONCE ENTERED, AN EMPLOYEE NUMBER
SHOULD NOT BE MODIFIED.

          FIELD   PAYROLL.ACTIVITY CODE

THE EMPLOYEE ACTIVITY CODE ELEMENT CONTAINS THE
NUMBER AND EMPLOYEE PAY CODE AND STATUS CODE

          FIELD   PAYROLL.EMPLOYEE CODE

EMPLOYEE CODE IS ONE CHARACTER FIELD THAT CONTAINS
EMPLOYEES' PAY TYPE. IT SHOULD CONTAIN "H" FOR HOURLY
OR "S" FOR SALARY. THIS IS USED FOR PAY RATE AND YEAR
INFORMATION.

Figure 11-8
Example of data
dictionary report.
(Courtesy ADR.)

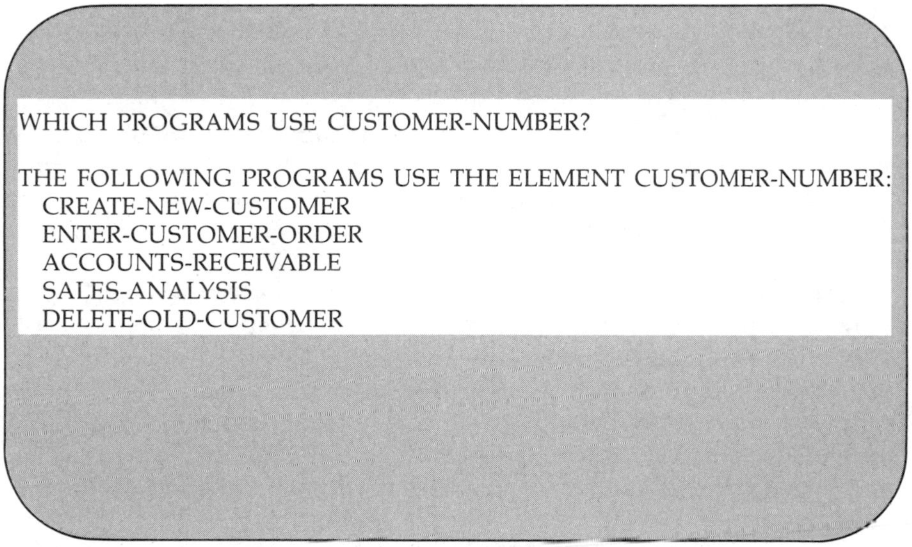

Figure 11-9
Typical DD/D query.

WHICH PROGRAMS USE CUSTOMER-NUMBER?

THE FOLLOWING PROGRAMS USE THE ELEMENT CUSTOMER-NUMBER:
CREATE-NEW-CUSTOMER
ENTER-CUSTOMER-ORDER
ACCOUNTS-RECEIVABLE
SALES-ANALYSIS
DELETE-OLD-CUSTOMER

An example of a standard user-oriented report produced from a DD/D (ADR's DATADICTIONARY) is shown in Figure 11-8. This report uses an indented format to show the entities (area, file, records, and fields) that make up a Human Resources data base. A comprehensive DD/DS is the source of much of the documentation required in a data base system.

Query Processing. In addition to standard reports, the DD/D manager must provide a high-level query language interface so that users can easily formulate requests for dictionary data. A typical request for such data is shown in Figure 11-9. In this example, the user has requested a list of all programs that use the data item CUSTOMER-NUMBER. Using the associations between data dictionary entities, the query processor produces a list of five programs that use this element (you should examine the data structure diagram in Figure 11-5 and identify how this particular query is processed). The type of "where used" display shown in Figure 11-9 is very useful in **impact analysis** – analyzing the impact of a proposed change to one entity on other entities.

Software Interfaces. Finally, the DD/D manager must accept requests for metadata from other software components (e.g., the DBMS or TP monitor). It must prepare the metadata in a format that can be accepted and used by the requesting program.

Implementing a DD/DS

Most data dictionary/directory systems used today are called active systems. An **active** DD/DS is one in which the DD/D is the sole source of metadata in the data management system (Allen, Loomis, and Mannino 1982). That is, all users and all software components obtain the metadata they require from a single source: the DD/D. This ensures a high degree of control over data definitions and standards. The Integrated Data Dictionary portrayed in Figure 11-1 is an active DD/DS.

An active DD/DS stands in contrast to earlier systems, which were passive. A **passive** DD/DS is one in which a dictionary of definitions is maintained for human users. However, these definitions are not used by the various software components. Each software product (such as the DBMS) generates and/or stores its own metadata. With a passive DD/DS, there is no assurance that the same definitions are used throughout the system.

Actually, the term *active* is a relative term in comparing DD/D systems. Vendors use different approaches in implementing their DD/DS, depending on their marketing strategy and other factors (for a comparison of these approaches, see Allen, Loomis, and Mannino 1982). The trend in data management systems today is to fully integrated, active data dictionary/directory systems that provide a single source of metadata for all users (human and software).

USING A DBMS

In this section, we will describe the operations of a typical DBMS in managing a user data base. The major components of DBMS software are introduced, and their functions are described.

DBMS Software Components

The major software components in a DBMS operational environment are shown in Figure 11-10. This diagram shows how the DBMS interfaces with other software components such as user programs and access methods.

System Components.   A DBMS has two major operating components: a data base control system and a data base storage system. The **data base control system** (DBCS) is a module that interfaces with user programs. It accepts calls for data (such as READ and WRITE commands) and examines the external and conceptual schemas to determine what conceptual records are required to satisfy the request. The DBCS then places a call to the DBSS to fill the request.

The **data base storage system** (DBSS) manipulates the underlying storage files. It establishes and maintains the lists and indexes that are defined in the internal schema. If hash files are used, the DBSS calls on a hashing

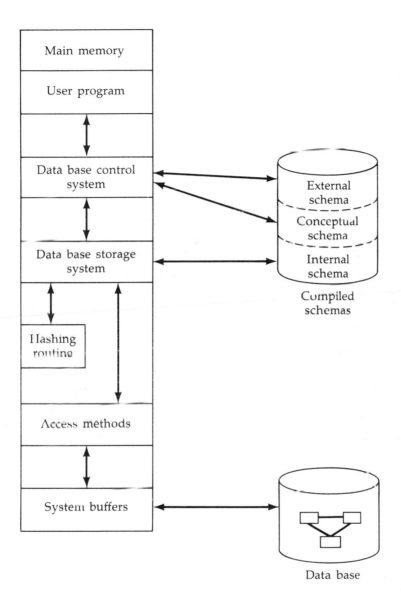

Figure 11-10
DBMS software
environment.

routine to generate record addresses. However, the DSS does *not* manage the physical input and output of data. It passes requests on to the appropriate access methods, which read data into and out of the system buffers.

The terms *data base control system* and *data base storage system* are generic and do not necessarily apply to a given DBMS. However, most DBMS products do have the equivalent of these operational modules.

Loading the DBMS. In preparation for processing a data base, all the software components shown in Figure 11-10 are loaded into main memory. Precompiled versions of all the software modules—user programs, DBCS,

DBSS, hashing routines, and access methods—are stored on a system disk. Also, compiled versions of the three schemas—external, conceptual, and internal—are stored in a disk library. When a program is to be run, all these components are loaded into main memory. They are linked together by an operating system module (sometimes called the linkage editor) so that they can communicate with one another. Also, system buffers are created by the operating system at this time. The resulting software system is represented in Figure 11-10.

Binding Times. An important event that occurs in loading the DBMS is the linking of a user program to its external schema (normally each user program has one external schema). The process of linking an application program to its external schema (and therefore its data definitions) is referred to as **binding**, and the time when this occurs is called **binding time**. Binding time is an important consideration for a DBMS because until the instant that binding occurs, changes can be made to data definitions without changing any process. For example, a data item length or type could be changed without the need to repeat the linking process. However, once binding occurs, any change to a data definition requires that the binding process be repeated.

In our description of the loading process, binding occurs during linkage editing (this is typical of contemporary data base management systems). However, binding may also occur at the following times:

1. When a program is written (such as when a constant is coded in the program logic).
2. When a program is compiled (such as a conventional application program that contains its own data descriptions).
3. When a program is linkage edited.
4. When a data base is opened (readied for processing).
5. When a user program is executed (user supplies data definitions at run time).

These alternatives may be diagrammed as follows:

In general, late binding promotes data independence, since data definitions can be changed up until the time the program is executed. However, binding at execution time is normally too costly in terms of human and computer resources and is used only in exceptional situations.

Processing a Data Base

Let us now examine how the components in Figure 11-10 communicate with one another in processing a data base. We will illustrate each step by means of an example. Suppose that a user program called NEWORDERS is being used to update the ORDER-ACCOUNTING data base. This program uses the external schema USERVIEW1 (Figure 11-3). Assume that all the components shown in Figure 11-10 have been loaded in main memory and linked by the linkage editor. This includes the object (or compiled) versions of the three schemas. We assume that the name of the external schema (USER-VIEW1) is specified in the NEWORDERS program, so that the system will know which external schema to select from the library.

Now let us suppose that the NEWORDERS program requests an occurrence of USERVIEW1 by means of a READ statement. In particular, the program requests the record for customer A123. Following are the essential steps that are performed:

1. The program NEWORDERS issues a call to the data base control system to READ an occurrence of USERVIEW1. The key value (A123) is passed to the DBCS.

2. The DBCS examines the external schema and looks up the description of USERVIEW1. The DBCS notes that USERVIEW1 is derived from the CUSTOMER conceptual relation.

3. The DBCS examines the conceptual schema and looks up the description of the CUSTOMER relation.

4. The DBCS issues a request to the data base storage system to retrieve the CUSTOMER stored record with the primary key value A123.

5. The DBSS searches CUSTNO-INDEX and locates the relative address for customer A123.

6. The DBSS now issues a call to the access method to read the stored record at the relative address. The access method reads the stored record (including any pointer fields) and places it in the system buffer (if records are blocked, more than one record is placed in the buffer.)

7. The DBCS extracts the required data items from the system buffer and moves them to the user work area (UWA) for the program NEWORDERS (pointer fields are not moved to the UWA). The user work area now contains the following data:

| A123 | 5000 |

8. Required status information (such as error indications) are transferred from the DBCS to the user program, as required.

9. While the system is performing these steps, the computer operating system has transferred control to another program. When the I/O operation is completed, control may be transferred back to NEWORDERS.

Considering the preceding steps, you may well wonder about the performance of a data base management system. Nine steps to obtain two data items! True, individual input/output operations are often slower with a DBMS than with a conventional file processing system. Yet, overall productivity is often much higher. Remember that the overall goal is to improve the productivity of human resources, not to conserve machine cycles or byte positions.

Interactive Data Base Processing

In a typical data base environment, many users may be interacting with a data base from remote terminals. Some of the users want to interrogate the data base, while other users want to update the data base. More sophisticated data management software is required to supervise such interactive data base processing. We describe two such components in this section: query language processors and teleprocessing monitors.

Query Language Processors.   A query language processor (QLP) provides a high-level language that allows end users to easily access the data base. INTERACT and ONLINE QUERY (pictured in Figure 11-1) are examples of such query languages. We can illustrate the use of a query language by referring to USERVIEW1 (see Figure 11-3a). Following is a typical query language statement:

    SELECT CUSTOMER#
    FROM USERVIEW1
    WHERE CREDIT-LIMIT > 10,000

This query requests a list of customer numbers whose credit limit exceeds 10,000. Referring to Figure 11-3a, we see that there is only one such customer, C039.

When this query is input from a terminal, the QLP analyzes the query and constructs a simple retrieval program. This program then interacts with the DBMS to retrieve the requested data, which are displayed by the program. If a particular query is used frequently, the retrieval program can be stored (thereby speeding up subsequent retrievals).

Teleprocessing Monitors.   When several on-line users are accessing a data base concurrently, a teleprocessing (TP) monitor is required to schedule and control the various activities. The TP monitor polls terminals for messages,

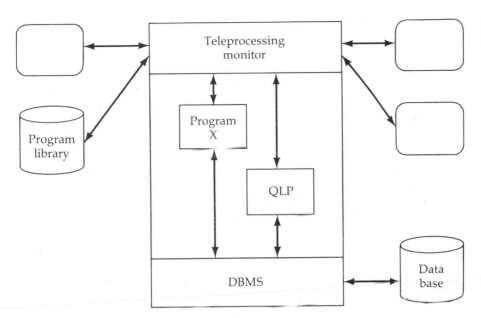

Figure 11-11
Using a TP monitor.

places messages in an incoming message queue, and schedules the execution of programs that process the messages and produce output.

The use of a TP monitor in a data management system is illustrated in Figure 11-11. Clearly, the TP monitor is a vital component of the data management system, and it is important that the TP monitor be designed to interface with the DBMS and other system components.

SECURITY MECHANISMS

The problem of computer security is entertainingly illustrated in a popular movie called *War Games*. On a visit to his principal's office, a high school computer whiz easily obtains a password to the school's computer (it is scrawled on a piece of paper on the principal's desk). From his home computer, the student dials up the school computer and, using the password, logs on and alters his grades (favorably, of course). Using his new-found knowledge, he then penetrates other computer systems. Ultimately, he logs on to a national defense computer, where he nearly perpetrates a nuclear disaster. (The end of the movie is predictable; the student uses his computer knowledge to save the day.) Although fictional, the story does illustrate some important points concerning security. First, simple passwords are often ineffective security devices. Second, regardless of how rigorous the safeguards, no computer system is completely safe in the face of a determined adversary. And finally, the impact of a security violation may range from simple mischief to organizational disaster.

Data base security is defined as protecting the data base against accidental or intentional loss, destruction, or misuse. As noted in Chapter 10, data administration is responsible for developing overall policies and procedures to protect data bases. Data administration uses several facilities provided by data management software in carrying out these functions. The most important security features of data management software are the following:

1. External schemas, which restrict user views of the data base.
2. Authorizations and controls, which identify users and restrict the actions they may take against the data base.
3. User-defined procedures, which define additional constraints or limitations in using the data base.
4. Encryption procedures, which encode data in an unrecognizable form.

External Schemas

External views and schemas promote security by restricting user views of the data base. Any data that are not included in a particular user view are presumably unknown to that user and cannot be accessed by a program that uses the external schema for that view. For example, USERVIEW1 shown in Figure 11-3 contains only the attributes CUSTOMER# and CREDIT-LIMIT. It does not contain information about other attributes in the CUSTOMER relation and it does not contain any information about the ORDER relation. Any user that uses USERVIEW1 cannot access these remaining attributes.

Although user views promote security, they are not adequate security measures. Unauthorized persons may gain knowledge of or access to a particular view. Also, several persons may share a particular view; all may have authority to read the data, but only a restricted few may be authorized to update the data. Finally, with high-level query languages, an unauthorized person may gain access to data through simple experimentation (as in *War Games*). As a result, more sophisticated security measures are normally required.

Authorization Rules

Authorization rules are controls incorporated in the data management system that restrict access to data and also restrict the actions that people may take when data are accessed. For example, a person who can supply the password JEDI may be authorized to read any record in a data base but cannot necessarily modify any of those records.

Fernandez, Summers, and Wood (1981) have developed a conceptual model of data base security. Their model expresses authorization rules in the

Subject	Object	Action	Constraint
Sales Dept.	Customer Record	Insert	Credit limit LE $5000
Order trans.	Customer record	Read	None
Terminal 12	Customer record	Modify	Balance due only
Acctg Dept.	Order record	Delete	None
Luke Skywalker	Order record	Insert	Order amt LT $2000
Program AR4	Order record	Modify	None

Figure 11-12
Authorization matrix.

form of a table (or matrix) that includes subjects, objects, actions, and constraints. Each row of the table indicates that a particular subject is authorized to take a certain action on an object in the data base, perhaps subject to some constraint. An example of such an authorization matrix is shown in Figure 11-12. This table contains several entries pertaining to records in the ORDER-ACCOUNTING data base. For example, the first row in the table indicates that anyone in the Sales Department is authorized to insert a new Customer record in the data base, provided that the customer's credit limit does not exceed $5000. The last row indicates that the program AR4 is authorized to modify Order records without restriction.

Subjects. Subjects are organizational entities that can access the data base. Examples of subjects are individuals, departments (or groups of people), terminals, transactions, and applications (all of these are illustrated in Figure 11-12). Also, subjects may be combinations of entities—for example, a particular person entering a certain transaction at a particular terminal.

Positive identification of subjects is a continuing problem in computer security. In most systems today, individuals are identified by passwords (often in conjunction with names and account numbers). However, passwords are unreliable, as *War Games* clearly illustrates. More positive identification techniques, such as fingerprints and voiceprints, are being introduced to control access to sensitive data.

Objects. Objects are data base entities to be protected by the security system. Examples of objects are records, relations, data items, programs, and data bases. In Figure 11-12, the objects are records.

In designing a security system, we must decide on the **granularity**, or size, of object to be protected by the system. A security system that permits (or denies) access to an entire data base is said to have large granularity, while a system that grants access to individual data items (or attributes) has small granularity. A system with large granularity exercises gross control over the data base. Individual users are either allowed access to the entire data base or else denied access. Systems with small granularity exercise close control: a user may be authorized to modify one data item in a record type but not authorized to modify another data item in the same record type. Such systems increase processing overhead, since the system must exercise a security check every time a user attempts to access any data item. Most security systems compromise by providing security at the record level.

Actions.   The third attribute in the authorization table is the action that can be taken by the subject against the object. Typical actions that can be taken are shown in Figure 11-12: Read, Insert, Modify, and Delete. Additional actions that can be defined are Create (add a new record type, data item type, or other entity type to the data base) and Destroy (delete an entity type from the data base). These two actions require changes to the metadata and authority is generally restricted to persons in data administration. Other data base actions may be defined by users and included in the authorization matrix.

Constraints.   Constraints on authorization rules are specified in the last column of the authorization matrix. For example, the fifth row of the table in Figure 11-12 indicates that a particular person (Luke Skywalker) can insert new Order records into the data base only if the amount of the order is less than $2000.

Implementing Authorization Rules.   Most contemporary data base management systems do not implement an authorization matrix such as the one shown in Figure 11-12. Instead, simplified versions are normally used. There are two principal types: authorization tables for subjects and authorization tables for objects. An example of each type is shown in Figure 11-13. In Figure 11-13a, for example, we see that salespersons (who are probably identified by passwords) are allowed to modify Customer records but not delete these records. In Figure 11-13b, we see that Order records can be modified by persons in Order Entry or Accounting but not by salespersons. A given DBMS product may provide either one or both of these types of facilities.

Authorization tables such as those shown in Figure 11-13 are attributes of an organization's data and their environment and therefore are properly viewed as metadata. Thus, the tables should be stored and maintained in the data dictionary/directory. Since authorization tables contain highly sensitive data, they themselves should be protected by stringent security rules. Normally, only selected persons in data administration have authority to access and modify these tables.

	Customer records	Order records
Read	Y	Y
Insert	Y	N
Modify	Y	N
Delete	N	N

(a)

Figure 11-13
Implementing
authorization rules.
(a) Authorizations for
    subjects
    (salespersons).
(b) Authorizations for
    objects (Order
    records).

	Salespersons (password JABBA)	Order entry (password HUTT)	Accounting (password QUILL)
Read	Y	Y	Y
Insert	N	Y	N
Modify	N	Y	Y
Delete	N	N	Y

(b)

User Procedures

Some DBMS products provide user exits (or interfaces) that allow system designers or users to define their own security procedures in addition to the authorization rules we have just described. For example, a user procedure might be designed to provide positive user identification. In attempting to log on to the computer, the user might be required to supply a procedure name in addition to a simple password. If a valid password and procedure name are supplied, the system then calls the procedure, which asks the user a series of questions whose answers should be known only to that password holder. Other user procedures can be used to enforce constraints in authorization rules (such as those in Figure 11-13).

Encryption Procedures

For highly sensitive data (such as company financial data), data encryption can be used. **Encryption** is the coding (or scrambling) of data so that they cannot be read by humans. Some DBMS products include encryption routines that automatically encode sensitive data when it is stored or transmitted over communications channels. Other DBMS products provide exits that allow users to code their own encryption routines.

Any system that provides encryption facilities must also provide complementary routines for decoding the data. These decoding routines must of course be protected by adequate security, or else the advantages of encryption are lost. These routines also require significant computing resources.

CONCURRENCY CONTROL

In most systems, several users can access a data base concurrently. The operating system switches execution from one user program to another to minimize waiting for input/output operations. With this approach, transactions are often interleaved; that is, several steps are performed on transaction A, then several steps on transaction B, followed by several more steps on transaction A, and so on. When transactions are interleaved, errors will occur in updating unless the DBMS has features to prevent interference between transactions.

Effects of Concurrent Updates

The effects of concurrent updates without concurrency control are illustrated in Figure 11-14. Two users are in the process of updating the same record, which represents a Savings Account record for customer A. At the present time, customer A has a balance of $100 in her savings account.

User 1 reads this record into the user work area, intending to post a customer withdrawal of $50. Next, user 2 reads the same record into that user work area, intending to post a customer deposit of $25. User 1 posts the withdrawal and stores the record, which now indicates a balance of $50. User 2 then posts the deposit (increasing the balance to $125) and stores this record on top of the one stored by user 1. The record now indicates a balance of $125 (customer A will be delighted by this turn of events!). In this case, the transaction for user 1 has been lost because of interference between the transactions.

Resource-Locking Mechanism

To prevent erroneous updates, the DBMS must incorporate a resource-locking mechanism. That is, any data that are retrieved by one user with the intent of updating must be "locked" or denied to other users until the update is completed.

Usually, data required by a program are locked when a transaction begins and released when the transactions is either completed (and committed) or aborted. Thus, to administer resource locking, the DBMS requires two pieces of information:

USER 1

CUST	BAL
A	100

USER 2

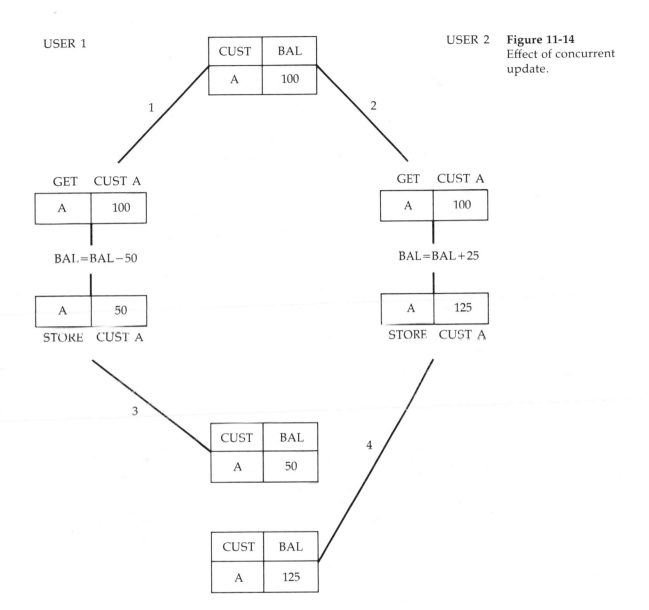

Figure 11-14
Effect of concurrent update.

GET   CUST A

A	100

BAL=BAL−50

A	50

STORE   CUST A

GET   CUST A

A	100

BAL=BAL+25

A	125

STORE   CUST A

CUST	BAL
A	50

CUST	BAL
A	125

1. Intention to update—whether a particular program (or terminal session) will require updating the data base.
2. Transaction boundaries—when a transaction begins and ends (discussed earlier).

   An important consideration in evaluating the locking mechanism is the **lock level**, or granularity. The choices, which are the same as for security,

Figure 11-15
Example of the deadly
embrace.

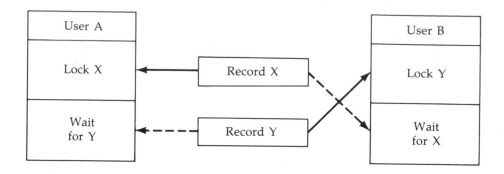

are the data base, file (or relation), record (or tuple), or data item (or attribute).

At one extreme, the DBMS could lock the entire data base for each user update request. This is generally unacceptable, since most transactions would have to wait for the data base locks. At the other extreme, the DBMS could lock individual data items so that two data items in the same record occurrence could be updated concurrently by two different users. This approach would provide the fewest conflicts, but would increase processing overhead. Locking at the record level is the most common approach with contemporary systems.

Deadly Embrace

Resource locking (say, at the record level) solves the problem of erroneous updates, but it may lead to another problem: the deadly embrace. The **deadly embrace** (or "deadlock") is an impasse that results when two users each lock certain resources, then request resources locked by the other user. An example of this situation is shown in Figure 11-15. User A is waiting for record Y (locked by user B), and user B is waiting for record X (locked by user A). Unless the DBMS intervenes, both users will wait indefinitely.

There are two basic ways to resolve the deadly embrace: deadlock prevention and deadlock resolution.

Deadlock Prevention.   When deadlock prevention is employed, user programs must lock all records they will require at the beginning of a transaction (rather than one at a time). In Figure 11-15, user A would have to lock both records X and Y before processing the transaction (if either record is already locked, the program must wait until it is released).

Locking records in advance prevents deadlock. Unfortunately, it is often difficult to predict in advance what records will be required to process a transaction. A typical program has many processing paths and may call other programs. As a result, deadlock prevention is not often practical.

Deadlock Resolution. The second (and most common) approach is to allow deadlocks to occur, but to build mechanisms into the DBMS for detecting and breaking the deadlocks. Essentially, this is how these mechanisms work: The DBMS maintains a matrix of resource usage, which, at a given instant, indicates what subjects (users) are using what objects (resources). By scanning this matrix, the computer can detect deadlocks as they occur. The DBMS then resolves the deadlocks by "backing out" one of the deadlocked transactions. Any changes made by that transaction up to the time of deadlock are removed, and the transaction is restarted when the required resources become available. We will describe the procedure for backing out shortly.

DATA BASE RECOVERY

Data base recovery is data administration's response to Murphy's law. Inevitably, data bases are damaged or lost because of some system failure. Such failures are caused by human error, hardware failure, incorrect or invalid data, program errors, and natural catastrophes. Since the organization depends so heavily on its data base, the data management system must provide mechanisms for restoring a data base quickly and accurately after loss or damage.

Basic Recovery Facilities

A data base management system should provide four basic facilities for backup and recovery of a data base:

1. Backup facilities, which provide periodic backup copies of the entire data base.
2. Journalizing facilities, which maintain an audit trail of transactions and data base changes.
3. A checkpoint facility by which the DBMS periodically suspends all processing and synchronizes its files and journals.
4. A recovery/restart facility by which the DBMS restores the data base to a correct condition and restarts processing transactions.

Backup Facilities. The DBMS should provide an automatic dump facility that produces a backup copy (or "save") of the entire data base. Typically, a backup copy is produced at least once per day. The copy should be stored in a secured location where it is protected from loss or damage. The backup copy is used to restore the data base in the event of catastrophic loss or damage.

Figure 11-16
Data base journals and
backup copy.

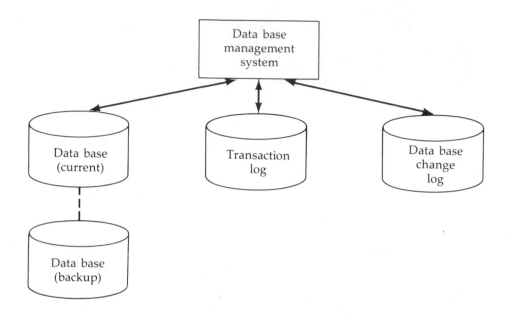

Journalizing Facilities. A DBMS must provide an audit trail of transactions and data base changes. As shown in Figure 11-16, there are two basic journals or logs. First, there is the **transaction log**, which contains a record of the essential data for each transaction that is processed against the data base. Data that are typically recorded for each transaction include the transaction code or identification, time of the transaction, terminal number or user ID, data values input, records accessed, and records modified.

The second kind of log is the data base change log, which contains before and after images of records that have been modified by transactions. A **before image** is simply a copy of a record before it has been modified, while an **after image** is a copy of the same record after it has been modified.

Checkpoint Facility. A checkpoint is a facility by which the DBMS periodically refuses to accept any new transactions. All transactions in progress are completed and the journal files are brought up to date. At this point, the system is in a "quiet state" and the data base and transaction logs are synchronized. The DBMS writes a special record (called a checkpoint record) to the log file. The checkpoint record contains information necessary to restart the system, including message queues and internal control blocks.

A DBMS may perform checkpoints automatically (which is preferred) or in response to commands in user application programs. Checkpoints should be taken frequently (say, several times an hour). When failures do occur, it is often possible to resume processing from the most recent checkpoint. Thus, only a few minutes of processing has to be repeated, compared with several hours for a complete restart of the day's processing.

Recovery/Restart Facility.   The recovery/restart facility (or manager) is a module of the DBMS that restores the data base to a correct condition when a failure occurs and resumes processing user requests. The type of restart used depends on the nature of the failure. The recovery/restart facility uses the journal files shown in Figure 11-16 (as well as the backup copy, if necessary) to restore the data base.

Recovery and Restart Procedures

The type of recovery procedure that will be used in a given situation will depend on the nature of the failure, the sophistication of the DBMS recovery facilities, and operational policies and procedures. Following is a discussion of the techniques that are most frequently used.

Restore/Rerun.   Restore/rerun involves reprocessing the day's transactions (up to the point of failure) against the backup copy of the data base. The most recent copy of the data base (say, from the previous day) is mounted, and all transactions that have occurred since that copy (which are stored on the transaction log) are rerun.

The advantage of restore/rerun is its simplicity. The DBMS does not need to create a data base change journal, and no special restart procedures are required. However, there are two major disadvantages to restore/rerun. First, the time to reprocess transactions may be prohibitive. Depending on the frequency of making backup copies, several hours of reprocessing may be required. Processing new transactions will have to be deferred until recovery is completed, and if the system is heavily loaded, it may be impossible to catch up. The second disadvantage is that the sequencing of transactions will often be different from when they were originally processed. This may lead to quite different results. For example, in the original run, a customer deposit may be posted before a withdrawal. In the rerun, the withdrawal transaction may be attempted first and may lead to sending a "not sufficient funds" notice to the customer.

For these reasons, restore/rerun is not a sufficient recovery procedure and is generally used only as a last resort in data base processing.

Backward Recovery.   Backward recovery (also called "rollback") is used to back out unwanted changes to the data base. As shown in Figure 11-17a, before images of the records that have been changed are applied to the data base. As a result, the data base is returned to an earlier state (the unwanted changes are eliminated). Backward recovery is used to reverse the changes made by transactions that have aborted, or terminated abnormally.

Forward Recovery.   Forward recovery (also called "rollforward") starts with an earlier copy of the data base. By applying after images (the results of

Figure 11-17
Basic recovery techniques

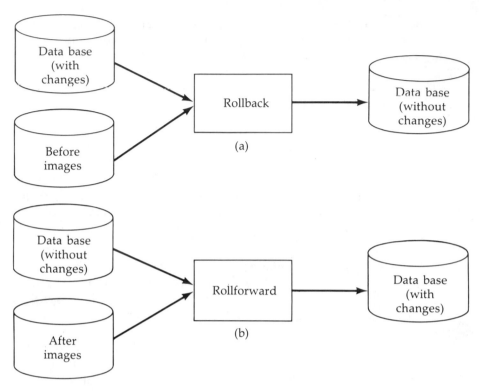

good transactions), the data base is quickly moved forward to a later state (see Figure 11-17b). Forward recovery is much faster and more accurate than restore/rerun, for the following reasons:

1. The time-consuming logic of reprocessing each transaction does not have to be repeated.

2. Only the most recent after images need to be applied. A data base record may have a series of after images (as a result of a sequence of updates). However, only the most recent "good" after image is required for rollforward.

3. The problem of different sequencing of transactions is avoided, since the results of applying the transactions (rather than the transactions themselves) are used.

Types of Data Base Failure

A wide variety of failures can occur in processing a data base, ranging from the input of an incorrect data value to complete loss or destruction of the data base. Four of the most common types of errors are aborted transactions, incorrect data, system failure, and data base loss or destruction. Each of these types of errors is described below, and the most common recovery procedure is indicated.

Aborted Transactions.   As we noted earlier, a transaction frequently requires a sequence of processing steps to be performed. Often, a transaction that is in progress will abort, or terminate abnormally. Some reasons for this type of failure are human error, input of invalid data, and hardware failure. A common type of hardware failure is the loss of transmission in a communications link when a transaction is in progress.

When a transaction aborts, we want to "back out" the transaction and remove any changes that have been made (but not committed) to the data base. The recovery/restart facility accomplishes this by backward recovery (applying before images for the transaction in question). This function should be accomplished automatically by the DBMS, which then notifies the user to correct and resubmit the transaction.

Incorrect Data.   A more complex situation arises when the data base has been updated with incorrect, but valid, data. For example, an incorrect grade may be recorded for a student, or an incorrect amount input for a customer payment.

Incorrect data are difficult to detect and often lead to complications. To begin with, some time may elapse before an error is detected and the data base record (or records) corrected. By this time, numerous other users may have used the erroneous data, and a chain reaction of errors may have occurred as various applications made use of the incorrect data. In addition, transaction outputs (such as documents and messages) based on the incorrect data may be transmitted to persons. For example, an incorrect grade report may be sent to a student, or an incorrect statement to a customer.

When incorrect data have been introduced, the data base may be recovered in one of the following ways:

1. If the error is discovered soon enough, backward recovery may be used. (However, care must be taken to ensure that all subsequent errors have been reversed.)

2. A series of compensating transactions may be introduced through human intervention to correct the errors if only a few errors have occurred.

3. If the first two measures are infeasible, it may be necessary to restart from the most recent checkpoint before the error occurred.

Any erroneous messages or documents that have been produced by the erroneous transaction will have to be corrected by appropriate human intervention (letters of explanation, telephone calls, and so on).

System Failure.   With a system failure, some component of the system fails, but the data base is not damaged. Some causes of system failure are power loss, operator error, loss of communications transmission, and system software failure.

When the system crashes, some transactions may be in progress. The first step in recovery is to back out those transactions using before images (backward recovery). However, it may not be possible to restart from this point after a system crash, since status information in main memory will likely be lost or damaged. The safest approach is to restart from the most recent checkpoint before the system failure. The data base is rolled forward by applying after images for all transactions that were processed after that checkpoint.

Data Base Destruction.   In the case of data base destruction, the data base itself is lost or destroyed or cannot be read. A typical cause of data base destruction is a disk drive failure (or head crash).

A backup copy of the data base is required for recovery in this situation. Forward recovery is used to restore the data base to its state immediately before the loss occurred. Any transactions that may have been in progress when the data base was lost are restarted.

SUMMARY

We conclude this chapter by summarizing some of the important considerations in evaluating and selecting data management software. For a more detailed discussion of selection criteria, see Martin (1983).

Integrated Data Dictionary/Directory System.   The foundation of a modern data management system is an integrated (or built-in) data dictionary/directory. Ideally, the DD/DS should be fully active—that is, it should provide a single source of metadata for all users and software components. Also, the DD/DS should be interactive and user-friendly.

Data Independence.   The system should afford a high level of data independence by providing clear boundaries between logical and physical data management. The three-level DBMS architecture described in this chapter provides this facility.

Data Base Recovery.   The DBMS must provide adequate mechanisms for recovery and restart following some system failure or data base loss. These mechanisms include transaction logs, data base change files, backward and forward recovery, and automatic system restarts.

Security Mechanisms.   The software should provide comprehensive controls to protect the data base. These controls include passwords, authorization tables, and audit trails.

Integrity Controls.   The software should provide at least the following controls over data integrity: concurrency controls, validity checks, and automatic range checks. More comprehensive integrity control mechanisms are under development but are not yet available in most systems today.

User-Oriented Languages.   The data management system *must* include high-level, user-oriented languages (query languages, report and graphics generators, spreadsheet programs, and so on). These languages must be easy to learn and use and should be supported by computer-assisted instruction in their use.

On-line User Facilities.   The data management system should provide a number of facilities for on-line users: integrated teleprocessing monitor, on-line query language, and support for local area networks and distributed data bases (if appropriate).

Qualified Vendor.   The data management software vendor should be chosen very carefully. Some things to look for are financial stability, an excellent reputation for support, a full range of training courses, a sound commitment to an evolving product line, and satisfied customers.

The concepts described in this chapter provide a framework for the next four chapters, which describe implementations of specific data management systems.

CHAPTER REVIEW

Review Questions

1. Give a concise definition for each of the following terms:

   a. data base management system
   b. transaction
   c. schema
   d. data definition language
   e. logical data independence
   f. data dictionary/directory

   g. impact analysis
   h. active DD/DS
   i. data base control system
   j. binding time
   k. deadly embrace

2. Contrast the following terms:
    a. DBMS; DD/DS
    b. DBCS; DBSS
    c. data dictionary; data directory
    d. external schema; internal schema
    e. active data dictionary; passive data dictionary
    f. deadlock prevention; deadlock resolution
    g. backward recovery; forward recovery

3. List and briefly describe six software components of a typical data management system.

4. List and briefly describe eight functions of a DBMS.

5. What is meant by the term *transaction integrity*? How is it achieved?

6. Explain the purpose of each of the following:
    a. conceptual schema
    b. external schema
    c. internal schema

7. What is the "extensibility" feature of a DD/DS? Why is it important?

8. List and briefly describe six functions of a DD/D manager.

9. Why is the execution time for a query language processor likely to be slower than for a prewritten program?

10. Describe three important functions of a TP monitor.

11. Describe four basic DBMS facilities that are required for backup and recovery of a data base.

12. Why is forward recovery generally faster and more accurate than restore/rerun?

13. List and briefly describe four common types of data base failure.

Problems and Exercises

1. For each of the following changes to the ORDER-ACCOUNTING data base, describe the changes that are required to the schemas (Figures 11-2, 11-3, and 11-4). Indicate whether each change provides an example of physical or logical data independence.
    a. Add a new relation (or record type) called ORDER LINE to the conceptual schema. This relation contains the following attributes: PRODUCT#, ORDER#, QTY-ORDERED.

    b. Expand USERVIEW1 to include the attribute CUSTOMER-NAME.

    c. Change the representation for the attribute BALANCE-DUE from "FLOAT" to "INTEGER."

    d. Change the index CUSTOMER-NAME from a secondary key index to a primary key index.

    e. Change the blocking factor for ORDER records from five to ten records per block.

2. Refer to the description of the movie *War Games* in the chapter. What type of security violation (or deficiency) is evidenced by each of the following incidents, and how could they be corrected?

    a. The student finds the computer password written on the principal's desk.

    b. Using the principal's password, the student is able to modify student grade information.

3. Fill in the following authorization tables for Mountain View Community Hospital with Y (for yes) or N (for no), based on your own assumptions

a.

	Patient records	Patient charges	Physician records	Employee records
Read				
Insert				
Modify				
Delete				

Authorizations for Nurses

b.

	Nurses	Physicians	Admissions	Administrator
Read				
Insert				
Modify				
Delete				

Authorizations for Patient Records

4. Fill in the following authorization tables for Pine Valley Furniture Company (Y or N), based on your own assumptions.

a.

	Customer records	Employee records	Product records
Read			
Insert			
Delete			
Modify			

Authorizations for Salespersons

b.

	Accountants	Quality inspectors	Personnel Department	President
Read				
Insert				
Modify				
Delete				

Authorizations for Employee Records

5. Write a conceptual schema (similar to the one in Figure 11-2c) for the following data model, which was extracted from the Mountain View Community Hospital conceptual model.

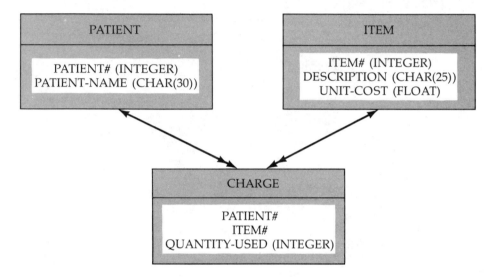

6. Develop two user views based on the conceptual model shown in Problem 5. For each user view, write an external schema similar to those shown in Figure 11-3.

7. Develop sample data dictionary entries (similar to those in Figure 11-6) for the conceptual model shown in Problem 5.

8. Explain what data base recovery technique is most appropriate for each of the following situations:

   a. A phone disconnection occurs while a user is entering a transaction.

   b. A disk pack is dropped and is damaged so that it cannot be used.

   c. A lightning storm causes a power failure.

   d. An incorrect amount is entered and posted for a student tuition payment. The error is not discovered for several days.

9. For the concurrent update situation shown in Figure 11-14, what balance would be shown if the transaction for user 2 was processed and the results stored before the transaction for user 1?

10. For the deadly embrace example pictured in Figure 11-15, what action should be taken by the DBMS?

11. Suppose that you are evaluating data management software for your own personal computer. Classify the factors named in the Summary as being of high (H) or low (L) importance.

12. Visit an organization that is using data management software.
    a. Which of the software components shown in Figure 11-1 are being used?
    b. Evaluate the procedures that are used for security and for data base recovery.

References

Allen, Frank W., Mary E.S. Loomis, and Michael V. Mannino, 1982. "The Integrated Dictionary/Directory System." *Computing Surveys* 14 (June): 245–286.

Codd, E.F. 1982. "Relational Database: A Practical Foundation for Productivity." *Communications of the ACM* 25 (February): 109–117.

Fernandez, Eduardo B., Rita C. Summers, and Christopher Wood. 1981. *Database Security and Integrity.* Reading, Mass.: Addison-Wesley.

Martin, James. 1983. *Managing the Data-Base Environment.* Englewood Cliffs, N.J.: Prentice-Hall.

Auerbach Publishers. 1981. *Practical Data Base Management.* Princeton, N.J.: Auerbach Publishers.

12

Hierarchical Data Base Systems

INTRODUCTION

The earliest data base management systems were based on the hierarchical data model. As data base requirements have become better understood, these systems have had to evolve to handle a broader range of data structures. However, many organizations today continue to use hierarchical data base management systems because of the investment they have in these products and the related application programs. In fact, the use of these products continues to grow.

Two hierarchical systems frequently used today are IBM's Information Management System (IMS) and INTEL's System 2000. Of these, IMS is by far the most widely used. Therefore, we devote most of this chapter to describing the main features of IMS. A brief description of System 2000 (a more recent hierarchical product) is provided at the end of the chapter.

IMS was developed during the mid-1960s in response to the data processing needs of the aerospace industry. This development was undertaken as a joint project between IBM and North American Aviation. Since its introduction in the late 1960s, IMS has evolved through several versions. The current version is IMS/VS (Information Management System/Virtual Storage). IMS is widely used among installations with IBM mainframe computers.

The IMS development team chose the hierarchical structure because they agreed with the philosopher who observed that all views of life are hierarchical in nature. They began by developing a physical hierarchical view, which unfortunately does not always mirror life. Finally, through logical relationships and other improvements, IMS was able to model life by becoming a logical hierarchical system.

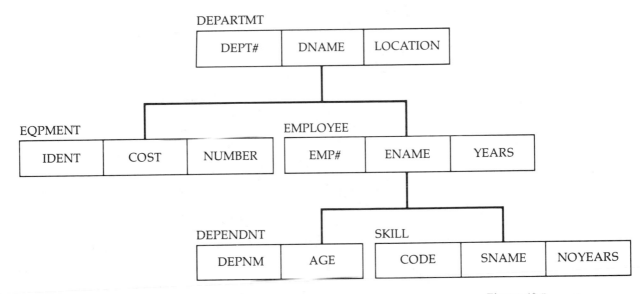

Figure 12-1
IMS physical data base record.

IMS PHYSICAL DATA BASES

The physical data base record is a basic building block in IMS. A **physical data base record** (PDBR) consists of a hierarchical arrangement of segments. A **segment**, in turn, consists of a set of related fields. The top segment (or entry point) in a PDBR is called the **root** segment. A PDBR then consists of a root segment plus a hierarchical arrangement of subordinate segments called **child** segments.

A typical IMS physical data base record is shown in Figure 12-1. This PDBR contains information about departments, about equipment that is assigned to each department, and about employees assigned to each department. DEPARTMT is the name of the root segment type for this PDBR, and EQPMENT and EMPLOYEE are child segment types. The EMPLOYEE segment, in turn, has two child segments, DEPENDNT and SKILL. These segments contain information about each employee's dependents and skills, respectively.

PDBR Occurrences

The physical data base record shown in Figure 12-1 is a PDBR *type*. An occurrence of this PDBR type is shown in Figure 12-2. This occurrence represents data for one department (ACCTG) and contains two EQPMENT segments and two EMPLOYEE segments. The first employee (Evans) has three dependents and two skills. The second employee (Thomas) has one skill and no dependents.

Figure 12-2
An occurrence of the
PDBR.

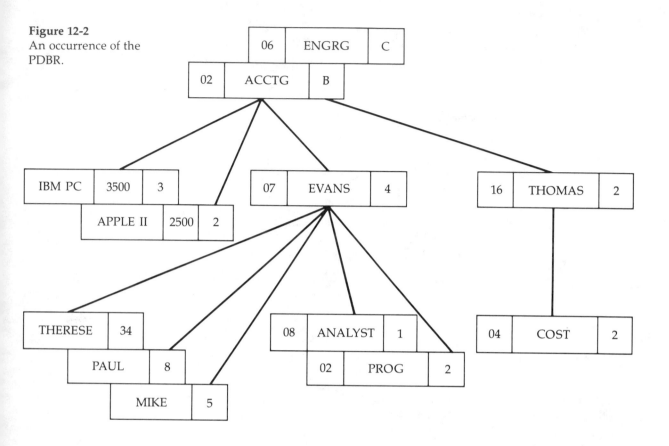

Each occurrence of a root segment represents one PDBR occurrence. Thus, all the segments constitute one such PDBR occurrence (the ENGRG root segment shown would constitute a second occurrence of this record type).

Data Base Description

Each IMS physical data base record type is defined by a **data base description** (DBD). The DBD appears as a set of macro statements that define the segments and fields within a PDBR. These macro statements are coded by a programmer or data base analyst and then assembled into object form and stored in a library by the IMS control program.

A skeleton DBD for the department data base is shown in Figure 12-3. The statements have been numbered for reference in the following discussion; normally, these statement numbers are omitted.

Statement 1 assigns the name DEPTDB to the data base shown in Figure 12-1. Statement 2 then defines the root segment. This segment type is

```
 1   DBD     NAME=DEPTDB
 2   SEGM    NAME=DEPARTMT, BYTES=27, PARENT=0
 3   FIELD   NAME=(DEPT#, SEQ), BYTES=3, START=1
 4   FIELD   NAME=DNAME, BYTES=20, START=4
 5   FIELD   NAME=LOCATION, BYTES=4, START=24
 6   SEGM    NAME=EQPMENT, PARENT=DEPARTMT, BYTES=29
 7   FIELD   NAME=(IDENT, SEQ), BYTES=15, START=1
 8   FIELD   NAME=COST, BYTES=10, START=16
 9   FIELD   NAME=NUMBER, BYTES=4, START=26
10   SECM    NAME=EMPLOYEE, PARENT=DEPARTMT, BYTES=42
11   FIELD   NAME=(EMP#, SEQ), BYTES=10, START=1
12   FIELD   NAME=ENAME, BYTES=30, START=11
13   FIELD   NAME=YEARS, BYTES=2, START=41
14   SEGM    NAME=DEPENDNT, PARENT=EMPLOYEE, BYTES=32
15   FIELD   NAME=(DEPNM, SEQ), BYTES=30, START=1
16   FIELD   NAME=AGE, BYTES=2, START=31
17   SEGM    NAME=SKILL, PARENT=EMPLOYEE, BYTES=28
18   FIELD   NAME=(CODE, SEQ), BYTES=6, START=1
19   FIELD   NAME=SNAME, BYTES=20, START=7
20   FIELD   NAME=NOYEARS, BYTES=2, START=27
```

Figure 12-3
Data base description
(DEPTDB).

assigned the name DEPARTMT and is defined as 29 bytes in length. All names in IMS are limited to a maximum length of eight characters.

Statements 3 to 5 define the three field types that are included in DEPARTMT. Each FIELD definition statement defines the name, length, and starting position within the segment. Statement 3 contains the clause NAME=(DEPT#,SEQ). This clause defines DEPT# to be the sequence field for the DEPARTMT root segment type. As a result, physical data base record occurrences within the DEPTDB data base are sequenced in ascending department number sequence.

Statement 6 defines the EQPMENT segment type. The clause PARENT=DEPARTMT in this statement defines EQPMENT as a child segment of DEPARTMT. The segment is 27 bytes in length.

Statement 7 defines the IDENT field type within the EQPMENT segment type. The clause NAME=(IDENT,SEQ) means that for each occurrence of a parent DEPARTMT segment type, occurrences of the child EQPMENT segment type are stored in ascending sequence according to the IDENT field. Thus, for example, in Figure 12-2, the segment for APPLE II occurs before the segment for IBM PC. All occurrences of child segments of a particular parent occurrence are referred to as **twins**.

Statements 8 to 20 define the remaining segment types and field types in the department data base. Multiple physical data bases will often be needed to represent a given conceptual data base model effectively and efficiently.

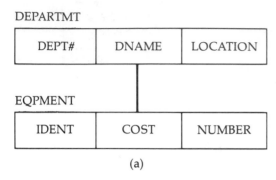

DEPARTMT

DEPT#	DNAME	LOCATION

EQPMENT

IDENT	COST	NUMBER

(a)

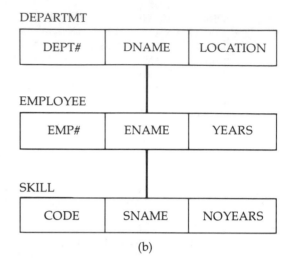

DEPARTMT

DEPT#	DNAME	LOCATION

EMPLOYEE

EMP#	ENAME	YEARS

SKILL

CODE	SNAME	NOYEARS

(b)

Figure 12-4
Examples of logical data
base records.
(a) Equipment LDBR.
(b) Personnel LDBR.

IMS LOGICAL DATA BASES

External views of individual users in IMS are reflected in logical data base records (LDBRs). A **logical data base** (LDB) consists of all occurrences of a logical data base record (LDBR) type. Each LDBR type is a subset of a corresponding PDBR type (or more than one PDBR type). An LDBR may differ from the corresponding PDBR in the following ways:

1. Any segment type (except the root segment) of a PDBR may be omitted from an LDBR. If any segment type in the PDBR is omitted, then all of its dependents are also omitted.

2. Any field types that occur in a PDBR may be omitted in the corresponding LDBR. Also, the fields in a PDBR may be rearranged within the LDBR segment type.

Example LDBRs

Two examples of logical data base records derived from the department physical data base are shown in Figure 12-4. Figure 12-4a is an "equipment" LDBR that contains the DEPARTMT and EQPMENT segment types. Figure 12-4b is a "personnel" LDBR that contains the DEPARTMT, EMPLOYEE, and SKILL segment types. Each of these LDBR types represents the view of a different user. Notice that each LDBR type contains DEPARTMT as its root segment, as required.

Although not shown in Figure 12-4, any of the fields in a PDBR segment may be omitted in the corresponding LDBR segment. For example, the

```
1    PCB       TYPE=DB, DBDNAME=DEPTDB, KEYLEN=19
2    SENSEG    NAME=DEPARTMT, PROCOPT=G
3    SENSEG    NAME=EMPLOYEE, PROCOPT=G
4    SENSEG    NAME=SKILL, PROCOPT=G
```

Figure 12-5
Program communication
block for personnel LDBR.

YEARS field in the EMPLOYEE segment could be omitted in the LDBR shown in Figure 12-4b. Also, the order of the fields EMP# and EMPNAME could be reversed if desired.

Program Communication Block

Each LDBR type is defined by a series of statements called a **program communication block** (PCB). The PCB for the personnel LDBR is shown in Figure 12-5.

Statement 1 defines the program communication block. The clause TYPE=DB is required for each PCB that defines a data base (as opposed to an on-line transaction). The clause DBNAME=DEPTDB specifies that the DBD for the underlying data base is DEPTDB (as defined in Figure 12-3).

The clause KEYLEN=19 defines the maximum length of the concatenated key for the hierarchical path in this LDBR. In the LDBR shown in Figure 12-4b, the hierarchical path consists of the DEPARTMT, EMPLOYEE, and SKILL segment types. The fields on which these segments are sequenced, and the field lengths, are the following: DEPT#, 3 bytes; EMP#, 10 bytes; and CODE, 6 bytes. Thus, KEYLEN=3+10+6, or 19 bytes. The KEYLEN clause is used by IMS to reserve space for concatenated keys in retrieving segments.

Statements 2 to 4 define the segments from the PDBR that are to be included in this LDBR. The term SENSEG means "sensitive segment." Segments from the PDBR that are included in an LDBR are said to be "sensitive" (the term can also be applied to fields that are to be included). In this PCB, the sensitive segments are, of course, DEPARTMT, EMPLOYEE, and SKILL.

The term PROCOPT in Figure 12-5 stands for "processing options." The PROCOPT clause specifies the operations that a user of this LDBR can perform against each segment. In Figure 12-5, the clause PROCOPT=G specifies that a user can only "get" (G) or retrieve each segment occurrence. Other options that can be specified are I ("insert"), R ("replace"), and D ("delete"). Also, any combination of these options may be specified.

Caution must be used in specifying and using the delete (D) option in IMS. When an occurrence of a sensitive segment is deleted, all children of that segment are also deleted, whether they are sensitive or not. For example, the LDBR in Figure 12-4b is sensitive to the EMPLOYEE and SKILL segment types, but not to the DEPENDNT segment type. Suppose that a user deletes an EMPLOYEE segment occurrence. All DEPENDNT segment occurrences for that employee are also deleted, even though the user may not be aware of their existence.

The sensitive segment feature of IMS offers two significant advantages:

1. Data independence: a new type of segment can be added to the data base without affecting existing users. The LDBR for the existing user is not sensitive to this new segment type.
2. Data security: a user cannot access particular segment types if the user view (LDBR) is not sensitive to those segment types.

Program Specification Block

Each user may have one or more program communication blocks. The set of all PCBs for a given user is called a **program specification block** (PSB). The PSB for each user is assembled and stored in a system library by the IMS control program. The control program extracts the PSB from the library when a user program is executed.

IMS INTERNAL MODELS

IMS offers the user a wide variety of physical data organizations and access methods. Choosing the best internal model for each application requires a detailed knowledge of both IMS and the pattern of data usage defined during physical design. In this section, we provide only a brief overview of the IMS data structures.

Overview of IMS Internal Model

An overview of the IMS data structures and access methods that constitute the internal model is shown in Figure 12-6. As shown in this illustration, IMS supports four types of data bases:

- Hierarchical Sequential Access Method (HSAM)
- Hierarchical Indexed Sequential Access Method (HISAM)
- Hierarchical Direct Access Method (HDAM)
- Hierarchical Indexed Direct Access Method (HIDAM)

The IMS control program contains routines to process each of these four data structures. Also, each of these routines "calls" (or uses) one of several standard access methods. The access methods used by IMS (and shown in Figure 12-6) are the following:

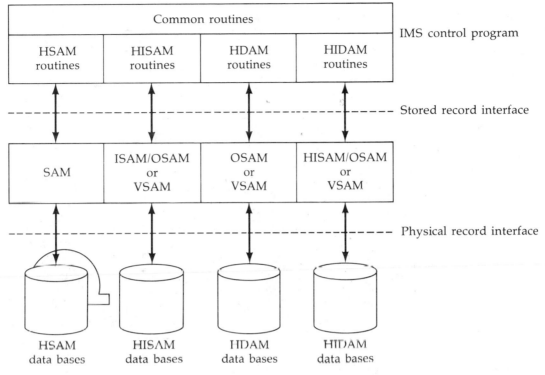

Figure 12-6
Overview of IMS internal
models.
(Source: Date 1981, 312.)

- Sequential Access Method (SAM)
- Indexed Sequential Access Method (ISAM)
- Virtual Storage Access Method (VSAM)
- Overflow Sequential Access Method (OSAM)

The function of each of these access methods is to retrieve a physical record (possibly containing several stored records) and to present a stored record to the IMS control program.

HSAM

The simplest IMS data structure is the Hierarchical Sequential Access Method (HSAM). With this organization, the segments that make up a physical data base record are stored in physical sequence within one or more stored records. The root segment is stored first, followed by its dependent segments. The segments are stored in **hierarchical sequence**, which is a "top-to-bottom, left-to-right" ordering within the PDBR. Thus, the hierarchical sequence is represented by physical adjacency in HSAM.

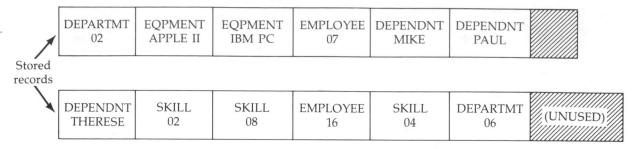

Stored
records

Figure 12-7
HSAM organization for
DEPTDB.

An HSAM organization for the department data base (DEPTDB) is shown in Figure 12-7. The segment occurrences in this figure are taken from the PDBR occurrence shown in Figure 12-2. The segment occurrences are stored in two fixed-length stored records. First, the root segment (DEPARTMT 02) is stored, followed by the two EQPMENT segments in sequential order. The remaining segments are stored in hierarchical sequence as they appear within the PDBR. When the first stored record is filled, the remaining segments continue in the next stored record. Since fixed-length stored records are used, some unused space often results.

Although simple, HSAM has the same disadvantages as any physical sequential organization of records. Locating a particular segment requires an extensive sequential scan (each stored segment has a code that identifies the segment type for retrieval). Also, insertions and deletions are difficult to manage. As a result, HSAM has very limited use in most IMS installations. Normally, this method is used for historical or archival files.

HISAM

The Hierarchical Indexed Sequential Access Method (HISAM) provides an indexed sequential organization for segments. As a result, the segments of a physical data base record can be retrieved either sequentially or by direct access. HISAM uses either ISAM or VSAM as its underlying access method (ISAM and VSAM are described in Chapter 4). ISAM is used with a special IMS access method called OSAM (Overflow Sequential Access Method).

A HISAM organization for the department data base is shown in Figure 12-8. In this example, two data sets (or physical storage files) are used, an ISAM data set and an OSAM data set. Each of these data sets is divided into fixed-length stored records. When an IMS data base is first loaded, each root segment that is stored causes a new ISAM stored record to be created. This root segment is stored at the front of the record (in Figure 12-8, DEPARTMT 02 is the first root segment). The remainder of that record is then filled with additional dependent segments in hierarchical sequence (in Figure 12-8, the first EQPMENT segment for department 02 is placed in the ISAM record.)

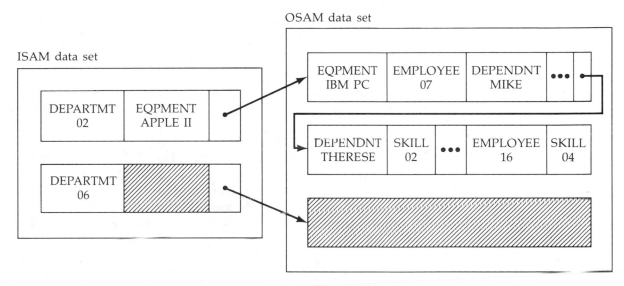

Figure 12-8
HISAM organization for
DEPTDB.

If all dependent segments for a particular root segment fit into one ISAM record, then no OSAM record is required. However, if the dependent segments overflow this record (as in Figure 12-8), then they are stored in hierarchical sequence in an OSAM record. A pointer containing the relative address of that OSAM record is placed in the last ISAM segment. If the first OSAM record is filled, a second record is created, and so on. As shown in Figure 12-8, one ISAM record and two OSAM records were required for all the segments for department 02.

The segments in a physical data base record may be processed sequentially by following the pointers such as those shown in Figure 12-8. Also, each root segment can be located by direct access using the ISAM index. Thus, HISAM provides the advantages of both sequential and direct access.

When VSAM is used, the ISAM data set is replaced by a VSAM key-sequenced data set. Also, the OSAM data set is replaced by a VSAM entry-sequenced data set. Thus, the segments are stored within VSAM control intervals and managed by the VSAM indexes.

HISAM is not often used in most IMS installations. It should be used only when no logical relationships exist and adds and deletes are minimal (i.e., the data base is not volatile).

HDAM and HIDAM

HDAM and HIDAM are both direct access methods. Both permit direct access to the root segment of a PDBR occurrence and therefore are frequently used. The dependent segments of that occurrence can then be accessed directly by following pointer chains. The main difference between

HDAM and HIDAM is in the technique for addressing root segments, as we will now explain.

Pointer Structures.   HDAM and HIDAM both use pointers to represent the hierarchical sequence of segments within a PDBR occurrence. As shown in Figure 12-9, the hierarchical sequence may be represented either by hierarchical pointers or by child/twin pointers.

The use of hierarchical pointers is shown in Figure 12-9a. These pointers are simply "threaded" through the segments in hierarchical sequence. The last segment in the PDBR occurrence (in this case, 04 COST 2) does not contain a pointer to the next root segment. Hierarchical pointers are most efficient when the segments within a PDBR are normally processed in hierarchical sequence.

The use of child/twin pointers is shown in Figure 12-9b. Each parent segment contains a pointer to its first child segment occurrence. Each child segment occurrence then contains a pointer to the next twin segment (if one exists). Also, each parent may optionally contain a pointer to the last (as well as first) child occurrence. Child/twin pointers are most efficient when only certain parent/child occurrences within a PDBR are normally processed each time (rather than the entire sequence).

Although not shown in Figure 12-9, both hierarchical and child/twin pointers may be bidirectional. That is, between any two segments, backward as well as forward pointers may be used.

HDAM.   Hierarchical Direct Access Method (HDAM) provides direct access to root segments by means of a hashing algorithm. Segments are stored in fixed-length stored records. The hashing algorithm generates a relative record address that provides the location of a root segment occurrence. The dependent segments may then be accessed by following the segment pointers (hierarchical or child/twin).

When an HDAM data base is initially loaded, the root segments may be loaded in any order (key sequence is not necessary). However, all dependent segments for each root segment must be loaded in hierarchical sequence after the root segment. Dependent segments are stored as closely as possible to the root segment (recall our discussion of clustering in Chapter 9).

When two root segments collide (hash to the same relative address), the second root segment is placed in the next available stored record that contains sufficient space. A pointer to the second root segment is then placed in the first root segment (several colliding root segments may be linked by such a pointer chain).

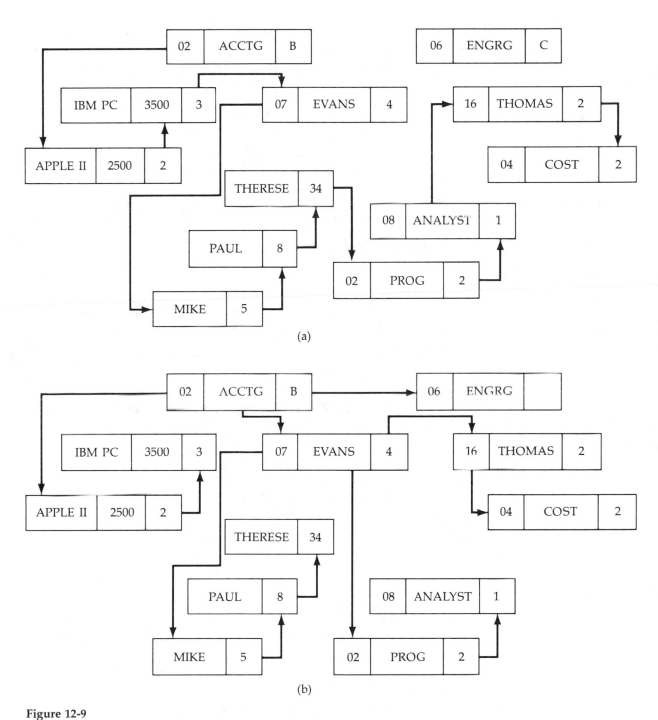

Figure 12-9
HDAM and HIDAM pointer structures.
(a) Hierarchical pointers. (b) Child/twin pointers.

HIDAM.   Hierarchical Indexed Direct Access Method (HIDAM) also provides direct access to root segments. However, instead of using a hashing
algorithm, HIDAM uses a dense index to locate root segment occurrences. Root segments are linked to dependent segments by pointers, as
with HDAM.

The main advantage of HDAM (compared with HIDAM) is the speed of
access where direct access is required. HDAM should be used where random access is required almost exclusively. Sequential processing with
HDAM is difficult or inefficient.

On the other hand, the main advantage of HIDAM is that both random
and sequential access are handled effectively. Thus, HIDAM is probably the
most frequently used of all access methods in IMS.

Specifying the Internal Model

In IMS, the mapping of a physical data base into storage is defined by adding
additional statements to the data base description (such as the one in Figure
12-3). For example, if HISAM is to be used, the following statement would
be added to DBD:

ACCESS = HISAM

Additional entries are required to define the access method (such as
VSAM versus ISAM) and the type of pointers to be used (hierarchical versus
child/twin). Full specification of the internal model is often quite complex
and is beyond the scope of this text.

IMS DATA MANIPULATION

The IMS data manipulation language is called Data Language I (DL/I). DL/I
consists of a set of commands that are used with a host language (COBOL,
PL/I, or assembler language). The application program invokes (or uses)
these commands by means of subroutine calls.

An overview of the DL/I commands is shown in Table 12-1. We describe
and illustrate each of these commands below. The syntax is simplified in the
following examples for ease of presentation. The examples are based on the
department data base (Figure 12-2).

GET UNIQUE (GU)

This command is used to retrieve a specific segment occurrence. The segment may be a root segment or a dependent segment. The segment desired
is specified in parentheses by a qualifying condition, called a segment search

Table 12-1
Summary of DL/I Operations
Source: Date 1981: 297

Operation	Explanation
GET UNIQUE (GU)	Direct retrieval of a segment
GET NEXT (GN)	Sequential retrieval
GET NEXT WITHIN PARENT (GNP)	Sequential retrieval under current parent
GET HOLD (GHU, GHN, GHNP)	As above, but allow subsequent DLET/REPL
INSERT (ISRT)	Add new segment
DELETE (DLET)	Delete existing segment
REPLACE (REPL)	Replace existing segment

argument (SSA). For example, suppose that we want to retrieve the segment for department 06 (a root segment). The following command would be used:

GU DEPARTMT (DEPT# = '06')

In this example, the SSA is DEPT# = '06'. The GU command will retrieve the *first* segment that satisfies the SSA (presumably there is only one occurrence for each department).

Now suppose that we want to retrieve the segment for EVANS (EMP# = 07) in ACCTG (DEPT# = 02). The following commands would be used:

GU DEPARTMT (DEPT# = '02')
    EMPLOYEE (EMP# = '07')

In this example, a hierarchical path is specified. The GU command will retrieve only the segment at the *bottom* of this path. Thus, the employee segment for EVANS (but not the parent department segment) will be retrieved.

The SSA may be omitted from a DL/I command. For example, consider the following commands:

GU DEPARTMT
    EQPMENT (IDENT = 'APPLE II')

With this command, DL/I will retrieve the *first* occurrence of an EQPMENT segment that satisfies the indicated SSA. It will scan DEPARTMT segments sequentially until this first dependent segment is located.

GET NEXT (GN)

GET NEXT is used for sequential retrieval of occurrences of a particular segment type. For example, suppose that we use the following commands:

```
GU DEPARTMT (DEPT# = '02')
    EQPMENT
GN EQPMENT
```

The GU command will cause the first EQPMENT segment (APPLE II) for DEPARTMT 02 to be retrieved. The GN command will then cause the next EQPMENT segment (IBM PC) to be retrieved.

The GN command cannot be executed until a "current position" has been established in the data base. In the preceding example, the GU command establishes the starting position by retrieving the first EQPMENT segment.

Now suppose that we add another GN command to the above example:

```
GU DEPARTMT (DEPT# = '02')
    EQPMENT
GN EQPMENT
GN EQPMENT
```

These commands will attempt to retrieve a third EQPMENT segment. However, referring to Figure 12-2, we see that there are only two such segments under DEPARTMT 02. Will this result in an error condition? The answer is that it will not. Instead, DL/I will retrieve the next EQPMENT segment in the data base under a new root segment. In fact, we can retrieve *all* EQPMENT segments in the data base with the following commands:

```
        GU DEPARTMT
            EQPMENT
MORE GN EQPMENT
            GO TO MORE
```

GET NEXT WITHIN PARENT (GNP)

Like GET NEXT, GET NEXT WITHIN PARENT causes sequential retrieval of segment occurrences. However, unlike GN, only occurrences under the current parent segment are retrieved. For example, suppose that we wish to retrieve all DEPENDNT segments for EVANS in ACCTG. The following commands would be used:

```
GU DEPARTMT (DEPT# = '02')
    EMPLOYEE (EMP# = '07')
    DEPENDNT
```

```
NEXT GNP DEPENDNT
        GO TO NEXT
```

In this example, the GU command retrieves the first DEPENDNT segment for this employee. The GNP then sequentially retrieves the remaining segments for the same employee (EVANS has three dependents). When the last segment is retrieved, DL/I will return a status message indicating that there are no more subordinate DEPENDNT segments for this employee.

The GNP command can be used to retrieve *all* subordinate segment occurrences under a current parent. For example, suppose that we wish to retrieve all segment occurrences for DEPARTMT 02:

```
        GU DEPARTMT (DEPT# – '02')
NEXT GNP
        GO TO NEXT
```

Since no segment type is specified for GNP, the loop will cause all subordinate segments to be retrieved in hierarchical sequence. DEPARTMT 02 has ten subordinate segments (see Figure 12-2).

GET HOLD

There are three GET HOLD commands: GET HOLD UNIQUE (GHU), GET HOLD NEXT (GHN), and GET HOLD NEXT WITHIN PARENT (GHNP). These commands function in exactly the same manner as GU, GN, and GNP, respectively. However, the GET HOLD versions must be used to retrieve segments that are going to be deleted (DLET) or replaced (REPL).

Replacement (REPL)

The replace (REPL) command is used to replace a segment occurrence with an updated version of the same segment. First, the segment must be retrieved by using one of the GET HOLD commands. The segment is then modified, and the REPL command writes the updated segment.

Look again at Figure 12-2. Suppose that we wish to change the age of the DEPENDNT PAUL from 8 to 9. The following commands could be used:

```
GHU DEPARTMT (DEPT#='02')
        EMPLOYEE (EMP#='07')
        DEPENDNT (DEPNM='PAUL')
        MOVE '9' TO AGE
        REPL
```

Deletion (DLET)

A segment to be deleted must first be retrieved by using one of the GET HOLD commands. For example, suppose that we wish to delete the skill PROG for EVANS in ACCTG. The following commands would be used:

```
GHU DEPARTMT (DEPT#='02')
    EMPLOYEE (EMP#='07')
    SKILL (CODE='02')
DLET
```

A DLET command deletes not only a particular segment, but all of its subordinate children (there are some exceptions to this rule, but they are beyond the scope of this text). For example, the following command will delete the root segment for DEPARTMT 02 plus all ten of its subordinate segments:

```
GHU DEPARTMT (DEPT#='02')
DLET
```

As a result, caution must be exercised in using this command. In general, the processing options (PROCOPT) specification in the PCB should limit the delete operation to only a few qualified users.

Insertion (ISRT)

ISRT allows the user to insert a new segment into the data base. To insert a new subordinate segment, the parent segment must already exist in the data base. For example, suppose that we wish to insert a new DEPENDNT occurrence for EVANS in ACCTG. The following commands could be used:

```
MOVE 'CHRIS' TO DEPNM
MOVE '0' TO AGE
ISRT DEPARTMT (DEPT#='02')
    EMPLOYEE (EMP#='07')
    DEPENDNT
```

First, the new segment to be inserted is built in the application program output area (indicated by the first two statements above). Next, the ISRT statement defines the hierarchical path to the segment to be inserted. The new segment occurrence is inserted in sequence among the existing child occurrences for the specified parent.

ADVANCED IMS FEATURES

So far, we have described the basic features of IMS. All these features are based on a purely hierarchical data model. In this section, we describe two additional features that extend IMS beyond this hierarchical model. These two features are logical data bases and secondary indexing.

Logical Data Bases

Earlier in this chapter, we defined a logical data base record (LDBR) as a subset of an IMS physical data base record (PDBR). More generally, an LDBR may be defined as a subset of one or more PDBRs. In this section, we describe how an LDBR can be defined as a subset of two PDBRs.

Suppose that the department data base (DEPTDB) illustrated in Figure 12-1 already exists. Now suppose that the organization wants to create a project data base (PROJDB). The structure of this proposed data base is shown in Figure 12-10a. The root segment type is PROJECT, and the dependent segment is EMPLOYEE.

One possible approach is to create a new PDBR type with the structure shown in Figure 12-10a. However, the new EMPLOYEE segment occurrences will contain the same data that already exist in the EMPLOYEE segments within the department data base. A better approach (which avoids this redundancy) is to link the new PROJECT segment with the existing EMPLOYEE segment by means of a logical pointer segment (see Figure 12-10b). There are two PDBR types in this figure: DEPTDB and PROJDB. The logical pointer segment (called EMPLPROJ) links the two data bases. EMPLPROJ is the *physical* child of PROJECT and the *logical* child of EMPLOYEE.

As shown in Figure 12-10c, the new PROJECT data base may now be represented as a logical data base. The LDBR type in this figure is a subset of the two PDBR types shown in Figure 12-10b. The logical data base shown in Figure 12-10c does not actually exist. However, a user application program may process the data as if they existed in this form.

Data Base Description.   Building a logical data base is a three-step process. The first step is defining a physical data base description of the project data base. In Figure 12-11a, statements 1 to 4 are similar to those in Figure 12-3 and the project segment is defined with two fields. Statement 5 is the description of the EMPLPROJ pointer segment. This statement identifies PROJECT as the physical parent, and EMPLOYEE (in DEPTDB) as the logical parent. The "P" in this entry denotes that the pointer in EMPLPROJ is a logical pointer. If there are data related to the combination of a project and an employee (called intersection data), this data can be stored in the EMPLPROJ segment.

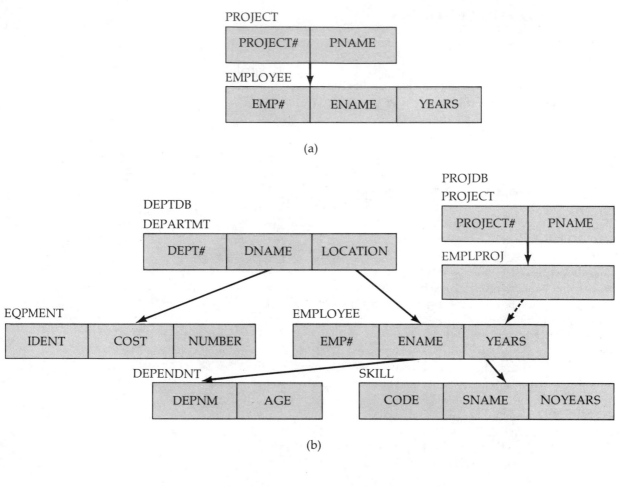

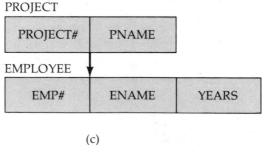

Figure 12-10
Logical data bases.
(a) Proposed project data base.
(b) Two linked PDBRs.
(c) One LDBR based on the first two PDBRs (PROJEMP).

The second step is to amend the Department physical data base description (Figure 12-3) by adding an LCHILD (logical child) statement, as shown in Figure 12-11b. Statement number 11 in this figure indicates that EM-

```
1   DBD        NAME=PROJDB
2   SEGM       NAME=PROJECT, BYTES=27, PARENT=0
3   FIELD      NAME=(PROJECT#, SEQ), BYTES=7, START=1
4   FIELD      NAME=PNAME, BYTES=20, START=8
5   SEGM       NAME=EMPLPROJ, PARENT=((PROJECT), (EMPLOYEE, P, DEPTDB))
```

(a)

```
10  SEGM       NAME=EMPLOYEE, PARENT=DEPARTMT, BYTES=42
11  LCHILD     NAME=(EMPLPROJ, PROJDB)
```

(b)

```
1   DBD        NAME=PROJEMP, ACCESS=LOGICAL
2   DATASET LOGICAL
3   SEGM       NAME=PROJECT, SOURCE=(PROJECT, DATA, PROJDB)
4   SEGM       NAME=EMPLOYEE, PARENT=PROJECT,
               SOURCE=((EMPLPROJ, DATA, PROJDB), (EMPLOYEE, DATA, DEPTDB))
```

(c)

Figure 12-11
Building the logical data base.
(a) Physical DBD.
(b) Change to EMPLOYEE segment of DEPTDB data base.
(c) Logical DBD for PROJEMP logical data base.

PLOYEE has a logical child called EMPLPROJ in the PROJDB data base. This statement is then followed by the FIELD statements for EMPLOYEE.

The third step in building our logical data base is to define the logical data base itself. As seen in Figure 12-11c, this process is rather straightforward. In statements 1 and 2, the data base is named and is defined as logical. In statement 3, the PROJECT segment is defined and the source of the data to be used is shown to be the PROJDB. In statement 4, the EMPLOYEE is defined and the source of its data is the EMPLOYEE segment in the DEPTDB data base and the EMPLPROJ segment in the PROJDB data base.

There are two important restrictions in defining logical data bases:

1. The root of a logical data base must also be the root of a physical data base. In Figure 12-10, PROJECT is the root of the PROJEMP (logical data base) and PROJDB (physical data base).

2. A logical child segment must have one physical parent and one logical parent. In Figure 12-10, EMPLPROJ is the physical child of PROJECT and the logical child of EMPLOYEE.

In this section, we have presented a simplified description of IMS logical data bases. In reality, additional entries would be required. For a complete discussion of this topic, see IBM Corp.

Processing a Logical Data Base. A logical data base is accessed in exactly the same way as a physical data base. The programmer does not have to know whether the data base is physical or logical.

Loading a logical data base is another matter. Again, it is a three-step process, assuming the logical data base has been correctly defined. First, the data must be loaded onto the first physical data base (DEPTDB in our example). Second, the data must be loaded onto the other physical data base (PROJDB). Finally, an IMS utility is run that causes the two data bases to be logically connected.

Once the logical data base has been loaded, a user can process it exactly as if it were a physical data base. That is, DL/I commands can be used to retrieve and manipulate the logical data base. For example, suppose that we wish to retrieve all EMPLOYEE segments for employees who are assigned to PROJECT ABCD. The following DL/I commands would be used:

```
        GU PROJECT (PROJECT#='ABCD')
             EMPLOYEE
NEXT GNP EMPLOYEE
          GO TO NEXT
```

Notice that in filling this request, the program will retrieve segments from two physical data bases.

Secondary Indexing

One of the important features of IMS is the ability to access data bases using multiple keys. As an example, we normally access the DEPTDB by department number. If we now need to access the DEPTDB by location, we could use a logical data base, but a better approach would be to use a secondary index. Like HIDAM data bases, secondary indexes are implemented by means of a physical index data base. To implement a secondary index, the DBD of the data base to be indexed (DEPTDB in our example) needs to be changed.

The following two statements would need to be added to the DBD (Figure 12-3) immediately after the LOCATION field statement:

```
LCHILD NAME=(LOCINDX, LOCDB), POINTER=INDX
XDFIELD NAME=XLOCN, SRCH=LOCATION
```

The first (or LCHILD) statement specifies that this data base (DEPTDB) is indexed by a segment called LOCINDX (location index). That index is defined in a data base called LOCDB. The POINTER=INDX entry specifies that LOCINDX is indeed an index (not a data record). The second (or XDFIELD) statement identifies the field that is indexed; in this example, it is LOCATION, as specified by the SRCH=LOCATION entry. The NAME= XLOCN entry specifies that the variable name XLOCN will be used in referring to the indexed field.

```
1   DBD       NAME=LOCDB, ACCESS=INDEX
2   SEGM      NAME=LOCINDEX, BYTES=4,
3   FIELD     NAME=LOCATION, BYTES=4, START=1
4   LCHILD    NAME=(DEPARTMT, DEPTDB), INDEX=XLOCN
```

Figure 12-12 .
DBD for secondary index.

Defining a Secondary Index.   The secondary index data base is described as shown in Figure 12-12. Statement 1 is a regular DBD statement and assigns the name LOCDB to this data base. Statement 2 assigns the name LOCINDX to the segment in an index, and statement 3 defines the field (LOCATION) on which the secondary index is defined. This is the only field in the LOCINDX segment. Statement 4 is the LCHILD that connects the index data base to the LOCATION field in the DEPTDB. A secondary index data base such as this one is loaded using IMS utilities.

Using a Secondary Index.   When an IMS data base is loaded, any secondary indexes that have been defined by the user are automatically constructed by IMS. Also, IMS automatically maintains the secondary indexes as the data base is modified.

To use a secondary index, the user specifies DL/I commands that invoke the variable names for the indexed field. To return to our original example, suppose that we wish to retrieve the segment for the department whose location is B100. The following statement will be used:

GU DEPARTMT (XLOCN = 'B100')

This statement will cause IMS to retrieve the B100 index segment within LOCDB. That segment contains a pointer to the B100 data segment within DEPARTMT, which is the target segment.

In this example, we assume that values of the indexed field are unique (e.g., there is only one B100 segment). However, an IMS secondary index may also be defined for fields that do not have unique values. For example, there may be more than one department at a given location. Therefore, a secondary index for LOCATION must accommodate nonunique values. Minor modifications are required in the secondary index definition for this case (for details, see IBM Corp.).

Mountain View Community Hospital

CASE EXAMPLE

In this section, we illustrate the use of IMS to implement a data base for Mountain View Community Hospital. A structure of a data base for this hospital is shown in Figure 9-11 and again in Figure 12-13 for ease of reference.

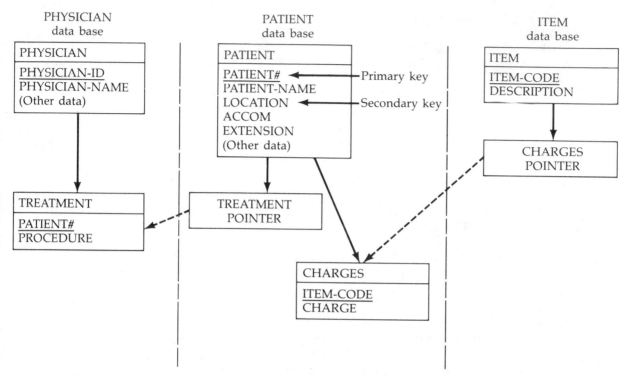

Figure 12-13
IMS data base structures (hospital).

Data Base Definition

Three distinct physical data bases are shown in Figure 12-13. These data bases are linked together by logical pointers for reasons already described. A DBD for the PHYSICIAN data base is shown in Figure 12-14 (we will ask you to develop DBDs for the remaining data bases in the chapter problems).

Two segment types are defined in the PHYSICIAN data base: PHYSICN (for physician) and TREATMT (for treatment). Notice that in statement 8, a logical child is defined for the TREATMT segment. This logical child is the treatment pointer (TREATPTR) in the PATIENT data base (PATNTDB). This pointer links the PATIENT and PHYSICIAN data bases.

Data Base Manipulation

In this section, we illustrate use of DL/I statements to retrieve data from the hospital data bases. All the statements are based on the data base structures shown in Figure 12-13.

Simple Retrieval.   To retrieve patient data for patient number 1234, we use the following command:

   GU PATIENT (PATIENT# = '1234')

```
1   DBD      NAME=PHYSDB
2   SEGM     NAME=PHYSICN, BYTES=17, PARENT=0
3   FIELD    NAME=(PHYSID, SEQ), BYTES=10, START=1
4   FIELD    NAME=PHYPHONE, BYTES=7, START=11
5   SEGM     NAME=TREATMT, PARENT=PHYSICN, BYTES=19
6   FIELD    NAME=(PATIENT#, SEQ), BYTES=4, START=1
7   FIELD    NAME=PROCEDUR, BYTES=15, START=5
8   LCHILD   NAME=(TREATPTR, PATNTDB)
```

Figure 12-14
DBD for PHYSICIAN data base.

Indexed Retrieval.   To retrieve patient data for the patient in location 4321, we use the following command:

    GU PATIENT (XLOCN – '4321')

This command assumes that there is a secondary index for the LOCATION field. Also, we assume that XLOCN is the variable name for the indexed field LOCATION.

Retrieval of Child Segments.   To calculate total charges for patient number 1234, we use the following commands.

```
        MOVE 0 TO TOTAL
        GU PATIENT (PATIENT#='1234')
            CHARGES
            ADD CHARGE TO TOTAL
MORE GNP CHARGES
            ADD CHARGES TO TOTAL
            GO TO MORE
```

The GET UNIQUE (GU) statement retrieves the first CHARGES segment for this patient (if one exists). The amount of the CHARGE is added to the running total (TOTAL). The GNP statement is then executed repeatedly to retrieve additional charges, and TOTAL is updated until there are no more charges for that patient.

Retrieval Using Logical Records.   To retrieve all TREATMT segments for patient number 1234, we use the following commands:

```
        GU PATIENT (PATIENT#=1234)
            TREATMT
MORE GNP TREATMT
            GO TO MORE
```

In this retrieval, the PATIENT and TREATMT segments exist in separate data bases. However, use of the Treatment Pointer (TREATPTR) allows the user to manipulate the TREATMT segment as a child of PATIENT.

SYSTEM 2000/80

System 2000/80 is a data base management system marketed by INTEL Systems Corporation. This DBMS evolved from the earlier System 2000 developed by MRI Systems Corporation, which became a division of INTEL in 1979.

System 2000/80 is fundamentally a hierarchical DBMS. However, it has features to support other data models as well. For example, to model a relational data base, there is a WHERE clause that allows the user to relate any given field to any other field in the data base. Also, there is a LINK command that allows the user to create network structures by establishing relationships between record types. System 2000/80 provides a variety of add-on features, including a screen-oriented query/update facility (QueX), a report writer, and a communications interface. System 2000/80 is available for mainframe computers, including those from CDC, IBM, and UNIVAC.

Data Base Definition

As with IMS, a System 2000/80 data base consists of a hierarchical arrangement of records (the term *segment* is not used in System 2000/80). Each record, except the root record, has one and only one parent, and each record is composed of data fields called **items**.

The schema definition language in system 2000/80 is called DEFINE. This language is used to describe the records and items in the data base. Figure 12-15 shows the DEFINE language used to describe the DEPARTMENT data base (see Figure 12-1).

There are five record types in the DEPARTMENT data base. These are identified in components 1, 4, 8, 12, and 15 in Figure 12-15. For record types that are immediately below the root segment (such as EQUIPMENT and EMPLOYEE), the parent record type need not be defined. However, for all records at a lower level, the parent record must be defined. Thus, the entry RECORD IN 8 for component 12 indicates that the parent of the DEPENDENT record type is EMPLOYEE (described in component 8).

We describe each item in a record immediately below the record definition by defining the item name, data type, and whether or not the item is indexed (KEY versus NONKEY). Ten possible character types are allowed in System 2000/80. They are CHARACTER, INTEGER, TEXT, DECIMAL, MONEY, DATE, REAL, DOUBLE PRECISION, BINARY, and OCTAL/HEXADECIMAL. Field lengths can be specified by using COBOL picture clauses. For example, the entry EMP NAME (NAME X(30) IN 8) specifies that the EMP NAME item is data type NAME and has a length of 30 characters.

A data item may be key or nonkey (the default is key). A key data item is one that is indexed, so that the record (or records) containing a data item

```
        DATA BASE NAME IS DEPARTMENT:
        1* DEPARTMENT NO (NAME X(3)):
        2* DEPT NAME (NAME X(20)):
        3* LOCATION (CHARACTER X(4)):
        4* EQUIPMENT (RECORD):
            5* IDENT (NAME X(15) IN 4):
            6* COST (NON-KEY MONEY 9(7).9(2) IN 4):
            7* NUMBER (NON-KEY INTEGER 9(4) IN 4):
        8* EMPLOYEE (RECORD):
            9* EMPLOYEE NO (NAME X(10) IN 8):
           10* EMP NAME (NAME X(30) IN 8):
           11* YEARS (NON-KEY INTEGER 99 IN 8):
           12* DEPENDENT (RECORD IN 8):
               13* DEP NAME (NAME X(30) IN 12):
               14* DEP AGE (NON-KEY INTEGER 99 IN 12):
           15* SKILL (RECORD IN 8):
               16* CODE (NAME X(6) IN 15):
               17* SKILL NAME (NAME X(20) IN 15):
               18* NO YEARS (NON-KEY INTEGER 99 IN 15):
```

Figure 12-15
System 2000/80 example schema.

occurrence can be accessed directly. Inspecting Figure 12-15, you will notice that component 14 (DEP AGE) is specified NONKEY. Therefore, it is not possible to access a DEPENDENT record occurrence directly given a value for DEP AGE. However, LOCATION (component 3) contains no key specification. Thus, by default there is an index for LOCATION, and given a value for LOCATION, we can directly access the associated DEPARTMENT record (or records).

Data Base Manipulation

System 2000/80 provides users with several languages for accessing and manipulating their data bases. For conventional programming application, there is a facility called Programming Language Extension (PLEX). PLEX consists of a set of commands for data base manipulation that are embedded in a host language such as COBOL or PL/I. In addition, there is an End User Facility that includes three languages that permit end users to access data bases without programming skills:

1. QUEUE, a query language that allows users to create, retrieve, and modify data (an expanded version called QUEST is also available).

2. Query/Update by Example (QueX), a screen-oriented, menu-driven facility that provides user-friendly access to data.

3. REPORT, a report writer facility.

System 2000/80 commands consist of an action to be performed followed by an optional WHERE clause that specifies the qualifying criteria for that action. We will now illustrate the use of the query language QUEUE in retrieving data from the DEPARTMENT data base. Consider the following command:

LIST DEPARTMENT NO, DEPT NAME, LOCATION:

This command produces a display of data for all departments (no WHERE clause is used).

Now consider the following:

LIST EMPLOYEE NO, EMP NAME, YEARS WHERE YEARS GE 10:

This command produces a list of employee data for employees who have worked ten years or more.

And consider the following:

LIST EMPLOYEE NO, EMP NAME, YEARS ORDERED BY EMP NAME WHERE YEARS GE 10:

This command produces the same result as the previous command, except that the list is sorted in alphabetical order by employee name.

Now let us consider more complex queries that require access to more than one record type.

Query 1: "Find the names of all employees who work in departments that own at least one IBM personal computer."

LIST ENAME WHERE DEPARTMENT HAS IDENT EQ IBM PC:

Query 2: "Find the identification of all equipment for departments whose employees have the 'programmer' skill."

LIST IDENT WHERE DEPARTMENT HAS SNAME EQ PROGRAMMER:

These queries illustrate the power and simplicity of the System 2000/80 query language in data retrievals.

SUMMARY

In this chapter, we have presented an introduction to data base management systems that are based on the hierarchical data model. Of these, by far the most widely used is Information Management System (IMS), an IBM software product. In IMS, data are viewed as hierarchical arrangements of segments. A data manipulation language called Data Language I (DL/I) allows the user to retrieve data by traversing the tree structure.

Although the design of IMS dates from the late 1960s, a stream of enhancements has been added to provide new features. Thus, through the use of logical data bases, the user can model limited networks. Also, secondary indexing permits access on fields other than primary keys. However, because these features tend to be quite complex, IMS tends to be used only in relatively sophisticated data processing shops where considerable technical expertise is available.

System 2000/80 is a somewhat newer DBMS product marketed by INTEL Corporation. It is based fundamentally on the hierarchical data model, but it is also capable of modeling network and relational views of data. One of the best features of System 2000/80 is a powerful query language that allows users to retrieve data using natural language commands.

Many other hierarchical DBMS products (not described in this chapter) are also available. Two of the more recent hierarchical products are FOCUS and DB Master. Although it represents older technology, the hierarchical model remains a viable alternative for DBMS implementations. However, it should be evaluated against the more recent network and relational systems.

CHAPTER REVIEW

Review Questions

1. Give a concise definition for each of the following terms:

a. segment	d. physical data base record
b. root segment	e. data base description
c. logical data base record	f. program communication block

2. Contrast the following terms:

   a. physical data base record; logical data base record

   b. program communication block; program specification block

   c. root segment; child segment

   d. hierarchical pointers; child/twin pointers

3. Define each of the following acronyms:

a. IMS	f. GNP
b. PDBR	g. LCHILD
c. LDBR	h. PLEX
d. PCB	i. SENSEG
e. PSB	

4. Describe each of the following access methods briefly, and indicate the conditions favoring its use:

a. HSAM	c. HDAM
b. HISAM	d. HIDAM

5. What are the three end-user-oriented languages in System 2000/80?

6. Describe two ways in which an LDBR may differ from a PDBR.

7. Describe two advantages of the "sensitive segment" feature in IMS.

8. Why must caution be used in deleting a root segment with the DL/I DLET Command?

9. Describe two restrictions in defining logical data bases.

10. Identify whether each of the following terms applies to IMS or System 2000/80.
    a. segment
    b. item
    c. DL/I
    d. QUEST
    e. PCB
    f. End User Facility

Problems and Exercises

Problems 1 to 6 are based on the following hierarchical data base structure for Pine Valley Furniture Company.

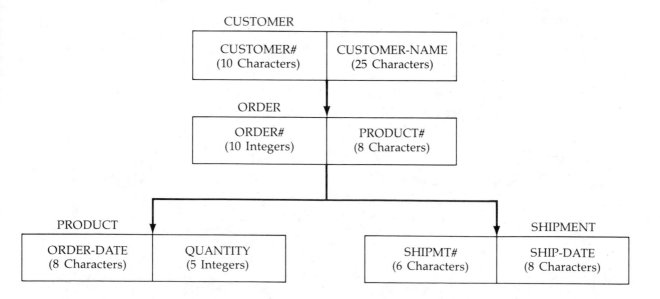

1. Write an IMS data base description (DBD) for the data base shown here.

2. Based on the DBD in Problem 1, write a program communication block (PCB) for a logical data base record that contains the CUSTOMER, ORDER, and PRODUCT segments (but omits the SHIPMENT segment).

3. Write DL/I statements for each of the following retrievals:
   a. CUSTOMER segment for customer number ABCD.
   b. ORDER segment for order number 1234, customer number ABCD.
   c. All ORDER segments for customer number ABCD.
   d. All PRODUCT segments for customer number ABCD, order number 1234.

4. Write DL/I statements for the following updates.
   a. Change the QUANTITY for product number 10 in order number 1234 for customer number ABCD from 3 to 2.
   b. Delete shipment number WXYZ for order number 6789 from customer number ABCD.
   c. Add shipment number CDEF to order number 6789 from customer number ABCD (shipment date is 6/18/8X).

5. Write a System 2000/80 schema for the data base structure shown here.

6. Write System 2000 QUEUE statements for each of the following retrievals:
   a. CUSTOMER record for customer number ABCD.
   b. PRODUCT segment for product number 12, order number 6789, customer number CDEF.
   c. All ORDER segments for customer number CDEF.
   d. SHIPMENT segments for all orders that order product number 24.

7. Write an IMS data base description for the ITEM data base in Figure 12-13 (include logical pointer CHARGES). Assume the following data item characteristics:

   ITEM CODE   10 Characters
   DESCRIPN   25 Characters

8. Write an IMS data base description for the PATIENT data base (Figure 12-13). Include the logical pointers. Assume the following data item characteristics:

   PATIENT#   10 Characters
   PATNAME   25 Characters
   LOCATION   5 Characters
   ACCOM   6 Characters
   EXTENSN   4 Integers
   ITEMCODE   10 Characters
   CHARGE   Decimal XXXX.XX

9. In Figure 12-13, LOCATION is identified as a secondary key in the PATIENT segment. Write an IMS secondary index DBD for this field.

10. One logical data base record derived from the hospital data base (Figure 12-13) appears as follows:

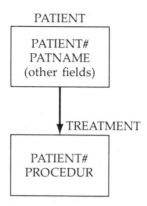

Write an IMS DBD for this logical record.

11. Write DL/I statements for the following retrievals in the hospital data base (Figure 12-13):

    a. CHARGE segment for item number 1234, patient number ABCD.

    b. All CHARGE segments for patient number ABCD.

    c. All TREATMENT segments for patient number ABCD performed by physician number P10.

12. Write a System 2000/80 schema for the PATIENT data base (Figure 12-13). Ignore the logical pointer (TREATMENT). Use the data item characteristics specified in Problem 8.

13. Write a System 2000 QUEUE statement to retrieve the TREATMENT record for patient number ABCD performed by physician number P12 (Figure 12-13).

14. Referring to Figure 12-2, what segment(s) will be retrieved for each of the following statements?

    a.   GU DEPARTMT (DEPT#='02')
              EQPMENT (IDENT='APPLE II')

    b.   GU DEPARTMT (DEPT#='02')
              EMPLOYEE (EMP#='07')
              SKILL (CODE='02')

    c.   GU DEPARTMT (DEPT#='02')
              EMPLOYEE (EMP#='07')
              DEPENDNT (DEPNM='THERESE')

        NEXT GNP DEPENDNT
              GO TO NEXT

15. Referring to Figure 12-2, what record will be retrieved in response to the following System 2000/80 QUEUE commands?

   a. LIST ENAME WHERE DEPARTMENT HAS IDENT EQ IBM PC:

   b. LIST SNAME WHERE DEPARTMENT HAS IDENT EQ APPLE II:

References

Atre, Shaku. 1983. *Data Base Management Systems for the Eighties.* Wellesley, Mass.. QED Information Sciences, Inc.

Date, C.J. 1981. *An Introduction to Data Base Systems.* 3d ed. Reading, Mass.: Addison-Wesley.

IBM Corp. *Information Management System/Virtual Storage General Information Manual.* IBM Form No. GH20-1260.

Tsichritzis, D.C., and F.H. Lochovsky. 1977. *Data Base Management Systems.* New York: Academic Press.

13

Network and CODASYL Implementations

INTRODUCTION

The implementation of the network data model is an interesting example of the influence of industry standards in the computing field and of the influence of individual vendors. In preliminary form in 1969 and in an updated and better-outlined form in 1971 (CODASYL 1971), the COnference of DAta SYstem Languages (CODASYL), through its Data Base Task Group (DBTG), issued descriptions of languages for defining and processing data. These reports and updates in 1978 and 1981 define the general characteristics for all but a few network DBMSs (ANSI X3H2 1981; CODASYL COBOL Committee 1978; CODASYL Data Description Language Committee 1978).

Although represented on the original DBTG, IBM Corporation did not sign or endorse these standards and to this day has not implemented a network DBMS. But many other hardware vendors and numerous software firms have chosen to develop systems following the CODASYL guidelines (even for IBM computers). At the same time, IBM has installed IMS, its hierarchical DBMS, in many of its customers' data centers. Again, these events indicate that variety is the hallmark of data base.

The CODASYL Committee is a voluntary group of individuals who represent hardware and software vendors, universities, and major developers and users of data processing systems. Their original charge had been to discuss changes to the COBOL programming language and to write position papers in this area. Member organizations were in no way bound to implement these positions in their program products. It had become clear that COBOL needed radical extension to support multiple-file (data base) data processing, and the DBTG was formed.

In 1963, General Electric (later Honeywell Information Systems) began to market Integrated Data System (IDS), the forerunner of network DBMSs. The generally accepted leader of the development of IDS was Charles Bachman. Although Bachman was not on the DBTG itself, several individuals from Honeywell were represented, along with Richard Schubert of B.F. Goodrich Chemical Company, a primary user of IDS. Through these individuals and because IDS was the most fully developed DBMS by this time, the structure of IDS (and the ideas of Charles Bachman) greatly influenced the deliberations of the DBTG. Even today, many organizations draw "Bachman diagrams" to represent network data bases.

Although pleased with the capabilities of IDS, B.F. Goodrich worked on expanding these functions to meet more of the DBTG guidelines. Interest grew in the computing community in bringing a DBTG network DBMS to the marketplace. John Cullinane approached B.F. Goodrich and purchased the rights to further develop and market their initial DBTG implementation along with the existing CULPRIT reportwriter product. He named his new product Integrated Database Management System (IDMS), which is still, today, the leading DBTG DBMS on IBM (and other) computers. Charles Bachman has been, at various times, a consultant with Cullinane Database Systems (now Cullinet Software).

Many network DBMSs exist today. Most of these are DBTG implementations, but several significant exceptions have appeared. Table 13-1 lists many of these network DBMSs and pertinent information about them. Since DBTG network DBMSs dominate, most of this chapter reviews the definition and processing of data using these DBMSs; aspects of other network DBMSs are briefly covered. Also addressed are recent extensions to network DBMSs that provide nonnetwork views of a data base managed by a network DBMS. This latter topic is an important development that creates much confusion in making distinctions between DBMSs.

There are actually three official versions of the DBTG guidelines (1971, 1978, and 1981 reports); we have chosen to emphasize the 1978 report because most DBTG DBMSs today come closest to following these guidelines. Some exceptions will be noted when appropriate. Because of its prominence among IBM computer installations, we will draw heavily on IDMS as an example of a DBTG implementation. For greater depth on the DBTG model, Olle (1980) provides an excellent coverage of these guidelines through several minor modifications published in 1973.

INTRODUCTION TO CODASYL DBTG GUIDELINES

To begin to understand the DBTG guidelines and implementations of this data model, we must start by analyzing the concept of a DBMS that underlies the work of the DBTG. Figure 13-1 shows the conceptual data base

Table 13-1
Summary of Some Network DBMSs

Package	Vendor	Equipment	Comments
CODASYL DBMSs			
IDMS	Cullinet Software	IBM 360/370, 30xx, 43xx, variety of operating systems, several minis and a few other mainframes	Various related packages, including: Integrated Data Dictionary, CULPRIT reportwriter, ONLINE ENGLISH natural language, distributed data base facility, and Application Development System (ADS/O)
PR1ME DBMS	PR1ME Computer	Various PR1ME mini and supermini computers under PR1MOS operating system	On-line query facility called QUERY/DBMS (VISTA)
DMS-170	CDC	Variety of hardware under NOS operating system	
DBMS 10	DEC	DEC 10 under TOPS operating system	PDP 11 version called DBMS 11
IDS II	Honeywell Information Systems	Variety of HIS computers	Extension of first network DBMS
SEED	International Database Systems	PDP minis and CP/M operating system based micros	Has several associated reportwriters and query languages
DMS-1100	Univac	Exec 8 and more recent operating systems for Univac 1100 computer family	Popular nonprocedural language MAPPER
Limited network DBMSs			
TOTAL	CINCOM Systems, Inc.	IBM 360/370, 30xx, 43xx, System/3, Harris, NCR, Honeywell, and CDC computers	ENVIRON/1 teleprocessing utility, SOCRATES report generator

Table 13-1 continued
Summary of Some Network DBMSs

Package	Vendor	Equipment	Comments
IMAGE	Hewlett-Packard	HP3000 and other HP minicomputers	Basically same as TOTAL in design and function
Complex network/extended CODASYL DBMSs			
DMS II	Burroughs	B1900 and higher, integrated with MCP operating system	Includes ALGOL host language interface
MDBS III	Micro Data Base Systems	CP/M and MS-DOS operating systems on micros and a few minis	Also hierarchical package HDMS; query language; BASIC, FORTRAN, and COBOL interfaces

management system envisioned by the DBTG. This diagram indicates that a DBMS is conceived as software that works in conjunction with an operating system to service multiple, concurrently executing user programs.

DBMS Operation

To comprehend the nature of a DBTG DBMS, it is important to understand the operational sequence of events that occurs when using such a DBMS. This sequence is depicted with numbered arrows in Figure 13-1 and can be summarized as follows:

1. A user program "calls" the DBMS with a request for service (retrieval, maintenance, and so on), which has been written using special data manipulation language (DML) statements. These statements are included in a host language (e.g., COBOL) user program.

2. The DBMS analyzes the request for service by matching the parameters of the request with a stored version of a definition of the data base (called a schema) and a definition of the part of the data base applicable to this program (called a subschema). These two data definitions have been predefined via data description languages (DDLs) and are maintained and stored separate from user programs in a library of data definitions.

3. As long as the request for service contains no inadmissible components (e.g., improper security passwords or references to data outside the

Figure 13-1
CODASYL conceptual
data base management
system.
(Source: CODASYL 1971.)

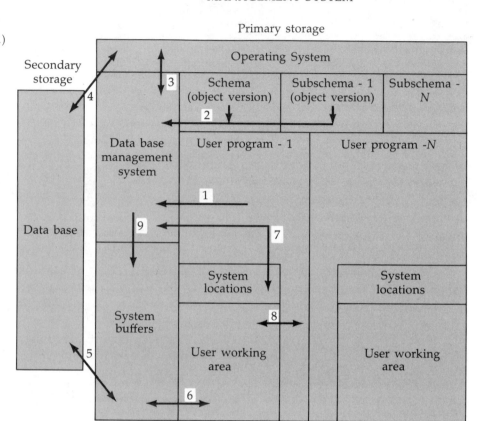

CONCEPTUAL DATA BASE
MANAGEMENT SYSTEM

invoked subschema), the DBMS composes a series of I/O commands for the access methods of the operating system.

4. The operating system interacts with secondary storage devices to initiate data base access.

5. The operating system performs the appropriate retrieval or modification of data base contents, using data buffers managed by the DBMS. These buffers contain blocks of data transferred between main and secondary memory in which data are formatted as defined by the schema.

6. In the case of data retrieval, data are then moved from the system buffers to a user work area or data section of the calling user's program (steps 5 and 6 are reversed for maintenance). This transfer also often includes the reformatting of data and the elimination of data in blocks not included in the subschema.

7. The DBMS then sets status-variable values in the user program with messages and error codes to indicate the nature of any problems, if any, that arose during data base interaction.

8. The user program is then free to further manipulate the data it has received from the data base or to compose new records for data base maintenance.

9. While each user program is executing, the DBMS manages the system buffers so that, for example, if a request for data is made that asks for data already in a system buffer, the DBMS can bypass steps 3 to 5 and provide the data immediately to the calling program.

Although the outline of this interaction could be interpreted in several ways, the resulting guidelines specified an implementation in which user calls occur at the record level; that is, the user program includes DML statements to retrieve or write *each* record required for processing, one at a time from each data base file.

DBTG Languages

The DBTG guidelines also specified or implied various new languages. First is a **schema data description language** (schema DDL), used to define the global data base. As previously mentioned, this is a combination of implementation-independent and -dependent statements. Since the schema DDL does not, however, cover all internal/physical declarations, a **device media control language** (DMCL) was proposed to specify assignment of data to particular devices, data block contents and format, data base update audit trail options, and so on.

Also proposed were standards for a **subschema data description language** (subschema DDL) for specification of data base structure to program compilers. Several user programs are allowed to share the same subschema. Originally, only a COBOL subschema DDL was proposed, but today a FORTRAN subschema DDL also exists. Each language requires its own subschema DDL, since the idea was to define the external data base in a syntax that can be easily translated into the data definitions of a programming language.

Finally, standards for a **data manipulation language** (DML), also host-language-specific, were proposed. Initially, only a COBOL version was outlined, but today a FORTRAN version also exists. The DBTG assumed a host language environment in which there would be extensions to an already existing language (as opposed to defining a new self-contained language for data base manipulation). These extensions would be handled either by vendors creating new language compilers to translate the expanded vocabulary or by preprocessors that would translate only the new language statements within a program into standard language sentences (usually CALL statements with parameters derived from the raw DML statement). The output from the DML preprocessor would then be given to a standard language compiler.

The DBTG proposals also called for extensive capabilities to define security controls in the schema DDL. Many initial implementations of the DBTG model chose not to include these capabilities, since it was felt that given computing power in the early 1970s, data base processing performance would be seriously deterred by such overhead. Today, inclusion of security controls is a standard feature of DBTG implementations. Also standard today are nonprocedural (non-record-at-a-time) query languages for DBTG implementations that permit retrieval (but often *not* update) to be accomplished in fewer statements and less programming time than in conventional procedural languages like COBOL or FORTRAN.

This, then, is an overview of the DBTG DBMS environment. The following sections address the DBTG model and its languages in greater detail.

DBTG SCHEMA DDL: THE CONCEPTUAL/INTERNAL DATA BASE

The DBTG schema DDL uses some familiar terminology but has certainly done its part to create new terms. On occasion, this terminology has been disturbing enough to cause CODASYL to change terms to clarify usage of the data model. The schema DDL has many clauses and various options in most of the clause parameters. It is beyond our purpose here to cover all features of the schema DDL, so only the most salient and frequently used features and parameters will be shown. The general structure of a DBTG schema definition is shown in Figure 13-2. The structure illustrated here generally obeys the 1978 DBTG guidelines; exceptions are indicated with footnotes.

A **schema** (definition) is a named collection of record types and pairwise associations (sets) between owner and member record types, which are located in specified, named regions of secondary memory (areas or realms).

The structure shown in Figure 13-2 can be broken into three general segments. The first segment defines contiguous physical storage regions, called areas, into which all data values will be located. Because this deals with the physical or metaphysical data base, the 1981 guidelines have dropped this segment (and related clauses) to make the schema more of a conceptual data base definition (at least more independent of implementation).

The second segment describes all the record types or files and the data item contents that compose the data base. The third segment defines the data base representation, called sets, of all pairwise record type rela-

```
        SCHEMA NAME IS _____
            [ON ERROR...]
            [PRIVACY LOCK...]
        {AREA NAME IS _____
            [ON ERROR...]
            [PRIVACY LOCK...]}*
        {RECORD NAME IS _____
            LOCATION MODE...
            [KEY IS...]**
            {WITHIN...}*
            [ON ERROR...]
            [PRIVACY LOCK...]
            [level-no data-base-data-name
            |((|PICTURE...| or |TYPE...|)
                |OCCURS...|) or
                (| SOURCE...|)|
                |RESULT...|
                |CHECK...|
                | FOR (ENCODING or DECODING)...|
                [ON ERROR...]
                [PRIVACY...]|}
    [SET NAME IS _____
        OWNER IS...
        |SET IS DYNAMIC or PRIOR|
        ORDER IS...
        [ON ERROR...]
        [PRIVACY LOCK...]
        {MEMBER IS _____
        INSERTION IS _____
        RETENTION IS _____
        [KEY IS...|
        |SEARCH KEY IS...|
        |CHECK IS...|
        |SET SELECTION...|
        [ON ERROR...]
        [PRIVACY LOCK...]}]
    END SCHEMA
```

Figure 13-2
General structure of
DBTG schema definition.

    *Deleted in 1981 CODASYL revision, but still a part of most DBMSs
    **Added in 1981 version, but not yet present in most DBMSs
        [...]—0, 1 or many occurrences of clause
        {...}—1 or many occurrences of clause
        |...|—0 or 1 occurrences of clause

tionships designed in the conceptual data base. The data model is a simple network, and link and intersection record types (called junction records by IDMS) may exist, as well as sets between them. Thus, the complete network of relationships is represented by several pairwise sets; in each set some (one) record type is owner (at the tail of the network arrow) and one or more record types are members (at the head of the relationship arrow). Usually, a set defines a 1:M relationship, although 1:1 is permitted.

Two types of clauses that can appear at various points in a schema will not be addressed in detail here; these are the ON ERROR and PRIVACY clauses. ON ERROR can be used to indicate that certain user-defined procedures are to be invoked in case of specified errors in data or commands. PRIVACY LOCKs specify passwords or procedures that are to be used to verify that certain data base manipulations are authorized for users of the data base.

Before we explain the schema DDL, it is worth mentioning that you may have the most trouble understanding three components of the DDL: LOCATION MODE, SET SELECTION, and set membership clauses. Carefully study examples and discussions that involve these most frequently misunderstood parts of a DBTG data base definition.

CASE EXAMPLE   Pine Valley Furniture

Areas or Realms

Consider the Pine Valley Furniture data base of Figure 2-10. If this data base were large enough to require many disk cylinders or disk packs, processing this data base could become very expensive. If it were realized that a significant amount of data processing were related to customer geographical regions (e.g., sales reports produced by region or new orders batched by region), then it might be advantageous to cluster CUSTOMER and ORDER records (at least) from a common geographical region close together in the physical data base for more rapid access between these records. Similarly, suppose that marketing applications concentrate record usage to CUSTOMER and ORDER records and that production applications primarily use PRODUCT and ORDER-LINE record types. In this case, it is advantageous to cluster CUSTOMER and ORDER records close together, but separate from a cluster of PRODUCT and ORDER-LINE records, to provide rapid access between records that are used together in data processing.

An **area** (or **realm** in recent CODASYL terminology) is a named, contiguous portion of secondary memory. Operationally, this is equivalent to a range of adjacent pages of some physical disk file. The purpose of the area designation is to control physical proximity of records, as illustrated in the Pine Valley Furniture cases of geographical regions and segregated data processing. The data base of a schema will reside in one or more areas. Each area is named in the schema, and the definition of each record specifies which area or areas will hold records of that type (the WITHIN clause).

A skeleton of a schema for this Pine Valley Furniture situation would be:

```
        AREA NAME IS SOUTH
        . . .
        RECORD NAME IS CUSTOMER
        . . .
          WITHIN SOUTH, EAST, WEST AREA-ID IS CUST-REGION
        . . .
          1 CUST-REGION ; TYPE IS CHARACTER 10
        . . .
        RECORD NAME IS ORDER
        . . .
          LOCATION MODE IS VIA ORDERS-FOR-CUSTOMER SET
          WITHIN AREA OF OWNER
        . . .
        SET NAME IS ORDERS-FOR-CUSTOMER
          OWNER IS CUSTOMER
        . . .
          MEMBER IS ORDER
        . . .
```

In this example, it is assumed that three areas were desirable: SOUTH, EAST, and WEST (area definitions for EAST and WEST are similar to the one for SOUTH). CUSTOMER records are automatically placed in the proper area by the DBMS when a new record is stored. The customer's region (and area) name, loaded into the CUST-REGION field of a CUSTOMER record instance by a data entry program, is used to specify proper placement. ORDER records are placed in the same region as their associated CUS-TOMER record (i.e., their owner is the ORDERS-FOR-CUSTOMER set). Thus, if data processing requirements frequently require ORDER records associated with a given CUSTOMER record, then these records will be able to be accessed more rapidly than if placement is not controlled. For this reason, a set is said to define an access path to "walk" through a data base from owner record to members (or vice versa). This placement of ORDER records near their related CUSTOMER record is controlled by the WITHIN clause of the ORDER record (makes all ORDERs closer to all CUSTOMERs than to other records) and the LOCATION MODE clause of the ORDER record (places a specific ORDER close to its particular CUSTOMER record instance).

Records

The second major data construct in the DBTG model is that of a record. A **record** is a named entity, instances of which describe individual occurrences of the entity. We define a record by specifying how the physical location of a record instance is determined (LOCATION MODE clause) and by a list of data element (or data-base-data-name) definitions.

Table 13-2
DBTG Record Placement Control Using LOCATION MODE

LOCATION MODE	Explanation	Examples
CALC	Indicates that a record instance will be placed and may be accessed in secondary memory based on a value for a primary or secondary key. Usually, this is implemented by key value hashing, but index methods are possible. That is, data base can be entered directly at a given record if a CALC key value is known.	RECORD NAME IS PRODUCT LOCATION MODE IS CALC USING PRODUCT# DUPLICATES NOT ALLOWED – defines a single, primary key – – – – – – – – – – – – – – – – – RECORD NAME IS CUSTOMER LOCATION MODE IS CALC USING CUST-ZIP DUPLICATES ARE FIRST – defines a single, secondary key
VIA	Indicates that a record instance will be placed in secondary memory close to its parent record instance for *one* specified set. This helps to improve performance when used with frequently referenced set. VIA and CALC may not both be used on same record; use of VIA prevents access to record on a key value.	RECORD NAME IS ORDER-LINE LOCATION MODE IS VIA ITEMS-ON-ORDER SET . . . SET NAME IS ITEMS-ON-ORDER OWNER IS ORDER . . . MEMBER IS ORDER-LINE – specifies that an ORDER-LINE instance should be stored close to its ORDER owner instance

LOCATION MODE of a Record. LOCATION MODE is a physical construct that has been removed in recent guidelines, but which is still present in most commercial implementations. **LOCATION MODE** specifies the method that will be employed to determine the precise disk address of an instance of a record when it is stored. Two methods are popular: CALC and VIA. Table 13-2 briefly summarizes the use of each of these methods.

Data processing frequently requires referring to records by logical key value. For example, a data entry operator may input a product number from a sales form and expect to see associated data in order to complete the entry of a customer order. The CALC LOCATION MODE would be appropriate to support this need.

The CALC LOCATION MODE can be illustrated with the following partial record definitions:

RECORD NAME IS PRODUCT
LOCATION MODE CALC USING PRODUCT# DUPLICATES NOT
    ALLOWED
. . .
    1 PRODUCT# ; PICTURE 9999.
. . .

RECORD NAME IS ORDER-LINE
LOCATION MODE CALC USING PRODUCT#, ORDER#
    DUPLICATES NOT ALLOWED
. . .
    1 PRODUCT# ; PICTURE 9999.
    1 ORDER# ; PICTURE 9999.
. . .

CALC was designed to specify that record instances will be stored and found by hashing on key values. For the preceding PRODUCT record, PRODUCT# is a primary key (since DUPLICATES NOT ALLOWED); for the ORDER-LINE record given here, the concatenated key is PRODUCT# plus ORDER#, which is also unique. If duplicates are allowed, then the DBMS will permit two or more records to have the same hash key value. Otherwise, when not allowed, the DBMS will enforce, during storing and modification, the primary key property by returning error codes for data manipulation commands that would cause a violation of the duplicates clause.

Some DBTG systems permit only one LOCATION MODE clause; others permit several LOCATION MODE or the more recent KEY IS clauses. Some DBTG systems even permit a data base designer to use other than hashing methods for implementing CALC mode (e.g., indexes). In general, the CALC mode must be interpreted as any keyed access method (entry point into a data base) using primary or secondary keys, as allowed by the DBMS. Use of CALC does not prohibit accessing a record by its association with other records; it simply says that records will be *physically placed* (and can be found) based on key values.

On other occasions, users of an information system do not know primary key values for desired records, but instead know the key for some associated record. For example, we might know a PRODUCT# but not know the CUSTOMER#s of customers who have open orders for this product. The second LOCATION MODE alternative, designed to provide efficient record access by association, is VIA.

VIA means that a record will be placed as close to its associated owner record instance as the DBMS can find *for the specified set*. Use of VIA in the DBTG model prevents a user from accessing a record directly by a key value. LOCATION VIA should be used for a given record when much data processing of this record involves first accessing an associated owner record before instances of this type are required (i.e., access via relationships between records, since records to be retrieved are only known by their association with other records).

Consider again the ORDER-LINE record type. Although each of these record instances could be identified by a concatenated key of ORDER# plus PRODUCT#, careful review of data processing might indicate that ORDER-LINE records are retrieved or stored only after first retrieving associated PRODUCT or ORDER records. After additional review, it is determined that ORDER-LINE records are more often processed along with ORDER records than with PRODUCT records. The following LOCATION MODE clause could then be used in the definition of the ORDER-LINE record:

```
RECORD NAME IS ORDER-LINE
LOCATION MODE IS VIA ITEMS-ON-ORDER SET
. . .
SET NAME IS ITEMS-ON-ORDER
OWNER IS ORDER
. . .
MEMBER IS ORDER-LINE
. . .
```

A record can be located VIA only one set in the DBTG model, so ORDER-LINEs cannot also be specified to be placed close to PRODUCT. It should be emphasized here that VIA does not establish which owner record instance is, in fact, the owner of a given member instance, but only that a member instance will be *placed* close to its owner instance. The SET SELEC-TION clause in the SET definition controls the method of determining ownership; we will discuss this clause later.

In the most recent CODASYL guidelines, LOCATION MODE has been eliminated in favor of a more general and logical clause called KEY IS. Under the latest guideline, not yet implemented in all commercial systems, each record type may have one or more single or concatenated primary or second-ary keys with either ascending or descending logical orderings maintained. For the primary key of CUSTOMER# in the CUSTOMER record of Figure 2-10, we could include (in place of the LOCATION MODE clause)

```
KEY CUSTOMER# IS ASCENDING CUSTOMER#
DUPLICATES ARE NOT ALLOWED
```

and for the secondary key of PRODUCT# in the ORDER-LINE record, we could include

```
KEY PRODUCT# IS ASCENDING PRODUCT#
DUPLICATES ARE FIRST
```

DUPLICATES ARE NOT ALLOWED specifies a primary key. The use of FIRST or LAST indicates how to sequence records for storage and retrieval with duplicate secondary key values. FIRST means that a new record with a duplicate value will be stored as the first record (first on a chain) among any with the same value for PRODUCT#; use of LAST would tell the DBMS to store the new record last (in this key sequence) after all existing records (on a chain) with this same PRODUCT# value. A KEY IS clause will cause some type of key access method, like hashing or indexing, to be employed, depending on the implementation.

Although not part of the most current CODASYL guidelines, LOCA-TION MODE has been presented here because most DBTG systems use some form of this clause, even if the KEY IS clause is also supported.

Data Elements in a Record Definition. A record type may have no data elements, which is the case of a link record. Link records are possible because the DBTG data model can be classified as a simple network model. In most cases, a record type will have one or more data elements, or data-base-data-names, as part of its definition.

The schema not only defines what data elements are to be in each record, but also their format of representation in the data base (which may be different from that for corresponding fields in user working storage). Thus, each data element must have exactly one of the following as part of its definition:

- PICTURE clause
- TYPE clause
- SOURCE clause
- OCCURS clause
- OCCURS and PICTURE clauses
- OCCURS and TYPE clauses

and any of the other clauses shown in Figure 13-2, with a few limitations.

The PICTURE format is similar to that used in COBOL. Both character and numeric formats are supported. A PICTURE is used to define a display format for data elements. Consequently, data are stored using the computer's typical coding scheme (e.g., EBCDIC or ASCII). TYPE is used to cause more efficient storage formats to be used. TYPE can specify base (BINARY or DECIMAL), scale (FIXED or FLOAT), and mode (REAL or COMPLEX); length specifications for arithmetic data, or BIT or CHARACTER strings; or DATA-BASE-KEY. For example, the PRODUCT file of Figure 2-2 could be defined as a DBTG record type as follows:

```
RECORD IS PRODUCT
LOCATION MODE CALC USING PRODUCT#
    . . .
```

```
1 PRODUCT# ; PIC 9999.
1 DESCRIPTION ; PIC X(20).
1 FINISH ; PIC X(8).
1 ROOM ; PIC X(2).
1 PRICE ; TYPE DECIMAL 6,2.
```

Here most data elements are to be used for display purposes. PRICE will be stored in the computer system's DECIMAL format, with four integer digits and two decimal places (some DBTG systems have a DOLLAR TYPE in which TYPE DOLLAR 4 would be identical to this specification).

An OCCURS clause may be used with PICTURE or TYPE to indicate a repeating group of elementary data items. In addition, an OCCURS clause may appear by itself to specify a repeating data aggregate. For example, we could expand the definition of PRODUCT in Figure 2-10 to include a set of PRICEs, depending on quantity purchased. Part of the record definition might then look like this:

```
RECORD IS PRODUCT
   . . .
1 PRICE-SCHEDULE ; OCCURS 3 TIMES.
   2 QTY-UPPER ; PICTURE 99999.
   2 QTY-PRICE ; DECIMAL 6,2.
```

In this example, a three-tiered price schedule capability has been designed for each Product. If different Products have a different number of quantity-price breaks, then

```
RECORD IS PRODUCT
   . . .
1 NO-BREAKS ; TYPE IS DECIMAL 2.
1 PRICE-SCHEDULE ; OCCURS NO-BREAKS TIMES.
   2 QTY-UPPER ; PICTURE 99999.
   2 QTY-PRICE ; DECIMAL 6,2.
```

would allow for 0 to 99 different quantity-price breaks for each PRODUCT.

Actual and Virtual Record Data Elements.   Some users of a data base may want to manipulate the price and quantity ordered of products; other users, in accounting, perhaps, may only want to see the derived product amount due. But can we be sure that all accounting user programs will calculate amount due correctly?

The DBTG guidelines introduced the concept of virtual data, or data that appear to exist in a record but which do not physically reside in an instance of that record. Two clauses, the SOURCE and the RESULT clauses, deal with the distinction between ACTUAL and VIRTUAL data elements. These clauses and options together allow the data base to appear to contain data that, at least in the form or location perceived, do not actually exist.

If the SOURCE clause is associated with a given data element definition, it signifies that a value for that data element is to be the same as a specified data element from its owner in a designated set. For example, ORDER# in an instance of an ORDER-LINE record from Figure 2-10 must have the same value as the ORDER# in its associated ORDER record. SOURCE provides a form of integrity control of the data base. Use of SOURCE prohibits use of PICTURE or TYPE on the same data element, since these are implied from the "source" data element. An appropriate SOURCE clause for this example would be

RECORD IS ORDER-LINE

. . .

1 ORD# ; ACTUAL SOURCE IS ORDER# OF OWNER
          ITEMS-ON-ORDER SET.

In this case, ACTUAL specifies that ORD# is to be redundantly stored again in the ORDER-LINE record. Use of VIRTUAL instead of ACTUAL would tell the DBMS to allow use of ORD# as if it were a data element of the ORDER-LINE record, but retrieve it from the associated ORDER record instead (and save the redundant space).

The RESULT clause also utilizes the ACTUAL and VIRTUAL designations. The RESULT clause says that the data element to which it applies is to be calculated or derived from a procedure involving other data elements from the same record; from all members for this record, in which the owner is some set (e g , to calculate a total across all members, the equivalent of a class attribute in the semantic data model); or from some more general calculation. If ACTUAL RESULT is specified, then the derived value is constantly maintained and stored in the record. If VIRTUAL RESULT is specified, then the derived value is calculated each time a record instance is retrieved and appears to be included in the physical record but actually only exists in the user's working storage area (or subschema).

Other Data Element Clauses. Any data element can be further defined in a schema by CHECK and coding clauses. A CHECK clause specifies validation criteria to be checked each time the associated data element changes value or a new value is added. Implementations vary, but most permit specification of a list of legitimate values or ranges of values or the execution of a more general user procedure.

Coding clauses inform the DBMS what to do to ENCODE or DECODE a data element value. Again, implementations vary, but the effect of such clauses is to define code tables so that long, standard character strings that are input can be converted to more compact codes to save storage space (and vice versa for reporting). For example, coding could be used for the DE-SCRIPTION of the PRODUCT record. Such coding could equate TABLE with a stored value of TA, WALL UNIT with a stored value of WU, and so on, to reduce space and eliminate wasted characters (if variable-length records are not supported). Entry of WALL UNIT for DESCRIPTION would result in only WU being stored; display of a TA stored value would result in TABLE actually being reported.

Relationship Definitions: Sets

A **set** is the definition of a directed relationship from an owner record type to one or more member record types. A set usually defines a 1:M relationship, say, an ORDERS-FOR-CUSTOMER set from CUSTOMER as owner to ORDER as member. A set may also define a 1:1 relationship, but this is unusual. A set may not define an M:N relationship, since the DBTG model prescribes a simple network data model. One can generally assume that a set is implemented as a ring data structure with the owner at the head of the chain and with the last member pointing to the owner. Other structures (bidirectional chains, pointer arrays, owner pointers, and so forth) can be defined in clauses not being considered here.

The Pine Valley Furniture data base of Figures 2-10 and 6-9 would result in three set definitions. The more extensive data base of Figure 6-10b would require five sets (and a link record definition). Figure 13-3 illustrates part of the data base of Figure 6-10b and a skeleton of the schema DDL necessary to define this part of the data base. This figure includes a complete record definition for the PRODUCT-VENDOR-LINK record. Assuming that this is only a link record, no data elements are defined, although some "data about data" (e.g., pointers to maintain sets) may be allocated from the compilation of the schema DDL.

The inclusion of a set, say, from PRODUCT to ORDER-LINE, in a schema for Figure 6-10b informs the schema DDL compiler to establish some type of data structure to permit rapid access from an instance of a PRODUCT record to instances of associated set ORDER-LINE members (and possibly vice versa). Whenever records are inserted, deleted, or modified in either of these files, the DBMS will perform much of the maintenance of the overhead data to continue correct record association. This schema in Figure 13-3 illustrates that a record type may be an owner of several sets and also a member of several sets; some DBTG systems even permit the same record type to be both owner and member of the same set!

However, a set is not the only means of relating records in the DBTG model. Consider the same PRODUCT to ORDER-LINE relationship just discussed. If both record types contain PRODUCT# and if this data element is used in a KEY IS clause in each record definition, then associated records may also be rapidly retrieved by accessing records by this logical key. Nevertheless, a set is the usual means employed in a DBTG data base to represent a relationship.

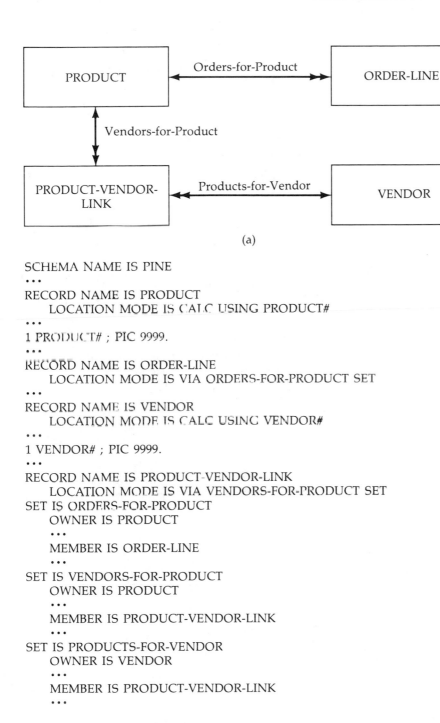

(a)

Figure 13-3
Skeleton of the schema
for part of Pine Valley
Furniture data base.
(a) Network diagram.
(b) Schema definition.

SCHEMA NAME IS PINE
. . .
RECORD NAME IS PRODUCT
    LOCATION MODE IS CALC USING PRODUCT#
. . .
1 PRODUCT# ; PIC 9999.
. . .
RECORD NAME IS ORDER-LINE
    LOCATION MODE IS VIA ORDERS-FOR-PRODUCT SET
. . .
RECORD NAME IS VENDOR
    LOCATION MODE IS CALC USING VENDOR#
. . .
1 VENDOR# ; PIC 9999.
. . .
RECORD NAME IS PRODUCT-VENDOR-LINK
    LOCATION MODE IS VIA VENDORS-FOR-PRODUCT SET
SET IS ORDERS-FOR-PRODUCT
    OWNER IS PRODUCT
       . . .
    MEMBER IS ORDER-LINE
       . . .
SET IS VENDORS-FOR-PRODUCT
    OWNER IS PRODUCT
       . . .
    MEMBER IS PRODUCT-VENDOR-LINK
       . . .
SET IS PRODUCTS-FOR-VENDOR
    OWNER IS VENDOR
       . . .
    MEMBER IS PRODUCT-VENDOR-LINK
       . . .

(b)

Figure 13-4
Alternative
representations of a loop
relationship in the
CODASYL model.
(a) Loop relationship with
the same owner and
member.
(b) Loop relationship
using two record
types.
(c) Loop relationship
using secondary key.

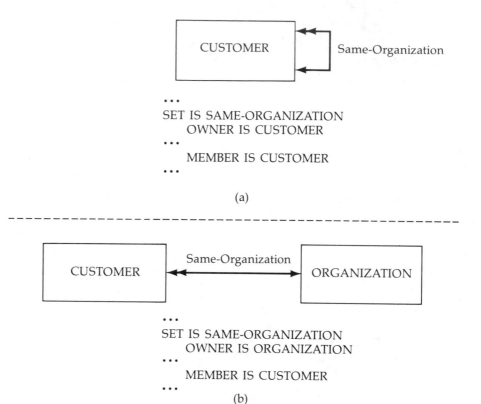

```
...
SET IS SAME-ORGANIZATION
    OWNER IS CUSTOMER
...
    MEMBER IS CUSTOMER
...
```

(a)

```
...
SET IS SAME-ORGANIZATION
    OWNER IS ORGANIZATION
...
    MEMBER IS CUSTOMER
...
```

(b)

```
...
RECORD IS CUSTOMER
LOCATION MODE IS CALC USING CUSTOMER#
KEY IS PARENT-ORG DUPLICATES ARE FIRST
...
1 CUSTOMER# ; PIC 9999.
1 PARENT-ORG ; PIC 9999.
...
```

(c)

Loop Relationship. Several types of 1:M relationships need special il-lustration if we are to explain their representation in schema DDL. The first is a loop relationship. Figure 13-4 reproduces such a relationship from Figure 6-14 and indicates a skeleton of the schema parts required to repre-

```
...
RECORD IS CUSTOMER
    LOCATION MODE IS CALC USING CUSTOMER#
...
1 CUSTOMER# ; PIC 9999.
1 CUST-ZIPCODE ; PIC 99999.
...
SET IS CUST-SORT
    OWNER IS SYSTEM
    ORDER IS SORTED BY DEFINED KEYS
    ...
    MEMBER IS CUSTOMER
    ...
    KEY IS ASCENDING CUST-ZIPCODE
        DUPLICATES ARE LAST
    ...
```

Figure 13-5
Example of a schema DDL for a singular set.

sent this relationship between customers under several different implementations in the DBTG model.

Figure 13-4a illustrates the basic loop relationship and the most direct way, if permitted, to represent this type of relationship. To do this requires that the DBMS support use of the same record type as both owner and member of the same set.

The approach of Figure 13-4b is to define an additional ORGANIZATION record type, instances of which own a set of CUSTOMER member instances for that parent organization. Data manipulation statements can be used to move from one member to another in a given set instance or from a member instance to the associated owner instance. The approach of Figure 13-4c is, if permitted by the particular DBMS, to define a secondary key on the PARENT-ORG data element of the CUSTOMER record type; data manipulation statements can then be used to access all CUSTOMER records with a common value for this secondary key. In all of these cases, it is still possible to define a primary key of CUSTOMER# for the CUSTOMER record.

Singular Sets. Singular or system relationships (called one-of-a-kind in IDMS) are easy to represent in a DBTG schema. The purpose of a singular relationship is to arrange all the instances of some record type into sorted sequence under a common owner, the "system."

Suppose we wanted to arrange all CUSTOMER records into ascending order by CUST-ZIPCODE to avoid the cost of sorting all CUSTOMER records for each mailing. Figure 13-5 illustrates the skeleton of the definition of a singular set that accomplishes this desired sequencing. CUSTOMER records can all be retrieved as members under one common parent (the singular system) in the zip code order because of the use of the ORDER IS SORTED clause and the KEY IS clause of the member specification for the set.

Singular sets can also be used to logically group together records with a common characteristic (e.g., all customers who have exceeded their credit limit); that is, not all record instances from the set member record type *must* be included in the set. In IDMS, this type of set must be designed using an artificial record type (one-of-a-kind) as the owner, rather than the implicit "system" owner. Release 10.0 of IDMS (IDMS/R 10.0) allows system-owned sets.

Sets with Multiple Member Types.   Any set definition contains reference to only one owner record type but may include several member record type clauses. This capability permits the representation of class relationships or any relationship in which a single owner record instance can be associated with many member instances, each of different types. Some DBTG systems permit all members to be sorted by such options as record name (all members of the same type sorted together under a common parent), data base key (i.e., physical address sequence, which is convenient for efficiently traversing a member chain), or key values in each member record type.

Figure 13-6 illustrates a typical situation where CUSTOMER records are related to both OPEN- and CLOSED-ORDERs. The CUSTOMER-ORDERS set definition places into a common set instance all OPEN- and CLOSED-ORDERs, in ORDER# sequence, for each CUSTOMER owner. The sorting option is used here simply to facilitate reporting of order data. A hazard of such a set with multiple members is that long member chains can be created; if individual sets are not established from owner to each member type (e.g., CUSTOMER to only OPEN-ORDER), processing for only one of the member type records can be degraded by having to access unwanted set members.

Multiple Relationships Between Records.   Any number of sets may be defined between the same pair of record types. For example, if Pine Valley Furniture writes both blanket and special orders (blanket means an order for a series of deliveries over some extended time period, and special means a one-time, stand-alone order), then we might want to define two sets between CUSTOMER and ORDER: Blanket-for-Customer and Special-for-Customer. In this way, users interested in only one type of customer order could use the specialized set to find only orders of the desired type without wasted accesses to unwanted types. Multiple sets between the same pair of record types can also be used to handle different sorting sequences (e.g., orders by sale date, or orders by due date).

Many-to-Many Relationships.   Because the CODASYL network standard is a simple network architecture, many-to-many relationships have to be implemented using link records. Figure 13-7 illustrates, by way of an instance diagram, the result of representing an *M:N* relationship between

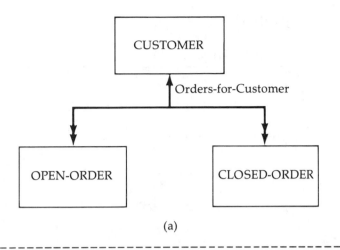

(a)

Figure 13-6
DBTG schema for a set with two member record types.
(a) Example of a class relationship.
(b) Schema DDL for class relationship.

RECORD IS CUSTOMER
• • •
RECORD IS OPEN-ORDER
• • •
1 O-ORDER# ; PIC 9999.
• • •
RECORD IS CLOSED-ORDER
• • •
1 C-ORDER# ; PIC 9999.
• • •
SET IS ORDERS-FOR-CUSTOMER
OWNER IS CUSTOMER
ORDER IS SORTED BY DEFINED KEYS
    DUPLICATES NOT ALLOWED
• • •
MEMBER IS OPEN-ORDER
• • •
    KEY IS ASCENDING O-ORDER#
        DUPLICATES ARE NOT ALLOWED
• • •
MEMBER IS CLOSED-ORDER
• • •
    KEY IS ASCENDING C-ORDER#
        DUPLICATES ARE NOT ALLOWED
• • •

(b)

PRODUCT and VENDOR. In this case, an intersection record containing the Vendor's PRICE for that Product is used to link a PRODUCT to a VENDOR when that Vendor supplies that Product. Note that each VENDOR and PRODUCT record is stored only once, but a PRODUCT-VENDOR-LINK record instance appears each time a Vendor can supply some Product. As will be seen later, the three record types and two sets of this figure can be

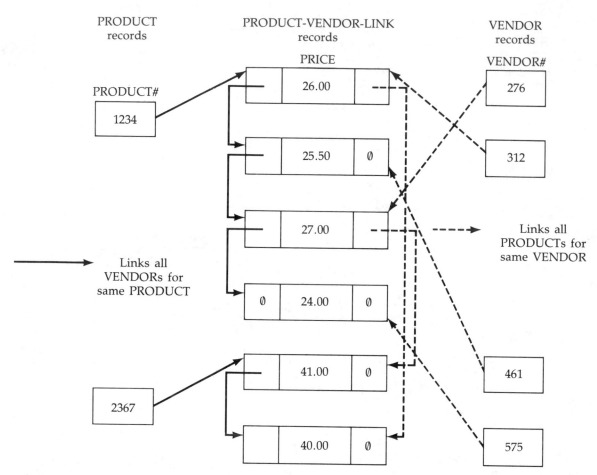

Figure 13-7
Example of records and
sets implementations for a
many-to-many
relationship.

used to find both the Vendors of a given Product and the Products of a given Vendor. That is, sets may be processed from either owner to member or member to owner.

Set Qualifications. A set may optionally be defined to be DYNAMIC or PRIOR. DYNAMIC means that this set has no specific member record type, but an instance of any record other than of the owner type may become associated in this set to a given owner instance. Use of DYNAMIC is rare. PRIOR, on the other hand, can be an important feature. Specification of SET IS PRIOR causes the DBMS to implement for the associated set a method that allows the set to be processed as efficiently in the backward (prior) direction as in the forward (next) direction. The effect is to create a bidirectional chain capability, although the guidelines do not specify that a bidirectional chain is *the* way PRIOR must be implemented.

Set Member Definition.   The set membership clauses are an important part of a schema. Not only do they provide a necessary companion to the OWNER IS clause, but they are instrumental in set integrity control and hence relationships in a data base. In addition, this section of a schema is important to study carefully because three of its clauses—INSERTION, RETENTION, and SET SELECTION—typically are difficult to understand for people getting their first exposure to data base management. Further, you should be aware that INSERTION is called CONNECTION and RE-TENTION is called DISCONNECTION by some DBTG systems.

Any set may have one or more MEMBER IS and associated clauses, one each for each record type related to the set owner in the relationship represented by the set. In explaining these clauses, we will use sets with only *one* member record type.

For the purpose of explaining set membership clauses, consider the data base shown in Figure 13-8a and a possible schema definition for this data base shown in Figure 13-8b. The situation depicted here is an inventory accounting data base for unique, serial-numbered, limited-life products stored at various warehouses. For this situation, we will assume that the organization permits transshipment of products between warehouses. This example would be typical of certain chemical or pharmaceutical products. This situation is another example of an *M:N* relationship and illustrates how such a relationship would be defined in the DDL.

The STORAGE set relates a generic product to particular serial-numbered instances of that product stored in warehouses. An analysis of reporting requirements involving records of this set indicates that no special set ordering of INVENTORY members for the associated PRODUCT owner is necessary, so ORDER IS FIRST is chosen to speed member record creation (since a new record would be inserted in a chained set at the beginning of the chain, which we have seen is the easiest point to insert in a single-directional chain).

Controlling Member Insertion.   Since an INVENTORY record may not logically exist unless it is for an already existing PRODUCT, INSERTION IS AUTOMATIC is used. This means that the DBMS will automatically link a new INVENTORY record to its associated PRODUCT owner when we store a new INVENTORY record in the data base.

The other choice for INSERTION IS is MANUAL, which means that we would have to explicitly and separately program when to connect a new INVENTORY record in a data entry program. AUTOMATIC saves a minimal amount of program coding. MANUAL would be appropriate if a member record might not have an owner record in a set when initially stored in a data base. For example, a set from department to employee might have INSER-TION IS MANUAL, since many employees when hired are not immediately assigned to a department.

Figure 13-8
Illustration of set membership clauses.
(a) Sample inventory data base.
(b) Schema DDL for inventory data base.

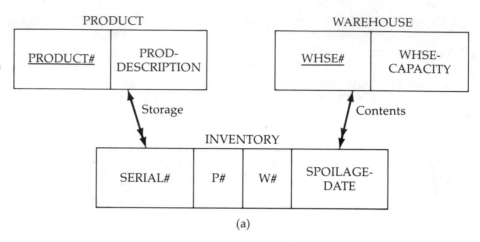

(a)

```
SCHEMA IS INVENTORY
AREA NAME IS STOCK
RECORD NAME IS PRODUCT
    LOCATION MODE IS CALC USING PRODUCT#
    1 PRODUCT# ; PIC 9999.
    1 PROD-DESCRIPTION ; PIC X(20).
RECORD NAME IS WAREHOUSE
    LOCATION MODE IS CALC USING WHSE#
    1 WHSE# ; PIC 99.
    1 WHSE-CAPACITY ; PIC 999999.
RECORD NAME IS INVENTORY
    LOCATION MODE IS VIA STORAGE SET
    1 SERIAL# ; PIC 99999.
    1 P# ; PIC 9999.
    1 W# ; PIC 99.
    1 SPOILAGE-DATE ; PIC 999999.
SET NAME IS STORAGE
    OWNER IS PRODUCT
    ORDER IS FIRST
    MEMBER IS INVENTORY
        INSERTION IS AUTOMATIC
        RETENTION IS FIXED
        CHECK IS PRODUCT# IN PRODUCT=P#
        SET SELECTION IS BY VALUE OF PRODUCT#
SET NAME IS CONTENTS
    OWNER IS WAREHOUSE
    ORDER IS SORTED BY DEFINED KEYS
    MEMBER IS INVENTORY
        INSERTION IS AUTOMATIC
        RETENTION IS MANDATORY
        KEY IS ASCENDING P# DUPLICATES ARE FIRST
        CHECK IS WHSE# IN WAREHOUSE=W#
        SET SELECTION IS STRUCTURAL WHSE#=W#
END SCHEMA
```

(b)

The CONTENTS set also uses INSERTION IS AUTOMATIC, since it is assumed that a particular serial-numbered part must reside in some warehouse. The INSERTION IS clause is an effective mechanism for enforcing certain semantic data requirements (i.e., existence dependencies upon original entry of a record). The appropriate value of AUTOMATIC or MANUAL for any given set can be established only after a careful analysis of the meaning of data and relationships involved in a set.

Controlling Member Retention.   Similar to the INSERTION IS clause is the RETENTION IS clause. In the STORAGE set, RETENTION IS FIXED is used. This means that once a serial number is associated to a generic PRODUCT record, it must be *permanently* associated with the same PRODUCT. The only way to change the association to another PRODUCT would be to delete the INVENTORY record and reenter it under a new owner PRODUCT.

On the other hand, since individual parts may be transshipped from one warehouse to another, RETENTION IS MANDATORY is used in the CONTENTS set. MANDATORY says that the member record, in order to exist, must always have some WAREHOUSE owner (the part has to be somewhere!), but that the particular owner may change. In terms of the data manipulation language to be introduced later, MANDATORY allows us to RECONNECT INVENTORY records as required to indicate current location of a part.

A third option for RETENTION IS, not illustrated here, is OPTIONAL. This choice means that we may actually DISCONNECT a member record from any owner and leave the member unowned for as long as is appropriate. For example, a part is not really in any warehouse during transshipment. To permit an INVENTORY record to have no WAREHOUSE owner during this period, we would use RETENTION IS OPTIONAL. OPTIONAL also permits the deletion of an owner record without having to delete members. For example, if a warehouse is closed, the associated part records will still exist until the parts are moved to a new location.

RECONNECTing records can have a subtle effect on data base performance. If, for example, INVENTORY records are located VIA the CONTENTS set instead of the STORAGE set, an INVENTORY record that changed its association to other than its original WAREHOUSE would *not* be physically moved to now be near its current WAREHOUSE owner record in the physical data base.

The RETENTION IS clause also provides a method to include semantic controls, after original loading of data, on proper data base record associations and data manipulation. Table 13-3 summarizes the impact of various combinations of INSERTION and RETENTION options. But be aware that the terms FIXED, MANDATORY, and OPTIONAL have not had the same meanings in all versions of the DBTG guidelines. Until 1978, FIXED did not exist and MANDATORY meant FIXED. If you are using a DBTG DBMS, read

Table 13-3
Summary of DBTG Semantic Controls in Set Membership Clauses

	INSERTION	
RETENTION	AUTOMATIC	MANUAL
FIXED	Member record *must* have an owner when it is stored and will continue to have *same* owner until member is deleted. DBMS will automatically CONNECT member to owner, based on SET SELECTION clause, when member is stored.	Member record is permitted to *not* have an owner when it is stored, but once CONNECTed to an owner, it *must* keep same owner until member is deleted. DBMS will *not* CONNECT member to owner until told to do so by user program.
MANDATORY	Member record *must* have an owner when it is stored, but member can be RECONNECTed to other owners as required. DBMS will automatically CONNECT member to owner, based on SET SELECTION clause, when member is stored.	Member record is permitted to *not* have an owner when it is stored, and once CONNECTed may be RECONNECTed to other owners as required. DBMS will *not* CONNECT member to owner until told to do so by user program.
OPTIONAL	Member record *must* have an owner when it is stored, but member can be RECONNECTed to other owners or DISCONNECTed from any owner as required. DBMS will automatically CONNECT member to owner, based on SET SELECTION clause, when member is stored.	Member record is permitted to *not* have an owner when it is stored; once CONNECTed, if ever, it may be RECONNECTed or DISCONNECTed as required. DBMS will *not* CONNECT member to owner until told to do so by user program.

the reference manuals carefully to determine what is implemented by that vendor.

Cross-Reference Key Control. The CHECK IS clauses provide yet another level of semantic control on record associations. Each of these clauses in the example of Figure 13-8 requires that key values in both member and owner of a set instance must be identical. These clauses provide an extra protection that the correct semantic connection occurs when records are originally inserted into the data base or CONNECTed to an owner. To fully appreciate the usefulness of the CHECK IS clause, the function of the SET SELECTION clause must be understood.

Determining a Member's Owner.   Whereas the INSERTION and RETEN-TION clauses control *when* and *whether* a record type must have an owner, the SET SELECTION clause determines *which instance* of the owner record type of a set should become the "proud parent."

For the STORAGE set in Figure 13-8, SET SELECTION IS BY VALUE OF PRODUCT# means that when a new INVENTORY record is stored in the data base (if INSERTION IS AUTOMATIC) or CONNECTed to a PRODUCT owner, the DBMS will use the current value in PRODUCT# from user working storage as a key to find the appropriate owner. Thus, PRODUCT must have a keyed access (e.g., LOCATION MODE IS CALC or a KEY IS clause, whichever the DBMS uses) on the data element referenced (in this case, PRODUCT#). This type of SET SELECTION clause forces the DBMS to find the owner record automatically and forces the DBMS user to make sure that the correct PRODUCT# is in memory. As long as P# is correctly recorded, the CHECK IS clause on this set is a validity check that set selection was done properly. This form of the SET SELECTION clause is more often used when the member record type does *not* contain the key of the owner record.

The SET SELECTION clause of the CONTENTS set is the one that is more appropriate when a member record contains the key of the associated owner record instance. SET SELECTION IS STRUCTURAL means that the DBMS is to find the associated owner record for a new member when it is stored (if INSERTION IS AUTOMATIC) or CONNECTed by using the value of a data element in the member (e.g., W#) as the key value of the owner (e.g., WAREHOUSE#). In this case, the CHECK IS clause is of no operational value, since the SET SELECTION clause guarantees that the check will not be violated.

Proper use of INSERTION, RETENTION, CHECK, and SET SELEC-TION clauses requires practice. Although use of these clauses forces a data base designer to deal with many details, these clauses provide valuable tools for semantic controls of the data base maintenance and processing. A data base programmer also needs to be aware of these clauses in order to interpret error messages that indicate breaches of these integrity constraints.

Many DBTG DBMSs also permit a SET SELECTION THRU CURRENT OF SET option. This version is difficult to understand until one understands the DBTG data manipulation language and a construct used there called currency indicators. Basically, this form differs from the others in that the DBMS does not have to find the owner record, but rather uses the last owner record instance retrieved. This is, in fact, often the most efficient choice for SET SELECTION, especially in interactive programs. For example, if when entering a new INVENTORY record the program first finds the record for the WAREHOUSE indicated for the part, why make the DBMS find it again in order to store the INVENTORY record? The proper WAREHOUSE owner is "current"ly in working storage and does not need to be refound.

A SET SELECTION clause is not found in certain DBTG systems. In these (in particular, IDMS), the owner for a new member record being inserted into the data base is essentially the most recently retrieved record of each set, which must be an instance of the proper owner record type for each set.

Sorting Members. Finally, the ORDER IS SORTED clause for the CON-TENTS set needs to be explained. An analysis of reporting requirements from this data base indicated that warehouse contents frequently were desired in PRODUCT# (P#) sequence for easy reading. The ORDER IS SORTED and KEY IS clauses cause the data base to automatically maintain member INVENTORY records in this sequence (usually via a sorted list), thus avoiding sorting of records or report lines for each report.

Other Set Member Clauses. Not illustrated in Figure 13-8 but appearing in Figure 13-2 is the SEARCH KEY IS clause of the member section of a set definition. The set itself establishes a method (usually a chain) to access all member instances, possibly in a sorted sequence, under a common owner record instance. The SEARCH KEY IS clause defines direct access from an owner instance to a member with a specific key value. That is, SEARCH KEY IS establishes functionally a key index in each owner record that points to each member record. For example, in the data base of Figure 13-8a, we might want to create a way to identify/access for each WAREHOUSE the IN-VENTORY that will spoil each day. To do so, we would include in the member clause of the CONTENTS set the clause

SEARCH KEY IS SPOILAGE-DATE DUPLICATES ALLOWED.

 As a summary of this section on DBTG schema definition, Figure 13-9 contains the IDMS schema DDL for the Mountain View Community Hospital network data base of Figure 9-7.

DBTG SUBSCHEMA DDL: EXTERNAL DATA BASES

Figure 13-9 (opposite) IDMS schema for Mountain View Community Hospital (see data base in Figure 9-7).

Each user of a data base usually wants to use only a portion of a global, conceptual data base. This portion may strictly be a subset but may also redefine, into more local terminology and different structures, selected components (records, data elements, sets) of the data base. Further, as a means to secure the data base against accidental damage by naive users or to ensure legislated, organizational, or personal privacy, a particular user may be limited in what components of the data base he or she may use and what data manipulations may be performed on the visible data.

```
**********************************************************
    SCHEMA DESCRIPTION.
**********************************************************
    SCHEMA NAME IS MVCH.
(1) FILE DESCRIPTION.
    FILE NAME IS MVCHFILE                 ASSIGN TO MVCHDS
                                          DEVICE TYPE IS 3380.
    FILE NAME IS JOURNAL                  ASSIGN TO SYSJRNL.
**********************************************************
    AREA DESCRIPTION.
**********************************************************
(2) AREA NAME IS MVCH-CHG                 RANGE IS 770351 THRU 770420
                                          WITHIN FILE MVCHFILE
                                             FROM 1 THRU 70.

    AREA NAME IS MVCH-PHY                 RANGE IS 770421 THRU 770586
                                          WITHIN FILE MVCHFILE
                                             FROM 71 THRU 160.
**********************************************************
    RECORD DESCRIPTION.
**********************************************************
    RECORD NAME IS ROOM.
(3) RECORD ID IS 100.
    LOCATION MODE IS CALC                 USING LOCATION
                                          DUPLICATES NOT ALLOWED.

    WITHIN MVCH-PHY AREA.
       02 LOCATION                        PIC 9999.
       (other data items)
    ************
    RECORD NAME IS PATIENT.
    RECORD ID IS 101.
    LOCATION MODE IS CALC                 USING PATIENT-NO
                                          DUPLICATES NOT ALLOWED.

    WITHIN MVCH-CHG AREA.
       02 PATIENT-NO                      PIC 9999.
       (other data items)
    ***************
    RECORD NAME IS PHYSICIAN.
    RECORD ID IS 102.
    LOCATION MODE IS CALC                 USING PHYSICIAN-ID
                                          DUPLICATES NOT ALLOWED.

    WITHIN MVCH-PHY AREA.
       02 PHYSICIAN-ID                    PIC X(10).
       02 PHYSICIAN-PHONE                 PIC 9(7).
    ***************
    RECORD NAME IS ITEM.
    RECORD ID IS 103.
    LOCATION MODE IS CALC                 USING ITEM-CODE
                                          DUPLICATES NOT ALLOWED.

    WITHIN MVCH-CHG AREA.
       02 ITEM-CODE                       PIC 999.
       02 DESCRIPTION                     PIC X(15).
    ***************
```

```
            RECORD NAME IS TREATMENT.
            RECORD ID IS 104.
       (4) LOCATION MODE IS VIA                    TREATED SET.
            WITHIN MVCH-PHY AREA.
                02 PHYSICIAN-ID                    PIC X(10).
                02 PATIENT-NO                      PIC 9999.
                02 PROCEDURE                       PIC X(15).
          ★ ★ ★ ★ ★ ★ ★ ★ ★ ★ ★ ★ ★
            RECORD NAME IS CHARGES.
            RECORD ID IS 105.
       (5) LOCATION MODE IS VIA                    INCURRED SET.
            WITHIN MVCH-CHG AREA.
                02 PATIENT-NO                      PIC 9999.
                02 ITEM-CODE                       PIC 999.
                02 CHARGE                          PIC 9999V99 COMP-3.
    ★ ★ ★ ★ ★ ★ ★ ★ ★ ★ ★ ★ ★ ★ ★ ★ ★ ★ ★ ★ ★ ★ ★ ★ ★ ★ ★ ★ ★ ★ ★ ★ ★ ★ ★ ★ ★ ★ ★ ★ ★ ★ ★ ★ ★ ★
            SET DESCRIPTION.
    ★ ★ ★ ★ ★ ★ ★ ★ ★ ★ ★ ★ ★ ★ ★ ★ ★ ★ ★ ★ ★ ★ ★ ★ ★ ★ ★ ★ ★ ★ ★ ★ ★ ★ ★ ★ ★ ★ ★ ★ ★ ★ ★ ★ ★ ★
            SET IS ASSIGNED.
            ORDER IS FIRST.
       (6) MODE IS CHAIN.
       (7) OWNER IS ROOM                            NEXT DBKEY POSITION IS 1.
       (8) MEMBER IS PATIENT                        NEXT DBKEY POSITION IS 4
                                                    LINKED TO OWNER
                                                       OWNER DBKEY POSITION IS 5
       (9)                                          OPTIONAL AUTOMATIC.
          ★ ★ ★ ★ ★ ★ ★ ★ ★ ★ ★ ★ ★
            SET IS RECEIVED.
      (10) ORDER IS LAST.
      (11) MODE IS CHAIN                            LINKED TO PRIOR.
            OWNER IS PATIENT                        NEXT DBKEY POSITION IS 1
                                                    PRIOR DBKEY POSITION IS 2.
            MEMBER IS TREATMENT                     NEXT DBKEY POSITION IS 1
                                                    PRIOR DBKEY POSITION IS 2
                                                    LINKED TO OWNER
                                                       OWNER DBKEY POSITION IS 5
      (12)                                          MANDATORY MANUAL.
          ★ ★ ★ ★ ★ ★ ★ ★ ★ ★ ★ ★ ★
            SET IS TREATED.
      (13) ORDER IS SORTED.
            MODE IS CHAIN                           LINKED TO PRIOR.
            OWNER IS PHYSICIAN                      NEXT DBKEY POSITION IS 1
                                                    PRIOR DBKEY POSITION IS 2.
            MEMBER IS TREATMENT                     NEXT DBKEY POSITION IS 3
                                                    PRIOR DBKEY POSITION IS 4
                                                    LINKED TO OWNER
                                                       OWNER DBKEY POSITION IS 6
                                                    MANDATORY AUTOMATIC
                                                    ASCENDING KEY IS PATIENT-NO
                                                       DUPLICATES ARE FIRST.


          ★ ★ ★ ★ ★ ★ ★ ★ ★ ★ ★ ★ ★
```

Figure 13-9, continued.

SET IS INCURRED.
ORDER IS SORTED.
MODE IS CHAIN.
OWNER IS PATIENT   NEXT DBKEY POSITION IS 3.
MEMBER IS CHARGES   NEXT DBKEY POSITION IS 1
                                   MANDATORY MANUAL
                                   ASCENDING KEY IS ITEM-CODE
                                   DUPLICATES ARE LAST.

★ ★ ★ ★ ★ ★ ★ ★ ★ ★ ★ ★
SET IS PROVIDED.
ORDER IS LAST.
MODE IS CHAIN.
OWNER IS ITEM   NEXT DBKEY POSITION IS 1.
MEMBER IS CHARGES   NEXT DBKEY POSITION IS 2
                                   LINKED TO OWNER
                                      OWNER DBKEY POSITION IS 3
                                   MANDATORY AUTOMATIC.

(1) Logical file names used in schema are matched with physical data set names and devices.

(2) Areas are assigned to page ranges in logical files. In this schema, we have chosen to have two areas: MVCH-CHG, which contains those record types related to a patient bill, and MVCH-PTY, which contains all other record types.

(3) RECORD ID simply assigns a number to identify each record type uniquely in the data dictionary.

(4) VIA is chosen here to group TREATMENT records close to PHYSICIAN records, since it is assumed that these related records are frequently used together in programs.

(5) Similar assumption as in (4), but this time for PATIENT and CHARGES records.

(6) This is a mandatory clause that simply says to create a chain from owner through members.

(7) The NEXT DBKEY POSITION clause specifies which relative pointer in the record associated with this clause (in this case, ROOM) is to be used for the next in chain pointer for this set.

(8) Again, the NEXT DBKEY POSITION clause specifies the pointer position (in this case in PATIENT); the LINKED TO OWNER indicates that each member record is to have a pointer (the pointer in the position specified) to its owner record to support rapid access to owner.

(9) OPTIONAL AUTOMATIC is used to allow PATIENTs to exist without being assigned a hospital location, but originally a PATIENT record can only be entered if the patient is admitted and placed in some location. The reader should note that IDMS does not have a SET SELECTION clause, as noted in the text.

(10) ORDER IS LAST is used to keep TREATMENT records in approximately ascending order by treatment date.

(11) LINKED TO PRIOR establishes backward chaining as well as forward chaining. The PRIOR clauses in the OWNER and MEMBER definitions indicate where in these records to find the PRIOR pointers.

(12) MANDATORY MANUAL is used here and in the INCURRED set to handle emergency treatment situations in which treatment is performed (and charges incurred) before the patient is admitted.

(13) ORDER IS SORTED is used to keep TREATMENT records grouped together by PATIENT (see ASCENDING KEY clause in member definition); DUPLICATES ARE FIRST is used in the member clause to keep TREATMENT records in reverse chronological order under each PATIENT.

Figure 13-9, continued.

Figure 13-10
IDMS subschema for
Patient Bill in Mountain
View Community
Hospital.

```
ADD SUBSCHEMA PATIENT-BILL
    OF SCHEMA MVCH.
ADD AREA . . .
ADD RECORD PATIENT
    ELEMENT PATIENT-NO.
    . . .
ADD RECORD ITEM
    ELEMENTS ARE ALL.
ADD RECORD CHARGES
    ELEMENTS ARE ALL.
ADD SET INCURRED.
ADD SET PROVIDED.
```

The CODASYL Data Base Task Group provided for these capabilities by the specification of subschemas. A **subschema** is a defined subset of an associated data base that gives a program invoking the subschema a customized view of the data base. The view of the data base as seen from a subschema may differ from the data base definition in that selected data elements, records, sets, and areas may be omitted; data elements, records, sets, and areas may be renamed using terms more understandable to a class of users; and data element formats (PICTURE, TYPE, length) may be changed to suit specialized data processing needs. Subschema capabilities in some DBTG systems even permit the subschema to define logical records that are combinations of data elements from several related schema records; this capability is similar to the "view" concept in relational data bases and can be considered the result of an implicit combination of record joins.

Subschemas provide a mechanism for data independence, since they yield a consistent view of the data base to a group of programs; if the schema changes but the local view is unaffected, then programs (which use a subschema, not the schema) are also unaffected.

Since subschemas are the definition of the view of a data base assumed by an application program, the subschema DDL is dependent on the programming language used in the application program. Over the years, subschema DDLs have been developed for COBOL, FORTRAN, PL/I, and Assembler languages. A subschema is defined separate from any application program that uses it; a subschema is stored in a subschema library, managed by the DBMS, and can be invoked or included in an application program when that program is compiled, link edited, or loaded, depending on the DBMS.

Figure 13-10 illustrates the IDMS subschema DDL via the Patient Bill user view of Figure 9-8 for the Mountain View Community Hospital schema definition in Figure 13-9. Each subschema is named and is matched to a particular schema.

Areas, records, data elements, and sets to be included in the subschema are defined along with restrictions on the use of data manipulation commands on these structural components. Also, depending on the features of

```
       ADD LOGICAL RECORD IS DETAILED-BILL
           ELEMENTS ARE PATIENT, CHARGES, ITEM
       ADD LOGICAL PATH OBTAIN DETAILED-BILL
           SELECT FOR FIELDNAME EQ PATIENT-NO
           FIND PATIENT WHERE CALCKEY IS
               PATIENT-NO OF REQUEST
           OBTAIN EACH CHARGES WITHIN INCURRED
           OBTAIN OWNER WITHIN PROVIDED
```

Figure 13-11
Example of IDMS logical record definition in a subschema.

the DBMS, this division may include privacy specifications and explanations of derivation of logical records as combinations of base records from the subschema. Some DBTG systems permit data names to be redefined into localized terms.

IDMS is one such DBTG DBMS that has a facility to define logical records and the process of deriving them (called a logical path). Figure 13-11 illustrates how the logical record concept could be used to define a DE-TAILED-BILL logical record for an identified patient.

In this case, the DBMS would automatically and transparently construct a DETAILED-BILL record for each CHARGES instance of each PA-TIENT record instance (i.e., DETAILED-BILL represents the complete printed line item on the patient bill depicted in Figure 8-9). We derive a DETAILED-BILL logical record by first using the current value of PATIENT-NO to FIND (i.e., locate but do not load any PATIENT data in working storage) a uniquely identified PATIENT; the application programmer must make sure that the proper PATIENT-NO is in working storage before requesting a DETAILED-BILL record. Then the DBMS would OBTAIN (i.e., transfer data element values into working storage) a CHARGES record for this PATIENT and conclude by OBTAINing the ITEM owner of this CHARGES in the PROVIDED set.

The operational benefit of a logical record, as will be seen later, is to reduce the application programmer's burden by creating virtual data that do not have to be constructed step by step in the application program. The result is less program coding (hence, faster development), less chance of erroneous data processing (since common, complicated data accesses can be coded into the subschema by a senior data base programmer), and often a more understandable data model presented to the programmer (since excessive details have been masked from the programmer).

COBOL DML: RETRIEVING AND MAINTAINING DATA

We choose to illustrate here the data processing capabilities in the COBOL programming language for accessing and manipulating a DBTG data base. As mentioned before, this is not the only procedural language possible, but it is the one most likely encountered in business data processing. As will be seen in the next section, nonprocedural language access is also possible with many DBTG systems.

Procedural, step-by-step (record-by-record) processing of a data base requires frequent reference to some relative position in the data base from which to move. Recall the data structure processing procedures from Chapter 6. These procedures were based on knowing some current position in order to find the next record on a chain or in order to identify a position for record insertion or deletion. This same logic is an integral part of processing a DBTG data base.

Currency Indicators

The term used in the DBTG data manipulation language (DML) for relative position is *currency indicator*. In fact, the DBMS is constantly keeping track of numerous currency indicators. A **currency indicator** is a variable that holds the physical address (data base key) of the record instance most recently accessed or manipulated in a specified category of records. These categories result in the following currency indicators important in various DML statements:

1. Current of run-unit: the most recent instance of any data base record referenced (i.e., retrieved or maintained by some DML command, such as FIND, OBTAIN, CONNECT, or STORE).

2. Current of record type: for each record type in the subschema, the most recent record instance referenced.

3. Current of set: for each set in the subschema, the most recent set record instance (owner or member) referenced.

4. Current of area: for each area in the subschema, the most recent record occurrence referenced.

Currency indicators are updated each time a record instance is accessed. Currency indicator updating may be suppressed, under application program control, to maintain a desired reference point. An application programmer must be well aware of the effect that each DML command has on currency indicator status.

Figure 13-12 contains a network diagram and an accompanying table that illustrates the maintenance of currency indicators. The situation illustrated here depicts part of the data processing necessary to produce a summary of the customers handled by each salesperson at Pine Valley Furniture. There is no need to sort the data in any way, so the process begins by accessing the first salesperson on file. To understand Figure 13-12, it is important to remember that user working storage contains only one instance of each record type at a time. Each time we OBTAIN (read) another

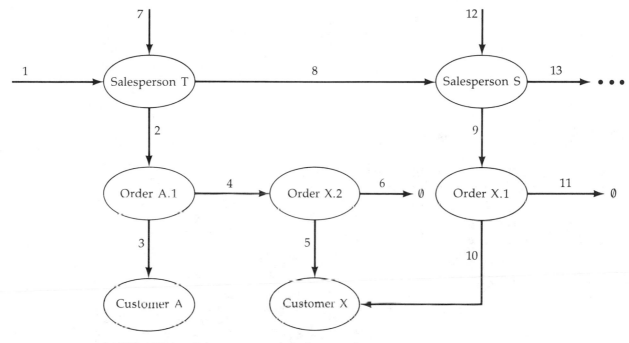

SALES-AREA: Salesperson and Order records
CLIENT-AREA: Customer records
SOLD-SET: Owner-Salesperson ; Member-Order
BOUGHT-SET: Owner-Customer ; Member-Order

(a)

Figure 13-12
Example of currency
indicator maintenance in a
DBTG DBMS.
(a) Sample data base.
(b) Currency indicators.
(Continued on page 454.)

ORDER record, for example, the prior ORDER record in main memory is overwritten.

In Figure 13-12b, a currency indicator is highlighted each time it is updated. A circle indicates that the currency indicator actually changes value; a box signifies that it was updated but no value change occurred. Logical values for currency indicators are used for clarity; currency indicators, in practice, are physical or relative disk addresses. Numbers on the arrows in the diagram (Figure 13-12a) correspond to the movement through the data base caused by execution of the DML statements in the table.

Several events shown in Figure 13-12 require explanation. The first step in the table can occur without any currency indicator values established, since it accesses an absolute, not relative, record (the first SALESPERSON record found in the SALES-AREA). All the OBTAIN NEXT ORDER commands require that there be an established value for CURRENT OF SOLD-SET. Since there is no NEXT ORDER after orders X.2 and X.1, the DBMS would return an error message to the calling program and leave currency indicators unchanged after execution of these commands. The OBTAIN CURRENT SALESPERSON is necessary in step 7 to establish the proper

DML command	CURRENT OF RUN-UNIT	Records CURRENT OF SALESPERSON	CURRENT OF ORDER	CURRENT OF CUSTOMER	Sets CURRENT OF SOLD-SET	CURRENT OF BOUGHT-SET	Areas CURRENT OF SALES-AREA	CURRENT OF CLIENT-AREA
1 OBTAIN FIRST SALESPERSON WITHIN SALES-AREA	T	T			T		T	
2 OBTAIN NEXT ORDER WITHIN SOLD-SET	A.1	T	A.1		A.1	A.1	A.1	
3 OBTAIN OWNER WITHIN BOUGHT-SET	A	T	A.1	A	A.1	A	A.1	A
4 OBTAIN NEXT ORDER WITHIN SOLD-SET	X.2	T	X.2	A	X.2	X.2	X.2	A
5 OBTAIN OWNER WITHIN BOUGHT-SET	X	T	X.2	X	X.2	X	X.2	X
6 OBTAIN NEXT ORDER WITHIN SOLD-SET	X	T	X.2	X	X.2	X	X.2	X
7 OBTAIN CURRENT SALESPERSON	T	T	X.2	X	T	X	T	X
8 OBTAIN NEXT SALESPERSON WITHIN SALES-AREA	S	S	X.2	X	S	X	S	X
9 OBTAIN NEXT ORDER WITHIN SOLD-SET	X.1	S	X.1	X	X.1	X.1	X.1	X
10 OBTAIN OWNER WITHIN BOUGHT-SET	X	S	X.1	X	X.1	X	X.1	X
11 OBTAIN NEXT ORDER WITHIN SOLD-SET	X	S	X.1	X	X.1	X	X.1	X
12 OBTAIN CURRENT SALESPERSON	S	S	X.1	X	S	X	S	X
13 OBTAIN NEXT SALESPERSON WITHIN SALES-AREA	—	—	—	—	—	—	—	—

(b)

Figure 13-12, continued.

value for CURRENT OF RUN-UNIT so that step 8 will work as desired (if CURRENT OF RUN-UNIT remained X.2, step 8 would actually access Salesperson T again).

In addition to currency indicators, special data elements defined automatically in the user working area by the subschema compiler can be used for application program control. These data elements include the following:

- DB-STATUS: a code that is set after each DML command and that contains a value indicating the type of error, if any, that occurred; although implementation-dependent, this code is usually composed of an indicator for the type of command on which the error occurred (e.g., FIND) and several other characters symbolizing the specific error encountered (e.g., no next record found in set).

- DB-RECORD-NAME, DB-SET-NAME, DB-AREA-NAME, and DB-DATA-NAME: codes in which the DBMS places the subschema names for the record, set, area, and data element (where applicable) for the error that has just occurred (e.g., step 6 in Figure 13-12 would result in DB-

Table 13-4
Typical COBOL DML Commands

Retrieval	
FIND	Locates record in data base.
GET	Transfers record to working storage.
OBTAIN	Combines FIND and GET.

With each command, we can retrieve

- unique record
- duplicate record
- next or prior record in set or area
- owner of a member record

Modification	
STORE	Puts a new record into data base and links it to all sets in which it is an automatic member.
MODIFY	Changes data values in an existing record.
CONNECT	Links an existing member record into a set occurrence.
DISCONNECT	Removes (unlinks) an existing member record from its current set occurrence.
RECONNECT	A combination of DISCONNECT and CONNECT to unlink a record from its current set and link it to a new set occurrence of the type.
ERASE	Deletes record from data base, DISCONNECTs it from all set occurrences in which it participates, and deletes other records for which this is an owner in set.

Control	
COMMIT	Makes permanent all data base updates made since last COMMIT command executed.
ROLLBACK	Aborts all updates since last COMMIT and restores data base to status at time of last COMMIT.
KEEP	Places concurrent access controls on data base records.

RECORD-NAME equaling ORDER, DB-SET-NAME equaling SOLD-SET, DB-AREA-NAME equaling SALES-AREA; DB-DATA-NAME is applicable only on operations involving data elements (usually for violations of CHECK clauses on data values).

The DBTG COBOL DML commands can be divided into three categories: retrieval statements, modification statements, and control statements. Table 13-4 lists the various DML commands included in each of these categories.

Data Retrieval

In record-at-a-time processing, records can be retrieved on the basis of:

- Unique key or address value.
- Next with same or duplicate key value.
- Next or prior in set or area (with or without some key value or in a specified order).
- Owner of a member record in a set.

Further, since retrieval is the basis for navigating/moving through a data base, we might want to (1) only locate the position of a record to verify its existence or as a reference point for subsequent movement (FIND); (2) once located (i.e., current of run-unit), put the record's data into working storage for processing (GET); or (3) combine the first two steps into one for both data manipulation and subsequent movement (OBTAIN). In addition, we may want to retain exclusive access to data while retrieving in order to prohibit other programs from updating data. (The need to do this depends on the concurrency control of the DBMS; see Chapter 11.)

To understand some of these data retrieval capabilities, consider again the subschema in Figure 13-10 for the Mountain View Hospital Patient Bill user view. Recall that the DBTG COBOL DML contains statements that extend the standard COBOL examples; all the following examples represent parts of a COBOL program necessary to perform the data retrieval function specified (the IDMS COBOL DML is used as an example DML; IDMS uses the variable ERROR-STATUS instead of DB-STATUS).

Suppose we simply wanted to retrieve data for a specified patient (PATIENT-NO 1234). To do so, we need to store the desired key value (1234) in the PATIENT-NO field of the PATIENT record in working storage and then issue the proper DML OBTAIN command. This would be accomplished by

```
MOVE '1234' TO PATIENT-NO IN PATIENT.
OBTAIN CALC PATIENT.
IF ERROR-STATUS=0 THEN NEXT SENTENCE
    ELSE...error routine...
```

The preceding OBTAIN command would make the PATIENT record for PATIENT-NO 1234 current of run-unit, current of PATIENT record type, and current of INCURRED set. If we then wished to calculate this patient's total charges, we could

```
            MOVE 0 TO TOT-CHARGE.
LOOP.
            OBTAIN NEXT CHARGES WITHIN INCURRED.
            IF ERROR-STATUS=error code for no next record
               THEN GO TO B.
            IF ERROR-STATUS=some other error code
               THEN GO TO error routine.
            ADD CHARGE IN CHARGES TO TOT-CHARGE.
            GO TO LOOP.

   B.
               . . .
```

In this example, CHARGES record instances related to the current of INCURRED set are (logically) sequentially retrieved and processed as required. At the first iteration, the set PATIENT owner (PATIENT-NO 1234) is current of set. The looping terminates when ERROR-STATUS indicates that there are no more CHARGES records within this set instance; any other error code in ERROR-STATUS indicates an unexpected error in the data base, which may require user intervention or even termination of the program. It is highly advisable to fully use the error monitoring capabilities of the DBMS after every DML statement (some implementations have ON ERROR clauses as part of each DML command).

As a final example of retrieval statements, consider a reporting requirement to display the description of all the items charged to a specified patient (again, PATIENT-NO 1234). In this case, all three subschema records have to be accessed, but no data from the CHARGES record for this patient are desired. The following DML statements could be used to retrieve the necessary data:

```
            MOVE '1234' TO PATIENT-NO IN PATIENT.
            OBTAIN CALC PATIENT.
            IF ERROR-STATUS=0 THEN NEXT SENTENCE
               ELSE...error routine...
            Display or print desired PATIENT data.
LOOP.
            FIND NEXT CHARGES WITHIN INCURRED.
            IF ERROR-STATUS=error code for no next record in set
               THEN terminate this procedure.
            IF ERROR-STATUS=some other error code
               THEN...error routine...
            OBTAIN OWNER WITHIN PROVIDED.
            IF ERROR-STATUS=any error code
               THEN...error routine...
            Display or print DESCRIPTION IN ITEM.
            GO TO LOOP.
```

In this example, note that current of INCURRED set was not affected by accessing a CHARGES owner in the PROVIDED set. CHARGES records act like link records in this example; since link records have no meaningful contents, only FIND needs to be used to retrieve them.

Data Maintenance and Control

Data maintenance within the DBTG model, although limited to only six commands (see Figure 13-13), requires careful development because of the various semantic controls that may be specified in a DBTG schema (refer to Table 13-3 for a summary of these controls). Further, to ensure the integrity of a data base against concurrent record update and abnormal program termination in the middle of a set of update statements, data maintenance routines require careful design.

When a data base (or data base area) is opened by a program, most DBTG DMLs require a specification of the mode of processing to be performed by the program (retrieval or update). If the mode is retrieval, then the DBMS will prohibit use of any data modification command in the program. If the mode is update, then two options are often permitted. The first, PROTECTED, means that concurrent update is prevented but that concurrent retrieval is allowed. The second, EXCLUSIVE, prevents any concurrent use of the data base (or area).

In addition, many DBTG DMLs permit record-level controls, called locks, to maintain a finer level of concurrent update management. In IDMS, for example, a program can place a SHARED lock on a record to prevent other run-units from updating a record temporarily while permitting retrieval. An EXCLUSIVE lock prohibits any other activity on a record until the lock is released. Exclusive locks are implicitly placed on a record that is altered by a STORE, MODIFY, or ERASE DML command.

Further control can be imposed to protect the integrity of a data base from abnormal termination of a program during the middle of a series of related maintenance statements. Consider the situation of entering a new customer order into the Pine Valley Furniture data base. Roughly, the procedure to enter this information into the data base would be as follows:

1. Accept order header data and enter a new ORDER record.
2. Accept PRODUCT#, QUANTITY-ORDERED, and so on, for a LINE-ITEM and store the Line Item.
3. If there are more LINE-ITEMs, then repeat step 2.

Suppose that after accepting and storing the ORDER data and several LINE-ITEM records, an on-line order entry operator realizes that she has been reading data from several order forms. She then decides to abort this "logical transaction" and wants to delete all the previously entered data for this order. Using the ORDER# in working storage and the set between ORDER and LINE-ITEM, the program could ERASE these records. But a simpler approach in which the DBMS automatically performs these deletions is frequently available. The beginning of the logical transaction is indicated by some special DML control statement (a START TRANSACTION, COMMIT, or some other command). If during the logical transaction a user wishes to abort processing or if a fatal data base error occurs, the transaction can be aborted and the data base will be restored automatically to its state at the time the transaction began (the command ROLLBACK is used in IDMS).

Storing a New Record. The data modification statements will be illustrated using the Mountain View Community Hospital subschema of Figure 13-9 and some variations. Consider the situation of storing the charge for an additional procedure performed on a patient. Since CHARGES is an AUTOMATIC member of both the INCURRED and PROVIDED sets, we will not have to use a CONNECT command, only STORE. Further, since the SET SELECTION clause of the INCURRED set implies THRU CURRENT OF SET, we will have to first make the proper PATIENT record current. The DML for this update for PATIENT# 1234 would be as follows:

```
MOVE '1234' TO PATIENT-NO IN PATIENT.
FIND CALC PATIENT.
IF ERROR-STATUS=0 THEN NEXT SENTENCE
    ELSE...error routine...
MOVE 150 TO CHARGE IN CHARGES.
MOVE '1234' TO PATIENT-NO IN CHARGES.
MOVE 307 TO ITEM-CODE IN CHARGES.
STORE CHARGES.
IF ERROR-STATUS=0 THEN NEXT SENTENCE
    ELSE...error routine...
```

If CHARGES were a MANUAL member of the PROVIDED set, then we would have to append to the preceding commands

```
CONNECT CHARGES TO PROVIDED.
IF ERROR-STATUS=0 THEN NEXT SENTENCE
    ELSE...error routine...
```

Deleting an Existing Record. The schema for this data base (see Figure 13-9) indicates that CHARGES is a FIXED member of both sets. We may simply delete a CHARGES in the case of misbilling by first FINDing the desired record and then ERASEing it. If we wanted to delete the CHARGES entered earlier, we would

```
MOVE '1234' PATIENT-NO IN CHARGES.
MOVE 307 TO ITEM-CODE IN CHARGES.
FIND CALC CHARGES.
IF ERROR-STATUS=0 THEN NEXT SENTENCE
    ELSE...error routine...
ERASE CHARGES.
IF ERROR-STATUS=0 THEN NEXT SENTENCE
    ELSE...error routine...
```

Changing a Member Record's Owner. RETENTION IS FIXED prevents us from moving a CHARGES to a different owner record, which is natural in this case. If, however, we had indicated RETENTION IS MANDATORY for CHARGES in the PROVIDED set, we could then RECONNECT (but not DISCONNECT) CHARGES records. Suppose we wanted to move the CHARGES given earlier to the 413 ITEM-CODE. Assuming temporarily that we had used MANDATORY, not FIXED, we would

```
MOVE 413 TO ITEM-CODE IN ITEM.
FIND CALC ITEM.
IF ERROR-STATUS=0 THEN NEXT SENTENCE
    ELSE...error routine...
MOVE 307 TO ITEM-CODE IN CHARGES.
MOVE '1234' TO PATIENT-NO IN CHARGES.
OBTAIN KEEP EXCLUSIVE CALC CHARGES.
IF ERROR-STATUS=0 THEN NEXT SENTENCE
    ELSE...error routine...
RECONNECT CHARGES TO PROVIDED.
IF ERROR-STATUS=0 THEN NEXT SENTENCE
    ELSE...error routine...
MOVE 413 TO ITEM-CODE IN CHARGES.
MODIFY CHARGES.
IF ERROR-STATUS=0 THEN NEXT SENTENCE
    ELSE...error routine...
COMMIT.
```

The KEEP EXCLUSIVE clause on the OBTAIN command prevents any other run-unit from retrieving or modifying this CHARGES record while this run-unit is updating it. The COMMIT command releases this concurrency lock and makes the updates permanent (i.e., the updates may not be aborted and undone after this point). KEEP EXCLUSIVE and COMMIT are vocabulary particular to IDMS but are representative of the data maintenance controls available in DBTG COBOL DMLs.

To illustrate DISCONNECT, suppose that miscellaneous charges (ITEM-CODE 999) do not have an ITEM record and that to support storage of such charges, we had made CHARGES an OPTIONAL member of the

PROVIDED set. We could then change the charge for ITEM-CODE 413 to 999 by

```
MOVE '1234' TO PATIENT-NO IN CHARGES.
MOVE 413 TO ITEM-CODE IN CHARGES.
OBTAIN KEEP EXCLUSIVE CALC CHARGES.
IF ERROR-STATUS=0 THEN NEXT SENTENCE
    ELSE...error routine...
DISCONNECT CHARGES FROM PROVIDED.
IF ERROR-STATUS=0 THEN NEXT SENTENCE
    ELSE...error routine...
MOVE 999 TO ITEM-CODE IN CHARGES.
MODIFY CHARGES.
IF ERROR-STATUS=0 THEN NEXT SENTENCE
    ELSE...error routine...
COMMIT.
```

Note that in this and the prior example, we had to OBTAIN, not just FIND, CHARGES in order to MODIFY its contents.

Special Maintenance Considerations.   In addition to deleting a record instance, the ERASE command can have a much broader effect on data base contents. Assuming the original schema and subschema from Figures 13-9 and 13-10, respectively, consider deletion of an ITEM record occurrence. Since CHARGES are FIXED members of the PROVIDED set (the same would be true of MANDATORY), they cannot exist without an ITEM owner. If we ERASE an ITEM record in this case, the CHARGES records associated with this ITEM would also automatically be erased by the DBMS.

If CHARGES were an OPTIONAL member of the PROVIDED set, then we would have a choice on what to do with CHARGES members (and members of any other set owned by ITEM) when deleting an ITEM owner. If we were to use

    ERASE ITEM PERMANENT MEMBER.

then any MANDATORY or FIXED member for a set owned by ITEM would also be ERASEd, but OPTIONAL members (like CHARGES under the preceding assumption) would only be automatically DISCONNECTed. If we

    ERASE ITEM SELECTIVE MEMBER.

then all MANDATORY or FIXED members would be ERASEd, but OPTIONAL members would also be ERASEd *if* they do not currently have a member in any other set (e.g., INCURRED) occurrence. In the case of CHARGES records, since each must be a member of some INCURRED set, none would be ERASEd. This would only apply to members that are OP-TIONAL members of other sets. All members can be ERASEd irrespective of other set membership by using ERASE ITEM ALL.

Logical Record Processing in IDMS

In Figure 13-11, we introduced the IDMS logical record construct that can be defined in a subschema. The purpose of a logical record is to define a simple view of the data base that consolidates several data base records into one virtual record. Logical records can be used to simplify OBTAIN, STORE, MODIFY, and ERASE processing by permitting *one* such DML statement to implicitly retrieve and appropriately process a group of related records.

Figure 13-11 contains a definition for a DETAILED-BILL logical record. We can use this logical record to produce a listing of all charges for a given PATIENT (say, PATIENT# 1234) by

```
PRINT-LIST.
    OBTAIN NEXT DETAILED-BILL WHERE PATIENT-NO = '1234'
        ON LR-NOT-FOUND GO TO AFTER-LIST.
    Display or print data from CHARGES and ITEM records
        (but not PATIENT, since logical record definition uses FIND for
        PATIENT record)
    . . .
    GO TO PRINT-LIST.
AFTER-LIST.
    . . .
```

The ON error clause also represents a logical/symbolic way to check data base error codes instead of detailed IF statements involving ERROR-STATUS and other variables.

DEVICE MEDIA CONTROL LANGUAGE

Although the schema DDL specifies some internal data base characteristics, the schema still has a great deal of data independence from the internal data base. The device media control language (DMCL) is used to complete the data base definition.

Because the DMCL is used to prescribe physical data base charac-teristics, use of the DMCL should be limited to the data base administrator. PR1ME Computer, in fact, has made this implicit by calling their version of the DMCL for their DBTG DBMS the Data Base Administrator Control Program (DBACP) and by requiring that a user have special computer system privileges to perform most of the DBACP functions.

In IDMS, the DMCL is used to:

- Specify the number of secondary memory pages to keep in a main memory buffer area (this would specify the size of the system buffers block in Figure 13-1).
- Specify the characteristics of each area, such as the number of characters per page in the area, space for expansion of variable-length records, and alias names for the area.
- Define the physical characteristics of journal files used to store record and transaction images useful in data base recovery.

Similar functions are performed by most DMCLs or equivalent utilities. In general, these functions allocate physical space for the data base, specify which options to use (if any) for representing sets, name all the various physical operating system files and/or data sets used to construct the data base, and indicate whether and how to create audit trails and data modification journals.

NONPROCEDURAL ACCESS: QUERY AND NATURAL LANGUAGES

Most vendors of DBTG systems provide nonprocedural query languages for ad hoc, interactive retrieval of data and/or reportwriter programs for nonprocedural production of customized reports. For example, PR1ME provides DBMS/Query (or VISTA) with its DBTG DBMS. Cullinet provides OnLine Query (OLQ) as a query language, IDMS/CULPRIT as a reportwriter, and OnLine English (OLE) as a natural language processor. (OnLine English is marketed by Cullinet, but is one version of Intellect, a product of Artificial Intelligence Corp.) Further, Cullinet now has a new version of IDMS, IDMS/R, which includes a relational-like query language. Their claim is that this marriage of network data storage with relational access provides both high performance and ease of access.

Query Languages

Query languages permit an interactive programmer, often a non-data processing professional, to write record retrievals using expressions that specify what records are desired, not the process of record-by-record retrieval. Often such query languages resemble relational calculus; thus, it is possible to give an end user a relational-like view of a network data base.

As an example of a query language for a network data base, we will present a few sample queries using Cullinet's OnLine Query (OLQ). For this illustration, consider the inventory data base of Figure 13-8. We could retrieve the first sequential PRODUCT record in the data base by

(1) GET FIRST SEQUENTIAL PRODUCT RECORD

and OLQ would immediately display the contents of this record on the terminal. We could then retrieve the first INVENTORY for this PRODUCT by

(2) GET FIRST INVENTORY BELONGING TO THIS PRODUCT

and could continue to retrieve other INVENTORY records one by one using

(3) REPEAT WITH LAST

Otherwise, if we wanted to see all the INVENTORY records for this PROD-UCT, we could issue the following command immediately after (1):

(4) GET ALL INVENTORY BELONGING TO THIS PRODUCT

Such query languages are helpful in that they can rapidly produce the result of a simple end user question, check on the contents of a data base after a series of COBOL data maintenance program executions, or provide a user with a prototype of the type of report that could be produced in a fancier format by a batch reportwriter or COBOL report program. These languages do, however, have a precise grammar and syntax that must be learned by anyone who wishes to write a query. Release 10.0 of OLQ from Cullinet has a menu-driven front end for end users.

Natural Languages

Natural language processors eliminate the need to learn a specific grammar, vocabulary, and syntax. Cullinet explains their package OnLine English (OLE) in this way (Cullinet 1982b):

> OnLine English (OLE) is an English-language query system that enables users to obtain computer-stored information by means of simple request. OLE accepts and interprets a freely worded request, retrieves the appropriate data, and performs all processing necessary to display the results in a meaningful format. The capacity to accept everyday English phrases is a powerful feature of OnLine English that distinguishes it from traditional query systems.

Consider again the inventory data base of Figure 13-8. After signing on and being greeted by OLE, Figure 13-13 illustrates some possible dialogue between OLE and the user. In this figure, OLE prompts and responses are shown in capital letters and user questions in lowercase. Prior to processing each English question, OLE displays a structured query version of its interpretation of the original question. The user can abort the processing at this point in order to restate the query if OLE has misinterpreted the question. If

PLEASE ENTER YOUR FIRST REQUEST

What are the fields in the inventory file?

FIELDS IN THE INVENTORY FILE

S#   P#   W#

NEXT REQUEST

What is the S# and P# of all inventory in 04 warehouse?

PRINT THE S# AND P# OF ALL INVENTORY WITH W#=04
THE NUMBER OF RECORDS TO RETRIEVE IS 3

S#	P#
12345	1234
72843	5436
92371	3476

NEXT REQUEST

Where is part 1234 stored?

PRINT THE W# OF ALL INVENTORY WITH P#=1234
THE NUMBER OF RECORDS TO RETRIEVE IS 2

W#

04

12

NEXT REQUEST

How many warehouses are there?

COUNT THE WAREHOUSE
ANSWER: 16

NEXT REQUEST

...

Figure 13-13
Example of IDMS OnLine English dialogue.

the user uses key words such as average, minimum, or bar graph, OLE will generate the appropriate result.

Given that such nonprocedural languages exist for access to a network data base, why should we ever program in COBOL? First, most of these facilities are limited to only data retrieval and reporting; data update is usually not supported. Second, the computer time required to dynamically translate query or English statements into the record-level commands adds significant overhead to computer processing. A prewritten procedural language routine would execute the same type of retrieval much faster (but, of course, would take significantly more time to code). The trade-off, basically, is between machine efficiency and programmer efficiency. When rapidly developed, ad hoc, frequently modified, or one-time reports are desired, nonprocedural languages are suitable; if high-volume transaction processing or repeated rapid response queries characterize the computing work load, then procedural languages will be more appropriate for processing the network data base.

Figure 13-14
Example of an IMAGE
data base schematic.

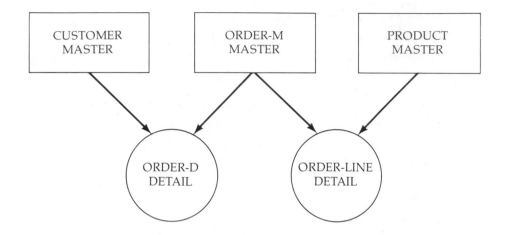

LIMITED NETWORK IMPLEMENTATIONS

DBMSs have also been developed that conform to the general architecture of the limited network data model. Although there is no industry standard like the DBTG model for these systems, there is a practical standard. TOTAL, developed and marketed by CINCOM Systems (CINCOM Systems, Inc. 1982) for IBM and other hardware, is this default standard. Various computer manufacturers (NCR, Harris, Hewlett-Packard, and others) provide DBMSs that were originally developed by CINCOM or that were developed under the advice and consent of CINCOM. We introduced the generic characteristics of the limited network model in Chapter 6; the purpose of the current section is to illustrate briefly the features of a DBMS under such a model. We have chosen to use IMAGE, the Hewlett-Packard version of TOTAL, for these illustrations (Hewlett-Packard 1983).

IMAGE Data Definition

Figure 13-14 is an adaptation of Figure 6-11 for a limited network data base for Pine Valley Furniture. In Figure 13-14, master record types are represented by rectangles and detail record types are represented by circles. Master record types are entry points into the data base. Each master record has one hash key, called a **search item** (e.g., CUSTOMER-NO, ORDER-NO or PRODUCT-NO), which provides direct record access. Detail records may be accessed only via chains from master records. A detail record may have only one master instance for each master with which it is associated. Detail records cannot exist without an associated master.

To implement a relationship from master to detail, both records must have a common search item. A detail may have up to 16 search items; that is, a detail may be related to up to 16 different master record types.

There are two types of master record types, both of which are illustrated in Figure 13-14. A **manual** master (e.g., CUSTOMER) need not have a related detail and may contain not only a search item but also additional data items. An **automatic** master (e.g., ORDER-M) must be related to at least one detail and may not contain any data other than the search item; the rest of the data on this type of entity is in one of the associated details (e.g., the ORDER-D). An automatic master is automatically added or deleted when a related (one-to-one related) detail is added or deleted. For example, insertion (or deletion) of an ORDER-D record for some CUSTOMER would automatically create (or delete) an ORDER-M record with the same ORDER-NO search key; however, insertion of an ORDER-LINE detail would not cause such action.

One of the relationships entering a detail can be designated as the **primary path**. This designation can be used by several DBMS utility programs to periodically reorganize the data base; during reorganization, records on the primary path from a common master instance are stored in contiguous secondary memory locations. Relationships may also have **sort items** so that detail records may be kept in a specified sequence under a master.

Figure 13-15 illustrates an IMAGE schema definition. Passwords can be specified and then referenced in item and set (record) definitions to control access to data. All the data base data elements (items) are listed together, along with a type code for each. Only two type codes are illustrated. The I code designates a one- to four-digit integer; X signifies an alphanumeric string of the length indicated.

Set is the IMAGE term for record type. In Figure 13-15, we have chosen to define the three master files first. CUSTOMER is defined as a manual set, which forces a CUSTOMER record to be manually entered into the data base before any associated records (ORDER-D) are entered. The CUSTOMER set has two data items; one of these, CUSTOMER-NO, is the key and has only one path (relationship) for which this is a common key (the relationship to ORDER-D). ORDER-M, on the other hand, has ORDER-NO as the key, but ORDER-M has two related sets (relationships). ORDER-M was defined as automatic, so that instances of this record type would be automatically created each time a new ORDER-D or ORDER-LINE was entered for a new ORDER-NO. Note also that the automatic set has only one item, the key ORDER-NO. The capacity specifications indicate the number of logical records for which space should be allocated for each set.

ORDER-D is defined as a detail record with three data items. CUS-TOMER-NO is the common item used to relate ORDER-D to a CUSTOMER record; the exclamation point specifies that this is the primary path, as already explained. The ORDER-DATE argument in the CUSTOMER-NO entry here defines a sort key; that is, ORDER-D records will be stored in sequential order by ORDER-DATE under their associated master CUS-TOMER record. ORDER-D is also related to ORDER-M records via the common item ORDER-NO. Similarly, the ORDER-LINE detail record is

Figure 13-15
Skeleton of an IMAGE
schema.

```
BEGIN DATA BASE PVF;
PASSWORDS:
    • • •
ITEMS:
    CUSTOMER-NO,  I;
    CUST-ADDR,      X20;
    ORDER-NO,       I;
    ORDER-DATE,    X6;
    PRODUCT-NO,   I;
    QTY-ORDERED,  I;
    QTY-ON-HAND,  I;
SETS:
    NAME:  CUSTOMER,MANUAL;
    ENTRY:  CUSTOMER-NO(1),
            CUST-ADDR;
    CAPACITY:  100;

    NAME:  ORDER-M,AUTOMATIC;
    ENTRY:  ORDER-NO(2);
    CAPACITY:  1000;

    NAME:  PRODUCT,MANUAL;
    ENTRY:  PRODUCT-NO(1),
            QTY-ON-HAND;
    CAPACITY:  200;

    NAME:  ORDER-D,DETAIL;
    ENTRY:  CUSTOMER-NO (!CUSTOMER(ORDER-DATE)),
            ORDER-DATE,
            ORDER-NO(ORDER-M);
    CAPACITY:  1000;

    NAME:  ORDER-LINE,DETAIL;
    ENTRY:  PRODUCT-NO(PRODUCT),
            ORDER-NO(ORDER-M),
            QTY-ORDERED;
    CAPACITY:  5000;
END.
```

related to both PRODUCT (via the PRODUCT-NO item) and ORDER-M (via the ORDER-NO item). There is no primary path or record sorting specified for ORDER-LINE records.

IMAGE Data Manipulation

Data manipulation in IMAGE involves both record retrieval and modification. Record retrieval commands are DBFIND (locate a record) and DBGET (move record to working storage); modification commands are DBUPDATE (rewrite with new values), DBPUT (add a new record), and DBDELETE (delete an existing record).

There are four methods for retrieving data:

1. *Direct*: relative record number addressing of either master or detail records.

2. *Serial*: physical sequential record accessing, either forward or backward, in either master or detail files.

3. *Calculated*: search key access to a master file record (using hashing).

4. *Chained*: accessing detail records under a common master (DBFIND is used to find the correct master and DBGET is used to "walk" the chain).

The DML is actually specified as arguments in COBOL CALL statements. It is beyond the scope of this chapter to cover all commands in detail; we will illustrate the general structure of a DML CALL via two examples that appear in Figure 13-16. Figure 13-16a indicates the necessary steps to add a new CUSTOMER record to the data base defined in Figure 13-15. Figure 13-16b illustrates retrieval of ORDER-D records for a specified customer.

The arguments necessary for a DBPUT are, in order of reference:

- *Base-name*: essentially the name of the data base; the two-character prefix is a code for the data base returned when the data base was opened (data base opening not shown).

- *Set-name*: the name of the record type being added.

- *Mode*: a code that controls the type of record accessing and the locking of records for concurrent access (e.g., a mode 1 declares the intention to add records to the data base and prohibits concurrent access to the record being added).

- *Statuss*: a data aggregate from working storage into which the DBMS will place error codes and messages to indicate the status of the command execution (CONDTN-WORD is one of the elementary data items in STATUSS).

- *Item list*: a variable that contains the item names that are to be manipulated; the code @ signifies that all items are to be manipulated.

- *Buffer*: a data aggregate from working storage that contains the data item value being manipulated.

In Figure 13-16a, CU-BUFF-NO and CU-BUFF-ADDR are the elementary items in the CUSTOMER record buffer. The IF statements after the CALL determine if any error has occurred, and depending on the type of error, appropriate action is taken.

Many of the same arguments from DBPUT are common to other DML commands. DBFIND, in Figure 13-16b, uses Base-name, Set-name, Mode, and Statuss; in addition, DBFIND requires the following:

Figure 13-16
Example of image DML.
(a) Add CUSTOMER 1234
    to CUSTOMER file.
(b) Display ORDER-M
    Records for
    CUSTOMER 1234.

```
MOVE 'xxPVF' TO PVF.
MOVE 'CUSTOMER' TO CUST.
MOVE 1 TO MODE1.
MOVE '@' TO ALL-ITEMS.
MOVE 1234 TO CU-BUFF-NO.
MOVE '123 ADAMS' TO CU-BUFF-ADDR.
CALL "DBPUT" USING PVF, CUST, MODE1, STATUSS, ALL-ITEMS,
                     CU-BUFFER.
IF CONDTN-WORD=43 DISPLAY "DUPLICATE CUSTOMER"
        GO TO RE-ENTER.
...
```

(a)

```
        MOVE 'CUSTOMER-NO' TO SEARCH-KEY.
        MOVE 1234 TO KEY-VALUE.
        CALL "DBFIND" USING PVF, CUST, MODE1, STATUSS, SEARCH-KEY,
                             KEY-VALUE.
        Error checks placed here.
READ.
        MOVE 'ORDER-M' TO ORD.
        MOVE 5 TO MODE5.
        MOVE SPACES TO ORD-M-BUFFER
        CALL "DBGET" USING PVF, ORD, MODE5, STATUSS, ALL-ITEMS,
                             ORD-M-BUFFER.
        IF CONDTN-WORD=15 DISPLAY "END OF CHAIN"
             GO TO C.
        Other error checks placed here.
        Display or print record.
        GO TO READ.
C.
        ...
```

(b)

- *Search-key*: a variable that contains the name of the item on which the calculated search (hashing) is to be performed.

- *Key-value*: a variable that contains the value of the search item.

In Figure 13-16b, DBFIND establishes the head of chain to the proper CUSTOMER record (CUSTOMER-NO 1234). DBGET is then used to retrieve detail ORDER-M records in chained sequence under this common CUSTOMER. It is MODE5 that indicates that chained forward access is to be performed. As in Figure 13-16a, all data items in the ORDER-M record are to be retrieved, this time into the ORD-M-BUFFER. When the CONDTN-WORD of STATUSS has value 15, the end of the chain has been reached.

SUMMARY

This chapter has reviewed the major network data model implementations, the CODASYL DBTG model (and IDMS, a leading commercial product), and the limited network model of TOTAL (and IMAGE, the Hewlett-Packard product). Although the discussion has been dominated by record-level access to data, we have also shown example query languages for access data in network data bases. Such query and natural languages can provide a relation-like front-end view of a network data base.

The network data model has been much maligned since the introduction of the relational model. Criticisms have primarily focused on issues of ease-of-use and processing complex queries, which generally favor the relational model. However, in practice, the network data model DBMSs have continued to be popular data management technologies, usually because of the better performance possible by the explicit record-level processing. Today, because of relational-like query language front ends, we can "have our performance and ease of use, too."

CHAPTER REVIEW

Review Questions

1. Define each of the following terms:

   a. CODASYL DBTG
   b. IDS
   c. DDL
   d. DML
   e. DMCL
   f. schema
   g. subschema
   h. area
   i. host language
   j. location mode
   k. manual insertion
   l. automatic insertion
   m. fixed retention
   n. mandatory retention
   o. optional retention
   p. CALC location mode
   q. virtual data
   r. currency indicator
   s. search key
   t. IDMS logical record
   u. natural language
   v. master record (set) in TOTAL
   w. detail record (set) in TOTAL

2. Contrast the functions of the three DBTG retrieval commands FIND, GET, and OBTAIN.

3. Discuss the advantages of using a network DBMS with a relational-like query language.

4. Describe the use of the system buffers shown in Figure 13-1. When are data moved in and out of these buffers? What effect would paging in a virtual memory operating system have on buffer contents?

5. Describe the role of a computer operating system in data base access under the DBTG guidelines.

6. Explain why there are different subschema DDLs, one for each host programming language.

7. Explain why a record may not have a CALC key and also be located VIA some set.

8. Explain the factors to consider for selecting among FIRST, LAST, and SORTED for the ORDER IS clause of a set definition.

9. Explain why two Order files are necessary in Figure 13-14.

10. Explain the benefit of the IDMS logical record construct.

11. Explain the purpose of the IDMS COMMIT command and discuss where in a program this command can be usefully placed.

12. Under what circumstances (data base schema characteristics) is the DML command RECONNECT permitted?

Problems and Exercises

1. Consider the entities of Agent, Policy, Client, Beneficiary, and Insurance Company in an independent insurance agency. Design a DBTG network diagram for this situation.

2. For the data base designed in Problem 1, suggest several data processing requirements for which use of more than one area would be beneficial in the schema.

3. Specify the LOCATION MODE clause for each record type in Problem 1 and justify your choice of mode and duplicates specification.

4. For each of the sets in your answer to Problem 1, specify and justify INSERTION and RETENTION clauses. Write complete set definitions for this problem.

5. Consider the entities of Project, General Task, and Employee in a project management or job shop organization. Design a DBTG network diagram for this situation.

6. For the situation in Problem 5, assume that there is a need to report the employees working on a project in order by their job classification. Write the schema DDL necessary to support this requirement through the data base structure.

CODASYL COBOL Committee. 1978. *COBOL Journal of Development*. Available from Federal Department of Supply and Services, Hull, Quebec, Canada.

CODASYL Data Description Language Committee. 1978. *DDL Journal of Development*. Available from Federal Department of Supply and Services, Hull, Quebec, Canada.

Cullinet. 1983. *IDMS Programmer's Reference Guide—COBOL*. Revision 1.0. Westwood, Mass.: Cullinet, April.

————. 1982a. *IDMS Database Design and Definition Guide*. Revision 0.0. Westwood, Mass.: Cullinet, September.

————. 1982b. *ONLINE ENGLISH User's Guide*. Revision 0.0. Westwood, Mass.: Cullinet, May.

Hewlett-Packard. 1983. *IMAGE Database Management System Reference Manual*. Cupertino, Calif.: Hewlett-Packard, March.

Olle, T. William. 1980. *The CODASYL Approach to Data Base Management*. Chichester, Eng.: Wiley.

7. Consider the situation of an automobile dealership and entities Owner, Vehicle, Sale, and Salesperson. Assume all the usual relationships between these entities plus the association of a sale to vehicles traded in on that sale. Design a DBTG network diagram for this situation and write the schema DDL, using data items of your choice.

8. In the situation in Problem 7, assume that the dealership's general manager frequently sends promotional mailings to owners of vehicles on file. To minimize mailing costs, she wishes this to be printed in customer zip code order. Add to your schema and network diagram for Problem 7 the constructs necessary to support this data processing.

9. Review the alternatives of representing a loop relationship presented in Figure 13-4. Evaluate each of these and suggest situations in which each would be a desirable approach.

10. For the data base schema of Problem 7, write the COBOL and DML commands necessary to change ownership of a vehicle. Assume any data elements you believe are essential; include skeletons of data base error checks.

11. For the data base of Problem 1, write the COBOL and DML commands required to enter a new policy into the data base. Assume any data elements you believe are essential; include skeletons of data base error checks.

12. Consider again the data base of Problem 1. Write the COBOL and DML commands required (skeleton of the code is all that is necessary) to produce a report of the policy numbers and anniversary dates for each policy of each client. The policy numbers and dates are to be grouped by client; the clients are not to be printed in any particular logical order.

13. In the preceding data base design problems, you were not given much information about the data processing requirements of the situation, but instead were asked to design the data base in more general terms. Specifically, what clauses of a DBTG schema are affected by knowledge of particular data processing requirements?

14. Consider again the data processing required in Problem 12. Design some sample data for this problem and develop an illustration of currency indicator maintenance, as in Figure 13-12, for your sample data and the program fragment you wrote for Problem 12.

References

ANSI X3H2. 1981. *Proposed American National Standard for a Data Definition Language for Network Structured Databases*. American National Standards Institute.

CINCOM Systems, Inc. 1982. *TOTAL Reference Manual*. Cincinnati: CINCOM.

CODASYL. 1971. *Data Base Task Group April 71 Report*. New York: Association for Computing Machinery.

14

Relational Implementations

INTRODUCTION

Data base management systems built for the relational data model (see Chapter 6) are abundant and rapidly increasing in number. As with the network data model implementations, there is not just one type of relational DBMS available. Although the basic relational data model is rather consistently used in all products, the style of relational data manipulation languages varies across several categories. The purpose of this chapter is to review these various styles, using example relational DBMS products to illustrate their features.

A RELATIONAL DBMS: AN OVERVIEW

Many DBMSs are said to be relational. In fact, without even trying to generate an exhaustive list, we can safely say that there are more data management products claiming to be relational than there are claiming to be all other data models combined. Although for practical purposes it does not matter (if the DBMS has the features required for our data processing, why should we care what it is called?), an attempt to carefully distinguish relational from nonrelational systems will highlight the important features of relational implementations.

Kim (1979) has listed nine "requisite features for a hypothetical, comprehensive relational system," many of which are general features of any true DBMS (see Chapter 11), but several, which we will emphasize here, are unique to relational systems. These nine features are as follows (Kim 1979, 185, 186):

475

1. An interface for a high-level, nonprocedural data language that provides the following capabilities for both application programmers and non-technical users: query, data manipulation, data definition, and data control facilities.

2. Efficient file structures in which to store the data base and efficient access paths to the stored data base.

3. An efficient optimizer to help meet the response-time requirements of terminal users.

4. User views and snapshots of the stored data base.

5. Integrity control—validation of semantic constraints on the data base during data manipulation and rejection of offending data manipulation statements.

6. Concurrency control—synchronization of simultaneous updates to a shared data base by multiple users.

7. Selective access control—authorization of access privileges to one user's data base to other users.

8. Recovery from both soft and hard crashes.

9. A report generator for a highly stylized display of the results of interactions against the data base and such application-oriented computational facilities as statistical analysis.

Since many of these features are, in fact, general characteristics of DBMSs, it is essential that a true relational DBMS be, first, a true DBMS. This may seem trivially obvious, but an evaluation of some "relational DBMS" products will indicate deficiencies in these essential features. Several of these nine points require elaboration to be made specific to relational DBMSs.

In his ACM Turing lecture, Codd (1982) states that relational data definition is via the construct of flat files or tables and that data can be manipulated, explicitly or implicitly, via at least three operators: select, project, and join. Further, to be truly relational, *any* table column must be able to be manipulated with these operators, independent of the existence of data structures, like indexes, to make these manipulations efficient. The use of the word *join* in defining the minimal characteristics is somewhat unfortunate, since it is not essential that such a verb actually be present in the DML. Rather, what is essential is that it be possible in one DML statement to refer to data in related records (tuples in relational terminology) from different tables. This was illustrated in Chapter 6 (see "Data Processing with the Relational Data Model), where two relational DML styles were introduced: relational algebra (explicit join) and relational calculus (implicit join).

In this chapter, we will also present illustrations of other languages for manipulating relational data bases: tabular/graphical and host language interfaces. Although Kim states that both application programmers and nontechnical users are addressed by relational DBMSs, the primary emphasis has always been nontechnical users. Some relational DBMSs do not have special procedural languages or interfaces to general-purpose programming languages used to develop many data processing programs.

Any DBMS attempts to provide efficient access paths to data. With relational DBMSs, this is typically achieved via B-tree key indexes (see Chapter 5) on data elements (*roles*, in relational terminology). Obviously, efficient access to data is a function of both the data structures used and the data processing work load. Relational DBMSs are designed for data processing environments in which data are to be retrieved based on a variety of possibly complex multiple-key qualification statements (Boolean expressions). Often, such retrieval requests cannot be anticipated, but rather arise ad hoc as new business problems or new insights to old problems occur. Multiple-key indexes are easy to combine in various Boolean patterns and are therefore practical structures to use in such an environment. Thus, the combination of Boolean statements and multiple-key indexes makes it possible for relational systems to support more complex ad hoc inquiry into a data base compared to other types of DBMSs.

The user view feature cited by Kim may have two dimensions for a truly relational DBMS. Minimally, it means that data are viewed in tables (files), with possibly many rows/tuples (records) and columns/roles (attributes). Even the result of a DBMS manipulation must be a table. Values in the cells of these tables are restricted to certain domains (valid value sets). For more richly developed relational DBMSs, there may also exist customized user views (external data bases). Such user views also conceptualize data into tables; these tables may be subsets of the complete data base (generated from SELECTions and PROJECTions from the complete data base), or a user view may include tables that are combinations of related tables from the original data base (generated from JOINing tables). The more these tables can be manipulated without knowledge of their physical implementation (e.g., whether an index exists or not), the more relational the DBMS is. However, as pointed out in Chapter 6, such logical manipulation often requires the user to know what data are in common between two or more tables (i.e., what roles relate to the same domain). In network DBMSs, it is sufficient to simply ask for a related record without knowing the linking data name.

The last of Kim's relational DBMS features to require elaboration here is integrity control. We saw in Chapter 13 that network DBMSs include semantic and integrity controls in CHECK clauses and in various SET definition statements. In relational DBMSs, this is accomplished by means of integrity assertions. As explained by Kim (1979, 203):

> Integrity assertions may describe either valid states (state assertions) or valid state transitions (transition assertions). For example, the assertion "no employee should earn less than 10K" describes a valid

state; while the assertion "no employee should be given a pay cut" constrains a state transition.

Integrity assertions may be imposed on individual tuples (as above) or on groups of tuples of relations. For example, the state assertions "average salary of employees in any department should not exceed 20K" and "salary of employees in any department with 100 employees should not exceed 30K" are applied to groups of tuples. . . .

Not illustrated here is the typical network system set integrity capability, also present in many relational DBMSs, to restrict values across record types (e.g., a department number may not appear in an employee record unless there exists a department record [tuple] with that number). Thus, more powerful integrity constraints have been implemented in relational DBMSs than in other types of systems.

Not only have relational DBMSs been implemented in the classical fashion of DBMSs as software utilities, but also numerous special-purpose DBMS machines have been developed in laboratories (see Banerjee et al. 1978; Schuster et al. 1978; Su and Lipovski 1975) and for commercial sale (see Britton-Lee Corporation 1982). Data base computers will be discussed in detail in Chapter 15. Basically, such a special "back-end" computer is attached to a general-purpose computer. The data base computer receives a stream of requests for data base processing from the host computer's operating system (generated from application programs). These requests are queued, sequenced for efficient processing, and satisfied in parallel to the host CPU doing non-data-base tasks. The data base computer is configured in ways to optimize data base processing (e.g., special architectures like array or associative processors, fast channels for data transfer, and DBMS functions built in hardware or firmware). Relational DBMSs implemented in hardware are just emerging in commercial applications, and their progress requires attention.

As stated earlier, the number of relational DBMSs is large and rapidly increasing. A definitive list of such products is not feasible here. Table 14-1 summarizes examples of leading relational products under different categories; these categories will be explained and illustrated in later sections of this chapter. Microcomputer implementations will be discussed in Chapter 15.

RELATIONAL DATA DEFINITION LANGUAGES

There is not much variety among relational data definition languages, since the relational data model is rather simple and standardized. Significant differences occur in embellishments such as inclusion of integrity and security constraints, definition of user views (external data bases), and implementation clauses to indicate, for example, creation of a key index. The process of designing a relational data base has been covered elsewhere in

Table 14-1

Summary of Some Relational Systems

Package	Vendor	Equipment	Comments
Relational algebra systems			
RIM	Boeing Commercial Airplane Company	PR1ME 750	Host language interfaces to FORTRAN, PASCAL, and COBOL; logical views not supported, integrity assertions supported; typical algebra operators, including INTERSECT
dBASE II	Ashton-Tate	Variety of micros under CP/M and MS/DOS	Special procedural language as well as typical algebra operators
Relational calculus systems			
SQL/DS	IBM	S/370, 3033; DOS/VSE operating system	Host language interfaces to COBOL, PL/I, and assembler; logical views supported; query language: SEQUEL
INGRES	Relational Technology	DEC VAX-11; VMS and UNIX operating systems	Host language interfaces to C, PASCAL, FORTRAN, BASIC, and COBOL; logical views supported; query language: QUEL
ORACLE	Relational Software	DEC PDP-11, VAX (VMS, UNIX, RSX, RSTS), and IBM S/370 and 3033 (VM/CMS)	Host language interfaces to COBOL, PL/I, FORTRAN, C, BASIC, and assembler; logical views supported; query language: SEQUEL
Knowledge Man	Micro Data Base Systems	Various micros under MS/DOS	QUEL-like query language and special procedural language; query commands may be embedded in simple spreadsheet cells; views not supported
Graphical/tabular systems			
Query-by-Example	IBM	S/370 and 3033	Unique graphical, fill-in-the-blanks query language

(Continued)

Table 14-1 (Continued)

Package	Vendor	Equipment	Comments
Relational-like			
NOMAD	National CSS	IBM S/370 and others	Hierarchical and relational models; limited logical views; special query language
Model 204	Computer Corp. of America	IBM S/370 and others	Inverted file organization; no logical views; special query language; host language interfaces to COBOL, PL/I, FORTRAN, and assembler
ADABAS	Software AG	IBM S/370 and others	Inverted file organization with some network constructs; several query and reportwriter languages

this text (see "Relational Data Model" in Chapter 6 and Chapter 7); normalization is used to derive the relations to be defined. This section will assume that this design has occurred and will concentrate on the translation of these relations into DDL.

CASE EXAMPLE **Mountain View Community Hospital**

To illustrate the use of typical relational DDLs, we will again refer to the Mountain View Community Hospital data base of Figures 8-13 and 9-7. Figure 14-1 contains a definition of this data base using the DDL of SQL/DS.

Various data definition commands are possible. In SQL/DS (see IBM Corp. 1982), seven are frequently used (these are typical of many relational DBMSs):

CREATE TABLE: Defines a new table and its columns.

DROP TABLE: Destroys a table (definition and contents).

ALTER TABLE: Adds a new column to a table (in some DBMSs this would also permit deleting columns).

CREATE INDEX: Defines an index on a column that enables rapid access of the rows of a table in a sequence or randomly by key value; a table may have many indexes.

```
CREATE TABLE ROOM
     (LOCATION              CHAR(4) NOT NULL,
      ACCOM                 CHAR(2),
      EXTENSION             SMALLINT,
      PATIENT#              SMALLINT)
CREATE TABLE PATIENT
     (PATIENT#              INTEGER NOT NULL,
      DATE-DISCHARGED       INTEGER,
      ••• Other data elements •••)
CREATE TABLE PHYSICIAN
     (PHYSICIAN-ID          CHAR(10) NOT NULL,
      PHYSICIAN-PHONE       CHAR(8)
CREATE TABLE ITEM
     (ITEM-CODE             SMALLINT NOT NULL,
      DESCRIPTION           CHAR(15))
CREATE TABLE TREATMENT
     (T-PHYSICIAN-ID        CHAR(10) NOT NULL,
      T-PATIENT#            INTEGER NOT NULL,
      PROCEDURE             CHAR(15))
CREATE TABLE CHARGES
     (C-PATIENT#            INTEGER NOT NULL,
      C-ITEM-CODE           SMALLINT NOT NULL,
      C-CHARGE              DECIMAL(6,2))
```

Figure 14-1
SQL/DS data definition for Mountain View Community Hospital.

DROP INDEX: Destroys an index.

CREATE VIEW: Defines a logical table from one or more tables or views.

DROP VIEW: Destroys a view definition.

Table Definition

Most relational systems allow dynamic table definition. This is relatively easy to permit, since there are no physical links between tables; rather, indexes are used to support retrieving associated records (see "Implementation of the Relational Data Model" in Chapter 6). In SQL/DS, the Item relation from Figure 14-1 would be defined by

```
CREATE TABLE ITEM
     (ITEM-CODE          SMALLINT NOT NULL,
      DESCRIPTION        CHAR (15))
```

Various data types are possible besides CHARacter; these include two different integer sizes, decimal, floating point, and variable and very long character strings. NOT NULL is a semantic control that informs the DBMS not to permit any tuple in the ITEM table to have a null value for ITEM-CODE; this will be enforced on all data manipulation statements.

Security Controls

Tables and views (to be discussed shortly) may also be given security restrictions (at the table level). For example,

GRANT INSERT ON ITEM TO INV-MANAGER

gives the user identified as INV-MANAGER privilege to insert tuples in the ITEM relation, and

REVOKE UPDATE ON ITEM FROM STOCKROOM

denies update capability to the ITEM table for the user identified as STOCK-ROOM. Data-element (column)-level restrictions are only possible by creating views with different column combinations and applying GRANTs and REVOKEs to views.

INGRES (see Relational Technology, Inc. 1982) has an interactive command, PERMIT, to specify who (by user name) can do what (by DML command) under certain conditions (e.g., time of day, day of week). A PERMIT is applied to a table and is checked each time that table is used. Suppose we wanted to allow only retrieval and adding new CHARGE data (APPEND command) by Billing Clerks in the accounts receivable office (terminal TTA4) only during normal business hours from Monday through Friday. The PERMIT command for this situation would be

DEFINE PERMIT RETRIEVE, APPEND ON CHARGE
    TO BILLING-CLERK AT TTA4 FROM 8:30 TO 17:50
    ON MON TO FRI

Other options can be used to restrict access to certain columns and to data in specified ranges of values (e.g., to permit an employee to be able to see only her own salary history).

View Definition

The major purpose of a view is to simplify query commands, as was the case with the logical record concept in IDMS (see Figure 13-11). Consider the Patient Bill of Figure 9-8. Construction of the lines of this bill requires access to three tables: PATIENT, CHARGES, and ITEM. A view allows this association to be defined once as part of the data base, so that each user does not have to reconstruct the joining of data to produce the report. In SQL/DS, this view would be defined as

CREATE VIEW DETAILED-BILL
    AS SELECT (PATIENT-NO, ITEM-CODE, DESCRIPTION, C-
            CHARGE, PATIENT-NAME and other columns as
            required)

    FROM PATIENT, CHARGES, ITEM
    WHERE PATIENT-NO = C-PATIENT-NO
    AND ITEM-CODE = C-ITEM-CODE

The SELECT clause (same as the DML SELECT command) indicates what data elements (columns) to include in the view table. The FROM clause lists the tables involved in the view development. The WHERE clause specifies the names of the common columns used to join CHARGES to ITEM and to PATIENT.

    After this view definition is added to the data base, the DETAILED-BILL table may be used as any other (base) table. This view table is not maintained as real data; rather, it is constructed as needed automatically by the DBMS. Therefore, a view is a virtual table. A view can be a SELECTion or a PROJECTion of a base table or may simply reorder the columns of a base table. As above, it may join multiple tables together and it may contain derived (or virtual) columns. Access to this view may be restricted with GRANT and REVOKE statements. Further, view tables may not be updated; only the associated base tables are updated (then update of the view table is implicit); virtual columns in views also may not be directly updated. INGRES, on the other hand, permits some update operations to data in a view, as long as the update is confined to *one* of the base tables in the view.

Index Definition for Rapid Data Retrieval

Indexes may be created in SQL/DS to provide rapid random and sequential access to tuples. Although not directly referenced by the user, SQL/DS recognizes when existing indexes would improve query performance. Indexes can be created for both primary and secondary keys (SQL/DS makes no distinction) and on single or concatenated keys. For example, to create an index on the TREATMENT relation for T-PHYSICIAN-ID, we would

    CREATE INDEX T-PHYS
        ON TREATMENT
        (T-PHYSICIAN-ID)

and to create a concatenated key index on the CHARGES relation for C-PATIENT-NO and C-ITEM-CODE, we would

    CREATE INDEX C-PAT-ITEM
        ON CHARGES
        (C-PATIENT-NO, C-ITEM-CODE)

When tables, views, or indexes are no longer needed, the associated DROP statements may be used. For example, to delete the preceding T-PHYS index, we would use

DROP INDEX T-PHYS

The maintenance of indexes varies among different relational systems. For example, in dBASE II (see Ashton-Tate 1981), when you specify that you want to USE a data base file, you may choose to also USE *one* of the indexes on that file. Only that index will be updated by tuple additions, deletions, and modifications; other indexes have to be redefined/rebuilt after data modifications. In INGRES, all indexes are maintained with *any* data maintenance.

Further, in INGRES, a user has control over the file organization of each file. A file can be organized as a heap (new tuples added to end of file), sorted/sequential, hashed, or ISAM; a file may be dynamically reorganized, but each such reorganization requires indexes to be rebuilt (since the pointers to tuples need to be changed to refer to the new addresses).

Data Integrity Control

Integrity assertions are not implemented in SQL/DS. INGRES does provide such a data definition facility (see Relational Technology, Inc. 1982). Suppose we wanted to limit the amount of a charge to a patient. If we wanted to restrict the C-CHARGE column in the CHARGES relation to be greater than $9.99 (charges less than this are recovered as overhead) but less than $1000.00 (requires special handling), we would include the following integrity definitions in the data base description:

Define integrity on charges is charge > 9.99

Define integrity on charges is charge < 1000.00

Cross-table integrity controls can also be specified using the Visual Forms Editor (VIFRED) of INGRES. For example, if we wanted to guarantee that a C-ITEM-CODE assumed an ITEM-CODE value of only existing ITEMs, then in VIFRED the C-ITEM-CODE would be defined including the following clause:

c-item-code in item.item-code

Such integrity constraints may become very complex, but INGRES does not permit them to include any of the data aggregation functions like sum or average. These integrity constraints may be issued at any time; if issued after affected data have been entered into the data base, INGRES will not accept the integrity definition if any existing tuple violates the restriction. Subsequently, whenever new data are appended or existing data modified, INGRES will not process any such update that would result in the violation of some integrity definition.

Summary of Data Definition

The preceding remarks describe the salient, typical data definition features of relational DBMSs. As can be seen, except for some syntactical differences, DDL features are rather uniform across these systems. However, this is not true for data manipulation languages. For this reason, it will take several sections to explain these different styles. We will begin with the first DML style to be developed: relational algebra.

DATA MANIPULATION: RELATIONAL ALGEBRA

Relational data manipulation languages in general, and relational algebra languages in particular, are all special-purpose languages. That is, they are basically self-contained, new languages that are by themselves sufficient for a wide variety of data retrieval and maintenance operations. These languages are relation-at-a-time (or set) languages, in which all tuples, possibly from several relations, are manipulated in one language statement without explicit looping. Some relational DBMSs also provide reportwriters, screen- or forms-oriented languages for dialogue management and procedure development, and interfaces so that querylike statements can be embedded in host procedural languages like FORTRAN or COBOL.

The basic relational algebra commands were introduced in the first major paper published by Codd (1970) on the relational model and are common to all relational algebra systems (e.g., RIM [Boeing Commercial Airplane Company 1982] and dBASE II [Ashton-Tate 1981]). SELECT (originally called restriction), PROJECT, and the equi-JOIN were described in Codd's paper and have been discussed in Chapter 6. Other relational algebra operators are union, difference, intersection, and product.

Union.   With **union**, two tables that have corresponding columns with identical domains can be merged into one table with duplicate tuples eliminated. Two tables that have the same number of columns and for which corresponding columns have identical domains are called **union-compatible**.

Difference.   The **difference** of two tables, A−B, is a third table, C, which contains the tuples that are in A but not in B. We can only perform difference if the two tables are union-compatible. Clearly, A−B does not equal B−A. RIM (Boeing Commercial Airplane Company 1982) has such an operator, called SUBTRACT. With RIM, the difference can be restricted to selected columns, in which case only the relations defined by projection on these selected columns need to be union-compatible. Difference (SUBTRACT) is often useful to compare the difference between two tables that are the result of other data manipulation statements. For example, in the relational data base of Figure 14-1, we might first derive table A, which is a list of those patients treated by physician WILCOX, and then derive a similar table, B, for physician HENRY. The difference A−B would be those patients treated by WILCOX but not treated by HENRY.

Intersection.   The **intersection** of two tables is a third table that contains those tuples that are common to both original tables. Again, the tables must be union-compatible. RIM provides a rather general form called INTER-SECT, in which selected columns (not all columns) may be used to define common tuples. For example, assume the following two instances of relations:

	EMPLOYEE				SALARY		
NAME	DEPT	JOB		DEPT	JOB	PAY
Smith	A	Writer		A	Writer	1000
Jones	C	Prgmr		B	Writer	700
Smith	B	Writer		C	Writer	600
Franks	C	Writer				

Then the command

    INTERSECT EMPLOYEE WITH SALARY FORMING CLASSIFIED
        USING DEPT NAME JOB

would produce the following table:

CLASSIFIED		
DEPT	NAME	JOB
A	Smith	Writer
B	Smith	Writer
C	Franks	Writer

When not all the columns of the intersected tables are used, duplicate rows can result; in this case, RIM provides the DELETE DUPLICATES command for the user (if desired) to eliminate duplicate tuples.

Product.   The **product** of two relations is a table that contains tuples that are every pairwise concatenation of the original table tuples. That is, if table A has *r* rows and table B has *s* rows, then the result of the product of A with B will have *r*×*s* rows. Product is not often used because of the indiscriminate "joining" of tuples. When it is desired to concatenate tuples that only have some specified column relationships, then one of the JOIN operators is appropriate.

JOIN: The Heart of Relational Algebra

The JOIN operator requires special attention for two reasons. First, it is the most powerful of the algebra operators frequently implemented in relational DBMSs. Second, although only two types of JOINs, the equi-JOIN and the natural JOIN, appear in most relational algebra implementations (and are implied in many relational calculus implementations), other more general JOIN operators have been defined.

   JOIN is actually a combination of PRODUCT, SELECT, and PROJECT. With the equi- and natural JOINs, tuples from the two relations being joined (i.e., JOIN is a binary operator) are concatenated only if they have common values in matching columns (matching columns must have the same domains and, in some systems, must also have the same column name). With the natural JOIN (e.g., dBASE II), these common columns are redundantly kept in the resulting relation; with the equi-JOIN (e.g., RIM), only one of the redundant columns is kept. PROJECTion can be combined into this concatenation by restricting the resultant table to only certain columns. Some systems will, in this case, automatically eliminate duplicate tuples; others, like RIM, leave this to the discretion of the user to use the DELETE DUPLICATES command. Some examples of the equi-JOIN are shown in "Data Processing with the Relational Data Model" in Chapter 6.

   It is also permitted in many algebra-based systems to JOIN on other than equality conditions. Although the need for such an inequality capability is rare, the requirement may arise. Consider the following two relations:

CURRENT-SALES			PAST-SALES	
PRODUCT#	SALES-YTD		YEAR	AVG-TOTAL-SALES
1234	10000		1980	9000
3256	8000		1981	11000
5426	12000		1982	10500
6788	9500			
7392	6600			

If we wanted to know what products, to date, have exceeded prior average total product sales, in RIM we could

      JOIN CURRENT-SALES USING SALES-YTD
          WITH PAST-SALES USING AVG-TOTAL-SALES
          FORMING WINNERS WHERE GT

and the resulting table would be

WINNERS

PRODUCT#	SALES-YTD	YEAR	AVG-TOTAL-SALES
1234	10000	1980	9000
5426	12000	1980	9000
5426	12000	1981	11000
5426	12000	1982	10500
6788	9500	1980	9000

There are other types of JOINs, but they are not usually implemented in commercial packages. Refer to Codd (1970), Date (1981), and Ullman (1980) for a discussion of these other types. In addition, these references define other relational algebra operators that are also not typically implemented.

Algebra Modification Statements

Data base modification commands in relational algebra vary in name among DBMSs. In RIM, the modification commands include the following:

LOAD:	Enters additional tuples into a table.
CHANGE:	Changes existing values in tuples that satisfy a selection clause.
DELETE ROWS:	Deletes selected rows from a table.
DELETE DUPLICATES:	Removes duplicate rows from a relation.

Also found in algebra and other relational languages are commands to display table definitions. For example, in RIM, the LISTREL command lists the names of relations in the data base and LISTREL relation-name displays the complete table definitions for the named relation.

DATA MANIPULATION: RELATIONAL CALCULUS

Some authors (e.g., see Date 1981; Kroenke 1983; Ullman 1980) distinguish between three different but related forms of relational calculus: tuple calculus, domain calculus, and transform languages. INGRES (Relational Technology, Inc. 1982) and the query language on which it is based, QUEL (Stonebraker et al. 1976), are representative of tuple calculus. A few rare implementations of domain calculus exist (see Date 1981 for a discussion).

Several popular products—SQL/DS and ORACLE, for example—are based on the transform language SEQUEL (Chamberlin et al. 1976). Since INGRES, SQL/DS, ORACLE, and their imitations are most frequently found, we will discuss aspects of both tuple calculus and transform languages. Because the differences are subtle, we will not dwell on these distinctions. As pointed out by Date (p. 224), the underlying concept of both of these forms is the same. Therefore, we will freely mix examples of both INGRES and SQL/DS to illustrate relational calculus.

Structure of Relational Calculus

There are two fundamental differences between relational algebra and calculus: (1) calculus combines the SELECT and PROJECT commands into one RETRIEVE (or similar) statement that lists the column names to appear in the result (PROJECT) and uses a WHERE clause to specify the selection criteria; and (2) calculus also uses the WHERE clause to specify the intertable associations used for implicitly JOINing relations in the RETRIEVE command. Thus, whereas the JOIN operator of the relational algebra is a binary operator (and a table that is the combination of n relations must be generated in $n-1$ JOINs), one RETRIEVE command can JOIN numerous tables (implicitly). Several examples of relational calculus were given in Chapter 6.

   SQL/DS divides most data manipulation statements into three clauses:

SELECT: Lists the columns to be projected.

FROM: Identifies the tables used.

WHERE: Includes the conditions for tuple selection within a single table or between tables implicitly joined.

For example, we can display the patient charges from the CHARGES relation of Figure 14-1 for C-PATIENT-NO=1234 by

    SELECT C-CHARGE
      FROM CHARGES
      WHERE C-PATIENT-NO=1234

AND, OR, and NOT operators can be used to create complicated WHERE clauses. If the user does not wish to see duplicate tuples in the result, then SELECT DISTINCT may be used. All the columns of the referenced tables can be displayed by use of SELECT *, where * is shorthand for all columns. Functions such as COUNT, MAX, SUM, and AVG can also be used in place of column names in the SELECT clause. If the resulting tuples are desired in a sorted sequence, an ORDER BY clause may be added to the query to achieve ascending or descending sequence with major and several minor sort keys. A GROUP BY clause can be used to have functions performed on groups of rows with common values. INGRES has similar constructs.

We can produce a list of the total charges per patient for major medical items (item codes in the range 500–800) by

SELECT C-ITEM-CODE, SUM(C-CHARGE), C-PATIENT-NO
 FROM CHARGES
 WHERE C-ITEM-CODE > =500
  AND C-ITEM-CODE < =800
 GROUP BY C-PATIENT-NO
 ORDER BY C-PATIENT-NO

Here the GROUP BY clause is used to specify subtotal control breaks. This query will display a subtotal of C-CHARGE for each patient, as well as producing a grand total. The ORDER BY phrase simply sorts the output into patient number sequence for easier scanning. Some relational languages require ORDER BY to accompany each GROUP BY phrase. This is used to sort tuples together with the same GROUP BY value to facilitate subtotal calculations.

Functions may also be used in WHERE clauses. If we wish to display all the patient numbers for patients who have had charges above the average charge, we would

SELECT C-PATIENT-NO, C-CHARGE
 FROM CHARGES
 WHERE C-CHARGE > AVG(C-CHARGE)

Implicit JOINs in Relational Calculus

Queries may also be written in SQL/DS that use multiple relations. SQL provides two different syntaxes for formulating such queries: the subquery technique involves placing one query (SELECT, FROM, WHERE) within another query; the joining technique uses one SELECT, FROM, WHERE and uses the WHERE clause in specifying the linking columns. This second approach is essentially identical to that found in INGRES.

Suppose we wanted to display the ITEM-CODE and DESCRIPTION for all work performed on PATIENT-NO 1234 in Mountain View Community Hospital. In SQL's subquery approach, we would

SELECT ITEM-CODE, DESCRIPTION
 FROM ITEM
 WHERE ITEM-CODE=
  (SELECT C-ITEM-CODE FROM CHARGES
   WHERE C-PATIENT-NO=1234)

This approach is appropriate when only data from the relation in the outer query are to be displayed. This nesting can be many levels deep.

The joining technique is appropriate when data from several relations are to be retrieved and displayed. Suppose we augment the preceding query so that we also want to display the actual CHARGE values for the specified patient. In this case, more than just the linking column is required from the CHARGES table; thus, the subquery approach is not feasible. The joining approach would be

> SELECT ITEM-CODE, DESCRIPTION, C-CHARGE
>   FROM ITEM, CHARGES
>   WHERE C-PATIENT-ID=1234
>   AND C-ITEM-CODE=ITEM-CODE

As already mentioned, with only slight syntactical changes, this joining approach is identical to the transform language format in INGRES. One difference between INGRES and SQL/DS relates to what the DBMS does with the result of a SELECT (or RETRIEVE in the case of INGRES). With SQL/DS, the result is simply displayed, whereas in INGRES, the user has the option to name a new table into which the results are to be temporarily stored. This resultant table can then be manipulated like any other table (it is essentially a dynamically created view), but unless explicitly SAVEd by the user, it will disappear after some period (usually seven days) when a PURGEDB command is issued.

Special Retrieval Features

The SQL/DS joining and the INGRES transform approaches permit the construction of some very long WHERE clauses to implicitly join many relations. Suppose we wanted to know the telephone numbers of the physicians who have treated the patient in location with telephone extension X4372 and who was discharged on September 30, 1983. To answer this query, we must access the CONTROL, PATIENT, TREATMENT, and PHYSICIAN relations, in that sequence. In the INGRES syntax, we would write this query as:

> RANGE OF C IS CONTROL
> RANGE OF P IS PATIENT
> RANGE OF T IS TREATMENT
> RANGE OF H IS PHYSICIAN
> RETRIEVE (H.PHYSICIAN-PHONE)
>   WHERE C.EXTENSION=4372 AND
>   C.LOCATION=P.LOCATION AND
>   P.DATE=DISCHARGED=093083 AND
>   P.PATIENT#=T.PATIENT# AND
>   T.PHYSICIAN-ID=H.PHYSICIAN-ID

In INGRES, the RANGE statement is used to define a shorthand reference to table names (more precisely, the range variable stands for a set of qualified tuples). The first WHERE condition selects the proper location tuple; the second WHERE condition links the selected location to the patients who have been accommodated at this location; the third condition restricts these patients to those (probably one) who were (was) discharged on the desired date; the fourth condition finds the treatments performed on these (this) patient(s); and the fifth condition accesses the physician tuple for each of these treatments.

SQL/DS has two special operators that can be useful for complex qualifications. In WHERE clauses, the logical operators EXISTS and NOT EXISTS restrict tuple display to situations in which subqueries have and have not, respectively, any qualified tuples. For example, suppose we wanted to know the patient numbers of any patient that has been charged for both treatments 307 and 807. We would write this query as follows in SQL/DS:

```
SELECT  DISTINCT C-PATIENT#
FROM    CHARGES A
WHERE   EXISTS
        SELECT *
        FROM CHARGES B
        WHERE A.C-PATIENT#=B.C-PATIENT#
        AND A.C-ITEM-CODE=307 AND B.C-ITEM-CODE=807
```

In this example, both the outer query and the subquery refer to the same relation, CHARGES. To distinguish tuples from each, SQL permits assignment of unique names, A and B. Here, A and B are similar to range variables in INGRES. The subquery will be true if the same patient (qualified by the first WHERE clause of the subquery) has two CHARGES tuples, one for item 307 and another for item 807 (qualified by the second WHERE condition of the subquery).

Although not exclusively for retrieval support, relational systems frequently have elementary data dictionary functions to help a user recall the definitions of data. For example, with INGRES, a user may issue the following functions:

CATALOGDB: Lists the names of data bases created by the user.

HELP: Lists the names of relations in the data base currently being used.

HELP relation: Lists the column names and associated data formats for the specified relation as well as general relation statistics such as number of existing tuples and file organization.

Data Modification in Relational Calculus

The SQL/DS data maintenance operators are:

INSERT: Places a new row in a table.

UPDATE: Changes values in one or more qualified rows of a table.

DELETE: Deletes one or more qualified rows of a table.

INGRES has, in addition, a COPY command that permits tuples to be transferred between data base tables and external files. COPY is useful for batch loading of data, where the external file, containing new tuples, was created by a separate data entry or text editor program.

In SQL/DS, a new tuple could be added to the CHARGES relation by

    INSERT INTO CHARGES
        VALUES (1234,300,220.00)

In addition, tuples can be copied from one table to another. Suppose there were also an OUT-PATIENT relation in the data base of Figure 14-1, for patients receiving treatment without occupying a hospital sleeping room. When such a patient is admitted for overnight, we could copy (without destroying) the patient's demographic data by

    INSERT INTO PATIENT
        SELECT PATIENT-NO, ...
        FROM OUT-PATIENT
        WHERE PATIENT-NO = 1234

Whole groups of tuples can be copied when the WHERE clause involves secondary keys.

Similarly, tuples can be deleted individually or in groups. In addition, deletion must be done with care when tuples from several relations are involved. For example, if we delete a PATIENT tuple before deleting associated CHARGES, we will have an integrity violation. Suppose we wish to delete all treatments performed by physicians in a given department (these physicians have the same phone extension, X3422). In this case, we must first delete the TREATMENT tuples before we can delete the PHYSICIANs. Therefore, we would

    DELETE TREATMENT
        WHERE T-PHYSICIAN-ID =
            SELECT PHYSICIAN-ID
            FROM PHYSICIAN
            WHERE PHYSICIAN-PHONE = 'X3422'

    DELETE PHYSICIAN
        WHERE PHYSICIAN-PHONE = 'X3422'

To update data in SQL/DS, we must inform the DBMS what relation, columns, and tuples are involved. Suppose an incorrect charge were entered for patient no. 1234 and item no. 307. The following SQL/DS UPDATE statement would institute an appropriate correction:

```
        UPDATE CHARGES
          SET C-CHARGE=322.50
          WHERE C-PATIENT-NO=1234
          AND C-ITEM-CODE=307
```

Host Language Interface

Many relational DBMSs not only have a self-contained algebra or calculus language, but also permit access to the data base from a host procedural language. An interesting phenomenon has occurred: network DBMSs, designed primarily to work with procedural languages like COBOL and FORTRAN, have been expanded to include relational calculuslike query languages; and relational systems, originally designed with stand-alone query languages, have been enhanced to include procedural language interfaces.

Both SQL/DS and INGRES have host language interfaces. We will demonstrate this capability with the INGRES FORTRAN interface. This capability is called EQUEL, for Embedded QUEL; QUEL is the calculus language that is the basis for INGRES's query language. A programmer simply includes some query-language-like statements in a FORTRAN program, indicating each with a special symbol, ##, at the beginning of each query line. A precompiler translates the FORTRAN program with query statements in it into standard FORTRAN code by replacing the query commands with correctly argumented FORTRAN CALL statements to the INGRES DBMS. The translated program is then given to the standard FORTRAN compiler, as with any FORTRAN program. This process is very similar to the use of precompilers for network DMLs.

Suppose we wanted to write a FORTRAN subroutine to retrieve a PATIENT tuple and print the patient's name and address on the standard output device. In EQUEL, this could be done for PATIENT-NO 1234 in the following way:

```
        SUBROUTINE GETPATIENT
##      DECLARE
##      INTEGER        IPATNO
##      CHARACTER*30   PATNAM
##      CHARACTER*30   PATADD
        ID=1234
##      RETRIEVE (PATNAM=PATIENT.PATIENT-NAME,
##               PATADD=PATIENT.PATIENT-ADDR)
##        WHERE PATIENT.PATIENT-NO=ID
##        {
        WRITE(6,100)PATNAM,PATADD
100     FORMAT(' THE ADDRESS OF ', A, ' IS ', A)
##        }
        END
```

This capability to access a relational data base by a procedural language can be important. Often, the relational query language (calculus or algebra) is not capable of summarizing or printing data in the format we desire. Use of a procedural language will give us this ability, and yet we will still be able to use the high-level data retrieval facilities of a relational language.

DATA MANIPULATION: TABULAR/GRAPHICAL

Zloof (1977) has developed a unique form of relational data manipulation language called QUERY-BY-EXAMPLE, or QBE (IBM Corp. 1980). Not only is it visually quite different, but several research studies (e.g., Greenblatt and Waxman 1978; Thomas and Gould 1975) have also shown that even with relatively little training, student subjects formulated QBE queries in less time and with greater accuracy than did subjects using SQL or a relational algebra-based language.

A user interacts with QBE on a cathode-ray tube (CRT) terminal by filling in values in different cells of a table template. QBE displays a skeleton table, and the user enters values as indicated below.

Table name here	Column name here	Column name here
	Condition or examples in here	Condition or examples in here

The symbol P. may be entered in these cells to indicate what the user would like printed. For example, if we forget what columns there are in the PATIENT table, we can complete the table template as follows:

PATIENT P.			

QBE would respond with

PATIENT	PATIENT-NO	PATIENT-NAME	PATIENT-ADDR

If we do not know the names of any tables in the data base, we simply enter P. in the table name cell of the skeleton; QBE will then display under that column the names of the tables in the data base.

Suppose we wanted to determine what patients had been charged for item 307. With QBE, we would formulate this query by indicating the condition directly in a table. This particular query would be formulated as

CHARGES	C-PATIENT-NO	C-ITEM-CODE	C-CHARGE
	P.	307	

The result would be a display of a similar table, with only the C-PATIENT-NO data column, listing all the patient numbers for people who have had a charge for item 307. If we wanted patients charged for item 307 or 807, we would complete a table template with two rows (and an implied OR logical operator between these rows) as follows:

CHARGES	C-PATIENT-NO	C-ITEM-CODE	C-CHARGE
	P.	307	
	P.	807	

We can also write queries that involve AND conditions. Consider the situation in which we want to know if anyone has been charged between $550 AND $600 for item 807. To answer this in QBE, we would input as follows:

CHARGES	C-PATIENT-NO	C-ITEM-CODE	C-CHARGE
	P.2222	807	>550
	2222	807	<600

The second condition line specifies finding all CHARGES tuples with item code 807 and with a charge less than $600; the example value 2222 in the second line stands for whatever patient number is stored in a qualified tuple. The first condition line says print this patient number if the charge is also greater than $550. The example patient number is used to link these two joint conditions together.

Data maintenance is performed in a similar fashion. For example, we indicate update with a U. instead of a P. under the table name. To illustrate, if we wanted to increase the charge 10% for all people who have been charged for item 807, we would complete the template as follows:

CHARGES	C-PATIENT-NO	C-ITEM-CODE	C-CHARGE
U.		807	$\underline{500} \times 1.1$

In this case, the item underlined is an "example" of an existing value for C-CHARGE. QBE will take whatever value actually exists and multiply it by 1.1. It is from the use of such "example" data that QBE gets its name.

Other more complex queries are possible in QBE. Suppose we knew that the patient with number 1234 had been charged for item 450 and we wanted to know if anyone else had been charged more for this item than had patient 1234. This would be written in QBE as

CHARGES	C-PATIENT-NO	C-ITEM-CODE	C-CHARGE
	1234	450	$\underline{500}$
	P.	450	$> \underline{500}$

In this situation, we do not even need to know exactly what patient 1234 was charged for item 450; we simply use an example to relate the two tuples.

We can also pose even more complex conditions. When these conditions are too difficult to state by linking different condition rows, QBE supports a Condition Box, separate from the table template, for entry of such conditional statements. Refer to Zloof (1977) for an example of this capability.

As a final example of the capabilities of QBE, we will illustrate how two tables can be linked and queries written that place conditions on the related tables. Suppose we wanted to know the descriptions of the items for which patient 1234 had been charged. This query involves both the CHARGES and the ITEM tables. There is a way to get QBE to display two table templates. We would then fill these templates in as follows:

CHARGES	C-PATIENT-NO	C-ITEM-CODE	C-CHARGE
	1234	$\underline{333}$	

ITEM	ITEM-CODE	DESCRIPTION
	$\underline{333}$	P.

Here again, the example item code of 333 is used to link tuples.

QBE is especially interesting when we are using a color CRT. QBE is designed to highlight column names in different colors, depending on their usage (condition, example, printing, and so on).

RELATIONAL-LIKE DBMSs

There are numerous data base management systems that, although they are not really considered relational, have many relational characteristics. The purpose of this section is to introduce briefly a few of these relational-like DBMSs as examples of this class of DBMS.

NOMAD (see National CSS 1981) is available from National CSS as both a service on the NCSS time-sharing computer service and as a purchased product to be run at an organization's own data center. NOMAD uses a combination of relational and hierarchical data structures, so it cannot be classified as a pure relational system. With relational tables, joining is done dynamically as required to satisfy queries. When data will be frequently accessed in different tables that have nested 1:*M* relationships, the data base designer can define these files to have explicit pointers linking masters (owners) to segments (members). This allows the data base designer to structure the data base efficiently. The same data base may contain both relational tables and hierarchical structures.

NOMAD supports a variety of relational operators. The basic NOMAD DML command is LIST, similar to the RETRIEVE command in INGRES. With LIST, the user may project a table on specified columns and qualify which tuples to display in a WHERE clause. The LIST command is combined with the NOMAD relational operators to perform more complex manipulations. For example, if we wanted to list the items and their descriptions for which patient 1234 had been charged in Mountain View Community Hospital, we would in NOMAD say,

```
LIST BY C-ITEM-CODE WHERE C-PATIENT-NO=1234
     EXTRACT MATCH
   FROM ITEM ITEM-CODE
   ITEM-CODE DESCRIPTION
```

The EXTRACT MATCH phrase identifies the equivalent of a JOIN and the BY clause on the original table (CHARGES), and the column listed in the FROM clause are the columns to be matched for joining.

NOMAD also has graphics capabilities to plot data, and it can work with arrays and produce textual reports with data base contents embedded in the text. NOMAD can even be used to answer "what if" questions from the data base. By entering SAVE OFF, any changes to the data base are not permanent and will be undone at the end of the user's session. NOMAD can also calculate simple descriptive statistics (mean, median, and so on) and perform multiple regression, t-tests, chi-square tests, and others. Because such a variety of data management, analysis, and display functions are integrated into one high-level language, NOMAD can best be classified as a fourth-generation language, 4GL; like many other fourth-generation languages, a relational-like view of data is a feature.

Other systems, like Model 204 and ADABAS (see Computer Corporation of America 1982; Software AG of North America 1981), are also relational-like. These two products, in particular, view a data base as a set of inverted files or lists (see Chapter 5). Although many relational DBMSs also use inverted lists (key indexes) to support rapid access to data based on content (the tuple selection clause), many inverted-file-type systems restrict certain language commands to be used only when a data item is indexed. For example, Model 204 will use the inverted indexes only if *all* data elements mentioned in a FOR WHICH (WHERE-type) clause are indexed. Most relational systems would use whatever indexes were helpful and then resolve the rest of the qualifications after retrieving only the records found from the index searches.

Another difference between ADABAS and Model 204 and a relational DBMS is that ADABAS and Model 204 permit the definition of repeating groups in a record. This, of course, violates one of the basic rules of the relational data model, that of each column being a simple, single-valued data element.

ADABAS also differs from a relational system in that explicit linking of relations must be defined. In the relational model, when two relations have a domain in common, these relations may be joined without the DBMS being told about this commonality when the data base is defined. In ADABAS, however, data elements that are to be used to associate two files must both be indexed. For example, both ITEM-CODE and C-ITEM-CODE would have to be indexed to find associated records in the CHARGES and ITEM files. Further, C-ITEM-CODE would not only have to be defined to be a search key (the designation for indexed), but would also have to be declared as "coupled," since it is used to "couple" the CHARGES file to the ITEM file. That is, the record type that is the "many" member of a 1:*M* relationship requires a special indexing designation.

ADABAS organizes indexed data in an ingenious fashion, as depicted in Figure 14-2. Indexes themselves do not point directly to data records. Rather, indexes refer to an internal sequence number, ISN. This ISN is a cell number in a table that matches each ISN to a pointer to the associated data record. In this way, if a record changes physical position (e.g., because of file reorganization or because of file rewriting stemming from variable-length record changes), only the ISN table, called the associator, must be changed. Thus, no index needs to be updated except when records are added or deleted or when key values are changed.

Other systems, like FOCUS, RAMIS II, and DATACOM/DB (see Information Builders 1980; Mathematica, Inc. 1980; Applied Data Research 1976), can be classified as relational-like. The features of these systems will not be

Figure 14-2
ADABAS general data
base organization.

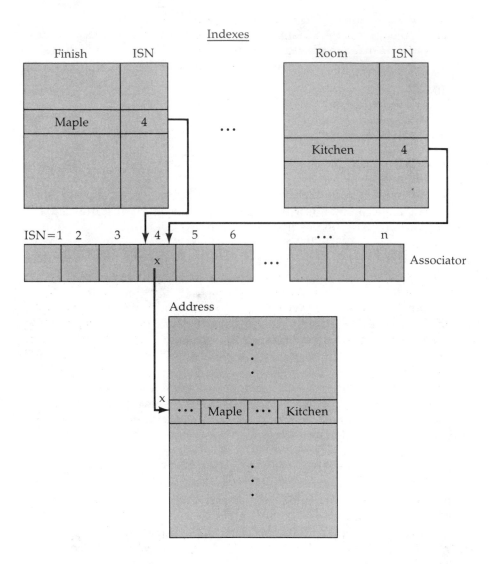

reviewed here. What is important is that we can achieve some of the benefits of data independence found in the relational data model or some of the ease of data retrieval found in relational query languages even in data base management systems that are not purely relational.

It is our suggestion that claims or labels are not as precise in practice as may be depicted in this or other textbooks. What is important for a prospective DBMS user is to know what his or her data processing requirements are and to determine what data modeling and manipulation will meet those needs. Whether a DBMS is hierarchical, network, relational, relational-like, or whatever is not the real problem.

SUMMARY

Relational DBMSs have been characterized in this chapter as viewing data in flat files or tables; manipulating data using commands that are, or are equivalent to, the relational algebra operators of PROJECT, SELECT, and JOIN; and providing an implementation-independent access to data (e.g., independent of the existence or nonexistence of key indexes).

Relational systems were criticized for many years because of their relative inefficiency compared to network systems. However, with recent performance improvements and with judicious use of key indexes, a data base designer is now able to construct relational data bases that can be efficiently processed. Host language interfaces to relational systems can be used to provide the detailed data processing controls still necessary for customized programming. Relational query languages can be used to develop a variety of information systems, but they are still most frequently used for information retrieval applications. Increasingly, relational systems are being used to develop and iteratively evolve all types of information systems.

It is our suggestion that no one DBMS architecture, even relational, will become dominant. First, different applications require different data management capabilities. Second, different organizations have various data processing traditions and skills that will naturally help to select different technologies. And finally, there is no reason to doubt that another Charles Bachman or Ted Codd is already at work on a new generation of DBMS. Some insights into the trends in the data base field will be presented in the next chapter.

CHAPTER REVIEW

Review Questions

1. Define each of the following terms:

   a. view
   b. relational algebra
   c. relational calculus
   d. host language interface
   e. index
   f. integrity assertion
   g. relational algebra intersection operator

   h. equi-JOIN
   i. natural JOIN
   j. SQL/DS subquery
   k. SQL/DS joining
   l. relational-like
   m. internal sequence number (ISN)

2. Explain the following statement regarding SQL/DS: Any query that can be written using the subquery approach can also be written using the joining approach, but not vice versa.

3. Explain the difference between features like LISTREL in RIM and HELP in INGRES and the capabilities of a data dictionary/directory.

4. Explain why JOIN is called a binary operator.

5. Drawing on material covered in prior chapters, explain the factors to be considered in deciding whether to create a key index for a table.

6. Explain why it is sometimes necessary to prefix a column name with a table name in query language statements.

7. Explain the difference between the INTERSECT and JOIN relational operators.

8. Explain why the DELETE DUPLICATES operator is necessary in RIM.

9. Explain the purpose of the RANGE statement in INGRES.

10. The section "Data Manipulation: Tabular/Graphical" illustrates two queries, one for an implied OR logical operator between the two rows of the query template and one for an implied AND logical operator between the two rows of the query template. What construct was used to distinguish between ORing and ANDing the conditions in two rows?

11. What is the benefit of the ISN in ADABAS?

Problems and Exercises

1. Suggest several alternative ways for a relational DBMS, like SQL/DS, to handle the ALTER TABLE command. Consider the possibility of both adding and deleting columns.

2. Write a relational-algebra-like query to answer the following question from the Mountain View Community Hospital data base of Figure 14-1: What physicians have performed a tonsillectomy?

3. Write a relational-calculus-like query to answer the question from Problem 2.

4. Write relational algebra commands to answer the following question from the data base of Figure 14-1: What patients (display PATIENT-NAME) have been charged for the item TELEVISION?

5. Write relational calculus commands to answer the question from Problem 4.

6. Show how you would complete QBE skeleton templates to answer the question of Problem 2.

7. Write an SQL/DS query to answer the following question about Mountain View Community Hospital: What patients (display PATIENT-NO) are being treated by both Drs. Wilcox and Franklin?

8. Write integrity assertions for INGRES to restrict DATE-DISCHARGED in Figure 14-1 to values greater than DATE-ADMITTED for each patient in the data base.

9. Use the SUBTRACT operator of RIM to find those physicians that have not yet treated any patients at Mountain View Community Hospital. *Hint*: The structure of SUBTRACT is very similar to the syntax of INTERSECT.

10. Assume that the ITEM relation of Figure 14-1 is altered to also include STD-CHG, the standard charge for an item. Write the RIM commands to display the patient numbers for those patients that have been charged above standard.

References

Applied Data Research. 1976. *DATACOM/DB: User's Guide*. Dallas, Tex.: Applied Data Research.

Ashton-Tate. 1981. *dBASE II User's Manual*. Culver City, Calif.: Ashton-Tate.

Banerjee, J., Richard I. Baum, and David K. Hsiao. 1978. "Concepts and Capabilities of a Database Computer." *ACM-TODS* (December): 347–384.

Boeing Commercial Airplane Company. 1982. *User Guide: RIM 5.0*. Seattle, Wash.: Boeing Commercial Airplane Company.

Britton-Lee Corporation. 1982. *IDM 500*. Los Angeles: Britton-Lee Corporation.

Chamberlin, D.D., M.M. Astrahan, K.P. Eswaran, P.P. Griffiths, R.A. Lorie, J.W. Mehl, P. Reisner, and B.W. Wade. 1976. "SEQUEL 2: A Unified Approach to Data Definition, Manipulation and Control." *IBM Journal of Research and Development* 20 (November): 560–574.

Codd, E.F. 1970. "A Relational Model of Data for Large Shared Data Banks." *Communications of the ACM* 13 (June): 377–387.

———. 1982. "Relational Database: A Practical Foundation for Productivity." *Communications of the ACM* 25 (February): 109–117.

Computer Corporation of America. 1982. *Model 204: User Language Manual*. Cambridge, Mass.: Computer Corporation of America.

Date, C.J. 1981. *An Introduction to Database Systems*. 3d ed. Reading, Mass.: Addison-Wesley.

Greenblatt, D., and J. Waxman. 1978. "A Study of Three Database Query Languages." In *Database: Improving Usability and Responsiveness*, ed. B. Shneiderman. New York: Academic Press, 1978.

IBM Corp. 1980. *Query-by-Example: Terminal User's Guide*. Form SH20-2078-1. Irving, Tex.: IBM Corp.

———. 1982. *SQL/Data System: Concepts and Facilities*. Form GH24-5013-1. Endicott, N.Y.: IBM Corp.

Information Builders. 1980. *FOCUS: Query Language Primer*. New York: Information Builders.

Kim, Won. 1979. "Relational Database Systems." *ACM-Computing Surveys* 11 (September): 185–211.

Kroenke, D. 1983. *Database Processing*. 2nd ed. Chicago: Science Research Associates, Inc.

Mathematica, Inc. 1980. *RAMIS II*. Princeton, N.J.: Mathematica, Inc.

National CSS. 1981. *NOMAD 2 Reference Manual*. Norwalk, Conn.: National CSS.

Relational Technology, Inc. 1982. *INGRES Reference Manual* (Version 1.4, VAX/VMS). July. Berkeley, Calif.: Relational Technology.

Schuster, S.A., H.B. Nguyen, E.A. Ozkarahan, and K.C. Smith. 1978. "RAP.2—An Associative Processor for Data Bases." *Proceedings of the Fifth Annual IEEE Symposium on Computer Architecture*. April.

Software AG of North America. 1981. *ADABAS Reference Manual*. Reston, Va.: Software AG of North America.

Stonebraker, M.R., Eugene Wong, Peter Kreps, and Gerald Held. 1976. "The Design and Implementation of INGRES." *ACM-TODS* 1 (September): 189–222.

Su, S., and G. Lipovski. 1975. "CASSM: A Cellular System for Very Large Data Base." In *Proceedings of the First Very Large Data Base Conference*. September: 456–472.

Thomas, J.C., and J.D. Gould. 1975. "A Psychological Study of Query by Example." In *Proceedings of National Computer Conference*. AFIPS Press.

Ullman, J.D. 1980. *Principles of Database Systems*. Potomac, Md.: Computer Science Press.

Zloof, M.M. 1977. "Query-by-Example: A Data Base Language." *IBM Systems Journal* 16 (4): 324–343.

## 15

Emerging Data Base Management Opportunities and Issues

INTRODUCTION TO THE FUTURE

The previous chapters of this book have concentrated on developing the principles of data management required for information systems analysis, design, and programming. We have tried in these chapters to illustrate these principles through the major data base management system technologies now in practice. Although the principles of data modeling and administration covered here should prevail well into the future, the data management technologies now in use are inevitably being replaced or enhanced by emerging equipment and software and ingenious combinations of DBMS with other technologies. The purpose of this chapter is to introduce some of these emerging technologies and to outline their role in effective data management in the future.

The technologies to be discussed in this chapter are distributed data bases, data base computers, personal or microcomputer data base management systems, and the Spatial Data Management System. Our goal is not to give a comprehensive review of these technologies, because each is a major topic itself. Rather, we present the salient features of these technologies and the opportunities and issues that these technologies bring to the data base management arena.

The technologies that we will review here are not speculative, but already exist in limited practice or are used but not well understood. All, we believe, are a definite part of the near future of data management in organizations.

Because these technologies are emerging, they are constantly evolving. Therefore, it would be useful to seek out additional information on these topics, since the actual implementation of these technologies is likely to change. However, the salient features, opportunities, and issues should remain the same.

DISTRIBUTED DATA BASES

It is important to distinguish between distributed and decentralized data bases. A **distributed data base** is one that is stored on secondary memory devices (usually disk) attached to *several* electronically connected computers and from which a user at one of the computers can, with varying degrees of ease, access data stored at any of the computers. The computers may be relatively far apart geographically, or they may be in adjacent rooms or even in the same room. The point is that there are two or more connected computers involved in managing parts of a single data base and that a single program can access data stored at the multiple nodes of the computer network.

A **decentralized data base** is a data base stored on secondary memory devices at separate, independent computers. A user at one computer cannot access in one computer program or query via one DBMS data stored at the multiple sites or nodes. Thus, although we can consider the data conceptually as one data base, a decentralized data base is really implemented as a set of data bases.

Structure of a Distributed DBMS Environment

To have a distributed data base, there must be a distributed data base management system that coordinates the access to data at the various nodes. Although each node may also have a DBMS managing the local data base at that site, a master DBMS is required to determine, from a distributed data dictionary, the location from which to retrieve the requested data; compose the response to the data request; possibly translate a request from one node using a local DBMS into the proper request to another node using possibly a different DBMS and different data model; and provide security, concurrency and deadlock control, recovery, and other data management functions across the various parts of the data base.

The general architecture of a distributed computer system with a distributed DBMS capability is depicted in Figure 15-1. This environment consists of local data bases with associated DBMSs at these sites. Interfaces between the local DBMS and the distributed DBMS may be necessary to translate data requests from a local syntax and data model to a meta or intermediate level (or vice versa) when a mixed DBMS configuration is supported. The nucleus of the distributed DBMS coordinates the internode communication of retrieval requests and data.

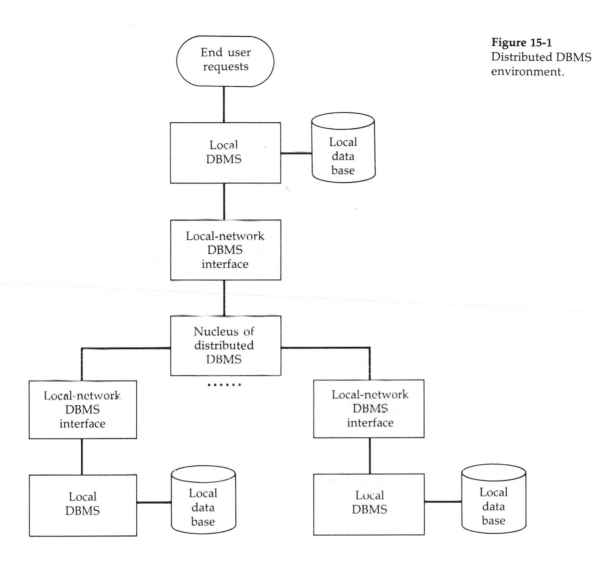

Figure 15-1
Distributed DBMS
environment.

Objectives and Hazards of a Distributed Data Base

The objective of a distributed DBMS is to provide data management services as transparently as possible so that the user does not realize that data are being accessed from multiple locations. That is, the data base should appear to be stored at one site, managed by the local DBMS at the user's node. Further, data maintenance from one site should be performed as if the data to be updated, added, or deleted were stored at only that site, whereas, in fact, it may be at one or more sites.

Distributed data bases permit both localized and centralized management in an organization. They reduce data communications traffic by storing data close to the location most frequently using the data, but also support convenient consolidation of data across locations. This reduced communications time should have a positive impact on processing throughput and response time. Data are more consistent, since a single DBMS coordinates synchronized updating of redundant data. Distributed systems permit specialization of hardware and DBMS software at each node to best suit the needs at that site without sacrificing integration of the information resource of the organization. Prudent redundant storage of data can achieve greater reliability and availability, since users are not dependent on data from only one site.

The achievement of these objectives does not come without significant costs and hazards. First, current distributed DBMS technologies permit less freedom of choice than may be hoped regarding the mixing of DBMSs at different sites. For example, the IDMS Distributed Database System supports only IDMS running at each site on an IBM or IBM-compatible computer. Second, distributed systems are expensive and not widely used; a user of a distributed DBMS is at the forefront of DBMS technology, with all the concomitant risks. Finally, complex design issues must be faced in order to provide an efficient distributed data base. These issues include network design, placement of data at nodes, replication of data, and how to process programs that require data at different sites.

Distributed Data Base Design Issues

There are four basic data placement designs. In a **centralized** system, a single copy of the data base files is stored at a centralized site, from which users at the remote sites may retrieve data. This alternative, frequently listed with the other choices, does not fit our definition and will not be considered further.

In a **partitioned** system, each network node is allocated disjoint subsets of the organization's data base, and access to data can be prohibited (purposely or as a result of network breakdown) by limiting access to the node at which the data are stored. A partitioned system can be appropriate when storage space is limited at some sites, but storage of some local data can greatly reduce communication costs and response delays.

In a **replicated** system, each network site retains a complete copy of the data base, and the distributed DBMS must extensively coordinate the synchronized updating of data. This approach is frequently used when infrequent updating is sufficient for data processing applications; updates at one node are periodically broadcast to other nodes. This strategy has great reliability, since reasonably current data can be accessed from any location, and has high data retrieval efficiency, since accessing is localized. The cost, of course, is for significant storage space.

In a **clustered** system, each node may have unique subsets of the data base as well as selected redundant copies of some files or subsets of files. For example, the Detroit office may contain customer records for contacts in that region, whereas computers at other offices contain their own regional customer data. The corporate headquarters may contain another customer file of general demographic customer data, extracted from the local data bases, for purposes of aggregate sales forecasting.

Date (1983) has developed an excellent yet simple example of the implications of another of the issues mentioned here: query processing. Consider the following situation adapted from Date (pp. 303–306):

A simplified procurement (relational) data base has the three relations

SUPPLIER(SUPPLIER#,CITY)   10,000 records, stored in Detroit

PART(PART#,COLOR)   100,000 records, stored in Chicago

SHIPMENT(SUPPLIER#,PART#) 1,000,000 records, stored in Detroit

and a query (in SQL/DS) to list the supplier numbers for Cleveland suppliers of red parts:

```
SELECT SUPPLIER.SUPPLIER#
FROM   SUPPLIER, SHIPMENT, PART
WHERE SUPPLIER.CITY        = 'Cleveland'
   AND  SUPPLIER.SUPPLIER# = SHIPMENT.SUPPLIER#
   AND  SHIPMENT.PART#     = PART.PART#
   AND  PART.COLOR         = 'Red'
```

Further, suppose that each record in each relation is 100 characters long, there are 10 red parts, a history of 100,000 shipments from Cleveland, and a negligible query computation time compared with communication time. Also, assume a communication system with a data transmission rate of 10,000 characters per second and a 1-second access delay to send a message from one node to another.

Date identifies six plausible query-processing strategies for this situation and develops the associated communication times; these strategies and times are summarized in Table 15-1. This example clearly indicates that choice of a poor strategy over a good strategy can result in much slower communication times. Although the last strategy is best, the fourth strategy may also be acceptable.

In general, this example would indicate that it is often advisable to break a query in a distributed data base environment into components that are isolated at different sites, then determine which site has the potential to yield the fewest number of qualified tuples/records, and then move this result to another site where additional work is performed. Obviously, more than two sites require even more complex analyses and more complicated heuristics to guide query processing. Bernstein et al. (1981) contains an excellent discussion of optimization of query processing in probably the most sophisticated distributed DBMS now available, SDD-1 from Computer Corporation of America. This vendor also has a videotape that summarizes

Table 15-1
Query-Processing Strategies in a Distributed Data Base Environment
(Adapted from Date 1983).

Method	Time
Move PART relation to Detroit and process whole query at Detroit computer.	16.7 minutes
Move SUPPLIER and SHIPMENT to Chicago and process whole query at Chicago computer.	28 hours
JOIN SUPPLIER and SHIPMENT at the Detroit computer, PROJECT these down to only tuples for Cleveland suppliers, and then for each of these, check at the Chicago computer to determine if associated PART is red.	2.3 days
PROJECT PART at the Chicago computer down to just the red items and for each, check at the Detroit computer to see if there is some SHIPMENT involving that PART and a Cleveland SUPPLIER.	20 seconds
JOIN SUPPLIER and SHIPMENT at the Detroit computer and PROJECT just SUPPLIER# and PART# for only Cleveland SUPPLIERs and move this qualified projection to Chicago for matching with red PARTs.	16.7 minutes
Select just red PARTs at the Chicago computer and move the result to Detroit for matching with Cleveland SUPPLIERs.	1 second

the features of this unique product. Compared to most other distributed DBMSs, SDD-1 does permit a limited mixture of different DBMSs to be operating at the different network nodes.

Summary of Distributed Data Bases

Distributed data base management, in some form, is a necessity in the data-communications-oriented world of the future. Recent introductions of DBMSs on personal computers that link a PC data base to an associated mainframe data base (see "Microcomputer DBMSs") provide a new dimension to distributed data bases. Whatever the form, distributed data bases will be necessary in many environments that are not efficient enough or reliable enough with only centralized data base processing. The discussion here should provide the basic principles and issues necessary to understand this emerging technology in data base management.

DATA BASE COMPUTERS

It is common practice to use specialized front-end communication processors to off-load computer network communication functions from a general-purpose host computer. Not only have these functions been separated into distinct machines, but these separate machines have been uniquely designed to handle the specific type of data processing in telecommunications. Simply from the viewpoint of symmetry, a back-end data base computer would seem able to handle the specialized and high-volume activity of data base processing.

It is not unusual in large data centers today to find separate general-purpose computers performing the bulk of the data base processing, especially data inquiry. Periodically, files are transferred to such separate, independent computers from others that perform transaction processing and data base maintenance. The growth in data base size and processing activity, estimated at 3% per month (Champine 1977), creates an expensive data processing burden that one centralized computer cannot safely handle by itself.

A major problem with this use of a general-purpose computer for data base processing is cost. Epstein (1983) has reported that typical mainframe computer technology costs from $100,000 to $400,000 per million of instructions per second (MIPS). However, with the use of special-purpose data base computers connected to a general-purpose host, data base processing cost can be reduced to as little as $10,000 per MIPS on a data base computer. Because of their special architecture to handle data base searching and query processing, data base computers can search as many as 30,000 records per second. Experience has shown that the use of data base computers is, in general, justified when an organization exhibits a steady, high-volume stream of data base transactions.

Data Base Computer Environment

Figure 15-2 depicts the difference between a conventional DBMS environment and a DBMS in a data base computer environment. We will discuss several alternative implementations of this general picture shortly, but basically the data base computer contains a customized operating system and the run-time components of the DBMS. Data dictionary, data definition, and other DBMS functions may or may not be moved to the data base computer (DBC).

Operationally, with the DBC present, data manipulation commands or DBMS calls are transferred via a high-speed data channel to the DBC as encountered in an application program in the host. These commands are interpreted and queued for processing in the DBC. The data base is searched

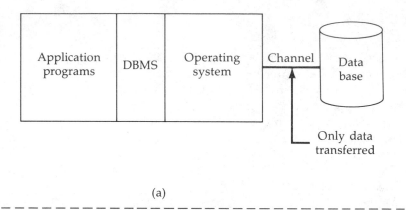

(a)

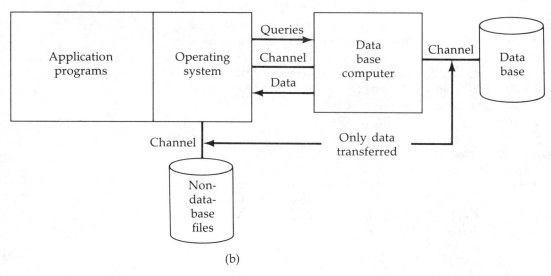

(b)

Figure 15-2
Comparison of conventional and data base computer configurations.
(a) Conventional DBMS configuration.
(b) Data base computer configuration.

for the required data and the requested data and/or DBMS messages are passed back to the host into the working storage area of the calling program. This whole process is transparent to the application program, since the DBMS call and the result apparently occur to the user as they would in the conventional environment.

Objectives and Hazards of Data Base Computers

There are a number of benefits provided by data base computers.

Portability.   The DBMS, residing in its own hardware, can be connected to a wide variety of general-purpose computers. This allows an application user to use a desired DBMS (on the separate DBC) even though that DBMS was not designed to run on the host computer being used. This not only gives users greater flexibility, but also opens up new markets for DBMS vendors.

Security.   Data security protection can be a costly overhead expense in a data base environment, since security enforcement consumes CPU cycles while other programs wait. A DBC allows extensive security controls to be used without interfering with the productivity of non-data-base processing. Further, since a DBC can be simultaneously connected to several hosts, a DBC can provide a centralized security service in a multiple mainframe computer environment.

Shared Data Base.   Since several mainframe host computers can all share the same DBC, an organization can achieve greater sharing of its data. Specialized department computers, laboratory computers, internal time-sharing service computers, and the like, can all share the same data base. The DBC handles concurrency control for all hosts, as well as providing an efficient data base processing service.

Cost Performance.   A DBC is specially designed and configured to provide rapid data searching and retrieval at an economical price. A special operating system can be utilized to concentrate on efficient secondary storage management. Some highly repetitive and stable DBMS functions can be built into the hardware or firmware of the DBC.

These benefits of DBCs are balanced by some potential hazards.

Vulnerability.   All the data in the data base attached to a DBC are accessible only through the DBC. If the DBC breaks down, all data base processing can cease, unless appropriate backup has been performed that will allow the hosts to take over data base retrieval and maintenance duties.

Applicability.   A DBC is not cost effective in all data base environments. Champine (1977) has estimated that at least 40% of the host work load should be data base accessing for a DBC to provide significant cost/performance improvements.

Complexity.   A DBC adds complexity to the data base environment. Additional hardware vendors may be necessary in the data center, one for the host computer and another for the DBC. Problems can go unresolved as different vendors try to blame each other. The DBC, because of its possibly different architecture, is not a widely understood technology. Special training, reliance on vendor personnel, and a small user base can all contribute to unexpected DBMS support costs.

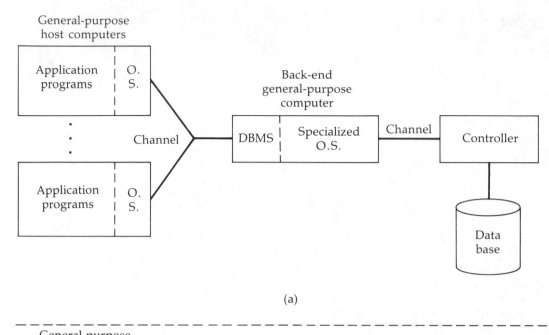

General-purpose
host computers

Back-end
general-purpose
computer

(a)

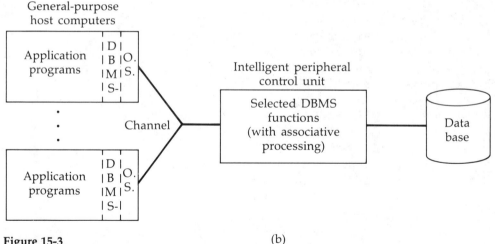

General-purpose
host computers

Intelligent peripheral
control unit

(b)

Figure 15-3
Alternative data base
computer (DBC)
configurations.
(a) Back-end general-
    purpose processor
    DBC.
(b) Intelligent peripheral
    control unit DBC.
(c) Special-purpose
    processor DBC.

Data Base Computer Architectures

Various technologies are being used for data base computers (see Banerjee et al. 1978; Champine 1977; Epstein 1983; Hawthorn 1981; Maryanski 1980). Some of the alternatives are depicted in Figure 15-3. These alternatives include the back-end general-purpose processor, the intelligent peripheral control unit, and the special-purpose processor.

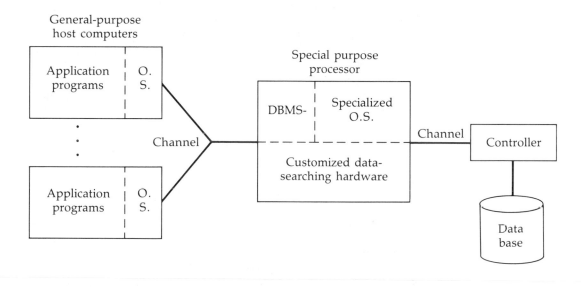

General-purpose
host computers

Application programs | O. S.

Application programs | O. S.

Channel

Special purpose processor

DBMS- | Specialized O.S.

Customized data-searching hardware

Channel

Controller

Data base

(c)

Figure 15-3, continued.

Back-End General-Purpose Processor. With the back-end general-purpose processor, a master host uses a dedicated slave general-purpose computer to perform the data base processing. The host may be a large mainframe and the slave may be a minicomputer, although other combinations are possible. This alternative achieves the advantages of simultaneous data base and other processing, but does not utilize a more cost-effective data base processing technology in the dedicated slave. When several hosts share the same dedicated slave data base computer, this DBC can be viewed as one node in a computer network.

Intelligent Peripheral Control Unit. With the intelligent peripheral control unit, highly repetitive and detailed functions of the DBMS are moved out of the host and placed in the logic of a mass storage unit controller device. This relieves the host from such processing steps. Such functions can include data content searching, sorting, data validation and error correction, data access scheduling, and even data recovery. Data may also be read in parallel across several surfaces of a multiple-surface secondary storage medium like magnetic disk. This type of associative storage and processing means that a whole disk cylinder can be searched for qualified data in approximately the time of one disk revolution. One version of this approach moves these data base processing functions literally to the read/write heads of the secondary storage devices. Some authors refer to this version as **logic-per-track**.

Special-Purpose Processor. The special-purpose processor is the rarest of the alternatives because of the cost to develop whole computers with customized architectures. The approach here is similar to the logic-per-track disk drives, except that such associative processing is done in the main memory of the special processor. Data are staged into the DBC main memory, where they can be searched rapidly in predetermined patterns; these patterns often correspond to certain relational operations such as SELECT or JOIN. Although specially designed hardware can be most cost effective in this case, existing array processor technology, such as the Goodyear Aerospace STARAN computer, has been used as a DBMS staging device (Maryanski 1980).

Summary of Data Base Computers

The Intelligent Database Machine (IDM) introduced by Britton-Lee in 1982 is the first major commercial DBC (Epstein 1983). Other ventures for ADABAS and IDMS and several research laboratory implementations preceded the Britton-Lee products. The IDM products, which utilize the data management approach of INGRES, are being marketed to first-time DBMS as well as existing INGRES users (see Relational Technology, Inc. 1982).

Because of the continued rapid advances in microcomputer and disk technologies, there is no clear trend in data base computers. Some of the developments in personal computer DBMS in which inquiry (especially ad hoc access) processing is being down-loaded to desk-top computers naturally reduce the data base work load on mainframes (see the next section for more details). This may reduce the need for data base computers as now defined. DBCs, however, still have a number of advantages, and high data base activity data centers should consider their application.

MICROCOMPUTER DBMSs

It is difficult to put boundaries around the topic of microcomputer DBMS. When IBM announces a desk-top S/370 with 4 million bytes of virtual storage and the capacity to run S/370 mainframe software, like that of DBMSs, it is difficult to limit one's discussion of microcomputer DBMS.

To a great extent, a microcomputer DBMS (referred to as PC-DBMS) mimics the capabilities of its mainframe ancestors. For example, we find hierarchical data models (HDMS) and network (e.g., MDBS III) and relational (e.g., dBASE II and KnowledgeMan) PC-DBMSs (see Micro Data Base Systems 1981a, 1981b, 1983; Ashton-Tate 1981). Further, we find that these products may also have screen formatters, reportwriters, query languages, multiple host language interfaces, and special procedural or command languages for data base processing.

Unique Features of a PC-DBMS

What makes a PC-DBMS unique from its mainframe counterpart? First, some DBMS functions are often missing in PC-DBMS products. For example, there is frequently no restart and recovery support, and many times there are no data security procedures. In dBASE II, for instance, copies of data base files are not automatically made by the DBMS, nor is any transaction log or audit trail maintained. If a user accidentally defines a new relational table to have the same name as an existing table, the existing table is destroyed and written over by the new data. Unless the user has explicitly made a backup copy of that file or diskette, the previous data base file is permanently lost.

The second difference between a mainframe system and a PC-DBMS is in the operating environment of data base processing. With mainframe systems, it is assumed that data base processing occurs in a multiprogramming, multiuser environment. Concurrent access to the data base must be controlled, and security protection is essential because of the shared data. In the PC arena, there are, in contrast, varying environments.

Single-User Stand-Alone Approach. The single-user stand-alone approach is today the most typical PC-DBMS environment. Here, a single user at a time uses a PC dedicated to that user's processing. The data base is private in the sense that the user can take the diskettes away after use to prohibit other users from accessing the data. The data base, too, is personal. Further, the data base on the PC is separate from any other data base, possibly on a mainframe from which the PC data base may have been extracted. Thus, data may be duplicated, and synchronization of updating is a problem with which to deal.

Multiuser Stand-Alone Approach. The multiuser stand-alone approach is different from the single-user stand-alone approach in that a hard-disk-based data base is usually shared among a number of concurrently executing users. These different users may all be using the same PC with a multiprogramming type of operating system, or they may be sharing a hard disk file server from several PCs. In either case, concurrency control and security are limited or handled at a very coarse level (e.g., file-level lockout for update control, rather than record- or element-level lockout). Here, as in the prior situation, the PC data base is maintained separately from any mainframe data base.

Mainframe Link Approach. The mainframe link is a relatively new but rapidly expanding class of PC-DBMS in which the same or very similar DBMS products are provided at both the PC and mainframe computers. A communications link (hardware and software) is provided as part of the PC package. From the PC, a user can access a mainframe data base as he or she would from a terminal (in so-called terminal emulation mode, in which the PC is made to act as a special terminal, like an IBM 327x). The user can also have selected data from the mainframe transferred to the PC (often using the same type of retrieval command as in any data access statement, but with an extra clause to indicate that the destination of the result is a file, data base, or table on the PC). And finally, the user can manipulate data at the PC using the same language and range of commands as on the mainframe. Thus, users familiar with the mainframe product need minimal training time to learn the PC version. The benefit is that the PC can be used to relieve a mainframe doing production data base processing from also having to perform ad hoc inquiry processing, which can be expensive to support and can degrade the performance of the production data base. New products such as PC/FOCUS, PC/204, and Cullinet Personal Computer Software are examples of this category of product (see Information Builders, Inc. 1983; *Computerworld* 1983; Cullinet Software, Inc. 1983). Other packages, such as MicroRIM (see MicroRIM, Inc. 1983a), represent a downsizing of a mainframe DBMS to a PC without the PC to mainframe linkage.

Multifunction Package Approach.   Multifunction packages include packages that have integrated DBMS functions along with other management support tools. For example, several spreadsheet packages combine some simple DBMS functions with spreadsheet and graphics capabilities. KnowledgeMan provides more relational DBMS functions with limited spreadsheet facilities (see Micro Data Base Systems 1983). This category of PC-DBMS should continue to expand as more general decision support system generators are created for personal computers.

Besides these environmental differences, the PC-DBMS differs from its mainframe predecessors in the size of a data base that can be managed by such products. For example, dBASE II (see Ashton-Tate 1981) is limited to 65,535 records per data base and 32 data elements per record type. Newer PC-DBMS products are beginning to relax such size constraints. For example, R:BASE 4000 from MicroRIM, Inc. (1983b) permits 100 billion records and 400 data elements per record type (obviously, the size of secondary storage can place more restrictive practical limits than those supported by the package). As word sizes and operating system capabilities on PCs expand, larger data bases will be created via PC-DBMS. A PC-DBMS is also limited by the processing speed of a personal computer, especially the time to access disk or diskette storage.

Role of PC-DBMS in Data Management

A PC-DBMS has several distinct features that make it attractive as part of a general data management strategy. First, it provides mainframe-like DBMS function for organizations or organizational units that do not require the power of a mini- or maxicomputer. Second, the PC-DBMS allows computer users in organizations that have an existing mainframe DBMS to develop data base applications that are truly independent of production data bases in a way that does not interfere with the performance of production data bases. Third, newer PC-DBMS technologies essentially permit an organization to create loosely coupled distributed data bases to achieve greater host performance as well as reduce communication traffic in the computer network. Fourth, for users already using personal computers for management support, a PC-DBMS provides an additional powerful tool to manage and present relevant data and information. And finally, a PC-DBMS is portable, since for many of these products, the DBMS and data bases can be easily transported by moving diskettes. This not only has benefit to mobile managers, but also means that the same DBMS and data base can be used on mixed, yet compatible, machines (e.g., several PCs running the CP/M operating system or the MS-DOS operating system). This portability also impacts education, since students learning a DBMS can do so at home or in a classroom or laboratory, and they can learn without disrupting other students (when their errors crash the DBMS or destroy a file of input transactions).

Summary of PC-DBMS Technology

Although it might be interesting at this point to give several examples of a PC-DBMS, most such systems are operationally very similar to mainframe systems that use the same data model, and so illustrations are not very enlightening. For example, dBASE II and MicroRIM are only slightly syntactically different from a mainframe relational algebra DBMS; MDBS III has practically all the features of any CODASYL network DBMS (it even supports an extension of the basic DBTG guidelines, including many-to-many relationships); and the data manipulation features of KnowledgeMan are similar to those in the relational calculus QUEL language of INGRES. Besides the differences already noted between a mainframe DBMS and a PC-DBMS, a PC-DBMS is no more operationally different from mainframe systems than any two data base management systems (with the same data model) differ from each other.

The principles of data base management hold whether we deal with mainframe or PC data bases. The major issues are sharability, integrity, consistency, security, and accessibility. PC and mainframe product alike should be measured on the same features and data processing requirements. As with many mainframe products, often the label DBMS is ascribed to a PC product that may only manage a single file of data or may only assist in producing stylized reports from single flat files. Care should be taken to apply the same stringent requirements for PC data management products as have been introduced elsewhere in this text for DBMS products in general. PC-DBMSs exist on a different type of computer but should provide the same functionality.

THE SPATIAL DATA MANAGEMENT SYSTEM

In Chapter 14, we introduced Query-by-Example as an example of a graphical relational DBMS (see Zloof 1977). Although QBE draws the skeleton of a relational table on the terminal screen, QBE is not capable of dealing with pictorial data. One rather unique DBMS, the Spatial Data Management System (SDMS) from Computer Corporation of America (see Herot 1980), is able to represent data in graphical format within a spatial context, as well as display numerical and textual data about the details of the picture.

A Spatial View of Data

Consider for a moment the following hypothetical example of data management possible with SDMS. Many knowledge workers in offices are accustomed to working with data within the spatial context of the office. Required data are found because we remember we placed it somewhere in the tall stack of papers in the far left-hand corner of our desk, because we remember that we received the report in an oversized green envelope, or because the letter had a certain red logo on it. We are used to locating data based on where we stored it or what the medium containing the data looked like. We can force an office worker to convert to a different framework for data management that requires highly formatted records and stylized content-based inquiries, or we can electronically reproduce the office to permit more rapid and natural access to data, even when we are not physically present in our "office."

The SDMS utilizes a combination of joystick, keyboard, and multiple touch-sensitive screens to simulate the environment in which data exist. One screen presents a "world-view" of the entire data environment; a second screen shows a magnified portion in which the user is currently searching (this same area, in less detail, is outlined in the "world-view" screen). The joystick can be used to move the "window" around the environment and to zoom in on certain segments. For example, as we would zoom in on our desk, the stack of indistinguishable papers on our desk would become more readable and letterheads and colors on each document could be discerned. When we find a file folder of interest, we can enter a query on the keyboard to search for desired information or we can scan the pages of the folder as we would manually.

Different objects (entities) in our office (data base) are associated with different icons or graphical symbols. Instances of these entities are placed on a data surface. An icon has both a relative size and color. At certain levels of detail, an entity is defined by tabular data; a class of entities can be defined so that data can be viewed in aggregation as well as in detail.

Unique Advantages of SDMS

As reported in Herot (1980), the SDMS has six advantages over the conventional DBMS.

Simple and Natural Movement Through Data Base. Because data can be accessed spatially and also by symbolic query languages, data retrieval can be by whatever method is natural at that moment. Content and structure are readily apparent, since data are present within their context. Data do not have to be abstracted to be retrieved.

Data Space Is Its Own Dictionary. The graphical data representation describes the data. If data are about a ship, then a ship icon is used. If we deal with ships in a convoy, then we see a group of ships traveling together. Abbreviated and obscure data names have been replaced by meaningful icons.

Browsing Is Encouraged. Because the combination of "world-view" and magnified screens shows more data than are requested at any point in time, the user is visually stimulated to ask questions about the relationship of objects that look alike or are physically close to one another.

Position Conveys Information. The physical, relative placement of icons can be used to convey information. Relative sizes or distances not only indicate relationships but also allow visual comparisons of such values.

Graphic Representation. When appropriately applied, graphic representations can be vivid and clear. Use of colors can effectively supplant numerical classifications. For example, all Canadian ships can be one color and all Liberian ships another color.

Unique Data Types. Illustrations and pictures stored on videodisks or other media can be incorporated into the data base.

Summary of SDMS: An Example of Things to Come

If our description has not been sufficiently graphic of the capabilities of SDMS, you may want to see a demonstration of SDMS. A 20-minute videotape is available from Computer Corporation of America; this tape illustrates several possible applications of SDMS.

A discussion of SDMS was included here to suggest that the structured record approaches of the hierarchical, network, and relational data models are not the *only* choices for viewing data. Although SDMS is still relatively experimental and is certainly expensive and rarely applied, advancements in computer graphics should make it more feasible.

Audio data bases exist for telephone directory assistance and bank account balance inquiries. Organizations contain not only numbers and text but also pictures, sounds, and even odors and tastes. Imagine accessing a restaurant guide data base in which we could select where to eat by the comparative aromas and tastes (a kind of "scratch and smell" data base). Remember, DBMSs are based on data models, and data models are abstractions of reality. Ideally, the abstraction eliminates inessential elements and represents meaningful elements in accurate and convenient forms. When pictures, sounds, odors, and tastes are essential, can they be abstracted into numerical form? SDMS may simply be an example to suggest that we should not become content with today's technology but should consider and encourage useful new data base management technologies.

SUMMARY

Many authors, futurists, and management thinkers believe that we are on the verge of an information society. It has been estimated that from 10% to 50% of payroll costs are being spent to collect, distribute, and maintain the organizational information resource. There is now discussion in the accounting profession on how to value the *information asset* of a business and how to include this asset in financial statements.

Data base management will play an important role in such an information society. Systems analysts, designers, programmers, and users alike will define, administer, protect, account for, and guarantee the accuracy of the information resource. And DBMS technology will permit a variety of data organizations that will facilitate cost-effective storage and access of this valuable resource. It is becoming increasingly more important that managers be able to use technology effectively to manage data. To be involved in the development of data bases in organizations places one in the center of an evolution of management practice. Best wishes on putting the principles of data management into practice!

CHAPTER REVIEW

Review Questions

1. Define each of the following terms:
   a. centralized data base
   b. distributed data base

    c. decentralized data base
    d. partitioned distributed data base
    e. data base computer
    f. logic-per-track
    g. mainframe link PC-DBMS
    h. icon

2. Explain the relative advantages of centralized, decentralized, and distributed data bases.

3. Describe the role of the interface module of a distributed data base management system.

4. Explain how distributed data bases help to achieve both centralized and decentralized data processing.

5. What are the costs of replicated data in a distributed data base?

6. Describe a situation in which a clustered distributed data base might be of benefit.

7. Explain how deadlock can occur in a distributed data base.

8. Explain the benefits of a special-purpose data base computer.

9. What are the unique characteristics of a PC-DBMS compared with mini and mainframe systems?

10. Explain the issues of data security for PC data bases.

References

Ashton-Tate, 1981. *dBASE II Users' Manual*. Culver City, Calif.: Ashton-Tate.

Banerjee, Jayanta, Richard I. Baum, and David K. Hsiao. 1978. "Concepts and Capabilities of a Database Computer." *ACM-TODS* 3 (December): 347–384.

Bernstein, Philip A., Nathan Goodman, Eugene Wong, Christopher L. Reeve, and James B. Rothnie, Jr. 1981. "Query Processing in a System for Distributed Databases (SDD-1)." *ACM-TODS* 6 (December): 602–625.

Champine, G.A. 1977. "Six Approaches to Distributed Data Bases." *Datamation* 23 (May): 69–72.

Computerworld. "CCA's 'PC/204' Links Its DBMS to IBM Micro." November 7, pp. 53, 62.

Cullinet Software, Inc. 1983. *Cullinet Personal Computer Software: Summary Description*. October. Westwood, Mass.: Cullinet Software, Inc.

Date, C.J. 1983. *An Introduction to Database Systems*. Vol. 2. Reading, Mass.: Addison-Wesley.

Epstein, Robert. 1983. "Why Database Machines?" *Datamation* 29 (July): 139, 140, 144.

Hawthorn, Paula. 1981. "The Effect of Target Applications on the Design of Database Machines." In *Proceedings ACM SIGMOD 1981,* available from Association for Computing Machinery.

Herot, Christopher F. 1980. "Spatial Management of Data." *ACM-TODS* 5 (December): 493–513.

Information Builders, Inc. 1983. *PC/FOCUS Product Description.* March. New York: Information Builders, Inc.

Maryanski, Fred J. 1980. "Backend Database Systems." *ACM-Computing Surveys* 12 (March): 3–25.

Micro Data Base Systems. 1981a. *Application Program Reference Manual: MDBS-DMS.* Lafayette, Ind.: Micro Data Base Systems.

————. 1981b. *HDMS Users' Guide.* Lafayette, Ind.: Micro Data Base Systems.

————. 1983. *KnowledgeMan Users' Guide.* July. Lafayette, Ind.: Micro Data Base Systems.

MicroRIM, Inc. 1983a. *MicroRIM Data Base Management System Tutorial.* March. Bellevue, Wash.: MicroRIM, Inc.

————. 1983b. *Tutorial: R:base 4000.* Bellevue, Wash.: MicroRIM, Inc.

Relational Technology, Inc. 1982. *INGRES Reference Manual.* Version 1.4 VAX/VMS. July. Berkeley, Calif.: Relational Technology, Inc.

Zloof, M.M. 1977. "Query-by-Example: A Data Base Language." *IBM Systems Journal* 16 (4): 324–343.

Index

Page numbers for definitions are in italics.